Applied Data Structures
with
C++

Peter Smith

California State University, Channel Islands

JONES AND BARTLETT PUBLISHERS

Sudbury, Massachusetts

BOSTON   TORONTO   LONDON   SINGAPORE

World Headquarters

Jones and Bartlett Publishers
40 Tall Pine Drive
Sudbury, MA 01776
978-443-5000
info@jbpub.com
www.jbpub.com

Jones and Bartlett Publishers
Canada
2406 Nikanna Road
Mississauga, ON L5C 2W6
CANADA

Jones and Bartlett Publishers
International
Barb House, Barb Mews
London W6 7PA
UK

Cover image © PhotoAlto Photography/Veer

Library of Congress Cataloging-in-Publication Data

Smith, Peter.
  Applied data structures with C++ / by Peter Smith.— 1st ed.
      p. cm.
  ISBN 0-7637-2562-5 (Paperback)
  1. C++ (Computer program language) 2. Data structures (Computer
science) I. Title.
  QA76.73.C153S662 2004
  005.13'3—dc22

                                            2003021167

Production Credits

Acquisitions Editor: Stephen Solomon
Production Manager: Amy Rose
Marketing Manager: Matthew Bennett
Editorial Assistant: Caroline Senay
Cover Design: Kristin E. Ohlin
Manufacturing Buyer: Therese Bräuer
Production Coordination: Jennifer Bagdigian
Technical Art: Smolinski Studios
Composition: Northeast Compositors
Printing and Binding: Malloy, Inc.
Cover Printing: Malloy, Inc.

Printed in the United States of America
08 07 06 05 04   10 9 8 7 6 5 4 3 2 1

For Laura

Preface

This book started as lecture notes for a third semester course in data structures in which the emphasis was on files and persistent structures. This is the material that is now in Part Two. The topics in Part One were added to make the text more balanced, and to provide instructors with more options in selecting topics for a one-semester course.

The data structures and algorithms are of primary interest in this text. However, rather than use pseudo-code in the algorithms, we chose to use C++ where possible and introduce features of the language as necessary either in the body of the text or, more often, in end-of-chapter notes. We use C++ rather than Java because of its superior file-handling capabilities. When there was a choice between clarity of exposition and efficiency of implementation in the code, for the most part we chose clarity. For the same reason, in those cases when an algorithm is so large that the C++ code is unwieldy, it is presented in a more concise pseudo-C++. Thus, there is scope for improving the C++ and for converting the pseudo-C++ into the real thing.

Prerequisites

It is assumed that students using this book will have an algorithms and programming background equivalent to a first semester course in Computer Science, will have written several programs in a high-level language (though not necessarily an object-oriented one), and will be familiar with simple data types and arrays.

Organization and Contents

The text is organized into two parts, each having seven chapters. Generally, Part One of the book deals with main memory structures and Part Two with file-based structures.

In Chapter 1, we introduce the concept of object-oriented design, show how it is different from algorithm-oriented design, and discuss the concept of persistence as a property of a data structure. The topics of recursion and Big-O notation are covered; this might be review material for some readers.

Chapter 2 covers linear lists, both simple lists and variants such as general lists and skip lists. After considering array-based implementations, we introduce dynamic storage allocation (and some of its pitfalls in C++).

Chapter 3 discusses sets, in particular the advantages and disadvantages of various ways to implement a set.

Chapter 4 looks at stacks and queues. We discuss their implementation and review applications that use these structures. We give an example of an algorithm that uses backtracking and show two ways to simulate an environment containing a queue.

Chapter 5 introduces the concept of a map as an abstract data structure that permits storage and retrieval of items by a unique key. In this chapter, we look at hash-based techniques for implementing maps.

Chapter 6 continues the discussion of maps and looks at tree-based implementations. In addition to the usual material on binary search trees, there is a section on tries, and how tries can be implemented using ternary trees.

Chapter 7 concludes Part One by examining the graph data structure. We look at ways in which a graph can be implemented and at some of the more useful graph algorithms.

With Chapter 8, we begin Part Two by looking at hardware foundations of files and the storage of persistent objects. This chapter can be considered optional material, although it includes aspects of secondary storage—for example the long access times and addressability, that influence the design of persistent and large-scale data structures.

Chapter 9 looks at files from a programmer's point of view, and gives some simple examples of programs that read from and write to files. The programmer's interaction with secondary memory generally will be through the interface to files provided in a high-level language. We give a brief introduction to file accessing methods and show how an object definition can include save/restore capabilities.

Chapter 10 covers sorting. Rather than divide the topic between two chapters, both internal and external sorting are covered here.

Chapter 11 looks at hash-based maps implemented using files. Thus, this chapter is the counterpart to Chapter 5.

Chapter 12 looks at indexed files, both static and dynamic. The tree-structured nature of indexed files means that this chapter can be considered to be the counterpart of Chapter 6.

Chapter 13 looks at the multimap. With multimaps, a key may be associated with multiple items, all of which should be returned by a retrieval operation. We look both at conventional indexing techniques and at the grid file organization.

Chapter 14 summarizes the structures covered in Part Two, presents a simple method that could be used to select the appropriate structure for a particular application, and then gives a very brief glimpse of database systems, comparing them with files.

Possible Course Structures

The text can be used in a second semester course, but an instructor may be hard-pressed to cover every chapter. In this case, chapters that could be skipped without great harm include Chapter 3 (Sets), Chapter 8 (Hardware Foundations), the External Sorting section of Chapter 10, and Chapter 14 (Persistent Structures and Databases).

If the text were to be used in a follow-on course from second semester course, an instructor might begin by selecting from Part One any topics not previously covered, and then go through the chapters in Part Two.

Exercises and Problems

I prefer to give open-book rather than closed-book examinations and quizzes, and this is reflected in the type of exercises that appear at the end of the chapters. Most require application and synthesis of ideas rather than memorization or simple reading comprehension. The problems that follow the exercises typically require some programming effort or a longer time frame to complete.

Acknowledgments

It has been a genuine pleasure to work with the publishing team at Jones and Bartlett. I would like to thank Toni Ackley-Zuccarini, Tracey Chapman, and Caroline Senay for all their efforts on my behalf.

I would like to acknowledge the assistance of current colleagues at California State University, Channel Islands and former colleagues at California State University, Northridge. In particular, my thanks are due to Mike Barnes, not only for permission to use material on which we hold a joint copyright, but also for his willingness to read and comment on numerous fragments of the text. Thanks, too, to dozens of students enrolled in courses that used preliminary versions of the material and who have, knowingly or not, field-tested many of the exercises.

The manuscript has passed through the hands of many reviewers. I would like to thank in particular those who read an almost complete version of the text: John Donath of Queens College, Hongjun Song of the University of Memphis, and Dana Wortman of Frostburg State University. Their comments and suggestions were most helpful.

Many thanks to my family, both human and animal members, for their patience and quiet, steady encouragement.

Peter Smith
Camarillo, California

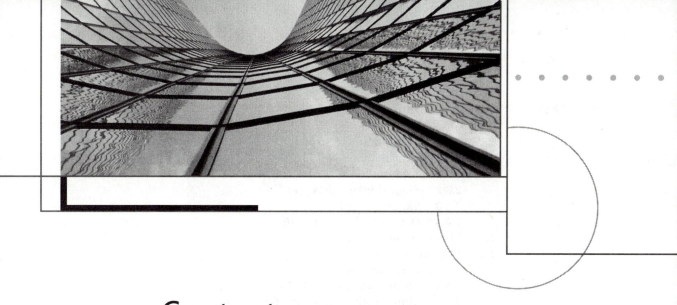

Contents

Transient Objects

Programming with Objects

1.1 Introduction

This chapter introduces some general aspects of object-oriented programming. Section 1.2 introduces the philosophy of the object-oriented approach and illustrates some of the advantages that it has over more traditional algorithm-oriented design. Section 1.2 also examines some aspects of simple object class definition and usage in the C++ programming environment. Programmers can use templates to write general object definitions; templates and the Standard Template Library are examined in Section 1.3.

One of the properties of an object is its duration, or persistence, which is often closely related to its scope. However, whereas scope defines the visibility of a variable (i.e., where it can be accessed from inside the code), duration refers to its lifetime. If an object in a program exists only in main memory, then it typically ceases to exist on exit from the program block that created it (which may be the entire program) if there is no longer an active pointer to it. Secondary memory can be used to make an object persist for longer than its normal duration. Secondary memory may also be required if the object is large. Examples of objects requiring secondary memory are provided in Section 1.4. Chapters 11, 12, and 13 examine the use of files to implement data structures.

The last two sections of this chapter cover material used in later chapters. These sections can be skipped by readers already familiar with the topics. Section 1.5 looks at some aspects of recursive definitions of functions and compares recursion with iteration. Finally, Section 1.6 examines measures of algorithmic complexity.

1.2 Object-Oriented Design

1.2.1 Definitions

An *object* is an entity that performs computation and has a local state (Stefik and Bobrow 1986). A simple example is a counter. The state of the counter includes information about the current value of the count. Computation enables us to change the value of the count and also determine the current value of the count.

Object-oriented design is an approach to system design that focuses on the objects being manipulated and on the operations that are defined on those objects. Non-object-oriented design tends to focus on algorithms and algorithmic decomposition rather than object decomposition.

As an example of object-oriented design, consider a system that generates crossword puzzles (i.e., diagrams filled with words). Such a system will have a dictionary of some form, thus the top-level design includes a dictionary object. The top level of the design will also have an object representing the diagram to be filled with words. As we refine the design, we identify capabilities required of the objects. For example, we would like to request from the dictionary the next word that matches "---y-l-n-". We also would like the diagram object to display its contents in some convenient format. Thus, the design focuses more on "what" than "how."

Electrical engineers are able to construct circuits using well-designed, tested, reliable components such as multiplexors, shift registers, and counters. They do not need to build each new circuit from scratch at the gate level. The goal of object-oriented design is to enable software engineers to do the same thing. Similar objects, such as queues, symbol tables, and matrices, occur in many different systems. Well-designed, reliable object definitions can be used and reused in many different programs, thus reducing the time that programmers must spend tinkering with and writing lines of code and enabling them to operate more at a component level, as electrical engineers do.

Figure 1.1 depicts a very simple software counter object.

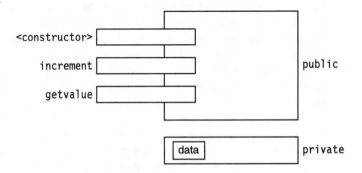

Figure 1.1 • Counter object

Data Abstraction

Data abstraction is the process of separating the specification of a data object from its implementation. Sometimes programmers use the term *abstract data type* (ADT) when referring to the essential properties of a data type independent of how objects of that type are implemented. For example, a stack has *pop* and *push* operations that have the appropriate effect on the stack contents regardless of whether the stack is implemented as an array, as linked storage, or as a file. The counter depicted in Figure 1.1 has mechanisms for incrementing the count and for determining the current value of the count; we are not concerned about how the object represents the count.

Data Encapsulation and Information Hiding

Data encapsulation and information hiding are mechanisms used to conceal the implementation of an object while making the appropriate features available. As exemplified in Figure 1.1, our notation depicts a public component as protruding from the box representing the object, whereas a private component is depicted as entirely within the box. Think of giving user information about a class on a "need-to-know" basis; a user of the counter class does not need to know how the count is implemented (e.g., you could use a simple scalar of a particular size or a linked list of digits).

In the case of our counter, the memory location containing the count is hidden and can be accessed only through the public functions that permit us to do the following:

- Create a counter with a particular initial value
- Increment the counter
- Read the current value

Information hiding enables us to change the implementation of an object without changing the functional interface (i.e., ways in which it can be used). For example, the implementation of a dictionary could be changed from a binary tree to a linked list to a hash table, and the interface that allows users to retrieve, add, and remove words would remain the same.

Inheritance

Consider a file in a computer system. All files have certain attributes. For example, every file has a name, a size, a creation date, and a location. Similarly, certain operations can be applied to any file (given appropriate permissions); it can be created, renamed, moved, or deleted.

It is common to divide files into two categories: text/ASCII and binary. An example of a text file is the source code for a program, which can be edited with a simple editor and listed on the screen. Examples of binary files are program executables and compressed archive files containing data in a proprietary format.

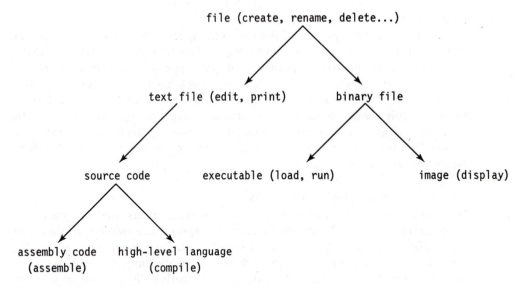

Figure 1.2 • Hierarchy of file classes

In addition to the operations that can be done on any file, each of the two file categories has particular operations that can be done on files in that category. Thus, we can define a *base class* called *file* and have *derived classes* called *text-file* and *binary file* that **inherit** aspects of the parent, such as the ability to be copied or renamed, and have additional attributes such as the ability to be loaded into memory and executed. Figure 1.2 illustrates a possible hierarchy of some file types with associated operations.

Objects in a well-designed object-oriented system are likely to be related to each other through inheritance. If an object library does not have precisely the object you need, you can probably find one on which to base it. A well-designed object hierarchy can often be extended to create an object for a specific task without having to design it from scratch. For example, our counter example could be the base for a more general counter having additional features that permit users both to decrement the counter and to set it to an arbitrary value.

Programming With and Without Objects
First, consider the following C++ program (without objects) that inputs integers until the user enters −1. It counts how many of the input numbers are odd and how many are multiples of three. The values of the two counts are output at the end.[1]

```
#include <iostream.h>

int main()
{
```

```
      int N,                    // input number
          counterofodds=0,      // count of odd numbers
          countermultiples=0;   // count of multiples of 3

   do
     {
       cout << "Enter number (-1 to finish): ";
       cin >> N;

       if (N != -1) // not the terminator
         {
           if (N%2 == 1) counterofodds++;      // odd number
           if (N%3 == 0) countermultiples++;  // multiple of 3
         }

     } while (N != -1);

  cout << "Number of odd numbers:" << counterofodds << endl
       << "Number of multiples of three:" << countermultiples << endl;

  return 0;
  }
```

Note two things about this program. First, the two counter variables are not protected. There is nothing to prevent them from being accessed or updated from anywhere in the main program. Second, the counter mechanism is not encapsulated in any way. The declaration, initialization, update, and access of the counter cannot be easily cut and pasted for use in another program.

In contrast, consider the following program:

```
#include <iostream.h>

class counter
{
 public : counter(int N=0)
             { data = N; }        // constructor. default initial is 0
          void increment(int D=1)
             { data += D; }       // increment is 1 by default
          int getvalue()
             { return data; }     // returns the current count

 private: int data;               // stores the count
};
```

```
int main()
{
  int N;                               // for input number
  counter counterofodds,               // for odd numbers
          countermultiples;            // for multiples of 3

  do
    {
      cout << "Enter number (-1 to finish): ";
      cin >> N;

      if (N != -1) // not the terminator
        {
          if (N%2 == 1) counterofodds.increment();     // Odd number
          if (N%3 == 0) countermultiples.increment();  // Multiple of 3
        }

    } while (N != -1);

  cout << "Number of odd numbers:" << counterofodds.getvalue() << endl
       << "Numbers of multiples of 3:" << countermultiples.getvalue() << endl;

  return 0;
}
```

In this program, we define a class of object called *counter* that corresponds to Figure 1.1.[2] The components of the class are either public or private. Public components can be accessed by users of objects of the class. Private components are hidden and are accessible only within the object (e.g., from the public functions). The compiler enforces this information hiding. In the case of the counter, we designate the variable that contains the current counter value as private and provide three public functions:

1. The constructor function *counter*. Constructor functions always have the same name as the class. They are called automatically when an object of the class is created. (Destructor functions are covered in Chapter 2.) The constructor is used to initialize the counter variable. The user is free to specify an initial value; we have specified that the default initial value is zero. By having the constructor function do the initialization, the counter variable can never be in an undefined state.

2. The updating function *increment*. The public functions are permitted to access the private class components. Increment adds an amount (one by default) to the counter.

3. The accessing component *getvalue*. When called, *getvalue* returns the current value of the counter. This is the only mechanism for determining the current value. We cannot access *data* directly because it is in the private section.

The *counter* class definition presented here should not be considered "industrial strength." A more robust version would include checks to ensure that the value of the counter remains inside any limits imposed by its implementation and would report failure if an attempt is made to change it beyond those bounds.

1.3 Templates and the Standard Template Library

1.3.1 Templates

C++ is a typed language; therefore, if you need different kinds of counters (e.g., short integer, regular integer, and long integer), it would seem that you would need three separate class definitions. However, the **template** mechanism (generally available in all but the oldest C++ compilers) enables us to write just one generic definition. Here is that definition:

```
template <class Type>
class counter
{
 public : counter(Type N=0) { data = N; }
          void increment(Type D=1) { data += D; }
          Type getvalue() { return data; }

 private: Type data;
};
```

We indicate in the first line that a class definition follows with *Type* as the "parameter." In the definition, we use *Type* where we previously had *int*. When we declare an object of class *counter*, we must now specify an appropriate type.[3] This is illustrated in the next example.

Let us assume that we have put the text of our template counter definition into header file *counter.h*. Suppose we decide that our counter of multiples of three need only be a short integer, whereas the count of odd numbers should be a full integer; our program now becomes:[4]

```
#include <iostream.h>
#include "counter.h"

int main()
 (
```

```
            int N;
            counter<int> counterofodds;        // for odd numbers
            counter<short> countermultiples;    // for multiples of 3

            do
              {
                cout << "Enter number (-1 to finish): ";
                cin >> N;

                if (N != -1)  // not the terminator
                  {
                    if (N%2 == 1) counterofodds.increment();      // odd number
                    if (N%3 == 0) countermultiples.increment();  // multiple of 3
                  }

          } while (N != -1);

          cout << "Number of odd numbers:" << counterofodds.getvalue() << endl
               << "Numbers of multiples of 3:" << countermultiples.getvalue() << endl;

          return 0;

        }
```

Inheritance

We mentioned earlier that being able to set a counter to an arbitrary value and also to decrement the value of the count by an arbitrary value would make our counter more general. Here is a definition of a *general_counter* class based on the *counter* class in the previous section.[5]

```
template <class Type>
class general_counter : public counter<Type>        // base on class counter
{
  public : general_counter(Type N=0) : counter(N) {}
           void setcounter(Type N=0) { data = N; }   // now can set value
                                                      // at any time
           void decrement(Type D=1) {  data -= D; }  // now can decrement too

};
```

The following program uses the *general_counter* class. It uses the counter to record the difference between the number of positive numbers and the number of negative numbers in an input data stream terminated by zero.

```
#include <iostream.h>
#include "counters.h"

int main()
{
  general_counter<int> difference;
  int N;

  do
    {
      cout << "Enter a number (0 to finish): ";
      cin >> N;

      if (N != 0)  // not the terminator
        {
          if (N<0)
              difference.decrement();    // negative number read
          else  difference.increment();  // positive number read
        }

    } while (N != 0);

  cout << "Number of positive entered minus number of negative: "
      << difference.getvalue() << endl;

  return 0;
}
```

A Stack Example

Our second example definition is for a class of objects with which you may already be familiar—stacks (stacks are covered in detail in Chapter 4). A stack ADT has *pop* and *push* operations defined, and the data component can be implemented in many ways. We have added two more public functions to our stack definition: *isempty* and *gettop*. Neither function is a primitive because each can be implemented in terms of *pop* and *push*, but their inclusion will make a later example more readable. Without loss of generality, we assume that the stack has a count that keeps track of the number of items it contains. Our stack object is depicted in Figure 1.3.

Following is the first part of a class definition for a stack. To improve readability, we have put only the prototypes of functions inside the class definition; the rest of the function definitions will follow.[6] Again, we use templates so that we may easily declare different types of stack objects.[7] The *pop* and *gettop* functions will fail if the stack is empty; the *push* function may similarly fail if there is no way to make the stack bigger. Each of these three functions returns a *bool: true* if it succeeds and *false* if it fails.

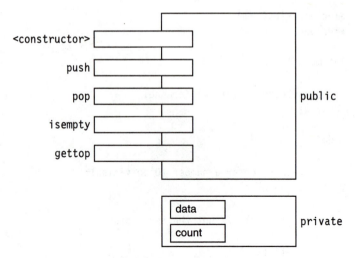

Figure 1.3 • Stack object

```
template <class Entry>
class stack
{

   public: stack();               // constructor
          bool push(Entry);        // push item onto stack
          bool pop (Entry&);       // pop from stack into item
          bool isempty();          // check if stack is empty
          bool gettop (Entry&);    // get top without popping it

   private: int count;             // count of items in stack
          Entry data[100];         // to hold the items. Top is data[count-1].
};
```

The rest of the definition fully defines the functions:

```
template <class Entry>
stack<Entry>::stack(): count(0) {}

template <class Entry>
bool stack<Entry>::push(Entry item)
  {
    if (count==100)
        return false;              // stack full
    else
```

```
        {
          data[count] = item;        // insert item
          count++;
          return true;
        }
    }

template <class Entry>
bool stack<Entry>::pop(Entry& item)
  {
    if (isempty())
        return false;                // stack empty
    else
        {
          count--;
          item = data[count];        // get item
          return true;
        }
  }

template <class Entry>
bool stack<Entry>::isempty() {return count==0;}

template <class Entry>
bool stack<Entry>::gettop(Entry& item)
{
  if (isempty())
      return false;
  else
      {
        item = data[count-1];
        return true;
      }
}
```

Example of an Application that Uses Stacks
Stacks are useful in evaluating arithmetic expressions. The following is a program for evaluating an infix expression consisting of operators (with various priorities), operands, and parentheses. Note the use of two different stacks, one for operands and one for operators. If the expression is well formed, its value is left as the only item in the operand stack.[8]

```
// fragile evaluator of well-formed infix expressions
// assumes tokens are separated by white space
```

```
#include <iostream.h>
#include <stdlib.h>                              // for the atoi function
#include "stack.h"

stack<char> operatorstack;
stack<int> operandstack;

enum symtype {oprand,openparen,closeparen,oprator};  // the 4 token types

symtype classify(char sym[])
{
  // determine which type of symbol we have
  if (strcmp(sym,"(")==0) return openparen;
  if (strcmp(sym,")")==0) return closeparen;
  if (   strcmp(sym,"+")==0 || strcmp(sym,"-")==0
      || strcmp(sym,"*")==0 || strcmp(sym,"/")==0) return oprator;
  return oprand;
}


void apply (char op)
{
  // apply the operator to the top two stack items and replace them
  // by the result of the operation
  int one, two;
  operandstack.pop(two);
  operandstack.pop(one);
      if (op=='+') operandstack.push(one+two);
  else if (op=='-') operandstack.push(one-two);
  else if (op=='*') operandstack.push(one*two);
  else if (op=='/') operandstack.push(one/two);
}

int priority (char op)
{
 // determine the priority of the operator
 if (op == '*' || op == '/') return 2;
 if (op == '+' || op == '-') return 1;
 return 0;
}

int main()
{
  int result;                                   // for result of expression
```

```
    char OP;                                // temporary for operator symbol
    char symbol[100];                       // to store expression symbols

    while (cin >> symbol)                   // while more input
      {
        int symboltype = classify(symbol);
        switch (symboltype)
          {
          case oprand: operandstack.push(atoi(symbol));   // operand is pushed
                    break;                  // on operand stack

          case openparen: operatorstack.push('(');        // open paren is pushed
                    break;                  // on operator stack

          case closeparen: while(true)     // pop and apply operators
                      { operatorstack.pop(OP);    // until open paren is
                        if (OP=='(') break;       // found. Pop it.
                              else apply(OP);
                      }
                    break;

          case oprator: while(true)
                      {                            // pop and apply
                        if (operatorstack.isempty()) break;   // operators
                        operatorstack.gettop(OP);             // until stack is
                        if(priority(OP) < priority(symbol[0]))  // empty or top
                            break;                            // has lower
                        operatorstack.pop(OP);                // priority than
                        apply(OP);                            // operator just
                      }                                       // read
                    operatorstack.push(symbol[0]);
          }
      }

    while (operatorstack.pop(OP)) apply(OP);    // pop and apply any operators
    operandstack.pop(result);                   // top operand is result
    cout << result;

    return 0;
}
```

Table 1.1 traces the algorithm as it evaluates the expression

$(6 + 4) * (3 + 17)/8$

● **TABLE 1.1** Trace of Program Evaluating (6 + 4) * (3 + 17)/8

Input	operandstack	operatorstack
(		(
6	6	(
+	6	+ (
4	4 6	+ (
)	10	
*	10	*
(	10	(*
3	3 10	(*
+	3 10	+ (*
17	17 3 10	+ (*
)	20 10	*
/	200	/
8	8 200	/
<end>	25	

Each line shows the state of the stacks (top to the left) after the algorithm has finished processing a particular input symbol.

Having determined the appropriate objects for an application, we turn our attention to implementation issues. Of greatest importance are questions concerning the size and life spans of the data. These aspects may determine more than any others how the object is implemented. These issues are examined in Section 1.4.

● 1.3.2 The Standard Template Library

The Standard Template Library (STL) is a C++ library of adaptors, algorithms, containers, function objects, and iterators; its principal authors are Alexander Stepanov and Meng Lee (Stepanov and Lee 1995). The STL contains many of the fundamental data structures used in programs (stacks, queues, strings, maps, and so on), as well as efficient versions of commonly used algorithms, including sorting and searching. STL components are highly parameterized. The STL has been adopted as a standard by the International Organization for Standardization (ISO/IEC) and by the American National Standards Institute (ANSI). However, current implementations of the STL vary from platform to platform; therefore programs using STL are not completely portable.

The use of STL components will be examined in the chapters that follow.

● 1.4 Objects and Secondary Memory

One aspect of an object in a particular application is its **persistence**, which is its life span. Some categories of persistence are:

- The object exists only during the execution of a particular statement block.
- The object exists only during the execution of a particular subprogram or function.
- The object exists only during the run of a particular program.
- The object exists indefinitely.

Consider, for example, the various stack objects in the following program.

```
#include <iostream.h>

stack C;            // lifespan: program

void test(int i)
{
stack B1;           // lifespan: execution of test

 if (i<100)
    {
        stack A1; // lifespan: program block
        ...
    }
  else { ... }
}

int main()
{
  stack B2;         // lifespan: execution of main
  int N;
  cin >> N;
  test(N);

  return 0;
}
```

The stacks in this program and, in general, the objects in the first three categories, are termed **transient**. They are typically implemented using main memory.

In Part Two of this book, we examine the implementation of objects that involve secondary memory in some way, either because the objects are large, because they are required to persist beyond the run of a program, or both. The following are some example of objects using secondary memory.

- Transient objects created and used by a compiler—perhaps holding intermediate code or parse trees. Although the objects are naturally transient, they may be too large to store in main memory and must therefore be implemented in secondary memory. They are typically discarded after compilation is complete.
- Objects manipulated by document processing software. Such software might need to store arbitrarily large clipboards, buffers containing deleted text (for possible restoration later), and stacks enabling unlimited use of an *undo* command. The user may wish to retain some of these objects to paste into other applications.
- Files of student records held by a college or an inventory database used by a business. These are both objects that have a long lifetime and are typically too large to store in main memory.
- Small and persistent objects. These are objects that are small enough to fit in main memory and that are held there when the program is running because of main memory's shorter access times. They are saved to secondary storage so that they are preserved. They can then be loaded back into memory for further processing. A spreadsheet is an example of such an object.

In the remaining chapters of Part One, we look at other objects that are usually implemented in main memory. In particular, we consider various implementations of the map abstract data type.

In the final two sections of this chapter, we look at two aspects of object implementation that appear throughout the text. Readers already familiar with recursion (Section 1.5) and measures of complexity, such as Big-O notation (Section 1.6), may wish to skip these sections.

1.5 Recursion

A recursive function is one that is defined, either directly or indirectly, in terms of itself. A simple example of a directly recursive function is *factorial*(N), which returns the product of the first N integers. The *factorial* function is defined for non-negative N as follows:

factorial(0) = 1
factorial(N) = 1 * 2 * 3 * ... N ($N > 0$)

Thus, we can define *factorial*(N) in terms of a simpler problem:

factorial(0) = 1
factorial(N) = N * *factorial*($N - 1$)   ($N > 0$)

This formulation leads to the following function definition:

```
int factorial (int N)
    {
        if (N==0)
            return 1;
        else return N * factorial (N-1);
    }
```

Note that there must be at least one nonrecursive path through the function in order to avoid infinite recursion. The nonrecursive paths typically correspond to the base cases. For comparison, here is an iterative version of the *factorial* function.

```
int factorial (int N)
{
    int result = 1;
    for (int i=2; i<=N; i++) result *= i;
    return result;
}
```

• 1.5.1 Examples of Recursion

Recursive functions do not have to be arithmetic. Each of the following recursive functions could be used to print N asterisks on the output ($N > 0$).

```
void printstars_1 (int N)
    {
        if (N>1) printstars_1(N-1);
        output("*");
    }

void printstars_2 (int N)
    {
        output("*");
        if (N>1) printstars_2(N-1);
    }
```

You may be interested in an algorithm that operates on a data structure. Consider the binary or logarithmic search for integer *Target* in a section ($A_{first}...A_{last}$) of an array of integers arranged in ascending order. Getting the terminating condition correct in an iterative solution to this problem can be tricky (Bentley 1983). In the following recursive function, we probe the middle of the array, then narrow the search area to approximately half of the original.

```
bool Search (int Target, int A[], int first, int last)
    {
```

```
    if (first>last) // nothing to search
        return  false;
    else
        {
        int mid = (first + last) / 2;
        if (A[mid]==target) return true; // found at the probe point
        if (A[mid]< target)
              return Search(Target,A,mid+1,last); // search first half
        else return Search(Target,A,first,mid-1);// search last half
        }
    }
```

A call to a recursive function may generate more than one recursive call, as shown in the following function that computes a binomial coefficient (think Pascal's triangle or the number of ways in which we can select k items from n items).

```
int bincoeff (int n,  int k)
{
   if (k==0) return 1;
   if (k==n) return 1;
   return  bincoeff(n-1,k) + bincoeff(n-1,k-1);
  }
```

A nonbase case spawns two additional calls. Another example of this multiple spawning is a recursive function to return the Nth integer in the Fibonacci sequence. The Fibonacci sequence is

1 1 2 3 5 8 13 21 34 ...

The first two integers (Fib_0 and Fib_1) are 1; thereafter, each term is the sum of the two previous terms. We might be tempted to write

```
int Fib (int N)
{
    if  (N <= 1)
                    return    1;
              else return Fib(N-1)+ Fib(N-2);
    }
```

but the number of calls required to compute $Fib(N)$ is large; it is at least as large as $Fib(N)$ itself (see Exercises). An iterative function to compute $Fib(N)$, although not as simple, is still straightforward (see Exercises) and much faster than the recursive one for large N.

Indirect Recursion

All of the examples in this section have been of a function directly calling itself. It is possible to have indirect recursion, in which function F_1 calls function F_2, which calls the next function, and so on, until at some point function F_i calls function F_1. Consider the following grammar rules for a very simple arithmetic expression:

expression → term + term | term − term | term

term   → factor * factor | factor /factor | factor

factor   → (expression) | letter | digit

We might design a parser in which there is a function for each nonterminal symbol in the grammar (*expression, term, factor*). Thus, when parsing the input, the function checking for *expression* might call the function checking for a *term*, which in turn calls the one checking for a *factor*, which, having seen a parenthesis, might call the function to check for an *expression*.

1.5.2 Iteration or Recursion?

Theory tells us that for any recursive function there is an equivalent iterative function, and vice versa (see the previous factorial example). So why might we choose one formulation of an algorithm over the other?

Advantages of Recursion

The following are some reasons why we might choose a recursive form for an algorithm.

1. A function cast in recursive form may be simpler or more elegant or more obviously correct. Consider the following function to fund the largest value in the first N elements of array A ($A_1 \ldots A_N$).

```
int biggest( int A[], int N)
    {
        if (N==1)
                return A[N];  // array only has one element
        else  return max( A[N], biggest(A,N-1) );
    }
```

2. A function has a natural recursive form. An example of a highly recursive function is Ackermann's function A, defined as follows.

$$A(m,n) = n + 1 \qquad\qquad \text{if } m = 0$$
$$= A(m - 1,1) \qquad\quad \text{if } m \neq 0 \text{ and } n = 0$$
$$= A(m - 1,A(m,n - 1)) \quad \text{if } m \neq 0 \text{ and } n \neq 0$$

We will return to Ackermann's function in Chapter 2. The Towers of Hanoi problem also has a short recursive solution. The problem is to move a stack of N discs, arranged smaller on top of larger, from one corner (*Source*) of a triangle to another corner (*Destination*), moving only one disc at a time. At no time is a larger disc permitted to be on top of a smaller one.

We define the solution in terms of a slightly smaller problem (moving $N - 1$ discs). After moving $N - 1$ discs from *Source* to the third corner (*Temp*), we can move the largest disc from *Source* to *Destination* and then move the $N - 1$ discs from *Temp* to *Destination*. The problem of moving $N - 1$ discs involves moving $N - 2$ discs, and so on. The following function will output a list of required moves.

```
void Hanoi (int N, int Source, int Destination, int Temp)
    {
    if (N>1) Hanoi (N-1, A, Temp, B);
    output("Move disc on ", A, "to", B);
    if (N>1) Hanoi (N-1, Temp, B, A);
    }
```

3. The recursive form of an algorithm matches well with the problem domain. Later chapters will demonstrate that some data structures (e.g., lists, trees) are recursive in nature and that some algorithms on these structures (e.g., searching) can be written very concisely using recursion.

Disadvantages of Recursion

Most of the disadvantages of recursion have to do with the efficiency of the compiled code. A function call has overheads of time and space (typically on the run-time stack). If space requirements are too great (e.g., the function is called with a very large parameter, resulting in many simultaneously active calls), the program may fail.

However, if our recursive definition has **tail recursion**, it can be modified by a clever compiler. The *printstars_2* function shown earlier is an example of tail recursion in that the recursive call comes at the end (tail) of the function body. Because the function exits immediately on returning from the recursive call, it is not necessary to retain the calling environment. A clever compiler can identify a tail recursive function and compile it into an iterative loop in which the recursive call is replaced by a jump back to the beginning of the loop. Typically, parameters are held in registers whose contents are updated on each iteration.

1.6 Measures of Complexity

It is important to be able to characterize the space and time requirements of an algorithm independent of its implementation on a particular system. This enables us to estimate the resources needed to process a particular data set and to compare algorithms. In some cases, it might be helpful to know the worst-case behavior of an algorithm as well as its best-case and average behavior. For example, if an algorithm has to be completed within a particular period of time, we may prefer algorithm A over algorithm B even though the average run time of A is longer if the worst-case behavior of A is not as bad as that of B.

• 1.6.1 Big-O and Related Analyses

Big-O and related analyses show how the run time and space requirements of an algorithm increase as the size of the data set increases. Here we will look only at time. Informally, if the run time of an algorithm is characterized as $O(n)$, it means that the run time is proportional to the size of the data set; if the size of the set doubles, we would expect the run time to double also. If the algorithm is $O(n^2)$, doubling the size of the data set would result in a fourfold increase in run time.

Big-O

More formally, Big-O notation provides a way to describe the upper bound on the time requirement of an algorithm.[9] For nonnegative functions f and g

$f(n)$ is $O(g(n))$[10] if there exist positive constants c and n_0 such that
$$f(n) \leq c * g(n) \text{ for all } n \geq n_0$$

This means that for sufficiently large n, the run time is bounded above by $g(n)$. Table 1.2 gives some example functions.

Figure 1.4 shows the relationship between f and g pictorially.

For Big-O analysis, we are interested in what we might think of as the least upper bound on f. Thus, although it is true that $f(n) = 5n + 17$ is $O(n)$ and $O(n^2)$ and $O(n^3)$

• TABLE 1.2 Example Bounds on Functions

Function	is	because	for all	c	n_0
$5n + 17$	$O(n)$	$5n + 17 \leq 6n$	$n \geq 17$	6	17
$20n^2 + 15n + 7$	$O(n^2)$	$20n^2 + 15n + 7 \leq 21n^2$	$n \geq 16$	21	16
$7 * 2^n + n^2$	$O(2^n)$	$7 * 2^n + n^2 \leq 8 * 2^n$	$n \geq 4$	8	4

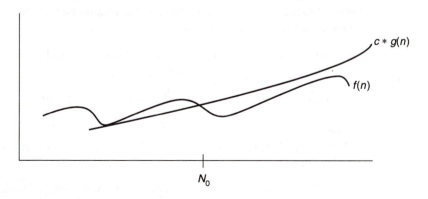

Figure 1.4 • f(n) is O(g(n))

● TABLE 1.3 Common Characteristic Functions

		$n = 4$	$n = 64$	$n = 1,024$
O(1)	constant	1	1	1
O(log N)	logarithmic	2	6	10
O(N)	linear	4	64	1024
O(N log N)		8	384	10,240
O(N^2)	quadratic	16	4,096	$2^{20} \approx$ 1 million
O(N^3)	cubic	64	262,144	$2^{30} \approx$ 1 billion
O(2^N)	exponential	16	2^{64}	2^{1024}

and so on, we characterize it as O(n) because we want the closest bound. Normally, the constant factors are not important. For example, if the run time for algorithm A is $100n + 50$ and for algorithm B it is $n^2 + 5$, we would not use algorithm B unless we were dealing with only small data sets. The seven most common algorithm characterizations are shown in Table 1.3.

Little-o
The difference between Big-O and Little-o is that a Little-o function has to be strictly greater than $f(n)$, thus

$f(n)$ is o($g(n)$)   if there exist positive constants c and n_0 such that
$$f(n) < c * g(n) \text{ for all } n \geq n_0$$

Big-Omega
We can also describe the lower bound on run time; that is, the time the algorithm would require to run even in the most favorable circumstances. We use Ω (Greek Omega) rather than O and define

$f(n)$ is $\Omega(g(n))$ if there exist positive constants c and n_0 such that
$$f(n) \geq c * g(n) \text{ for all } n \geq n_0$$

Figure 1.5 shows this relationship between f and g pictorially.

Little-Omega
If the bounding function is strictly less than $f(n)$ then we use ω (little omega) rather than Ω.

$f(n)$ is $\omega(g(n))$ if there exist positive constants c and n_0 such that
$$f(n) > c * g(n) \text{ for all } n \geq n_0$$

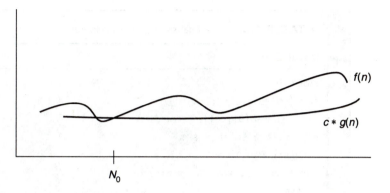

Figure 1.5 • $f(n)$ is $\Omega(g(n))$

Big-Theta

Big-Theta (Θ) bounds a function both from above and from below, thus we need two constants.

$f(n)$ is $\Theta(g(n))$ if there exist positive constants c_1, c_2, and n_0 such that

$$c_1 * g(n) \le f(n) \le c_2 * g(n) \text{ for all } n \ge n_0$$

This relationship between functions f and g is shown pictorially in Figure 1.6.

What Are We Measuring and How Do We Determine It?

We typically measure the steps in the algorithm. In the algorithm, there are likely to be sections with different complexity measures. Generally speaking, we take the highest-order component to characterize the behavior of the algorithm as a whole. The first column of Table 1.4 contains a pseudocode algorithm to find which row in the $N \times N$ matrix M has the highest total of entries. The corresponding entries in

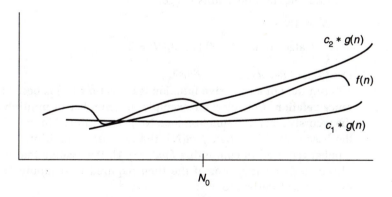

Figure 1.6 • $f(n)$ is $\Theta(g(n))$

● **TABLE 1.4** Matrix Analysis Algorithm and Instruction Counts

Instruction	Count
sum = 0	1
for (col=0; col<N; col++)	$N + 1$
sum+=M[0][col]	N
highesttotalsofar = sum	1
highestrowsofar = 0	1
for (row = 1; row <N; row++)	N
sum = 0	$N - 1$
for (col=0; col<N; col++)	$(N + 1)(N - 1)$
sum+=M[row][col]	$N(N - 1)$
if (sum>highesttotalsofar)	$N - 1$
highesttotalsofar = sum	$N - 1$
highestrowsofar = row	$N - 1$
output(highestrowsofar)	1

the second column are the number of times the line will be executed (in the case of the conditional statements, we give the worst case).

We could characterize the run time based on the sum of the line counts as

$$2N^2 + 6N$$

and hence as $O(n^2)$ ($c = 3$, $N_0 = 6$) and as $o(n^2)$ ($c = 3$, $N_0 = 7$).

Table 1.5 contains another algorithm with instruction counts. The algorithm in Table 1.5 is part of a selection sort of elements 1 through N of array AR.

Summing the line counts we get

$$2N^2 + 4N - 4$$

thus the algorithm is $O(n^2)$ ($c = 3$, $N_0 = 3$).

What About Recursive Algorithms?

The run time of a recursive function (see Section 1.5) is best expressed by a **recurrence relation**. Consider, for example, the number of multiplications required by the recursive factorial function *fact*. None are required in *fact*(0) or *fact*(1); these are the base cases. For other *fact*(N), the number of multiplications is one plus the number required in computing *fact*(N − 1). We assume that the number of multiplications is an indicator of the time required to compute *fact*(N), and thus we express this time as follows:

$$T(n) = T(n - 1) + 1 \text{ for } n > 1$$

● **TABLE 1.5** Selection Sort Algorithm and Instruction Counts

Instruction	Count
`for (i=1; i<N; i++)`	N
`  indexsmallest = i`	$N - 1$
`  smallest = AR[i]`	$N - 1$
`  for (j=i+1; j <= N; j++)`	$N(N + 1)/2$
`        if AR[j] < smallest`	$N(N - 1)/2$
`                indexsmallest=j`	$N(N - 1)/2$
`                smallest = AR[j]`	$N(N - 1)/2$
`AR[indexsmallest] = AR[i]`	$N - 1$
`AR[i] = smallest`	$N - 1$

We typically wish to replace a recurrence relation by a closed form solution. One approach is repeated substitutions into the right-hand side as follows.

$$T(n) = T(n - 1) + 1$$
$$= (T(n - 2) + 1) + 1 \qquad = T(n - 2) + 2$$
$$= (T(n - 3) + 1) + 1) + 1 \qquad = T(n - 3) + 3$$
$$= (T(n - 4) + 1) + 1) + 1) + 1 \qquad = T(n - 4) + 4$$
$$\cdots$$
$$= (T(n - (n - 1)) + (n - 1)$$
$$= T(1) + n - 1$$
$$= n - 1$$
$$= O(n)$$

The following example is the time necessary to mergesort an array of n items (see Chapter 10). No time is required if there is only one item to sort, so $T(1) = 0$; otherwise, we sort the two halves of the array and then merge them together.

$$T(n) = 2T(n/2) + n \qquad n > 1$$

Substituting, we get

$$T(n) = 2T(n/2) + n$$
$$= 2(2T(n/4) + n/2) + n \qquad = 4T(n/4) + 2n$$
$$= 4(2T(n/8) + n/4) + 2n \qquad = 8T(n/8) + 3n$$
$$= 8(2T(n/16) + n/8) + 3n \qquad = 16T(n/16) + 4n$$
$$\cdots$$
$$= 2^i T(n/2^i) + i * n$$

$$= nT(1) + \log n * n$$
$$= n\log n$$
$$= O(n \log n)$$

The final example of a recurrence relation is presented without an associated algorithm (see Exercises).

$$T(1) = 1$$
$$T(n) = T(n - 1) + n \quad n > 1$$

Substituting, we get

$$T(n) = T(n - 1) + n$$
$$= T(n - 2) + (n - 1) + n$$
$$= T(n - 3) + (n - 2) + (n - 1) + n$$
$$= T(n - 4) + (n - 3) + (n - 2) + (n - 1) + n$$
$$\cdots$$
$$= T(n - (n - 1) + (n - (n - 2)) + \ldots (n - 1) + n$$
$$= T(1) + 2 + 3 + \ldots n$$
$$= 1 + 2 + 3 + \ldots n$$
$$= n(n + 1)/2$$
$$= O(n^2)$$

1.6.2 Complexity of Problems

Theoreticians are interested in discovering lower bounds on the complexity of problems; that is, what is the inherent work that must be done by any algorithm that solves the problem. Consider the problem of multiplying two N by N matrices. We know that a multiplication algorithm must be at least $O(N^2)$ because it must access each of the matrix elements. We know it is no worse than $O(N^3)$ because we can easily write an $O(N^3)$ algorithm. So the question is, what is the inherent complexity of matrix multiplication? At present, the best-known algorithm for determining the complexity of a multiplication algorithm is the one devised by Coppersmith and Winograd (1990); it is $O(N^{2.376})$.

Consider the problem of sorting an array of N items into order. It can be shown that any sorting method based on key comparisons must be at least $O(N \log N)$. This is based on considering the sorting algorithm as traversing a binary decision tree. The number of leaves in the tree is the number of permutations of the N items to be sorted (i.e., $N!$). The height of the tree is $\log(N!)$, which is $\Omega(N \log N)$. Thus, the number of decisions/comparisons is $\Omega(N \log N)$; therefore, we cannot find a key-comparison sorting algorithm that runs faster than $O(N \log N)$.

Various classes of problem have been defined; we consider some of them next.

Class P

Interest in identifying those problems for which there is a "fast" solution predates modern computers. Edmonds (1965) argues that polynomial-time is a good formalization of efficient computation. Thus, we arrive at the class P of problems, where for each problem there exists a polynomial $P(n)$ such that the number of computing steps required on input x of length n is bounded above by $P(n)$. Examples of problems in the class P include sorting an array, multiplying two matrices, and computing $factorial(x)$.

Class NP

The class NP (nondeterministic polynomial) was identified by Cook (1971). A problem is in NP if one can verify a solution in polynomial time. Whether P equals NP is an open question that some would argue is the most important unanswered question in computer science. The set NP-P contains problems (such as the Traveling Salesman, discussed later) for which no polynomial time solution is currently known. However, we cannot yet prove that no polynomial time solution can exist.

Problem Reduction

If any instance of problem A can be reduced to an instance of problem B, then we can say that B is at least as difficult as A. Two examples of this follow.

1. We can reduce multiplication to the problem of squaring a number by observing that

   $$A * B = ((A + B)^2 - (A - B)^2) / 4$$

   Thus squaring is at least as difficult as multiplying, because if it were easier, we could obtain a faster multiply by converting all multiplications to squarings (plus linear time overheads).
2. Consider the problem of finding a combination of values on its N inputs that makes a certain Boolean circuit output true. (This is the satisfiability problem, which will be discussed in detail later.) We can use this problem to determine if an N-bit integer X is prime as follows. We design a circuit that has $2*N$ inputs representing two N-bit binary integers. The circuit multiplies the two integers and reports whether the result is X and neither input number is 1. We have reduced testing the primeness of X to an instance of the satisfiability problem. Thus, satisfiability is at least as difficult as finding a prime.

Class NP-Complete

NP-complete problems are the most difficult NP problems. All NP-complete problems are equivalent (with polynomial time transformation). If any NP-complete problem is in P, then all NP problems are in P. The first problem identified as NP-complete was the satisfiability problem just described. Cook showed that all NP

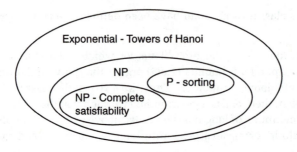

Figure 1.7 • Classes of Problems

problems could be transformed to an instance of the satisfiability problem. Other NP-complete problems include the following:

- Traveling salesman. Given a set of cities and the distances between them, find the shortest path that visits each city exactly once.
- Clique. Find the size of the maximal complete subgraph of a graph.
- Knapsack. Given a set of items each with a certain size and value, find a subset that will fit in a backpack of size B and have total value of at least K.

Figure 1.7 shows the currently known relationships among the various classes of problems.

In addition to P, NP, and NP-complete, Figure 1.7 also shows problems known not to have a polynomial time solution. Examples of such problems are the Towers of Hanoi and finding the best move in a game of chess. Not shown are the undecidable problems, such as the halting problem, for which we can prove that no algorithm can exist.

● Chapter Summary

This chapter introduced the concept of an object and contrasted the object-based approach to program design with the algorithmic approach. The former permits the construction of reusable components and may enable software engineering to become somewhat more like electrical engineering in terms of component use. Hierarchies of objects can be defined. If a needed object is not already defined, it may be possible to derive it from a more general object using an inheritance mechanism.

A characteristic of the C++ object implementation is the use of templates that enable programmers to parameterize an object definition. The Standard Template Library (STL) is a collection of highly parameterized objects and algorithms, further reducing the need for programmers to write programs and algorithms from scratch.

One of the characteristics of an object is its persistence. Within a program, there might be short-lived objects and longer-lived objects. Persistence is one of the factors that determines whether an object is implemented in main memory or in secondary memory. Part Two of this text considers file-based objects.

We also looked at the concept of a recursive algorithm and noted some of the advantages (elegance, natural match with the problem domain) and disadvantages (run-time overhead) of using such algorithms.

Finally, we described a notation that enables programmers to characterize the run-time behavior of an algorithm independent of its implementation platform. We noted that there is a class of problem for which no polynomial-time algorithm is known, and it is not known whether such an algorithm can exist.

● Exercises

1. How does inheritance enable software engineers to build software more quickly?

2. How does information hiding ease the modification of existing software?

3. Consider a bank account abstract data type (class).

    a. What would be the public components of such a type?

    b. What would be the private components?

4. Show that the number of calls required to compute $Fib(N)$ is at least as large as $Fib(N)$ itself.

5. Write an iterative function to compute $Fib(N)$.

6. Devise an iterative function $Hanoi$ for the Towers of Hanoi problem. A call to function $Hanoi(N,A,B,temp)$ should output the sequence of moves required to move a pile of N discs from corner A to corner B using third-corner $temp$ as required.

7. Write a recursive function to find the greatest common divisor (GCD) of two positive integers. For example, $GCD(63, 108) = 9$

8. Find the simplest example you can of an algorithm that has the characteristics of the third example of a recurrence relation.

9. Fill in the blanks in the following table.

Function	is	because	for all	c	n_0
$5n^3 - n^2 + 7$					
$20n^4 + 100$					
$3n - 5$					

10. We defined Big-Theta but not Little-theta. How would you define Little-theta? Is Little-theta useful?

● Problems

1. Modify the expression evaluation program so that it handles ill-formed expressions gracefully. Examples of such expressions are:

   6 * (4 − 7

   6 + * 3

) * 3

2. Define an industrial-strength version of the counter class.

3. Modify the expression evaluation program so that it evaluates Boolean expressions with AND, OR, and NOT operators.

4. Extend the stack definition presented in Section 1.2 so that a user can

   a. Find out how many items there are in the stack.

   b. Replace the top item on the stack with a new one without affecting the other items.

   c. "Wipe out" the stack (remove all items).

   Show how these extensions can be implemented by

   a. Writing a new stack definition from scratch

   b. Deriving a definition from the existing one

5. Add to the stack definition a facility for giving a stack a name (or an appropriate default). Both the constructor and destructor should output the name when called. Modify the stack example program presented in Section 1.4 so that it traces the construction and destruction of stacks.

6. Suppose you were designing a class for a two-dimensional array abstract data type. What operations would you permit and what benefits might a user get from using your class rather than the built-in data type?

7. Symmetric square arrays occur in many applications. In such an array, the element in row i column j has the same value as the element in row j column i. Thus, we only need to store a triangular array. However, programming languages do not allow us to declare triangular arrays. Suppose we define a class *symmetric* that can be used in a program in the following way:

```
symmetric M (10,10);     // declaration of 10 3 10 symmetric array


X = M.getvalue(i,j);     // get value from row i column j and store in X


M.putvalue(p,q,99);      // put value 99 in row p column q
```

Outline an appropriate definition for the class *symmetric*. Your answer should include:

a. How the required space is computed and allocated

b. Details of either *putvalue* or *getvalue*

8. Using the stack definition of Section 1.2 as a guide, write a C++ class definition for a queue.

9. A *deque* is a linear data structure that permits items to be added and removed from either end (in contrast to a stack, in which all activity takes place at one end). Write and test a class definition for a deque derived from the base class *stack*.

● References

Bentley, J. 1983. Programming pearls: Writing correct programs. *Communications of the ACM* 26(12): 1040–1045.

Cook, S. A. 1971. The complexity of theorem proving procedure. *Proceedings of the 3rd ACM Symposium on the Theory of Computing*, 151–158.

Coppersmith, D., and S. Winograd. 1990. Matrix multiplication via arithmetic progressions. *Journal of Symbolic Computing* 9: 251–280.

Edmonds, J. 1965. Paths, trees, and flowers. *Canadian Journal of Mathematics* 17: 449–467.

Stefik, M., and D. Bobrow. 1986. Object-oriented programming: Themes and variations. *AI Magazine* 6(4): 40–62.

Stepanov, A., and M. Lee. 1995. *The Standard Template Library.* Hewlett-Packard Technical Report, HPL-94-34.

● Notes

[1]The *include*d header file *iostream.h* includes definitions of *cin* and *cout*. These are objects that permit interactive input and output, respectively.

- In C++, the main program appears as a function called *main*.

- We can combine declaration (e.g., of *counter1*) with initialization.

- The "not equal" operator is !=. The test for equality is ==. (Yes, this does cause problems!)

- *A%B* yields the remainder on dividing *A* by *B*.

- The effect of *i++* is to increase the contents of *i* by 1.

- The endl item in the output stream causes a new line to be taken in the output.

[2]In C++, all subprograms are termed *functions*. The general form of a function definition (optional components in italics) is:

type-of-value-returned name (*parameter-list*) {*body-of-function*}

- The constructor function has the same name as the class itself.

- In specifying a parameter, you can also specify a default value that the parameter takes if omitted from a call of the function. Here the default value of the parameter of the constructor is 0.

- Type *void* indicates that the function does not return a value.

- The effect of *i* += *j* is to add *j* to *i*.

- The *return* statement exits the function. If followed by a value, that value is the one returned by the function.

[3]Because of the way we have used variables in our definition, *Type* may be replaced only by types for which 0 and 1 are meaningful values and for which the assignment and += operators have been defined.

[4]If the file name following #*include* is enclosed in double quotes rather than angle brackets, then the compiler looks for it in the current directory rather than in the system directory of header files.

[5]The base class (*counter*) on which we are basing *general_counter* is specified in the class heading. In order for *general_counter* to be legal, we have to recategorize the *data* member of *counter* as *protected* rather than *private*. Protected is an intermediate category between public and private. Protected members can be accessed by members of derived classes.

[6]This approach may also reduce the space required by instances of the class. A function prototype is just the function heading giving the type of value returned, the name of the function, and the type of any parameters. It gives enough information to enable the compiler to detect whether a call of the function is valid.

[7]• *Push* and *pop* will each return true if they succeed and false if they fail (e.g., if we try to pop from an empty stack).

- The parameter of *pop* is passed by reference, thus we can update it. This is indicated by the ampersand following the type specification.

- We choose to fix the stack size at 100. Later we will see better ways of defining the size of and allocating space for data components.

- Text from // to the end of the line is commentary.

[8]• The *switch* statement implements a multiway branch. Here we are branching on the value in *symtype*. The *break* statement transfers control to the statement following the switch and is necessary to avoid falling into the next case. Optionally, you can have a "catch-all" *default* case.

- The *atoi* function (found in header *stdlib.h*) converts a string of digits to the corresponding integer.

[9]Big-O has a long history and is actually Big (Greek) Omicron.

[10]Read this as "f of n is big oh of g of n."

Lists and Strings

2.1 Introduction

This chapter examines two relatively simple, linear data structures. Section 2.2 introduces the list abstract data type, then Section 2.3 looks at ways in which it might be implemented. The STL supports lists, and Section 2.4 examines some of the STL's components. Section 2.5 examines the types of structures that result if elements of a list are lists themselves. Section 2.6 explores three applications of lists. In Section 2.7, (character) strings, another linear data structure, are considered, and in Section 2.8 we look at implementation and support for strings through libraries. Finally, string applications are presented in Section 2.9.

2.2 Basic List Operations

A **list** is an ordered sequence of data items of the same type. The sequence is ordered in the sense that we can talk about the fourth item preceding the fifth item. The sequence is not necessarily ordered in the sense that the value of the fourth item has any particular relation to the value of the fifth item. The list abstract data type has the following operations defined:

Getlength()	Returns the number of items in the list.
Findposition(*item*)	Returns the position of the item or an indication that the item is not present. If there are duplicate items, it returns the location of the first.
Finditem(*position*)	Returns the item in the given list position; undefined if the position does not exist.
Remove(*position*)	Removes the item in the given position; fails if the position is not defined for the list.
Insert(*item,position*)	Puts the item in the specified position; fails if the position is not defined for the list.

Thus, if our list *L* is [*p b r n a h*] and we assume that elements are numbered from zero upwards:

L.Getlength()	returns 6
L.Findposition(*a*)	returns 4
L.Finditem(3)	returns *n*
L.Remove(4) makes the list [*p b r n h*]	
L.Insert(*f*,1) makes the list [*p f b r n h*]	

2.3 List Implementations

This section looks at ways of implementing lists, beginning with array-based methods and then introducing linked storage.

2.3.1 Arrays

Figure 2.1 shows one way in which the final list *L* could be implemented using an array.

We have allocated an array (*data*) having *max* elements to hold the list data items. The current number of list elements is stored separately in variable *count*. The size of the array is an upper bound on the growth of the list. Two of our list operations are fast: *getlength* and *finditem* are both O(1). However, *findposition* requires a linear search of the array, and both *remove* and *insert* may require items

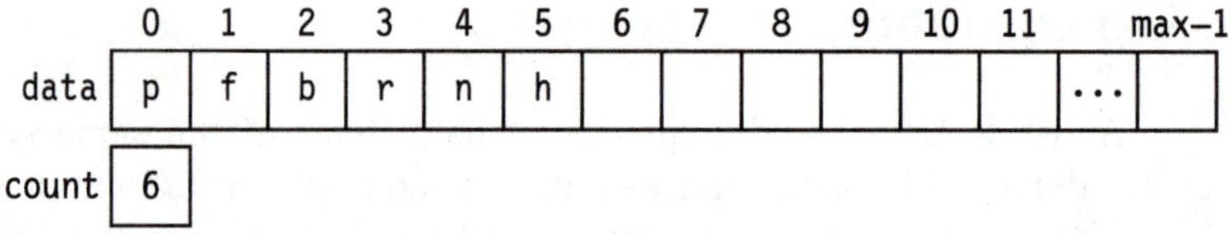

Figure 2.1 • An array implementation of list [*p f b r n h*]

0 1 2 3 4 5 6 7 8 9 10 11 max−1
data
p f r n h ...
count
5

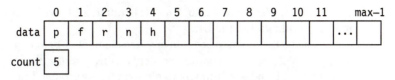

Figure 2.2 • The list shown in Figure 2.1 with *b* removed

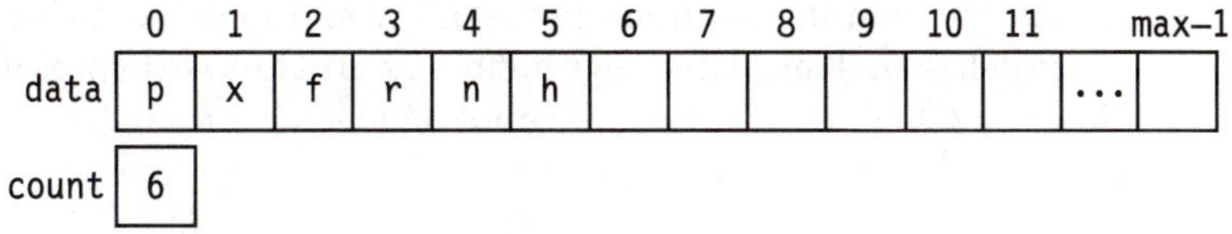

0 1 2 3 4 5 6 7 8 9 10 11 max−1
data
p x f r n h ...
count
6

Figure 2.3 • The list from Figure 2.2 with *x* inserted

to be shuffled in the list; these three operations are O(*N*). For example, if we call *remove*(2) on the list in Figure 2.1, we get the list shown in Figure 2.2.

It was necessary to move *r*, *n*, and *h* to the left. Similarly, if we call *insert*(*x*,1) on the list from Figure 2.2, we need to move *f*, *r*, *n*, and *h* to the right, resulting in the list shown in Figure 2.3.

An Alternative Array Implementation

Figure 2.4 shows an alternative way to use arrays that does not require elements to be moved during an insert or remove operation.

In this representation, the data items need not be adjacent or in order; they are placed in arbitrary locations in *data*. The value in *root* is the index of the first item in the list. Thereafter, each element points to the next in the following manner. The value in *next*[*i*] indicates the location of the item that follows *data*[*i*] in the list or it contains the "impossible" location value of −1 if *data*[*i*] is the last item in the list.

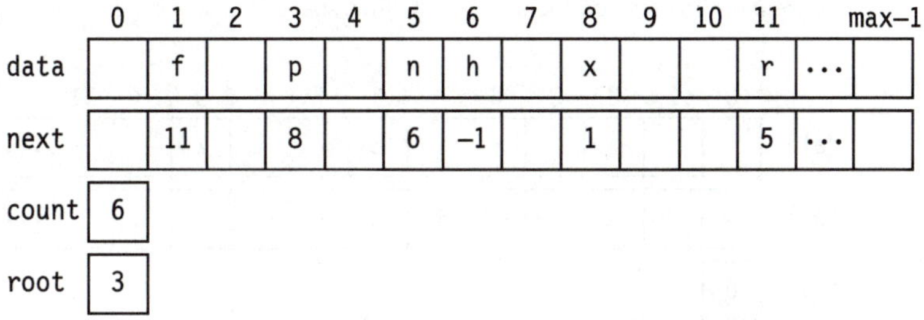

0 1 2 3 4 5 6 7 8 9 10 11 max−1
data
f p n h x r ...
next
11 8 6 −1 1 5 ...
count
6
root
3

Figure 2.4 • An alternative way to use arrays to store the list [*p x f r n h*]

For example, f is in *data*[1] and *next*[1] contains 11, which is the location of r, the item that follows f in the list.

To insert a new item, place it in any free element of *data* and update *next* appropriately. Figure 2.5 shows a possible result of calling *insert*(w,3) on the list from Figure 2.4.

We have placed w arbitrarily in element 9 and arranged for it to point to r by setting *next*[9] to 11. We updated the pointer from f so that it points to w and not to r. How do we know that a particular element of *data* is available for use? We can use a reserved value (perhaps −2) in *next*[j] to signify that *data*[j] is available. Figure 2.6 shows what the list from Figure 2.5 would look like using this convention.

To delete an item, just arrange for the chain of links to bypass it and set the unneeded link to −2. Figure 2.7 shows the result of deleting x from the list in Figure 2.6.

	0	1	2	3	4	5	6	7	8	9	10	11	max−1
data		f		p		n	h		x	w		r	···	
next		9		8		6	−1		1	11		5	···	
count	7													
root	3													

Figure 2.5 • The list from Figure 2.4 with w inserted, yielding [p x f w r n h]

	0	1	2	3	4	5	6	7	8	9	10	11	max−1
data		f		p		n	h		x	w		r	···	
next	−2	9	−2	8	−2	6	−1	−2	1	11	−2	5	···	−2
count	7													
root	3													

Figure 2.6 • The list from Figure 2.5 with "free space" markers in *next*

	0	1	2	3	4	5	6	7	8	9	10	11	max−1
data		f		p		n	h		x	w		r	···	
next	−2	9	−2	1	−2	6	−1	−2	−2	11	−2	5	···	−2
count	6													
root	3													

Figure 2.7 • The list from Figure 2.6 with x deleted: [p f w r n h]

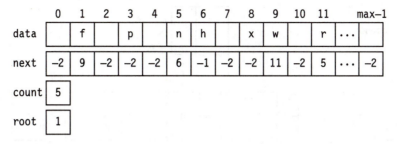

	0	1	2	3	4	5	6	7	8	9	10	11	max−1
data		f		p		n	h		x	w		r	...	
next	−2	9	−2	−2	−2	6	−1	−2	−2	11	−2	5	...	−2

count | 5

root | 1

Figure 2.8 • List from Figure 2.7 with the first item removed: [*f w r n h*]

The chain of links now goes from *p* to *f* instead of from *p* to *x* to *f*. Note that *x* is still in *data*, but the fact that *next*[9] is −2 indicates that *data*[9] is available for use by an *insert* operation. Figure 2.8 shows what happens when the first item in a list is deleted. This is the only kind of deletion that causes the *root* variable to change.

Rather than have two arrays, we could have a single array in which each element is a (data,link) pair, but such a list would still be bounded and be a waste of space when the list is less than its maximum length. For these reasons, lists are usually implemented using linked dynamic storage; we look at one version of this method in the next section.

2.3.2 Single-Linked Lists

In a linked dynamic storage implementation, we allocate as many list **nodes** as we need to store the list. Nodes are allocated from the heap at run time. Each node contains a data item and, in the single-linked version, either a pointer to the next item in the list or a recognizable end-of-list (*NULL*) value. A root pointer points to the first node of the list. Figure 2.9 shows how the list [*p b r n a h*] might be stored using single-linked nodes.

This type of structure is known as a single-linked list because each node has a single link to an adjacent one. Although these lists do not provide fast direct access to a particular element, as occurs with arrays, the memory allocated to the list can grow and shrink with the size of the list and is bounded only by the available heap space.

If we have a pointer to the appropriate list node, then an insertion or a deletion at that point can be done in constant time. Suppose, for example, we call *insert*(*g*,3) on the list from Figure 2.9. If we have a pointer to the insertion point (the current third node), then the insertion operation is

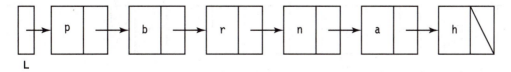

Figure 2.9 • Single-linked implementation of list [*p b r n a h*]

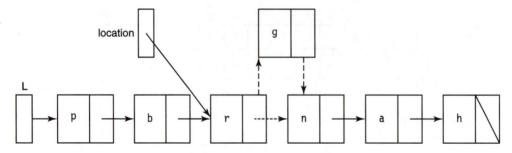

Figure 2.10 • Item *g* inserted into the list from Figure 2.9

1. Create a node containing *g* and a copy of the pointer in the third node.
2. Change the pointer in the third node to point to the new node.

This is illustrated in Figure 2.10, where *location* is the pointer.

Without pointer *location* identifying the insertion point, we would have to traverse the list to that point; this is an O(*N*) operation.

Similar adjustments allow us to remove an item from a list. If the current list is as shown in Figure 2.9, a call *remove*(*2*) changes a pointer so that the second element is removed, as shown in Figure 2.11. Again, with a pointer (*location*) to the existing node that will be modified, this is an O(1) operation.

Removing the first item in a linked list is a special case. There is no need for *location,* and the value in the root pointer (*L*) changes to point to the second item in the list.

Memory Allocation and Deallocation
When space is needed for a new node, we invoke a mechanism to allocate that space from the heap memory pool. When an allocated section of memory is no longer needed (as in the case of a node deleted from a list), it should be returned to the heap by the program. This memory reclamation process in C++ contrasts with

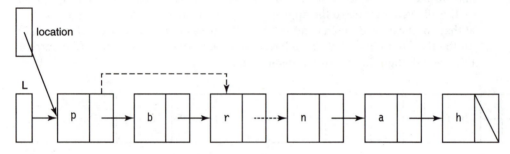

Figure 2.11 • Item *b* removed from the list from Figure 2.9

some other programming language environments (e.g., Java) that provide automatic garbage collection. A **garbage collector** is a program that runs in the background and identifies and returns the free space storage that can no longer be reached from any active memory location. C++ does not have a garbage collector, so it is the responsibility of the programmer to explicitly return unused memory. Failure to do so results in the program having a **memory leak**, which may prevent successful operation of the program due to heap space becoming exhausted.

Implementation: Node and Linked List

Our implementation of a single-linked list will involve two class definitions: one for a node and one for the list itself. We use templates to define a generic linked list class. Our first version of the node class is:

```
template <class Entry>
class listnode
{
  private: Entry data;
           listnode *next;
};
```

Our first version of the list class will have just the basic interfaces discussed earlier.

```
template <class Entry>
class linkedlist
{
  public: linkedlist();          // constructor - initialize root
          ~linkedlist();         // destructor - reclaim memory
          int Getlength();
          int Finditem(Entry X);   // return position or -1
          bool Finditem(int i,Entry& X);  // get ith item. False if none
          bool remove (int i);        // remove ith list element
          bool insert (Entry X,int i);    // insert new item

  private: listnode<Entry> *root;
};
```

Now we can have, for example:

```
linkedlist<int> numbers;
linkedlist<char> char_list;
```

and so on.

Some functions (e.g., *insert* and *remove*) will return *false* if they fail to perform the required operation. For instance, *remove* would return *false* if we call it to remove an item that does not exist; *insert* would return *false* if there is no more free space or if the position into which we are trying to insert is not defined.

Friend Classes

Normally, the private components of a class are not accessible by functions in another class. However, the functions in the *linkedlist* class need to be able to access the *data* and *next* components of objects of the *listnode* class. A solution is to designate *linkedlist* as a friend class of class *listnode*. In general, if class A is a friend of class B, then the functions of A are permitted to access the private components of objects in class B.

Recursion and Linked Lists

A linked list is a recursive structure because a list is either empty or it can be regarded as a first item (head) followed by a list (tail). For instance, note how the following list

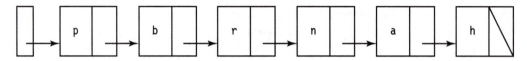

can be regarded as

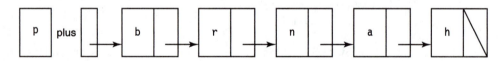

which in turn can be regarded as

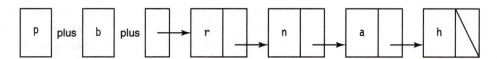

Thus, if *print(L)* prints the contents of the list rooted in *L*, then *print(L→next)* prints the tail of that list.[1] We can devise compact, elegant, recursive functions for performing common operations on lists. For instance, the following function returns the length of a list:

```
int llength (listnode *L)
    { // returns length of list rooted in L
      if (L == NULL) return 0;
              else return 1+llength(L->next);
    }
```

A corresponding iterative function is

```
int llength (listnode  *L)
    {
      listnode *P=L;
      int count = 0;

      while (P != NULL) { count++;   P=P->next;}
      return count;
    }
```

As a second example, consider the problem of printing the list in reverse. Assuming that the data items being stored in the list have the stream-insertion operator (<<) defined in order to display their contents, the recursive function is simply

```
void printlistbackwards(listnode *L)
    {
    if (L != NULL)
        {
          printlistbackwards(L->next);
          cout << L->data;
        }
    }
```

The corresponding iterative function is not as simple, and is left as an Exercise. A third example of recursion is a function that returns the last item in a nonempty list.

```
Entry lastone(node *L)
    {
      if (L->next == NULL)  // single-element list?
          return L->data;
      else   return lastone(L->Next);
    }
```

Construction of an equivalent iterative function is also left as an Exercise.

Although the definition of a recursive function can be compact, and recursive definitions might be more apparently correct, there are disadvantages to recursive functions. The overheads associated with function calls are likely to make a call that requires several levels of recursion that take significantly longer to execute than an equivalent call that uses iteration. In addition, the run-time space requirements of recursion may limit applicability; for example, a recursive call to find the length of a list with hundreds of elements may exhaust system resources.

Now let us turn to the function definitions for our *linkedlist* class. We use recursion, despite the caveats just mentioned, in order to keep the definitions simple.

Typically, a public driver function calls a private recursive function. This arrangement keeps the number of parameters of the public function to a minimum. For example, consider function *finditem* that returns the position in the list of a given item (or −1 if the item is not in the list). The public function is

```
int Finditem(Entry X) {return find_aux(0,X,root);}
```

and the corresponding private function *find_aux* does all the work.

```
int find_aux(int N, Entry X, listnode* L)
  {
   if (L == NULL)    return -1;      // list is empty
   if (X == L->data) return N;       // item is the first in list
   return find_aux(N+1,X,L->next);   // search rest of list
  }
```

Constructor and Destructor Functions

The constructor function will simply set the root node to NULL. The destructor function is responsible for deallocating the space used by the list and returning it to the heap. In an environment with a garbage collector, you could set the root to NULL, and the space used by the list would later be identified as unreachable and returned to the heap. Unfortunately, in C++, you need to be more involved in the space release. In particular, you need to be careful not to delete the only pointer to a node before you have deallocated that node. Deallocation can be done recursively, thus we have the destructor

```
~linkedlist() { release_aux(root); }
```

In the private section, we have a function that releases the space pointed to from the current node before releasing the current node itself.

```
void release_aux(listnode<Entry> *&t)
 {
  if (t != NULL)
   { release_aux(t->next);
     delete t;
   }
```

Copy Constructor: The Problem and a Solution

The Problem—There are places in a C++ program where a copy of an object is made either explicitly or implicitly. Examples are:

- An object is passed by value as the parameter of a function call.
- An object is returned as the result of a function.

- An object is assigned from one variable to another.

Normally, these copy operations work correctly. However, if objects of a class contain dynamically allocated storage, the built-in operators that copy objects do not work correctly. They only perform a top-level (shallow) copy rather than a correct (deep) duplication.

Consider a *linkedlist* object. Instead of creating a new list that is a copy of the old one, the default copy operation will create a new object having a root pointer that points to the old list. This causes a problem if the list being copied is then destroyed (e.g., by the action of a destructor function). Consider the following:

```
linkedlist<char> X;

void dummy()
{
        linkedlist<char> Y;

        Y.insert('a',1); Y.insert('t',1); Y.insert('c',2);

        X = Y;
}
```

After the calls to *insert*, list *Y* (local to function *dummy*) contains three characters, as depicted in Figure 2.12.

During a call to *dummy*, list *Y* appears to be assigned to list *X*, but all that happens is that the root pointer in *Y* is copied to the root pointer in *X*, as shown in Figure 2.13.

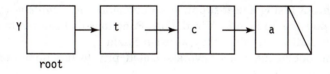

Figure 2.12 • Local list *Y*

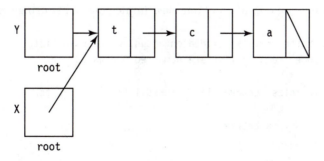

Figure 2.13 • Shallow copy of *Y* to *X*

Public Function	Private Function
Getlength	llength
Finditem(X)	find_aux
Finditem(I,X)	find_aux2
insert	insert_aux
remove	remove_aux
destructor, replicator	release_aux

• **TABLE 2.1** Public and Corresponding Private Functions in the *Linkedlist* Class

On exit from the function call, the destructor of the local variable Y is invoked, the list pointed to from Y is reclaimed, and, as a consequence, the root pointer in X is left pointing to space that has been returned to the heap. (It is worth noting that most other object-oriented languages do not have this problem of shallow copying.)

A Solution—To deal with contexts in which you truly need to duplicate an object, you need to have (1) a replicator method (copy constructor) and (2) an overloaded assignment operator as part of the class definition. These will be used in place of the system defaults. You must ensure that the replicator makes a full copy of the storage. The final version of the *linkedlist* class (see the next section) has these features.

In the *linkedlist* class, we give the user two ways to find an item in a list: *Finditem* with a single parameter (X) returns the position in the list of the item that matches X (using a user-supplied == operator) and *Finditem* with two parameters (i,X) puts the ith item in X in the list. Functions that can fail in some way return a *bool* to indicate whether they were successful.

The public functions have associated private functions that do the work, as shown in Table 2.1.

Single-Linked List Class Definition
The following definition of our class implements a list using single-linked storage.

```
// operator == is defined on actual objects in list
// assume items in list are numbered 0 upwards

template <class Entry> class linkedlist;        // forward declaration

template <class Entry>
class listnode
{
  friend class linkedlist<Entry>;
```

```
   private: Entry data;
           listnode *next;
};

template <class Entry>
class linkedlist
{
  public: linkedlist();           // constructor - initialize root
          ~linkedlist();          // destructor - reclaim memory
          linkedlist(const linkedlist& rhs);  // replicator
          linkedlist& operator = (const linkedlist&); // assignment
          void clear();   // clear the list
          int Getlength();
          int Finditem(Entry X);  // return position or -1
          bool Finditem(int i,Entry& X);  // get ith item. False if none
          bool remove (int I);            // remove Ith list element
          bool insert (Entry X,int i);    // insert new item

  private: listnode<Entry> *root;
          void copylist (listnode<Entry> *&newlist,     // for use by
                         listnode<Entry> *oldlist);     // replicator
          int llength(listnode<Entry> *L);              // actual counter
          int find_aux(int N, Entry X, listnode<Entry> *L);
          bool find_aux2(int N, Entry& X, listnode<Entry> *L);
          bool insert_aux(Entry X, int i, listnode<Entry> *&L); // inserter
          bool remove_aux(int i, listnode<Entry> *&L); // actual deleter
          void release_aux(listnode<Entry> *&L);        // actual space
                                                        // reclaim
};

template <class Entry>
linkedlist<Entry>::linkedlist()
{
   root = NULL;
}

template <class Entry>
linkedlist<Entry>::~linkedlist()
{
   release_aux(root);
}

template <class Entry>
void linkedlist<Entry>::clear()
```

```
{
    release_aux(root);
    root = NULL;
}


template <class Entry>
void linkedlist<Entry>::release_aux(listnode<Entry> *&L)
{
  if (L!=NULL)
    {
      release_aux(L->next);
      delete L;
    }
 }



template <class Entry>
int linkedlist<Entry>::Getlength()
{
    return llength(root);
}



template <class Entry>
int linkedlist<Entry>::llength(listnode<Entry> *L)
{
    if (L==NULL) return 0;
          else return 1+llength(L->next);
}



template <class Entry>
void linkedlist<Entry>::copylist (listnode<Entry> *&newlist,
                    listnode<Entry> *oldlist)
{
 newlist = NULL;
 if (oldlist!=NULL)
    { newlist = new listnode<Entry>;
      newlist->data = oldlist->data;
      copylist(newlist->next,oldlist->next);
    }
}



template <class Entry>
```

```
linkedlist<Entry>::linkedlist(const linkedlist &rhs)
{
  copylist(root,rhs.root);
}


template <class Entry>
linkedlist<Entry>& linkedlist<Entry>::operator = (const linkedlist& rhs)
{
  // overloaded assignment operator
  if (this!=&rhs) // not assigning to self
      {
        release_aux(root);  // to stop memory leak
        copylist(root,rhs.root);
      }
  return *this;
}



template <class Entry>
int linkedlist<Entry>::Finditem(Entry X)
    { // looking for an item by its contents
       return find_aux(0,X,root);
    }



template <class Entry>
int linkedlist<Entry>::find_aux(int i, Entry X, listnode<Entry> *L)
    {
        if (L==NULL)    return -1;     // list empty
        if (X==L->data) return i;      // found the item
        return find_aux(i+1,X,L->next); // look in the rest of the list
    }

template <class Entry>
bool linkedlist<Entry>::Finditem(int i, Entry& X)
    { // looking for an item by its position
       if (i<0) return false;      // bad parameter
       return find_aux2(i,X,root);
    }

template <class Entry>
bool linkedlist<Entry>::find_aux2(int i, Entry& X, listnode<Entry> *L)
    { // put into X the ith item in L
        if (L==NULL) return false;     // empty list
```

```
            if (i==0)                          // return first item
                {
                  X = L->data;
                  return true;
                }
            return find_aux2(i-1,X,L->next);
        }


template <class Entry>
bool linkedlist<Entry>::remove(int i)
{ // remove the ith item
  if (i<0) return false;      // bad parameter
  return remove_aux(i,root); // does the removal
}

template <class Entry>
bool linkedlist<Entry>::remove_aux(int i,listnode<Entry> *&L)
{ // remove ith item from list L
  if (L==NULL) return false;       // list is empty
  if (i==0)                        // remove front item
        {
          listnode<Entry> *temp = L;
          L = temp->next;
          delete temp;
          return true;
        }
  return remove_aux(i-1,L->next);
}

template <class Entry>
bool linkedlist<Entry>::insert(Entry X,int i)
 { // insert X at ith position
   return insert_aux(X,i,root);
 }


template <class Entry>
bool linkedlist<Entry>::insert_aux(Entry X, int i, listnode<Entry> *&L)
  {
    if (i<0) return false;    // off the front
    if (i==0)
              {
                  listnode<Entry> *temp = new listnode<Entry>;
```

```
              if (temp==NULL) return false; // out of space
                 temp->data = X;
               temp-> next = L;
             L = temp;
            return true;
          }
      if (L==NULL) return false;  // off the end;
      return insert_aux(X,i-1,L->next);
  }
```

Variants of the Single-Linked List

Self-Organizing Search—When searching an unordered list of N items for a particular item, the average number of comparisons for a successful search is $N/2$;
for an unsuccessful search, the number of comparisons is N. In some applications, there is a locality of retrievals; that is, the retrieval of a particular item
means it is likely to be retrieved again in the near future. The average time for a
successful search can be reduced by rearranging the list after a retrieval. For
instance, you can

- Move the retrieved item to the front of the list.[2]
- Move the item k places towards the front.
- Exchange the item with the one in front of it ($k = 1$).

This reduces the number of comparisons required to find the item next time.
New items are inserted at the front of the list. Figure 2.14 illustrates a move-to-
front strategy.

Over time, the most frequently retrieved items will move toward the front of the
list, and the average number of comparisons in a successful retrieval will tend to be
less than $N/2$. See Hester and Hirschberg (1985) for a comparison of algorithms that
modify the search order of linear lists. A move-to-front strategy is seen in some systems that use drop-down menus; an option that the user has selected before may
now be closer to the beginning of the list.

Circular Lists—Instead of terminating a list with a NULL pointer, we could have the
last element point back to the first, creating a circular list. Consider a round-robin
application that processes each item in a list in turn; after the last item, the application returns to the beginning. For example, a chess master may play many oppo-
nents simultaneously, making a move at each board in turn. Similarly, a
multitasking operating system runs several tasks at once, giving each a small allocation of CPU time. By making the list circular, no special check is needed to deal
with the end of the list. Figure 2.15 shows a circular list.

List Cursor—You are familiar with the idea of a cursor representing a current activity position; for example, a cursor on a computer screen might show the current

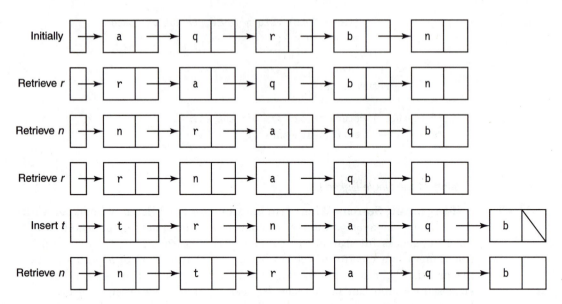

Figure 2.14 • Move-to-front strategy

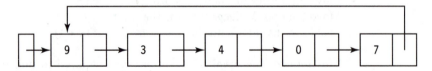

Figure 2.15 • Circular list

typing position in a word-processed document. We used the idea of current location in Figures 2.10 and 2.11. We can use the same idea to represent the current processing point in a list. If we wish to process all the elements of a list (*X*) in order, the following code will work, although it is inefficient.

```
length = X.llength();

for (int i=1; i<=length; i++)
    {
        X.finditem(i,temp);
        // ith item is in temp
            . . .
    }
```

The code is inefficient because each time the code retrieves the *i*th item, it counts from the beginning of the list. A better solution would be something like this

```
length = X.llength();
X.finditem(1,temp);
...

for (i=2; i<length; i++)
    {
            X.getnextitem(temp);
            // next item is in temp
            ...
    }
```

where *getnextitem* returns the data element following the one previously retrieved. An efficient implementation of *getnextitem* would use a pointer in the private section of the object; it would then update the pointer appropriately. Implementation of this idea is left as an Exercise.

2.3.3 Skip Lists

Let us change our representation of a linked list and rotate each node 90 degrees. Figure 2.16 shows a linked list of integers in the new format.

In this particular example, the list elements are in order. If an ordered list contains *N* items, then both an unsuccessful search and a successful search require, on average, *N*/2 comparisons between the search target and a list element. **Skip lists** were proposed by Pugh (1990) as a way to speed up searches at a cost of a little extra storage and increased complexity in the retrieval, insertion, and deletion algorithms.

The idea is to enhance the list with additional pointers that enable the program to move faster along the list and to skip over elements that cannot contain the data it needs. Figure 2.17 shows the list from Figure 2.16 with additional pointers in some of the nodes.[3]

Retrievals
Following is a pseudocode search algorithm for a skip list. It assumes that the pointers in a node are in an array *next*, with *next*[0] being the lowest level and *next*[*max_level*] being the highest level. It also assumes that *root* is a pointer to an array of header pointers, as shown in Figure 2.17.

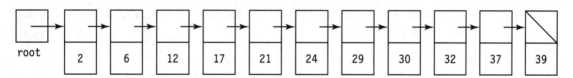

Figure 2.16 • Ordered, single-linked list

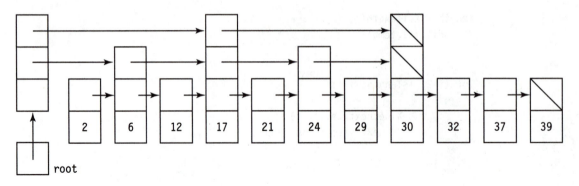

Figure 2.17 • Skip list: Enhanced, ordered list

```
bool retrieve (Entry target)
{
  node *current = root;
  int level = max_level;

  if (current == NULL) return false;     // empty list case

  while ( level >= 0)
    {        // search current level for target and
             // stop at match or node before if no match

             while (     current->next[level] != NULL
                    && current->next[level]->data <=target
                  )
                      current = current->next[level];

             if (current->data == target)
                      return true; // found at this level
             level--;                      // not found yet, try next lower level
    }

return false;     // no more levels to search
}
```

Consider the following searches of the list from Figure 2.17; two are successful and two are unsuccessful.

```
Search for 29:   At level 2, 29 is compared with 17 and 30.
                 At level 1, 29 is compared with 17, 24 and 30.
                 At level 0, 29 is compared with 24 and 29 (succeed).
```

Search for 12:   At level 2, 12 is compared with 17.
                 At level 1, 12 is compared with 6.
                 At level 0, 12 is compared with 6 and 12 (succeed).

Search for 50:   At level 2, 50 is compared with 17 and 30.
                 At level 1, 50 is compared with 30.
                 At level 0, 50 is compared with 32, 37, and 39 (fail).

Search for 22:   At level 2, 22 is compared with 17 and 30.
                 At level 1, 22 is compared with 17 and 24.
                 At level 0, 22 is compared with 17, 21, and 24 (fail).

Note the similarity between the locations of the comparisons and the elements that would be examined during a binary search of an array containing the same numbers.

Insertions

To insert a new node, we create a node containing the new data item and a random number of link fields. Every skip list has a fixed, user-determined, associated probability p that is used to determine the number of links that a particular node has. The probability p is the fraction of nodes with a level i pointer that also have a level $i + 1$ pointer. For example, if p were 0.5, approximately 50% of nodes would have one link, 25% would have two links, 12.5% would have three links, and so on.

In addition, the user may wish to cap the number of links (e.g., at *max_level*). This value could be provided to the constructor function and used to create the array of pointers pointed to by the root. Another useful variable is *current_max*, which would contain the largest number of links currently in any node.[4]

We insert the new node into the appropriate place in the ordering and then complete the linkage. For example, suppose we insert a node with data 27 into the list shown in Figure 2.17, and our random process determines that the node has two link fields. Figure 2.18 shows what the resulting list will look like.

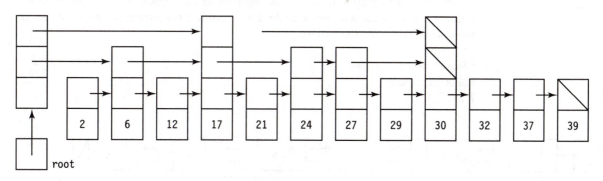

Figure 2.18 • List from Figure 2.17 following insertion of a node with 27 and two links

We may wish to cap the maximum number of links that can be generated. The limit can be based on how long we expect the list to get in the future or it could be based on the current list length. But what about the root, how many pointers should it have? It clearly needs as many pointers as are contained in the largest node, and again, this could be capped.

Deletions

To delete a node from a skip list, we unlink it from its location. If it is the only node that has the largest number of links, then we have the option of reducing the size of the array pointed to by the root. For example, if we deleted both 17 and 30 from the list in Figure 2.18, the array pointed to by the root need contain only two pointers. However, it is probably not worth reclaiming the small amount of pointer space in the root if we anticipate that the root will grow again later.

Performance of Skip Lists

Because of the random factor in node creation (the number of links in a new node), a skip list structure is probabilistic, and performance will therefore vary. Pugh (1990) suggests using $p = 0.5$ if bounds on performance are important; otherwise, use $p = 0.25$. Worst-case behavior is bad but unlikely to occur. Pugh reports that when $p = 0.5$ and the number of nodes is 4096, the probability of the number of comparisons being greater than three times the expected value is less than one in two million. Note that a search need not start at the *current_max* level. Pugh suggests that it should start at level $L = \log_{1/p} n$, where n is the number of elements in the list. For example, if n is 300 and we have $p = 0.5$, we start at level 8 ($\log_2 300$). On the other hand, if p is 0.25 we would start at level 4 ($\log_4 300$).

2.3.4 Double-Linked Lists

Skip lists demonstrate that having multiple pointers in a node can be beneficial. A simple way to augment a linked list is to have each node point to its predecessor as well as to its successor. Figure 2.19 illustrates such a *double-linked list.*

Space for an additional pointer is required in each node. Now we have both a pointer (*next*) to the successor node and a pointer (*previous*) to the predecessor node. Here is a node definition:

```
template <class Type>
class dlistnode
{
```

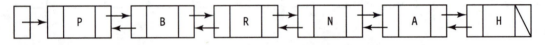

Figure 2.19 • A double-linked list

```
    friend class dlinkedlist<Type>;

private: Type data;
        dlistnode *next;
        dlistnode *previous;
};
```

What advantages does the double-linked list have? Earlier we saw the notion of a list cursor (current position). Double-linking a list permits us to insert and delete at the cursor position with ease and also to move the cursor back and forth in a simple way.

Insertions

Figure 2.20a shows the insertion of a new element at the front of a list, and Figure. 2.20b shows the insertion of a new element after the element pointed to by *location*. The variable *temp* points to the new element, and new links are shown as dashed arrows.

The following is a function to insert a new element at position *i* in a double-linked list; it is similar to the function shown earlier for the single-linked list. The comments following some of the assignments reference the appropriate links in Figure 2.20.

```
template <class Type>
bool dlinkedlist<Type>::insert(Type X, int i)
```

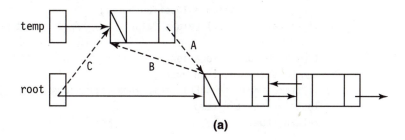

(a)

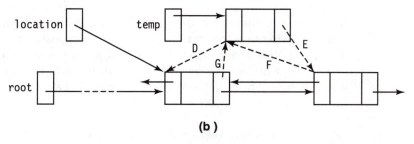

(b)

Figure 2.20 • Insertion into a double-linked list (a) at front, (b) not at front

```
{
        if (i<0) return false;  // bad parameter

        dlistnode<Type> *location,*temp = new dlistnode<Type>;

        if (temp==NULL) return false;  // out of space

        temp->data = X;          // values in
        temp->previous = NULL;   // the new
        temp->next = NULL;       // node

        if (i==0)   // new first element in the list?
          {
            temp->next = root;                          // LINK A
            if (root != NULL) root->previous = temp;    // LINK B
            root = temp;                                // LINK C
            return true;
          }

        // more general insertion

        location=root;
        while (i>1 && location !=NULL)
           { i--; location = location->next; }
        if (location==NULL) return false;          // list not long enough

        temp->previous = location;                  // LINK D
        temp->next = location->next;                // LINK E
        if (temp->next != NULL) {temp->next->previous = temp;}  // LINK F
        location->next = temp;                      // LINK G
        return true;
}
```

Deletions

If we have a pointer to a node, we can remove that node from a double-linked list without having to search for the predecessor. Suppose, for example, that pointer *deletethis* points to the node to be removed, as shown in Figure 2.21a.

The following two assignments result in the list shown in Figure 2.21b. (We would normally need to test to see if the node to be removed is either the first or the last in the list—see Exercises.)

```
deletethis->previous->next = deletethis->next;  // LINK H
deletethis->next->previous = deletethis->prev;  // LINK I
```

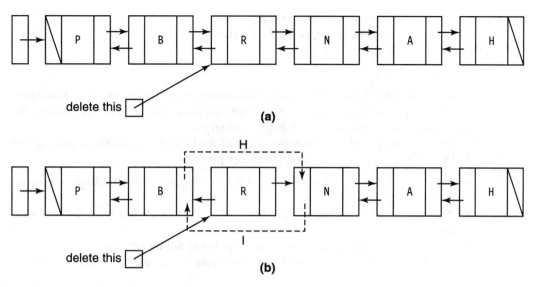

Figure 2.21 • Double-linked list (a) before deletion, (b) following deletion

Note that although the node containing *R* has been removed from the list, as long as we do not return it to the heap (using *delete*) and still have pointer *deletethis*, it can be restored easily to its original place in the list with the following assignments:

```
deletethis->previous->next = deletethis; // replaces LINK H
deletethis->next->previous = deletethis; // replaces LINK I
```

(Again, special action is need for the two end nodes.) Hitotumatu and Noshita (1979) use this technique in speeding up Dijkstra's (1972) back-tracking algorithm for solving the *N*-queens problem.

2.4 Lists and the STL

A list is one of the container classes supported by the STL (others include the vector and deque). Containers in general have iterators associated with them. An **iterator** is a pointer-like object that lets us move through a structure without worrying about details of how to move from one item to the next. In the STL, the member function *begin*() returns an iterator that accesses the first item in the container, and *end*() denotes the end of the collection. The following is a generic function to find an item in a container:

```
iterator find (iterator first, iterator last, Entry& target)
    {
```

```
            iterator iter = first;
            while (iter != last && *iter != target) ++iter;
            return iter;
    }
```

The function returns either the end-of-container iterator or one that references the item we were searching for. We could call *find* with parameters suitable for searching a list, a vector, a set, a deque, and so on.

The following program illustrates some of the facilities available to users of the STL *list* class. Note the following about this program.

- In function *showlist*, a loop similar to the one in *find* is used to display the contents of a list.
- An item can be added to the front of a list (*push_front*) or to the back (*push_back*).
- The first item (*pop_front*) or the last (*pop_back*) can be removed.
- Function *remove* can be used to delete from a list all items that match the parameter.
- Function *erase* can be used to get rid of a single element.
- Function *sort* can be used to arrange items into ascending order. (Function *reverse* is available to reverse the order of elements.)
- Function *merge* can be used to merge two ordered lists.

```
#include <list>
#include <iostream.h>

void showlist(list<int> L)
{
 cout << "[ ";
 for (list<int>::iterator i = L.begin(); i != L.end(); i++)
      cout << *i << " ";
 cout << "]\n";
}


main()
{
 list<int> A,B,C;

 A.push_front(2); A.push_back(7); A.push_front(5);
 A.push_back(8); A.push_front(3);
 showlist(A);                            // should be 3 5 2 7 8

 // find 7 and replace by 5
 list<int>::iterator l = A.begin();
 while (*l != 7) l++;
```

```
*l = 5;

// make a copy of the list
B=A;
showlist(B);                        // should be 3 5 2 5 8

// get rid of the 5s
B.remove(5);
showlist(B);                        // should be 3 2 8

// find the 2 and remove it
l = B.begin();
while (*l != 2) l++;
B.erase(l);
showlist(B);                        // should be 3 8

// add new numbers to the front
B.push_front(12); B.push_front(9); B.push_front(20);

// remove last element
B.pop_back();
showlist(B);  // should be 20 9 12 3

// sort, then output the list
B.sort();
showlist(B);  // should be 3 9 12 20

// create C then sort
C.push_front(4); C.push_front(11); C.push_front(5); C.push_front(7);
C.sort();

B.merge(C);
showlist(B); // should be 3 4 5 7 9 11 12 20
}
```

Here is the output when this program runs:

```
[ 3 5 2 7 8 ]
[ 3 5 2 5 8 ]
[ 3 2 8 ]
[ 3 8 ]
[ 20 9 12 3 ]
[ 3 9 12 20 ]
[ 3 4 5 7 9 11 12 20 ]
```

2.5 General Lists

Thus far, we have only examined linear lists; what about lists in which the elements may themselves be lists? Using brackets to delimit a list, the simple linear list of Figure 2.22 could be represented as [*a b c d*].

Using the same notation, the list of Figure 2.23 could be denoted as [*p* [*q r*] *b* [*a t* [*m n*] *g*] *v*{[*x*]}].

Implementation of a General Node
The first component of a node in a general list is either a data item or a pointer to a sublist. This is reflected in our definition of a generalized list node (*glistnode*).

```
template <class Entry>
class glistnode
{
    friend class glinkedlist<Entry>;

    private: bool isatom;
             union { Entry data; glistnode *list; };
             glistnode *next;
};
```

The *isatom* component is a flag that indicates whether the node is an atomic element or a pointer to a list. The second field will be either a data value or a

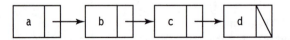

Figure 2.22 • Simple linear list

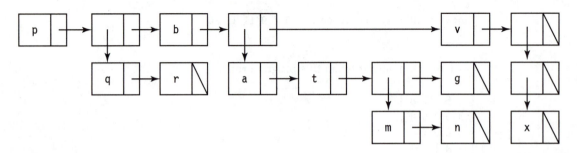

Figure 2.23 • List with sublists

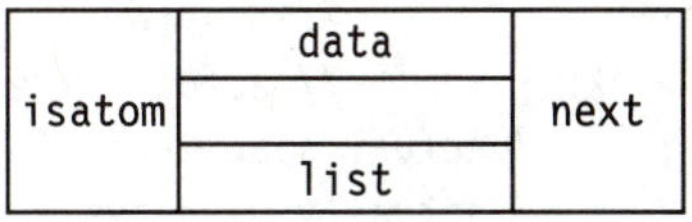

Figure 2.24 • A generalized list node

pointer to a sublist. The *union* feature of C++ enables us to allocate only the space needed by the larger of these two types. Figure 2.24 depicts a generalized list node.

Implementation of the General List Class

A definition of the *glinkedlist* (general linked list) class differs in some aspects from the earlier linear *linkedlist* class. Many variations are possible; the approach we take here has the following features:

- A retrieval function to search a specific list
- A general retrieval function to search the whole structure
- Insertion functions for both simple data and lists
- A *showlist* function to depict the list structure

These changes lead to the following top-level class definition:

```
template <class Entry>
class glinkedlist
{
  public: glinkedlist();                      // constructor
          ~glinkedlist();                     // destructor
          glinkedlist(const glinkedlist& rhs);  // replicator
          glinkedlist& operator = (const glinkedlist&);
          bool Finditem(Entry X,int& i,glistnode<Entry> *&L,
                  glistnode<Entry> *LR);
          bool Finditem(Entry X,int& i,glistnode<Entry> *&L);
          bool remove (int I);           // remove Ith list element - top level
          bool insert (Entry X, int i); // insert new atom at top level
          bool insert (glinkedlist<Entry> L, int i);// insert new list:top level
          void showlist();                       // show list contents

  private: glistnode<Entry> *root;
          void copylist (glistnode<Entry> *&newlist,
                    glistnode<Entry> *oldlist);  // for use by replicator
          bool find_aux(Entry X,int& i,glistnode<Entry> *&L,
                  glistnode<Entry> *LR);
          bool insert_aux(Entry X, int i, glistnode<Entry> *&L); // inserter
          bool insert_aux2(glinkedlist<Entry> L, int i,
```

```
                    glistnode<Entry> *&L);                //inserter
        bool remove_aux(int i, glistnode<Entry> *&L);        // actual deleter
        void release_aux(glistnode<Entry> *&L);     // actual space reclaim
        void show_aux(glistnode<Entry> *L);          // actually displays
};
```

Many functions are similar to their counterparts in the *linkedlist* class of Section 2.3.2.

Although iteration was a reasonable approach for functions operating on a linear list, recursion is particularly useful for functions operating on the more general structure. This is illustrated in the *copylist* function, which has been modified here to duplicate a list at all levels.

```
template <class Entry>
void glinkedlist<Entry>::copylist (glistnode<Entry> *&newlist,
                                   glistnode<Entry> *oldlist)
{
 newlist = NULL;
 if (oldlist != NULL)
    {
      newlist = new glistnode<Entry>;
      newlist->isatom = oldlist->isatom;
      if (newlist->isatom)                      // current node an atom?
          newlist->data = oldlist->data;        // yes – simple copy
      else
          copylist(newlist->list,oldlist->list);// no – copy list
      copylist(newlist->next,oldlist->next);    // rest of the list
    }
}
```

Use of recursion also leads to a simple definition of a function to display the contents of a list. Here are *showlist* and the associated *show_aux* function.

```
template <class Entry>
void glinkedlist<Entry>::showlist()
{
    show_aux(root);
}

template <class Entry>
void glinkedlist<Entry>::show_aux(glistnode<Entry> *L)
{
 cout << "[ ";
```

```
   while (L!=NULL)
      {
       if (L->isatom)
            cout << L->data;
       else show_aux(L->list);
       cout << " ";
       L=L->next;
      }
  cout << "]";
}
```

The following public function (and the private auxiliary function) is used to insert a new list at position *i* in the top level of a general list.

```
template <class Entry>
bool glinkedlist<Entry>::insert(glinkedlist<Entry> L,int i)
{
   return insert_aux2(L,i,root);
}
```

```
template <class Entry>
bool glinkedlist<Entry>::insert_aux2(glinkedlist<Entry> newL, int i,
                                     glistnode<Entry> *&L)
  {
    if (i<0) return false;    // off the front
    if (i==0)
            {
                glistnode<Entry> *temp = new glistnode<Entry>;
                if (temp==NULL) return false; // out of space
                copylist(temp->list,newL.root);
                temp->isatom = false;
                temp-> next = L;
                L = temp;
              return true;
            }

    if (L==NULL) return false;  // off the end;
    return insert_aux2(newL,i-1,L->next);
  }
```

These functions are used in the following program, which creates the list structure shown in Figure 2.23.

```
#include "gllist.h"
#include <iostream.h>

int main()
{
 glinkedlist<char> final,temp1,temp2,temp3,temp4,temp5;
 glistnode<char> *temp;
 int i;

 final.insert('p',1);
 final.insert('b',2);
 final.insert('v',3);

 temp1.insert('q',1); temp1.insert('r',2);
 final.insert(temp1,2);

 temp2.insert('a',1); temp2.insert('t',2); temp2.insert('g',3);
 temp3.insert('m',1); temp3.insert('n',2);
 temp2.insert(temp3,3);
 final.insert(temp2,4);

 temp4.insert('x',1);
 temp5.insert(temp4,1);
 final.insert(temp5,6);

 final.showlist();
 cout << endl;

}
```

When run, the program produces the following output:

```
[ p [ q r ] b [ a t [ m n ] g ] v [ [ x ] ] ]
```

2.6 List Applications

Linked lists are versatile data structures; this section looks at four list applications. In the first, a linked list is used by a function to store previously computed results. If the function is a complex one, being able to avoid recomputing an old result may save time. The second application shows how linked lists can be used to store very large integers. Such an application can be used to combine the range of floating point numbers with the precision of integers. The third application is a generalization of the second, and shows one way in which polynomials can be stored using a list. Finally, the fourth application shows how a sparse vector—one in which most of the elements are zero—can be stored compactly using a list.

2.6.1 Memo Functions

Memo functions were proposed by Donald Michie (Michie 1968). A memo function is one that remembers results of prior calls, and when called upon to compute a value, checks to see if the result was previously computed and is already known. If the result is not known, then after being calculated, it is added to the collection of known values. This memo component of a function can save time if the computation required by the function is extensive.

Consider the example of Ackermann's function A, defined as follows:

$$
\begin{aligned}
A(m,n) \quad &= n + 1 & &\text{if } m = 0 \\
&= A(m - 1,1) & &\text{if } m \neq 0 \text{ and } n = 0 \\
&= A(m - 1,A(m,n - 1)) & &\text{if } m \neq 0 \text{ and } n \neq 0
\end{aligned}
$$

As you can see, the function is highly recursive; for example, it requires 42,438 calls to compute A(3,5). However, on many occasions, a value of $A(m,n)$ is called for that has already been computed earlier in the recursion.

The following is a definition of class *memo* to which a user may add components appropriate for a particular function. We show those appropriate for Ackermann's function. Parameter-parameter-result triples are stored in a linked list L. We have added code that enables us to record the number of function calls.

```
class memo
{
public: memo() {L.clear();}
        int ackermann(int m, int n)
            { calls = 0; return ackermann_aux(m,n); }
        void showcalls() {cout << calls << endl; }

private:
        class triple
          {
            public: triple(int M=0, int N=0, int V=0)
                        {m=M; n=N; value = V;}
            int getvalue() { return value; }
            bool operator == (triple T)
              {
              return (m==T.m) && (n==T.n);
              }
            private: int m,n,value;
          };
```

```
linkedlist<triple> L;
int calls;

bool ackermann_lookup(int m,int n,int& res)
    {
        triple temp(m,n);
        int pos = L.Finditem(temp);
        if (pos == -1) return false; // not in triples list
        L.Finditem(pos,temp);        // get from position pos
        res = temp.getvalue();       // the remembered value
        return true;
    }

void ackermann_remember(int m,int n,int val)
    { // adding a new triple to the list
      triple temp(m,n,val);
      L.insert(temp,0);        // at the front
    }

int ackermann_aux(int m,int n)
    {
      int res;

      if (ackermann_lookup(m,n,res)) return res; // already known

      // compute the value into res
          if (m==0)    res =  n + 1;
      else if (n==0) res = ackermann_aux (m-1, 1);
      else res = ackermann_aux (m-1, ackermann_aux(m,n-1));

      // remember parameters and res for future reference
      ackermann_remember(m,n,res);
      return res;
    }
};
```

Note that you can add other functions to the *memo* class (with their corresponding lists).

Table 2.2 shows for various values of *m* and *n* the value of $A(m,n)$, the number
of calls needed to compute the value when there is no memo list, and the number of
calls needed after adding a memo capability.

m	n	A(m,n)	Calls without *memo*	Calls with *memo*
TABLE 2.2	Ackermann's Function With and Without *Memo*			
1	1	3	4	4
1	2	4	6	6
1	3	5	8	8
1	4	6	10	10
1	5	7	12	12
1	6	8	14	14
2	1	5	14	11
2	2	7	27	17
2	3	9	44	23
2	4	11	65	29
2	5	13	90	35
2	6	15	119	41
3	1	13	106	38
3	2	29	541	88
3	3	61	2,432	186
3	4	125	10,307	380
3	5	253	42,438	766
3	6	509	172,233	1536

2.6.2 Multilength Arithmetic

An integer variable normally has a relatively small range. For example, the range of a 32-bit integer is approximately $\pm 2 \times 10^9$. For some applications this is inadequate. By storing a number as a list of digits, you can represent and manipulate arbitrarily large values. For example, you could treat an integer as a base 10,000 number where each digit is in the range 0 to 9999. An integer A with value 3,421,479,047,216 could be represented by the list shown in Figure 2.25.

In practice, in order to save space, you would arrange for the capacity of each element to be as large as possible so that each element could hold as much as a normal integer variable rather than just the four decimal digits shown in Figure 2.25.

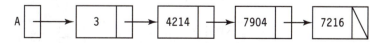

Figure 2.25 • Linked list representation of integer 3,421,479,047,216

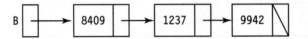

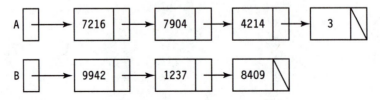

Figure 2.26 • Linked list representation of integer 840,912,379,942

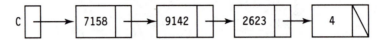

Figure 2.27 • Linked integers with least significant digits first

Figure 2.28 • Result of addition of integers of Figure 2.27

Consider the addition of A with the similarly represented integer B of Figure 2.26.

Because addition begins with the least significant digits of the operands, the algorithm would be simpler if numbers were stored with the least significant component first, as in Figure 2.27.

Addition proceeds down the lists with components appended to the result, yielding list C, shown in Figure 2.28.

Outputting the digits of a number in the correct order is not a problem; earlier we saw one way to print a list backwards.

2.6.3 Polynomials

You can generalize the idea of storing integers to the concept of storing polynomials. For example, you could represent $3.5x^6 - 19.75x^2 + 4.8$ by an ordered linked list of (coefficient, power) pairs, as shown in Figure 2.29.

What are the fundamental operations on a polynomial abstract data type? What methods might be included in a *polynomial* class definition?

We would expect to have arithmetic operators that take two polynomials and produce a third polynomial as a result. Operations specific to polynomials would

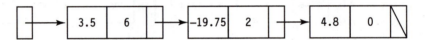

Figure 2.29 • Polynomial as linked list of (coefficient, power) pairs

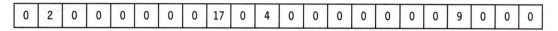

Figure 2.30 • Sparse array

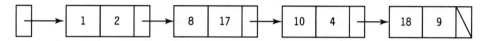

Figure 2.31 • The array from Figure 2.30 as a list of (index, nonzero value) pairs

include evaluation (given x, find the value of the polynomial) and differentiation (changing the polynomial or generating a new one).

The way in which some list operations work would be modified. For example, inserting a term into a polynomial would either create a new list element if the coefficient did not already exist (e.g., inserting $4.5x^3$ into the example of Figure 2.29), change an existing element (e.g., inserting $1.1x^6$ changes the coefficient from 3.5 to 4.6), or remove an existing element (e.g., inserting -4.8 makes the constant zero and eliminates it).

2.6.4 Sparse Vectors and Matrices

Note that we do not bother to store those terms in the polynomial that have a coefficient of zero. We can extend this idea to arrays in general. A **sparse array** is one in which a large percentage of the elements have the same value (typically zero). Depending on how sparse the array is, we may be able to save space by recording information about only the nonzero elements. The array shown in Figure 2.30 could be represented by the list shown in Figure 2.31, in which each element contains an (index, value) pair for one of the four nonzero elements.

The sparse representation idea can be extended to multidimensional arrays. Applications of sparse matrices include information retrieval systems and equation solving; many spreadsheets are sparse matrices. Using an appropriate class definition, we can hide details of storage from the user while providing a normal array interface.

2.7 Basic String Operations

You are familiar with character strings from their use in statements such as

```
cout << "end of program run\n";
```

Fundamental operations on a string are similar to those for a list. We would expect to be able to perform functions such as:

- Find the length of a string.
- Determine the *i*th character in a string.
- Replace the *i*th character in a string.
- Append one string to another.
- Extract a substring from a string.

We can build more powerful operations, such as sorting strings and searching for one string inside another, using these primitives.

2.8 String Implementation

2.8.1 C-Style Strings

In C++, we can declare "C-style" strings such as

```
char X[] = "hello";
char Y[] = "apricot";
```

Strings are stored in character arrays as null-terminated sequences. Thus, from the previous code, *X* is stored as

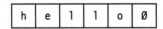

where the final byte is the ASCII NUL (null) character represented by the value 0. This style of string storage and manipulation is termed *C-style* because it is derived from the C language, which, although it enables the storage of strings, does not provide any operators for operating on a string as a unit (Kernighan and Ritchie 1978). Strings can be passed as parameters to functions. The following function determines whether a string is a palindrome.

```
bool palindrome_test (char S[])
{
        char *front=S, *back=S;

        while (*back !='\0') back++;   // move pointer to
        back--;                        // last character

        while (   front<back    // pointers haven't met or crossed
              && *front==*back  // characters pointed to are the same
```

```
        )
    {
      front++;               // move front pointer forward
      back--;                // and back pointer back
    }

      return front>=back;    // is palindrome if pointers
                             // meet or cross over
  }
```

This style of string is also often termed a "second-class" object in contrast with, for example, *int* and *float*, which are "first-class" objects. First-class objects have built-in operators for their assignment and comparison. Comparisons between C-style strings do not work as expected. Given our two strings

```
char x[] = "hello";
char y[] = "apricot";
```

if we write

```
if (X<Y) ...
```

we are comparing the addresses of the two strings in memory, not their contents. In addition, if we attempt to copy a string, as in

```
char *Z = Y;
```

we only copy a pointer to the string. After the assignment, both *Z* and *Y* reference the same string.

2.8.2 The *String.h* Header File

The *string.h* header file includes functions that enable us to perform true comparisons (*strcmp*) and assignments (*strcpy*). In addition, functions are available that enable us to find the length of a string (*strlen*), to perform concatenation (*strcat*), and to perform tokenization (*strtok*).[5] The following program demonstrates the use of *strtok*.

```
#include <iostream.h>
#include <string.h>




main()
{
```

```
char x[] = "this, (is a) string!";
char *symbol;

symbol = strtok(x," ,;.!?");
cout << symbol << endl;

while ( (symbol = strtok(NULL," ,;.()!?")) !=NULL )
    cout << symbol << endl;

cout << "x at the end is :" << x << ": with length " << strlen(x) << "\n";

}
```

The second parameter of *strtok* is a string containing what we want to be regarded as token delimiter characters. Only the first call to *strtok* uses the string to be tokenized. The function calls put null characters in the string, and subsequent calls use these markers to start tokenization where the previous call left off. As you can see from the last line of the following output, the nulls inserted into *x* change irreparably. Thus, it is advisable to work with a copy of the string to be tokenized.

When the program runs, it outputs the following:

```
this
is
a
string
x at the end is :this: with length 4
```

You can use the *strlen* function in *string.h* to shorten the palindrome function.

```
bool palindrome_test (char S[])
{
    char *front=S, *back=S+strlen(S)-1;

    while (front<back && *front==*back)
        {front++; back--}

    return front>=back;
}
```

However, the functions in *string.h* are somewhat awkward to use when compared with the built-in operators. For example, instead of

```
if (X<Y)
```

we write

```
if (strcmp(X,Y)<0)
```

In addition, if we do a string copy, we have to be sure that the destination array is big enough to hold the string. Another disadvantage of C-style strings is that they cannot be used with template classes (e.g., to make a list of strings).

2.8.3 Strings and the STL

We could define our own *string* class and provide the functionality that would make it a first-class object. However, including the string file from the STL does just that. We can write

```
string A,B("dog"),C,D;
```

and later

```
A = "cat";
C = A+B;    //  "catdog"
D = C;      //  also "catdog"

if (D<A)    //  will be false because cat precedes catdog
```

We can be confident that if

```
linkedlist<int> L;
```

works, then so does

```
linkedlist<string> L;
```

The palindrome-testing routine can now be written using iterators, rather than pointers, as follows:

```
bool palindrome_test(string S)
{
  string::iterator front=S.begin(), back=S.end()-1;

  while(front<back && *front==*back)
      {front++;back--;}

  return front>=back;
}
```

2.9 String Applications

This section looks at two applications of strings. The first uses a list of strings to determine the frequency of words in a text. The second looks at the general problem of locating instances of one string in a second (generally much longer) string.

2.9.1 Word Frequencies

Lists and strings can be used to determine the frequencies of words in a piece of text. Each element in our list will be an object that contains a string and its frequency. We read text a token at a time. If the token is already in our list, the count is bumped by one; otherwise, a new object with count equal to one is inserted. A class definition for our list member follows:

```
class wordcounter
{
 public: wordcounter(string S="")
         {
           W = S;          // remember word parameter
           count = 1;     // initial frequency
         }
         void bumpcount() { count++; }
         int getcount()    { return count; }
         string getword() { return W; }

 private: string W;
          int count;
};
```

We choose to ignore both punctuation and case when counting words, so all of the following will be treated as instances of *where*:

Where where? "Where where... where. Where?!"

Function *cleanup* returns a string that is the same as its parameter except that nonletters have been removed and letters have been mapped into lowercase. Thus, *cleanup*("Where?!..") returns *where*.

```
string cleanup(string S)
{
 string result="";

 for (int i=0; i<S.length(); i++)
    if (isalpha(S[i]))              // if an alphabetic character
```

```
        result+= tolower(S[i]);  // append the lower case version

 return result;
}
```

In the code fragment that follows, only the methods developed for our linked list class are used. Efficiency could be improved if other methods were available, such as a version of *Finditem* that returns a pointer to a node and a version of *insert* that lets us insert at a given pointer position.

```
string T,cleanT;

linkedlist<wordcounter> L;

while (cin >> T)  // get next token to T
  {
    cleanT = cleanup(T);  // clean it up
    if (cleanT != "")      // any characters left?
       {
          wordcounter temp(cleanT);     // make an object for list
          int pos = L.Finditem(temp);   // see if already present
          if (pos != -1)
             {
               L.Finditem(pos,temp);   // yes, get it
               L.remove(pos);          // and remove from list
               temp.bumpcount();       // increase frequency count
             }
          L.insert(temp,1);            // new or replacement node
       }
  }
```

After the list is created, a simple loop will print out its contents. For the following text,

```
Here is some text to test the program.
"A horse, a horse, my kingdom for a horse!"
"To be or not to be, that is the question"
Punctuation?! Do we really need punctuation?
```

the program output is

```
punctuation 2
need 1
```

```
really 1
we 1
do 1
question 1
the 2
is 2
that 1
be 2
to 3
not 1
or 1
horse 3
a 3
for 1
kingdom 1
my 1
program 1
test 1
text 1
some 1
here 1
```

See the Exercises for some suggested improvements and enhancements to this frequency counter.

2.9.2 String Searching

A common problem is to find the first or all occurrences of a string $P(P_1 \ldots P_M)$, termed the *pattern*, in a text string $T(T_1 \ldots T_N)$, where, generally, $N \gg M$. Algorithms for solving this problem have applications in virus checkers, editors, document processors, and information retrieval systems.

A Naïve Algorithm

A simple approach to this problem is to compare the pattern first with $T_1 \ldots T_M$, comparing character pairs left-to-right. If there is a mismatch, then compare the pattern with $T_2 \ldots T_{M+1}$, and if this fails, with $T_3 \ldots T_{M+2}$, and so on. Conceptually, we begin by aligning the pattern and the text at their first characters; if a mismatch is detected, we shift the pattern rightward one place. The following function implements this algorithm and returns the index in *Text* of the first location of *Pattern* or -1 if there is no match.

```
int find (char Pattern[], int M, char Text[], int N)
{
        int index=0, text_index, pattern_index;
```

```
while ( index < N-M+1 ) // more alignments to try
  {
      index++;
      text_index=index;
      pattern_index=1;

      while (Pattern[pattern_index]==Text[text_index])
        {
          if ( pattern_index==M )
              return index; // matched all of Pattern

          text_index++;        // move to next pair of
          pattern_index++;     // characters to compare
        }
  }

  return -1;          // no match found
}
```

In the worst case, the algorithm can be very slow. Suppose the pattern is *xxxxxxy* and the text is composed entirely of the character *x*. In each alignment, we would not find a mismatch until the last character pair, and the number of comparisons for the entire search is O($M*N$). In practice, we would expect most mismatches to be detected quickly and the number of comparisons for the entire search to be O(N).

Boyer–Moore–Horspool Algorithm

The Boyer–Moore–Horspool (BMH) algorithm (Horspool 1980) improves on the naïve algorithm by enabling us to shift the pattern more than a single place rightward after a mismatch is detected. It does this by matching character pairs right-to-left rather than left-to-right and by using information at the first mismatch location to determine the extent to which the pattern can be shifted without missing any possible matches. Consider the pattern/text alignment of Figure 2.32.

Matching right-to-left, the (*e,e*) and (*h,h*) pairs match and then a mismatch occurs between the *t* and the *c*. If we know that the pattern does not contain *t*, then we can slide it past the *t* in the text and get the alignment shown in Figure 2.33.

In this position, the (*e,e*) pair matches, and then once again the first mismatch is with a *t* in the text. We are able to slide to the alignment shown in Figure 2.34.

```
Text:        These are the text characters
Pattern:              cache
```

Figure 2.32 • Pattern/text alignment 1

```
Text:        These are the text characters
Pattern:                cache
```

Figure 2.33 • Pattern/text alignment 2

```
Text:        These are the text characters
Pattern:                  cache
```

Figure 2.34 • Pattern/text alignment 3

More generally, the text character in the mismatch may appear somewhere in the pattern; therefore, we shift the pattern to align it with the rightmost instance of that character. In Figure 2.34, for example, a mismatch occurs between c in the text and e in the pattern. The character c is in the pattern, thus our next alignment is as shown in Figure 2.35.

However, we never move the pattern backwards. If the rightmost instance of the character has been passed, we just shift one place. Figure 2.36 shows a sequence of alignments that illustrate the various cases.

To determine how far the pattern can be shifted, the algorithm requires the computation of a **skip table** that is derived from the pattern before the search begins. We use the text character in the mismatch to access the table, which yields the distance that the pattern can be shifted. The following is an implementation of the Boyer–Moore–Horspool algorithm.

```
Text:        These are the text characters
Pattern:                    cache
```

Figure 2.35 • Pattern/text alignment 4

```
Text: ... and this also uses only a small ...
Pattern:    bakes
Pattern:      bakes
Pattern:        bakes
Pattern:            bakes
Pattern:             bakes
Pattern:                bakes
```

Figure 2.36 • Sequence of pattern alignments (BMH)

```
int findBMH (char Pattern[], int M, char Text[], int N)
{
  int index=M, text_index, pattern_index;

  while (index <= N)
     {
       text_index = index;
       pattern_index = M;

       // test this alignment, right to left
       while ( pattern_index > 0 &&
               Text[text_index] == Pattern[pattern_index]
             )
        {
          pattern_index--;
          text_index--;
        }

       if (pattern_index==0)
           return text_index+1; // complete match, return position

       index = index + skip_table(Text[index]);  // shift the pattern
     }

  return -1;  // no instance of pattern found
}
```

If a character does not appear in the pattern, then its skip-table entry is M (the pattern length); otherwise it is $M - j$, where j is the index of the rightmost occurrence of the character. The last character in the pattern is not processed. Thus, assuming our alphabet consists of the 26 lowercase characters plus the space character, the string *procedure* would have the skip table shown in Table 2.3.

● **TABLE 2.3** Skip Table for *Procedure*

A	B	C	D	E	F	G	H	I	J	K	L	M	N	O	P	Q	R	S	T	U	V	W	X	Y	Z	Sp
9	9	5	3	4	9	9	9	9	9	9	9	9	9	6	8	9	1	9	9	2	9	9	9	9	9	9

```
Text:  ... and this also uses only a small ...
Pattern:    bakes
Pattern:         bakes
Pattern:          bakes
Pattern:               bakes
Pattern:                    bakes
Pattern:                         bakes
```

Figure 2.37 • Sequence of pattern alignments (Sunday's variant)

Sunday's Improvement

Sunday's insight into the string-matching problem (Sunday 1990) was to observe that if the pattern does not match the currently aligned text fragment, then the text character just beyond the current alignment (T_{k+M}) must be aligned with the pattern in its next position (unless the pattern is shifted right past it). He uses this text character to determine the shift amount, again using a skip table precomputed from P. If T_{k+M} is in P, then it is aligned with its right-most instance.

Using T_{k+M} to determine the shift distance has two consequences. First, if the character is not in P, we can shift the pattern right past it. Thus, the greatest distance we can shift the pattern is one greater than the greatest shift possible with Boyer–Moore–Horspool. Figure 2.37 shows some example shifts.

Second, when examining the current pattern-text alignment, character pairs can be compared in any order. In particular, we can first test the pair that gives the best shift if there is a mismatch, or first test the pair that seems most likely to result in a mismatch. For example, characters can be compared in ascending order of their *a priori* frequency in the language. Sunday termed this approach the Optimal Mismatch (OM) technique. His experiments showed that it results in fewer character comparisons than the Boyer–Moore–Horspool algorithm (though the percentage improvement declines with increasing pattern length).

• Chapter Summary

This chapter examined the properties of the list abstract data type as well as array-based and linked storage implementations. We noted the problem of shallow copying in the C++ environment and saw that the skip list variant can be used to speed up searches at the cost of extra storage. Double-linking a list also requires extra storage, but has reliability benefits and also improves the efficiency of certain operations. The STL includes the *list* type. We looked at lists where the elements themselves can be lists and saw that recursion is particularly useful in processing general lists.

Finally, we looked at strings, which are also a linear structure with STL support. We looked at facilities provided in various libraries. An example application showed how to determine word frequencies in a text. We concluded the chapter by examining string searching algorithms.

Exercises

1. Write an iterative function that uses a list pointer as a parameter and displays the contents of the list in reverse order.

2. Write a recursive function that returns the data item in the last element of a single-linked list.

3. Write a function that creates a list *B* derived from list *A*. Each element in *B* is the result of applying function *F* to the corresponding element of *A*.

4. Describe how the contents of a linked list could be sorted using additional pointer variables but only one additional list element. Then describe how to do this without the storage for the additional list element.

5. Write a function to apply function *G* to every element of single-linked list *L*.

6. Write a function to reverse the order of the elements in single-linked list *L* using minimal additional space.

7. Outline an algorithm for multiplying two arbitrarily large integers stored as linked lists of digits.

8. Suggest guidelines for determining whether it is worth memorizing a function.

9. Devise a function that determines whether two single-linked lists are identical. They could be the same list or different lists with equal elements at corresponding positions.

10. Create a list containing *N* elements and compare the run times of the iterative and the recursive functions to find the length of the list. Try values of *N* = 100, 200, 400, 800, and so on. Is there a value of *N* for which the recursive function fails?

11. Add accessing and updating methods to the linked list class that make it more efficient to change the contents of a node.

12. Write a function that takes a list *L* and determines whether *L* contains any repeated items.

13. Write a function that takes an ordered list *L* and eliminates duplicate items.

14. Write a function that takes a list *L* and creates a second list containing those items that appear exactly once in *L*.

15. Write a function that takes an ordered list of integers *L* and creates a list containing the first-order differences. Thus, if *L* is [6 11 13 18 18 49 42], the new list is [5 2 5 0 31 −7].

16. Write a function that takes two parameters: a list (*L*) and a Boolean function (*B*) that operates on the items in *L*. The function creates two lists: one contains those items in *L* for which *B* returns true and the second contains those items for which *B* returns false.

17. Write a function that takes a list *L* and item *X* and creates a list containing those items in *L* that immediately follow an occurrence of *X*.

18. Counting function calls is only one measure of the effectiveness of a memo function. Compare the times required to compute each of the values of Ackermann's function in Table 2.1 without the memo mechanism and with the memo mechanism.

19. Discuss the relative strengths and weaknesses of an array and a double-linked list.

20. Suppose we have a double-linked list rooted in L, but only the forward links are filled in. Sketch an algorithm for filling in the backward links. Your algorithm should work on lists of any length.

21. Devise a method for a single-linked list class that enables a user to retrieve the item following the one most recently retrieved. Similarly, devise a method for a double-linked list class that permits a user to retrieve the item that precedes or the item that follows the one most recently retrieved. Your methods should act appropriately if the requested items are undefined.

22. Create a code that deletes the node pointed to by *deletethis* from a double-linked list. Your code should work correctly for any node in the list.

23. Under what circumstances might one choose to use a double-linked list rather than a single-linked list?

24. A double-linked list could be implemented using three arrays: data, forward pointer, and back pointer. Devise a way in which the two pointer arrays could be combined into a single array, yet still preserve the double-linking.

25. The *cleanup* function used in the word frequency application does not deal correctly with strings having "internal" punctuation, as in *multi-processor*, *don't*, and *o'clock*. Modify the function so that internal nonletter characters are retained.

26. Devise a function similar to that of Exercise 6 that operates on general lists.

27. Modify the palindrome checking function so that it accepts strings that are palindromic only if case and nonletter characters are ignored. Examples of such strings are:

    A man, a plan, a canal - Panama!

    Madam, I'm Adam

28. A string is prime if it is not empty and if it is lexicographically less than all of its proper suffixes. (A proper suffix is a suffix that is at least one character long but shorter than the string itself.) For example, "abbab" is not prime because of the ordering: "ab" "**abbab**" "b" "bab" "bbab." The string "abbac" is prime because of the ordering: "**abbac**" "ac" "bac" "bbac" "c."

    Write a function *prime* that takes string parameter S and returns true if S is prime and false otherwise.

29. For each of the following, give an example of a pattern/text alignment with the specified properties:

    (a) The shift made by Boyer–Moore–Horspool is greater than the shift made by Sunday's variant.

(b) The shifts made by the two algorithms are the same.

(c) The shift made by Sunday's variant is greater then the shift made by the Boyer–Moore–Horspool algorithm.

30. One way to translate a word into its Pig Latin equivalent is:

```
If the first letter is a consonant,
            move it to the end and add ay (welcome becomes elcomeway),
else        add way to the end of the word (eat becomes eatway).
```

Write a function that takes a word (string) as a parameter and returns the Pig Latin equivalent.

31. Software used to generate form letters often has problems with names. For example, Hank Williams, Jr. may be addressed as *Dear Mr. Jr.* What problems do you foresee in developing an algorithm that takes a string containing a name and generates the appropriate salutation? For example, R. M. Jones, Sr. M.D. should be greeted as *Dear Dr. Jones.*

● Problems

1. Implement a multilength arithmetic class. The user should be able to declare objects of the class and perform basic input/output, assignments, and arithmetic operations.

2. A sparse array is one in which a very high percentage of the elements have the same value (typically zero). Space can be saved by storing data only about the "interesting" elements. Implement a class definition for a sparse matrix. Provide the usual functionality of two-dimensional arrays—the ability to read from and write to element $M[i][j]$.

3. Investigate the performance of various move-to-front strategies for retrievals from a linked list. Use at least the following two environments:

   a. The input is a typical piece of English text, the list is a list of (word, frequency) pairs, and we wish to determine word frequencies.

   b. The list is a list of integers (range 0–99) and the input is provided by a random number generator.

4. Write a memo function *ISPRIME(N)* that returns true if N is a prime number and false otherwise.

5. Goldbach's conjecture is that every integer greater than four is the sum of two primes. To date, no counterexample has been found. Write and test a function *GOLDBACH* that takes as a parameter an integer (N) greater than four and returns a pair of primes that sum to N.

6. The decimal expansion of any fraction of the form $1/N$ is either a terminating decimal or a decimal sequence that repeats. Write a program that inputs N and outputs the decimal expansion of $1/N$. If the fraction repeats, the program should clearly identify the repeating sequence.

7. A surveyor measures an irregularly shaped field by starting at point $P1$ on the perimeter and measuring the direction and distance to a second perimeter point $P2$. From point $P2$, he measures the distance and direction of point $P3$, and so on. He thus creates a list

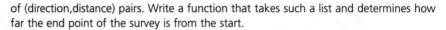

of (direction,distance) pairs. Write a function that takes such a list and determines how far the end point of the survey is from the start.

a. Assume initially that each direction is either north, south, east, or west.

b. Write a more general function in which a direction is a heading in the range 0 to 359 degrees.

8. Write a function that takes a polynomial as a parameter and generates a list of its prime factors.

9. Write a function that takes an arbitrarily large integer, represented as a linked list of *int* variables, and prints it in decimal with commas inserted in the correct place; for example, 4,262,391,427,158.

10. Complete the definition of a double-linked list class. Provide functions similar to those of the single-linked list.

11. Add a function to the general list class that enables a user to remove the *i*th item from a particular sublist. What parameters will the function need?

12. Add to the general list class a function that enables a user to insert a simple entry into a particular sublist at position *i*.

13. Add to the general list class a function that enables a user to insert a list into a particular sublist at position *i*.

14. Write a function *string_edit* that takes three strings, *A*, *B*, and *C*, as parameters. It returns a string that is identical to *A* except that each occurrence of *B* has been replaced by *C*.

15. Write a Boolean function *Anagram* that takes two strings *A* and *B* and returns true if one is an anagram of the other, and false otherwise. Ignore nonletter characters in the strings.

16. Create a list of strings *CROWLIDIETS* in which each string is the scrambled name of a city somewhere in the world. A user inputs a string, and the program reports whether the input string is an anagram of any of the strings in *CROWLIDIETS*.

17. A simple buzzphrase generator uses a list of sets of strings. It constructs a buzzphrase by concatenating a random selection from each set. For example, if we have the following three sets, a buzzphrase might be "web-based automatic interface."

a. S1: [web-based hyper]

b. S2: [proactive mindless automatic eclectic]

c. S3: [interface synergy environment]

The list of sets of strings can be represented by a general list structure. Write a function that takes such a structure and, depending on the parameters, (a) generates a random phrase and (b) outputs all possible phrases.

How can you detect if an arbitrary phrase is one that might be have been produced by your generator?

18. Every string S has a unique prime factorization $S = L_1 + L_2 + \ldots + L_N$, where each L_i is a prime string (see Exercise 28) and N is minimized. Write a function *factorize* that takes string S as a parameter and produces a list of the prime factors of S. Note that AB is prime if A is prime, B is prime, and $A < B$. For example, the prime factorization of MISSISSIPPI is M + ISS + IS + IPP + I.

19. By generating random strings and testing them for primeness, estimate the proportion of n-character strings that are prime for each n from 5 to 20.

20. Implement Sunday's variant on the Boyer–Moore–Horspool algorithm and run experiments to compare the performance of the two algorithms in a variety of searches. Measure the number of character–character comparisons each algorithm uses, and measure the run time of each.

● References

Dijkstra, E. W. 1972. Notes on structured programming. In *Structured Programming*, pp. 1–82. New York: Academic Press.

Hester, J. H., and D. S. Hirschberg. 1985. Self-organizing linear search. *ACM Computing Surveys* 17(3): 295–311.

Hitotumatu, H., and K. Noshita. 1979. A technique for implementing backtrack algorithms and its application. *Information Processing Letters* 8(4): 174–175.

Horspool, R.N.S. 1980. Practical fast searching in strings. *Software: Practice and Experience* 10(6): 501–506.

Hume, A., and D. Sunday. 1991. Fast string searching. *Software: Practice and Experience* 21(11): 1221–1248.

Kernighan, B. W., and D. M. Ritchie. 1978. *The C Programming Language.* Upper Saddle River, NJ: Prentice-Hall.

Michie, D. 1968. Memo functions and machine learning. *Nature* 218: 19–22.

Pugh, W. 1990. Skip lists: A probabilistic alternative to balanced trees. *Communications of the ACM* 33(6): 668–676.

Sunday, D. M. 1990. A very fast substring search algorithm. *Communications of the ACM* 33(8): 132–142.

● Notes

[1] $E{\rightarrow}N$ denotes the N component of the item pointed to by E.

[2] This is equivalent to a least recently used algorithm because the least recently accessed item is the one at the end of the list.

[3] Our version of skip lists differs from that of Pugh (1990), who assumed that every list is initialized with a special element containing a key greater than any legal key. This element thus acts as a list terminator. For generality, we avoid using such an element, although the algorithms may not be as efficient.

[4]Assuming that the *rand*() function returns a value evenly distributed in the range 0.0 to 1.0, the following code uses p to determine the number of levels of links in a new node (adjusted to stay within the *max_level* bound):

```
level = 1;
```

```
while (rand()<p && level < maxlevel) level++;
```

Pugh mentions the possibility of avoiding large increments in *current_level* by not allowing *current_level* to increase by more than one, but notes that it "destroys our ability to analyze the resulting algorithms."

In the special case where $P = 0.5$, an alternative way to determine the number of levels is to generate a random *max_level*-bit integer, count the number of trailing zeros, and add one.

[5]By tokenization, we mean the process of breaking a string up into tokens or symbols. Typically, tokens are delimited by white-space characters (e.g., space and tab), and possibly by punctuation. The punctuation characters themselves may be tokens. Tokenization is a low-level task performed by translation programs such as assemblers and compilers. For instance, the following line

A[I] = max(r,a+b)

might be broken up into the following 13 tokens

A   [I   ]   =   max   (r   ,   a   +   b   )

3

Sets

3.1 Introduction

A set is a very general and useful data structure. This chapter looks at the fundamental operations on the set abstract data type and at two ways in which a set might be implemented. Set implementations in the STL and two example applications of sets also are presented.

A **set** is a collection of objects of the same type. If S is a set of objects of type T, then any object of type T is either in S or not in S.[1] T is the **base type** of S. Thus, we could have sets of integers:

Set1: [1 3 5 6 8 10 15 17 20]

Set2: [2 6 7 11 15 16 17 29]

As well as a set of characters:

Set3: [a y o u i e]

In our depiction of a set, there is no significance in the ordering of the items. For example,

[2 9 4 6 8], [8 6 4 9 2], and [4 9 8 6 2]

all represent the same set.

Set A is a **subset** of set B if all the members of A are members of B. Set A is a **proper subset** of set B if A is a subset of B and there is at least one member of B that is not a member of *A*. In the following example, both *Set4* and *Set5* are subsets of *Set6*; however, *Set4*, but not *Set5*, is a proper subset of *Set6*.

Set4: [a b c]
Set5: [a b c d]
Set6: [a b c d]

3.2 Basic Set Operations

There are three basic operations on a set:

- Tests for membership
- Insertion of an item
- Removal of an item

It is also useful in practice to be able to find the number of items in a set.

Three fundamental set operators may be applied to two compatible sets (i.e., two sets with the same base type). These are *union*, *intersection*, and *difference*. Other set-set operations can be defined in terms of these three.

- *Union.* The result of *SetA union SetB* (which can be denoted *SetA* $\cup$ *SetB*) is a set that contains the items that are in either *SetA* or *SetB*, or both. Using the example sets offered earlier,

  Set1 $\cup$ Set2 is [1 2 3 5 6 7 8 10 11 15 16 17 20 29]

- *Intersection.* The result of *SetA intersection SetB* (which can be denoted *SetA* $\cap$ *SetB*) is a set that contains the items that are in both *SetA* and *SetB*. For example,

  Set1 $\cap$ Set2 is [6 15 17]

- *Difference.* The result of *SetA difference SetB* (which can be denoted *SetA* $-$ *SetB*) is a set that contains those items that are in *SetA* but not in *SetB*. For example,

  Set1 $-$ Set2 is [1 3 5 8 10 20]

An example of a set-set operator that can be defined in terms of these fundamental operators is *symmetric-difference*. *Symmetric-difference* is somewhat like the *exclusive-or* operator on Boolean values. The result of

SetA symmetric-difference SetB

is the same as the result of

SetB symmetric-difference SetA

(hence the name). The result is the set of items that are in either *SetA* or *SetB*, but not in both. The operation is defined as follows:

SetA symmetric-difference SetB ≡ (*SetA* ∪ *SetB*) − (*SetA* ∩ *SetB*)

For example,

Set1 symmetric-difference Set2 is [1 2 3 5 6 7 8 10 16 20 29]

Few programming languages have sets as a built-in type, although the very high-level language SETL is based on sets (Schwartz and Dewar 1986) and Pascal lets a user define, declare, and manipulate sets (with some restrictions on base type) (Jensen and Wirth 1974). In an object-oriented language, however, a general set class can be defined.

3.2.1 Class Definition

The following class definition includes the three fundamental set operations (*is_member*, *insert*, and *remove*). An *insert* operation may fail due to lack of available memory, in which case the function returns *false*. (However, if we try to insert an item that is already in the set, the function quietly does nothing.) Similarly, if we try to remove an item that is not in the set, *remove* returns *false*.

Our class definition includes a function (*size*) that returns the current number of set members (as well as function *empty* for convenience), a function (*show*) to display the contents of the set (along with an optional string to label them), and a function (*extract*) that removes a randomly selected element from the set (returning *false* if the set is empty). The latter could be called repeatedly to process the items in the set in an arbitrary order. The top level of our class definition follows:

```
template <class Entry>
class set
{
 public: set();                         // constructor - empty set
         ~set();                        // destructor - reclaim space
         set(const set& x);             // copy constructor
         set& operator =(const set&);   // assignment operator
         bool is_member (Entry E);      // check for membership
         bool insert(Entry E);          // add new member
         bool remove (Entry E);         // remove member
         bool empty();                  // is set empty?
         int size();                    // current set size
         void show(ostream&,char[]="");// contents to output stream
         bool extract(Entry& E);        // take out arbitrary member

 private: // implementation specific
};
```

3.2.2 Set-Set Operators

The following implementation of a *difference* operator uses only the public functions; the operator is thus independent of the set implementation. However, operator definitions that are implementation-specific are likely to be more efficient; examples of this are presented in Section 3.3.

```
template <class Entry>
set<Entry> operator - (set<Entry> A, set<Entry> B)
// difference A minus B
{
  set<Entry> result;
  Entry temp;

  // get members of A and see if they are in B
  while (A.extract(temp))
      if (!B.is_member(temp)) result.insert(temp);

  return result;
}
```

We can define operators for *union* and *intersection* in a similar manner.

3.3 Implementation of Sets

This section looks at two ways in which a set might be implemented. The first uses a single-linked list; the second uses an array of bits. Each method has advantages and disadvantages.

3.3.1 Linked List

An unordered list can represent a set in a simple way. For example, the set

[a y o u i e]

can be represented by the list shown in Figure 3.1.

A new item can be inserted anywhere in the list. In particular, it can be inserted at the front, so this operation is O(1). However, membership checking and removal of a particular item from the set both require a linear search and are thus O(*N*). The

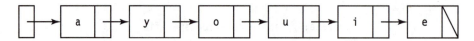

Figure 3.1 • A set as an unordered list

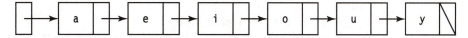

Figure 3.2 • A set as an ordered list

set-set operators are $O(N^2)$ because for each of the N items in one of the operands there is an $O(N)$ membership-checking process on the second operand.

If an ordering is defined on the items in the base type, then we can represent a set as an ordered list. Figure 3.2 shows our example set as an ordered list.

Insertion is now an $O(N)$ operation. Membership checking and remove operations are a little faster on average than with the unordered list [though still $O(N)$]. Set-set operations can be performed efficiently. For example, the *union* operation is the merge of two ordered lists, and the time required is proportional to the sum of the sizes of the sets. The time required to perform one of the three set-set operations is $O(N)$ rather than $O(N^2)$.

The following is a definition of class *set_llist* that implements a set using an ordered linked list. We assume that the operator < is defined for the base type. Note that this operator is sufficient to test for set membership because

```
A==B        ≡        !(A<B) && !(B<A)
```

If the user wishes to call function *show* to output the contents of a set, then the stream insertion operator << must be defined on the set items.

```
#include <stdlib.h>  // for rand – see extract function

template <class Entry> class set_llist;    // forward declaration


template <class Entry>
class set_llist_element     // class definition for linked list element
{
 friend class set_llist<Entry>;

 public:  set_llist_element()  { next = NULL;}

 private: Entry data;
         set_llist_element<Entry> *next;
};

template <class Entry>
class set_llist
```

```
{
// set as ordered linked list
// assumes that operator < is defined on set elements

public: set_llist();                        // constructor - empty set
        ~set_llist();                       // destructor - reclaim space
        set_llist(const set_llist& x);       // copy constructor
        set_llist& operator =(const set_llist&); // assignment operator
        bool is_member (Entry E);     // check for membership
        bool insert(Entry E);         // add new member
        bool remove (Entry E);        // remove member
        bool empty();                 // is set empty?
        int size();                   // current set size
        void show(ostream&,char[]="");// insert items into output stream
        bool extract(Entry& E);       // take out arbitrary member

private:int count;
        // for copy constructor
        void copylist(set_llist_element<Entry> *&,
            set_llist_element<Entry>*);
        void cleanup(set_llist_element<Entry> *&L);  // actual space
                                                     // reclaiming
        set_llist_element<Entry> *root;   // pointer to members in asc. order
};

template <class Entry>            // constructor
set_llist<Entry>::set_llist()
{
count = 0;
root = NULL;
}


template <class Entry>
void set_llist<Entry>::cleanup(set_llist_element<Entry> *&L)
{
if (L != NULL)
    { cleanup(L->next);
      delete L;
    }
}

template <class Entry>           // destructor
set_llist<Entry>::~set_llist()
```

```
{
  cleanup(root);
}

template <class Entry>
void set_llist<Entry>::copylist (set_llist_element<Entry> *&newlist,
                            set_llist_element<Entry> *oldlist)
{
 //
 newlist = NULL;
 // the first element
 if (oldlist != NULL)
    { newlist = new set_llist_element<Entry>;
      newlist->data = oldlist->data;
      newlist->next = NULL;
      oldlist=oldlist->next;
    }
 // remaining items
 set_llist_element<Entry> *endlist = newlist;
 while (oldlist != NULL)
    {
     endlist->next = new set_llist_element<Entry>;
     endlist->next->data = oldlist->data;
     endlist->next->next = NULL;
     endlist = endlist->next;
     oldlist=oldlist->next;
    }
}

template<class Entry>
set_llist<Entry>& set_llist<Entry>::operator = (const set_llist<Entry>& x)
{
  if (this != &x) // not assigning to self
    {
      count = x.count;
      cleanup(root);          // avoid memory leak
      copylist(root,x.root);
    }
  return *this;

}

template<class Entry>
set_llist<Entry>::set_llist<Entry>(const set_llist<Entry> &x)
```

```
{
 //  copy constructor
 count = x.count;
 copylist(root,x.root);
}


template<class Entry>
bool set_llist<Entry>::is_member(Entry E)
{
  // returns true if E is in the list, false otherwise
  set_llist_element<Entry> *L=root;
  while(L!=NULL)
   {
     if (  !(L->data<E) && !(E<L->data) ) return true;
     L = L->next;
   }
  return false;
}


template<class Entry>
bool set_llist<Entry>::insert(Entry E)
{
  // attempt to insert E in the correct place in the ordered list

  if (is_member(E)) return true;    // already in, no duplication is permitted

  set_llist_element<Entry> *t = new set_llist_element<Entry>;
  if (t==NULL) return false;  // out of space for new items

  t -> data = E;
  if (root == NULL || E < root->data)  // new first element
        {
           t->next = root;
           root=t;
           count++;      // number of items in set
           return true;
        }
  // find insert place
  set_llist_element<Entry> *L = root;
  while (L->next !=NULL && (L->next)->data < E) L=L->next;

  // update the list
  t->next = L->next;
```

```
    L->next = t;
    count++;                // number of items in set
    return true;
}


template<class Entry>
bool set_llist<Entry>::remove(Entry E)
{
    // attempt to remove E from the ordered list

    set_llist_element<Entry> *L = root;
    if (L == NULL) return false;     // list is empty
    if ( !(L->data<E) && !(E<L->data) )   // first item is the one to remove
      {
        root = L->next;
        delete L;
        count--;            // number of items in set
        return true;
      }
    // search for item with L pointer to item before it in the list
    while ( (L->next!= NULL) && (L->next->data < E) ) L=L->next;

    if (L->next == NULL) return false;   // E is not in the list
    if ( !(E<L->next->data) )            // found it
      {
        set_llist_element<Entry> *temp = L->next;
        L->next = temp->next;
        delete temp;           // reclaim space
        count--;               // number of items in set
        return true;
      }
    return false;  // E not found
}

template<class Entry> bool set_llist<Entry>::empty() { return count==0;}

template<class Entry> int set_llist<Entry>::size() { return count;}

template<class Entry>
void set_llist<Entry>::show(ostream &s, char message[])
{   // output set members with message and count

    set_llist_element<Entry> *L=root;
    s << message << count << " elements: ";
```

```
      while(L!=NULL)
        { s << L->data << " ";
          L = L->next;
        }
      s << endl;
    }



template<class Entry>
bool set_llist<Entry>::extract(Entry& R)
{
  // remove a random element from the set and put in R

  if (count==0) return false;      // set is empty

  int location = rand()%count;     // get random index 0..count−1
  set_llist_element<Entry> *L=root;

  if (location==0)  // we are removing the first item
    {
      R = L->data;
      root = L->next;
      delete L;
      count--;       // number of items in set
      return true;
    }
  // move down list to deletion point
  while (location>1) { location--; L=L->next; }
  // extract
  set_llist_element<Entry> *temp = L->next;
  R = temp->data;
  L->next = temp->next;
  delete temp;           // reclaim space
  count--;               // number of items in set
  return true;
}


template <class Entry>
set_llist<Entry> operator + (set_llist<Entry> A, set_llist<Entry> B)
{
  // union: implementation independent, uses extract and insert
  set_llist<Entry> result; Entry temp;
```

```
      while (A.extract(temp)) result.insert(temp);
      while (B.extract(temp)) result.insert(temp);
      return result;
}


template <class Entry>
set_llist<Entry> operator - (set_llist<Entry> A, set_llist<Entry> B)
{
   // difference A minus B: implementation independent, uses extract,
   // is_member and insert

   set_llist<Entry> result; Entry temp;
   while (A.extract(temp))
         if (!B.is_member(temp)) result.insert(temp);
   return result;
}

template <class Entry>
set_llist<Entry> operator * (set_llist<Entry> A, set_llist<Entry> B)
{
   // intersection: implementation independent, uses extract,
   // is_member and insert

   set_llist<Entry> result; Entry temp;
   while (A.extract(temp))
         if (B.is_member(temp)) result.insert(temp);
   return result;
}
```

3.3.2 Bit Map

Each of the insertion, removal, and set-membership operations on an ordered linked list of N items takes O(N) time. Thus, the time required to perform these operations on a set implemented using lists increases as the set size increases. We can do better. In this section, sets will be implemented in such a way that these operations can be done in O(1) time; that is, the time is independent of the number of items in the set.

If members of the base type can be cast to the *int* type, then the set can be represented by a Boolean array in which element k of the array contains *true* if the kth member of the base type is in the set, and contains *false* otherwise. However, on many C++ implementations, a *bool* variable occupies a byte or multiple bytes in order to make the assembly code for accessing and updating operations simple.[2] Our implementation will use a single bit for each element, even though this makes the accessing and updating functions more complex. Such an array of single bits is variously denoted as a **bit map**, **bit vector**, or **bit list**. This book uses the term *bit map*.

The size of the array of bits is determined by the number of possible values in the base type of the set, therefore this implementation is feasible only if the underlying base type has a relatively small range. For example, it is suitable for days of the year (366 possible members), U.S. states (50 members), lottery numbers (perhaps 60 members), or students in a college (perhaps 30,000 members), but it would not be a good choice for a set of 32-bit integers (2^{32} possible members). Although Pascal was one of the first programming languages to include a set type, a typical Pascal implementation (Turbo Pascal) limits sets to those in which the base type has fewer than 256 values, although some implementations (GNU Pascal) have no such limitations.

Examples of Sets Represented as Bit Maps
Consider the following set *V_SYMM*. It contains those uppercase letters that have vertical symmetry

V_SYMM:[A H I M O T U V W X Y]

If the base type is restricted to uppercase letters, this set could be represented by the bit map shown in Figure 3.3 (annotated to show the correspondence between bits and set members).

If an array of bytes is used to store a bit map, rather than an array of words or some larger object, the amount of space wasted is minimized when the size of the underlying domain is not a multiple of the array element size. For instance, a set of both uppercase and lowercase letters (52 potential members) occupies 7 bytes (56 bits), and just 4 bits are wasted.

When a set is implemented using a bit map, the set-membership, insertion, and removal operations are very fast. Because only 1 byte is involved, the time required to perform the operation is independent of both the current size of the set (number of bits that are 1) and the size of the underlying domain (number of bits in the bit map). In the following expression, we assume that *bits* is an array of unsigned bytes and that *CHAR_BIT* is the number of bits in a byte (usually 8). The following expression yields true if element *k* is in the set, and *false* otherwise:

```
( bits[k/CHAR_BIT] & (1<<(CHAR_BIT-1-k%CHAR_BIT)) ) != 0
```

A	B	C	D	E	F	G	H	I	J	K	L	M	N	O	P	Q	R	S	T	U	V	W	X	Y	Z
1	0	0	0	0	0	0	1	1	0	0	0	1	0	1	0	0	0	0	1	1	1	1	1	1	0

Figure 3.3 • Annotated bit map representing *V_SYMM*

If we number both the bytes and the potential members of the set from zero upwards, then $k/CHAR\_BIT$ identifies the element of *bits* that we are interested in. The bit of interest within this byte is isolated by performing a *bitwise-and* (&) on the byte and a bit mask. The bit mask is

10000000 for the leftmost bit (bit 0)
01000000 for bit 1
00100000 for bit 2, and so on.

The appropriate bit mask is achieved by shifting 1 leftwards (1 <<) an appropriate number of places. The result of the *bitwise-and* operation will be zero (false) if the bit we are interested in is 0, and will be nonzero (true) if the bit is set to 1.

Membership Testing: First Example
Figure 3.4 shows the set from Figure 3.3 (*V_SYMM*) padded out to 4 bytes with the byte boundaries identified and the bytes numbered.

Suppose we wish to find out if the letter *S* is in our set of vertically symmetric letters. We start the alphabet with A = 0, therefore the membership of *S* is represented by bit 18 (i.e., $k = 18$). Assuming *CHAR_BIT* is 8, then the appropriate elements of *bits* is *bits*[18/8] = *bits*[2], which is

Q	R	S	T	U	V	W	X
0	0	0	1	1	1	1	1

The value of $CHAR\_BIT - 1 - k\%CHAR\_BIT$ is $8 - 1 - 18\%8 = 7 - 2 = 5$, and the result of 1 << 5 is

0	0	1	0	0	0	0	0

Performing a *bitwise-and* between this bit mask and *bits*[2] yields

0	0	0	0	0	0	0	0

Because this is zero, we know that *S* is not in our set of vertically symmetric letters.

A	B	C	D	E	F	G	H	I	J	K	L	M	N	O	P	Q	R	S	T	U	V	W	X	Y	Z						
1	0	0	0	0	0	0	0	1	1	0	0	0	1	0	1	0	0	0	1	1	1	1	1	0	0	0	0	0	0	0	0

bits[0]   bits[1]   bits[2]   bits[3]

Figure 3.4. • *V_SYMM* bit map in an array of bytes

Membership Testing: Second Example

We wish to see if letter O is in *V_SYMM*. The membership of O is represented by bit 14 (i.e., $k = 14$). The appropriate elements of *bits* is *bits*[14/8] = *bits*[1], which is

I	J	K	L	M	N	O	P
1	0	0	0	1	0	1	0

The value of $CHAR\_BIT - 1 - k\%CHAR\_BIT$ is $8 - 1 - 14\%8 = 7 - 6 = 1$, and the result of $1 << 1$ is

0	0	0	0	0	0	1	0

Performing a *bitwise-and* between this bit mask and *bits*[1] yields

0	0	0	0	0	0	1	0

Because this is nonzero, we know that O is in our set of vertically symmetric letters.

The *insert* and *removal* operations are implemented in a similar manner. The following code adds element k to a set represented by array *bits*:

```
bits[k/CHAR_BIT] |= (1<<(CHAR_BIT-1-k%CHAR_BIT))
```

Here we use *bitwise-or* (|) rather than *bitwise-and*. Note that if the bit is already set, this operation leaves it unchanged. Thus, in contrast to the linked list implementations of a set, the *insert* operation does not need to check for existing membership (unless we wish this to be reported to the user).

The following code removes element k from a set represented by *bits*:

```
bits[k/CHAR_BIT] &= ~(1<<(CHAR_BIT-1-k%CHAR_BIT))
```

For example, suppose we decide that the letter M does not really meet our definition of vertical symmetry and we wish to remove it from *V_SYMM*. The membership of M is represented by bit 12 in *bits*[1]. The byte *bits*[1] is currently

I	J	K	L	M	N	O	P
1	0	0	0	1	0	1	0

We shift 1 to the left three places $(8 - 1 - 12\%8)$, which yields

0	0	0	0	1	0	0	0

The complement of this is

1	1	1	1	0	1	1	1

The result of *bitwise-and*ing this with *bits*[1] is

I	J	K	L	M	N	O	P
1	0	0	0	0	0	1	0

and *M* is removed.

Implementation of Set-Set Operators

In addition to fast membership test, insertion, and removal operations, the *union*, *intersection*, and *difference* operations can also be performed quickly using bitwise operators. Such operators are typically implemented very efficiently at the machine-code level. Recall that the set-set operators are defined only if the underlying base types of the sets are the same; thus, it follows that the bit maps representing the two operands must be the same size. The time required to perform a set-set operation is proportional to the size of the domain and independent of the number of members in either set.

To illustrate how the set-set operators work, we have a second set of uppercase letters. *H_SYMM* contains those letters having horizontal symmetry. The set

   H_SYMM: [B C D E H I O X]

is represented by the bit map shown in Figure 3.5.

A	B	C	D	E	F	G	H	I	J	K	L	M	N	O	P	Q	R	S	T	U	V	W	X	Y	Z
0	1	1	1	1	0	0	1	1	0	0	0	0	0	1	0	0	0	0	0	0	0	0	1	0	0

Figure 3.5 • Bit map representing *H_SYMM*

Union   We perform a *bitwise-or* on the two arrays to get the union of the two sets that they represent. Where there is a bit set to 1 in either operand, the corresponding bit is set to 1 in the result. If there are *N* bytes in each of arrays *A* and *B*, then the result is computed as follows:

```
for (int i=0; i<N; i++) result[i] = A[i] | B[i];
```

For example, we can find the letters that have either vertical or horizontal symmetry by performing a *union* between *V_SYMM* and *H_SYMM*. The result is

   V_SYMM union H_SYMM: [A B C D E H I M O T U V W X Y]

which is represented by the bit map shown in Figure 3.6.

Intersection   We perform a *bitwise-and* between the two bit maps. Only where a particular bit position contains a 1 in both operands will that bit position be a 1 in the result. The loop is similar to the union operation

```
for (int i=0; i<N; i++) result[i] = A[i] & B[i];
```

We can find the letters that have both vertical and horizontal symmetry by performing an intersection operation on the two sets. The result is the set

   H_SYMM intersection V_SYMM: [H I O X]

which is represented by the bit map shown in Figure 3.7.

Difference   To find the difference between two sets, we perform a *bitwise-and* between one bit map and the inverse of the other. Thus, where there is a bit in

A	B	C	D	E	F	G	H	I	J	K	L	M	N	O	P	Q	R	S	T	U	V	W	X	Y	Z
1	1	1	1	1	0	0	1	1	0	0	0	1	0	1	0	0	0	0	1	1	1	1	1	1	0

Figure 3.6 • Bit map representing *H_SYMM union V_SYMM*

A	B	C	D	E	F	G	H	I	J	K	L	M	N	O	P	Q	R	S	T	U	V	W	X	Y	Z
0	0	0	0	0	0	0	1	1	0	0	0	0	0	1	0	0	0	0	0	0	0	0	1	0	0

Figure 3.7 • Bit map representing *H_SYMM intersection V_SYMM*

the first but not in the second there will be a bit in the result. The loop to produce $A - B$ is

```
for (int i=0; i<N; i++) result[i] = A[i] & ~B[i];
```

We can find letters that have vertical but not horizontal symmetry by performing a difference operation on the two sets. The result is the set

$V\_SYMM - H\_SYMM$:   [A M T U V W Y]

which is represented by the bit map shown in Figure 3.8.

Space Requirements for a Bit Map Representation

You have seen that operations on bit maps are fast and independent of set size. How do the space requirements of a bit map implementation compare with those of a linked list implementation? Each of the V_SYMM and H_SYMM sets requires only 4 bytes. A linked list representation requires more space than that whenever the set has two or more members (assuming 4 bytes for the root pointer and 4 bytes for the pointer field in each node). More generally, consider a set of 4-byte integers. If the domain of integers is D, then the bit map implementation requires approximately $D/8$ bytes, whereas a linked list implementation requires 8 bytes per element (4 for the integer field and 4 for the *next* pointer). Thus, our two set-representation schemes require approximately the same amount of space for a set when the set size is $D/64$. For example, if the domain of the integers is 0 through 2047, then a linked list takes up less space when there are fewer than 32 members in the set and more space when there are more than 32.

The setsize Function

In order to determine the size of a set represented using a bit map, we need to count the number of bits set to 1. If the array of bytes is large, it is worth investigating techniques for fast bit counting; see, for example, Berkovich et al. (2000).

The following definition of class *set_bitmap* implements a set using a bit map. The definition includes function *showones*, which outputs a list of the locations where a bit is set to 1. We get the value of *CHAR_BIT* (the number of bits in a *char*) from the system header file *limits.h*.

A	B	C	D	E	F	G	H	I	J	K	L	M	N	O	P	Q	R	S	T	U	V	W	X	Y	Z
1	0	0	0	0	0	0	0	0	0	0	0	1	0	0	0	0	0	0	1	1	1	1	0	1	0

Figure 3.8 • Bit map representing $V\_SYMM - H\_SYMM$

```
#include <limits.h>          // for CHAR_BIT : number of bits in a char

template <class Entry>
class set_bitmap
{
 // requires that Entry can be cast to int

  friend set_bitmap<Entry> operator +<> (set_bitmap<Entry>, set_bitmap<Entry>);
  friend set_bitmap<Entry> operator *<> (set_bitmap<Entry>, set_bitmap<Entry>);
  friend set_bitmap<Entry> operator -<> (set_bitmap<Entry>, set_bitmap<Entry>);

  public: set_bitmap(int N=1024);        // allocate space - default 1K bits
          ~set_bitmap();                 // destructor - reclaim space
          set_bitmap(const set_bitmap& x); // copy constructor
          set_bitmap& operator =(const set_bitmap&);  // assignment operator
bool is_member(Entry);        // check for membership
          bool insert(Entry);          // add new member
          bool remove (Entry);         // remove member
          int setsize();       // current set size
          void show(ostream&); // output locations of the 1 bits

  private:unsigned char *bits;
          int elements;  // number of array elements in bitlist
          int size; // number of potential elements in set
};

// constructor
template <class Entry>
set_bitmap<Entry>::set_bitmap(int N=1024)
{
  size = N;
  // figure how many bytes needed
  if (N%CHAR_BIT==0)
        elements = N/CHAR_BIT;
    else elements = N/CHAR_BIT+1;
  bits = new unsigned char [elements];  // allocate from heap
  for (int i=0; i < elements; i++) bits[i] = 0;  // and set to 0
}

// destructor
template <class Entry>
set_bitmap<Entry>::~set_bitmap()
{
  delete[] bits;
}
```

```
template<class Entry>
set_bitmap<Entry>& set_bitmap<Entry>::operator = (const set_bitmap<Entry>& x)
{
  if (this!=&x)
    {
     elements = x.elements;
     size = x.size;
     delete[] bits;     // to avoid memory leak
     bits = new unsigned char [elements];
     for (int i=0; i < elements; i++) bits[i] = x.bits[i];
    }
  return *this;
}


template<class Entry>
set_bitmap<Entry>::set_bitmap<Entry>(const set_bitmap<Entry> &x)
{
 //  copy constructor
  elements = x.elements;
  size = x.size;
  bits = new unsigned char [elements];
  for (int i=0; i < elements; i++) bits[i] = x.bits[i];
}


template<class Entry>
bool set_bitmap<Entry>::is_member(Entry E)
{
      int i = (int)E;
      if (i < 0 || i > size-1) return false;    // index out of range
      if (  ( bits[i/CHAR_BIT] & ( 1 << ((CHAR_BIT-1)-i%CHAR_BIT))) != 0 )
             return true;
        else return false;
}

template<class Entry>
bool set_bitmap<Entry>::insert(Entry E)
{
      int i = (int)E;
      if (i < 0 || i > size-1) return false;  // index out of range
      bits[i/CHAR_BIT] |= ( 1 << ((CHAR_BIT-1)-i%CHAR_BIT));
      return true;
}
```

```
template<class Entry>
bool set_bitmap<Entry>::remove(Entry E)
{
      int i = (int)E;
      if (i < 0 || i > size-1) return false;  // index out of range
      if (!is_member(E)) return false;         // not in set
      bits[i/CHAR_BIT] &= ~( 1 << ((CHAR_BIT-1)-i%CHAR_BIT));
      return true;
}


template<class Entry>
int set_bitmap<Entry>::setsize()
{
  // code to count the number of bits set to 1 in the array
  int sum = 0;
   for (int i=0; i< elements; i++)
     {
      int tempbyte = bits[i];         // copy for destructive testing
      for (int j=0; j<CHAR_BIT; j++)
        {
          if (tempbyte&1==1) sum++;  // test rightmost bit
          tempbyte = tempbyte >> 1;  // then shift right
        }
     }
  return sum;
}

template <class Entry>
set_bitmap<Entry> operator + (set_bitmap<Entry> A, set_bitmap<Entry> B)
{
  // union – logical or
  set_bitmap<Entry> result;

  for (int i=0; i< A.elements; i++) result.bits[i]= A.bits[i] | B.bits[i];

  return result;
}

template <class Entry>
set_bitmap<Entry> operator * (set_bitmap<Entry> A, set_bitmap<Entry> B)
{
```

```
// intersection - logical and
set_bitmap<Entry> result;

for (int i=0; i< A.elements; i++) result.bits[i]= A.bits[i] & B.bits[i];

return result;
}

template <class Entry>
set_bitmap<Entry> operator - (set_bitmap<Entry> A, set_bitmap<Entry> B)
{
  // difference A minus B
  set_bitmap<Entry> result;

  for (int i=0; i< A.elements; i++) result.bits[i]= A.bits[i] & ~B.bits[i];

  return result;
}

template<class Entry>
void set_bitmap<Entry>::show(ostream &s)
{
// inside square brackets, indices of the 1 bits in ascending order are
// inserted into stream s
s << "[";
for (int i=0; i<elements; i++)
     if (bits[i] != 0)
          for (int j=0; j<CHAR_BIT; j++)
            if ((bits[i] & (1<<((CHAR_BIT-1)-j)))!=0 )
               s << i*CHAR_BIT+j << " ";              // the index of a 1
s << "]\n";
}
```

Testing set_bitmap

The following program tests the bit map implementation of the set abstract data type:

```
#include "set_bitmap.h"
#include <iostream.h>

int main()
{
```

```
set_bitmap<char> A, B, C;
set_bitmap<char> X,Y,Z,S,T,U;

A.insert('x'); cout << A.setsize(); A.show(cout);
A.insert('P'); cout << A.setsize(); A.show(cout);

B.insert('Q'); cout << B.setsize(); B.show(cout);
B.insert('R'); cout << B.setsize(); B.show(cout);
B.insert('P'); cout << B.setsize(); B.show(cout);
B.insert('V'); cout << B.setsize(); B.show(cout);
B.insert('H'); cout << B.setsize(); B.show(cout);

if (B.is_member('P')) cout << "OK"; else cout << "bad"; cout << endl;
if (!B.is_member('M')) cout << "OK"; else cout << "bad"; cout << endl;
if (!B.is_member('W')) cout << "OK"; else cout << "bad"; cout << endl;
if (B.is_member('H')) cout << "OK"; else cout << "bad"; cout << endl;

C = B;
C.show(cout);
cout << C.setsize(); C.show(cout);
C=C;
cout << C.setsize(); C.show(cout);

if (C.remove('V')) C.show(cout); else cout << "bad remove\n";
if (C.remove('D')) C.show(cout); else cout << "bad remove\n";
if (C.remove('H')) C.show(cout); else cout << "bad remove\n";

X.insert('g'); X.insert('f'); X.insert('e');
X.insert('d'); X.insert('c'); X.insert('a');

Y.insert('c'); Y.insert('f'); Y.insert('r'); Y.insert('t');

Z.insert('a'); Z.insert('c'); Z.insert('d');

S = X * Y; cout << S.setsize(); S.show(cout);
T = Y + Z; cout << T.setsize(); T.show(cout);
U = X - Y; cout << U.setsize(); U.show(cout);

return 0;
}
```

• **TABLE 3.1** Time Complexity of Set Operations for Various Implementations			
	Unordered List	**Ordered List**	**Bit Map**
Insert	O(1)	O(N)	O(1)
Remove, Is-member	O(N)	O(N)	O(1)
Union, intersection, difference	O(N^2)	O(N)	O(B)

The output from a run of the program follows:

```
1[120 ]
2[80 120 ]
1[81 ]
2[81 82 ]
3[80 81 82 ]
4[80 81 82 86 ]
5[72 80 81 82 86 ]
OK
OK
OK
OK
[72 80 81 82 86 ]
5[72 80 81 82 86 ]
5[72 80 81 82 86 ]
[72 80 81 82 ]
bad remove
[80 81 82 ]
2[99 102 ]
6[97 99 100 102 114 116 ]
4[97 100 101 103 ]
```

Table 3.1 shows the time complexity of operations on a set for the three set implementations that we have considered. *N* is the number of items in the set, and *B* is the number of potential items (the size of the base type).

3.4 Sets in the STL

The STL supports the *bitset* class (storing sets using the bit map method), the *set* class, and the *multiset* class. As you might expect, given our discussion of bit maps, when using a *bitset*, the user specifies the number of bits in the representation rather than the type of the items to be stored, thus:

bitset S<600>

The following program illustrates some of the facilities available with the *bitset* class:

```
#include <limits.h>
#include <stdlib.h>
#include <bitset>
#include <iostream>

int main()
{
 bitset<50> A,B,C,D;

 // set 20 random bits in A
 for (int i=0;i<20; i++) A.set(rand()%50);

 cout << "number of bytes: " << sizeof(A) << endl;
 cout << "number of bits: " << A.size() << endl;
 cout << "number of 1s: " << A.count() << endl;
 cout << "A          " << A << endl;

 // set 20 random bits in B
 for (int i=0;i<20; i++) B.set(rand()%50);
 cout << "B          " << B << endl;

 C = A & B; cout << "C=A&B      " << C << endl;
 D = C << 5; cout << "D=C<<5     " << D << endl;
 D.flip(4); cout << "D.flip(4)  " << D << endl;

 return 0;
}
```

In our local C++ implementation, space is allocated in multiples of 4 bytes, therefore each *bitset* in this program takes up 8 bytes rather than the 7 bytes it actually needs. The *size* function returns the number of bits in the set in contrast with *count*, which returns the number of bits that are set to 1. The stream-insertion operator is defined so we can see the contents of the set (bits are inserted in descending order of index, i.e., bit 0 is inserted last). We can perform *bitwise-and* and *bitwise-or* operations and, maybe less usefully, shift the bits in a set to the left or right. The *flip* function changes the specified bit. The program produces the following output:

```
number of bytes: 8
number of bits: 50
number of 1s: 19
A          10000010001111011000001010000010111011010100000010
B          00011100000001000110010001000000110000100000111110
C=A&B      00000000000001000000000000000000110000000000000010
D=C<<5     00000000100000000000000000011000000000000001000000
D.flip(4)  00000000100000000000000000011000000000000001010000
```

The number of 1s is reported as 19, even though we set 20 random bits in A; therefore, two of them must have been the same.

A *multiset* is a set that can contain multiple instances of the same item. In the STL, both sets and multisets are stored using a data structure that requires that there be an ordering function defined on the items.[3] By default the < operator must be defined; the user is free to substitute an alternative ordering function.[4]

3.5 Applications of Sets

This section looks at two applications of sets and multisets and uses components from the STL. The first application uses multisets to hold the prime factors of two integers in order to find their highest common factor. The second application shows how sets could be used to process lottery tickets.

3.5.1 Factorization

A multiset can hold the prime factors of an integer. The set of prime factors of 180, for example, is [2 2 3 3 5]; for 4096 it is [2 2 2 2 2 2 2 2 2 2 2 2]. If we take the intersection of such sets derived from integers *A* and *B*, then the resulting set contains the prime factors of the highest common factor (HCF) of *A* and *B*. For example,

prime factorization of 600 = [2 2 2 3 5 5]

prime factorization of 270 = [2 3 3 3 5]

$$[2\ 2\ 2\ 3\ 5\ 5] \cap [2\ 3\ 3\ 3\ 5] => [2\ 3\ 5]$$

The product of 2, 3, 5 is 30, which is the HCF of 600 and 270.

The following program prompts the user for two integers, derives sets (actually multisets) of their prime factors, computes the intersection of the sets, and then reports the product of the elements in the intersection—the HCF.

```
#include <set>
#include <algorithm>    // for intersection
#include <iostream.h>
```

```
multiset<int> factorize (int N)
{
 // return a multiset containing the prime factors of N

     multiset<int> factors;
     int f=2;                   // current factor
     while (N >= f)
       {
       while (N%f==0) { factors.insert(f); N/=f; } // all instances of f
       f++;
       }

     return factors;
}

int main()
{
 multiset<int> FA,FB,FHCF; // for factors
 int A,B,HCF=1;

 cout << "Numbers please :"; cin >> A >> B;

 FA = factorize(A);
 FB = factorize(B);

 // FHCF = intersection FA, FB using STL method

 set_intersection(FA.begin(),FA.end(),
                  FB.begin(),FB.end(),
                  inserter(FHCF,FHCF.begin())
                 );

 // multiply HCF by each member of FHCF using iterator a

 for (multiset<int>::iterator a = FHCF.begin();
      a != FHCF.end();
      a++
     ) HCF*=*a;

 cout << "hcf of " << A << " and " << B << " is " << HCF << endl;

 return 0;
}
```

The following output is from some runs of the program:

```
$ hcf
Numbers please :600 30
hcf of 600 and 30 is 30
$ hcf
Numbers please :600 270
hcf of 600 and 270 is 30
$ hcf
Numbers please :4096 65536
hcf of 4096 and 65536 is 4096
$ hcf
Numbers please :53 97
hcf of 53 and 97 is 1
```

3.5.2 Processing Lottery Tickets

In the pseudo-C++ that follows, a lottery ticket is represented by a set of integers; there is a list (*L*) of such sets. For each ticket, we determine the number of integers it has in common with *winning* (the set of winning numbers) and update a frequency distribution. We assume that the prize money will be allocated based on this distribution. The following fragment shows how the frequency distribution might be determined.[5]

```
// generate the five winning numbers
count = 0;
while (count < 5)
    {
      N = rand(50);                  // pick a number
      if (!winning.is_member(N))  // is number already picked?
        {
          winning.insert(N);    // no, add it to the set
          count++;
        }
    }

// process tickets - list L of sets
while (L != NULL)
    {
      tick = L->data;          // the current ticket
      L = L->next;
      temp = tick * winning;   // intersection operation
      match = temp.size();     // number of winning numbers on this ticket
      Histogram[match]++;      // update counter
    }
// now figure winnings
```

Following is an implementation of the lottery program using the *<list>* and *<set>* classes from the STL. Function *makeset* generates a set of numbers within specified bounds and is used to generate both the set of winning numbers and the tickets. Each ticket in the list is then compared with the winning set, and a distribution of matches is stored in *histogram*. The *figureprizes* function determines the winnings for tickets with five correct numbers, those with four correct numbers, and so on, based on the distribution of matches and on the available jackpot.

```
#include<list>
#include<set>
#include<algorithm>  // for set_intersection

#include <stdlib.h>  // for rand
#include <iostream.h>

typedef set<int> SET_NUM;

const int NUMTIX = 10000;     // the number of tickets
const int JACKPOT = 6000000;  // prize money


void makeset(SET_NUM &T, int sz, int range)
{
 // make set with sz members each in the range 1..range

 T.clear();
 while (T.size()<sz) {T.insert(rand()%range+1);}
}

void showset(SET_NUM T)
{
 for ( SET_NUM::iterator start=T.begin(); start!=T.end(); ++start)
      cout << *start << " ";
}

void figureprizes(int& jpot,int dist[], int prizes[])
{
 // somewhat arbitrary calculation of winning amounts

 jpot = jpot - dist[3] * 5;  // money left after $5 winners
  if (dist[5]>0) // match all, get 90% of money left
      {
          prizes[5] = ( 9*jpot/10 ) / dist[5];
```

```
                jpot = jpot/10;
            }
    if (dist[4]>0) // match 4 of 5, get 20% of money left
        {
            prizes[4] = ( 2*jpot/10) / dist[4];
            jpot = 8*jpot/10;
        }
}


int main()
{
 list<SET_NUM> tickets;         // list of customer tickets
 SET_NUM winningnums,           // the winning numbers
         ticket,
         intersection;

 int histogram[] = {0,0,0,0,0,0}; // how many tickets with 0,1,2 ... correct
 int prize[] = {0,0,0,5,0,0};     // always win $5 for 3 numbers correct
 int prizepool = JACKPOT;

 srand(123);                             // seed the random number generator

  // generate the tickets
  for (int i=0; i<NUMTIX; i++)
    {
      makeset(ticket,5,50);             // make a ticket and
      tickets.push_back(ticket);        // append to the list
    }

  // generate winning numbers
  makeset(winningnums,5,50);
  cout << "!! WINNING NUMBERS: ";
  showset(winningnums);
  cout << "!!\n";

  // process tickets, evaluate each and create distribution of winners
  for (list<SET_NUM>::iterator sta = tickets.begin();
       sta !=tickets.end(); ++sta
      )
       {
         ticket = *sta;
         // form intersection of ticket and winning numbers
         intersection.clear();
```

```
            // following function is from the STL
            set_intersection(ticket.begin(),ticket.end(),
                         winningnums.begin(),winningnums.end(),
                         inserter(intersection,intersection.begin())
                         );
            // get size of the intersection and bump appropriate histogram entry
            histogram[intersection.size()]++;
          }

  // figure out how much each type of ticket is worth
  figureprizes(prizepool,histogram,prize);

  // report results
  for (int i=5; i>=0; i--)
    {
     if (histogram[i]>0 && prize[i]>0.0)
         cout << "Number of tickets with " << i << " numbers correct: "
              << histogram[i] << ". Each worth $" << prize[i] << endl;
    }
  cout << "rolling over $" << prizepool << " to next draw\n";

  return 0;

}
```

The following output is from a run of the program.

```
!! WINNING NUMBERS: 9 11 16 17 43 !!
Number of tickets with 4 numbers correct: 1. Each worth $1199956
Number of tickets with 3 numbers correct: 44. Each worth $5
rolling over $4799824 to next draw
```

● Chapter Summary

This chapter examined the set abstract data type, the operations possible on a single set, and those operations defined between compatible sets. Sets can be implemented in many ways. We saw the advantages and disadvantages of an implementation using linked lists and an implementation using an array of bits. The STL includes class definitions for sets and multisets. We saw how these could be applied to factorization and to the processing of lottery tickets.

● Exercises

1. Consider the following strategy for extracting a random member of a set implemented as a linked list. We traverse the list, and for each node we encounter we generate a

random probability P $(0.0 \leq P < 1.0)$. If $P > 0.5$, we extract the current node and exit; otherwise, we continue. What are the flaws in this approach?

2. Suppose we have the following two sets

    A: [1 3 4 6 8]

    B: [2 3 5 6 7 8 9 10]

    What is the result of each of the following?

    a. $A \cup B$

    b. $A \cap B$

    c. $A - B$

    d. A *symmetric-difference* B

3. Suppose we define *restricted-multiset-k* as a type of multiset in which no item can appear more than k times (thus a set is a *restricted-multiset*-1). How would you define *union*, *intersection*, and *sum* operations on this type of set? Justify your reasoning.

4. Outline a method for extracting a random member of a set that is implemented as a bit map.

5. An online bookstore implements gift certificates. Each certificate has a monetary value and a unique identification number. Devise a class of objects that enables a user to:

    a. Create a new certificate with a specified value V.

    b. Determine the value left on certificate N.

    c. Reduce the value remaining on certificate N by an amount X, and when the value becomes zero, remove the certificate from the certificate set.

6. Outline an algorithm that inputs two integers X and Y $(X < Y)$ and reports which integer I $(X < I < Y)$ has the largest set of prime factors. The number 30, for example, has three factors (2, 3, 5), 80 has two (2, 5), and 49 has one (7).

7. Design and test a function that reverses an arbitrary *bitset*. Thus, if A is 010010001110011, then *reverse(A)* is 110011100010010.

8. Certain book-indexing software uses *bitsets* to store the numbers of pages on which certain terms appear. Write a function that takes a *bitset* as a parameter and outputs an appropriate string suitable for an index. For example, if the *bitset* is

    011001011101110010

    then the string might be

    1, 4–6, 8–10, 12, 15–16.

9. Write and test a function that processes a string of page references as it might appear in an index and returns a *bitset* containing the numbers of pages referenced. (This is the inverse of the previous exercise.) Thus, if the input were

2–5, 7, 8, 13–15, 19

the result would be the bitset

10001110000110111100

10. Write and test a function that processes a string of integers and (possibly overlapping) integer ranges and returns a *multiset* containing the integers referenced. (This is a generalization of the previous exercise.) For example, if the input were

2–4, 1–6, 5, 3–7

the result would be the multiset

[1 2 2 3 3 3 4 4 4 5 5 5 6 6 7]

11. Write a function that takes a multiset as a parameter and outputs a representation of its contents as a string. Try to make the string as short as possible. (This is the inverse of the previous exercise.)

12. Devise an algorithm that permits a user to enter a string of uppercase letters and determines if

   a. The string will look the same when upside-down (e.g., NOON).

   b. The string will look the same when viewed in a mirror (e.g., TOYOT).

13. Devise an algorithm that permits a user to enter a character string and then determines if the string can be typed using

   a. Only the left hand.

   b. Only the right hand.

   c. Both hands (assuming a conventional mapping of typewriter keys to hands).

14. We can define the Hamming distance between two bitsets as the number of bits in one bitset that have to be flipped in order to make it identical to the other. Write a function *Hamming* that takes two bitsets as parameters and returns the Hamming distance between them.

15. Write a function *flip* for our *set_bitmap* class. The effect of *flip()* is to change all the bits in the set. The effect of *flip(i)* is to change only the *i*th bit.

16. Write a function *Int_to_bitset* that takes as parameters integers K and N. *Int_to_bitset* returns a bitset that, when printed, resembles the N-bit binary representation of K. For example

```
cout << Int_to_bitset(-7,9)   outputs   111111001
```

17. Write a function *Bitset_to_int* that takes a bitset and returns the signed integer that it would represent if its contents were viewed as a signed binary number. For example, if bitset B were [11011011000] then *Bitset_to_int(B)* should return -296.

18. How would you use sets to find the least common multiple of positive integers A and B, that is, the smallest number of which both A and B are factors?

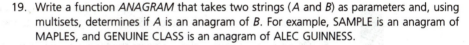

19. Write a function *ANAGRAM* that takes two strings (*A* and *B*) as parameters and, using multisets, determines if *A* is an anagram of *B*. For example, SAMPLE is an anagram of MAPLES, and GENUINE CLASS is an anagram of ALEC GUINNESS.

20. How many proper subsets are there of a set with *N* members? Suggest a way to systematically generate the proper subsets of set *S*.

21. Write a function *COMBINATION* that takes as parameters an integer *k* and a set *S* with *N* members. The function outputs all the different subsets of *S* having exactly *k* members.

22. Suppose we have 100 flags numbered 1 through 100 and that initially all the flags are raised. We then take down each odd-numbered flag. Then we reverse the position (up to down or down to up) of flags 3, 6, 9, and so on. Then we reverse the position of flags 4, 8, 12, and so on. We proceed in this manner until the final modification is made just to flag 100. What are the numbers of the flags still flying? Write an algorithm that uses a bitset to solve this problem.

23. Suppose that bills in a legislature each have a unique four-digit number. The voting record of a legislator can be represented by a set of the numbers of the bills that he or she voted for. A certain lobbying group wishes to identify the legislators whose voting record most closely match their interests. If *x* is the set of bills that the group supports and *legislator*[*I*] is the set of bills supported by legislator *I*, sketch an algorithm that identifies the five legislators of most interest to the lobbyists. Show how you break ties.

24. If main memory space were not at a premium, how could we rewrite *setsize* (for the bit map implementation) so that it runs faster than the current version?

Problems

1. Assume the existence of a set of words *DIR*. Write a program that lets a user input a set of characters and identifies the longest word in *DIR* that can be made from just the letters input (repeating letters as often as necessary).

2. Write a program that identifies those words in *DIR* (see Problem 1) that

   a. look the same when a mirror is placed halfway across them. An example is

      CHECKBOOK

   b. look the same when a mirror is placed halfway along them. An example is

      TOOT

3. Write a function *SIMILAR* that takes two words *S1* and *S2* as parameters and determines how similar they are. If the words are identical, the function returns 0. For other pairs of words you might consider the number of transformations (insert a letter, remove a letter, transpose adjacent letters, double a letter) required to turn *S1* into *S2*. For example, *pool* might be considered similar with a score of 1 to *polo*, *pol*, and *tool* and similar with a score of 2 to *peel* and *moon*.

4. Use *SIMILAR* (see Problem 3) in a program that enables a user to enter a misspelled word (*W*) and reports which words in *DIR* (see Problem 1) are most similar to *W*.

5. Implement set-set operations for an implementation of sets that uses ordered linked lists. Your implementations should operate directly on the lists themselves.

6. On a system of your choice, compare the time required to insert and remove items from a *bitset* with the time required to perform the same operations on a *set*. Test a variety of set sizes.

7. Rewrite the lottery program so that it uses the *bitset* class instead of the *set* class.

8. Consider the different relationships there can be between two sets A and B (e.g., A and B are identical, A is a proper subset of B, and so on). Write and test a function that takes two sets as parameters and returns a value that indicates their relationship.

9. Primes from 2 to N can be found using the following sieve method created by Aristosthenes.

   a. Mark integers 2 through N.

   b. Examine each number in turn from 2 through N. If the number is marked, output it and unmark all its multiples.

   Write a program that inputs N and outputs the primes from 2 to N using a bitset and this sieve method.

10. Investigate *multisets*. How are the following operations defined: *intersection, union, sum*, and *difference*?

11. A certain set (E) of positive integers has the property that

    a. 1 is in E.

    b. Whenever x and y are in E (the case $x = y$ being allowed), $2x + 5y$ is in E.

    Write a program that reads a positive integer N and constructs the largest set E where all the elements are less than N.

12. An N-bit Gray code is an ordering of the 2^N N-bit binary numbers in which each number differs from the previous one in only one bit position. Thus, a 3-bit Gray code might be

    000 001 011 010 110 111 101 100

    Note how the sequence wraps around. Design and test a function $Gray(N)$ that uses a bitset and outputs an appropriate sequence of N-bit codes.

13. A certain bitset M contains N bits. The members of the set are the numbers of those blocks on a disc currently in use. For example, M with 70 bits is

    1111111111111111111100001110011100001111110011111000001110000001100

    Write and test two functions:

    a. *first_fit(M,N,k)* returns the starting point of the first sequence of consecutive integers at least k long, none of which is in M. By "first" we mean the sequence with the smallest starting point. The function should return -1 if there is no such sequence. Recall that bits are numbered from 0 upwards, right-to-left. In the case of our example, *first_fit(M,70,3)* returns 4 (the index of the sequence of six zeroes).

b. *best_fit(M,N,k)* returns the address of the shortest sequence of integers at least *k* long, none of which is in *M*. If there are multiple smallest sequences, it should return the lowest possible address. Again, −1 should be returned if there is no sequence that satisfies the requirements. With our example bitset, *best_fit(M,70,3)* returns 33 (the start of the first of the two sequences of length 4).

14. Use a bitset of 366 entries to investigate the "Birthday Paradox." Start with an initially empty bitset, and use a reliable source of random integers in the range 1 through 366. Insert random integers into the set until an integer is found that is already in the set. Record the number (*I*) of iterations it took to find a duplicate. Run your program a significant number of times and plot the distribution of *I*.

References

Berkovich, S., G. M. Lapir, and M. Mack. 2000. A bit-counting algorithm using the frequency division principle. *Software: Practice and Experience* 30(14):1531–1540.

Jensen, K., and N. Wirth. 1974. *Pascal: User Manual and Report.* Berlin: Springer-Verlag.

Schwartz, J. T., and R. B. K., Dewar. 1986. *Programming with Sets—An Introduction to SETL.* Berlin: Springer-Verlag.

Notes

[1]A *bag* is also a collection of items of some type, but in the case of a bag, an object may appear multiple times. For example, a particular bag of integers could be denoted

(4, 274, 65, −99, 274, 36, 0, −99)

A *multiset* is also a collection in which multiple occurrences are permitted (i.e., it is another name for a bag).

[2]On the system used by the author, a *bool* variable occupies 4 bytes, that is, 32 times as much space as theoretically required!

[3]A balanced search tree is used. We look at balanced trees in Chapter 6.

[4]Set functions test to see if $A == B$ by checking that both $A < B$ and $B < A$ are false.

[5]Appendix A discusses random number generation and describes the weaknesses of using a single seed generator to pick lottery numbers. Here, where we pick 5 from 50, using a 32-bit seed is OK because only about 2.1 million different tickets are possible.

Stacks and Queues

● 4.1 Introduction

A **deque** (pronounced "deck") is a linear structure in which items can be removed and added only at the ends. Figure 4.1 is a depiction of a deque.

The arrows in Figure 4.1 indicate the permissible insertion and removal operations. This chapter looks at two subclasses of deques that are of particular interest because of their use in many applications. These subclasses are the **stack,** depicted in Figure 4.2a, and the **queue,** depicted in Figure 4.2b.

Note that in a stack, insertions and removals take place at the same end, whereas in a queue, items are inserted at one end and removed at the other.

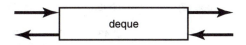

Figure 4.1 • Deque

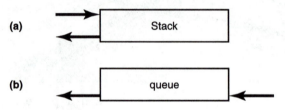

Figure 4.2 • Stack (a) and queue (b)

4.2 Stacks

To understand how a stack operates, think of a stack of books or dishes, where a new item may be added only at the top and the only item that can be removed is the top one. A stack is sometimes called a LIFO (last-in, first-out) structure because the most recently added item (the last one in) is the one that is removed first (the first out).

4.2.1 Basic Stack Operations

Conventions vary as to the number and the effect of the fundamental operations associated with the stack abstract data type. We will assume for the present that there are two operations:

- *Push(X)*: Pushes the value *X* onto the stack
- *Pop(Z)*: Pops the top item off the stack and stores it in *Z*

Figure 4.3 shows a sequence of stack operations.

In addition to routines that implement the fundamental operations, we have chosen two convenient ones, and arrive at the following top-level definition of a stack class.

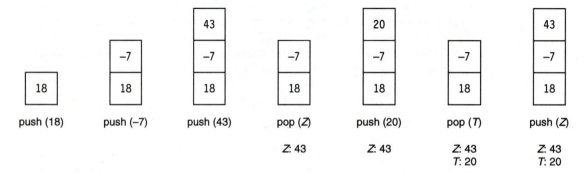

Figure 4.3 • Stack operations

```
template <class Entry>
class stack
{
  public: stack();               // constructor
        ~stack();                 // destructor
          bool push(Entry);       // push item onto stack
          bool pop (Entry&);      // pop from stack into item
          bool isempty();         // check if stack is empty
          bool get_top (Entry&);  // get top without popping it
  private: // implementation specific
};
```

The *pop*, *push*, and *get_top* functions each return *false* if the operation cannot be performed successfully. For example, *pop* is undefined if the stack is empty; *push* will fail if the stack cannot be expanded.

You may be aware that when a typical program runs and calls a subprogram or function, information about the calling environment (register values perhaps) is saved on a stack. The stack is a good place to keep local variables, to store parameters passed into a function, and to store results passed back to the calling environment. Figure 4.4 depicts this run-time stack during the execution of function *C*, which has been called from function *B*, which in turn has been called from function *A*.

A stack is an appropriate data structure to use for this purpose because of the nested nature of function calls. When the call of *C* terminates, we pop off its parameters and local variables and resume the call of *B*. Similarly, when the call of *B* finishes, its data are popped from the top of the stack.

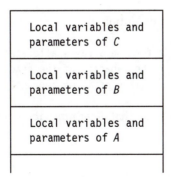

Figure 4.4 • Partial stack during call of *C*, called from *B*, called from *A*

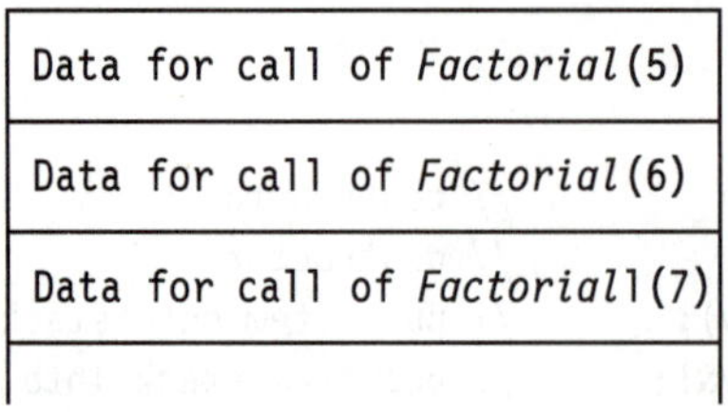

| Data for call of *Factorial*(5) |
| Data for call of *Factorial*(6) |
| Data for call of *Factoriall*(7) |
| |

Figure 4.5 • A partial stack during a call of *Factorial*(10)

If a function is recursive, many levels on the stack may correspond to different instantiations of the function. For example, the following defines a *Factorial* function recursively:

```
Factorial (N): if N is 1 or 0
               return 1
otherwise      return N * Factorial(N-1)
```

Figure 4.5 depicts part of the stack during a call of *Factorial*(10).

This space and time overhead of multiple function calls is the reason that recursion, although elegant, is not as efficient as the equivalent iteration.

4.2.2 Stack Implementations

An array (e.g., *data_values*) of a certain fixed size (e.g., *stack_size*) can hold the stack items, and a counter (e.g., *count*) can record the number of items currently in the stack. To minimize data movement during *pop* and *push* operations, we will adopt the convention that *data_values*[0] contains the item at the bottom of the stack and that *data_values*[*count*−1] holds the top item. Now we do not need to move existing items when a new one is pushed onto the stack or when the top item is removed.

The private section of the class definition is

```
private: Entry *data_values;  // for the array — allocated dynamically
         int stack_size;      // the capacity of the stack
         int count;           // number of items currently in the stack
```

We give the constructor a parameter that determines the stack size, perhaps with a default value, thus:[1]

```
template <class Entry>
stack<Entry>::stack(int capacity = 15)
{
    stack_size = capacity;                    // remember parameter value
```

```
    data_values = new Entry[stack_size]; // allocate space
    count = 0;                           // stack initially empty
}
```

Figure 4.6 shows how the rightmost stack of Figure 4.3 might be stored using the array method.[2]

Implementation of the stack functions is straightforward. For example, the definition of *pop* is:

```
template <class Entry>
bool stack<Entry>::pop(Entry& item)
  {
    if (count==0)
        return false;          // stack empty
    else
        {
        count--;                       // reduce count and
        item = data_values[count];   // get item
        return true;
        }
  }
```

However, with many applications, we may not be able to determine the maximum stack space necessary or we may not wish to waste unused space in the array. Dynamic linked storage is an alternative way to hold the stack elements. For example, the stack from Figure 4.7a can be represented by the single-linked list of Figure 4.7b.

The linked list representation could be very similar to the single-linked lists defined in Chapter 2. That linked list class can be reused, thus:

```
#include "llist.h"

template <class Entry>
class stack
```

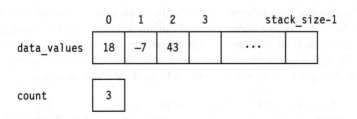

Figure 4.6 • Array implementation of a stack

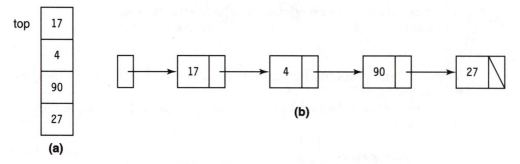

top

(a)

(b)

Figure 4.7 • An abstract stack (a) and implementation as a linked list (b)

```
{  public: stack();              // constructor
          ~stack();              // destructor
          bool push(Entry);      // push item onto stack
          bool pop(Entry&);      // pop from stack into item
          bool isempty();        // is empty?
          bool get_top(Entry&);  // get top without popping it
private: linkedlist<Entry> data; // list of items
          int count;
};
```

The definition of the *pop* function for this implementation is:

```
template <class Entry>
bool stack<Entry>::pop (Entry& item)
{
  if (count==0) return false;  // stack is empty
  data.Finditem(0,item);
  data.remove(0);
  count--;
  return true;
}
```

• 4.2.3 Stack Applications

The following sections illustrate the usefulness of stacks with three applications. The first checks a string to see if the bracket characters are well formed. The second shows how an arithmetic expression can be evaluated with the aid of two stacks. The third application shows how a stack is useful in implementing an algorithm that may have to retrace its steps in finding a solution to a problem.

Stack Application 1: Bracket Checking
Suppose we wish to check a text string *T* to see if the bracket characters it contains are well formed. We use the term *brackets* here to include character pairs with dis-

tinct opening and closing characters such as { }, < >, and ( ). The brackets are well formed if the number of openers is the same as the number of closers and, reading the string from left to right, the number of closers never exceeds the number of openers. Thus, for example,

()()() is well formed.
((())) is well formed.
(()())) is not well formed.
(()))()(is not well formed.

If the text uses only one opener character and one closer character, then we can accomplish the checking with a simple count, as in the following function:

```
bool bracket_check (string T, char opener, char closer)
{
        int N = T.length(), count = 0;

        for (int i=0; i<N && count >=0; i++)  // stop at end or negative count
          {
                if (T[i]==opener) count++;
           else if (T[i]==closer) count--;
          }
return (count==0);  // count is zero at end for well-formed string
}
```

Thus,

bracket_check ("(()   (( )))", '(', ')') returns *true*
bracket_check ("< < > < > > >", '<', '>') returns *false*
bracket_check ("{ { } } } { }", '{', '}') returns *false*

However, if multiple opener/closer pairs are used, then we need a stack in order to know, for example, what sequence of closers is permitted after text such as

(then { f(ar[Q[j ...

We will have a list of opening characters and a list of corresponding closing characters and arrange matters so that a closing bracket character occupies the same position in the list *closers* as the corresponding opening character does in the list *openers*. The following are example lists:

openers: (< { [
closers:) > }]

Lists, rather than strings, are used so we can easily add multicharacter delimiters such as /* and */, *begin* and *end*, and *if* and *endif*. The following function uses the lists to check a string:

```
bool bracket_check2 (string T,
                     linkedlist<char> openers, linkedlist<char> closers
                     )
{
     const int N = T.length();
     stack<char> S;

     for (int i=0; i<N; i++)
       {
         // if current character is opener, push on stack
         if (openers.finditem(T[i]) != -1)
             S.push(T[i]);
         else
           { // see if it is a closer
             int position = closers.finditem(T[i]);
             if (position != -1)
                { // yes, check stack top to see if it matches
                  char temp;
                  if (S.pop(temp))
                   {
                     if (openers.finditem(temp)!=position)
                         return false;  // last opener not the right one
                   }
                  else return false; // there was no opener to check
                }
           }
       }
     return (S.size()==0);   // bad matching if stack not empty. There
                             // were more openers than closers
}
```

Thus,

```
bracket_check2 ( "( < > { (<><>) })", openers, closers) returns true
bracket_check2 ( "( { < >()(( ))))", openers, closers) returns false
bracket_check2 ( "< [ ]{{}} > >", openers, closers)       returns false
```

Stack Application 2: Expression Evaluation
An algorithm to translate an infix arithmetic expression into the corresponding bracket-free postfix expression uses a stack. An example translation is

$$(a * b) + (c * d) / e * f \quad \text{to} \quad ab * cd * e/f * +$$

Postfix form may be more useful if we want to evaluate the expression using a calculator or translate the expression into a sequence of assembly code instructions. (Postfix form is sometimes referred to as Reverse Polish notation.)[3] The translation algorithm reads the input a symbol at a time. Operands are passed straight through to the output, whereas parentheses and operators are put on a stack. The operators are popped to the output at the appropriate time.

We can also use a stack to evaluate a postfix expression, for example:

ab * *cd* * *e*/*f* * +

with

$a = 3, b = 6, c = 4, d = 2, e = 4, f = 5$

is 28.

The postfix expression is read a symbol at a time. If the symbol is an operand, its value is pushed onto a stack. If the symbol is an operator, the appropriate operation is applied to the top two stack items, which are then replaced by the result of the operation. Figure 4.8 shows the processing of the example expression. Above each symbol of the input is a depiction of the stack after that symbol has been processed.

As you might expect, the translation algorithm and the evaluation algorithm can be combined into a single algorithm that evaluates an infix expression using two stacks (one for operators and one for operands). Here is that algorithm:

```
while more input
    {
        Get symbol S
        If S is an operand push its value on the operand stack
        If S is an opening parenthesis push it onto the operator
                stack with precedence 0.
        If S is a closing parenthesis, pop operators off the
                operator stack (and apply them to the operand stack)
                until we reach an opening parenthesis. Pop the
                opening parenthesis.
        If S is an operator, pop operators off the operator stack
                (and apply them to the operand stack) until the
                precedence of the top item is lower than the
                precedence of S. Push S on the operator stack.
    }
Pop and apply any operators remaining on the operator stack.
```

				2		4		5		
	6		4	4	8	8	2	2	10	
3	3	18	18	18	18	18	18	18	18	28
a	b	*	c	d	*	e	/	f	*	+

Figure 4.8 • Evaluation of a postfix expression

● **TABLE 4.1** Operator Precedence	
Operator	**Precedence**
* /	2
+ −	1

The precedence of operators determines the order in which they are applied within an expression. Our example implementation uses very few operators and assumes the precedences shown in Table 4.1.[4]

The following program is an implementation of the expression evaluation algorithm. It assumes that the expression consists of integers, parentheses, and operators (with various priorities). If the expression is well formed, its value is left as the only item on the operand stack.[5]

```cpp
// fragile evaluator of well-formed infix expressions
// assumes tokens are separated by white space
// tokens are: ( ) operators and integers

#include <string>
#include <iostream>
#include <cstdlib>
#include "stack.h"

typedef stack<int> intstack;

enum symtype {oprand,openparen,closeparen,oprator};




int valueof(string integer)
{
// atoi only on C-style strings?
char temp[100]; int i=0;
string::iterator j=integer.begin();
while (j<integer.end()) { temp[i++] = *j; j++; }
temp[i]='\0';
return atoi(temp);
}
```

```
symtype classify(string sym)
{
  if (sym=="(") return openparen;
  if (sym==")") return closeparen;
  if (   sym=="+" || sym=="-" || sym=="*" || sym=="/") return oprator;
  return oprand;
}

void apply (string op, intstack& OS)
{
  int one, two;
  OS.pop(two);
  OS.pop(one);
        if (op=="+") OS.push(one+two);
  else if (op=="-") OS.push(one-two);
  else if (op=="*") OS.push(one*two);
  else if (op=="/") OS.push(one/two);
}

int precedence (string op)
{
 if (op == "*" || op == "/") return 2;
 if (op == "+" || op == "-") return 1;
 return 0;
}


int main()
{
  int result;
  bool go_on;
  string OP, symbol;

  stack<string> operatorstack;
  intstack operandstack;

  while (cin >> symbol)
    {
      int symboltype = classify(symbol);
      switch (symboltype)
        {
        case oprand: operandstack.push(valueof(symbol));
                  break;
```

```
                  case openparen: operatorstack.push("(");
                          break;

              case closeparen: go_on = true;
                          while(go_on)
                            { operatorstack.pop(OP);
                              if (OP=="(")
                                       go_on=false;
                              else    apply(OP,operandstack);
                            }
                          break;

              case oprator: while(true)
                          {
                            if (!operatorstack.pop(OP)) break;
                            if (precedence(OP) < precedence(symbol))
                                {operatorstack.push(OP); break; }
                            apply(OP,operandstack);
                          }
                          operatorstack.push(symbol);
              }
          }

      while (operatorstack.pop(OP)) apply(OP,operandstack);
      operandstack.pop(result);
      cout << result;

      return 0;
  }
```

This program assumes that the input expression is well formed. Some errors can be detected by remembering the type of the preceding symbol and comparing it with the type of the current symbol. For example, the symbol immediately following an opening parenthesis must be another opening parenthesis or an operand. In addition, as described previously, a simple counter can detect ill-formed parentheses.

Stack Application 3: Backtracking Algorithm

Stacks are useful in applications that need to backtrack to a previous state of some kind in order to move forward in a different direction. Think of solving a maze. On encountering a dead end, we need to backtrack to the last place where we had a choice of paths to follow and move in a different direction than the one that led to the dead end. A stack is an appropriate structure on which to keep information about decision points because the data is accessible in the order in which we may need to backtrack; the most recent choice point is on top, the one before that is the second stack item, and so on.

The problem of finding a knight's tour around a chessboard can be used to illustrate the use of backtracking. A **knight's tour** is a sequence of moves made by a knight chess piece that visits each square on the board exactly once. In each move, the knight moves two squares horizontally then one vertically, or two squares vertically then one horizontally. (In a chess game, its move cannot be blocked by another piece.) The eight squares that a knight may reach in a single move from a particular square S are marked ♞ in Figure 4.9.

If S is close to an edge of the board, there may be fewer than eight reachable squares. The reader is encouraged to attempt to find a knight's tour of a four-by-three board before looking ahead at Figure 4.10, which shows one possible tour beginning at the square marked 1 and continuing to squares 2, 3, . . . , 12. However, be aware that for certain starting squares, no tour of a four-by-three board is possible.

In a **reentrant knight's tour**, it is possible to move from the last square back to the first with a single additional move.

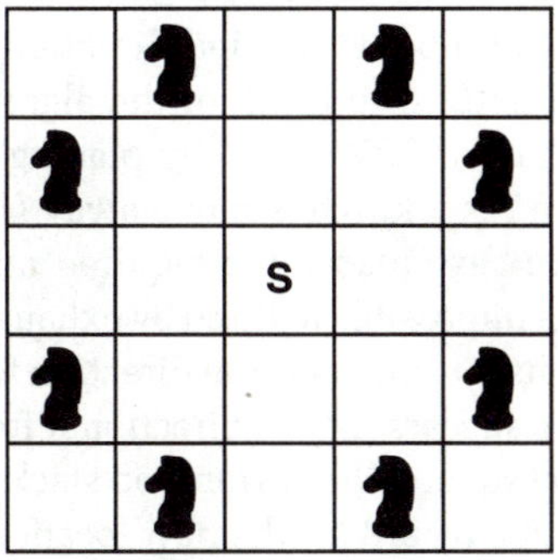

Figure 4.9 • The eight squares reachable in a single knight moves from square S

1	4	7	10
8	11	2	5
3	6	9	12

Figure 4.10 • A knight's tour on a four-by-three board

Figure 4.11 • Numbering of potential directions for the knight's move

Information about a decision point on the stack is stored as a triple:

column, row, direction-to-try-next

in which we number directions as in Figure 4.11. When we have a choice of moves to try, we will choose the lowest-numbered untried direction.

Rather than a tour, it may be helpful to think of the algorithm as placing numbered knights (1, 2, 3, . . .) on the board. We start by placing the first knight on an arbitrary square; thereafter, piece I is a knight's move away from piece $I - 1$.

Our algorithm iterates until we have placed the required number of pieces on the board or have determined that it is impossible to do so by exhausting all possible paths. When we place a piece, we stack its location and the direction to try if we ever need to backtrack to that point. If we move successfully in direction K from a particular square, we update the stack record for that square (the current top stack item) so that next time we try direction $K + 1$. We also put a record for the new location on the stack.

Consider an attempt to tour a four-by-four board starting at row 1 column 1.[6] The board and stack are shown in Figure 4.12. Depictions of the stack will show triples. Next to each triple, in square brackets, the stack will show the number of the knight that it represents.

We successfully place the second knight in direction 4 from the first one so that the board and the stack are as shown in Figure 4.13. The stack entry for the first decision point (where to place the second knight) has been updated so that if we need to backtrack that far we try direction 5 next.

Figure 4.14 shows the location of the third knight and the state of the stack.

We can continue in this manner until we reach the configuration shown in Figure 4.15. For space reasons, we omit all except the top few stack items. We have no square on which to place knight 15.

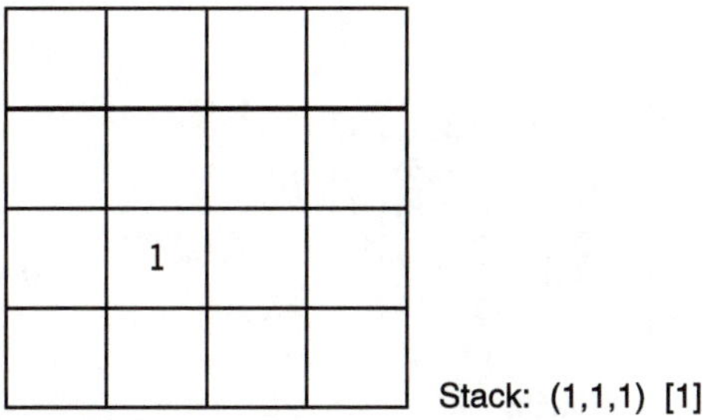

Stack: (1,1,1) [1]

Figure 4.12 • Placement of first knight

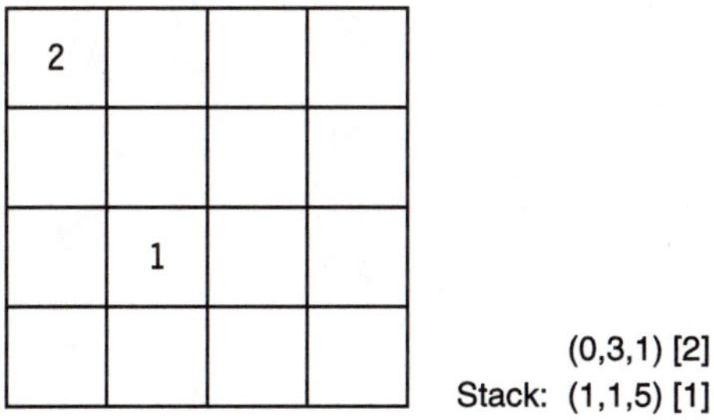

(0,3,1) [2]
Stack: (1,1,5) [1]

Figure 4.13 • Placement of second knight

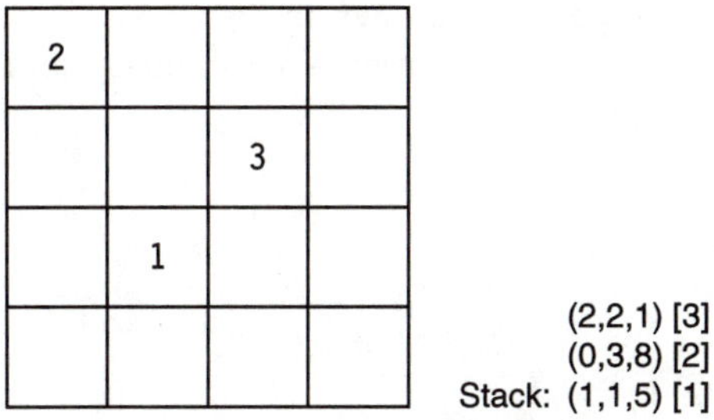

(2,2,1) [3]
(0,3,8) [2]
Stack: (1,1,5) [1]

Figure 4.14 • Placement of third knight

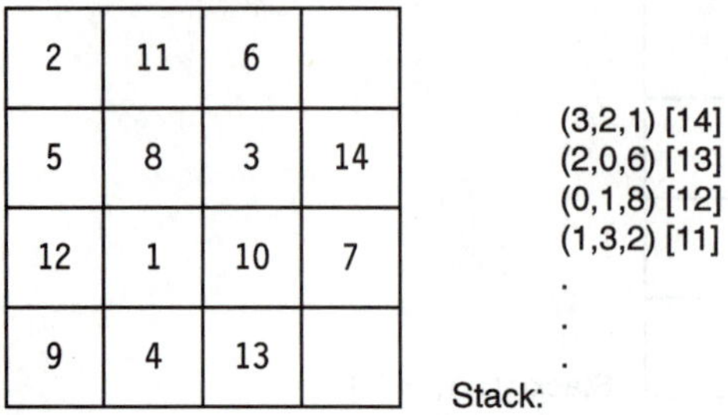

2	11	6	
5	8	3	14
12	1	10	7
9	4	13	

(3,2,1) [14]
(2,0,6) [13]
(0,1,8) [12]
(1,3,2) [11]
.
.
.
Stack:

Figure 4.15 • Configuration before backtracking

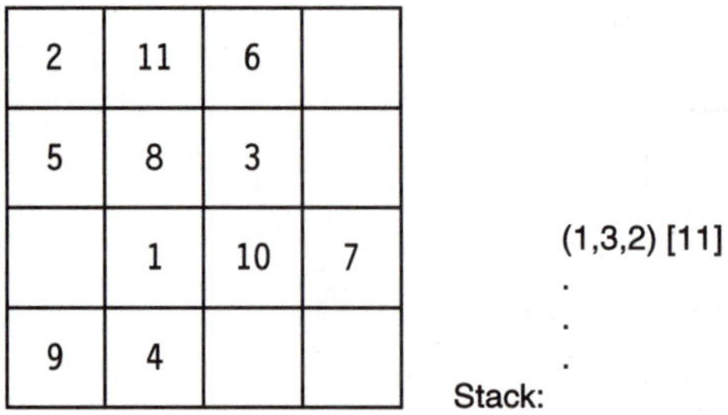

2	11	6	
5	8	3	
	1	10	7
9	4		

(1,3,2) [11]
.
.
.
Stack:

Figure 4.16 • Backtracking

We remove knight 14, but there is no other square on which to place it, so we remove knight 13. However, there is no other square on which to place knight 13 either. We remove knight 12, leaving the board as in Figure 4.16.

We now move forward and try the next possible direction from knight 11 (this is direction 7) and place knight 12 as shown in Figure 4.17.

It turns out that there is no tour possible for a four-by-four square, so eventually we exhaust all possible paths.

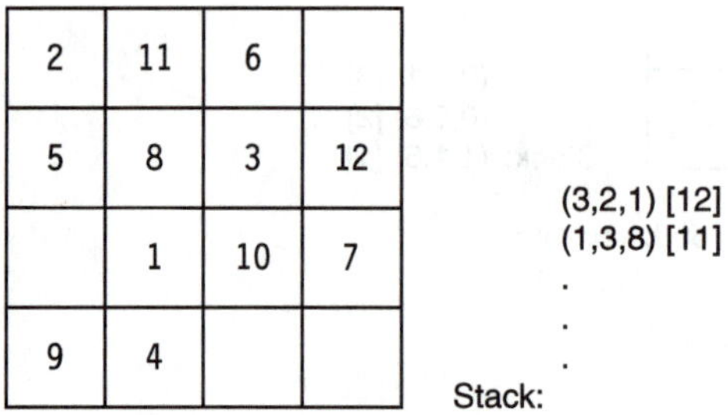

2	11	6	
5	8	3	12
	1	10	7
9	4		

(3,2,1) [12]
(1,3,8) [11]
.
.
.
Stack:

Figure 4.17 • Moving forward again

In the following program, the user defines the dimensions of the board (*numrows* by *numcols*) and also the length (*goal*) of the path required (for a full tour, *goal* = *numrows* * *numcols*). The user supplies the coordinates of the start square at run time. In the array representing the board, we use zero to indicate an empty square and a value *I* to indicate that a square is occupied by the *I*th knight.

```cpp
#include <iostream.h>
#include <iomanip.h>
#include <stdlib.h>
#include <stack>

const int NUMROWS = 5;
const int NUMCOLS = 5;
const int GOAL = NUMROWS * NUMCOLS; // for a complete tour

bool move (int col, int row, int dir,
           int& newcol, int& newrow, int board[][NUMROWS])
{
  switch(dir)
    {
        case 1: if (col>0 && row>1 && board [col-1][row-2]==0)
                  {
                    newcol = col-1; newrow = row-2; return true;
                  }
                  return false;
        case 2: if (col>1 && row>0 && board [col-2][row-1]==0)
                  {
                    newcol = col-2; newrow = row-1; return true;
                  }
                  return false;
        case 3: if (col>1 && row<NUMROWS-1 && board [col-2][row+1]==0)
                  {
                    newcol = col-2; newrow = row+1; return true;
                  }
                  return false;
        case 4: if (col>0 && row<NUMROWS-2 && board [col-1][row+2]==0)
                  {
                    newcol = col-1; newrow = row+2; return true;
                  }
                  return false;
        case 5: if (col<NUMCOLS-1 && row<NUMROWS-2 && board[col+1][row+2]==0)
                  {
                    newcol = col+1; newrow = row+2; return true;
                  }
```

```
                          return false;
          case 6: if (col<NUMCOLS-2 && row<NUMROWS-1 && board[col+2][row+1]==0)
                       {
                          newcol = col+2; newrow = row+1; return true;
                       }
                       return false;
          case 7: if (col<NUMCOLS-2 && row>0 && board[col+2][row-1]==0)
                       {
                          newcol = col+2; newrow = row-1; return true;
                       }
                       return false;
          case 8: if (col<NUMCOLS-1 && row>1 && board[col+1][row-2]==0)
                       {
                          newcol = col+1; newrow = row-2; return true;
                       }
                       return false;
    }
}
void showboard(int b[][NUMROWS])
{
 for (int r=NUMROWS-1; r>=0; r--)
  {
    for (int c=0; c<NUMCOLS; c++)
        cout << setw(4) << b[c][r];
    cout << endl;
  }
}


class stackdata
{ // the triples that are stored on the stack
public: stackdata(){setup(0,0,0);}
        void setup(int C, int R, int D){ col = C; row=R; dir=D;}
        void extract(int& C, int& R, int& D){ C=col; R=row; D=dir;}
private: int col, row, dir;
};


int board[NUMCOLS][NUMROWS];

int main(int argc, char* argv[])
{
 // imagine we are trying to place 'GOAL' knights and each must be a
 // knight's move from the last one placed.
 //
 //
```

```
// Command line parameters supplied by the user:
//
//    column number of starting square            (in argv[1])
//    row number of starting square               (in argv[2])
//

    stack<stackdata> thestack;
    stackdata temp;
    int col, row, dir, newcol, newrow, knightnumber = 0;

    // start square - supplied by user
    col=atoi(argv[1]); if (col<0 || col>=NUMCOLS) exit(1);
    row=atoi(argv[2]); if (row<0 || row>=NUMROWS) exit(1);

    // place the first knight
    board[col][row]= ++knightnumber;

    // prime the stack
    temp.setup(col,row,1); thestack.push(temp);

    // now see if we can place the knights
    while (knightnumber < GOAL && !thestack.empty())
        {
         temp=thestack.top();temp.extract(col,row,dir);
         while (dir<9 && !move(col,row,dir,newcol,newrow,board))
             dir++;

         if (dir!=9) // an appropriate empty square found
               {
                    // update direction field in backtrack point
                    thestack.pop();            // pop current stack top
                    temp.setup(col,row,dir+1); // expand components
                    thestack.push(temp);        // and put back modified
                    // place a knight
                    board[newcol][newrow] = ++knightnumber;
                    // put new backtrack point on the stack - this location
                    temp.setup(newcol, newrow, 1);
                    thestack.push (temp);
               }
          else // backtrack
                {
                 thestack.pop();  // pop current stack top
                 board[col][row]=0;    //remove last piece
```

```
                        knightnumber--;  // number of pieces on board is reduced
                        }
                }

        if (knightnumber!=GOAL)
          cout << "no solution\n";
        else
                {
                cout << "success\n";
                // show board
                showboard(board);
                }

        return 0;
        }
```

Some runs of the program (in this case, a full tour on a five-by-five board) follow.

```
$ knighttour 0 0
success
    3  12   7  18  25
    6  17   4  13   8
   11   2  19  24  21
   16   5  22   9  14
    1  10  15  20  23
$ knighttour 1 1
success
   21   8   3  14  23
    2  13  22   9   4
    7  20  15  24  17
   12   1  18   5  10
   19   6  11  16  25
$ knighttour 0 1
no solution
$ knighttour 2 1
no solution
$ knighttour 2 0
success
   21   8  13   4  23
   14   3  22   7  12
    9  20   5  24  17
    2  15  18  11   6
   19  10   1  16  25
```

4.3 Queues

You are probably familiar with queues, having waited in line at a store, bank, or movie theater. A queue is sometimes called a FIFO (first-in, first-out) structure because, in a well-behaved queue, the first item to enter the queue is also the first to leave.[7]

4.3.1 Basic Queue Operations

There are two fundamental operations defined on the queue abstract data type:

- *Enqueue*(*X*): Adds *X* to the end of the queue
- *Dequeue*(*Z*): Removes the front item from the queue and stores it in *Z*

Figure 4.18 shows a sequence of queue operations; the head of the queue is to the left.

Our class definition is similar to that for a stack.

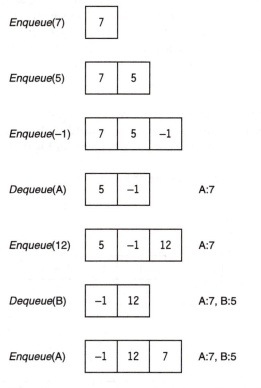

Figure 4.18 • Queue operations (head of queue is to the left)

```
template <class Entry>
class queue
{
  public: queue();              // constructor
          ~queue();             // destructor
          bool enqueue(Entry);   // add item to queue
          bool dequeue(Entry&);  // remove from queue into item
          bool isempty();        // check if queue is empty
          bool isfull();         // appropriate if queue is bounded
          bool getfront(Entry&); // get front without removing it

  private: // implementation specific
};
```

4.3.2 Queue Implementations

We can use an array to store queue elements as we did with a stack. To avoid moving items unnecessarily during an *enqueue* or *dequeue* operation, we maintain two indices—one is the position of the front item in the queue and the other is the position of the last item. (We also keep a count of items to simplify detection of full queues.) Suppose that after a sequence of *enqueue* and *dequeue* operations, our queue (with *g* at the head) is

g k a w b t r

It might be stored in an array as shown in Figure 4.19.

Note that the queue may wrap around the end of the array. For example, if we first enqueue *m* and then enqueue *f* to the queue in Figure 4.19, we get the queue shown in Figure 4.20.

Figure 4.21 shows two examples of full queues.

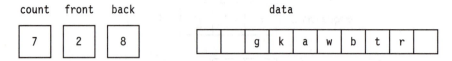

Figure 4.19 • Representation of queue *gkawbtr*

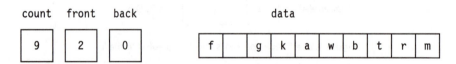

Figure 4.20 • A queue wrapped around in an array

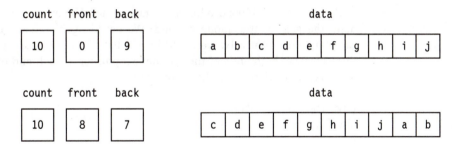

Figure 4.21 • Full queues

Checking the value of *count* rather than the relationship between *front* and *back* is the simplest way to see if a queue is full.

The *enqueue* operation for our array-based implementation is:

```
template <class Entry>
bool queue<Entry>::enqueue(Entry item)
  {
    if (isfull())
        return false;           // queue is full
    else
       {
         back = (back + 1) % queuesize; // may wrap around
         data_values[back]=item;       // store item
         count++;
         return true;
       }
  }
```

The *dequeue* function is:

```
template <class Entry>
bool queue<Entry>::enqueue(Entry& item)
  {
    if (isempty())
        return false;           // queue is empty
    else
       {
         item = data_values[front];     // get item from queue
         front = (front + 1) % queuesize; // may wrap around
         count--;
         return true;
       }
  }
```

As with stacks, if we use linked storage rather than arrays, we do not have to estimate the size of the queue needed. We could again reuse our linked list from Chapter 2. Alternatively, we could have a list of *queue_nodes* and, because operations occur at both ends of the list, have a pointer to each end of the list. Here is a top-level definition using this approach:

```
template <class Entry>
class queue
{
  public: queue();                  // constructor
         ~queue();                  // destructor
          bool enqueue(Entry);      // add item to queue
          bool dequeue(Entry&);     // remove from queue into item
          bool isempty();           // check if queue is empty
          bool getfront(Entry&);    // get front without removing it

  private: queue_node *first, *last;

};
```

Here is the *enqueue* function for a linked storage implementation:

```
template <class Entry>
bool queue<Entry>::enqueue(Entry item)
{ // add item to queue

  queue_node *temp = new queue_node;
  if (temp==NULL) return false;        // no space available
  temp->data = item;
  temp->next = NULL;
  if (count==0)                        // is this the first item?
      first = temp;                    //yes
  else
      last->next = temp;               // no, so append it
  last = temp;                         // either way it is now the last
  count++;                             // and the queue is one item longer
  return true;
}
```

4.3.3 Queue Applications

We now look at two applications to illustrate the use of queues. The first is a simulation in which the queue is used to hold representations of customers waiting for service. A supermarket or bank may use such simulations to determine the number of checkers/tellers required in order to keep customers from having to wait too long. The second application uses both a queue and a stack to check to see if a string of tokens is a palindrome.

Queue Application 1: Clock-Driven Simulation

The queue ADT is useful in simulations. In the example that follows, we simulate the processing of customers in an environment where there is a single queue and multiple servers; this might be similar to a bank or post office. For example, at a bank there might be a single waiting line and five tellers. We give the simulation parameter values that determine:

- *P:* The probability in a given unit-time interval of a new customer arriving
- *NUMSERVERS:* The number of servers
- *MAXSERVICE:* The maximum amount of service required by a customer[8]

Each *Person* in our simulation is represented by a two-field structure. One field holds the time at which the person enters the line and the other holds the amount of service time the person requires. The latter is sampled from a uniform distribution of 1 to *MAXSERVICE*; in other words, each value from 1 to *MAXSERVICE* is equally likely to be chosen. We use the queue to represent the people waiting in line.

We have an array of server objects. Each server object has a timer that indicates how much service time remains to be given to the customer that the server is currently dealing with. If this timer is 0, then the server is available to help the next person in line.

The simulation in this example can be classified as *synchronous* or *fixed-time increment*. At each iteration of the main loop, the variable *clock* (representing the current time) advances by one regardless of the events, or lack of them, that happen at that time. An alternative approach to simulation is provided in Section 4.4.

In each iteration of the main loop, we first see if a new customer arrives, then we check each server in turn. If the server is free, we dequeue the head of the line (if any) and begin service for the new customer; otherwise, we decrement the service time remaining for the current customer. In pseudocode this is

```
for each clock tick
{
    if (random_function) add new customer to queue

    for each server
        {
            if (free)
                take customer from queue
            else
```

```
                              give a unit of service to current customer
                    }
          }
```

We are interested in the behavior of the system as various factors change:

- The number of servers
- The probability of a customer arriving during a particular time interval
- The average service requirements of a customer

We include metrics in the program so that we are able to determine:

- The average and maximum queue lengths
- The average time that a customer had to wait in line
- The longest time that a customer had to wait in line

The program is as follows:

```cpp
#include <iostream.h>
#include <stdlib.h>
#include "queue.h"

#define MAXCLOCK 120              // time limit for the simulation

struct Person {int arrival_time; int service_time;};


class server
{
 public: server() {time = 0;}
         void settime(int N) { time = N;}
         bool free() { return time == 0;}
         void decrement() { time--; }

 private: int time; // service time for current customer
};

int main(int argc, char *argv[])
{
  //
  // parameters of the simulation are passed as command line arguments
  //
  // argv[1]    P    probability of an arrival during a time interval
  // argv[2]    NUMSERVERS     number of servers
  // argv[3]    MAXSERVICE     largest service time for a customer
  //
```

```
        server *servers;
        Person tempperson;
        queue<Person> Q;  // the queue of customers

        float P = atof(argv[1]);   // first argument conversion, string to float
        int NUMSERVERS = atoi(argv[2]);     // second is number of servers
        int MAXSERVICE = atoi(argv[3]);      // third is max. service time

        int totwaits = 0, waitcount = 0, wait, maxwait = 0,
            maxqt, totq = 0, maxq = 0, clock = 0;

        srand(123);          // initialize random number generator

        servers = new server[NUMSERVERS];  // the servers

    while (clock<MAXCLOCK)
      {
      if (  ((float)rand() / (float)RAND_MAX ) < P) // person arrives?
        {
          tempperson.arrival_time = clock;
          // determine an amount of service
          tempperson.service_time = rand() % MAXSERVICE + 1;
          Q.enqueue(tempperson);
        }

      // check the servers
      for (int i=0; i<NUMSERVERS; i++)
        {
          if (servers[i].free())
            {// server is available
             if (!Q.isempty())
               { // dequeue first person to server
                 Q.dequeue(tempperson);
                 servers[i].settime(tempperson.service_time);
                 // how long was this person waiting?
                 wait = clock - tempperson.arrival_time;
                 // do waiting statistics
                 totwaits+=wait;
                 waitcount++;
                 if (wait > maxwait) maxwait = wait;
               }
            }
          else servers[i].decrement(); // serve current customer some more
        }
```

● **TABLE 4.2** Results from Simulator Runs

P	NUMSERVERS	MAXSERVICE	Avg. Q	Max. Q	Avg. Wait	Max. Wait
0.7	3	7	5.0	10	7.6	14
0.7	**2**	7	16.7	33	25.7	51
0.7	**4**	7	0.3	3	0.4	3
0.6	3	7	0.5	3	1.0	4
0.8	3	7	16.0	31	19.6	35
0.7	3	**6**	1.8	6	2.7	8
0.7	3	**8**	9.0	18	13.5	26

```
// do queue length statistics
if (Q.length() > maxq) {maxq = Q.length(); maxqt = clock;}
totq += Q.length();
clock++;
}

// results
cout << "average queue " << (float)totq/(float)clock << endl;
cout << "max queue " << maxq << " at time " << maxqt << endl;
cout << "max wait " << maxwait << endl;
cout << "average wait " << (float)totwaits/(float)waitcount << endl;

return 0;
}
```

Table 4.2 shows results from multiple runs of the simulator. The first three columns are the parameter values set by the user, and the last four columns are the results displayed by the program.

The first row of the table represents a "baseline" run of the program. The remaining six rows show the effect of changing one of the three parameters. The value that differs from the baseline run is in bold. The simulation appears to be sensitive even to small changes in any of the three parameters. For example, adding another server to the original three reduces the length of the longest queue from 10 to 3, but if we take one away instead, the queue is as long as 33. If we change the probability of a customer arriving from 0.7 to 0.8, the effect is similar to taking away one of the servers.

Queue Application 2: Palindrome Checking
One type of application that uses both a stack and a queue is a palindrome checker, which determines whether the input stream reads the same backwards as forwards.

One strategy is to store the input both in a stack and in a queue. Then we read the stack items (representing the input in reverse order) and the queue items (the sequence in the original order). If they match, then the input is palindromic. In pseudocode this is

```
while more input
     { get symbol; Stack.push(symbol); Queue.enqueue(symbol);
     }

while stack not empty
     { Stack.pop(Y); Queue.dequeue(Z);
       if (Z != Y) return false;
     }
return true;
```

For example, suppose that the input is the seven-character stream

A B C D C X A

Figure 4.22a shows the stack after the reading phase and Figure 4.22b shows the queue (head to the left as usual).

Figure 4.23 shows the stack and queue after one iteration of the checking loop. As you can see, the next iteration will *pop X* and *dequeue B*, and detect that the input is not a palindrome.

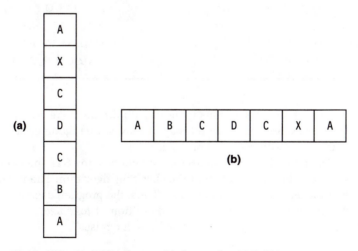

Figure 4.22 • Stack (a) and queue (b) after reading *ABCDCXA*

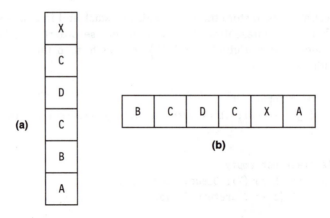

Figure 4.23 • Stack (a) and queue (b) after one iteration of checking loop

	TABLE 4.3	Types of Palindromes			
Type	**Tokens**	**Ignore Spaces?**	**Ignore Punctuation?**	**Example(s)**	
1	Words	No	No	SO PATIENT A DOCTOR TO DOCTOR A PATIENT SO	
2	Words	No	Yes	ALL GAVE SOME, SOME GAVE ALL	
				GIRL, BATHING ON BIKINI, EYING BOY, FINDS BOY EYING BIKINI ON BATHING GIRL	
3	Characters	No	No	RATS LIVE ON NO EVIL STAR	
4	Characters	No	Yes	ABLE WAS I, ERE I SAW ELBA	
5	Characters	Yes	Yes	MADAM, I'M ADAM	
				A MAN, A PLAN, A CANAL – PANAMA!	

Table 4.3 shows various types of palindromes.[9] We assume that case is ignored, that spaces and punctuation may or may not be ignored, and that the unit of tokenization is either a word or a character.

The following program uses components of the STL (more on the STL in Section 4.5) in an implementation of the checking algorithm. The program tokenizes at the word level, ignoring punctuation. Thus, the program can check for type 1 and type 2 palindromes. By changing the definition of *tokenize*, we can make the program check for types 3, 4, and 5 instead (see Exercises).

```
#include <string>
#include <stack>
```

```
#include <queue>
#include <list>

#include <iostream.h>

void tokenize(string &X, string separators, list<string> &words)
{ // extracts tokens from X, puts them in list
 int length = X.length();
 int first=X.find_first_not_of(separators,0);

 while (first>=0 && first<length)
    {
     int last = X.find_first_of(separators,first);
     // check for last token on line
     if (last<0 || last>length) last = length;
     // append token to list
     words.push_back(X.substr(first,last-first));
     first = X.find_first_not_of(separators,last+1);
    }
}

bool palinstring(string &line)
{
 // returns true if line contains palindrome

 stack<string> S;
 queue<string> Q;
 list<string> the_words;
 string one,two;

 tokenize(line," ,;:",the_words); // tokenize the input line

 list<string>::iterator start=the_words.begin();
 list<string>::iterator stop=the_words.end();

 while (start != stop)
    {// put current token on stack and queue
     S.push(*start);
     Q.push(*start);  // this is the enqueue operation.
     start++;
    }

 // now check to see if we have a palindrome
 while (!Q.empty())
```

```
      {
        one = S.top(); S.pop();
        two = Q.front();Q.pop();
        if (one!=two) return false;
      }
    return true;
    }




main()
{
 string line;

 while (getline(cin,line))
    {
      cout << line << " <= is ";
      if (!palinstring(line)) cout << "not ";
      cout << "a palindrome\n";
    }
}
```

A run of the program produces the following output:

```
$ palinstring < palindromes
so patient a doctor to doctor a patient so <= is a palindrome
rats live on no evil star <= is not a palindrome
this is a palindrome <= is not a palindrome
able was i, ere i saw elba <= is not a palindrome
a man, a plan, a canal, panama <= is not a palindrome
all gave some, some gave all <= is a palindrome
```

We will see further applications of stacks and queues in other chapters. For example, when trying to find a path through a graph (Chapter 7), we need to put aside information for later use during the search. Both a stack and a queue are reasonable structures to use. Choosing one over the other affects the way the search progresses and characteristics of the path found.

4.4 Priority Queues

A variation on the general queue is one where each queue element has a value associated with it. When we dequeue, we remove the element with the smallest value.[10] We could think of the dequeue operation as *getmin*. One application of such **prior-**

ity queues is in multiprogramming environments where the operating system scheduler has to pick the next task to be given some CPU time. A priority queue might be found in real life in a friendly supermarket where customers with fewer items are allowed to check out ahead of those having more items.

4.4.1 Priority Queue Implementation

An unordered list or array could hold the items. This makes *enqueue* an O(1) operation because we can put the new item anywhere; however, *getmin* requires a search of the items and is thus an O(N) operation. Alternatively, we could keep the items in ascending order of value. The item with the smallest value is thus easy to find, so *getmin* is O(1) but *enqueue* is O(N). An alternative approach is to use a "heap" (see Chapter 10). With a heap, both *getmin* and *enqueue* are O(log N) operations. Compared with a linked list, a dynamic storage implementation of a heap uses an additional pointer for each item in the queue.

4.4.2 Priority Queue Applications

The following sections look at two applications of priority queues. The first is a simple list of tasks to be done; the tasks are ordered by perceived importance. We leave details of the implementation of this structure as an Exercise. The second application illustrates a different approach to simulation than that of Section 4.3.3. In addition to the queue of customers, the simulation maintains a queue of events ordered by the times at which they happen.

Priority Queue Application 1: "To Do" List
Items in a "to do" list are ranked in order of priority or, if you like, are ranked by a procrastination factor (How many days can I put off doing this?). Figure 4.24 represents such a list.

Insertion of item "grade exams" with priority 6 changes the list to the one shown in Figure 4.25.

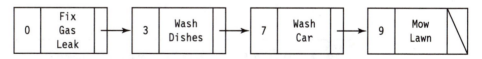

Figure 4.24 • "To do" list as a priority queue

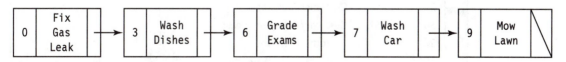

Figure 4.25 • Updated "to do" list

Priority Queue Application 2: Event-Driven Simulation

In Section 4.3.3, we saw an example of a simulation that was classified as *synchronous* or *fixed-time increment*. The main loop iterated for each value of the *clock* variable even if there was no significant change in the state of the simulation—no arrival of a customer, no movement from queue to server, no departure when service was complete. The time required to run this kind of simulation is proportional to the time limit set on *clock*. If the time interval is refined by a factor of 10 (e.g., changing from minutes to tenths of minutes), then even though the number of events remains the same, the simulation would take 10 times longer to run and our only benefit would be more precise measurements of waiting times.

An alternative approach to simulation is one in which time jumps from event to event and skips over those intervals where nothing happens. This type of simulation is termed *asynchronous* or *event driven*. The time to run the simulation depends on the number of events. Thus, if Table 4.4 represents the clock-driven approach, Table 4.5 represents the same time interval with an event-driven approach.

● **TABLE 4.4** Fragment of a Clock-Driven Simulation

Clock	Event
29	Customer 5 arrives
30	Customer 2 begins service
31	
32	Customer 6 arrives
33	
34	
35	
36	Customer 2 ends service

● **TABLE 4.5** Fragment of an Event-Driven Simulation

Clock	Event
29	Customer 5 arrives
30	Customer 2 begins service
32	Customer 6 arrives
36	Customer 2 ends service

In event-driven simulation, event records are held in a priority queue arranged by the time at which they happen. Events are processed in the order in which they occur, and an event may trigger one or more future events. Records for these future events are then inserted into the priority queue. Suppose, for example, that at time 116 a customer arrives at a server and needs 12 units of service. This generates a record with time 128 representing the completion of the service and the departure of the customer. An event-driven simulation runs until there are no more events to process.

In the following program, we revisit the simulation of Section 4.3.3, this time using the event-driven approach and a priority queue. The structures in the priority queue have three fields:

- *time:* The time at which the event occurs.
- *etype:* The type of event (arrival or departure).
- *serv:* If the event is an arrival, then this field is used to store the required service time for the arriving customer. If the event is a departure, then this field holds the number of the server who has just finished.

In an event-driven simulation, we first prime the event queue with all the arrivals. The main loop of the algorithm in pseudocode is

```
while (the event queue is not empty)
{
      dequeue an event and set the clock
      if event is an arrival
            if there is a free server
                  mark the server as busy
                  add an end-of-service event to the event queue
            else put person in customer queue
      else
            mark server free
            if customer waiting
                  take first customer
                  mark server busy
                  add an end-of-service event to the event queue
}
```

The program is as follows:

```
#include <iostream.h>
#include <stdlib.h>

#include "queue.h"              // for the people
#include "priorityqueue.h"     // for the events
```

```
#define MAXCLOCK 120          // the time limit on the simulation

enum eventclass{arr,dep};     // the type of event

struct Person { int arrival_time; int service_time;};
struct Event { int time; eventclass etype; int serv;};

int operator < (Event E, Event E2)  // for ordering events
 { return E.time < E2.time; }

int main(int argc, char *argv[])
{
 //
 // parameters of the simulation are passed as command line arguments
 //
 // argv[1]   P   probability of an arrival during a time interval
 // argv[2]   NUMSERVERS    number of servers
 // argv[3]   MAXSERVICE    largest service time for a customer
 //

 bool *servers;
 priorityqueue<Event> eventlist;  // the event list
 queue<Person> Q;                 // the queue of customers

 Person tempperson;
 Event tempevent;

 float P = atof(argv[1]);         // probability of a customer arriving
 int NUMSERVERS = atoi(argv[2]);  // the number of servers
 int MAXSERVICE = atoi(argv[3]);  // the maximum service one person can
                                  // have.

 int totwaits = 0, waitcount = 0, wait, maxwait = 0, maxqt, totq = 0,
     maxq = 0;
 int service, servernum, clock = 0;

 srand(123);        // initialize the nrandom number generator

 servers = new bool[NUMSERVERS];  // the servers, false => free

 // prime the event queue with arrivals
 // these are all the arrivals that there will be during the course of the
 // simulation so, for each time interval, see if someone arrives at that time.
```

```
for (int i=0; i<MAXCLOCK; i++)
  {
    if (  ((float)rand() / (float)RAND_MAX ) < P)
      {
        // arrival record
        service = rand() % MAXSERVICE + 1;  // how much service
        tempevent.time=i;
        tempevent.etype=arr;
        tempevent.serv = service;
        eventlist.enqueue(tempevent);
      }
  }


// initialize the servers
for (int i=0; i<NUMSERVERS; i++)
      servers[i]=false;              // all servers are free initially


// main simulation loop
while (!eventlist.isempty())
  {
    eventlist.getmin(tempevent);  // get next event
    clock = tempevent.time;         // forward to the time it happens

    if (tempevent.etype==arr)
      {
        // event is an arrival. Any free servers?
        int freeserver = -1;
        for (int i=0; i<NUMSERVERS; i++)
            if (!servers[i]) freeserver = i;

        if (freeserver==-1)
          { // no server free, customer enters queue
            tempperson.arrival_time=clock;
            tempperson.service_time=tempevent.serv;
            Q.enqueue(tempperson);
            if (Q.length() > maxq) {maxq = Q.length(); maxqt = clock;}
          }
        else
          { // there is a server available
            servers[freeserver] = true; // server now busy
            // make end of service record
            tempevent.time=clock+tempevent.serv;
```

```
                      tempevent.etype=dep;
                      tempevent.serv = freeserver;
                      eventlist.enqueue(tempevent);
                      // wait stats - no waiting for this customer
                      waitcount++;
                  }
              }
          else

              {
               // event is an end of service
               servernum = tempevent.serv; // who was serving?
               servers[servernum] = false; // not now busy
               if (!Q.isempty())
                  { Q.dequeue(tempperson) ; // get first customer in line
                    // stats on waiting
                    wait = clock - tempperson.arrival_time; // how long waiting
                    waitcount++;
                    totwaits += wait;
                    if (wait>maxwait) maxwait = wait;

                    servers[servernum] = true; // server now busy
                    // make end of service record
                    tempevent.time=clock+tempperson.service_time;
                    tempevent.etype=dep;
                    tempevent.serv = servernum;
                    eventlist.enqueue(tempevent);
                  }
              }
          }

    // results

    cout << "max queue " << maxq << " at time " << maxqt << endl;
    cout << "max wait " << maxwait << endl;
    cout << "average wait " << (float)totwaits/(float)waitcount << endl;

    return 0;
    }
```

The output from a few runs of the program follows. Note that there is no measurement of the average queue length; this is left as an Exercise.

```
$ simulation2 0.7 3 8
max queue 12 at time 93
max wait 17
average wait 6.44828

$ simulation2 0.7 3 7
max queue 6 at time 93
max wait 5
average wait 1.86207

$ simulation2 0.8 3 7
max queue 16 at time 101
max wait 18
average wait 11.7053
```

These results are not directly comparable with the earlier simulation. In the earlier program, simulation stopped when the clock reached *MAXCLOCK*, at which time there could be many customers in the line. With this program, processing continues until all customers have been processed.

4.5 Stacks, Queues, and the STL

In the STL, stacks and queues are not fundamental classes; rather, they are implemented as *adaptors*. That is, they are built on top of other containers and adapt or modify the interface. For example, a *pop* operation for the stack might be a *pop_back* operation on the underlying container. Currently, STL implementations vary from system to system. The following illustrative programs run on the author's local system; aspects of this implementation of the STL may differ from other STL implementations.

4.5.1 Stacks

The following program illustrates how a user specifies the container to hold the stack. The choice could be based on the expected behavior of the stack. A vector implementation is faster but potentially uses more space; a list implementation is slower but uses space more efficiently. A deque is the default implementation. In the program, both stacks are stacks of integers; stack *One* uses a deque (the default) and stack *Two* uses a vector. The program illustrates basic stack operations.

```
#include <stack>
#include <vector>
#include <iostream.h>
```

```
int main()
{
 stack<int> One;
 stack< int, vector<int> > Two;

 One.push(60); One.push(20); One.push(50); One.push(10);
 cout << "Number of elements in One is: " << One.size() << endl;

 cout << "Top item is: " << One.top() << endl;
 One.pop();
 cout << "Top item is: " << One.top() << endl;

 // pour items from One to Two
 while (!One.empty()) { Two.push(One.top()); One.pop(); }

 cout << "Number of elements in Two is: " << Two.size() << endl;

 cout << "Contents of Two: ";
 while (!Two.empty()) { cout << Two.top() << " "; Two.pop(); }
 cout << endl;

 return 0;
}
```

Output from a run of the program follows:

```
Number of elements in One is: 4
Top item is: 10
Top item is: 50
Number of elements in Two is: 3
Contents of Two: 60 20 50
```

• 4.5.2 Queues

The following program illustrates queues. Adaptation for queues is similar to adaptation for stacks except that a vector cannot be used to implement a queue because the *pop_front* operation is not supported. Although the queue ADT permits access only to the front item, the STL *queue* class allows us to access both the first and the last queue elements.

In the program, after the first of the original characters in the queue is removed, the remaining items form a palindrome. We test for this using a stack and queue as we did in Section 4.3.3.

```
#include <queue>
#include <stack>
```

```
#include <list>
#include <iostream.h>

int main()
{
 stack<char> Three;
 queue<char, list<char> > Four;
 char a,b,c;
 bool palindrome;

 Four.push('x'); Four.push('a'); Four.push('b');
 Four.push('c'); Four.push('b'); Four.push('a');

 // see what's in the queue
 for (int i=0; i<Four.size(); i++)
   {
     c = Four.front(); cout << c;
     Four.pop();
     Four.push(c);
   }
 cout << endl;

 // the two end items
 cout << Four.front() << Four.back() << endl;

 // pop one item and check size
 Four.pop();
 cout << "Number of elements in queue is now: " << Four.size() << endl;

 // palindrome testing of the queue (non-destructive)
 for (int i=0; i<Four.size(); i++)
     {
       c = Four.front();
       Four.pop();
       Three.push(c);  // char to stack
       Four.push(c);   // and back in queue
     }

palindrome = true;
while (!Three.empty() & palindrome)
     {
       a = Three.top(); Three.pop();
       b = Four.front(); Four.pop(); Four.push(b);
```

```
            if (a != b) palindrome = false;
        }

    if (palindrome) cout << "palindrome\n";
                else  cout << "not palindrome\n";

    return 0;
}
```

A run of the program produces the following:

```
xabcba
xa
Number of elements in queue is now: 5
Palindrome
```

● Chapter Summary

Stacks and queues are forms of the general deque data structure. In a stack, insertions and deletions take place at the same end; in a queue, items are inserted at one end and removed at the other. Both structures can be implemented using arrays or with linked storage. Stacks are useful in applications where data are set aside in a nested manner. Some backtracking applications fall into this category. Queues are useful in simulations. The STL enables both stacks and queues to be defined in terms of a base data structure.

● Exercises

1. Using the C++ inheritance mechanism,

    a. Define a deque class derived from the stack class.

    b. Define a deque class derived from the queue class.

2. Consider Figure 4.1. How many different subclasses of deque are there? How many of them are useful?

3. Write a *push* function for a stack implemented as an array.

4. Write a *push* function for a stack implemented using linked storage.

5. Sketch an algorithm for

    a. Reversing the order of the items in a stack.

    b. Reversing the order of the items in a queue.

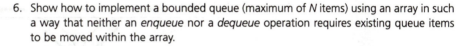

6. Show how to implement a bounded queue (maximum of *N* items) using an array in such a way that neither an *enqueue* nor a *dequeue* operation requires existing queue items to be moved within the array.

7. In what way would a stack be useful if you had to print an arbitrarily large integer one digit per line, most significant digit first?

8. Show how you could (nondestructively) test to see if two stacks are identical.

9. Show how you could remove from a stack all items satisfying a certain predicate. The relative positions of the remaining items should be unchanged.

10. Show how you could remove from a queue all items satisfying a certain predicate. The relative positions of the remaining items should be unchanged. Your solution should not require the use of any additional data structures.

11. Write an iterative factorial function that uses a stack to simulate recursion.

12. Give a pseudocode function for removing the *k*th item from a queue of *N* items. What special cases are there?

13. Show how you could map two stacks (of the same type) onto a single array so that a *push* operation fails only when all the space is used up.

14. Show how you could map *N* stacks (of the same type) onto a single array so that a *push* operation fails only when all the space is used up. What data are contained in a single element of your array?

15. Show how to print the contents of a queue, leaving the queue unaltered and without using auxiliary storage.

16. What is the flaw in the following code designed to print the contents of the stack *S*? (It does not matter that the contents of the stack are destroyed.)

    ```
    for (int I=0; I<S.size();I++)

        {

        cout << S.top();

        S.pop();

        }
    ```

17. How would you modify the knight's tour program so that it looks for reentrant tours?

18. How would you modify the event-driven simulation program so that it is able to output the average queue length?

19. Modify the palindrome program so that it recognizes type 3, 4, and 5 palindromes.

20. If we have the following railroad yard configuration where travel is permitted only in the directions shown

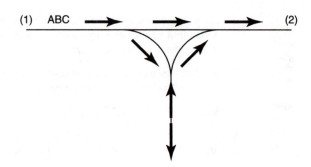

Wagons at (1) can go straight to (2) or be diverted into the siding (stack) and sent to (2) later.

a. List the permutations of the starting arrangement shown (*ABC*) that cannot be produced at (2).

b. Suppose we add a second siding (stack), as shown in the following figure:

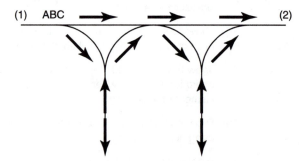

Are there any permutations of *ABC* that cannot be achieved at (2)? If so, which?

21. Suppose the railroad company of the previous exercise prefers queues to stacks.

a. List the permutations of *ABC* that cannot be achieved at (2).

b. Suppose we add a second queue, as shown in the following figure.

Are there any permutations of *ABC* that cannot be achieved at (2)? If so, which?

22. Suppose we have a stream of integers and need to identify which integers are the k most recently seen in the stream. For example, if we are interested in the five most recently seen and our number stream in part is

    . . . 4 1 5 9 8 2 3 7 3 1 2 4 2 1 9 4 8 2 1 2 3

    Then at the time the second 9 is read, the five most recently seen numbers are 9, 1, 2, 4, and 3. Algorithms such as this one are used in cache memories and virtual memory systems. Show how we could use a queue to identify the k most recently read numbers.

Problems

1. Modify the expression evaluation program so that it handles ill-formed expressions gracefully.

2. Change the initialization of the random number function so that instead of a constant, it uses a user-supplied value. Run the clock-driven simulator with a wider range of parameters than those reported in the text.

3. Augment either simulation program by adding an "express lane." Customers requiring Z or fewer units of service (where Z is an additional user-supplied parameter) have the option of entering a separate queue served by a single server in the manner of an express lane at a supermarket. How does the main loop determine whether an eligible customer stays in the normal line or goes to the express line?

4. Add a method to the queue class that enables an item other than the one at the head of the queue to be removed. Augment the simulation by adding a random impatience factor to the information stored about a person waiting in line. The higher the factor, the more likely a person is to leave the line before reaching its front.

5. In the clock-driven simulation program, change the initialization of the random number function so that it uses the current time of day, as in

   srand((unsigned)time(NULL));

   and arrange for the simulation to run 10 times using the same set of user-supplied parameters. The numbers reported at the end should be averages from the 10 runs.

6. Augment the simulation programs by having them output information about the servers. For example, what is the percentage of time that k servers are idle? For each server, what is the longest period that the particular server is idle?

7. A maze may be represented by a two-dimensional array of integers in which an element containing -1 represents a blocked square, an element containing 0 represents a free square, an element containing 1 represents the start, and an element containing 2 represents a destination. Write a program that takes such an array and finds a path, if any exists, from the start square to a destination square. A move from one square to the next must be either horizontal or vertical.

8. Modify the knight's tour program so that instead of determining whether a tour is possible, it counts the number of different tours (may be zero) that are possible from a particular starting location.

9. How might a knight move in a three-dimensional chessboard? What would need to be modified in the knight's tour program in order to adapt it for three-dimensional tours?

10. The binomial coefficient $B(n,k)$ for power n and term k is defined recursively as follows:

$$B(n,k) = 1 \quad \text{when } k = 0$$

$$B(n,k) = 1 \quad \text{when } k = n$$

otherwise $\quad B(n,k) = B(n-1,k) + B(n-1,k-1) \quad\quad 0 < k < n$

Write a function B that takes n and k and returns the value of $B(n,k)$. The catch? Your function must not itself be recursive. Instead it should use one or more stacks in some way.

11. We can use a stack to generate a permutation of an input stream. For example, if our input is 1, 2, 3, 4, 5, then the sequence of operations

push push pop push pop push push pop pop pop

where *push* pushes the next input on the stack and *pop* pops the top of stack to the output, results in output 2 3 5 4 1.

Not every permutation of the input can be produced in this way. Write and test a program that takes as input an integer N and a permutation of the integers 1 to N and determines whether the permutation could have been generated using the stack method if the input was the sequence 1, 2, . . . N.

12. Design and test a *priority_queue* class.

13. Design and implement a *to_do_list* class. What operations should a user be able to do on items in the list? How do you order items with the same priority? Should a user be allowed to change the priority of an item?

14. A small recursive function is sufficient to print out the moves required to solve the Towers of Hanoi problem (moving N discs from corner A to corner B of a triangle). Write a function *HanoiState* that takes four parameters (N,A,B,k) and outputs a representation of the configuration of the discs after k moves have been made. For example, the output of *HanoiState*(5,1,3,26) might be

Corner 1: Disc 3

Corner 2: Disc 2

Corner 3: Disc 5, Disc 4, Disc 1

15. Consider an information retrieval system (e.g., a Web search engine) that permits users to enter queries such as

find: A and (B or C) and not D

Each operand is a reference to a set containing the numbers of the documents in which the operand is found. Write and test a program that processes Boolean expressions such as the one just presented and creates a set of the numbers of the documents satisfying the expression. For example, if the sets are:

A: [2 6 12 17]

B: [3 8 9 12]

C: [2 8 10 12 17]

D: [5 12 13]

The result is the set [2 17].

16. Modify the bracket-checking program to permit multicharacter brackets such as /* and */.

17. Devise and implement a simulation that compares an *N*-server single queue environment with an *N*-server *N*-queue environment (arriving customers join the shortest queue). Suggest a way in which your program could permit customers to switch queues in the multiple-queue model.

Notes

[1] The default parameter would also have to be added to the constructor prototype.

[2] Elements 3 to *stack_size*−1, although not currently in use, do contain values; we just don't care what they are.

[3] In the 1920s, Jan Lukasiewicz (1878–1956), a Polish mathematician, developed a system that enabled mathematical expressions to be written without parentheses by placing the operators before the operands (prefix) or after the operands (postfix). Prefix notation became known as Polish notation, after Lukasiewicz, and postfix form became known as Reverse Polish.

[4] We could have used any values in the table provided that * and / have the same value, + and − have the same value (and a value less than * and /), and all operator precedences are greater than 0—the value we assign to opening parenthesis.

[5] The *switch* statement implements a multiway branch. Here we are branching on the value in *symtype*. The *break* statement transfers control to the statement following the switch and is necessary to avoid falling into the next case. Optionally, you can have a "catch-all" *default* case. The *atoi* function (found in header *stdlib.h* and used in *valueof*) converts a string of digits to the corresponding integer.

[6] We assume that 0,0 is the lower left-hand corner of the board consistent with the normal notation (a–h, 1–8) for identifying columns and rows on a chess board.

[7] Our queue is well-behaved. New items are permitted only at the end, and no item other than the one at the head of the queue is permitted to leave.

[8] To run the program, a user gives the filename followed by the parameters, as in

simulate 0.7 3 7

The value of integer *argc* (argument count) is the number of symbols on the command line (4 in our example). The symbols themselves are available as elements of *argv* (argument vector). Thus, in our example, *argv*[1] contains "0.7". We use library functions *atoi* and *atof* to convert a string to an integer and double-length float number, respectively.

[9]The "SO PATIENT . . . " and "GIRL BATHING . . . " examples were created by J. A. Lindon. The response to Adam's introduction is itself a palindrome: Eve.

[10]We use smallest in our examples; naturally, a priority queue could equally well be defined to return the largest value.

5

Maps: Hash Tables

5.1 Introduction

This chapter and the next look at various ways that maps can be implemented. A **map** is a very general abstract data structure capable of storing objects that consist of a primary key (a uniquely identifying component or combination of components) and, possibly, other nonkey components.

A map provides a mapping between the unique primary key and the nonkey values, thus:

$key_1 \rightarrow value_1$
$key_2 \rightarrow value_2$
.

.

$key_i \rightarrow value_i$

.

$key_n \rightarrow value_n$

Some examples of maps are a dictionary of words used by a spelling checker, a table of students used in a registration program, and a catalog of electronic components keyed by part number. Maps in the form of symbol tables are used extensively by translation programs such as assemblers and compilers. Maps are used to record information about identifiers used in the program being translated.[1]

A map viewed as an abstract data type permits users to:

- Determine whether an entry with a particular key is in the map
- Retrieve the entry having a particular key
- Insert a new entry (key-value pair)
- Modify an entry having a particular key
- Remove an entry having a particular key

What we have, in effect, is an **associative memory** or a **content-addressable memory** from which we retrieve according to content. This contrasts with an array or vector, for example, from which we retrieve by location. An analogy is identifying a house as "the one where Mr Green lives" compared with identifying a house as "50 Main Street."

The map abstract data type can be implemented in many ways. Properties of a particular map implementation include:

- The speed of retrieval operations
- The expandability of the structure
- Whether the entries can be accessed in key order

● 5.1.1 Primary Key

In many applications, it is quite difficult to devise a reasonable key from the normally occurring data. Suppose, for example, that we need to maintain a collection of student records where each record consists of the student's name, major, phone number, street address, and date of birth. No single field is likely to be unique. We cannot even be sure that a combination of two fields is unique.[2] However, if we make the key a combination of three or more fields, data operations become unwieldy. The solution is to create a unique key—the student ID number—and attach it to the data. Other examples of artificial keys are social security numbers, bank account numbers, International Standard Book Numbers, and vehicle identification numbers. No two objects in a map can have the same primary key.[3]

This chapter looks at hash table implementations of maps; the next chapter looks at implementations using trees.

● 5.1.2 Overview of Hashing

You are familiar with data structures in which a search for a particular object takes O(log N) time, where N is the number of objects in the structure. One example of such a structure is an array in which objects are ordered by key. The array is searched using a binary or logarithmic search that halves the search area at each iteration. With such a structure, if we double the number of objects, we would expect the average number of comparisons in a search to increase by one. Thus, as N increases, the search time also increases, although comparatively slowly.

We can devise structures in which even faster searches are possible, in which the search time is independent of N. If we characterize the searches in the previous paragraph as O(log N), then we can devise structures in which searches are O(1). Suppose, for example, that we are storing employee records and are using nine-digit social security numbers as the primary (unique) key field. We could create an array T with 10^9 entries. An employee record with social security number i would be stored in T_i. To retrieve the record for an employee with social security number j, we examine T_j. If the record is not there, we need not look anywhere else—it does not exist. In a similar way, a home-delivery pizza business might use a customer's seven-digit phone number as a primary key; a school district might use a six-digit student identification number when storing student records.

However, although insert and retrieval operations are fast, these structures are likely to be very sparsely filled and waste a lot of space. The pizza business storage structure, for example, has space for 10 million potential customers. To solve this problem, a **hash table** gives up the one-to-one correspondence between primary key and storage location but, if designed well, can retain most of the storage and retrieval speed of the larger structure.

The capacity of a hash table is based on the number of objects we expect to store. Typically, we set up an array of a particular size, say M elements. We then devise a function that maps primary keys (phone numbers, social security numbers, license plates, and so on) onto **addresses**, say 1 to M. We use the term *address* to represent a location where one (or more) objects can be stored. In a particular implementation, it might be an array index, the number of a disc sector, or possibly an actual memory address. The name "hash table" arose because, in many cases, the address is produced by chopping up (hashing) the primary key of the object in some way. The hash function should spread out objects across the table. Unlike the earlier array T, however, it is possible that two or more objects will map to the same address, thus we need a mechanism to deal with that.

The following is a simple example of a hash table. Later sections of this chapter will look at some of the design factors in more detail. The chapter concludes with C++ class definitions for two kinds of hash tables, and two example applications. The applications use both kinds of hash tables and one application shows another use of hashing.

5.1.3 Example of a Simple Hash Table

Suppose we wish to store seven names in a table. Instead of creating a table with just seven spaces, we should allow some extra room and create a table with 10 entries, so that the final insertion operations proceed reasonably quickly. For an analogy, compare the time it takes to park 2000 cars in (a) a parking lot with 2000 parking places and (b) a parking lot with 2500 places.

We need a function that maps names onto the integers 0 through 9; that is, the indexes of the table entries. Even with the assumption that names contain only letters,[4] there are many possibilities for a general name-to-address function. Here we use one that takes the rank in the alphabet of the first and last letters in the name (A = 1, B = 2, ..., Z = 26), adds them up, and uses the remainder on division by 10. Thus,

Hash(Peter) = (rank(P) + rank(r)) modulo 10
= (16 + 18) modulo 10
= 4

To see how this works, we will store the first names of recent U.S. presidents. These names, with corresponding values of the hash function in parentheses, are:

Bill (4), George (2), Ronald (2), Jimmy (5), Gerald (1), Richard (2), Lyndon (6)

In general, we would expect to have **collisions**—two or more keys mapping to the same address, as with George, Ronald, and Richard in our example.[5] If more names hash to a particular address than we can store at that address, we have **overflow**. A hash table implementation must include a method for resolving overflows.

Let us assume that:

- Table entries are initially space-filled.
- We can only store one name at each address.
- If we have overflow, we store the name in the next free location (treating the table as circular if necessary).

If we insert the names in the order listed, we get the table shown in Figure 5.1.

Bill and George each hash to their home address (the one given by the hash function). Ronald hashes to 2, which is full (George is there), and ends up at the next

0	
1	Gerald
2	George
3	Ronald
4	Bill
5	Jimmy
6	Richard
7	Lyndon
8	
9	

Figure 5.1 • Hash table

free address (3). Jimmy hashes to 5 and Gerald to 1, both of these home addresses are free. Richard hashes to 2, which is full, as are addresses 3, 4, and 5, so Richard ends up in 6. Finally, Lyndon hashes to 6, which is now occupied by Richard, so Lyndon ends up at address 7.

Retrievals

To retrieve an object, start at the address given by the hash function. If the object is not found there, follow the same overflow path used by the insertion algorithm until either the object or an empty space is found. In the latter case, the object being searched for is not in the table. Test this on a couple of names in our list. Try also to retrieve a name that is not in the table such as John (hash value 4).

Clearly, when designing a hash table, we have more factors to consider than when using a "canned" data structure such as a linked list or binary search tree. The following sections will look at four design factors:

1. Bucket size—the number of objects stored at each address
2. Packing density—how much extra space to allow
3. The hash function—mapping keys to addresses
4. Overflow resolution—where to place overflowing objects

5.2 Bucket Size

We use the term **bucket** for a space in memory having a particular address (though this term is usually associated with disc files). If we had chosen a bucket size of two for our name table, the hash table would look like Figure 5.2.

In this case, overflow happens only when a third object hashes to a particular address. However, when the table is in main memory, there is no compelling reason to store more than one object at each address (i.e., to have a bucket size greater than one) because in main memory we can access the next bucket just as quickly as the next space in the current bucket.[6] This is not the case when we are hashing to disc,

0		
1		
2		
3		
4		

Figure 5.2 • Hash table: Two entries per address

as we will see in Chapter 11. **Home buckets** are those with addresses that can be produced by the hash function (there may be other buckets used for overflow only).

5.3 Packing Density

The number of accesses required to perform an insertion or retrieval operation tends to rise as the table fills. This is understandable; if more of the slots are occupied, it is more likely that the hashing function will generate the address of an occupied slot during insertion or the address of a slot containing an unwanted object during retrieval. However, it may be economically undesirable to have tables containing a lot of empty space. We define **packing density** as follows:

Packing density = Number of items in the table/ Total capacity of home buckets

As a rule of thumb, overflows often become unacceptably frequent if the packing density exceeds 70 percent, although this depends on bucket size. Given the choices for bucket size and packing density, we can estimate the number of objects that will overflow the home buckets. We will investigate this further in Chapter 11.

5.4 Hash Function

The third design factor we consider is the function that transforms a key into an address. The function has three general considerations:

1. The function must be deterministic. We may be tempted to introduce a random element into the function in order to spread out addresses, but whenever we give the function a particular key, it must return the same address. This is because the function is used in both storing an item and in retrieving it later.
2. Some of the time needed to store and retrieve objects is taken up by the computation of the hash function. When hashing to secondary rather than primary memory, the time taken to compute the hash function is normally insignificant compared with disc access time, so it may be worth having a relatively complex mapping [though one that is still $O(1)$ and not $O(N)$] in order to minimize secondary storage accesses. When hashing to main memory, we may opt for a simpler, faster function. Ramakrishna and Zobel (1997) point out that in a binary search of a table of strings, most comparisons between a table entry and the target string fail after a few character pairs are examined, whereas when searching for strings in a hash table, the hash function is computed on an entire string at least twice.
3. The principal measure of goodness of a hash function is the uniformity of the mapping. That is, the expected set of keys should be mapped uniformly onto the addresses, with minimal collisions. If there is bias towards particular

addresses, then objects hashing to the favored addresses are likely to overflow home buckets and take longer to store and retrieve.

5.4.1 Example Hash Function

Suppose we need to map four-digit decimal integers onto addresses 0 through 99 and that, as far as we know, any four-digit number is as likely as any other to be in the set to be mapped. Denoting the decimal digits of a number as d_1, d_2, d_3 and d_4, here are four possible hash functions:

1. address = d_1 * 10 + rand(10) (where rand(10) yields a random integer 0 to 9)
2. address = d_3 * 10 + d_4
3. address = (d_1 * d_2 * d_3 * d_4) modulo 100
4. address = (d_1 + d_2 + d_3 + d_4) modulo 100

Of these, only the second is reasonable. The first function is nondeterministic; it does not always yield the same value given the same key. The third function produces 0 whenever any of the digits is 0. The last function can only produce 37 different values and, moreover, the distribution of the 37 is nonuniform (e.g., 670 different numbers hash to 18, but only 4 hash to 35). The second function essentially uses the last two digits of the key as the value of the function, thus all 100 values are possible and there is no bias towards any particular address.

We now look at a general approach to designing a hash function.

5.4.2 A General Hash Function

Rather than trying to devise a function that transforms the key directly into an address using knowledge of the domain of the keys, it may be easier in many cases to reduce the key-to-address transformation to bit-level operations. Martin (1977) suggests that an address be derived from the key with a sequence of three transformations:

1. Key to integer A without loss of information (not needed if key is already integer)
2. Integer A to integer B where the range of B is close to the address range
3. Integer B to address

Step 2 is normally the crucial one. Methods based on division, that is,

$$B = A \text{ modulo } T$$

often give good results. Ghosh and Lum (1975) showed that if goodness is measured in terms of overflows, division is better than the randomization method, which is theoretically perfect. The randomization method would hash a key to a particular bucket out of N buckets with probability $1/N$. More important, it would hash two consecutive keys to the same bucket with probability $1/N$. Why might division be better? In practice, the set of keys to be hashed may contain clusters of adjacent values. Typically, Step 1 of the three-part operation will produce clusters of consecutive integers. (This is the case, for example, if the key is considered a base K integer, where K is the size of the alphabet from which its characters are drawn.) The division method spreads out the clusters by ensuring that two consecutive values for A produce different values of B. Contrast this with a method that uses the high-order rather than the low-order bits of a key. Table 5.1 shows some keys and typical results for Steps 1 and 2. The A values are the keys considered as a base 38 number: Space = 0, Hyphen = 1, A to Z = 2 to 27, 0 to 9 = 28 to 37. The B values are the remainders when dividing the corresponding A values by 3001 (a large prime number; more on this later).

The set of original keys contains two subsets of clustered objects. Step 1 produces the set of A values containing two subsets of consecutive integers. However, we can see from the third column how the division method ensures that the integers in a cluster produce different B values.

Some values of the divisor T are better than others. Buchholz (1963) suggested that T be the largest prime number less than the number of buckets. Lum et al. (1971) tested a number of key-to-address transformation methods and found division to work well. They advise that although T need not be a prime number, it should not have a prime factor of less than 20.

Another method that can work well in deriving integer B from integer A is **folding**. The bits of A are divided into two or more sections, which are combined using addition or exclusive-or. (Think of a business letter being folded into thirds.) The length of the sections is determined by the required size of B. Every bit in A contributes to B, and often the transformation can be accomplished very efficiently. We use folding in our example implementation.

Trial and error may be a reasonable way of deriving a hash function. A representative sample of key values can be run through the function and the results considered for unacceptable bias (see Exercise 2 at the end of the chapter).

● **TABLE 5.1** Keys and Hash Values

Key	*A* Value	*B* Value
ASM0343L	290219317455	1919
ASM0343M	290219317456	1920
ASM0343N	290219317457	1921
T121-B	1726095549	1376
T121-C	1726095550	1377
T121-D	1726095551	1378
T121-E	1726095552	1379

Note that if we hash objects into a table, we typically lose the capability to process them in sequential order. However, certain techniques will preserve the order of the objects (see the note on order-preserving hashing at the end of Chapter 11).

Example of the Three-Step Design

Suppose we are designing a hash function for a mail-order catalog company. Each item in their catalog has a unique identifier of the form *dllddd-l*, where *d* is a digit and *l* is a lowercase letter. Examples of keys are *2nt758-y* and *0tv911-r*. Let us assume a table size of 1965, thus we are hashing the identifiers to addresses 0 to 1964.

Our hash function generally follows Martin's (1977) approach and

1. Transforms the key to an integer *A* without loss of information
2. Uses folding to transform *A* into an 11-bit integer *B* (0 to 2047)
3. Uses scaling to obtain the address from *B*

Step 1 Each character position (apart from the hyphen) has a particular number of choices (10 for digits, 26 for letters). We convert the key to an integer by mapping each character to a particular value (0 to 9 for digits and 0 to 25 for letters), multiplying it by an appropriate weight (the product of the number of choices to its right), and then summing the products. This is similar to converting a base *B* number to decimal, except that not every digit is using the same base. Consider the processing of our first example key.

Character	2	n	t	7	5	8	—	y
Choices	10	26	26	10	10	10	1	26
Value	2	13	19	7	5	8	—	24
Weight	17,576,000	676,000	26,000	2600	260	26	—	1

The value of *A* derived from *2nt758-y* is thus

$$2 * 17{,}576{,}000 + 13 * 676{,}000 + 19 * 26{,}000 + 7 * 2600 + 5 * 260 + 8 * 26 + 24 * 1$$

$$= 35{,}152{,}000 + 8{,}788{,}000 + 494{,}000 + 18{,}200 + 1300 + 208 + 24$$

$$= 44{,}453{,}732$$

Step 2 From these numbers, we can see that the largest possible value of *A* is 175,759,999, which is a 28-bit number. Our address range is a little less than 2^{11}. Thus, we can take three overlapping 11-bit sections of *A* and exclusive-or them together to get *B*. Picture the 28-bit string being folded as we might fold a letter, except that we do not reverse the order of the bits in the middle section. We take the most significant 11 bits, the least significant 11 bits, and 11 bits from the middle of *A*. Thus every bit of *A* contributes to *B*.

Step 3   Finally, we multiply *B* by 1964/2047 to get an address. This is just a linear scaling operation to get a number in the right range. The numerator is the range of addresses; the denominator is the range of integer *B*.

The three steps are embodied in the following functions.

```
int mapchar (char c)
{
  // returns 0 through 25 for lowercase letters
  // returns 0 through 9  for digits
  // returns -1  for other characters

  if (islower(c)) return c-'a';
  if (isdigit(c)) return c-'0';
  return -1;
}

int hash (char key[])
{
  // key assumed to be dllddd-1  No error checking.

  int A=0, B, i, cumulative_weight=1;
  int weights[] = {10,26,26,10,10,10,0,26};

  for (i = 7; i>=0; i--)
    {
      if (weights[i] != 0)
        {
          A += ( mapchar(key[i]) * cumulative_weight);
          cumulative_weight *= weights[i];
        }
    }
  // now fold 11-bit sections
  B = (A & 2047) ^ ( (A>>8) & 2047 ) ^ ( (A>>17) & 2047) ;
  // now scale to get return value
  return B * 1964 / 2047;
}
```

Table 5.2 shows some keys and the addresses to which they hash.

• 5.4.3 A Hash Function for Strings

A problem with our general function is that it requires large integers and, in Step 1, time-consuming operations. Ramakrishna and Zobel (1997) describe a class of func-

• **TABLE 5.2** Keys and Hash Values	
Key	**Address**
2nt758-y	115
7xx123-h	748
0tv911-r	379
0aa000-a	0
9zz999-z	1628
5mm555-m	1112

tions designed to hash strings quickly. In general, for a string S consisting of characters $C_1 \ldots C_m$ and seed integer v, the general form of their function is

$h_0 \leftarrow \text{init}(v)$

for C_i in S $h_i \leftarrow \text{step}(i, h_{i-1}, C_i)$

return $\text{final}(h_m, v)$

The v parameter enables us to derive multiple hash values from the same key (we will see in the section on overflow resolution that double hashing uses two such values). In particular, Ramakrishna and Zobel recommend the shift-add-xor class of functions. If we wish to hash string S to integers in the range 0 to $T - 1$, then the recommended function is of the form

$h_0 \leftarrow v$

for C_i in S $h_i \leftarrow h_{i-1} \oplus (\text{leftshift}_L(h_{i-1}) + \text{rightshift}_R(h_{i-1}) + C_i)$

return h_m modulo T

where leftshift_L is a shift of L places left, rightshift_R is a shift of R places right, and $\oplus$ is the exclusive-or operator. Each of these logical operations is fast.

In experiments to evaluate their class of functions, Ramakrishna and Zobel used $L = 5$ and $R = 2$, but found that similar results were achieved when L was in the range 4 to 7 and R was 1, 2, or 3. Using the experimental settings yields the following C++ function.

```
int hashstring(string S, int v, int T)
{
    string::iterator i = S.begin();
    int res = v;

    while (i<S.end())
        {
```

S	v	T	hashstring
cat	0	1000	24
frog	0	1000	979
mouse	0	1000	121
horse	0	1000	384
mouseketeer	0	1000	780
mouseketeer	15	1000	911
mouseketeer	25	1000	678

• **TABLE 5.3** Hashing Strings with a String-Hashing Function

```
        res = res ^ ((res<<5) + (res>>2) + *i);
        i++;
        }
    return abs(res % T);
}
```

The call of *abs* is required because *res* may overflow the *int* range and become negative. If *T* is a power of two, we can replace the *abs* and modulo operations on the last line by a faster & (*and*) operation.

Table 5.3 shows the results of calling the *hashstring* function with various parameter combinations.

5.5 Overflow Resolution

Overflow occurs when an object hashes to a full bucket. When this happens, the problem is (1) to find space for the object and (2) to arrange matters so that the object can be found when searched for.[7] We will look at two broad categories of solutions: open addressing and closed addressing (chaining). These solutions can be categorized, respectively, as a computational approach and a data-structure approach. With open addressing, addresses of buckets to search are calculated dynamically. With closed addressing, chains of overflow objects are rooted in the home buckets. Our earlier name table example used a simple instance of open addressing.

5.5.1 Open Addressing

The following mechanism can generate a list of bucket addresses from the key of the object:

$$A_i = f(i, key) \quad i = 0, 1, 2, \ldots$$

If, when storing the object, bucket A_i is full, bucket A_{i+1} is examined. The mechanism should stop if we ever try to access the home bucket a second time. Thus, a C++ function might be:

```
bool insert (keytype key)
{
  int probe = 0, A = f(probe,key), home = A;

  while (true)
    {
      if (room_in_bucket(A))
          {
            insert_in_bucket(A,key);
            return true;
          }
      probe++;
      A = f(probe,key);
      if (A == home) return false;
    }
}
```

When retrieving an object, buckets are examined until one is found that either contains the required object or has an empty space. An empty space indicates that the object being searched for is not in the file. The following C++ function implements this algorithm:

```
bool retrieve (keytype key)
{
  int probe=0, A=f(probe,key), home = A;
  bucket tempbucket;

  while (true)
    {
      get_bucket(A,tempbucket);
      if (object_is_in_bucket(key,tempbucket)
          return true;
      if (room_in_bucket(tempbucket))  // bucket is not full
          return false;

      probe++;
      A = f(probe,key);
      if (A == home) return false;
    }
}
```

This method of resolving overflow was proposed by Peterson (1957), who gave it the term **open addressing**. A good function f should ensure that each integer 0 through $N - 1$ (where N is the number of home buckets) appears in the generated list of bucket addresses before the addresses begin to repeat.

A simple class of address-generating functions is represented by

$$A_i = (i * step + hash(key)) \text{ modulo } N$$

This method of computing addresses is called a **linear probe**. We look at buckets spaced equally apart (the step size), treating the table as circular if necessary. If the value of *step* is chosen to have no factors in common with N (i.e., they are relatively prime), then the first N elements of the list will be all the possible bucket numbers.[8]

The linear probe method suffers from two forms of "clustering." That is, there are two ways in which objects tend to bunch together in particular buckets instead of being spread evenly throughout the file. Clustering is undesirable because it increases the average number of accesses required for storage and retrieval. The two forms of clustering are **primary clustering** and **secondary clustering**. There are a number of ways to minimize clustering.

Primary Clustering

Primary clustering occurs because buckets probed when processing an object hashing to the first bucket in a sequence are also used by objects hashing to the second and subsequent buckets in that sequence. For example, if the number of home buckets (N) is 31 (numbered from 0 to 30), a simple mechanism for generating a sequence of overflow addresses is

$$A_i = (i * 3 + hash(key)) \text{ modulo } 31$$

Table 5.4 shows the addresses of buckets probed for a number of different keys where

$$hash(key) = key \text{ modulo } 31$$

● **TABLE 5.4** Keys and Linear Probe Sequences

Key	Hash(key)	Probe Sequence					
1234	25	25	28	0	3	6	9 ...
245	28	28	0	3	6	9	12 ...
1054	0	0	3	6	9	12	15 ...
100	7	7	10	13	16	19	22 ...
1591	10	10	13	16	19	22	25 ...
323	13	13	16	19	22	25	28 ...

If bucket 25 overflows into bucket 28, for instance, then the probability that bucket 28 will overflow increases. Overflow from both buckets will compete for space in bucket 0, and so on. There is a tendency for clusters of filled locations to get larger. Our presidential names example used linear probe. Consider Figure 5.1. The probability that the next object hashed to the table will end up in slot 0 is 0.1. The probability of the next object hashing to slot 9 is 0.1; however, the probability of it ending up in slot 8 is 0.8 because if it hashes to any address in the range 1 through 8 it will be placed in slot 8.

A solution to the primary clustering problem is to use a nonlinear function to generate the sequence of probe addresses. Examples of such functions are:

$$A_i = (hash(key) + i * constant_1 + i^2 * constant_2) \text{ modulo } N$$

and

$$A_i = (hash(key) + i^2) \text{ modulo } N$$

Table 5.5 shows the sequences we get if we replace the linear probe of Table 5.4 by

$$A_i = (hash(key) + i * 3 + i^2 * 5) \text{ modulo } 31$$

Note how buckets having overlapping probe sequences in Table 5.4 (e.g., 7, 10, and 13) now have different sequences. However, a sequence may repeat without generating all possible addresses and may never generate some addresses. Using our example formula, the start value of the sequence appears again in positions 18, 31, 49, 62, 80, 93, and so on, and only 16 of the 31 possible addresses are generated.

Secondary Clustering

Using a nonlinear rather than a linear probe does not eliminate secondary clustering. Secondary clustering occurs with simple open addressing because all objects with the same original home bucket follow the same sequence of overflow buckets. Defects in the design of the original hash function are likely to be perpetuated. For

● **TABLE 5.5**   Nonlinear Probe Sequences

Key	Hash(key)	Probe Sequence (first 12 values)											
1234	25	25	2	20	17	24	10	6	12	28	23	28	12
245	28	28	5	23	20	27	13	9	15	0	26	0	15
1054	0	0	8	26	23	30	16	12	18	3	29	3	18
100	7	7	15	2	30	6	23	19	25	10	5	10	25
1591	10	10	18	5	2	9	26	22	28	13	8	13	28
323	13	13	21	8	5	12	29	25	0	16	11	16	0

example, suppose that the hash function of our two tables was poorly designed and that far too many objects hashed to bucket 25. From Table 5.5 we can see that if the nonlinear probe were being used, we would expect buckets 2, 20, 17, 24, and so on to become full quickly.

A solution to the secondary clustering problem is to use **double hashing**. With this method, the probe sequence is produced in the following way:

$$A_i = (hash(key) + i * hash2(key)) \text{ modulo } N$$

The function *hash2* should produce an integer that is relatively prime to N; that is, it has no factors in common with N. In this way, the probe sequence will include all bucket numbers from 1 through N. If N is prime, *hash2* could return any positive integer less than N, and each bucket would be probed. The two hash functions should be independent: if N is prime, the probability that *hash(key1)* will equal *hash(key2)* and *hash2(key1)* will equal *hash2(key2)* if *key1* is not the same as *key2* should be approximately $(1/N)^2$. [See Knuth (1973) section 6.4 for suggestions on the design of *hash2*.] Table 5.6 illustrates double hashing. It shows, for a small number of keys, the two hash values and part of the sequence of buckets probed. Again, we assume 31 home buckets. The two functions used in the example are:

$$hash(key) = key \text{ modulo } 31$$

$$hash2(key) = 1 + (truncate(key/31) \text{ modulo } 29)$$

Analysis of Overflow Methods

Knuth (1973) derived the following approximations for different overflow strategies where *PD* represents the packing density defined earlier:

U_n—the average number of comparisons in an unsuccessful search

S_n—the average number of key comparisons in a successful search

---

● **TABLE 5.6** Keys and Double Hashing

Key	Hash(Key)	Hash2(Key)	Probe Sequence						
1234	25	11	25	5	16	27	7	18	29 ...
366	25	12	25	6	18	30	11	23	4 ...
831	25	27	25	21	17	13	9	5	1 ...
100	7	4	7	11	15	19	23	27	0 ...
224	7	8	7	15	25	0	8	16	24 ...
4471	7	29	7	5	3	1	30	28	26 ...

Linear probe

$$U_n = \frac{1}{2}\left(1 + \left(\frac{1}{1-PD}\right)^2\right)$$

$$S_n \approx \frac{1}{2}\left(1 + \frac{1}{1-PD}\right)$$

Double hashing

$$U_n = \frac{1}{1-PD}$$

$$S_n \approx -\left(\frac{1}{PD}\right)\log_e(1-PD)$$

Table 5.7 shows some values for these formulas.

Based on these values, we would choose double hashing over linear probe. But what might experiments with actual data show?

Experiments In order to see how close actual performance comes to theoretical prediction, we ran some experiments. Using a hash table of 997 entries, we implemented linear probe:

```
Home = abs(key) % 997
Step size = 1
```

and double hashing

```
Home = key % 997
Step = abs(key)/997%996+1;
```

● **TABLE 5.7** Theoretical Hashing Parameters

PD	Linear Probe		Double Hashing	
	U_n	S_n	U_n	S_n
0.1	1.12	1.06	1.11	1.05
0.3	1.52	1.21	1.43	1.19
0.5	2.50	1.50	2.00	1.39
0.7	6.06	2.17	3.33	1.72
0.9	50.50	5.50	10.00	2.56

• **TABLE 5.8** Observed Hashing Parameters				
PD	**Linear Probe**		**Double Hashing**	
	U_n	S_n	U_n	S_n
0.1	1.12	1.05	1.11	1.05
0.3	1.52	1.21	1.43	1.19
0.5	2.49	1.50	2.01	1.39
0.7	6.01	2.17	3.35	1.72
0.9	42.08	5.17	10.20	2.56

Using a reliable source of random numbers (Marsaglia 2000), we generated two nonintersecting sets of 32-bit keys. One set was hashed and then both were searched for. The results of the experiments are summarized in Table 5.8 using the same form as in the theoretical figures of Table 5.7. Each reported figure is the average of 500 trials. As you can see, there is close agreement between theory and practice in most cases.

Deletions

Open addressing forces us to be careful with deletions. Consider the name table from Figure 5.1 and what happens if we first delete Jimmy and then look for Richard. If we make Jimmy's space empty, then the search for Richard that starts at address 2 ends prematurely at address 5. Two possible solutions to the problem are (1) "logical" deletion of objects and (2) rehashing.

Logical Deletion   Using logical deletion, we mark an object "deleted" in some way rather than removing it and making the space empty. For example, we could set the primary key to some "impossible" value, such as −1 for keys that are normally only positive integers. Locations that contain "deleted" objects are treated as empty by the insertion algorithm so that they can be reused. However, they are not considered empty by the retrieval algorithm, thus the retrieval continues. The difficulty with this solution is that once an object slot becomes nonempty, it never becomes empty again. There are only three possible transitions:

1. Empty to used
2. Deleted to used
3. Used to deleted

Unsuccessful searches terminate only when an empty object slot is found; therefore, searches take longer and longer as empty space becomes scarcer and scarcer.

To maintain the performance of the table, it may be necessary, from time to time, to replace the table with a new one that contains only empty and used object slots. This **periodic maintenance** could be done by first allocating an empty table of the appropriate size and then scanning the current table. Objects in nonempty slots that are not marked deleted are hashed into the new table.

Rehashing   Another solution to the deletion problem is to remove the object from the table in the usual way; that is, to make the slot empty, but then to "rehash" certain remaining objects in the table. Rehashing an object involves deleting it and then inserting it. A copy of the object is made, its slot is marked empty, and then the copy is reinserted into the table as if it were a new object. The problem here is knowing which objects to rehash. In a simple case where overflow is resolved using linear probe and a step size of 1, the only objects that need to be rehashed are those positioned between the deleted object and the next free space. These are the only objects that could have overflowed from the deleted space.

In the case of our example, after we delete Jimmy we look at the objects between the newly empty space and the next empty space. These are Richard and Lyndon. Although a more subtle algorithm is possible (see the Exercises), we remove these objects and rehash them back into the table. Figure 5.3 shows one possible result.

The same problem with deletions arises when the bucket size is greater than 1. A retrieval may stop prematurely because an empty space in a bucket is taken as evidence that the object being searched for is not in the file. Consider the file depicted in Figure 5.4.

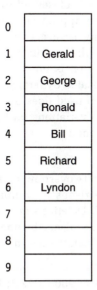

Figure 5.3 • Hash table after deletion and rehashing

Record #	Contents		
199			
200	A	P	
201	B	T	U
202	C	Q	L
203	W		
204	D	S	V
205	X		
206	Y	R	
207			

Figure 5.4 • Example hash file

Suppose that Q hashes to address 201. If we delete objects B, T, U, or C and just leave the slot empty, a search for Q will fail.

5.5.2 Closed Addressing (Chaining)

A second solution to the problem of overflows is **closed addressing**, in which lists of objects that have overflowed are rooted in appropriate home buckets. Closed addressing is sometimes referred to as **chaining** because of its use of linked storage. The overflow objects are put in a convenient place in the table, perhaps in a separate overflow area or in an arbitrary bucket that is not full. Alternatively, space could be found outside the table, perhaps allocated dynamically from heap storage. In contrast with open addressing, the location used does not typically depend on the contents of the object. We consider three variations on this idea: (1) separate lists, (2) coalescing lists, and (3) directory methods.

Separate Lists

The separate-lists method links together objects overflowing from the same home bucket. The list is rooted in that bucket. Comparisons are minimized during a search because only one list needs to be examined. Deletions are straightforward. If an object is deleted from a home bucket, it can be replaced by one on the overflow list. If an object on a list is deleted, it is removed from the list in the conventional way. Suppose we have the following keys:

120 191 132 22 81 140 70 63 21 41 181 90 11 980 51 72 101

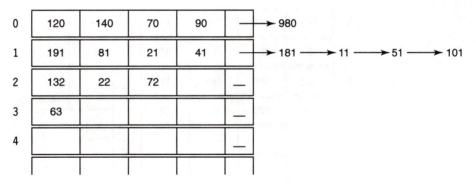

Figure 5.5 • Overflow with separate lists

and our hash function is

$Hash$ = key modulo 10

Using separate lists of overflow objects, we get the table shown in Figure 5.5.

Knuth's analysis of overflow resolution with separate chaining yields the following approximations.

$$U_n \approx PD$$
$$S_n \approx 1 + \frac{PD}{2}$$

Coalescing Lists

The separate-lists method requires a comparatively large amount of space for pointers. A second possibility is to store objects in spare space in home buckets. Each bucket has a single pointer pointing to the next bucket to try when searching. Pointers are established as objects overflow. This method reduces pointer overhead, but many more objects may have to be examined when searching because lists that begin separately may coalesce. Using our example keys, we get the table shown in Figure 5.6.

The efficiency of this structure is poor in this case because we have many overflows (e.g., when searching for 72, we would compare that target key with 132, 22, 181, 11, 63, 980, 51, and 72). Poor efficiency is generally acceptable if there are relatively few overflows. We can reduce coalescing by having two or more nonintersecting lists of free buckets.

Directory Methods

Again, with methods involving directories, room is allocated in a home bucket beyond that needed to store objects. A bucket holds C objects and N pointers. The first $N - 1$ overflows from a bucket are pointed to directly. Subsequent overflows

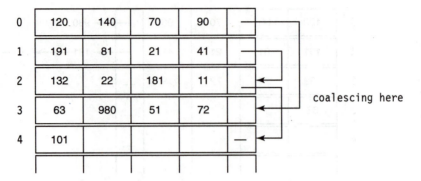

Figure 5.6 • Overflow with coalescing lists

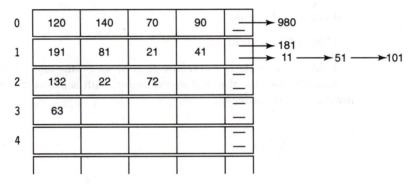

Figure 5.7 • Overflow with directory

are put on a list rooted in the Nth pointer. With our example keys and $N = 2$, we get the final table shown in Figure 5.7.

The principal difference between directories and separate lists is the location of the first $N - 1$ overflows. For example, a table with bucket size 8 and three pointers is logically equivalent to a table with bucket size 7 and four pointers.

5.6 Hash Table Implementations

In this section, two map classes that use a hash table implementation will be defined:

- *map_hash_bounded* will use open addressing to resolve overflows, and thus have a capacity bounded by the number of table entries that we specify.
- *map_hash_unbounded* will use closed addressing with separate lists, and thus have an unbounded capacity.[9]

The way in which we define the interfaces for *insert*, *retrieve*, and *remove* operations (both in the hashed-based maps in this chapter and the tree-based maps in the next) may appear unusual. Apart possibly from a pointer to a data structure, each of the three functions (*insert*, *remove*, and *retrieve*) takes a single parameter—an object (*X*) of the type being stored in the map.

- *Insert:* We attempt to insert *X* into the structure. If an object already exists with the same key as *X*, it is replaced by *X*. (Thus, we do not need a separate *modify* function.)
- *Remove:* If we find an object with the same key as *X*, we remove it.
- *Retrieve:* If we find an object with the same key as *X*, we overwrite *X* with that object.

This approach allows the functions to not be concerned about what parts of an object constitute the key. We only require that the user overloads the equality operator (==) that is used to determine if two objects have the same key.[10]

As usual, we will use a template to make the definitions as general as possible; the class of objects to be stored in the table will be the "parameter" of our class definitions. We assume for the objects to be stored that:

- An equality operator (==) is defined on them.
- A hash function (*H*) exists that we can invoke with table size as a parameter—*H* returns a bucket number.
- The stream-insertion operator (<<) is defined to display the object.[11] This is not really necessary except that we may wish to display the contents of the table.

In addition, our implementations assume the use of an assignment operator and a copy constructor (either user-defined or the system default, as appropriate).

5.6.1 *map_hash_bounded*

Here is the first part of our class definition for the hash table that uses open addressing; it consists of the function prototypes.[12] Note that because hashing is an implementation technique, the public component of the class definition is almost completely a generic map interface. Only the default argument in the constructor is particular to the hash table implementation.

```
template <class Entry>
class map_hash_bounded
{
 public:
        map_hash_bounded(int N=10);    // constructor - allocate memory
        ~map_hash_bounded();           // destructor - clean up memory
        map_hash_bounded(const map_hash_bounded &rhs);      // replicator
        map_hash_bounded& operator = (const map_hash_bounded&); // assignment
        void showmap(ostream&) const;  // display contents
        bool retrieve(Entry&);         // looks for key match, puts in
```

```
      bool insert(Entry);        // overwrites if key there
      bool remove(Entry);        // deletes one with same key
 private:
      enum hashtag {empty,full,deleted};
      void copytags (hashtag *&newtable, hashtag *oldtable, int N); // used by rep.
      void copyentries(Entry *&newtable, Entry *oldtable, int N); // used by rep.
      int size;                  // number of slots in table
      hashtag *tags;             // for tags
      Entry *entries;            // for the table entries
      int find(Entry);           // find entry with same key
      int findfree(Entry);       // find appropriate space for new key
};
```

Figure 5.8 is a depiction of an object of class *map_hash_bounded*.

Implementation Details

We will resolve overflows using linear probe and permit deletions to be made from the table. Thus, a technique is needed for representing the state of a particular table entry: *empty, full,* or *deleted.* In general, we do not know what kinds of keys our table entries have, so we cannot reserve particular key values to represent *empty* and *deleted.* Instead, we define an enumerated type *hashtag* having three possible

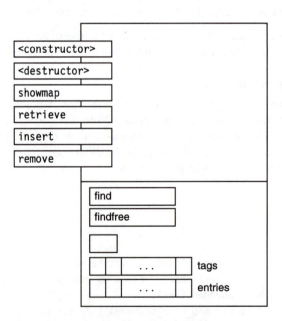

Figure 5.8 • Hash table object: Bounded table

values (*full*, *empty*, and *deleted*), and we use an array of tags in parallel with the array of table entries. The state of *entries[i]* is stored in *tags[i]*. The constructor function allocates dynamic arrays for the table entries and for the tags. The default size for these arrays is 10, but the user can specify any size. The destructor releases the allocated space.

The public functions make use of two utility functions, *find* and *findfree*, to find a particular undeleted key and to find a nonfull entry, respectively. These two functions do not need to be public. Here is the rest of the class definition:[13]

```
template <class Entry>
map_hash_bounded<Entry>::map_hash_bounded(int N=10)
        { // constructor: remember size of table, allocate space for array of tags
          // and array of entries. Initialize the array of tags
          size=N;
          tags = new hashtag[N];
          entries = new Entry[N];
          for (int i=0;i<N;i++) tags[i]=empty;
        }


template <class Entry>
map_hash_bounded<Entry>::~map_hash_bounded()
        { // destructor: reclaim space for array of tags and array of entries
          delete[] tags;
          delete[] entries;
        }


template <class Entry>
void map_hash_bounded<Entry>::copytags(hashtag *&newtable,
                                       hashtag *oldtable, int size)
{ // make a copy of the array of tags
 newtable = new hashtag[size];
 for (int i=0; i<size; i++) newtable[i] = oldtable[i];
}

template <class Entry>
void map_hash_bounded<Entry>::copyentries(Entry *&newtable, Entry *oldtable, int size)
{// make a copy of the array of entries
 newtable = new Entry[size];
 for (int i=0; i<size; i++) newtable[i] = oldtable[i];
}


template <class Entry>
```

```
map_hash_bounded<Entry>::map_hash_bounded(const map_hash_bounded &rhs)
{// copy constructor
 size = rhs.size;
 copytags(tags,rhs.tags,size);
 copyentries(entries,rhs.entries,size);
}


template <class Entry>
map_hash_bounded<Entry>& map_hash_bounded<Entry>::operator =
                                    (const map_hash_bounded &rhs)
{
  // overloaded assignment operator
  if (this!=&rhs) // not trying to assign to self
        {
         size = rhs.size;
         copytags(tags,rhs.tags,size);
         copyentries(entries,rhs.entries,size);
         return *this;
        }
}


template <class Entry>
void map_hash_bounded<Entry>::showmap(ostream &s) const
        { // to display the table in a simple way
          // requires << to be defined for objects being stored
          for (int i=0; i<size; i++)
            { s << i   << " " ;
              if (tags[i]==full) s << entries[i];
              s << endl;
            }
        }


template <class Entry>
int map_hash_bounded<Entry>::find(Entry target)
        {  // returns index in the table of undeleted target.
           // returns -1 if not present or present but deleted

           int home= target.H(size);  // hash function gives home address
           int pos = home;            // starting point for search

           while (  tags[pos]!=empty && !(entries[pos] == target))
                {
```

```
                    pos = (pos+1) % size;      // next location - circular
                    if (pos==home) return -1; // back at starting point - not found
                  }
                  if (tags[pos]==full) return pos;  //  stopped on target
              return -1;                             // found target but it was deleted
            }


template <class Entry>
bool map_hash_bounded<Entry>::retrieve (Entry& target)
          {
        int row=find(target);        // look for key match
         if (row==-1) return false; // not found

         target = entries[row];     // found: overwrite parameter
         return true;
         }



template <class Entry>
bool map_hash_bounded<Entry>::insert (Entry E)
          {
        int row=find(E);            // look for key match
         if (row>=0)
             { // already in - overwrite attributes
                entries[row]=E;
                return true;
              }
        else  { row=findfree(E); // not in, look for free space
                 if (row>=0)
                 { // free space found
                      entries[row]=E;
                      tags[row]=full;
                  return true;
                   }
                 else return false;     // table full
              }
          }
template <class Entry>
bool map_hash_bounded<Entry>::remove (Entry target)
          {
         int row=find(target);      // look for key match
          if (row=-1) return false; // not in the table
```

```
            tags[row] = deleted;      // found. mark deleted.
            return true;
        }


template <class Entry>
int map_hash_bounded<Entry>::findfree(Entry target)
        { // returns index of free space or -1 if none
            int home= target.H(size);  // H give home address
            int pos = home;            // start search there
          while (tags[pos] == full)
             {
               pos = (pos+1) % size;       // treat table as circular
               if (pos==home) return -1; // back at beginning - no free space
             }
          return pos;
        }
```

• 5.6.2 *map_hash_unbounded*

Our second hash table class deals with overflows by having a list of overflowing objects for each bucket. Because of the way that entry removal is implemented, our tags now need only two values: *empty* and *full*. In parallel with the array of tags and the array of table entries, we have an array of lists.[14] The first part of our class definition for the table using closed addressing follows.

```
#include <list>
#include <iostream.h>        //   for cout


template <class Entry>
class map_hash_unbounded
{

 public:
        map_hash_unbounded(int N=10);    // constructor - allocate memory
        ~map_hash_unbounded();           // destructor - clean up memory
        map_hash_unbounded(const map_hash_unbounded &rhs);  // replicator
        map_hash_unbounded& operator = (const map_hash_unbounded&);
        void showmap(ostream&) const;   // display contents
        bool retrieve(Entry&);          // looks for key match, puts in
        bool insert(Entry);             // overwrites if key there
        bool remove(Entry);             // deletes one with same key

  private:
        enum hashtag  {empty,full};
```

```
        typedef list<Entry> overflow;
        void copytags (hashtag *&newtable, hashtag *oldtable, int N); // used.
        void copyentries(Entry *&newtable, Entry *oldtable, int N); //  by
        void copyoverflows(overflow *&newtable, overflow *oldtable, int N); // rep.
        int size;              // number of slots in table
        hashtag *tags;         // for tags
        Entry *entries;        // for the table entries
        overflow *overflows;   // for the overflow lists
};
```

Figure 5.9 is a depiction of an object of class *map_hash_unbounded*.

Implementation Details

When an object hashes to a full slot, it is pushed to the front of the appropriate overflow list. The code for the *remove* function is left as an exercise for the reader, but note that it needs to deal with two cases: where the object to be removed is in the table and where the object is in an overflow list.

Here is the rest of the class definition.

```
template <class Entry>
map_hash_unbounded<Entry>::map_hash_unbounded(int N=10)
        { // constructor: remember the size, allocate space for array of tags,
          // array of entries and array of overflow lists. Initialize the array
```

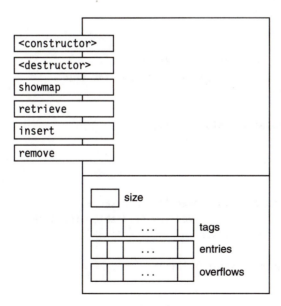

Figure 5.9 • Hash table object: Unbounded table

```
            // of tags
            size=N;
            tags = new hashtag[N];
            entries = new Entry[N];
            overflows = new overflow[N];
            for (int i=0;i<N;i++) tags[i]=empty;
        }


template <class Entry>
map_hash_unbounded<Entry>::~map_hash_unbounded()
        { // destructor: reclaim the space allocated for the three arrays
          delete[] tags;
          delete[] entries;
          delete[] overflows;
        }

template <class Entry>
void map_hash_unbounded<Entry>::copytags(hashtag *&newtable,
                                         hashtag *oldtable, int size)
{// make a copy of the array of tags
 newtable = new hashtag[size];
 for (int i=0; i<size; i++) newtable[i] = oldtable[i];
}


template <class Entry>
void map_hash_unbounded<Entry>::copyentries(Entry *&newtable,
                                            Entry *oldtable, int size)
{// make a copy of the array of entries
 newtable = new Entry[size];
 for (int i=0; i<size; i++) newtable[i] = oldtable[i];
}


template <class Entry>
void map_hash_unbounded<Entry>::copyoverflows(overflow *&newtable,
                                              overflow *oldtable, int size)
{// make a copy of the array of overflow lists
 newtable = new overflow[size];
 for (int i=0; i<size; i++) newtable[i] = oldtable[i];
}


template <class Entry>
```

```
map_hash_unbounded<Entry>::map_hash_unbounded(const map_hash_unbounded &rhs)
{// copy constructor
 size = rhs.size;
 copytags(tags,rhs.tags,size);
 copyentries(entries,rhs.entries,size);
 copyoverflows(overflows,rhs.overflows,size);
}


template <class Entry>
map_hash_unbounded<Entry>& map_hash_unbounded<Entry>::operator = (const map_hash_unbounded &rhs)
{
  // overloaded assignment operator
  if (this!=&rhs) // not trying to assign to self
      {
        size = rhs.size;
        copytags(tags,rhs.tags,size);
        copyentries(entries,rhs.entries,size);
        return *this;
      }
}



template <class Entry>
void map_hash_unbounded<Entry>::showmap(ostream &s) const
      { // function to display the table on stream s
        for (int i=0; i<size; i++)
          {
            s << i   << " " ;
            if (tags[i]==full)
              {
                s << entries[i];          // here is the entry
                if (!overflows[i].empty())
                    { // print the overflow list
                      overflow::iterator t = overflows[i].begin();
                      while (t!=overflows[i].end())
                          {
                            s << " " << *t;
                            t++;
                          }
                    }
              }
            s << endl;
          }
      }
```

```
template <class Entry>
bool map_hash_unbounded<Entry>::retrieve (Entry& target)
        {
        int row=target.H(size);              // the row of interest
         if (tags[row]==empty) return false; // nothing there
         if (entries[row]==target)
                { // found in the table
                  target = entries[row];  // overwrite parameter with table entry
                  return true;
                }
         if (overflows[row].empty()) return false; // no overflows to search
         // look in overflow list
         overflow::iterator i = overflows[row].begin();
         while (i!=overflows[row].end() && !(target==*i)) i++;
         if ( i==overflows[row].end()) return false;  // no match in list
         target = *i;                             // found in overflow list
         return true;
        }




template <class Entry>
bool map_hash_unbounded<Entry>::insert (Entry E)
        {
        int row=E.H(size);       // the row of interest
         if (tags[row]==empty)  // entry is currently empty
           {
              entries[row]=E;
              tags[row]=full;
              return true;
            }
         if (entries[row]==E)  // entry found with same key
           {
             entries[row]=E;    // overwrite with the new object
              return true;
             }
        // see if in overflow list
        overflow::iterator i = overflows[row].begin();
        while (i!=overflows[row].end() && !(E==*i)) i++;
        if (i!=overflows[row].end())
             *i = E;    // found so overwrite with new object
        else overflows[row].push_front(E); // not found, push at front of list
         return true;
        }
```

```
template <class Entry>
bool map_hash_unbounded<Entry>::remove (Entry target)
        {
        int row = target.H(size);             // the row of interest
        if (tags[row]==empty) return false;   // is empty so not in table
        if (entries[row]==target)             // is it the table entry?
            {
            if (overflows[row].empty())       // yes. any overflows?
              tags[row] = empty;              // no so this row is now empty
            else
              {       // yes so move first overflow to table
                      overflow::iterator i = overflows[row].begin();
                      entries[row] = *i;
                      overflows[row].pop_front();
              }
            return true;
            }
        else {       // see if object to be removed is in overflow list
            overflow::iterator i = overflows[row].begin();
            while (i!=overflows[row].end() && !(target==*i)) i++;
            if (i==overflows[row].end())
                    return false;      // no so remove fails
            overflows[row].erase(i); // yes get rid of it
                return true;
            }
        }
```

5.7 Applications

We illustrate uses of hash-based maps with two applications. The first is a simple spelling checker that uses maps to hold sets of words. The second is a password manager that uses a map to hold data on system users. This second application also illustrates another use for hash functions.

• 5.7.1 A Spelling Checker

A rudimentary spelling checker program might use two collections of words: a list of known correct words (the dictionary) and a list of words it encounters that are not in the dictionary. We would like the checking to proceed as quickly as possible, thus hash tables are a good choice. The check we implement here (see also Problems) is not interactive, thus the user is not able to add words to the dictionary on the fly. This makes the size of the dictionary fixed and predictable, thus we could use an object of our *map_hash_bounded* class. The number of entries in the collection of suspected bad words depends on the text being checked, thus it also makes sense to use an object of the *map_hash_unbounded* class.

Here is the class definition for the word objects that will be stored in the two tables.

```
class direntry
{
 public: direntry(string S=""){theword=S;}
         void setup(string A){ theword=A; }
         int H(int size)
           {// the hash function
            string::iterator t = theword.begin();
            int res = 1;
            while(t<theword.end())
                {
                  res = res ^ ( (res<<5) + (res>>2) + *t);
                  t++;
                }
            return abs(res%size);
           }
         void cleanup ()
           { // remove nonletters, map to lowercase
             string result="";
             for (int i=0; i<theword.length(); i++)
                  if (isalpha(theword[i])) result+= tolower(theword[i]);
             theword = result;
           }
         friend ostream& operator <<(ostream& outs, const direntry& X)
           { // stream-insert operator
             outs << X.theword;
             return outs;
           }
         bool operator == (direntry other) {return other.theword == theword; }
         int wordsize() { return theword.length(); }
         string getword() { return theword; }

 private : string theword;
};
```

The *H* function uses the string hashing algorithm of Ramakrishna and Zobel (1997). Because of the simple way in which tokens are read from the text, the *cleanup* function is needed to remove leading and trailing nonletter characters. In addition, it changes words to be checked to lowercase (all our dictionary words are entirely lowercase).

The spelling checker program follows. The dictionary is loaded with a list of the 1000 most frequently occurring words in the British National Corpus (1995). The *dictionary* table is allocated 1428 spaces, meaning that it will be about 70 percent full when the word list is loaded. For a useful spelling checker, we would normally want a much larger word list, but here we are just testing the algorithms.

```
#include <fstream.h>
#include <string>

#include "map_hash_bounded.h"
#include "map_hash_unbounded.h"

#include "direntry.h"

int main(int argc, char *argv[])
{
 fstream dir, text;
 int count = 0;
 map_hash_bounded<direntry> dictionary(1428); // fixed size dictionary
 map_hash_unbounded<direntry> badwords(25);   // variable number of bad words

 string S;

 // load directory
 dir.open("samplefordir",ios::in);
 while (dir >> S)
   {
     direntry temp(S);
     if (dictionary.insert(temp)) count++;
   }
 cout << "Number of words inserted into dictionary: " << count << endl;

 if (argc<2)
    cerr << "spellcheck: missing text file name\n";
 else
     {
       // open file to read
       text.open(argv[1],ios::in);
       while (text >> S)
         {
             direntry temp(S);
             temp.cleanup();
```

When Farmer Oak smiled, the corners of his mouth spread till they were
within an unimportant distance of his ears, his eyes were reduced to
chinks, and diverging wrinkles appeared round them, extending upon his
countenance like the rays in a rudimentary sketch of the rising sun.

His Christian name was Gabriel, and on working days he was a young man
of sound judgement, easy motions, proper dress, and general good character.
On Sundays he was a man of misty views, rather given to postponing, and
hampered by his best clothes and umbrella: upon the whole, one who felt
himself to occupy morally that vast middle space of Laodicean neutrality
which lay between the Communion people of the parish and the drunken section,
-- that is, he went to church, but yawned privately by the time the
congregation reached the Nicene creed, and thought of what there would be
for dinner when he meant to be listening to the sermon. Or, to state his
character as it stood in the scale of public opinion, when his friends and
critics were in tantrums, he was considered rather a bad man; when they were
pleased, he was rather a good man; when they were neither, he was a man whose
moral colour was a kind of pepper-and-salt mixture.

Figure 5.10 • Test data for the spelling checker

```
                      if (temp.wordsize()>0) // any characters left after cleanup?
                          if (!dictionary.retrieve(temp)) badwords.insert(temp);
          }
      cout << "\nbad words\n";
      badwords.showmap(cout);
          }
    }
```

Testing

Figure 5.10 shows the first two paragraphs of Thomas Hardy's *Far from the Madding Crowd* ([1874]1996).

Based on the text, the spelling checker produces the following output. The numbers at the beginning of each line are bucket numbers. (Because of the way in which our tokenizer works, hyphenated words are run together. See bucket 6 for an example.)

```
Number of words inserted into dictionary: 1000

bad words
0
1 corners scale
2 till nicene congregation hampered chinks distance
3 creed
```

4 farmer smiled oak
5 sermon
6 christian pepperandsalt reached communion judgement
7 dress middle
8 countenance yawned
9 ears neutrality diverging
10 rays clothes
11 spread mixture postponing misty sketch
12 wrinkles laodicean occupy
13 motions lay views
14 appeared
15 parish tantrums meant privately
16 reduced vast extending
17 sun moral umbrella
18 morally
19 rudimentary
20 listening critics opinion
21 sundays
22 rising dinner proper
23 drunken pleased
24 unimportant neither gabriel

5.7.2 A Password Manager

Our second application uses a hash table to store usernames and passwords, which means that when a user logs in, the retrieval operation is fast. However, rather than store the password string itself, the application stores three hash values derived from the password string, making it less important to keep the password table secret. A disadvantage of this arrangement, however, is that we could get a false match if some string other than the correct password happens to hash to the same three values. Here is the class definition for the table entries.

```
class userpass
{
 public: userpass() { username = ""; }
        void setup(string UN, string PWD)
          {
              username = UN;
              for (int i=0; i<3; i++) hashcodes[i]=hash(PWD,i);
          }
        int H(int size)
          {
              string::iterator t = username.begin();
             int res = 1;
```

```cpp
              while (t<username.end())

                  {
                    res = res ^ ( (res<<5) + (res>>2) + *t);
                    t++;
                    }
                return abs(res%size);
            }
    bool operator == (userpass other)
        { return other.username == username; }
    friend ostream& operator <<(ostream& outs, const userpass& X)
      {
        outs << X.username;
        for (int i=0; i<3; i++) outs << " " << X.hashcodes[i];
        return outs;
      }
    void show()
        {
          cout << username;
          for (int i=0; i<3; i++) cout << " " << hashcodes[i];
        }
    bool checkcodes(string test)
        {
          for (int i=0; i<3; i++)
              if (hashcodes[i]!=hash(test,i)) return false;
          return true;
        }

    private: string username;
             int hashcodes[3];
             int hash(string S,int v)
                { // similar to H except that there is a v parameter and
                  // it returns a 32-bit number
                  string::iterator t = S.begin();
                  int res = v;
                  while (t<S.end())
                  // can return any integer
                    {
                      res = res ^ ( (res<<5) + (res>>2) + *t);
                      t++;
                      }
                  return res;
                  }
};
```

We use the string function proposed by Ramakrishna and Vogel (1997) both to hash objects to the table (function *H*) and to obtain integer values from the password string (function *hash*). Experiments suggest that having more than one hash code reduces the possibility of a false match. Function *checkcodes* tests to see whether a particular string hashes to three stored integers.

Testing

The following program tests the class definition in an imitation of operating system facilities that enable us to

- Enter a new username/password (n)
- Log in and have the system check the password (1)
- Change a password for a user (need to know current password) (c)

In addition, we implement a command (s) to show us the table of usernames and stored data.

```
#include <string>
#include <iostream>

#include "map_hash_unbounded.h"
#include "userpass.h"

int main()
{
  map_hash_unbounded<userpass> users(8);
  userpass temp;
  char command,junk;
  string U, P;

  cout << "Command (x or X to exit): ";
  cin.get(command);
  cin.get(junk);            // consume the Enter character

  while(command !='x' && command != 'X')
    {
      switch(command)
      {
      case'n':  // new user
                cout << "enter username and password: ";
                cin >> U >> P; cin.get(junk);
                temp.setup(U,P);
                users.insert(temp);
```

```
                                  break;

                   case'l':  // log in
                             cout << "enter username and password: ";
                             cin >> U >> P; cin.get(junk);
                             temp.setup(U,P);
                             if (users.retrieve(temp)) // user exists?
                                {
                                  if (temp.checkcodes(P))
                                       cout << "login successful\n";
                                  else cout << "username/password invalid\n";
                                }
                             else cout << "username/password invalid\n";
                             break;

                   case'c':  // change password
                             cout << "enter username and password: ";
                             cin >> U >> P; cin.get(junk);
                             temp.setup(U,P);
                             if (!users.retrieve(temp)) { cout << "invalid\n"; break; }
                             if (!temp.checkcodes(P)) { cout << "invalid\n"; break; }
                             cout << "enter new password: ";
                             cin >> P; cin.get(junk);
                             temp.setup(U,P);
                             users.insert(temp);
                             break;

                   case's':  // show table
                             users.showtable(); break;

                  default: cerr << "Invalid command\n";
                 }
            cout << "Command (x or X to exit): ";
            cin.get(command); cin.get(junk);  }

        return 0;
        }
```

Output

Output from a run of the program follows. After setting up six users, we check to see that the password verification mechanism works, then test the password-changing function.

```
Command (x or X to exit): n
enter username and password: peter fido
Command (x or X to exit): n
enter username and password: sally london
Command (x or X to exit): n
enter username and password: kathy mnt1472
Command (x or X to exit): n
enter username and password: ben golakers
Command (x or X to exit): n
enter username and password: mike renzoid
Command (x or X to exit): n
enter username and password: robert denhaag
Command (x or X to exit): s
0
1 ben 1113422979 456719996 -1671740711
2
3 sally 109032802 612567462 2143438119
4 kathy -1994450781 -38920405 -1782752613 mike -2089973959 1393377330
                                                            -375961351
5 peter 3452888 4805633 5727935
6 robert -937592827 -1648233304 -894406755
7
Command (x or X to exit): l
enter username and password: kate dilbert
username/password invalid
Command (x or X to exit): l
enter username and password: peter rover
username/password invalid
Command (x or X to exit): l
enter username and password: peter fido
login successful
Command (x or X to exit): l
enter username and password: ben fido
username/password invalid
Command (x or X to exit): l
enter username and password: ben golakers
login successful
Command (x or X to exit): c
enter username and password: peter london
invalid
Command (x or X to exit): c
enter username and password: peter fido
```

```
enter new password: dusty
Command (x or X to exit): 1
enter username and password: peter fido
username/password invalid
Command (x or X to exit): 1
enter username and password: peter dusty
login successful
Command (x or X to exit): s
0
1 ben 1113422979 456719996 -1671740711
2
3 sally 109032802 612567462 2143438119
4 kathy -1994450781 -38920405 -1782752613 mike -2089973959 1393377330
                                                        -375961351
5 peter 115593649 156710724 189700431
6 robert -937592827 -1648233304 -894406755
7
Command (x or X to exit): x
```

● Chapter Summary

Hashing is a technique that stores data at an address derived in some way from the data itself. We typically use a key-to-address mapping function (the hash function) to determine the appropriate address. We use the same function both in storing an item and in retrieving it later. In favorable circumstances, storage and retrieval using hashing can be very fast—O(1) compared with O(N) or O(log N) of other methods.

However, a user is normally responsible for designing the hash function, and a good one (one that scatters data evenly over the address space) may be difficult to devise. In addition, we may have multiple data items mapping to the same address. If this is the case, we need to provide a mechanism for dealing with overflows.

Although hashing can be very fast when storing and retrieving individual items, the hash function typically scatters data in such a way that ordering is lost. Thus, it may be difficult to process the items in key order or to find those with keys in a certain range.

● Exercises

1. Names come in a variety of forms; some examples are:

    William B. Gates III

    Gregory Velasco y Trianosky

    Ronaldo

Basil d'Oliveira

Sir Ranulph Whykam-Twistleton-Fiennes

John F. Kennedy Jr.

Design a hash function that maps names to the integers 0 through 4999. Give your answer as a C++ or pseudocode function definition.

2. For each of the following key domains, devise two or more functions that map keys onto the integers 0 through 999. (You may have to investigate the ways in which keys are constructed.)

   a. License plates for your state

   b. International Standard Book Numbers (ISBNs)

   c. Social security numbers

   Devise a mechanism that evaluates hash functions and use it to determine your best function for each domain.

3. Double hashing is an effective way to handle overflows. We have two functions: hash1(key) yields the address of the home bucket and hash2(key) yields step size. What properties should the two functions have? Consider them independently and as a pair to be used together.

4. Our pizza business determines that a customer table with 1000 entries (numbered 0–999) is sufficient for its needs. In deriving a table index from a customer's seven-digit phone number, should it use (a) the first three digits, (b) the last three digits, or (c) three digits chosen at random? Give reasons for your answer.

5. Suppose we are hashing entries into a table using linear probe with a step size of 1. We wish to avoid the complications of having space marked "deleted." When an entry is removed:

   a. How can we tell if it is safe to leave it as "empty"?

   b. If it is not safe to leave it as empty, how can we determine which entries need to be moved to cover empty spaces correctly?

6. A certain state government issues drivers licenses with unique six-digit numbers. Numbers have been allocated sequentially from 1 upwards. There are currently about 50,000 licensed drivers. Which of the following would you use to hash license numbers onto addresses 0 through 999?

   a. address = license /1000

   b. address = license modulo 1000

   Give reasons for your choice.

7. Vehicles in a large company car pool are given unique five-digit identification numbers generated at random. Which of the following would you use to hash vehicle numbers onto addresses 0 through 999?

a. *key* modulo 1000

b. First digit * 100 + third digit * 10 + last digit

c. Sum of all digits * 1000 / 46

Give reasons for your choice.

8. Suppose that you need to hash names (lastname, firstname) into a table having 40,000 entries (each of which can hold one name). Give details of the hash function that you would use and give reasons for your choice.

9. Sketch a retrieval algorithm for a hash table that uses closed addressing with coalescing lists.

10. Sketch a deletion algorithm for a hash table that uses closed addressing with coalescing lists.

11. A video store wishes to create a hash table of the movie titles it has available for rental. At any time the store has room on the shelves for only 500 different titles. You have been assigned the task of setting up the computerized system.

   a. How large a hash table would you create (i.e., how many entries)?

   b. Give (in pseudocode or programming language) an algorithm that maps movie names to the address space from part a. (Note that movie titles may be numeric, e.g., 2001, 10, 8 1/2.)

12. The Unix spelling checker program *spell* uses Bloom filters (Bloom 1970) to store a dictionary of words. Instead of storing the words themselves, it uses several hash functions, H_1 through H_N, and an array of bits B initially full of zeros.

   To store a word (W), each hash function is applied to W, and the resulting hash values $i_1 \ldots i_N$ are used to index B. We set bits $B[i_1]$, $B[i_2]$ ... to 1.

   To check to see if a word (Y) is in the dictionary, we apply each hash function to Y yielding $j_1 .. j_N$. If all the bits $B[j_1]$, $B[j_2]$, .. $B[j_N]$ are 1, we assume the word is in the dictionary.

   a. Can the system ever report falsely that a word is in when it is not? Explain.

   b. Can the system ever report falsely that a word is not in when it is? Explain.

   c. What factors can be adjusted to reduce the number of errors of the type shown in part a.

   d. How can a word be deleted from the dictionary?

13. How might an addition operator be defined for two hash tables? The effect of $A = B + C$, where each of A, B, and C is a hash table, is to create hash table A containing the entries from B and those from C. Outline the algorithm for such an operation.

14. A weakness of our password-storing system is that it reveals if two people use the same password. Suggest a fix.

15. Would you classify a hash table that handles overflows with coalescing lists as bounded or as unbounded. Give reasons for your answer.

16. Suppose you are in charge of a large parking lot having numbered parking spaces. You decide that a vehicle is required to park in a space having a number derived from its license plate. How do you handle collisions (of the hashing variety)? What advantages and disadvantages does your parking policy have over a traditional free-for-all approach?

17. Suggest a way in which simple melodies can be hashed so that a change of musical key does not change the hash value.

18. Suppose we hash three-digit integers (> 100) into a 10-entry table using double hashing with the least significant digit providing the home address and the most significant digit providing the step size. Give a plausible sequence in which the contents of the following table could have been inserted.

0	482
1	110
2	802
3	
4	104
5	
6	262
7	301
8	
9	

● Problems

1. Modify the implementation of the *map_hash_bounded* class so that it expands the table when the current table is greater than 70 percent full. Entries should be hashed to a new, larger table and the old table discarded.

2. Compare different overflow strategies as follows:

   a. Store 1000 random integers in an array.

   b. Hash the integers into a hash table with space for 1500 integers using linear probe, then count how many accesses to the table are required to retrieve them.

   c. Repeat Step b, varying the size of the table (1400, 1300, 1200, and 1100 integers) and overflow method (quadratic probe, double hashing).

3. Compare the effect of different bucket sizes as follows:

    a. Store 1000 random integers in an array.

    b. Hash the integers into a table with bucket size M having room for 1200 integers, then count the number of table accesses required to retrieve the integers.

    c. Do Step b for $M = 1, 2, 3, 4, 5, 6, 8, 10,$ and 12, keeping the overflow strategy constant.

4. Complete the definition of the function that lets us remove an object from a hash table that uses overflow lists.

5. Enhance the spelling checker so that it reports the number of times that each unknown word appeared in the text.

6. Write a class definition for an unbounded hash table that uses a bucket size of zero (see note 14). Compare the run time of a spelling checker using this new class with the running time of the checker given in the text.

7. Design and test a hash table class that uses closed addressing with coalescing lists to handle overflows. Devise a sequence of insert/retrieve/remove operations with which to test an object of the class. Compare the time required to perform the sequence with the times required to perform the same sequence on (a) an object of type *map_hash_bounded* and (b) an object of type *map_hash_unbounded*.

8. Either analytically or experimentally, determine the probability that two different password strings hash to the same three integers (see class *userpass*).

9. Implement a dictionary class using Bloom filters (see Exercise 12). Modify a copy of the spelling checker program so that it uses an object of your class to hold the dictionary. Compare the results of running the two checkers on a variety of texts.

10. Compare the speed of the general hash function (*hash*) with the one specifically designed for strings (*hashstring*) in the following manner.

    a. Hash a variety of strings of each length from 4 to 20 characters using each of the two functions. For each length, measure the average time that each function takes to hash a string of that length. Use $T = 2000$.

    b. Change T to 2048, modify the last line of *hashstring* to use the & operator rather than *abs* and %, and rerun your tests. Do you notice any significant difference in the times compared with those for part a?

11. Modify the spelling checker so that it is interactive. When it encounters a word not in the dictionary, it should ask the user if the word should be added. Either change the nature of the dictionary or add a third map containing the new words.

● References

Bloom, B. H. 1970. Space/time trade-offs in hash coding with allowable errors. *Communications of the ACM,* 13 (7): 442–426.

British National Corpus. 1995. http://info.ox.ac.uk/bnc (accessed August 2003).

Buchholz, W. 1963. File organization and addressing. *IBM Systems Journal,* 2 (2): 86–111.

Cormack, G. V., R. N. S. Horspool, and M. Kaiserwerth. 1985. Practical perfect hashing. *The Computer Journal,* 28 (1): 54–58.

Fox, E. A., L. S. Heath, Q. Chen, and A. M. Daoud. 1992. Practical minimal hash functions for large databases. *Communications of the ACM,* 35 (1): 105–120.

Ghosh, S. P., and V. Y. Lum. 1975. An analysis of collisions when hashing by division. *Information Systems,* 1 (1-B): 15–22.

Hardy, T. [1874] 1996. *Far From the Madding Crowd.* New York: New American Library.

Knuth, D. E. 1973. *Sorting and Searching.* Vol 3, *The Art of Computer Programming.* Boston: Addison-Wesley.

Lum, V. Y., P. S. T. Yuen, and M. Dodd. 1971. Key-to-address transform techniques: A fundamental performance study on large existing formatted files. *Communications of the ACM,* 14 (4): 228–239.

Marsaglia, G. 1996. Diehard random number testing. http://stat.fsu.edu/~geo/diehard.html (accessed October 2002).

Martin, J. 1977. *Computer Data-Base Organization,* 2d ed. Upper Saddle River, NJ: Prentice-Hall.

Peterson, W. W. 1957. Addressing for random-access storage. *IBM Journal of Research and Development,* 1 (2): 130–146.

Ramakrishna, M. V., and J. Zobel. 1997. Performance in practice of string hashing functions. Proceedings of the Fifth International Conference on Database Systems for Advanced Applications, Melbourne Australia, April, 215–223.

● Notes

[1]High-level languages permit users to refer to variable memory locations by means of identifiers. The compiler keeps track of the name, type, and address of variables. For example, when compiling the following program

```
main()
 { int counter, total;
   char response;
   float average, number;
    .
    .
    .
 }
```

the compiler may construct the following symbol table

Name	Type	Address
counter	int	20
total	int	22
response	char	24
number	float	25
average	float	29

[2]The *Sunday Mail* (Queensland, Australia, March 10, 1996) reported the problems encountered by two women both named Belinda Lee Perry and both born on January 7, 1969. The *Ottawa Citizen* (Ottawa, Canada, November 23, 1992) reported the problems encountered by two men, both named Steven Reid, having the same birthdate and both living in Montreal and on the advice given by the police that one should change his name.

[3]A related structure called a **multimap** allows multiple values to be associated with a particular key.

[4]Sorry Sue-Ellen, R2D2, and Mike d'Abo.

[5]If we know the set of keys ahead of time, we could create a "perfect" hash function that maps each key to a different address. See, for example, Cormack et al. (1985). Even better, it is possible to devise a minimal perfect hash function that maps each of N keys to a different integer $0..N - 1$. See, for example, Fox et al. (1992).

[6]Not strictly true if we take into account the effects of a cache memory.

[7]Analogously, consider an address book in which a fixed number of pages are assigned to each letter. What do you do if a particular section fills up? Suppose, for example, you wish to enter more people with last name beginning H than the book allows room for? Where do you put the overflowing names and how do you know where to find them?

[8]If N and *step* have factors in common, then the number of different addresses in the list is N divided by the highest common factor of N and *step*.

[9]In practice, the capacity of the table is limited by the amount of heap space available for the overflow lists.

[10]C++ supports **operator overloading**; that is, users can define new contexts in which operator symbols such as ==, <, and >= apply. It makes code more readable and avoids the need for functions with names such as *equalkey*, *keylessthan*, and so on.

[11]Assume that the file *iostream.h* is included elsewhere.

[12]Notes on the definition:

- The name of the destructor member of the class is the class name preceded by a tilde (~). The destructor is invoked automatically when an object is destroyed, for example, when it goes out of scope. The destructor function is a convenient place to put code that tidies up memory, closes files, and so on.

- The parameter of *retrieve* is a reference parameter. The actual parameter will be the address of a variable of type *Entry*. The actual parameter points to an *Entry* variable having a certain value in its key field. If *retrieve* finds a table entry with the same key value, it overwrites the parameter variable with that table entry. This convoluted arrangement means that *retrieve* does not have to worry about what constitutes the key field or fields.

- A declaration of the form $X*Y$ declares Y to be a pointer to a variable of type X. Thus, for example,

int*P

declares P to be a pointer to an integer. We can assign an appropriate address to P and do arithmetic on it. Here, *hashtag*, for example, will be a pointer to a dynamically allocated array of tags.

- Each of *retrieve*, *insert*, and *remove* returns true if successful and false otherwise.

[13]Notes on the definitions:

- The *heap* is an area of memory from which a program can allocate space dynamically at run time and to which the space should be returned when no longer required. *new* is the built-in operator for allocating space from the heap. After the keyword *new*, the user specifies the type and amount of storage required, as in:

```
new int
new float[30]
new char[N]
```

If a block of memory of the requested size is available, the heap manager returns the address of the allocated space. If the request cannot be granted, a value of 0 is returned.

- *delete* is the storage deallocator. Users are responsible for returning space no longer needed to the heap; there is no automatic garbage collection as in Java.

[14]It is worth noting that the implementation would be simpler if we had a bucket size of 0; then we would have just an array of lists.

Maps: Binary Trees, Tries, and Ternary Trees

6.1 Introduction

Chapter 5 introduced the concept of a *map*—a data structure holding keyed data items. Users are able to retrieve an item in a map by specifying the item's unique key. We showed how a map can be implemented using a hash table. One of the characteristics of a hash table is that it typically does not store items in key order. In addition, some hash table implementations are fixed in size. This chapter looks at tree-based implementations of maps. Such implementations normally have no practical upper bound on their size and make it possible to process stored items in key order.

Section 6.2 provides a class definition for a map implemented as a binary search tree. However, such trees may be unbalanced, leading to slow retrievals. In Section 6.3, therefore, we look at a particular type of balanced binary tree—the AVL tree. An AVL tree is a height-balanced binary tree that has good worst-case behavior. Certain operations on trees may be faster if we decompose keys and search for a key section by section. This idea leads us to the trie data structure discussed in Section 6.4. One implementation of a trie has nodes with three descendants; these ternary trees are examined in Section 6.5. Finally, in Section 6.6, we illustrate the versatility of the binary tree by looking at two applications of binary trees that have nothing to do with the implementation of maps.

• 6.1.1 Overview of Trees

A linear search of an ordered array or linked list requires O(N) time. However, an ordered array can also be searched in O(log N) time using a binary search. What about a linked list? Suppose we change the structure of the list; consider, for example, the one shown in Figure 6.1.

Imagine lifting the list up by the middle element (16), and then doing the same with the middle of each of the two halves (10 and 28), and so on. After adding appropriate pointers, we get the structure depicted in Figure 6.2.

Most nodes now have two pointers (but if our original list were double linked, we would have two pointers anyway). Searches of this new structure are rapid and begin at the top. For example, when searching for 12 we compare it with 16, and because it is less than 16, we know that it is in the left side of the structure, so we move left to 10. Because 12 is greater than 10, our next move is right to 14, then left again to 12. These are the same comparisons that we would make during a binary search of an array containing the same numbers. Just as in a binary search, the space remaining to be searched halves with each step, and the time required for a complete search is O(log N). We have achieved fast searching of a dynamic structure.

Terminology

Figure 6.2 depicts a tree. In general, a **tree** is a set of nodes that is either empty or consists of a node called the **root** and disjoint sets of nodes T_1, T_2, . . ., T_N, where each T_i is itself a tree and is pointed to by the root. $T_1 \ldots T_N$ are the **subtrees** of the tree. In Figure 6.2, the node containing 16 is the root. The roots of the subtrees (10 and 28 in our example) are the **children** of the root. A link connects a node to each

$$4 \longrightarrow 7 \longrightarrow 9 \longrightarrow 10 \longrightarrow 12 \longrightarrow 14 \longrightarrow 15 \longrightarrow 16 \longrightarrow 22 \longrightarrow 23 \longrightarrow 26 \longrightarrow 28 \longrightarrow 31 \longrightarrow 37 \longrightarrow 38$$

Figure 6.1 • Ordered linear list

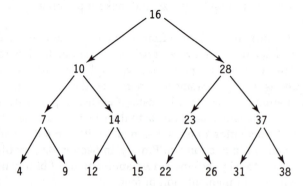

Figure 6.2 • The restructured list

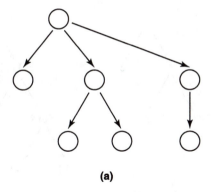
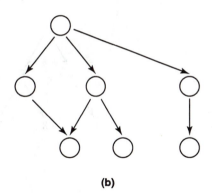

(a)   **(b)**

Figure 6.3 • (a) Tree and (b) nontree structures

of its children; the node is termed the **parent** of its children. In a tree, a unique path exists from the root to each nonroot node.[1] Nodes without children are termed **leaves**.[2] Figure 6.3a depicts a tree and Figure 6.3b depicts a structure that is not a tree because the subtrees are not disjoint.

The **bushiness** of a tree is the number of children of a nonleaf node. Thus, the bushiness of the tree in Figure 6.2 is two; the bushiness of the tree in Figure 6.3a varies from one to three. We define the **height** of a tree as being the length of (or the number of links in) the longest path from the root to a leaf. The height of the tree in Figure 6.2 is three; the height of the tree in Figure 6.3a is two. A tree with just one node has height 0, and an empty tree has height −1.

The tree in Figure 6.2 is a special case of a tree in that each parent has no more than two children; this is a **binary tree**. It is additionally special in that the items in the tree (and each subtree) are ordered (smaller to the left, larger to the right), making it a **binary search tree**. We study binary search trees in Section 6.2.

The tree structure provides both fast searching and the advantages of a dynamic structure. Note, however, that whereas the worst case in a binary search of an array is very close to the average case [both are O(log N)], a tree might become very unbalanced. It might have long paths from the root to some leaves and short paths to other leaves. In fact, a list is a special case of a tree, just as we will see in Chapter 7 that a tree is a special case of a graph. Like a list, a tree is a recursive structure in that the subtrees are themselves trees. This can lead to simple, elegant definitions for tree-processing functions.

• 6.1.2 Binary Trees

A binary tree is a tree in which each node has either zero, one, or two children. Figure 6.4 shows three examples: (a) another search tree, (b) an expression tree representing $A * B + 8$, and (c) an animals-question tree (see Problems).

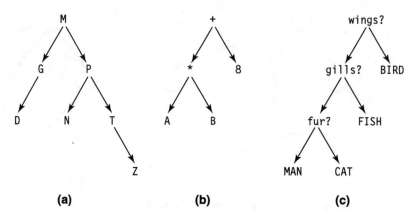

(a)   **(b)**   **(c)**

Figure 6.4 • Binary trees

Binary trees are of interest because they are the simplest possible tree (apart from a linear list), and we can change a general tree into a binary tree by applying what might be termed the "eldest sibling" transformation. For example, the trees in Figures 6.5a and 6.5b can be transformed into the binary trees of Figures 6.6a and 6.6b, respectively.

We have changed the tree by having the parent point not to each child directly, but just to the left-most (oldest) child in the original tree. The second pointer in the parent points to the parent's next-oldest sibling. For example, the 9 in Figure 6.5b now points down to 7 and across to 8.

Tree Traversals

A **tree traversal** is a systematic visiting of all the nodes in a tree. There are six traversals that can be defined simply in a recursive way. Consider the tree in Figure 6.7.

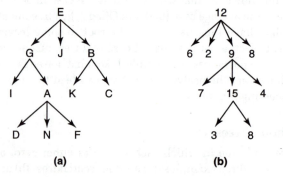

(a)   **(b)**

Figure 6.5 • General trees

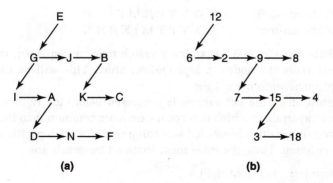

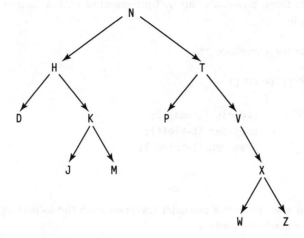

Figure 6.6 • General trees transformed into binary trees

Figure 6.7 • A binary tree

A traversal called *root-left-right* visits the root first, then the left subtree, and then the right subtree, and uses the same order recursively within the subtrees. For example, when processing the left subtree we would begin with its root, then go to its left subtree, and so on. This traversal strategy results in the nodes of Figure 6.7 being visited in the following order:

Root-left-right: N H D K J M T P V X W Z

Here are the other five traversals and the order in which each visits the nodes:

Root-right-left: N T V X Z W P H K M J D
Left-root-right: D H J K M N P T V W X Z
Left-right-root: D J M K H P W Z X V T N

Right-root-left: Z X W V T P N M K J H D
Right-left-root: Z W X V P T M J K D H N

Note that Figure 6.7 is a binary search tree; consequently, the left-root-right traversal visits the nodes in alphabetical order. This will be useful later when we implement maps using trees.

Most often, the left subtree is processed before the right subtree, therefore the three traversals in which this occurs are more common than the others. These three traversals are often identified according to the relative position of the root node in the ordering. Thus, the three most common traversals are:

- Inorder: Left-root-right
- Preorder: Root-left-right
- Postorder: Left-right-root

Each of these traversals can be implemented with a simple recursive function, for example,

```
void preorder (treenode *t)
{
        if (t != NULL)
               {
                 process (t->data);
                 preorder (t->left);
                 preorder (t->right);
               }
}
```

We can also achieve a preorder traversal with the following iterative algorithm that uses a stack of pointers:

```
void preorder()
{
        stack<treenode*>  S; treenode *temp;

        S.push(root);

        while ( !S.empty())
               {
                 S.pop(temp);
                 process(temp->data);
                 if (temp->right != NULL) S.push(temp->right);
                 if (temp->left != NULL) S.push (temp->left);
               }
}
```

Interestingly, if we replace the stack by a queue, we get yet another traversal.

```
void X()
{
    queue<treenode*>  Q; treenode *temp;

    Q.enqueue(root);

    while ( !Q.empty())
          {
            Q.dequeue(temp);
            process(temp->data);
            if (temp->right != NULL) Q.enqueue(temp->right);
            if (temp->left != NULL) Q.enqueue(temp->left);
          }
}
```

This traversal visits nodes level by level and is termed *breadth-first*. For the tree in Figure 6.7, the nodes are visited in the following order:

N T H V P K D X M J Z W

6.2 Binary Search Trees

Recall that a binary search tree is a binary tree in which all nodes in the left subtree of a node precede it in some ordering, whereas those in the right subtree follow it (or vice versa). Figures 6.2, 6.7, and 6.8 are examples of binary search trees. Binary search trees will be considered in this section.

A binary search tree implementation of a map is useful if we want the number of entries to be unbounded (or at least bounded only by available dynamic memory)

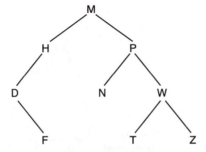

Figure 6.8 • Binary search tree of letters

or if we need to process the entries in key field order. For example, we may wish to see the contents of an address book in alphabetical order or the users of an assembler may wish to see an alphanumerically ordered list of the user-defined symbols found in a source program. If a hash-based implementation of a map is used, then a separate sorting operation is required to display an ordered list. If we use a binary search tree, then an inorder traversal gives us the items in order.

6.2.1 Implementation: *map_bst* Class

When we defined a linked list class in Chapter 2, we had one class for a list node and another class for the linked list. We will take a similar approach here; we will have one class for a tree node and another class for the entire tree. The *map_bst* class will be a friend class of the *treenode* class to permit access to the private node components. The following are the definitions of our *treenode* and *map_bst* classes; the *map_bst* definition is just a top-level definition containing function prototypes. Function definitions will be provided later.

```
template <class Entry> class map_bst;          // forward declaration

template <class Entry>
class treenode
{
  friend class map_bst<Entry>;

    public: treenode(const Entry& X)
             {
                  data = X;
                  left = NULL;
                  right = NULL;
             }

  private: treenode *left;
           Entry data;
           treenode *right;
};

template <class Entry>
class map_bst
{
  public: map_bst();           // constructor
          ~map_bst();          // destructor
          map_bst(const map_bst& rhs); // copy constructor
          map_bst& operator = (const map_bst&); // assignment
          void showmap(ostream&) const; // display contents
```

```
        bool retrieve(Entry&);  // looks for key match, puts in
        bool insert(const Entry&);    // overwrites if key there
        bool remove(const Entry&);  // deletes one with same key

private: treenode<Entry> *root;
         bool copytree (treenode<Entry> *&newtree,
                        treenode<Entry> *oldtree); // for use by replicator
         void destruct_aux(treenode<Entry> *t);     // actual destruct
         void inorder_aux(treenode<Entry> *t, ostream& s) const; //traverser
         bool insert_aux(Entry X, treenode<Entry> *&t); // inserter
         treenode<Entry>* retrieve_aux(Entry, treenode<Entry> *t);  // retriever
         bool remove_aux(Entry X, treenode<Entry> *&t);  // deleter
         void removenode(treenode<Entry> *&t);
         void getpredecessor(treenode<Entry> *t,Entry&);
};
```

As you would expect, the public components of *map_bst* are almost identical to the public components of the hash table implementations of the map (see Chapter 5), but here we do not need to specify a default size in the constructor. Again, we generalize our definition of a map class using templates so that map entries can be any kind of object. We require that the operator < be defined for the objects to be stored so that we can order them in the tree. If a user wishes to call *showmap* to display the contents of the map, then the stream-insertion operator (<<) must also be defined for the objects.

Like the linked lists that we saw earlier, a binary tree is a recursive structure; the subtrees of a binary tree are themselves binary trees. Tree operations have naturally recursive algorithms. As we did with linked lists, the following public function (e.g., *insert*) calls a private recursive function (*insert_aux*) that does the actual work. The *retrieve, insert,* and *remove* functions each return a *bool* value indicating if the action was successful. Here are the function definitions for all the operations except *deletion;* we leave details of deletions until Section 6.2.3.

```
template <class Entry>
map_bst<Entry>::map_bst()
 { // constructor - initialize root
   root = NULL;
 }


template <class Entry>
map_bst<Entry>::~map_bst()
 { // destructor - reclaim space
   destruct_aux(root);
 }
```

```
template <class Entry>
void map_bst<Entry>::destruct_aux(treenode<Entry> *t)
 {// actual space reclaimer
  if (t != NULL)
   { destruct_aux(t->left);      // reclaim left subtree
     destruct_aux(t->right);     // reclaim right subtree
     delete t;                   // and the node itself
   }
 }


template <class Entry>
bool map_bst<Entry>::copytree(treenode<Entry> *&newtree,
                              treenode<Entry> *oldtree)
{
  newtree = NULL;
  if (oldtree!=NULL)
    {
      newtree = new treenode<Entry>(oldtree->data);
      if (newtree==NULL) return false;  // out of space
      // return true if both subtrees copy ok
      return    copytree(newtree->left,oldtree->left)
             && copytree(newtree->right,oldtree->right);
    }
  return true;
}

template<class Entry>
map_bst<Entry>::map_bst(const map_bst& rhs)
{ // copy constructor
    copytree(root,rhs.root);
}


template<class Entry>
map_bst<Entry>& map_bst<Entry>::operator = (const map_bst& rhs)
{
  // overloaded assignment operator
  if (this!=&rhs) // not assigning to self
    {
      treenode<Entry> *temp;
```

```
        if (copytree(temp,rhs.root))
          {
            destruct_aux(root); // prevent possible memory leak
            root = temp;
          }
      }
  return *this;
}


template <class Entry>
void map_bst<Entry>::showmap(ostream &s) const
 { // to display tree contents - an inorder traversal
   inorder_aux(root,s);
 }


template <class Entry>
void map_bst<Entry>::inorder_aux(treenode<Entry> *t, ostream &s) const
 { if (t != NULL)
     { inorder_aux(t->left,s);
       s << t->data;
       inorder_aux(t->right,s);
     }
 }

template <class Entry>
bool map_bst<Entry>::retrieve (Entry& target)
 {
   //  if there is a map entry with the same key as target,
   //  we overwrite target with the entry

   treenode<Entry> *ptr = retrieve_aux(target,root);
   if (ptr==NULL) return false;  // not found
   // overwrite parameter
   target = ptr->data;
   return true;
 }



template <class Entry>
treenode<Entry>* map_bst<Entry>::retrieve_aux (Entry target, treenode<Entry> *t)
```

```
    {
       if (t==NULL)
               return NULL;      // empty tree
       if ( !(t->data<target) && !(target<t->data) )
               return t;  // found
       if (t->data < target)
               return retrieve_aux(target,t->right); // look in right subtree
          else
               return retrieve_aux(target,t->left);  // look in left subtree
    }

template <class Entry>
bool map_bst<Entry>::insert(const Entry& target)
 {
  // if we find an entry in the tree with the same key as target
  // (use < to determine this) then overwrite it with target.
  // Otherwise, try to insert new entry into tree

    treenode<Entry> *ptr=retrieve_aux(target,root);
    if (ptr != NULL)  // already in?
       {
         ptr->data = target;  // yes - overwrite
         return true;
       }
    else
         return insert_aux(target,root); // no - insert new entry
 }

template <class Entry>
bool map_bst<Entry>::insert_aux(Entry X, treenode<Entry> *&t)
  {
     if (t == NULL)  // empty root so put new entry here
       {
         t = new treenode<Entry>(X);
         if (t==NULL) return false;      // no heap space available
         return true;
       }
     else
       {
         if (X < t->data)
             return insert_aux(X,t->left);  // goes in left subtree
         else
             return insert_aux(X,t->right); // goes in right subtree
       }
  }
```

● 6.2.2 Random Trees

Theory tells us that if we have a minimally tall binary tree containing N nodes, then the largest number of comparisons required to retrieve a node from the tree is approximately $\log_2 N$, and the average number of comparisons is approximately $\log_2 N - 1$. Table 6.1 shows some actual worst-case and average-case values for **full binary trees**. A binary tree is full if it has the maximum number of nodes possible at each of its levels.

But what about trees in practice? Gonnet and Baeza-Yates (1991) report that the expected number of comparisons required to retrieve an item from a randomly constructed binary tree is approximately

$$1.3863 \log_2 N - 1.8456$$

Using a reliable source of random bits (Marsaglia 2002) we constructed random trees with N nodes (for various N) and measured the height and average node depth of each tree. The results are summarized in Table 6.2. (Results for a particular tree size are the averages from 7000 trees generated of that size.) For large N, there is a good match between the measurements and the formula.

Each point in Figure 6.9 represents two parameters of one of 7000 random trees with 1023 nodes. The parameters are tree height (which is the number of comparisons in a worst-case retrieval) and average node depth (which is the number of comparisons in an average-case retrieval). The worst-case value is plotted on the x-axis and the average-case value on the y-axis. The location of the point on each axis is the amount by which the parameter exceeds the best possible values for a 1023-node tree (worst case 10, average case 9.01).

● **TABLE 6.1** Retrieval Parameters of Some Full Binary Trees

N	Worst Case	Average Case
1	1	1
3	2	1.667
7	3	2.429
15	4	3.267
31	5	4.161
63	6	5.095
127	7	6.055
255	8	7.031
511	9	8.018
1023	10	9.010

● **TABLE 6.2** Retrieval Parameters of Random Trees			
N	Worst Case	Average Case	Formula for Average Case
1	1	1	−1.8456
3	2.627	1.891	0.351634
7	4.679	2.930	2.046236
15	6.820	4.069	3.570522
31	9.148	5.303	5.022402
63	11.626	6.613	6.440703
127	14.195	7.950	7.842814
255	16.757	9.292	9.236972
511	19.448	10.663	10.62719
1023	22.118	12.031	12.01545

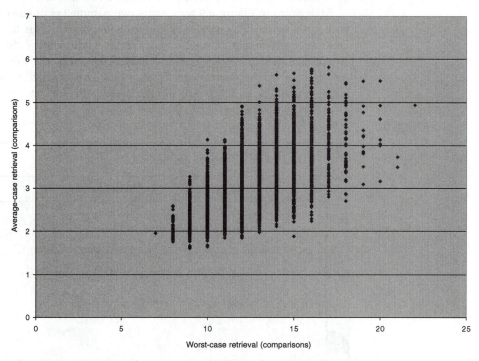

Figure 6.9 • 7000 1023-node trees compared with complete 1023-node tree

We see from Figure 6.9 that even the best of the random trees is significantly sub-optimal and that a few trees are three times the height of the optimal tree.

• 6.2.3 Deletions from a Binary Search Tree

The problem with deletions is that we cannot just remove a node that has one or two children because the children will be left unattached to the tree. Thus, three cases must be considered:

- The node to be deleted has no children.
- The node to be deleted has one child.
- The node to be deleted has two children.

If there are no children, we can just delete the node. If there is one child, we replace the node to be deleted by its only child. If there are two children, we replace the node by its predecessor in the tree (the node that would precede it in an inorder traversal) and delete the predecessor.[3] The predecessor is the right-most node in the left subtree of the node and will therefore have at most one child (you can verify this for yourself by looking at any binary search tree). Figure 6.10 illustrates the three deletion cases; we delete, in turn, nodes D, W, and T from an example tree.

Here are the function definitions associated with deletions to complete our implementation of a map as a binary search tree.

```
template <class Entry>
bool map_bst<Entry>::remove(const Entry& target)
{
 return remove_aux(target,root);
}


template <class Entry>
bool map_bst<Entry>::remove_aux(Entry X, treenode<Entry> *&t)
{
 // remove X from tree rooted at t
     if (t==NULL)
        return false;    // tree is empty
     if (X < t->data)
        return remove_aux(X,t->left);  // try left subtree
     if (t->data < X)
        return remove_aux(X,t->right);   // try right subtree
     removenode(t);          // root is to be deleted
     return true;
}
```

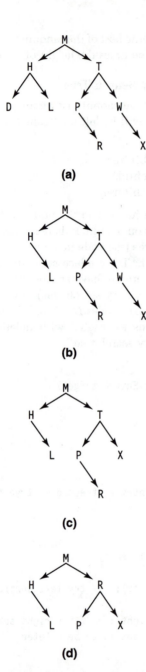

Figure 6.10 • Deletions from a binary search tree: (a) original tree, (b) the result of deleting *D* from (a) (no children case), (c) the result of deleting *W* from (b) (one-child case), (d) the result of deleting *T* from (c) (two-children case)

```
template <class Entry>
void map_bst<Entry>::removenode(treenode<Entry> *&t)
{
  // deletes node pointed to by t
  Entry tempdata;
  treenode<Entry> *tempptr;
  tempptr = t;   // second pointer to the node
      if (t->left == NULL)
          { // no left child, pointer to this node becomes pointer
            // to right child
            t = t -> right;
            delete tempptr;  // node deleted
          }
  else if (t->right == NULL)
          { // no right child, pointer to this node becomes pointer
            // to left child
            t = t -> left;
            delete tempptr;  // node deleted
          }
      else
          { // two children case
            // find predecessor (in left subtree)
            getpredecessor(t->left,tempdata);
            // overwrite current node with predecessor data
            t->data = tempdata;
            // and get rid of predecessor (it's in the left subtree)
            remove_aux(tempdata,t->left);
          }

}


template <class Entry>
void map_bst<Entry>::getpredecessor(treenode<Entry> *t, Entry& item)
{
 // predecessor is the rightmost node in tree rooted in t
 while (t->right != NULL) t = t->right;
 item = t->data;
}
```

• 6.2.4 Worst-Case Behavior

The height of an almost balanced binary search tree containing N items is approximately $\log_2 N$. Thus, approximately $\log_2 N$ operations are needed for typical retrieval, insertion, and removal operations. However, depending on the order in which items are inserted, the tree may have as many as *N* levels requiring *N* operations. Consider the following set of words (they are used in many examples in this chapter).

black blue dent mint the then there those

The tree shown in Figure 6.11 is typical of one in which words are inserted in random order into an initially empty tree. The worst-case retrievals (*black* and *then*) require 4 comparisons, and the average number of comparisons (each of the eight words being retrieved equally often) is 2.75.

However, inserting the words in alphabetical order into an initially empty tree results in the tree shown in Figure 6.12 (which is actually a linear list). The worst-case retrieval requires 8 comparisons, and the average required comparisons is 4.5.

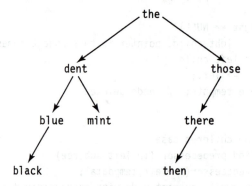

Figure 6.11 • Binary search tree of words

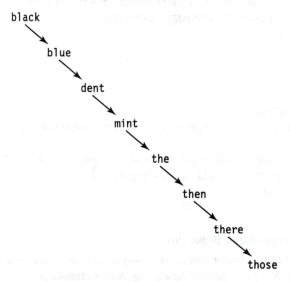

Figure 6.12 • A highly unbalanced binary tree

If we are concerned about minimizing worst-case behavior (perhaps in an environment where a retrieval must be completed within X milliseconds), we may wish to consider trees that have a guaranteed O(log N) behavior even in the worst case. We look at one such type of tree in the next section; in Chapter 13, we look at the B-tree family of trees.

6.3 AVL Trees

An AVL tree is a binary search tree balanced in the sense that the two subtrees of any node differ in height by no more than one (Adel'son-Vel'skii and Landis 1962). Note that we could define *balanced* in other ways. We could require all the leaves to be the same distance from the root (as in a B-tree) or we could define balanced in terms of the number of nodes in the two subtrees. Or the tree could be weight balanced in some way (see Huffman trees in Section 6.6). In Figure 6.13, tree (a) is an AVL tree, tree (b) is not an AVL tree because of the size of the difference in height of the two subtrees of the root.

Clearly, a binary search tree containing either no items or a single item is an AVL tree. The challenge is to devise an insertion algorithm that will, in no more than O(log N) time, insert an item into an AVL tree and make any necessary adjustments so that the new tree is still an AVL tree. The deletion problem is equally challenging.

We need to add data to each node to assist in tree balancing. The additional data could be an integer field recording the height of the tree for which the node is a root. Perhaps better, it could be a field (*balance_ factor*) indicating the relative heights of the two subtrees of the node. This might be a three-valued object:

- *EVEN* (or 0): Two subtrees are the same height.
- *RIGHT_HIGHER* (or +1): Height of right subtree is one greater than height of left subtree.
- *LEFT_HIGHER* (or −1): Height of left subtree is one greater than height of right subtree.

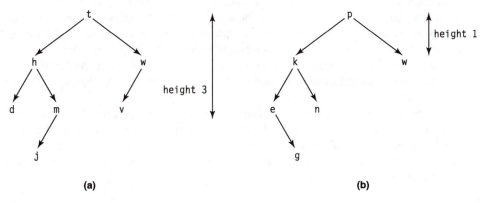

(a)   **(b)**

Figure 6.13 • Binary trees: (a) AVL, (b) non-AVL

or it could be an integer holding the value of

height of the right subtree − the height of the left subtree

In subsequent diagrams we will use this last height-difference integer scheme.

6.3.1 Insertion into an AVL Tree

During an insertion, we update height information if appropriate and, if the AVL property has been violated, we adjust the tree. This adjustment is accomplished by a **rotation** performed on the tree.

Suppose that a certain node (X) is found to violate the AVL tree property; that is, the heights of its two subtrees differ by more than one. Given that the tree was an AVL tree before the insertion, the imbalance is caused by one of four types of insertion:

1. Insertion into the left subtree of the left child of X (denoted by LL)
2. Insertion into the right subtree of the left child of X (RL)
3. Insertion into the left subtree of the right child of X (LR)
4. Insertion into the right subtree of the right child of X (RR)

As illustrated in the next section, we can fix cases 1 and 4 with a **single rotation**. Cases 2 and 3 require a **double rotation**. In either case, only one rotation is needed at some point in the tree to restore its AVL properties.

Single Rotation

This section looks only at the LL case, because the RR case is symmetric. Figure 6.14 shows an AVL tree before the insertion of a record into subtree A. An integer following a node is the value of the height-difference *balance_factor:* height(right subtree) − height(left subtree). Figure 6.15 shows the tree after the insertion.

The height of subtree A containing the recently inserted record is one greater than the height of subtree B. Subtrees B and C are the same height. This is the only situation that would allow the tree to be an AVL tree before the insertion into subtree A and allow node H to pass the balance test, now making node K the lowest out-of-balance (OOB) node in the tree and the one we have to deal with.

We restore the AVL property by a rotation that makes node H the root of the subtree currently rooted in the OOB node (K). The result of this rotation is shown in Figure 6.16.

Check the new arrangement and verify for yourself that ordering is preserved.

Comparing the tree in Figure 6.16 with the tree in Figure 6.14, we find that they are the same height. This means that if this were a subtree within a larger AVL tree then the tree would not require additional modification (such as updating height data or performing rotations).

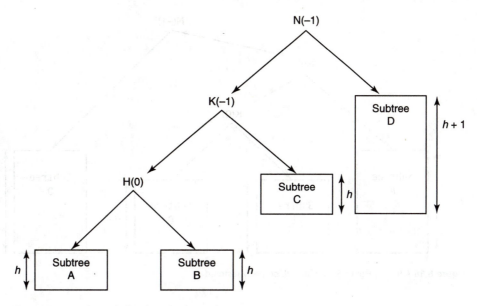

Figure 6.14 • AVL tree before insertion into subtree *A*

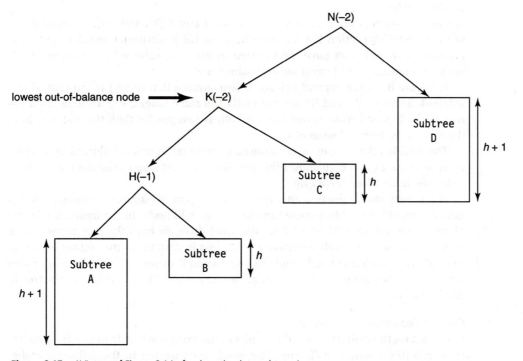

Figure 6.15 • AVL tree of Figure 6.14 after insertion into subtree *A*

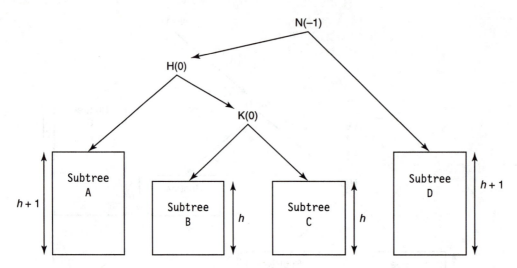

Figure 6.16 • Tree of Figure 6.15 with AVL property restored

Double Rotation

A single rotation is not sufficient to fix cases 2 and 3 (RL and LR); we need a pair of rotations. This section looks at case RL (case LR is similar). Consider the tree in Figure 6.17 in which we have just inserted an item into subtree B. As in Figure 6.15, we have identified the lowest out-of-balance node.

In Figure 6.18, we expand subtree B (we assume that node J is the root of this subtree). Subtrees B1 and B2 are not really the same height; the distance from the root to the lowest leaves of one but not both is two greater than the distance from the root to the lowest leaves of C.

The double rotation can be considered a single left rotation followed by a single right rotation. Figure 6.19 shows the tree after the first step in the double rotation; note how node J has moved up.

Figure 6.20 shows the tree after the second step in the double rotation. Node J is now the root of the subtree rooted in the lowest OOB node. In the figure, the leaves of one of the subtrees B1 and B2 are the same distance from the root as the leaves of A. The leaves of the other subtree are one less in distance. Thus, either both sub-trees of H are the same height and the subtrees of K differ in height by one or vice versa. As in the case of a single rotation, we do not need to go further up the tree to fix the imbalance.

Example Sequence of Insertions

Figure 6.21(a through h) shows the results of inserting the words in our example set into an initially empty AVL tree. The words are inserted in the following order: *dent, then, there, blue, mint, the, black, those.* In cases (c), (f), and (g), the tree

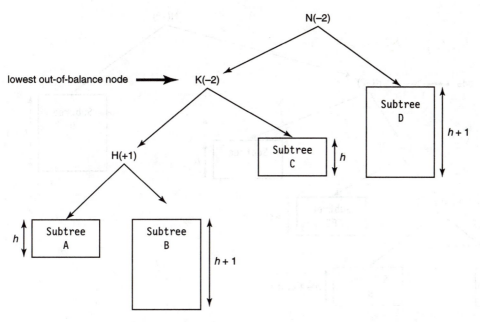

Figure 6.17 • Non-AVL tree before double rotation

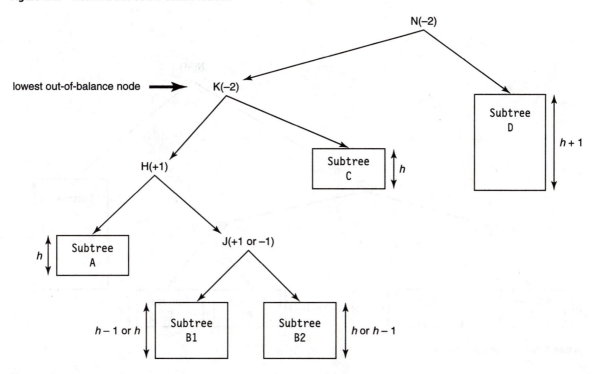

Figure 6.18 • Tree of Figure 6.17 in more detail

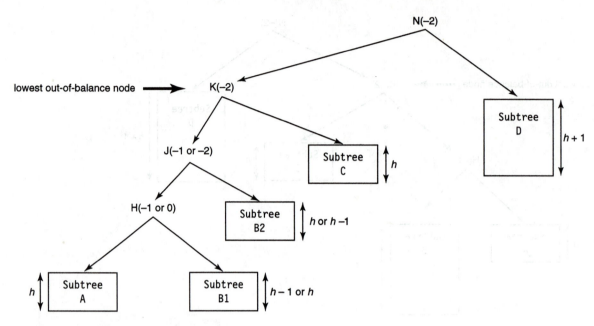

Figure 6.19 • Restoration of AVL property

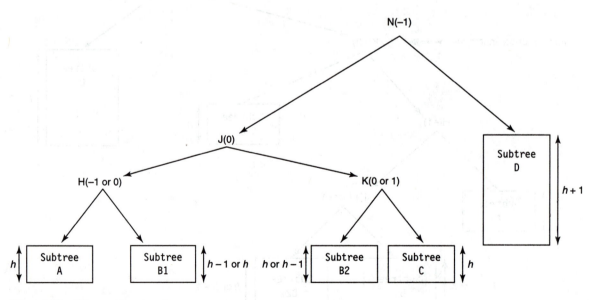

Figure 6.20 • AVL property restored

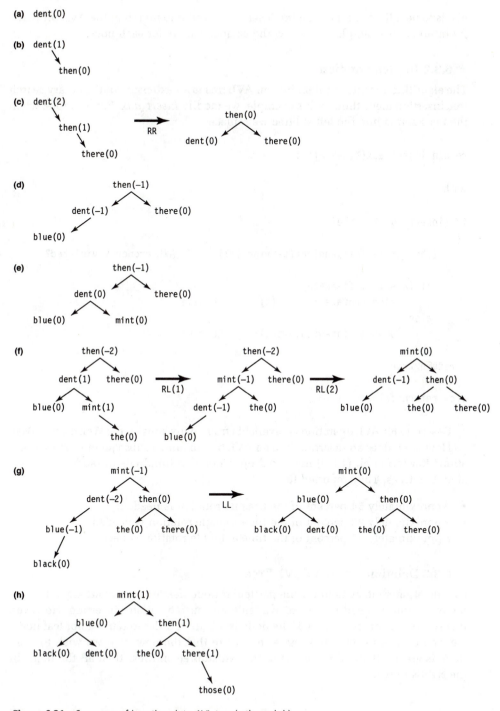

Figure 6.21 • Sequence of insertions into AVL tree (a through h)

needs to be adjusted following the insertion in order to maintain the AVL property. As in previous examples, we show the balance factors for each node.

6.3.2 Implementation

The algorithm to insert an item into an AVL tree is an extension of the binary search tree insertion algorithm. In this example, we modify *insert_aux*. For example, when the insertion is into the left subtree we replace

```
return insert_aux(X,t->left);
```

with

```
if (insert_aux(X,t->left))
 {
  if ( height(t->left)-height(t->right)>1)     // AVL property violated?
   {
     if (X < t->left->data)
           singlerotatewithleft(t);  // LL case
     else
           doublerotatewithleft(t);  // RL case
   }
  return true
 }
else return false;
```

C++ code for AVL operations is available from many sites on the World Wide Web.

How often does an insertion into an AVL tree require a subsequent rotation operation? Karlton et al. (1976) measured operations on hundreds of randomly generated AVL trees. They reported that

- Approximately 54 percent of the time no rotation is needed.
- Approximately 23 percent of the time a single rotation is needed.
- Approximately 23 percent of the time a double rotation is needed.

6.3.3 Deletions from an AVL Tree

One deletion strategy is to tag the particular node *deleted* and avoid any rebalancing operation. Deleted nodes are available for reuse by a later insertion. However, this solution is practical only if the node is a leaf. In order to reuse a nonleaf node, we would have to scan its subtrees to ensure that the new item we wish to store there is greater than all the items in the left subtree and less than all the items in the right subtree.

If a node is to be truly deleted, we begin by removing it from the tree using a binary tree deletion algorithm (see Section 6.2.3). Then we need to check to see if rotations are necessary in order to restore the AVL property. In contrast to the insert algorithm, we may need to perform multiple rotations. In the worst case, we may need a rotation at each level of the tree (we can imagine that fixing one imbalance produces another at the next level all the way up the tree); thus, as many as $O(\log N)$ rotations may be required.

Adel'son-Vel'skii and Landis (1962) do not address the deletion problem, but Knuth (1973), among others, sketches a solution. Following is a pseudocode algorithm for restoring the AVL property following a deletion:

```
t = parent of deleted node
while (true)
    {
      if (balancefactor(t) is 0)
         {
           update balance factor
           break                  // stop here
         }
      else if (balancefactor(t) not 0 and taller subtree was shortened)
             {
               balancefactor (t) = 0
               if (t is root) break else t = parent(t)
             }
      else // balancefactor not 0 && shorter subtree shortened
             {
               // AVL property violated at this node
               A = root of taller subtree of t
               if balancefactor(A) is 0
                  {
                    do a single rotate
                    update balance factor of A
                    update balance factor of t
                    break
                  }
               else if balancefactor (A) == balancefactor (t)
                  {
                    do a single rotate
                    balance factor of A = 0
                    balance factor of t = 0
                    if (t is root) break else t = parent(t)
                  }
```

```
else // balancefactor(A) != balancefactor(t)
{
    double rotate: round A then round t
    balance factor of new subtree root = 0
    update other balance factors
    if (t is root) break else t = parent(t)
}
}
}
```

Example Deletion from an AVL Tree

Consider the AVL tree shown in Figure 6.22. In our binary tree deletion algorithm, we replaced a node to be deleted with a copy of its predecessor in the tree. To show that using the successor works equally well, we will use the successor in our AVL deletion. Suppose we delete the node with key *T* from the tree of Figure 6.22.

We replace *T* with its successor (*W*), then delete the successor. This leaves us with the tree shown in Figure 6.23.

The AVL property is violated at the node pointed to by the arrow; the left subtree is height two and the nonexistent right subtree is height zero. The root of the taller subtree is the node containing P (balance factor 0). After a single rotation and adjustments, we get the tree shown in Figure 6.24.

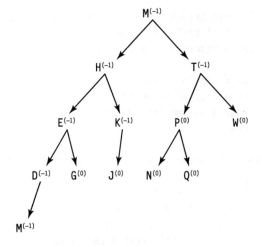

Figure 6.22 • AVL tree before deletion

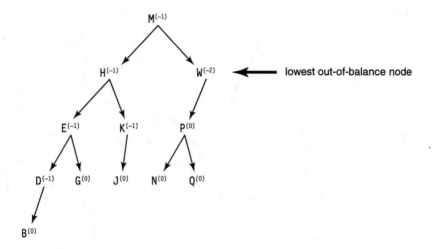

Figure 6.23 • AVL tree from Figure 6.22 after deletion of *T*

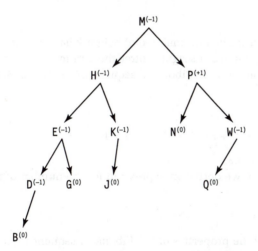

Figure 6.24 • Tree from Figure 6.23 with AVL property restored

● 6.3.4 Bounds on an AVL Tree

What are the benefits of maintaining the AVL property? Our motivation in looking at AVL trees was the worst-case behavior of a binary tree. What are the bounds on the height of an AVL tree (i.e., how high can such a tree be with N nodes)? Figure 6.25 shows AVL trees with the minimum number of nodes possible for various heights (h).

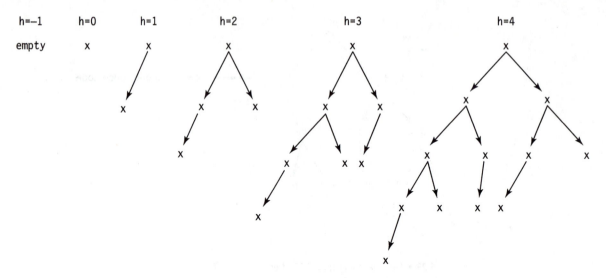

Figure 6.25 • Minimal AVL trees

Note the pattern: The minimal tree of height k has as its left subtree the minimal tree of height $k - 1$ and as its right subtree the minimal tree of height $k - 2$. This suggests a connection with the Fibonacci sequence: 0, 1, 1, 2, 3, 5, 8, 13, . . . , where

$Fib(0) = 0$
$Fib(1) = 1$
$Fib(i) = Fib(i - 2) + Fib(i - 1)$ $i > 1$

Consider Table 6.3.

From Table 6.3, we derive an expression for the number of nodes (N) in an AVL tree of height h.

$N \geq Fib(h + 3) - 1$

Knowledge of the properties of the Fibonacci sequence[4] yields:

$h \leq 1.44 \log_2(N + 1) - 1.328$

● **TABLE 6.3**   Sizes of Minimal AVL Trees and Fibonacci Numbers

h	−1	0	1	2	3	4	5
Fewestnodes(h)	0	1	2	4	7	12	20
Fib(h + 3)	1	2	3	5	8	13	21

Thus, the worst-case retrieval from an AVL tree requires only about 44 percent more comparisons than the average case. In practice, AVL trees will be better than the worst case, and the extra work needed to maintain the AVL property may be well worth it if the ratio of retrievals to insertions and deletions is high.

Recall our random binary search trees from Section 6.2.2. From the previous formula, the worst-case height of an AVL tree with 1023 nodes is 13. All of the trees we generated and plotted in Figure 6.9 were higher than this.

6.4 Tries

In each of the map implementations that we have considered thus far (the hash table of Chapter 5 and the binary trees of this chapter), the key has been treated as an atomic (indivisible) entity. If the key is complex, perhaps comprising several fields, significant time may be spent comparing two keys. Consider, for instance, the following multipart name and address key:

Zip	City	Street	Number	Last Name	First Name

However, practically any key can be decomposed into smaller components—into characters, digits or bits—and every component does not need to be the same size. This idea of key decomposition leads to another way to implement the map, as a trie,[5] in which comparisons involve only single components of the key. A **trie** is a tree in which branching at a particular level is determined by part of the key rather than the whole key.

6.4.1 Trie Variants

Consider again the following set of keys:

> black blue dent mint the then there those

One possible binary search tree containing these keys was shown in Figure 6.11. (We assumed that attributes associated with a key were stored in the same node as the key.) There are several variations on the trie concept; in the following discussion we use the same set of keys in presenting three trie variations and a class definition for one of the variations.

Trie: Variant 1
In the structure shown in Figure 6.26, we use the / character as an end-of-key marker.

A nonleaf node contains one or more key components and pointers to the next level (where the next component of the key may be found). A leaf node contains an end-of-key marker and attributes associated with a particular key. The trie contains

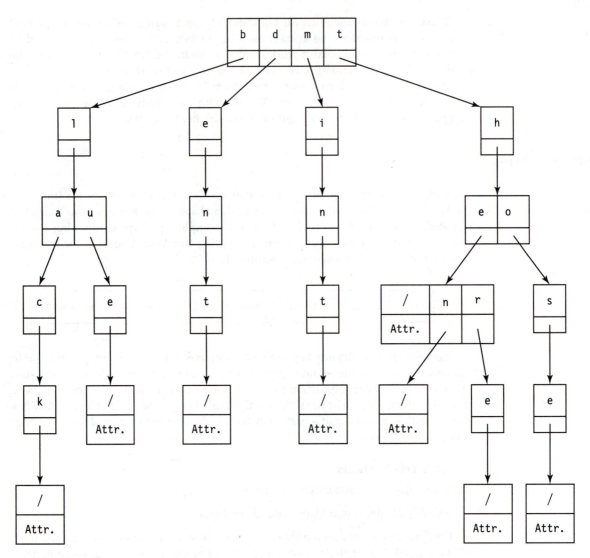

Figure 6.26 • Trie: Variant 1

our example set of keys and shows how those keys are decomposed into individual letters stored in consecutive levels. We assume that the end-of-key marker precedes other characters lexicographically, thus making it easier to output the trie entries in lexicographic order (e.g., because *the/* precedes *then/*).

Retrievals from a Variant 1 Trie   When searching the trie, we begin at the root and compare the entries there (*b,d,m,t*) with the first character of the target key.[6] If we find a match, we follow the appropriate pointer to the next level. At the second level, we compare entries with the second character of the target key, and so on. A search for the target succeeds if we match all the way to the end-of-key marker. A search for the target key fails if the current key component is not found in the node being searched.

Insertions into a Variant 1 Trie   As with many data structures, the insertion algorithm will begin by looking for the key we wish to insert. If it finds the key, then, consistent with the way that we have implemented insertions for maps in general, the algorithm overwrites the current attribute data with the given data. If the search does not find the key, then at the point at which the search fails, there will be a node that has to be augmented with a new key component. Thereafter, the remaining components of the key form a vertical list of new nodes.

Suppose, for example, that we wish to add the word *thorn* to the trie of Figure 6.26. Figure 6.27 shows the point at which the search for *thorn* fails; *r* is not found in the indicated node.

Figure 6.28 shows the final result of the insertion.

Deletions from a Variant 1 Trie   When deleting an entry from a trie, we remove those nodes that are part of the entry to be deleted but are part of no other entry. One way to determine the appropriate nodes is to search for the key and identify nodes that contain part of it. Then, starting at the leaf and working back up the trie, we remove those nodes that are not shared with other entries. The first shared node encountered is appropriately adjusted; then we exit.

Consider the deletion of the word *blue* from the trie of Figure 6.28. In Figure 6.29, the five nodes that are identified as holding part of *blue* are marked with an asterisk.

Figure 6.30 shows the trie of Figure 6.29 after we remove the two nodes that are used to store only parts of *blue* and then adjust the node that is shared with *black*.

Advantages of this trie over the binary tree include the following:

1. If we have a recognizable end-of-key marker, we can perhaps more easily accommodate arbitrarily long keys.
2. If we are searching for a key entered interactively, we can overlap entry of the key components with searching of the trie. You may notice this feature when using a help screen index or when searching online encyclopedias. Suppose, for example, that you are searching for *Edison*. Typing the *E* will cause the index display to show you the section for entries that begin with *E*. When you enter the *d*, it will move the display to the section where entries begin with *Ed*, and so on.

Trie: Variant 2
One of the difficulties of implementing tries like the ones we have termed variant 1 is the variety of nodes that a trie might contain. The trie shown in Figure 6.26, for instance, contains five different types of node. We can simplify matters by using the transformation discussed earlier (see Figures 6.5 and 6.6) to convert the variably

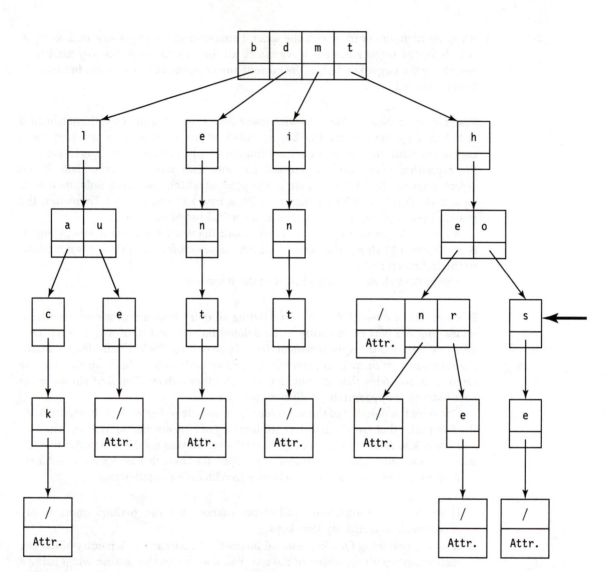

Figure 6.27 • Failure point for search for *thorn*

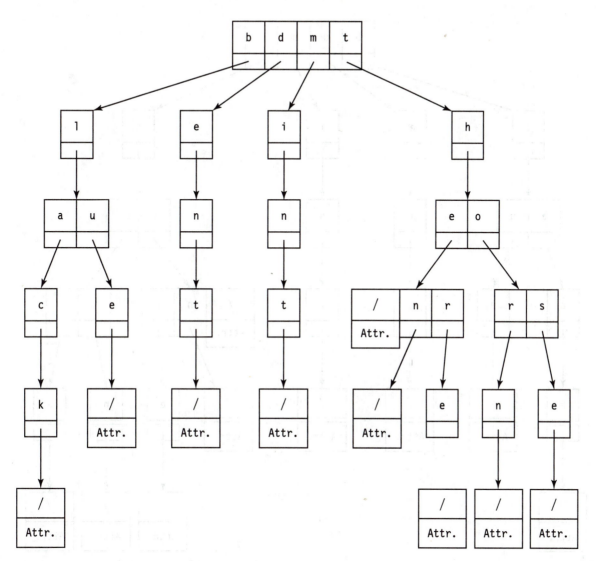

Figure 6.28 • Trie of Figure 6.27 after addition of *thorn*

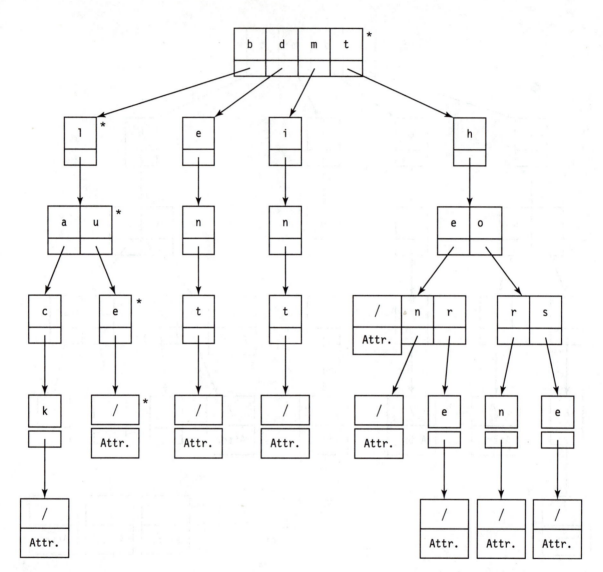

Figure 6.29 • Identification of nodes that are part of *blue*

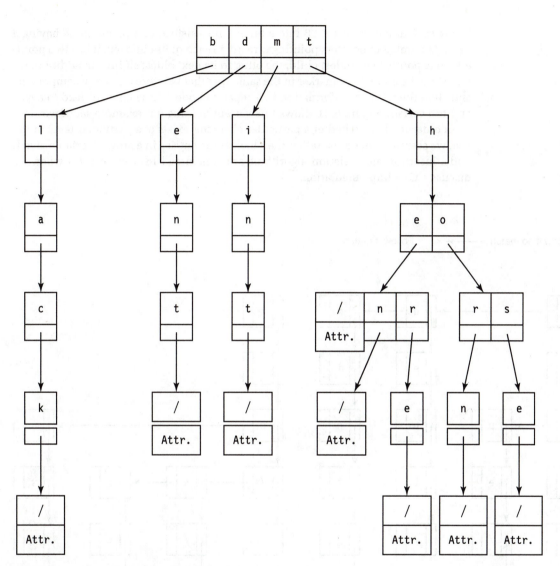

Figure 6.30 • Trie of Figure 6.29 after deletion of *blue*

bushy structure of Figure 6.26 into a binary one. Instead of a parent node having a variable number of pointers pointing directly to each of its children, it has two pointers—one points to its oldest child, the other to its next oldest sibling. In addition, we will store the end-of-key marker in the same way that we store other key components and store the attribute information in a separate node. These changes lead to a second trie variant. Figure 6.31 shows this variant holding our example set of words.

In order to check whether a particular character exists at a particular level in the trie, we search a linked list rather than look at the entries in a single (variable-sized) node. Insertion and deletion algorithms are considered in Section 6.4.3 when we discuss a C++ implementation.

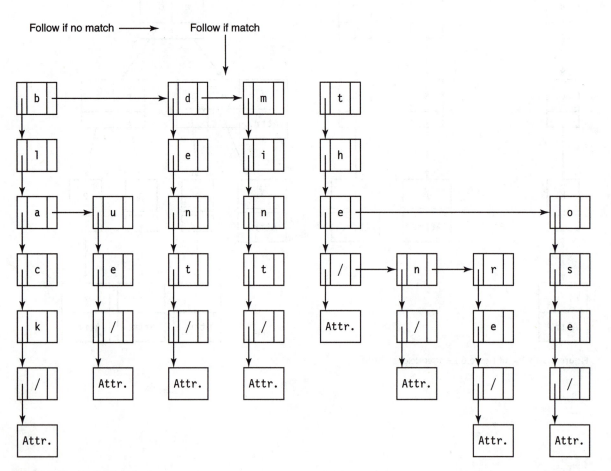

Figure 6.31 • Trie: Variant 2

Trie: Variant 3

A disadvantage of the variant 2 trie is that a lot of space is taken up by nodes that have no siblings. Our final trie variant shows one way in which a variant 2 trie can be compressed. Comparing Figure 6.32 with Figure 6.31, you will see that we have eliminated nodes with no siblings. Nodes at the beginning of a list now contain an integer showing the position within the keys of the items in the list. For example, we have [b,d,m,t] in position one and [/,n,r] in position four. This allows us to skip levels where there is no branching.

We need to store the full keys in the leaf nodes to guard against false matches because components in the target key may be skipped when we traverse down the trie. For example, in the trie shown in Figure 6.32, a search for *toe* or *tie* fails only when the target is compared with the contents of the leaf containing *the*. We assume that any attributes associated with a key are stored in the leaf containing the full key.

Insertions into a Variant 3 Trie We determine the values in the levels that have been skipped by examining the keys in the appropriate leaves. For example, if we were to insert a word such as *blind* into the trie of Figure 6.32, we would look at a leaf in the subtree rooted in the *b* node to discover that the (skipped) second-letter position for the words currently in the trie is also *l*. So we add a node to the third letter list to distinguish *blind* from *black*. The result is shown in Figure 6.33.

However, if instead we insert into Figure 6.32 a word such as *band*, we find by comparison with one of the entries in the appropriate subtree (e.g., *black*) that this will

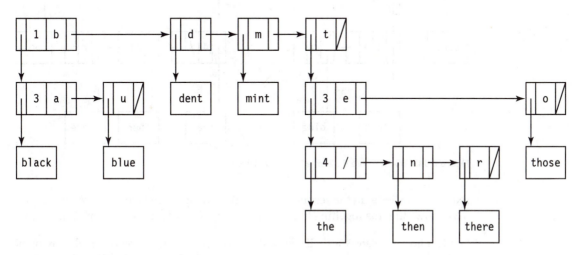

Figure 6.32 • Trie: Variant 3

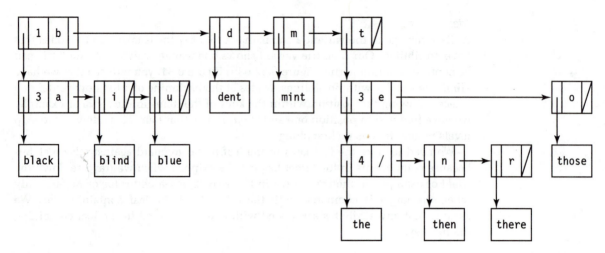

Figure 6.33 • Trie of Figure 6.32 with *blind* inserted

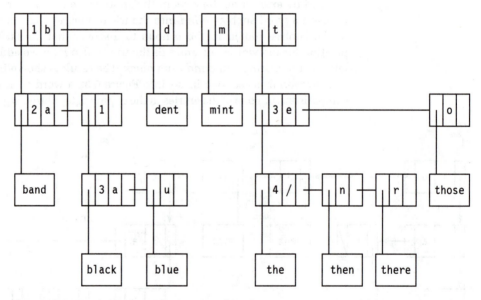

Figure 6.34 • Trie of Figure 6.32 after insertion of *band*

require a new letter in the second position. We will now need a list at level two. Figure 6.34 shows the tree resulting from the insertion of *band* into the tree of Figure 6.32.

Deletions from a Variant 3 Trie   If removal of a key results in an interior node having no siblings, then that node can be removed from the trie. For example, if we remove *those* from the trie of Figure 6.34, then all the words beginning with *t* have *e* in the third position. We can remove the node (3,*e*) leaving us with the trie shown in Figure 6.35.

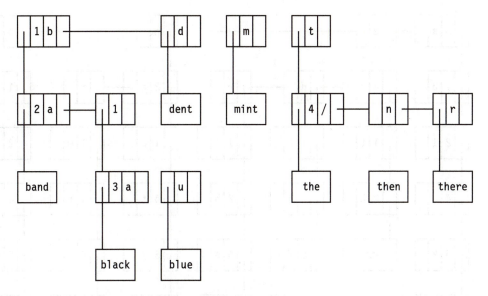

Figure 6.35 • Trie of Figure 6.34 after deletion of *those*

Key Sampling Order for Tries

If we are designing the trie for interactive searching, then we extract from the key in a left-to-right manner so that we can process key components in the order in which they are entered. However, in other applications we may be free to sample from the key in any order we wish. In particular, if we know the set of keys to be stored, we may choose a sampling order that reduces the size of a compressed trie or that reduces the average number of component comparisons, as we will see in an upcoming example. In such cases, where is the sampling order recorded? Perhaps it is recorded in the trie itself. If it is recorded as an additional data item in a node, then different subtrees are not required to use the same sampling order. Consider again our example set of words:

black blue dent mint the then there those

Figure 6.36 shows another variant 2 trie. In this instance, we record the component position in the node that begins each list.

We choose, somewhat arbitrarily, to begin comparisons at character position three. Different subtrees sample according to what best discriminates among the keys in that subtree. Consider, for example, the three words having *e* in the third position (*the*, *then*, and *there*). The first and second positions are the same for the three words, so we choose to test the fourth position next. This strategy pays off when we construct variant 3 tries (see the next section). Where there is only one word with a particular third letter (*blue*, *black*, *those*), we can sample the remaining characters in any order we choose.

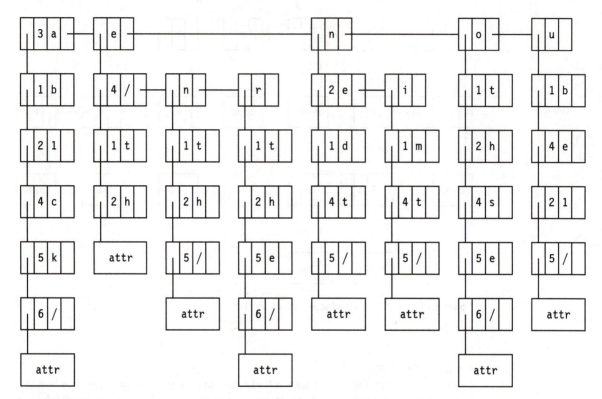

Figure 6.36 • Trie variant 2 with non-left-to-right sampling

Sampling for Variant 3 Tries   To minimize the total number of nodes in a compressed trie, intuition tells us that, at each position where we have a choice, we should select the most discriminating key component. For instance, if it turned out that each of our keys had a different fifth letter, then by testing that key component first we would immediately be able to tell potentially which trie entry could match. Thus, at each tree or subtree we should choose the position that best discriminates between candidate keys. Applying this strategy leads to the compressed trie of Figure 6.37. Figure 6.37 has two fewer nodes than the earlier compressed trie shown in Figure 6.32, but both require, on average, 4.625 component comparisons in successful retrievals.[7]

However, there are time-space trade-offs. For example, the trie of Figure 6.38 has one more node than the trie of Figure 6.37, but the average number of node comparisons is only 4.125.

Dynamic Tries

The previous discussion applies to situations where we know in advance the set of keys to be stored. If the keys are added on the fly, an algorithm could be devised

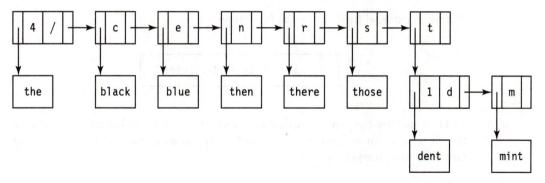

Figure 6.37 • Compressed trie

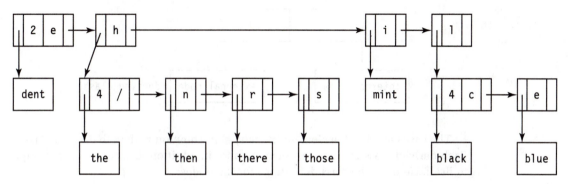

Figure 6.38 • A larger but faster compressed trie

that adjusts the tree so that the number of nodes or the average number of comparisons is minimal for the current set of keys. A trie implementation would have to weigh the costs incurred in the updates against any benefits due to faster retrievals.

6.4.2 Map Implementation

In order to present relatively simple algorithms, we choose to implement our map with trie variant 2 (e.g., see Figure 6.31). For compatibility with our other map implementations, we assume that leaves contain both full keys and attributes. We assume further that whatever form the key takes, we can transform components of it into integers.

We have two types of nodes and use a field (*nodetype*) to enable us to distinguish between instances of each type. An internal trie node (*nodetype* = 0) is thus

0	ptr	integer	ptr

and an external (leaf) trie node (*nodetype* = 1) is:

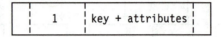

Thus, our trie has just two different types of nodes. Our implementation will use the class-inheritance feature of C++ and derive classes *internal_node* and *external_node* from base class *trienode*, thus:

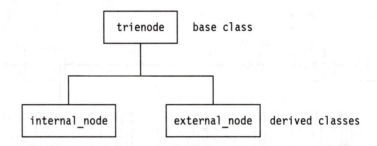

The base class has the element (*nodetype*) in common with both derived classes. Each derived class inherits this element and, in addition, has components unique to itself. Here are the class definitions for the nodes:

```cpp
template <class Entry> class map_trie;        // forward declaration

template <class Entry>
class trienode
{
   friend class map_trie<Entry>;
   protected: int nodetype;
};


template <class Entry>
class internal_node: public trienode<Entry>
{
   friend class map_trie<Entry>;
   private: int key_component;
            internal_node<Entry> *right;
            trienode<Entry> *down;
};
```

```
template <class Entry>
class external_node: public trienode<Entry>
{
    friend class map_trie<Entry>;
    private: Entry data;
};
```

Here is the top level of the class definition for the trie implementation of a map:

```
#include "stack.h"
#include <fstream.h>


template <class Entry>
class map_trie
{
  public: map_trie();         // constructor - initialize root
          ~map_trie();         // destructor - reclaim memory
          map_trie(const map_trie& rhs); // copy constructor
          map_trie& operator = (const map_trie&); // assignment
          void showmap(ostream&);      // driver for inorder traversal
          bool retrieve(Entry&);  // looks for key match, puts in
          bool insert(Entry);     // overwrites if key there
          bool remove(Entry);     // deletes one with same key

  private: internal_node<Entry> *root;
          void destruct_aux(internal_node<Entry> *&t); // actual destruct
          void traverse_aux(internal_node<Entry> *t, ostream& s);
          internal_node<Entry>* insertatthislevel
                              (internal_node<Entry>*&,int);
          void removefromlevel (internal_node<Entry>*& p,int component);
          internal_node<Entry>* searchlevel(internal_node<Entry>*p, int);
};
```

The definitions for the constructor and destructor functions follow:

```
template <class Entry>
map_trie<Entry>::map_trie()
 {
   root = NULL;
 }

template <class Entry>
map_trie<Entry>::~map_trie()
```

```
  {
    destruct_aux(root);
  }

template <class Entry>
void map_trie<Entry>::destruct_aux(internal_node<Entry> *&t)
  {
     if (t != NULL)
       {

          if ( t->down->nodetype==1)
                 delete t -> down;
          else
                 destruct_aux( (internal_node<Entry>*&)(t->down) );
          destruct_aux(t->right);
          delete t;
       }
  }
```

The following routines traverse the tree and output the data components in order. As with previous map implementations, the user needs to define the stream-insertion operator (<<) for the map objects in order to be able to use *showmap*.

```
template <class Entry>
void map_trie<Entry>::showmap(ostream& s)
  {
    traverse_aux(root,s);
  }

template <class Entry>
void map_trie<Entry>::traverse_aux(internal_node<Entry> *t, ostream& s)
  {
    if (t != NULL)
      { if (t->nodetype==1)    // t points to leaf
           { external_node<Entry> *temp;
             temp = (external_node<Entry>*) t;
             s << temp->data;
           }
         else
            {
              traverse_aux((internal_node<Entry>*)t->down,s);
              traverse_aux(t->right,s);
            }
      }
  }
```

• 6.4.3 Trie Algorithms

We now consider algorithms for retrieval, insertion, and deletion. We provide C++ code for the first two operations, and leave details of the deletion operation as an exercise.

Retrievals from a Variant 2 Trie

We look for the appropriate key component at the current level in the trie using the auxiliary function *searchlevel*. If we match every level up to the end of the key, then we can overwrite the parameter given to *retrieve* with the data from the tree. We assume that the objects stored by the user in the trie have two members:

keycomponent(i): A function that returns the value of the *i*th component of the key
end_of_key_mark: The integer value used to signify the end of a key

The definitions of functions *searchlevel* and *retrieve* follow:

```
template <class Entry>
internal_node<Entry>*
map_trie<Entry>::searchlevel(internal_node<Entry>* p, int component)
      {
        if (p==NULL)
           return NULL;
        else
            if (p->key_component == component)
                return p;
            else return searchlevel(p->right, component);
      }


template <class Entry>
bool map_trie<Entry>::retrieve (Entry& E)
      { internal_node<Entry> *ptr = root;
        int i = 1;

        while (true)
           {
           internal_node<Entry> *N = searchlevel(ptr,E.keycomponent(i));
           if (N==NULL)
                return false;  // not in trie
           else
                if (E.keycomponent(i)==E.end_of_key_mark)
                   {
                       external_node<Entry>* temp;
                       temp = (external_node<Entry>*) N -> down;
                       E = temp -> data;
                       return true;
                   }
```

```
                               else
                                  { ptr = (internal_node<Entry>*) N -> down;
                                    i++;
                                  }
                       }
               }
```

Insertions into a Variant 2 Trie

We search the trie component by component. If we find a complete match with our search target, then we overwrite the existing data with data supplied as part of the search parameters. Otherwise, at the point where the current trie diverges from the target, we insert the rest of the key followed by a leaf node containing the new data. Auxiliary function *insertatthislevel* inserts a node into a list. Here are the definitions of *insertatthislevel* and *insert*:

```
template <class Entry>
internal_node<Entry>* map_trie<Entry>::insertatthislevel
                        (internal_node<Entry>*&P, int component)
     {
       if (P==NULL)
           {
             P = new internal_node<Entry>;
             if (P==NULL) return NULL;              // no space left
             P -> nodetype = 0;
             P -> key_component = component;
             P -> right = NULL;
             P -> down = NULL;
             return P;
           }
       else if (P -> key_component > component)
               {
                 internal_node<Entry>* ptr = new internal_node<Entry>;
                 if (ptr==NULL) return NULL;        // no space left
                 ptr -> nodetype = 0;
                 ptr -> right = P;
                 ptr -> down = NULL;
                 ptr -> key_component = component;
                 P = ptr;
                 return P;
               }
           else
               return insertatthislevel(P->right,component);
     }
```

```cpp
template <class Entry>
bool map_trie<Entry>::insert(Entry E)     // overwrites if key there
      {
          internal_node<Entry> *ptr = root;
          internal_node<Entry> *temp, *above;
          external_node<Entry> *temp2;

          int i = 1;

          while (true)
            { internal_node<Entry> *N = searchlevel(ptr,E.keycomponent(i));
              if (N==NULL)
                 {  if (i==1)
                          N = insertatthislevel(root,E.keycomponent(i));
                    else
                          N = insertatthislevel(
                                          (internal_node<Entry>*&)above->down,
                                          E.keycomponent(i)
                                         );
                    if (N==NULL) return false;    // no space left
                    ptr = N;
                    do {
                          i++;
                        temp = new internal_node<Entry>;
                        if (temp == NULL) return false;  // no space left
                        temp -> nodetype = 0;
                        temp -> right = NULL;
                        temp -> down = NULL;
                        temp -> key_component = E.keycomponent(i);
                        ptr -> down = temp;
                        ptr = temp;
                      }
                    while (E.keycomponent(i) != E.end_of_key_mark);
                    // add the leaf data node
                    temp2 = new external_node<Entry>;
                    if (temp2 == NULL) return false;  // no space left
                    temp2 -> nodetype = 1;
                    temp2 -> data = E;
                    ptr -> down = (trienode<Entry>*) temp2;
                    return true;
                 }
```

```
     else
       {
         if (E.keycomponent(i)==E.end_of_key_mark)
           {
             temp2=(external_node<Entry>*) N->down;
             temp2 -> data = E;
             return true;
           }
         else
           {
             above = N;
             ptr = (internal_node<Entry>*) N -> down;
             i++;
           }
       }
   }
 }
}
```

Deletions from a Variant 2 Trie
To delete an element, those nodes that are on the path to the particular element and that are part of no other path must be deleted. In the absence of back pointers in the trie, we can stack pointers to nodes at each different trie level as we match them in searching for a key. Then, popping the pointers off the stack, we back up the trie and delete nodes. We stop either at the top of the trie or when we delete a node that is part of a multielement list.

Performance of Tries
If keys are length k on average and there are n items in a binary tree, then, on average, for reasonably balanced trees, key comparison time in a search is $O(k \log_2 n)$.

6.5 Ternary Trees

Generally, to be fast, tries must be space inefficient. A fast implementation uses the multiway branching of our trie version 1 with an array of pointers to the next level rather than the linked list of our trie version 3. When searching such a trie, we use the current key component to index the pointer array. However, this means allocating space for a pointer for each possible value of the key component. If key components are characters and we have a 26-character alphabet and 4 bytes per pointer, this gives us 104-byte nodes. What if the character set is even larger (e.g., 128-character ASCII)? The character set may be so large, for example the 49,194 characters of Unicode version 3.0 (Unicode 2002), as to prohibit this implementation approach altogether.

When we transformed a variant 1 trie into a variant 2 trie, we replaced a variable-sized node with a linked list of nodes. If we now replace this linear list with a binary tree, then we have a structure in which many of the nodes have three pointers, two to nodes at the current search level and one to a node at the next search level. We refer to this structure as a **ternary tree**. (Note that the term is also used to refer to other tree structures with three-way branching.) The ternary tree has advantages over both a hash table and a binary tree. Ternary trees are quite fast and yet space efficient no matter what the alphabet size. (AT&T uses them in a Unicode-based OCR system.) The structure appears to have originated in a paper by Clampett (1964). Bentley and Sedgewick (1997, 1998) have more recently compared its performance with hashing and binary trees.[8]

Each node in a ternary tree has a character (or, in general, a key component) and three pointers. Key-searching proceeds in a manner similar to searching a variant 2 trie except that at a particular level we are searching a binary tree rather than a linked list. If the character in the node matches the current key component, we follow the middle pointer to the next level down, where we look for the next key component. Otherwise, we follow the left or right pointer (in the manner of a binary search tree), continuing to look for a match with the current key component.

6.5.1 Example Ternary Tree

Suppose our variant 2 trie contained the fragment shown in Figure 6.39.

The corresponding fragment of the ternary tree might look like Figure 6.40.[9]

Following Bentley and Sedgewick's notation, we use solid lines for linking nodes at the same level and dashed lines for indicating a link to the next level. The four lists shown in Figure 6.39 become the four binary trees of Figure 6.40. For example, the linked list [a,c,d,f,m,p,t,w] at the top of Figure 6.39 becomes the

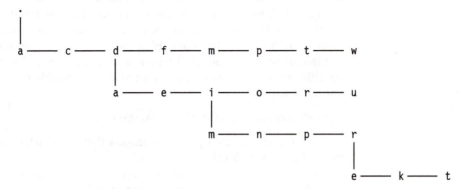

Figure 6.39 • A trie fragment

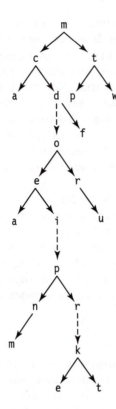

Figure 6.40 • A ternary tree fragment corresponding to Figure 6.39

binary tree at the top of Figure 6.40. A match with *d* in this tree leads to the binary tree at the next level down, which contains the same information as the list [*a,e,i,o,r,u*]. A match with *i* in the second tree leads to the third-level tree containing the same information as list [*m,n,p,r*]. Finally, a match with *r* at the third level leads us to the lowest tree containing the same data as list [*e,k,t*].

Like binary trees and unlike tries, a particular set of keys may be represented by different ternary trees. Figure 6.41 shows a possible ternary tree for our example set of words:

black blue dent mint the then there those

Table 6.4 shows the eight comparisons that occur when we search the ternary tree in Figure 6.41 for the word *there*.

We can define a *perfectly balanced* ternary tree as one in which each node contains the median of the appropriate set of values (i.e., the number of nodes in the left and right subtrees differ by at most one). Bentley and Saxe (1979) prove that the

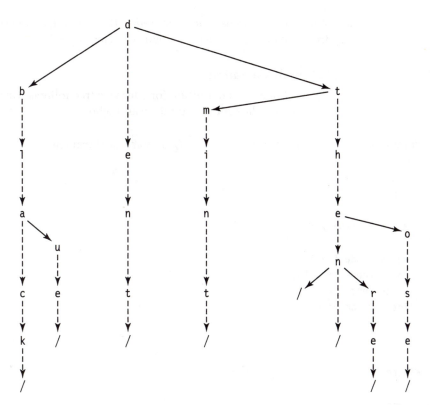

Figure 6.41 • Ternary tree for our example words

● TABLE 6.4	Trace of Search for *there*	
Key Component	**Compare With**	**Branch to Follow**
t	d	Right
t	t	Middle
h	h	Middle
e	e	Middle
r	n	Right
r	r	Middle
e	e	Middle
/	/	Match found

largest number of comparisons required to find a string in a perfectly balanced ternary tree containing n strings of length k is $\lfloor \log_2 n \rfloor + k$.

• 6.5.2 Implementation

The top level of a class definition for a ternary tree follows. Once more, we have a node class and a class for the structure as a whole.

```cpp
template <class Entry> class map_ternary;         // forward declaration

template <class Entry>
class ternarynode
{
  friend class map_ternary<Entry>;

  private: ternarynode *left;
           ternarynode *middle;
           ternarynode *right;
           int key_component;
};



#include <fstream.h>

template <class Entry>
class map_ternary
{
  public: map_ternary();         // constructor - initialize root
          ~map_ternary();        // destructor - reclaim memory
          map_ternary(const map_ternary& rhs);       // copy constructor
          map_ternary& operator = (const map_ternary&); // assignment
          void showmap(ostream&);       // driver for inorder traversal
          bool retrieve(Entry&);  // if key match update parameter
          bool insert(Entry);     // overwrites if key already there
          bool remove(Entry);     // deletes one with same key

  private: ternarynode<Entry> *root;
           void destruct_aux(ternarynode<Entry> *&t);      // actual destruct
           void inorder_aux(ternarynode<Entry> *t);        // actual inorder
           bool insert_aux(Entry X, ternarynode<Entry> *&t); // actual insert
           ternarynode<Entry>* retrieve_aux(Entry&, ternarynode<Entry> *t);
           void remove_aux(ternarynode<Entry> *&t);        // actual deleter
};
```

• 6.5.3 Comparisons with Hash Tables and Binary Trees

Ternary Trees and Hash Tables

Bentley and Sedgewick (1997) report that for successful searches, ternary trees are comparable in speed with hash tables in which overflow is handled with chaining. Ternary trees are significantly faster than hash tables when the search is unsuccessful (because they can stop without examining the whole key).

Although ternary trees typically take up more space than a comparable hash table, this space can be reduced. For example, if a subtree contains a single string, then the subtree can be replaced by the substring. A node now requires three single-bit fields indicating, for each pointer, whether it points to a node or to a substring. However, although space is reduced, the algorithms run slower.

Some operations that require linear time on a hash table, such as finding the successor or predecessor of a given key, can be performed very quickly on a ternary tree.

Ternary Trees and Binary Search Trees

Bentley and Sedgewick (1997) compared the times required to search a ternary tree of approximately 72,000 words with the times needed to perform a binary search of the same data set. The binary search represents a search on a perfectly balanced binary tree. They found that the binary search required about twice as much time as the search of the ternary tree.

• 6.5.4 Partial-Match Searches

Partial-match searches can be implemented elegantly on a ternary tree. We can identify two types of such searches: (1) those in which the search parameter may contain both normal key components and "wild card"/"don't care" positions and (2) *near-neighbor* searches in which we are looking for words that differ from the search string in no more than d positions. This type of search is useful in spell checking in which the checker suggests words close to the one not found in the dictionary.

Wild Card Searches

We modify the search algorithm so that if the current component is not a wild card and it matches the tree node, then we follow the appropriate branch down the tree. If the current component is a wild card (indicating it can be matched by any single component), then we recursively search all branches at the current level.

We can add to our *map_ternary* class the following function that outputs words that match E (E may contain wild card characters).

```
void show_partial(Entry E, ostream& outs)
  {
    partial_match_search(root,E,1,outs);
  }
```

The work is done by the following *partial_match_search* function, which is based on a function in Bentley and Saxe (1997).[10]

```
void partial_match_search (ternarynode<Entry> *p, Entry E,int i, ostream& outs)
{
  if (p==NULL) return;  // no more tree

  if (E.keycomponent(i)==E.wild || E.keycomponent(i) < p->key_component)
    partial_match_search(p->left,E,i,outs); // recursive search left

  if (E.keycomponent(i)==E.wild || E.keycomponent(i) == p->key_component)
    if (   p->key_component != E.end_of_key_mark
        && E.keycomponent(i) != E.end_of_key_mark
       )
        partial_match_search(p->middle,E,i+1,outs); // recursive search down

  if (   E.keycomponent(i) == E.end_of_key_mark
      && p->key_component == E.end_of_key_mark
     )
    outs << p->attribute; // found match

  if (E.keycomponent(i) == E.wild || E.keycomponent(i) > p->key_component)
    partial_match_search(p->right,E,i,outs); // recursive search right
}
```

The top levels of a trie tend to have higher branching factors than nodes further down. We would expect searches where the wild card is earlier in the string rather than later to take longer because there is a greater volume of tree to be searched. (Consider searching a phone book for everyone named *??son* versus searching it for everyone named *Mas??*). This was confirmed in experiments performed by Bentley and Sedgewick (1997).

Near-Neighbor Searches

Suppose we are interested in all words that differ from the search parameter in no more than *d* positions. This is useful if we are searching for a name and we are not quite sure of the spelling. It is also a useful way for a spell checker to suggest correct words when it finds a misspelling (although many typing errors are the result of transpositions). The following *neighborsearch* function is adapted from Bentley and Sedgewick (1997).

```
void neighborsearch(ternarynode *p, Entry E, int i, int distance, ostream& outs)
{
  if (p==NULL || distance < 0) return;  // no more matches possible
```

```
if (distance>0 || E.keycomponent(i) < p->key_component)
    neighborsearch(p->left,E,i,distance,outs);

if ( p->key_component==E.end_of_key_mark)
    {
      if  (E.numcomponents-i <= distance ) outs << p-> attribute;
    }
else neighborsearch(p->middle, E,
                    min(E.numcomponents,i+1),
                    E.keycomponent(i)==p->key_component? distance :distance-1,
                    outs
                    );

if (distance>0 || E.keycomponent(i) > p->key_component)
    neighborsearch(p->right,E,i,distance,outs);
}
```

6.6 Binary Tree Applications

Binary trees are versatile structures. To illustrate this, we look at two applications that have nothing to do with the map implementations of earlier sections: expression trees and Huffman code trees.

6.6.1 Expression Trees

As we saw in Figure 6.4b, we can represent an arithmetic expression as a binary tree. For example, the expression

$$(A + B) * ((C - D) / (E + F) * G)$$

can be represented by the tree shown in Figure 6.42.

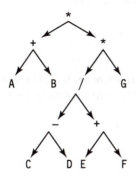

Figure 6.42 • Binary tree representing $(A + B) * ((C - D) / (E + F) * G)$

Note that two traversals of an expression tree are particularly useful. The postorder traversal gives us the postfix form of the expression (useful for entering the expression in certain kinds of calculators). For the tree in Figure 6.42, this is:

$$A\ B + C\ D - E\ F + / G * *$$

The preorder traversal gives us the prefix form. For our example tree, this yields:

$$* + A\ B * / - C\ D + E\ F\ G$$

We will devise a prototype class definition for an *exptree*. Methods of our class will enable us to:

- Construct a tree from a string containing the expression in infix form
- Evaluate a tree (with respect to a particular table of symbols and values)
- Generate assembly language instructions representing the evaluation of the expression

Our class will be very rudimentary—identifiers are single characters, expressions contain no constants, and there is little error checking in the functions. Enhancements to the class are left as exercises.

In order to be able to evaluate an expression, we need to be able to associate values with identifiers. First we have a symbol table class that lets a user enter (symbol,value) pairs and retrieve the current value of a symbol. The following version uses a binary search tree (*map_bst*). It is a simple matter to replace this with a hash table or other implementation.

In the class definition for a symbol table entry (*symtabentry*), *map_bst* requires the operator <, and *showmap* requires <<.

```
#include "map_bst.h"

class symtabentry
    {
    public: symtabentry(char s=' ', double v=0.0)
                { // constructor. Default symbol value is zero
                  sym=s;
                  val=v;
                }
            bool operator < (symtabentry X)
                { return sym < X.sym; }    // required ordering operator
            friend ostream& operator <<(ostream& outs, const symtabentry& X)
                {
                  outs << X.sym << " " << X.val << endl;
                  return outs;
                }
```

```
                 void setentries (char s, double v)
                       { // lets user create entry values
                         sym=s;
                         val=v;
                       }
                 double valuefield() { return val; }

         private: char sym;
                  double val;
       };


class symboltable
{
 public: double valueof(char id)
              { // returns the value associated with id
                symtabentry temp;
                temp.setentries(id,0.0f);
                symtab.retrieve(temp);
                return temp.valuefield();
              }
         void setvalue (char C, double F)
              { // makes or overwrites the entry for C
                symtabentry temp;
                temp.setentries(C,F);
                symtab.insert(temp);
              }
         void showsymbols(ostream& s)
              { // lists contents of symbol table
                s << "symbols and values\n";
                symtab.showmap(s);
              }

 private: map_bst<symtabentry> symtab;
};
```

Turning to the expression tree itself, first we have a definition for a node in the tree. There will be two types of node: (1) leaves holding identifiers and (2) internal nodes holding operators. In the following definition, we use the *union* feature to enable the identifier and the operator to share the same space. This may seem excessive in our simple case in which both these fields are type *char*, but in general, the fields might be quite different. For example, the identifier might be a string and the operator might be a pointer to a function.

```
class exptreenode
  {
  friend class exptree;

  private: bool isoperand;
          union { char oprator; char identifier;}};
          exptreenode *left, *right;
  };
```

Here is a top-level definition of our expression tree. Some aspects of this definition (e.g., destruction, copying, and assignment) are very similar to our earlier binary search tree.

```
class exptree
{
 public: exptree();           // constructor
         ~exptree();          // destructor
         exptree(const exptree& rhs);         // copy constructor
         exptree& operator = (const exptree&); // assignment
         double evaluate(symboltable);  // determine value of tree
         void codegen(ostream&);        // code from tree
         void buildtree (string);       // make tree from infix

 private: enum symtype {oprand,openparen,closeparen,oprator};
         void destruct_aux(exptreenode *t);      // actual destruct
         bool copytree (exptreenode *&newtree, exptreenode *oldtree);
         double evalnode(exptreenode*,symboltable);
         void codegennode (exptreenode*, ostream&);
         symtype classify(char);
         void apply(char);
         int priority(char);

         stack<char> operators;
         stack<exptreenode*> operands;

         exptreenode *root;
};
```

The three functions of particular interest are *buildtree*, *evaluate*, and *codegen*.

buildtree

Recall that in Chapter 4 we looked at an algorithm that processed an infix arithmetic expression and evaluated it using two stacks—one for operators and one for operands. We use the same algorithm in *buildtree* to construct the binary expression tree from an infix expression. As before, we will have a stack of operators, but this time the second stack, rather than being a stack of values, will be a stack of pointers to nodes. In the evaluation algorithm, whenever we popped an operator off the operator stack, we applied it to the top two items on the operand stack and replaced them by the result of the operation. Here, whenever we pop off the operator stack we create a node containing the operator and the top two items on the operand stack as its left and right links. Then we replace those two items by a pointer to the new node. At the end of processing, if the expression is well formed, there is a single pointer on the operand stack. We copy this to the root variable of the tree.

Figures 6.43, 6.44, and 6.45 show how the function processes the expression (*A* + *B*) * (*C* + *D*). For each of the 12 steps in building the tree (11 input characters plus end-of-string processing), the figure shows the input character, the operator stack, and the operand stack. For clarity, a stack is shown only when there is a change in its contents. In a tree node, *f* (false) and *t* (true) represent the value of the *isoperand* field.

The following are two of the auxiliary functions used by *buildtree*, which are similar to the functions found in Chapter 4.

```
exptree::symtype exptree::classify(char sym)
{ // return value indicates the class of character sym

  if (sym=='(') return openparen;
  if (sym==')') return closeparen;
  if (   sym=='+' || sym=='-' || sym=='*' || sym=='/') return oprator;
  return oprand;
}
```

```
int exptree::priority (char op)
{ // return value reflects precedence of operator "op"

 if (op == '*' || op == '/') return 2;
 if (op == '+' || op == '-') return 1;
 return 0;
}
```

The following code demonstrates the main difference between expression evaluation and tree building. Function *apply*, as defined here, constructs a tree rather than evaluate the expression.

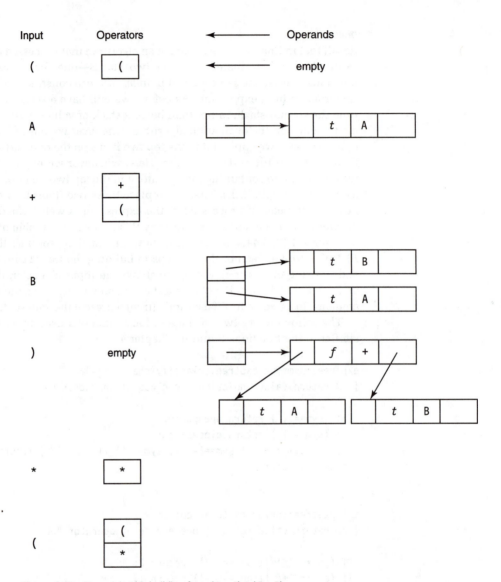

Figure 6.43 • Stage 1 in tree building from $(A + B) * (C + D)$

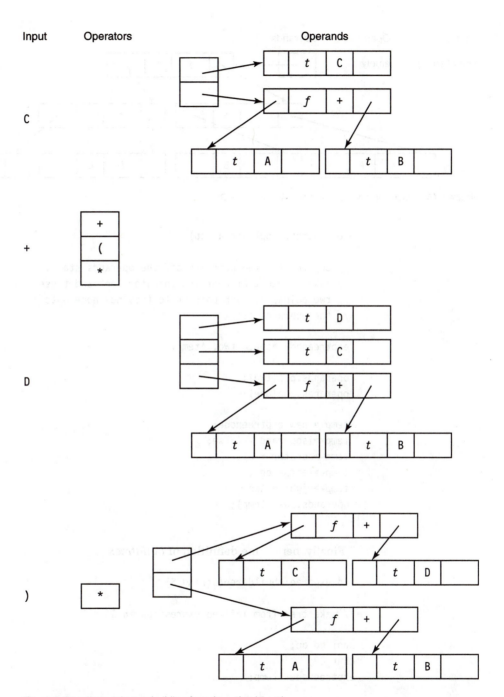

Figure 6.44 • Stage 2 in tree building from (A + B) * (C + D)

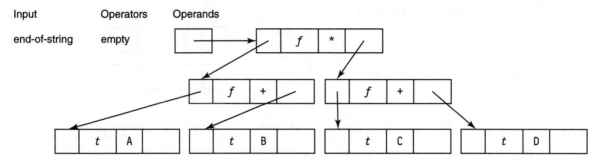

Figure 6.45 • Stage 3 in tree building from (A + B) * (C + D)

```
void exptree::apply (char op)
{
  // pop the top two pointers off the operands stack.
  // make a node that contains operator "op" and these
  // two pointers. Push pointer to this new node onto
  // the operands stack

  exptreenode *one, *two, *temp;

  operands.pop(two);
  operands.pop(one);

  temp = new exptreenode;
  temp->isoperand = false;
  temp->oprator = op;
  temp->left = one;
  temp->right = two;
  operands.push(temp);
}
```

Finally, here is the definition of *buildtree:*

```
void exptree::buildtree(string S)
{
 // make tree from infixed expression in S

 bool go_on;
 char OP;
 exptreenode *temp;
```

```
operators.clear();
operands.clear();
for (int i=0; i<S.length();i++)
  {
    // process character - either letter (operand) or operator or paren
    symtype symboltype = classify(S[i]);
    switch (symboltype)
      {
    case oprand: // make leaf containing the operand character
                temp = new exptreenode;
                temp->left=NULL;
                temp->right=NULL;
                temp->isoperand=true;
                temp->identifier=S[i];
                // and push pointer to it on the operand stack
                operands.push(temp);
           break;

    case openparen: operators.push('(');
           break;

    case closeparen: go_on = true;
           while(go_on)
             {
               operators.pop(OP);
               if (OP=='(') go_on=false;
                      else apply(OP);
             }
           break;

    case oprator: while(true)
             {
               if (!operators.pop(OP)) break;
               if (priority(OP) < priority(S[i]))
                   {operators.push(OP); break; }
               apply(OP);
             }
           operators.push(S[i]);
      }

  }
```

```
// at end of string process any operators outstanding
while (operators.pop(OP)) apply(OP);
// copy pointer to top of tree into root
operands.pop(root);
}
```

evaluate

The *evaluate* function is naturally recursive because the value of an expression tree is a function of the values in the two subtrees and the operator in the root. This applies recursively to the subtrees themselves. We make our *evaluate* function a little more general by enabling the user to specify which symbol table should be used to look up identifiers.

```
double exptree::evaluate(symboltable S)
{
// get value of the whole expression
return evalnode(root,S);
}


double exptree::evalnode (exptreenode *t, symboltable S)
{
// get value of tree rooted in t

if (t==NULL)
      return 0.0f;  // empty tree
if (t->isoperand)
      return S.valueof(t->identifier); // leaf - lookup in symbol table

// recursive case

   double L = evalnode(t->left,S);
   double R = evalnode(t->right,S);
   switch(t->oprator)
        {
        case '+': return L+R;
        case '-': return L-R;
        case '*': return L*R;
        case '/': return L/R;
         default: return 0.0f;  // really an error
        }

}
```

codegen

From an expression tree, we can generate a sequence of assembly code instructions that, when executed, computes the value of the expression. The function *codegen* outputs an instruction sequence for a generic architecture assumed to have both stack and three-register instructions. Again, this is a recursive process.

```
void exptree::codegen(ostream &s)
{
// generate the code for the entire tree to stream s
 codegennode(root,s);
}


void exptree::codegennode (exptreenode *t, ostream& outs)
{
// generate the code for the tree rooted in t

 if (t == NULL) return;   // empty tree
 if (t->isoperand)
      outs << "push " << t->identifier << endl;
 else
    {
      codegennode(t->left,outs);
      codegennode(t->right,outs);
      outs << "pop r2\n";
      outs << "pop r1\n";
        switch(t->oprator)
         {
          case '+': outs << "add r1,r2,r3\n"; break;
          case '-': outs << "sub r1,r2,r3\n"; break;
          case '*': outs << "mul r1,r2,r3\n"; break;
          case '/': outs << "div r1,r2,r3\n"; break;
           default: outs << "** unimplemented operator \n";
         }
      outs << "push r3\n";
    }
}
```

Testing the Class

The following program tests the functions *buildtree*, *evaluate*, and *codegen*. It builds a tree representing the expression $(A / B) * C + D$ and then evaluates it using two different symbol tables. Finally, it generates a sequence of assembly code instructions.

```cpp
#include <iostream.h>

#include "exptree.h"
#include "symboltable.h"

int main()
{
 exptree E,F;
 symboltable S,T;

 // make a small tree

 E.buildtree(  "(A/B)*C+D" );

 // make entries for the variables in S

 S.setvalue('C',8); S.setvalue('A',19); S.setvalue('D',-1);
   S.setvalue('B',17);
 S.showsymbols(cout);

 cout << "value of expression E wrt S is : " << E.evaluate(S) << endl;

 // change B to 30
 S.setvalue('B',30);
 S.showsymbols(cout);
 cout << "value of expression E wrt S is : " << E.evaluate(S) << endl;

 // copy the tree
 F = E;

 // make values for symbols in the second symbol table

 T.setvalue('C',8); T.setvalue('A',65); T.setvalue('D',42);
   T.setvalue('B',13);
 T.showsymbols(cout);

 cout << "value of expression F wrt T is : " << F.evaluate(T) << endl;

 cout << "code generated is : \n";
 F.codegen(cout);

 return 0;
}
```

The program produces the following output.

```
symbols and values
A 19
B 17
C 8
D -1
value of expression E wrt S is : 7.94118
symbols and values
A 19
B 30
C 8
D -1
value of expression E wrt S is : 4.06667
symbols and values
A 65
B 13
C 8
D 42
value of expression F wrt T is : 82
code generated is :
push A
push B
pop r2
pop r1
div r1,r2,r3
push r3
push C
pop r2
pop r1
mul r1,r2,r3
push r3
push D
pop r2
pop r1
add r1,r2,r3
push r3
```

• 6.6.2 Huffman Codes

Normal encoding of a file uses fixed-length codes (typically 8 bits, more recently 16 bits) for each character. However, we can save space by using a variable-length coding scheme with shorter codes for frequently occurring characters and longer codes

• **TABLE 6.5** Variable-Length Codes						
A	B	C	D	E	F	G
01	001	11	1001	1000	011	111

• **TABLE 6.6** Example Symbols and Frequencies	
Symbol (S_i)	Relative Frequency (P_i)
A	6
B	5
C	4
D	1
E	2
F	2
G	3

for those that are rarer. Some compression programs, such as the Unix utilities *pack* and *compact*, work in this manner.

The set of codes that we use must result in uniquely decodable files; that is, there must be an unambiguous decoding of the file. If the codes are all the same length, this is not a problem. The ASCII for BEAD is the following 32-bit string made up of four 8-bit character codes.

01000010010001010100000101000100

Consider the characters and binary codes shown in Table 6.5.

Using the codes in Table 6.5, BEAD is represented as 0011000011001. However, this binary string is ambiguous because it can be decoded both as BEAD and as BEFB. The problem arises because one code (01, the code for *A*) is the prefix of another (011, the code for *F*). We can eliminate the possibility of ambiguity and also arrive at an encoding that is in some sense optimal by employing a technique devised by Huffman (1952) that uses a binary trie.

Assume we have symbols S_1 . . . S_n with associated relative frequencies of P_1 . . . P_n. For illustrative purposes, we use the symbols and relative frequencies shown in Table 6.6.

Huffman's technique for deriving codes works as follows.

```
Make each symbol Sᵢ a single node with associated weight Pᵢ.
While (more than one parentless node)
      {
          Identify the two parentless nodes with the smallest
              weights (breaking ties arbitrarily)
          Create a new node, make it the parent of the two selected nodes
              and associate with it the sum of the weights of its children
      }
Label the branches of the tree: for each nonleaf node label one of its
      Branches with '0' and the other with '1'.
The code for a symbol is constructed by concatenating the characters
      ('0' or '1') on the path from the root to the symbol.
```

For example, from the data in Table 6.6, we first combine node D (weight 1) with either E or F (weight 2). Choosing E yields the structure shown in Figure 6.46.

We now combine node F (weight 2) with one of the nodes with weight 3. Choosing G gives us the tree shown in Figure 6.47.

The two nodes with the smallest weights now are node C and the node that resulted from our first construction. Joining these yields the structure shown in Figure 6.48.

We continue in this manner, finally arriving at the tree shown in Figure 6.49 (other trees are possible depending on how we break ties).

We now label the links. One of the links from a parent to its child will be labeled "1" and the other will be labeled "0," but it does not matter which is which. Figure 6.50 shows a possible tree after this labeling has been done.

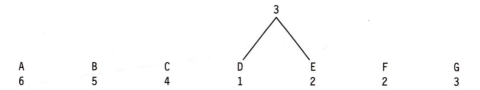

Figure 6.46 • Tree construction: Step 1

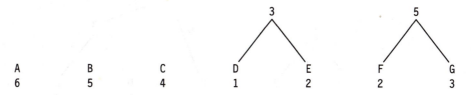

Figure 6.47 • Tree construction: Step 2

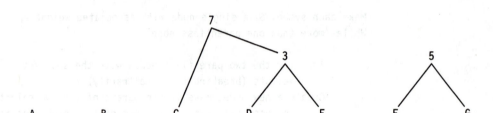

Figure 6.48 • Tree construction: Step 3

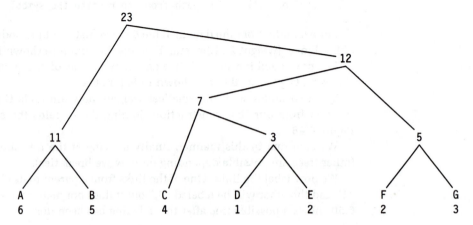

Figure 6.49 • Huffman tree before labeling

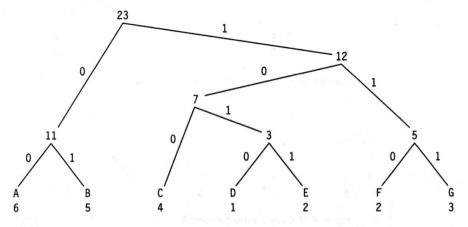

Figure 6.50 • Labeled Huffman tree

● **TABLE 6.7** Example Symbols and Codes	
Symbol	**Code**
A	00
B	01
C	100
D	1010
E	1011
F	110
G	111

The codes for each symbol are now derived by following paths from the root to the leaves. In essence, we have a trie because the code is the complete path and each edge represents only part of the symbol. The codes in this example are shown in Table 6.7.

To encode a character, we just replace it with the corresponding code, thus BEADED becomes 01101100101010111010.

To decode a string of bits, we start at the beginning of the string and with a pointer at the top of the code tree. When reading bits, we follow the appropriate paths down the tree. Whenever we reach a leaf, we output the corresponding symbol and reset the pointer to the root of the tree. Try it for yourself using the tree in Figure 6.50 to confirm that 100001101011 decodes to CAFE.

Optimality
The average weighted code length is determined using

$$\frac{\sum\left(P_i * codelength(S_i)\right)}{\sum P_i}$$

For our example, the average weighted code length is (6 * 2 + 5 * 2 + 4 * 3 + 1 * 1 + 2 * 2 + 2 * 3 + 3 * 3) / 25 = 61 / 25 = 2.44 bits.[11] Huffman coding is optimal in that there is no other assignment of codes to symbols that will have a shorter average weighted code length.

Static Versus Dynamic Huffman Encoding
What is outlined in the previous section is *static* Huffman encoding, in which a particular symbol has the same encoding throughout a file. We use some frequency data to determine the codes. For example, in a compression program we might read the file to be compressed twice: once to get the frequency distribution and a second

time to do the actual encoding. In this scheme, data about the (symbol,code) pairs would have to be preappended to the output (compressed) file so that it could be decompressed.

An alternative strategy for a file compression program is that it reads the file to be compressed only once. We start with an empty tree and add new symbols as they appear in the file. Frequencies of symbols and, consequently, the shape of the tree and the codes for the symbols are updated as the file is read. A particular character may have many different encodings at different points in the file (Vitter 1989). Although this *dynamic* Huffman encoding may not be globally optimal, it eliminates the need for encoding data to be preappended to a compressed file. Vitter (1987) shows that his adaptive Huffman algorithm compresses a file to between $S - n + 1$ and $S + t - 2n + 1$ bits where S is the number of bits required by the static Huffman method, t is the number of characters in the input, and n is the number of different characters in the input. Thus, it is never more than 1 bit per character worse than the static algorithm. The Unix utility *pack* uses a static Huffman method, whereas *compact* uses a dynamic Huffman algorithm. Although Huffman-based methods are generally simple to implement, there are other approaches that compress better (e.g., see Salomon 1998).

● Chapter Summary

This chapter and Chapter 5 considered three broad ways in which a map might be implemented: a hash table, a binary tree, and a trie. Factors to consider when choosing between these three implementations include:

- Relative frequency of insert, retrieve, and delete operations
- Available memory
- Speed requirements
- Whether entries need be ordered

A brief summary of each implementation follows:

- Hash table. Operations can be very fast. However, ordering of entries is normally destroyed and an implementation may require an estimation of the upper bound on the number of entries. Compared with the other structures, hash tables require more work to tailor an implementation for a particular application. In addition, space is likely to be allocated, but not used.
- Binary tree. Has simple algorithms and is an extendible structure. However, much time can be spent in key comparisons. Worst-case behavior can be very bad. Use of an AVL tree can greatly reduce the worst case, but AVL insertion and deletion algorithms are more complex and a little slower than their binary tree counterparts.
- Trie. Matching of partial keys rather than complete keys enables overlap of operations with key entry. Partial-match and near-neighbor searches are possible. Fast implementations may have high space requirements. The ternary tree imple-

mentation can be as fast as a hash table and occupy less space than a normal trie. Algorithms are comparatively complex.

Hash tables are good when one needs fast access to individual items. Hashing is commonly used to implement symbol tables in translator programs. In an operating system, a hash table could be used to look up user data quickly at log-in time. In each of these applications, an occasional slow retrieval, due to a long overflow chain, for example, is not problematic.

If, on the other hand, you wish to avoid bad worst cases, you might consider a balanced binary tree such as an AVL tree. An example application for this approach is when processing a real-time data stream (e.g., a sports or a stock market ticker, in which taking too long to process one item might result in the next item being missed or misread).

The advantage of a trie over both a hash table and a binary tree is that searching can be overlapped with key entry. Thus, in an interactive environment, the search algorithm can begin as soon as the user enters part of the key. In addition, the user can stop key entry when enough information has been entered to identify the entry uniquely or to indicate that there can be no match. An example application for tries is a user entering a search term into an online index such as a help file or a directory of people.

Exercises

1. A map can be implemented in different ways; two of these are the hash table and the binary tree. Give reasons for your choices.

    a. Give an example of an application in which you would choose to use the hash table rather than the binary tree implementation.

    b. Give an example of an application in which you would choose to use the binary tree rather than the hash table implementation.

2. What factors determine the speed with which a key is found in a map when the map is implemented as a:

    a. Binary tree

    b. Hash table

    c. Compressed trie

3. Construct a compressed trie for a given fixed set of words (e.g., the reserved words of C++). Your goal is to achieve a tree with as few nodes as possible. Explain how you would determine the order in which key components are sampled.

4. Suppose you knew ahead of time the set of keys that would be stored in a map (e.g., the set of reserved words in a programming language). For each of the three implementations covered in the text—binary tree, hash table, and binary trie—explain

how you could take advantage of this knowledge to improve the performance of the data structure.

5. Consider a trie that contains only key components (not complete keys). How could you traverse such a trie and output the keys that it contains?

6. Trace the insertion of the following sequence of single-character keys into an initially empty binary search tree. What does the final tree look like?

   t w v g d m k y f p

7. Outline an algorithm that determines whether a binary tree is a binary search tree; that is, the algorithm checks the ordering of the tree entries.

8. Outline an algorithm that determines whether an expression tree is well formed. What checks should your algorithm perform?

9. Add a method to *map_bst* that returns the height of the tree. See Figure 6.25 for examples of trees of various heights.

10. Extend the definition of an expression tree node to include constants as well as operators and identifiers. Modify the *evaluate* function appropriately.

11. A certain binary tree contains a single letter at each node. The sequence of nodes visited during an inorder traversal is:

    R C L T P M W H J D A S.

    The sequence of nodes visited during a preorder traversal is:

    M C R P L T A W J H D S.

    Draw the tree.

12. Sketch the logic of an operator that determines if two expression trees are identical.

13. Write a function that prints an expression tree in infix form using parentheses only where necessary.

14. From the data of Table 6.6, construct a Huffman tree that has a different shape than the one in Figure 6.49. Allocate codes and compute the average weighted code length. What do you conclude?

15. The adaptive Huffman method encodes the current character using the current tree and then changes the tree. Could you change the tree first and then encode the character? If so, why? If not, why not?

16. Suppose a Huffman-compressed file is corrupted—a few bits are changed. Can the expansion program detect this? If so, how?

17. Suppose you devise Huffman codes for a certain set of symbols. Under what circumstances will no two codes be the same length?

18. The following is a binary search tree with the identity of the nodes concealed.

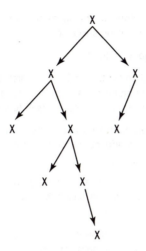

The tree actually contains nine characters: c, t, g, w, k, e, j, a, h.

a. Draw the tree so that an inorder traversal visits the characters in ascending alphabetical order.

b. Draw the tree as it appears after each operation in the following sequence:

   1. Insert v

   2. Insert d

   3. Delete a

   4. Delete w

   5. Delete g

● Problems

1. Modify the class definition for a map (any of the three implementations) so that entries record the frequency with which a key is entered. Thus, if a symbol entered has the same key as an existing entry, the count associated with the symbol is increased by one.

2. Test your solution to Problem 1 by including the modified class in a program that reads a file of text and outputs a list of the words in the text together with the frequency at which each occurred.

3. How many different binary trees contain exactly *k* nodes?

4. Complete the definition of the function that enables us to delete entries from a trie.

5. Write a program that generates a random binary tree with *N* nodes and determines its height (*h*). Run the program many times for a variety of values of *N* and plot *N* against *h*.

6. Add two functions to the *map_bst* class:

a. *getsuccesor(t)* returns a pointer to the successor in the tree to the node pointed to by *t*. It returns NULL if there is no successor.

b. *getpredecessor(t)* is similarly defined.

7. We could create a double-linked list from a binary search tree by performing an inorder traversal of the tree and appending each data item to an initially empty list. Instead, devise and test a recursive function that applies itself to subtrees.

8. Use the *map_bst* class in a program that maintains a set of student records. A user of the program should be able to add new students, remove students, and change the major of the student with Idnumber *N*.

   Extend the class definition so that you can find those map entries for which an arbitrary Boolean function *B* returns true. Use this facility to enable a user to find all students with a particular major.

9. Create a trie containing common English words. Use it in a program that enables a user to input lines of text. Your program should issue an audible or visible warning if the user appears to be entering a word that is not in your dictionary.

10. Extend your solution to Problem 9 so that if the user enters a word not currently in the trie, the program gives the option of adding it to the set.

11. Extend your solution to Problem 10 by adding a feature (that can be disabled) that lets the program suggest a word completion that the user can accept in a simple manner (e.g., by entering a space or other punctuation character) or reject by continuing to enter word characters.

12. Implement and test the algorithm that deletes a node from an AVL tree.

13. Write and test a function that reverses a binary search tree. For example, such a function would change tree (a) to tree (b) (see figures). Naturally, a second application of your function should change tree (b) to tree (a).

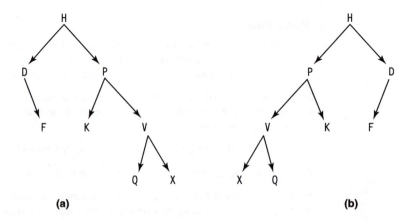

(a)   (b)

14. Devise and test a function that determines whether a binary tree contains two identical subtrees (such a function might be useful in simplifying expression trees).

15. Write and test a function that recursively builds a balanced tree from an ordered array of items.

16. Data about animals and their characteristics can be stored in a binary tree, as in the following example.

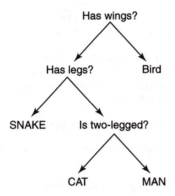

A program that adds a new animal to this tree might engage in the following dialogue with a user (user responses are italicized).

Has wings? *No*

Has legs? *Yes*

Is two-legged? *No*

Is it CAT? *No*

What is it? *COW*

Give me a characteristic that CAT has that COW does not have? *Has claws*

The program changes the tree to

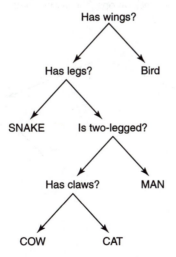

Write a program to maintain a tree of this type.

17. Write and test a function *LEVEL* that takes a tree *T* and integer *L* and reports the number of nodes at level *L* in *T* (assume the root is level zero, the children of the root are level one, and so on).

18. Write and test a function *LEVELPRINT* that takes as parameters a tree *T* and integer *L*. The function prints those nodes that are at level *L* in the tree.

19. Write and test a function that takes two strings of letters. One string represents an inorder traversal of a binary tree in which each node contains a letter; the second string represents a preorder traversal of the same tree. Assume no two nodes of the tree contain the same letter. The function is to

    a. Determine whether there can be such a tree.

    b. If there is a tree, by building the tree or otherwise, output a string representing a postorder traversal.

20. Write and test an operator that lets you combine two expression trees and a particular operator. For example, if the following are expression trees *E* and *F*, respectively:

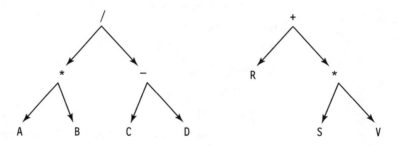

Then, given appropriate declarations, the assignment *G* = *E* * *F* should create the following expression tree *G*:

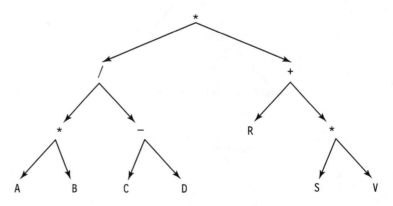

21. Improve the expression tree class by permitting identifiers to be strings of any length.

22. Add error checking to *treebuild* and make it a *bool* function that returns *true* only if a valid expression was read and a tree was built successfully.

23. Write and test a method for the *exptree* class that enables users to output the expression in a format of their choice.

References

Adle'son-Vel'skii, G. M., and E. M. Landis. 1962. An algorithm for the organization of information, English translation. *Soviet Math,* 3 (5): 1259–1263.

Bentley, J. L., and J. B. Saxe. 1979. Algorithms on vector sets. *SIGACT News,* 11 (9): 36–39.

Bentley, J. L., and R. Sedgewick. 1997. Fast algorithms for searching and sorting strings. Proceedings of the 8th Annual ACM-SIAM Symposium on Discrete Algorithms, New Orleans, January 5–7, 360–369.

Bentley, J. L., and R. Sedgewick. 1998. Ternary search trees. *Dr. Dobbs Journal,* 284: 20–22, 24, 25.

Clampett, H. A., Jr. 1964. Randomized binary searching with tree structures. *Communications of the ACM,* 7 (3): 163–165.

Fredkin, E. 1960. Trie memory. *Communications of the ACM,* 3 (9): 490–500.

Gonnet, G. H., and R. Baeza-Yates. 1991. *Handbook of Data Structures and Algorithms in Pascal and C,* 2d ed. Reading, MA: Addison-Wesley.

Huffman, D. A. 1952. A method for the construction of minimum-redundancy codes. *Proceedings of the I.R.E.,* 40 (9): 1098–1101.

Karlton, P. L., S. H. Fuller, R. E. Scroggs, and E. B. Kaehler. 1976. Performance of height-balanced trees. *Communications of the ACM,* 19 (1): 23–28.

Knuth, D. E. 1973. *Sorting and Searching.* Vol 3, *The Art of Computer Programming.* Reading, MA: Addison-Wesley.

Marsaglia, G. 2002. Diehard random number testing. http://stat.fsu.edu/~geo/diehard.html (accessed October 2002).

Salomon, D. 1998. *Data Compression: The Complete Reference.* New York: Springer-Verlag.

Unicode. 2002. http://www.unicode.org (accessed May 2003).

Vitter, J. S. 1987. Design and analysis of dynamic Huffman codes. *Journal of the ACM,* 34 (4): 825–845.

Vitter, J. S. 1989. Algorithm 673: Dynamic Huffman coding. *ACM Transactions on Mathematical Software,* 15 (2): 158–167.

Notes

[1]A tree is a special case of a **graph**. In a graph, we are free to have a link from any node to any other. We look at graphs in Chapter 7.

[2]Yes, the arboreal world is turned upside down in computer science. This is because operations on a tree typically begin with the root node, and it is easier to read down a page than up it.

[3]Using the successor instead of the predecessor would work equally well. The successor is the left-most node in the right subtree.

[4]*Fewestnodes*(h) = *Fib*(h + 3) − 1. From Fibonnaci theory

$$Fib(h) \approx \frac{\left[\dfrac{1+\sqrt{5}}{2}\right]^h}{\sqrt{5}}$$

therefore

$$Fewestnodes(h) \approx N \geq \frac{\left[\dfrac{1+\sqrt{5}}{2}\right]^{h+3}}{\sqrt{5}} - 1$$

from which we get

$h \leq 1.44 \log_2 (N + 1) - 1.328$

[5]The term *trie* (pronounced "try") is derived from retrieval and was suggested by Fredkin (1960).

[6]In practice, if the alphabet size is reasonably small, a trie is likely to have an array of pointers with an element for each possible character. This enables a search algorithm to use direct lookup to see if there is a pointer to the next level rather than a binary or linear search within a node as depicted in our figures.

[7]When we search Figure 6.37 for *mint*, we compare *t* with *c*, *e*, *n*, *r*, *s*, and *t* and then compare *m* with *d* and *m*. This is a total of eight comparisons. When we search for *there*, we compare *r* with *c*, *e*, *n*, and *r*, a total of four comparisons. The average over all eight words is 4.625 comparisons.

[8]For further details, see http://www.cs.princeton.edu/~rs/strings/.

[9]The trees shown are examples of those that could be constructed from the particular sets of elements.

[10]The test for *E.keycomponent(i)==wild* could be eliminated by defining the relational operators <, ==, and > so that a comparison with the wild card character always returns true.

[11]We can also get the 61 by adding up the weights on the nonleaf nodes of the tree.

chapter 7

Graphs

The definition of a tree (see Chapter 6) includes the requirement that subtrees be distinct. This means that each tree has a unique path from the root to a node. If we remove this restriction and permit links between any pair of nodes, then we have a **graph**. A tree is thus a special case of a graph, just as a linear list is a special case of a tree. Because of its generality, the graph data structure has many applications. This chapter examines the fundamental operations on a graph, ways in which a graph might be represented, and some common graph algorithms. Knuth (1993) created a set of general graph utilities and data files; the files of the Stanford GraphBase are available at *ftp://labrea.stanford.edu/pub/sgb*.

● 7.1.1 Terminology

Graph theory is rich in terminology; here we define some of the more important terms. A graph, in the data-structure sense, consists of a nonempty set of **vertices** (V) and a set (possibly empty) of **edges** (E). An edge E_{ij} has end points V_i and V_j, where i and j may be the same. We can distinguish between E_{ij} and E_{ji}. A graph in which there are multiple instances of edges with the same end points is a **multigraph**. For the most part, in this chapter we assume that the graph is not a multigraph. A graph is **complete** if every possible edge exists. Figure 7.1a depicts a

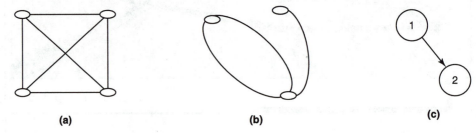

(a)   **(b)**   **(c)**

Figure 7.1 • Example graphs: (a) A complete graph with four vertices, (b) a complete graph with three vertices, (c) a two-vertex graph with one edge

complete graph with four vertices; Figure 7.1b depicts a multigraph with three vertices; and Figure 7.1c depicts a two-vertex graph in which there is an edge from V_1 to V_2, but not one from V_2 to V_1.

In a graph, a **path** exists from V_a to V_b if there is a sequence of edges starting at V_a and finishing at V_b in which the end vertex of one edge of the path is the same as the start vertex of the next. A **cycle** is a path in which the start and end points are the same. A graph containing a cycle is **cyclic**; one without a cycle is **acyclic**. A graph is **connected** if for each pair of distinct vertices there is a path from one member of the pair to the other; otherwise, the graph is **unconnected**.

In the graph shown in Figure 7.2a, the path from V_1 to V_4 goes via V_2, V_3, and V_5. Graph 7.2a is cyclic; for example, we can go from V_1 back to V_1 via V_2 or via V_2 and V_3. The graph depicted in Figure 7.2b is acyclic. Finally, by our definition, the graph of Figure 7.2b and the graph of Figure 7.2c are unconnected.

A graph is more general than a tree because there are no restrictions on the edges that can exist. (Recall that a tree may not contain multiple paths between vertices;

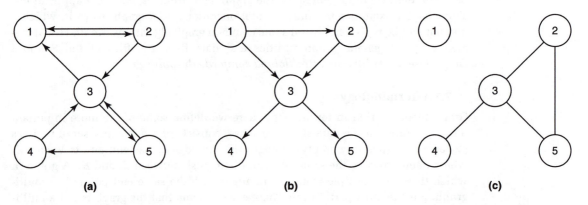

(a)   **(b)**   **(c)**

Figure 7.2 • Example graphs: (a) cyclic, (b) acyclic, (c) unconnected

therefore, it must be acyclic.) Graphs can be broadly categorized according to the characteristics of their edges:

- An **undirected** graph has edges with no associated direction. Figures 7.1a and 7.1b are undirected graphs.
- A **directed** graph is one in which the edges have a direction. Figures 7.2a and 7.2b are directed graphs. (A directed edge is sometimes termed an **arc**.) We can derive an undirected graph from a directed one by ignoring the directions on the edges.
- A **network** is a graph in which the edges have a weight or value associated with them.

In an undirected graph, the **degree** of a vertex is the number of edges that are attached to that vertex. In Figure 7.1a, all vertices are degree three, and in Figure 7.2c, V_5 is degree two. In a directed graph, we can distinguish between the **in-degree** of a vertex, which is the number of arcs that end at the vertex, and the **out-degree** of a vertex, which is the number of arcs that originate at that vertex. In Figure 7.2a, the in-degree of V_3 is three and the out-degree of V_3 is two.

7.1.2 Graphical Representations

The type of graph that should be used to represent an entity depends on the nature of the information that will be stored. The following sections describe four entities that might usefully be represented as graphs. Other entities that could be depicted as graphs, but that are not illustrated here, include the Internet, the phone system, the interstate freeway network, and the World Wide Web.

Airline Routes

A natural way to represent information about the routes that an airline flies is with a graph in which the vertices represent airports and the edges represent routes flown. Consider Figure 7.3. This is an undirected, connected graph in which the

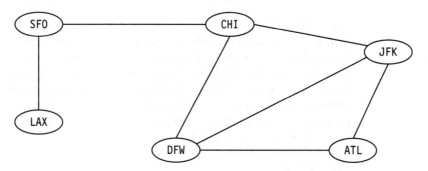

Figure 7.3 • Airline routes

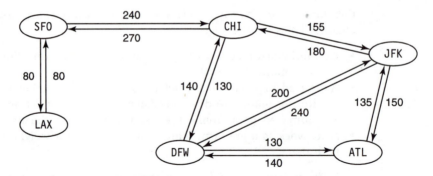

Figure 7.4 • Airports and flight times

degree of *SFO,* for example, is two, and the degree of *JFK* is three. In this instance, the degree of a vertex represents the number of cities with direct flights.

Alternatively, we could have a network such as that shown in Figure 7.4, in which scheduled flight time is associated with an edge.[1] Note that the value of E_{ij} is not necessarily equal to the value of E_{ji} (because of prevailing winds perhaps) and, on some graphs of this kind, might even be negative.

The graph of Figure 7.4 can be categorized as a directed network. A characteristic of this network (though not necessarily of all airline networks) is that the in-degree of a vertex is the same as its out-degree.

Family Trees

A multigenerational family tree of any size is likely to be, in reality, a "family graph" because a person may marry a distant relative and thus create two paths from any of their children to their parents' common ancestor. For example, in Figure 7.5, *Una* and *Victor* (the offspring of second cousins *Rose* and *Simon*) have two paths back to great-great-grandparents *Alice* and *Bill*. A family graph of the royal families of Europe has many instances of such multiple paths.

Program Graphs

A compiler can use a **precedence graph** to represent the order in which instructions have to be executed. In such a graph, edge E_{ij} indicates that, because of dependencies, the execution of instruction V_i must precede the execution of instruction V_j. The graph may enable the compiler to perform some optimizations. In a multiprocessor environment, the compiler may be able to assign instructions to different processors. Consider the following pseudocode program; Figure 7.6 shows the corresponding precedence graph.

```
100  f = 1.0
110  N = 0
120  read A,B
130  N = N+2
```

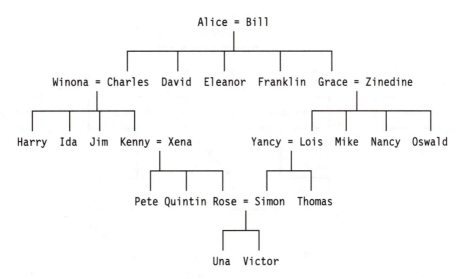

Figure 7.5 • A family graph

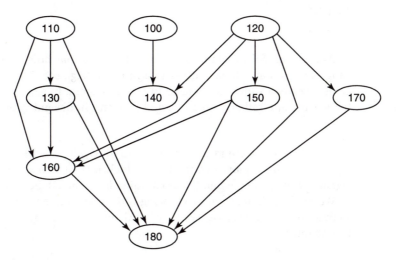

Figure 7.6 • Precedence graph

```
140 f = f * A * B
150 D = max (A,B)
160 N = N + D
170 Av = (A+B)*0.5
180 print Av,N
```

Only instructions 100 and 140 could be moved after 180 because the other six instructions directly or indirectly affect values used in instruction 180.

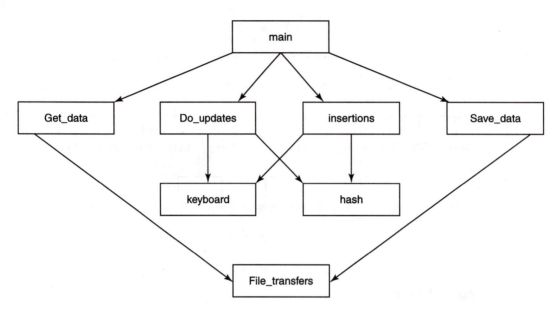

Figure 7.7 • Subprogram relationships

Another useful program-related graph is one that holds information about the subprograms that call each other in a program (e.g., see Figure 7.7) or the dependencies between software modules in a large system. In general, each of these structures is a graph rather than a tree and is useful in designing test sequences.

Circuits

Electronic circuits are rarely tree structured. Cycles are likely to be present, as in Figure 7.8, which shows a circuit for a clocked D latch, a simple 1-bit memory. The signal at *D* is latched when the clock value is 1. The latched value is available at *Q*.

We might be interested in knowing if the connections in a circuit can be routed so that no two wires cross. We look at this property of a graph in the last section of this chapter.

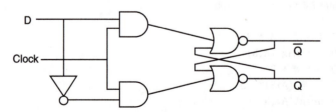

Figure 7.8 • Clocked D latch

7.2 Basic Graph Operations

The fundamental operations on the graph abstract data type are comparatively few:

- Add a vertex
- Delete a vertex
- Add an edge/arc
- Delete an edge/arc
- Get a list of the vertices directly reachable from vertex i

This list leads us to the following top-level definition for a *graph* class:

```
template <class vertex>
class graph
{
  public:  graph();        // constructor - initialize graph
           ~graph();        // destructor - tidy up any storage allocation
           bool isempty();  // true if no vertices
           int numvertices(); // return the number of vertices
           bool insertvertex (vertex v);
           bool deletevertex (vertex v);
           bool insertedge (vertex v1, vertex v2);
           bool deleteedge (vertex v1, vertex v2);
           list<vertex> adjacent(vertex v);

  private:
           // see implementation possibilities below
};
```

The template mechanism enables us to create a graph having objects of a particular class as its vertices. We could make our graph definition more general by enabling a value to be associated with an edge. This would require appropriate parameter changes to *insertedge* and possibly to *deleteedge*. As with earlier data structures, insert and delete operations return a *bool* value that indicates whether they succeeded. For example, if the graph is not a multigraph, then an attempt to add E_{ij} to a graph already containing E_{ij} will fail.

Other useful operations can be defined in terms of the fundamental ones. Examples are:

- *is-path*($v1,v2$): Indicates whether vertex $v2$ is reachable from vertex $v1$.
- *shortest-path*($v1,v2$): Returns the length of the shortest path from $v1$ to $v2$.
- *disconnected*(): Indicates if any part of the graph is isolated from the rest.

We next look at ways to implement a graph. Section 7.4 presents algorithms for common graph operations.

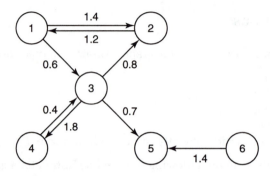

Figure 7.9 • Graph used for implementation methods

7.3 Graph Implementation

The six-vertex network shown in Figure 7.9 will be used to illustrate three ways to implement a graph: (1) using sets, (2) using an adjacency matrix, and (3) using linked storage.

7.3.1 Sets

We could take the formal definition of a graph literally and implement a graph using two sets, one of vertices and one of edges. Thus, the graph of Figure 7.9 would be represented:

Vertices [1 2 3 4 5 6]

Edges [(1,2,1.4) (2,1,1.2) (1,3,0.6) (3,2,0.8) (4,3,0.4) (3,4,1.8) (3,5,0.7) (6,5,1.4)]

Each member of the set of edges is a triple: (start vertex, end vertex, value). Operations defined on sets permit us to add and remove vertices and edges easily. However, constructing a list of the vertices that are connected directly to vertex i is not as straightforward.

7.3.2 Adjacency Matrix

The connectivity of an N-vertex graph can be represented by the entries in an N-by-N **adjacency matrix** M. Element M_{ij} contains information about edge E_{ij}. The information may be as simple as a *bool* value indicating whether the edge exists. It is worth noting that if the graph is undirected and the matrix contains only such connectivity data then $M_{ij} = M_{ji}$, the matrix is symmetric and thus we need to store only half of it. Alternatively, M_{ij} may contain a value or weight associated with E_{ij}. Figure 7.10 is an adjacency matrix for the network shown in Figure 7.9.

What entry is appropriate if there is no arc or edge E_{ij}? It depends on the semantics of the values. For example, if the value represents travel time and there is no route from V_i to V_j, then an entry of infinity might be appropriate. If M_{pq} represents

	1.4	0.6			
1.2					
	0.8		1.8	0.7	
		0.4			
				1.4	

Figure 7.10 • Adjacency matrix for the network in Figure 7.9

0	1	1	0	0	0
1	0	0	0	0	0
0	1	0	1	1	0
0	0	1	0	0	0
0	0	0	0	0	0
0	0	0	0	1	0

Figure 7.11 • Bit adjacency matrix for the network in Figure 7.9

the capacity in vehicles per hour of a road from V_p to V_q, and no such road exists, then zero is appropriate. If we want to represent just the existence of edges, M_{ij} need only be a single bit, as shown in Figure 7.11.

An advantage of using 1 and 0 rather than *true* and *false* is that the sum of the entries in column k gives us the in-degree of vertex V_k and the sum of the entries in row k gives us the out-degree of V_k. Furthermore, normal matrix multiplication gives us meaningful results. Multiplying the matrix of Figure 7.11 by itself gives us the matrix of Figure 7.12 (designated M^2).

Note that M^2_{ij} is the number of distinct paths of length two from V_i to V_j. For example, in Figure 7.11 we see that M_{32} is 1 and M_{42} is 0, indicating that a direct

1	1	0	1	1	0
0	1	1	0	0	0
1	0	1	0	0	0
0	1	0	1	1	0
0	0	0	0	0	0
0	0	0	0	0	0

Figure 7.12 • M^2: Square of the bit adjacency matrix of Figure 7.11

1	1	2	0	0	0
1	1	0	1	1	0
0	2	1	1	1	0
1	0	1	0	0	0
0	0	0	0	0	0
0	0	0	0	0	0

Figure 7.13 • M^3: Cube of the bit adjacency matrix of Figure 7.11

connection (path of length one) exists from V_3 to V_2, but that there is not a direct connection from V_4 to V_2. However, in Figure 7.12, we see that $M^2{}_{42}$ is 1 and $M^2{}_{32}$ is 0, indicating that a path of length two exists from V_4 to V_2, but no path of length two exists from V_3 to V_2.

If we cube the matrix of Figure 7.11, we get M^3, the matrix shown in Figure 7.13.

The matrix M^3 indicates where there are paths of length three. In general, $M^k{}_{ij}$ represents the number of paths of length k from V_i to V_j. For example, $M^3{}_{32}$ is 2; there are two paths of length three from V_3 to V_2 in the graph depicted in Figure 7.9, namely $V_3 \rightarrow V_2 \rightarrow V_1 \rightarrow V_2$ and $V_3 \rightarrow V_4 \rightarrow V_3 \rightarrow V_2$.

An adjacency matrix is a good way to represent a graph if the number of vertices is fixed, or at least bounded. But what if this is not the case?

• 7.3.3 Linked Storage

The matrix representation is awkward if the number of vertices can vary dynamically. Linked dynamic storage may be more convenient. We could have a linked list of vertex records and, rooted in each vertex record, a linked list of records representing the edges that originate in that vertex. We term this list an **adjacency list**. Each element in an adjacency list contains the number of the destination vertex and any weight associated with the edge. An alternative to using the vertex number of the destination is to use a pointer to the appropriate vertex. Figure 7.14 shows a linked list representation of the example graph from Figure 7.9.

If the graph is large enough, it may be beneficial to replace the linear lists with structures such as binary trees that can be searched faster. Other variations on the structure of Figure 7.14 are also possible. What if we need to quickly find those edges that end at a particular vertex? How would our list structure change if the graph were undirected?

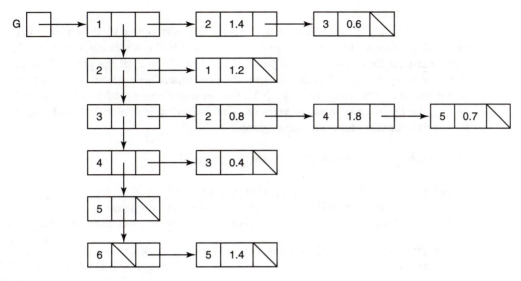

Figure 7.14 • Linked list representation of the network from Figure 7.9

If our graph is to be persistent, each of the representations that we have examined can be saved to a file and restored from a file in a straightforward manner.

7.4 Graph Algorithms

Because a graph is such a general structure, there are many algorithms of interest. This section looks at solutions to four problems:

1. Finding a path between two arbitrary vertices
2. Computing the transitive closure of a graph
3. Finding the shortest path between two vertices in a network
4. Finding a minimal spanning tree of a graph

7.4.1 Finding a Path

How can we tell if there is a path from V_i to V_j? Two possible approaches are a **breadth-first search** and a **depth-first search**.

Breadth-First Search

A *breadth-first* algorithm works outward from the start vertex V_i. It first examines the vertices adjacent to V_i, then the vertices adjacent to those vertices, and so on. In other words, it first checks all the paths of length one, then all the paths of length two, and so on. It stops if vertex V_j is reached or if there are no more vertices to be examined. If a path exists from V_i to V_j, the breadth-first approach finds the path having the fewest intermediate vertices. The following is a pseudo-C++ breadth-first search function for an *n*-vertex graph.

```
bool breadth_first_search (int i, int j, graph G)
  {
    queue<int> Q;              // vertices to check
    int n = G.numvertices();   // number of vertices in graph
    bool visited[n];           // whether or not vertex has been visited

    for (int k=0; k<n; k++) visited [k] = false; // mark all unvisited
    visited[i] = true;                           // except starting point

    Q.enqueue(i);              // start vertex

    while (!Q.empty())   // more vertices to check?
      {
        int current = Q.dequeue();  // first vertex number in the queue

        for (int k=0; k<n; k++)          // look at its neighbors
          if (G.exists_edge(current,k))    // edge to k?
            {
              if (k == j) return true; // found end-point, path exists

              if (!visited[k])
                {                          // haven't visited k yet
                  Q.enqueue(k);    // put it on the queue to visit
                  visited[k]=true; // and mark it
                }
            }
      }
    return false;  // no more to check, search for path is unsuccessful
  }
```

The algorithm works by maintaining a queue of vertices to visit. The starting vertex is the first to be queued. In the main loop, we dequeue a vertex and examine the vertices that are directly connected to it (its neighbors). If any of these vertices is the vertex we are trying to reach, we are done. Otherwise, we enqueue those neighbors that we have not yet visited. (We keep a simple map of which vertices have

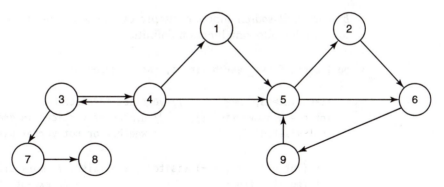

Figure 7.15 • Breadth-first path searches

been visited so that a vertex is not visited more than once.) If the queue becomes empty, then our search for a path has failed.

Consider the graph in Figure 7.15 and a search for a path from vertex 4 to vertex 9. The following is a trace of the function call *breadth_first_search(4,9,Fig7_15)*.

Enqueue 4

Current	Enqueued	Q (front on the left)
4	1, 3, 5	1 3 5
1	none - 5 already marked	3 5
3	7 (4 already marked)	5 7
5	2, 6	7 2 6
7	8	2 6 8
2	none - 6 already marked	6 8
6	none	

When we find an edge from vertex 6 to vertex 9, we know that a path from vertex 4 to vertex 9 exists.

Depth-First Search
An alternative path-finding strategy is a *depth-first* search. In a depth-first strategy, we follow one edge from each vertex until we reach the destination (and stop) or we reach a vertex that has already been visited. In the latter case, we back up to the last vertex at which we had a choice of edges to follow and then follow a different one. The strategy is similar to one we might adopt when trying to find a path through a maze. Note that we can create a *depth_first_search* function from the

breadth_first_search function simply by replacing the queue with a stack. This leads to the following function definition:

```
bool depth_first_search (int i, int j, graph G)
 {
   stack<int> S;             // vertices to check
   int n = G.numvertices();    // number of vertices in graph
   bool visited[n];            // whether or not vertex has been visited

   for (int k=0; k<n; k++) visited [k] = false; // mark all unvisited
   visited[i] = true;                      // except starting point

   S.push(i);

   while (!S.empty())    // more vertices to check?
     {
       int current = S.pop();  // top of the stack

       for (int k=0; k<n; k++)            // look at its neighbors
           if (G.exists_edge(current,k))    // edge to k?
             {
                 if (k == j) return true; // found end-point, path exists

                 if (!visited[k])
                   {                      // haven't visited k yet
                     S.push(k);       // push it on the stack to visit
                     visited[k]=true; // and mark it
                   }
             }
     }
   return false;  // no more to check, search for path is unsuccessful
 }
```

Using Figure 7.15 as our example graph, here is a trace of *depth_first_search* that was called to see if there is a path from vertex 3 to vertex 9.

Stack 3

Current	Pushed	S (top on the left)
3	4, 7	7 4
7	8	8 4
8	none	4
4	1, 5	5 1
5	2, 6	6 2 1
6	none	

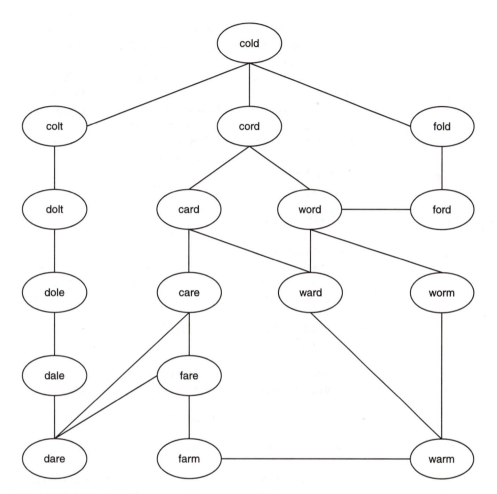

Figure 7.16 • Word graph

When an edge from vertex 6 to vertex 9 is found, we know that a path from vertex 3 to vertex 9 exists.

• 7.4.2 Identifying the Path

We might be interested both in the length of the path from V_i to V_j and in the particular vertices or edges in the path (as in the game *Six Degrees of Kevin Bacon*[2]). Consider Figure 7.16, which represents part of a graph of four-letter words. There is an edge between two words if they differ in exactly one letter position.

Graphs such as this are useful for solving *word-ladder* problems. The objective in a word-ladder problem is to find a sequence of words linking a particular start and finish pair, changing only one letter at a time. An example sequence linking *mark* to *coin* is

mark → park → pork → cork → corn → coin

Often the start and finish words are related. For example, we may wish to transform *cold* to *warm* changing only one letter at a time. This is equivalent to finding a path from *cold* to *warm* in Figure 7.16.

Our breadth-first search algorithm tells us whether a path exists between the start and finish vertices. However, if there is a path, how do we identify the intermediate vertices? One way is to have the search algorithm tag each vertex it visits with its distance from the start vertex. The following is an augmented version of our *breadth_first_search* algorithm that does just this. In addition to the queue of vertices, we maintain a parallel queue of tags. The tags are attached to vertices during the search process. As a side effect, we know the length of the shortest path, thus the revised algorithm returns the path length or −1 if there is no path.

```
int breadth_first_search2 (int i, int j, graph G)
 {
    queue<int> Q;                   // vertices to check
    queue<int> tags;                // parallel queue of tags for vertices
    int n = G.numvertices();        // number of vertices in graph
    bool visited[n];                // whether or not vertex has been visited

    for (int k=0; k<n; k++) visited [k] = false; // mark all unvisited
    visited[i] = true;                           // except starting point

    Q.enqueue(i);          // start vertex
    tags.enqueue(0);       // is distance 0 from itself

    addtag(i,0);           // put tag in start vertex

    while (!Q.empty())     // more vertices to check?
      {
        int current = Q.dequeue();   // first vertex number in the queue
        int currenttag = tags.dequeue(); // corresponding tag;

        for (int k=0; k<n; k++)              // look at its neighbors
          if (G.exists_edge(current,k))     // edge to k?
            {
              if (!visited[k])
                {
                  // haven't visited k yet
                  addtag(k,currenttag+1);// tag it with distance
                  if (k == j)              // is it the end-point?
                    return currenttag+1; // yes, return distance
                  Q.enqueue(k);     // put it on the queue to visit
                  tags.enqueue(currenttag+1); // and its distance
```

```
                    visited[k]=true; // and mark it
                }
            }
        }
    return -1;  // no more to check, search for path is unsuccessful
    }
```

Figure 7.17 shows the result of applying this tagging to the word graph in Figure 7.16. (There are other equivalent tagged graphs depending on the order in which vertices are visited.)

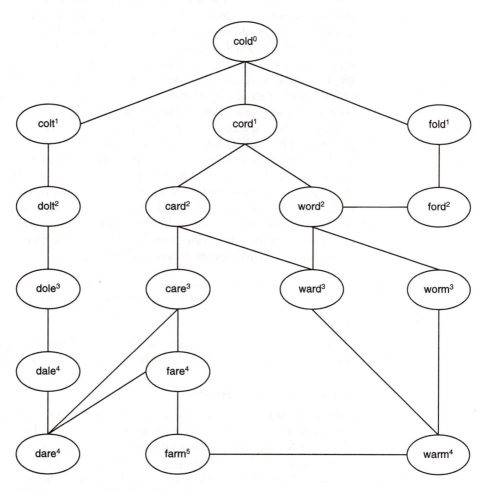

Figure 7.17 • Tagged word graph

To identify a path from *cold* to *warm*, we start at the end vertex (at *warm* with tag 4) and retrace a path to the beginning vertex (*cold* with tag 0), looking successively for vertices with tags 3, 2, 1, and 0. If there is a choice of vertices, it does not matter which one we select; it just means that there is not a unique path. As we find the vertices, we place them on a stack. When we have finished, popping the stack gives us a path from to *cold* to *warm*, for example:

cold → cord → word → ward → warm

7.4.3 Graph-Traversal Problem Solvers

The graph traverser once was a popular problem-solving paradigm in artificial intelligence research. Conceptually, the initial state of a problem is represented by one vertex on a graph, and one or more goal states are represented by other vertices. Additionally, if problem state A can be transformed into problem state B, then there is an arc from the vertex representing A to the vertex representing B. The role of the graph-traversal program is to find a path from the initial vertex to a goal vertex. Either a depth-first or a breadth-first strategy could be used (or we could even start concurrent searches at each end and try to find a common vertex in the middle).

Figure 7.18 is a graphical representation of a well-known puzzle. A farmer has to transport himself (*f*), a wolf (*w*), a goat (*g*), and a cabbage (*c*) across a river. The available boat is large enough to carry only the farmer and one other object or animal. However, if left unsupervised by the farmer, the goat will eat the cabbage; similarly, an unsupervised wolf will eat the goat. Wolves do not eat cabbages. In our representation of a vertex, the vertical bar separates those objects on the left bank of the river from those on the right. For example, if the farmer, goat, and wolf are on the left bank (with the cabbage on the right bank), and the farmer ferries the wolf across, the following representation can be used.

Note that there are two paths from the initial state to the goal state, as well as several dead ends when one or more items has been irreversibly eaten.

7.4.4 Transitive Closure

Note the transitive property of graph paths. That is, if there is a path from V_a to V_b and a path from V_b to V_c, then there is a path from V_a to V_c. The **transitive closure** of a graph G is a graph T_G having the same set of vertices as G. There is an arc E_{ij} in T_G if there is a path V_i to V_j in G. Figure 7.19 gives an example.

It is useful to know which vertices can be reached from which others. The transitive closure tells us, for example, if the graph is connected. If the out-degree of a ver-

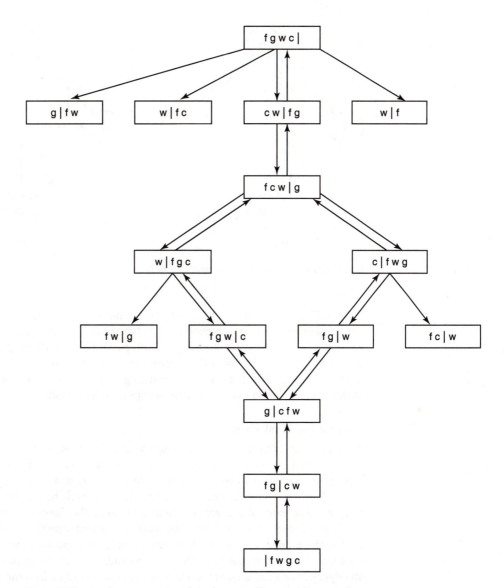

Figure 7.18 • Graph representation of the farmer-wolf-goat-cabbage puzzle

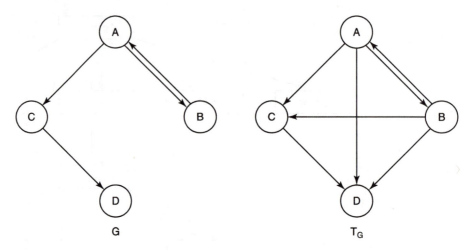

Figure 7.19 • Graph G and its transitive closure T_G

tex V in T_G is less than $N - 1$ (where N is the number of vertices), then there is at least one vertex that cannot be reached from V. Given an organizational chart of a company, we might be interested in knowing which people report (directly or indirectly) to a particular person. The transitive closure of the chart tells us this. We would expect the transitive closure of a graph representing airline routes to be complete. At the end of the next section is a short note on computing the transitive closure.

7.4.5 Shortest Path

A common problem is to find the shortest path between an arbitrary pair of vertices. If we need the path having the fewest edges, we can use the breadth-first search algorithm described in Section 7.4.1. More generally, a weight is associated with each edge in the graph, and we need to find the path having the smallest total of weights. For example, a graph might represent the layout of streets in a town. Vertices represent intersections and edges represent streets. If a distance is associated with an edge, then a shortest-path algorithm might help us identify the shortest route from our house to each local gas station. If travel time is associated with an edge, then a shortest-path algorithm helps paramedics find the fastest route from each intersection to the hospital.

Dijkstra (1959) devised an algorithm that finds the lengths of the shortest paths from a particular vertex V_i to each of the other reachable vertices. The algorithm can be generalized to find the length of the shortest path from any V_i to any V_j and extended to report the sequence of vertices found along that path.

Dijkstra's algorithm uses a set S of vertex numbers. The vertices in S are those for which we already know the length of the shortest path from the start vertex V_i. The algorithm uses an array *distance* with as many elements as the graph has vertices. The algorithm iterates as long as there are vertices not in S that are reachable from V_i. In each iteration, it adds a vertex v to S and then checks to see if any distance can be reduced by using edges originating at v. When the algorithm terminates, *distance*[k] will hold the length of the shortest path to from V_i to V_k. Here is a pseudo-C++ implementation of the algorithm.

```cpp
void dijkstra (int i, float distance[], graph G)
{  // Dijkstra's shortest path algorithm.
   // Vertices numbered V0 to VN-1

     set<int> S;
     int n = G.numvertices();

     S.insert(i);  // assume we know distance from i to itself

     for (int k=0; k < n; k++) // initialize distance with edge data
             if (k == i)               distance[k] = 0.0;
       else if (G.exists_edge(i,k)) distance[k] = G.weight(i,k);
                             else  distance[k] = infinity;

     while ( S.size() < n )
        {
          // get smallest element from distance that is associated
          // with a vertex not yet in S

          int v = smallest_distance_i_where_i_not_in_S();

          if (distance[v] == infinity) return;  // no more reachable

          S.insert(v); // now know smallest distance to v
          // see if any element of distance can be reduced
          for (int w = 0; w < n; w++)
            if (G.exists_edge(v,w) && !S.ismember(w))
              distance[w] = min( distance[w],distance[v]+G.weight(v,w) );
        }
}
```

As an example of how this algorithm works, consider the network shown in Figure 7.20.

Here is a trace of the shortest-path algorithm with $i = 3$. Initially,

	0	1	2	3	4	5	6
distance	20	∞	4	0	20	4	8

$S = [3]$

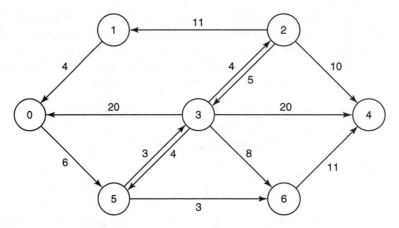

Figure 7.20 • Network to illustrate Dijkstra's shortest-path algorithm

The following shows what happens as we iterate around the *while* loop (changed array values are shown in bold).

	v = 2 *S* = [3 2] *w*. 1, 4, 3		*distance*	20	**15**	4	0	**14**	4	8

	v = 5 *S* = [3 2 5] *w*. 3, 6		*distance*	20	15	4	0	14	4	**7**

	v = 6 *S* = [3 2 5 6] *w*. 4		*distance*	20	15	4	0	14	4	7

	v = 4 *S* = [3 2 5 6 4] *w*. –		*distance* unchanged

	v = 1 *S* = [3 2 5 6 4 1] *w*. 0		*distance*	**19**	15	4	0	14	4	7

	v = 0 *S* = [3 2 5 6 4 1 0] *w*. 5		*distance*	19	15	4	0	14	4	7

A generalization of the shortest-path problem is to determine the shortest path between all possible pairs of vertices in *G*. The result will be a two-dimensional array in which $distance_{ij}$ represents the length of the shortest path from V_i to V_j. The algorithm in the following function was discovered independently by Floyd (1962) and Warshall (1962).

```
void floyd_warshall (float distance[][], graph G)
   {
```

```
int n = G.numvertices();

// initialize distance
for (int i=0; i< n; i++)
for (int j=0; j< n; j++)
      if (j == i)               distance[i][j] = 0.0;
 else if (G.exists_edge(i,j)) distance[i][j] = G.weight(i,j);
                    else      distance[i][j] = infinity;

// now see if any of the entries can be reduced
for (int i=0; i< n; i++)
for (int j=0; j< n; j++)
for (int k=0; k< n; k++)
   distance[j][k]= min(distance[j][k],
                         distance[j][i]+distance[i][k]
                       );

}
```

It is worth noting that when the algorithm terminates, the largest number in *distance* represents the **diameter** of the graph. This is the length of the longest shortest path between any two vertices in the graph.[3]

We can modify the Floyd–Warshall algorithm to produce the transitive closure as follows:

- Make *distance* a Boolean matrix.
- Initialize *distance*[i][j] to *true* if there is an edge V_{ij}, and *false* otherwise.
- Replace the assignment in the triple-nested loop by

```
distance[j][k] = distance[j][k] || (distance[j][i] && distance[i][k]);
```

When the function terminates, *distance*[i][j] is true if V_j is reachable from V_i, and false otherwise.

• 7.4.6 Spanning Tree

The **spanning tree** of a graph is a subset of the edges that forms a tree (i.e., is connected and contains no cycles) and includes every vertex. Often we are interested in the spanning tree having minimum total weight on its edges—the **minimum spanning tree**. Figure 7.21a is a network. Figure 7.21b is a subset of the edges of the network, but it is not a tree because it contains a cycle. Figure 7.21c is a spanning tree (total of the edge weights is 26), and Figure 7.21d is a minimum spanning tree. No spanning tree exists for the network of 7.21a having a smaller total edge length than the 22 of Figure 7.21d.

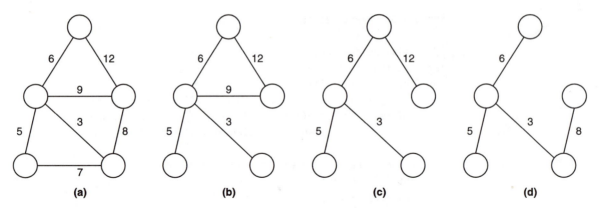

Figure 7.21 • (a) Network, (b) subset but no tree, (c) spanning tree, and (d) minimum spanning tree

Suppose we have a graph in which vertices represent cities, edges represent inter-city roads, and the distance between the end points of an edge represents the distance between cities. We want to upgrade some roads to freeway quality so that a driver can drive from any city to any other using only freeways, but we want to build the fewest total miles of freeway. We thus need to identify the minimum spanning tree of the graph; it will contain the roads that should be upgraded. A similar problem to which the minimum spanning tree provides a solution is that of finding the least wiring necessary to bring power to each component in a particular circuit board.

We look at two algorithms for finding a minimum spanning tree: the one devised by Kruskal (1956) and the one devised by Prim (1957). For a particular graph, the trees produced by each algorithm have the same total length; the algorithms differ in the way that a spanning tree is derived.

Kruskal's Algorithm

In Kruskal's (1956) minimum spanning tree algorithm, edges are considered in non-decreasing order of weight. They are added one at a time to what, in general, is a forest of trees, except that any edge that forms a cycle in an existing tree is rejected. The algorithm stops when a tree containing every vertex is identified by the algorithm or when it is found that no spanning tree is possible. If there are N vertices and the graph is connected, then there will be $N - 1$ edges in the spanning tree. Here is a pseudo-C++ function implementing Kruskal's algorithm in which T is a set of edges representing the spanning tree thus far. The function returns *true* if a spanning tree can be constructed and *false* otherwise.

```
bool kruskal (graph G, set<edge> T)
{
 int n = G.numvertices();
 graph temp = G;      // working copy of G from which we can delete edges
```

```
T.clear();          // make the set empty

while (T.size() < n-1 && temp.numedges() > 0)
  {
    edge e = temp.smallestedge();      // smallest in copy of graph
    temp.deleteedge(e);                // now delete from copy
    if (non_cyclic(T,e))               // see text for details
        T.insert(e);
  }
if (T.size() < n-1) return false; // no spanning tree possible
              else return true;  // minimum spanning tree edges are in T
}
```

How can we tell if the addition of an edge to an existing set of edges will form a cycle? One way is to maintain disjoint sets of vertices such that all vertices in the same set are connected. If the end points of our candidate edge are in the same set, then it is rejected because it will form a cycle. If its end points are in different sets, then it is added to the spanning tree and the two sets containing its end points are combined into one. Initially, we will have n vertex sets, each with one member. As we add edges, the sets will become fewer and larger until one set contains all n vertices.

Consider the seven-vertex undirected network shown in Figure 7.22. We will use it to illustrate Kruskal's and Prim's algorithms.

The following is a trace of Kruskal's algorithm applied to the graph of Figure 7.22 showing the order in which edges are considered.

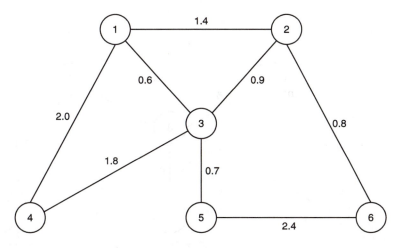

Figure 7.22 • Example undirected graph for spanning tree algorithms

```
Edge  Weight  Vertex sets                           T

1,3   0.6     [1 3]  [2]  [4]  [5]  [6]              [(1,3)]
3,5   0.7     [1 3 5]  [2]  [4]  [6]                 [(1,3)(3,5)]
2,6   0.8     [1 3 5]  [2 6]  [4]                     [(1,3)(3,5)(2,6)]
2,3   0.9     [1 2 3 5 6]  [4]                        [(1,3)(3,5)(2,6)(2,3)]
1,2   1.4     rejected: 1 and 2 are in same set
3,4   1.8     [1 2 3 4 5 6]                           [(1,3)(3,5)(2,6)(2,3)(3,4)]
```

The two longest edges—1,4 and 5,6—are not used. Figure 7.23 shows the spanning tree identified by the algorithm. It has a total weight of 4.8.

Prim's Algorithm

As with Kruskal's algorithm, Prim's algorithm (1957) represents the spanning tree by the set of edges (*T*) that comprise it. Again, edges are considered in nondescending order of weight. Prim's algorithm differs from Kruskal's in that the partial spanning tree is a single connected tree at all stages. An edge is rejected (as cycle forming) if both its ends are the ends of edges already in *T*. A pseudo-C++ implementation of Prim's algorithm follows.

```cpp
bool prim (graph G, set<edge> T)
{

int n = G.numvertices();
edge e;
```

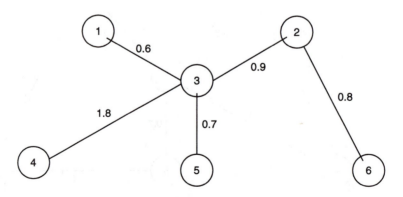

Figure 7.23 • Spanning tree for the graph in Figure 7.22

```
T.clear();              // make the set empty
T.insert( edge(i,j) )   // ij is the shortest edge

while (T.size() < n-1)
   {
     if (G.find_smallest_edge_one_end_in_T_other_not_in_T(e))
           T.insert(e);
     else
           break;                  // no candidate edges available
   }
if (T.size() < n-1) return false;   // no spanning tree possible
            else return true;   // minimum spanning tree in T
}
```

Here is a trace of Prim's algorithm on the graph from Figure 7.22.

```
Edge    Weight   T
1,3      0.6     [(1,3)]
3,5      0.7     [(1,3)(3,5)]
2,3      0.9     [(1,3)(3,5)(2,3)]
2,6      0.8     [(1,3)(3,5)(2,3)(2,6)]
3,4      1.8     [(1,3)(3,5)(2,3)(2,6)(3,4)]
```

We end up again with the tree shown in Figure 7.23. Note that equivalent trees (same total weight) are produced whether we use Kruskal's algorithm or Prim's algorithm. Additionally, if the algorithms are given the same ordering of the edges, they will produce identical trees.

7.5 Activity Networks

An **activity network** is a graph in which activities are associated with vertices, edges, or both. We consider two types of activity networks: (1) activity on vertex and (2) activity on edge.

7.5.1 Activity on Vertex

You are familiar with graphs of this kind if you have seen the requirements of a degree program presented as courses (vertices) with links representing prerequisites. Consider, for example, the network shown in Figure 7.24. The activity associated with a vertex is the taking of a particular course; an edge from X to Y means that course X must be taken before course Y.

A **topological ordering** of the vertices in a graph is a list in which V_i precedes V_j if there is an edge E_{ij}. Note that no such ordering is possible if the graph is cyclic.

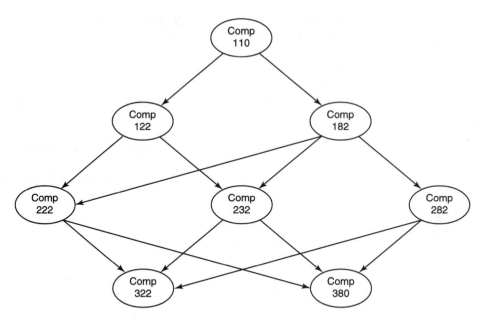

Figure 7.24 • An activity-on-vertex network

An acyclic graph may have many possible topological orderings. In the case of Figure 7.24, a topological ordering would show the order in which courses could be taken (taking one course at a time) while adhering to the prerequisites. A pseudocode algorithm to produce a topological ordering is:

```
while (any vertices left)
{
  identify a vertex (v) with no incoming edges
  if no v exists exit  // no ordering possible
  append v to the ordering
  remove v from the graph and all the edges that originate at v
}
```

Multiple orderings are possible if we have a choice of vertices. The following two orderings are among those possible for the graph in Figure 7.24.

110   122   182   222   232   282   322   380

110   182   282   122   232   222   380   322

• 7.5.2 Activity on Edge

Many projects can be broken down into subprojects, some of which can be completed in parallel whereas others have to be completed serially. For example, the network shown in Figure 7.25 represents the construction (greatly simplified) of a house. Activities in this type of graph are associated with edges rather than vertices. In Figure 7.25, numbers in parentheses represent the time units required to complete the activity.

Of interest here are the earliest and latest times that each activity can begin without delaying the project. Those activities for which these two times are the same are on the project's **critical path**. A delay in completing any activity on the critical path will delay the project as a whole.

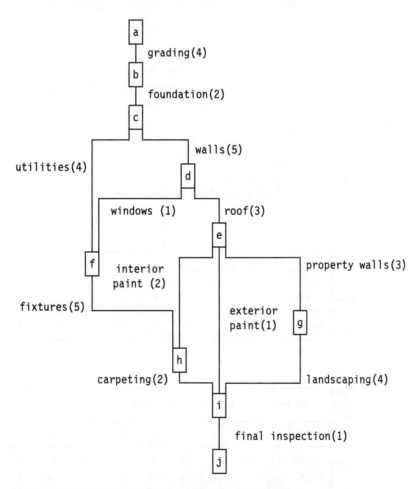

Figure 7.25 • House construction: An activity-on-edge network

Earliest Times

First we compute the earliest time at which each vertex can start. We do this by moving through the graph considering vertices in topological order V_0, V_1, V_2, . . . as defined in Section 7.5.1. The earliest start time of vertex V_0 is 0. For V_p ($p \neq 0$), it is the largest value of

$$earliest(V_k) + weight(E_{kp})$$

for those k where there is an edge E_{kp}. For the graph in Figure 7.25, this leads us to the data shown in Table 7.1.

For example, vertex i can be reached no earlier than time 21 because even though *exterior painting* can be completed as early as time 15 ($earliest(e) + 1$) and *carpeting* by time 19 ($earliest(h) + 2$), *landscaping* cannot be completed until time 21 ($earliest(g) + 4$).

Latest Times

The latest start time for each vertex is then computed by moving back through the graph in reverse topological order. The latest start time of vertex V_{max} is $earliest(V_{max})$. For V_p ($p \neq max$), it is the smallest of

$$latest(V_k) - weight(E_{pk})$$

for those k where there is an edge E_{pk}. For the graph in Figure 7.25, these calculations lead to the data shown in Table 7.2.

The critical path, in which start and finish times are the same, is a-b-c-d-e-g-i-j.

● **TABLE 7.1** Earliest Event Start Times Derived from Figure 7.25

Vertex	a	b	c	d	e	f	g	h	i	j
Earliest start time	0	4	6	11	14	12	17	17	21	22

● **TABLE 7.2** Earliest and Latest Times Derived from Figure 7.25

Vertex	a	b	c	d	e	f	g	h	i	j
Earliest start time	0	4	6	11	14	12	17	17	21	22
Latest start time	0	4	6	11	14	14	17	19	21	22

7.6 The Seven Bridges of Königsburg

Perhaps the seven bridges of Königsburg problem should have been the first topic in this chapter because it was Euler's consideration of this problem that many cite as the beginning of graph theory.

Figure 7.26 is a depiction of part of the Prussian city of Königsburg at the beginning of the 1700s; it shows the river Pregel, Kneiphof Island, and seven bridges labeled *a* through *g*.

Citizens were curious as to why they could not walk around the city crossing each bridge only once and return to their starting point. Imagine that you are the city bridge inspector. Pick an arbitrary starting point and try to carry out your inspection by crossing each bridge only once and returning to your starting point. For example, if you start on the island and cross bridges *a*, *b*, *e*, *f*, *d*, and *c*, you are now stranded on the north bank and cannot cross bridge *g* without first recrossing one of the bridges. Similarly, if you start on the north bank and cross bridges *c*, *d*, *b*, *a*, *e*, and *f*, then you are stuck on the island.

The problem came to the attention of the mathematician Euler (1736). He reduced the topology to the graph shown in Figure 7.27 in which each vertex represents one of the four land masses and each edge is one of the bridges.

The number shown in a vertex is the degree of that vertex because it is the degree of the vertices that determine whether a tour is possible. In graph theory terms, this tour is a **Eulerian cycle**. Traversing the graph, visiting each edge exactly once and starting and finishing at the same vertex, is possible only if all the vertices are of even degree (i.e., degree two, four, or six, etc.) This makes sense because if we enter a vertex by an edge, we need to be able to leave by a previously unused edge, thus

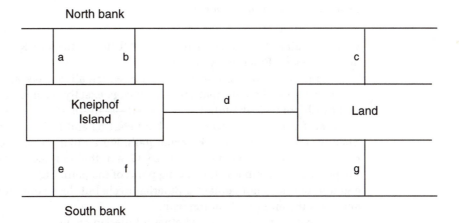

Figure 7.26 • Simplified depiction of Königsburg

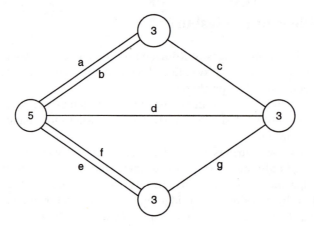

Figure 7.27 • Königsburg as a graph

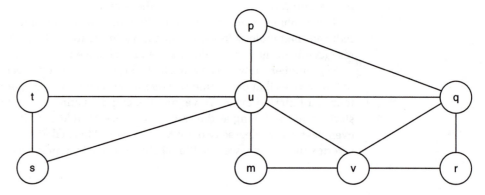

Figure 7.28 • Graph with a Eulerian cycle

we need pairs of edges at each vertex. All the vertices in Königsburg are of odd degree, thus no Eulerian cycle exists.

Figure 7.28 is an example of a graph in which all vertices are of even degree.

An example of a path that visits each edge exactly once (and has the same start and finish point) is the following: p→u→t→s→u→m→v→u→q→v→r→q→p

What if we relax the condition about starting and finishing at the same vertex? Then we are interested in a **Eulerian path**. For a Eulerian path to exist, all but two of the vertices must be of even degree. One of the odd-degree vertices is the starting point and the other is the ending point of the path. Figure 7.29 is an example of a graph that does not contain a Eulerian cycle but does contain a Eulerian path; *q* and *v* are the end points of the path.

We have a simple test for whether a Eulerian cycle or path is possible. Fleury's algorithm (1883) finds the actual path or cycle (see Exercises).

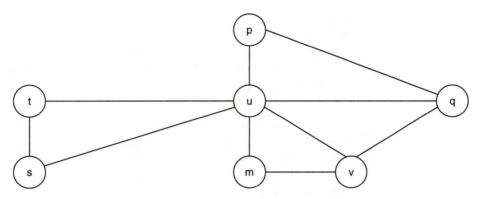

Figure 7.29 • Graph with Eulerian path but no cycle

7.6.1 Königsburg Today

The city that used to be Königsburg in Prussia is now the city of Kaliningrad in the Russian enclave between Lithuania and Poland; the river has been renamed the Pregolya. The original bridges were destroyed in the Second World War. Figure 7.30 shows the nonrail bridges in the part of Kaliningrad comparable with Figure 7.26.

Whether a cycle or a tour is now possible is left as an exercise.

7.6.2 Applications of Eulerian Paths and Cycles

Suppose our graph represents the road layout of part of a town—edges are streets and vertices are intersections. A weight on an edge might represent the number of houses in a street, the length of the street, or the time required to traverse it.

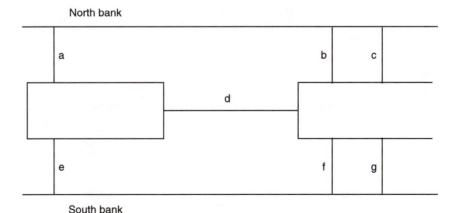

Figure 7.30 • The seven bridges of Kaliningrad

Consider the problem of finding a minimal-length route to be followed by a service that must visit every house; examples are trash pick-up and mail delivery.[4] If a Eulerian cycle or a Eulerian path exists, we can find a route that traverses each street exactly once. Finding the minimal-length route otherwise is an example of an NP-complete problem.

7.6.3 Hamiltonian Paths and Cycles

There is a dual concept to Eulerian paths and cycles. A **Hamiltonian path** is a path that visits each vertex in a graph exactly once, and a **Hamiltonian cycle** is a cycle that visits each vertex exactly once. In the Traveling Salesman problem (also NP-complete), vertices represent cities, each of which has to be visited by a salesperson. The problem is to find a route that minimizes the sum of the weights on the traversed edges (typically travel time or distance).

7.7 Planar Graphs

A **planar graph** is one that can be drawn on a plane (two-dimensional surface) with no edges crossing. It is useful when designing circuits to be etched onto chips, for example, to know whether a graph representing the components and their connections is planar. A necessary (but not sufficient) condition for a graph to be planar is:

number of edges ≤ (3 * *number of vertices*) − 6

Consider the problem of supplying three different utilities to three houses without any wires/pipes crossing. Try it using Figure 7.31.

It cannot be done. According to the inequality in the equation, a planar graph with six vertices can have up to 12 edges (3 * 6 − 6), but 4 of these are house-to-house or utility-to-utility connections, leaving us with a maximum of 8 utility-to-house edges, and we need 9.

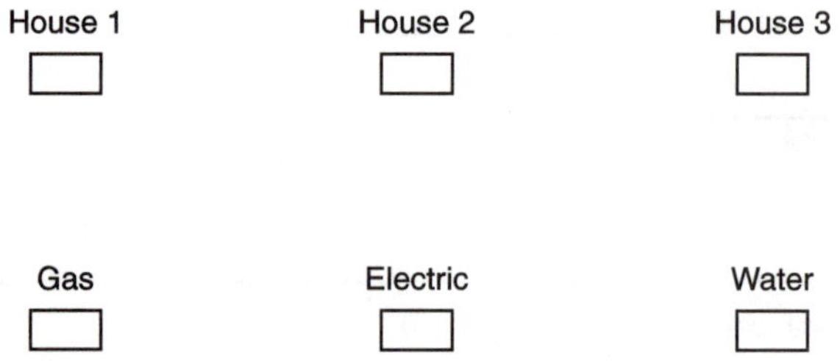

House 1   House 2   House 3

Gas   Electric   Water

Figure 7.31 • Three houses, three utilities problem

● Chapter Summary

This chapter examined the graph data structure. Because of its general nature, graphs can be used to represent a wide range of entities from transportation networks to family trees to electrical circuits to dependencies in a computer program.

Formally, a graph is a set of vertices and a set of edges, but graphs can be represented in a variety of ways. We saw how adjacency matrices and linked storage could be used. Graph algorithms were also examined, including those for finding a path between two vertices and for finding a tree that spans all the vertices.

Activity networks are a graph subclass that can be useful in planning projects and identifying critical subtasks. Finally, we considered the problem that led Euler to originate graph theory and noted that some graph-related problems are NP-complete.

This chapter concludes Part One of the text and our examination of simple, main memory-based data structures. In Chapter 1, we noted that some object implementations are likely to use secondary memory for space or persistence reasons. In Part Two of the text, we look at some aspects of persistent structures. In the next chapter, we look at secondary memory from the bottom up. First we consider characteristics of disc systems and then examine ways to improve the apparent performance of a disc drive. Finally, we look at how an operating system might use discs to store files.

● Exercises

1. How many edges are there in a complete graph with *N* vertices

   a. If the graph is undirected?

   b. If the graph is directed?

2. Is it possible to have an undirected graph in which there is an odd number of vertices of odd degree? If not, why not? If so, draw one.

3. Why might a graph showing aircraft flight times contain negative numbers?

4. Draw the precedence graph for the following sequence of instructions in a C-type language:

   1: a = 0

   2: read(b)

   3: c = a + b

   4: a++

   5: c++

   6: d = c - 5

   7: b++

   8: print a,c,d

   9: x = d / 2

   10: b = b + d

5. Choose one implementation of a graph and define an addition operator (+). The result of adding graphs *G1* and *G2* is a graph having the union of the vertices of *G1* and *G2* and the union of their edges.

6. How would Dijkstra's algorithm need to be modified to work correctly on multigraphs?

7. Would Dijkstra's algorithm work correctly if some weights are negative? What about the algorithm of Floyd and Warshall?

8. Apply Dijkstra's algorithm to vertices 1, 2, and 3 in the following graph.

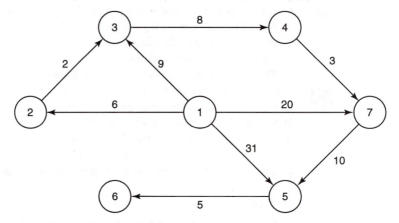

9. Dijkstra's algorithm enables us to find for a given vertex V_j the shortest distance from V_i to each of the other vertices. Sketch an algorithm that for a given vertex V_j lets us find the length of the shortest path from each of the other vertices to V_j. Note that it is not generally the case that the length of the edge from V_p to V_q is the same as the length of the edge from V_q to V_p.

10. Given a graph represented by an adjacency matrix, how can you tell whether the graph is cyclic?

11. Suppose you were empowered by the burghers of Königsburg to build additional bridges so that a tour would be possible. What is the fewest number of bridges you would need to build? Where would you build them?

12. Suppose the burghers of Königsburg let you move an existing bridge so that a tour would be possible. Which bridge would you move? Where would you move it to?

13. What is the fewest number of bridges that would have to be removed from Königsburg in order to make a tour possible? Give details to support your answer.

14. Is it possible to devise a Eulerian cycle or path using the bridges of Kaliningrad? Explain.

15. Suppose that we have an *N*-vertex directed graph. We represent the connectivity of the graph using an adjacency matrix (*M*) in which M_{ij} is 1 if there is an edge from V_i to V_j, and 0 otherwise. Give an algorithm (in C++ or pseudocode) that outputs a topological ordering of the vertices. Your algorithm may destroy the contents of the matrix if necessary.

16. Modify the topological ordering algorithm so that at each iteration it identifies (and outputs as a set) all the vertices of in-degree zero and then removes them from the graph. What is the output when this modified algorithm is applied to Figure 7.24?

17. Modify the topological ordering algorithm so that at each iteration it identifies up to k vertices of in-degree zero. What is the output when this algorithm is applied to Figure 7.24? How do you interpret this output?

18. Extend the modified topological sort algorithm of Exercise 16 so that it remembers the size of the largest set that it outputs. What is the significance of this number when you apply the algorithm to a dependency graph such as that in Figure 7.6?

19. Consider the circuit diagram in Figure 7.8 as a graph. How many vertices does it have? How many edges? Currently, edges cross; can it be redrawn without edges crossing?

20. Consider a generalization of the three-house, three-utilities problem. Write a function that takes two integer parameters, M and N, and determines if M houses can be connected to N utilities with a planar graph. Using this function, or otherwise, create a table showing which combinations are planar for N from 1 to 4 and M from 1 to 4.

21. Consider parts a through d in the following figure. Determine whether each part can be drawn by hand without taking the pen or pencil off the paper and without going over the same line more than once. What if the requirement is that you start and finish at the same point? Give reasons for your answers.

(a)　　　　　　(b)　　　　　　(c)　　　　　　(d)

22. Consider parts a and b in the following figure. For each, determine whether it is possible to draw a continuous line that crosses each line segment exactly once. What if it were required that the line be a closed curve? (Hint: Think how each figure might be represented as a graph and how the test for Eulerian cycles and paths would apply.)

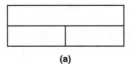 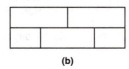

(a)　　　　　　　　　　(b)

23. Consider a groundskeeper marking soccer pitches as shown in the following figure. For each pitch, determine if it is possible to mark out the pitch without lifting the line-drawing machine off the ground and without going over any line more than once.

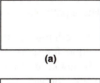 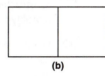

(a)　　　　　　　　　　(b)

 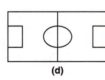

(c)　　　　　　　　　　(d)

24. Write and test functions *Eulercycle* and *Eulerpath*. Each takes an adjacency matrix as a parameter and determines whether the graph represented by the matrix contains an Eulerian cycle or an Eulerian path, respectively.

25. We considered Eulerian paths and circuits in undirected graphs. What are the conditions for a directed graph to contain (a) an Eulerian cycle or (b) an Eulerian path?

● Problems

1. Complete the definition of the *graph* class using an adjacency matrix implementation.

2. Complete the definition of the *graph* class using linked storage. Assume the existence of the *list* class.

3. Suppose that the vertices in a network represent subprograms in a program and the weight on edge V_{ij} represents the frequency with which subprogram i calls subprogram j during a program run. You need to partition the graph into two subgraphs, each with approximately the same number of vertices such that the sum of the weights on the edges that have end points in different subgraphs is minimized. Outline an algorithm to solve the problem.

4. Modify Dijkstra's algorithm so that the identity of the shortest path, as well as its length, is recorded.

5. Investigate techniques for representing sparse matrices and propose a third way to implement a graph.

6. Implement a depth-first search algorithm for finding a path between arbitrary vertices V_i and V_j.

7. Modify both the depth-first and breadth-first path-detection algorithms so that they return the length of the path found (or −1 if no path).

8. Modify both the depth-first and breadth-first algorithms by adding an integer parameter k. The algorithms are to consider only paths of length k or less.

9. A *word ladder* is a sequence of words in which successive words differ in exactly one letter position. An example ladder is *warm→ward→card→cord→cold*. Often, as in this example, the end words are related. The problem of constructing a ladder between two given end words can be regarded as finding a path between them on a suitably constructed graph. Write a program that reads a word list and constructs a graph. Add a facility for finding a path, if any exists, between two arbitrary words.

10. Write and test a program that constructs a graph representing the London Underground network. (The London Transport Web site at *http://www.londontransport.co.uk* has maps.) Your graph should record information about the different lines (e.g., *Bakerloo*, *Central*, *Victoria*) that connect stations. For example, three different lines connect the *South Kensington* and adjacent *Gloucester Road* stations. Your program should prompt the user for the names of two stations and print out the route between them that requires the fewest changes from one line to another.

11. Design a graph structure for representing a family tree. What information will you store in each vertex? What is the nature of an edge? Design a program that lets a user add information to a graph and determine the relationship between any two people in the graph.

12. Explore ways in which a dependency graph can be constructed from a sequence of assignment statements in a simple programming language. Write a graph construction program. What are the consequences of adding a loop construct to the language?

13. Obtain a copy of Knuth's set of five-letter words from the Stanford GraphBase (*ftp://labrea.stanford.edu/pub/sgb*). Create a graph in which each word is a vertex and there is an edge V_{ij} if V_i and V_j are the same in exactly four letter positions. What is the diameter of this graph? What does this result mean in terms of word ladders?

14. A *bipartite graph* is one in which the vertices can be divided into two disjoint sets, *VA* and *VB*, and every edge has one end in *VA* and the other in *VB*. Write a function that determines if an arbitrary graph (represented by adjacency matrix *M*) is bipartite.

15. Suppose *N*-vertex graphs *G1* and *G2* are represented by adjacency matrices *M1* and *M2*. Write a function that tests to see if the two graphs are isomorphic; that is, whether there is a one-to-one correspondence between the vertices of *G1* and *G2* that preserves adjacencies.

16. Paul Erdös (see note 2) investigated random graphs. Suppose we start with a set of *N* vertices and add edges at random. Erdös found that there is a jump in the size of the largest connected subgraph when the number of edges is roughly half the number of vertices. Write a program to generate random graphs and see this for yourself.

17. Devise an algorithm that, given a representation of a graph, tests to see if it contains a Eulerian path. If it does, the algorithm prints the path (as a list of vertices in the order in which they are visited).

18. Design and test a program that enables users to find travel directions between two arbitrary addresses in a very small city with a very simple road layout. Users should be able to choose between the shortest route and the fastest route. Describe the data structures used to represent the city.

References

Albert, R., H. Heong, and A-L. Barabási. 1999. Diameter of the World Wide Web. *Nature,* 401: 130–131.

Dijkstra, E. W. 1959. A note on two problems in connexion with graphs. *Numerische Mathematik,* 1: 269–271.

Euler, L. 1736. Solutio problematic ad geometriam situs pertinentis (The solution of a problem relating to the geometry of position). *Commetarii Academiae Scientiarum Imperialis Petropolitanae,* 8: 128–140.

Fleury, M. 1883. Deux problèmes de géométrie de situation, *Journal de mathématiques élémentaires,* pp. 257–261.

Floyd, R. W. 1962. Algorithm 97: Shortest path. *Communications of the ACM,* 5 (6): 345.

Knuth, D. E. 1993. *The Stanford GraphBase: A Platform for Combinatorial Computing.* ACM Press and Addison-Wesley, ftp://labrea.stanford.edu/pub/sgb.

Kruskal, J. B. 1956. On the shortest spanning subtree of a graph and the traveling salesman problem. *Proceedings of the American Mathematical Society,* 7 (1): 48–50.

Prim, C. 1957. Shortest connections networks and some generalizations. *Bell System Technical Journal* 36 (6): 1389–1401.

Warshall, S. 1962. A theorem on Boolean matrices. *Journal of the ACM,* 9 (1): 11–12.

● Notes

[1]Times are for nonstop flights. Data were taken from websites for United, Delta, and American Airlines during Spring 2001.

[2]Ithiel de Sola Pool floated the hypothesis that any two people can be linked via a chain of no more than five common acquaintances. Person A knows B who knows C, and so on. This has been termed "six degrees of separation." Kevin Bacon is an actor who has appeared in many movies. The idea of the game *Six Degrees of Kevin Bacon* is to identify the movies that associate Kevin Bacon with an arbitrary person. Consider Elvis Presley, for example. Elvis appeared in *King Creole* (1958) with Walter Matthau, and Walter Matthau appeared in *JFK* (1991) with Kevin Bacon. Walter Matthau thus has a *Bacon Number* of one and Elvis has a *Bacon Number* of two. The game is interesting because many people have Bacon Numbers less than or equal to six.

We can represent the associations between actors in a graph; vertices represent actors and edges are movies. There is an edge E_{ij} if actors i and j appeared in the same movie. The graph is likely to be a multigraph (consider Bob Hope and Bing Crosby, Walter Matthau and Jack Lemmon, for example). Using Kevin Bacon as the starting vertex in one of our path-detection algorithms, we can compute the Bacon Number of an arbitrary person. At the time of writing there is a commercially produced board game and a website at *http://www.cs.virginia.edu/oracle* with an interesting "how it works" section.

Paul Erdös (1913–1996) was a prolific Hungarian mathematician who wrote around 1500 papers. Mathematicians who co-authored a paper with Erdös are deemed to have an Erdös number of one. People co-authoring a paper with someone having an Erdös number of one have an Erdös number of two, and so on. Thus, a similar game could be devised: *Six Degrees of Paul Erdös.* A website on Erdös numbers is can be found at *http://www.acs.oakland.edu/~grossman/erdoshp.html.*

[3]Efforts have been made to estimate the diameter of the World Wide Web. However, despite the title of their paper, the value of 19 calculated by Albert et al. (1999) is an estimate of the average distance (number of links) between two randomly chosen documents *d1* and *d2* where such a link exists.

[4]In the literature, this is often referred to as the Chinese Postman problem.

part II

Persistent Objects

8

Hardware Foundations of Persistent Objects

8.1 Introduction

We assume that persistent objects reside on nonvolatile secondary memory at some point in their lifespan. Most likely they are in files stored on a disk that is accessible from programs via an operating system interface. This chapter examines how files can be implemented. We take a bottom-up approach, first examining the hardware and then the file system.

Section 8.2 looks at ways of improving the reliability of storage devices by using check data. This is particularly important for secondary memory that, because of its more mechanical nature, tends to be less reliable than primary memory. Section 8.3 looks at aspects of the operation of a disk drive and notes that read and write operations are very slow compared with main memory. We then look at RAID systems and cache memories. Both RAID techniques and cache memories can reduce the average time it takes to perform read and write operations on a disk. In addition, RAID techniques can improve reliability. The user's principal interface with secondary storage is likely to be through a file system maintained by an operating system. We look at some aspects of file system organization in Section 8.4.

8.2. Memory Reliability

When we read from a memory location (main memory or secondary memory), how confident can we be that the data we read are the same data that were written there?

Secondary memory is particularly vulnerable to data becoming corrupted because of the comparatively long times that may elapse between writing data and reading it back, the electromechanical nature of the storage devices and, in the case of offline storage, the environmental conditions in which the data are kept. The reader probably has personal experience of data on a removable medium, such as a floppy disk, becoming unreadable.

If every combination of bits in a storage location is a valid representation of a data item, then there is no way to detect whether the contents of the location have been altered since the last write operation. Therefore, error detection/correction schemes typically introduce redundancy by storing both data and check information derived from that data. When data are read back, the check data are recomputed and compared with the check data read from the storage location. This is illustrated in Figure 8.1.

The nature of the check function determines the possibilities for error detection and correction. Some schemes detect some types of error but not others; some schemes will correct certain types of errors. The costs of error detection/correction schemes are

- The space that the check information occupies that would otherwise be available for data
- The time needed to perform additional calculations[1]

Thus, a trade-off between space and time overheads and the ability to detect and/or correct errors is likely. No check system can eliminate the possibility of undetectable errors because any valid data/check combination in memory can be altered to such an extent that it forms another valid data/check combination.

The following sections describe three error-checking systems: simple parity, Hamming codes, and block check data. Section 8.3 offers examples of where each might be used.

8.2.1 Simple Parity

When storing data using a simple parity scheme, we append a 1 or a 0 to the data so that the number of stored bits that are 1 is an even number (even parity scheme) or odd (odd parity scheme). In what follows, we assume that we use an even parity scheme.

For example, suppose our data bits are 01101010. We have four 1s in the data. Four is an even number, so we do not need any more 1s. The parity bit will therefore be 0, and we store 011010100 (parity bit in bold). If, however, our data bits are 01100100, we have three 1s in the data. Three is an odd number, so the parity bit will be 1 to make the number of 1s stored an even number, and we store 011001001.

If, after the write operation, an odd number of stored bits are changed (e.g., 1 bit or 3 bits), we can detect that change because the parity of the group of bits will now be wrong. If an even number of stored bits are changed, then the data are still valid

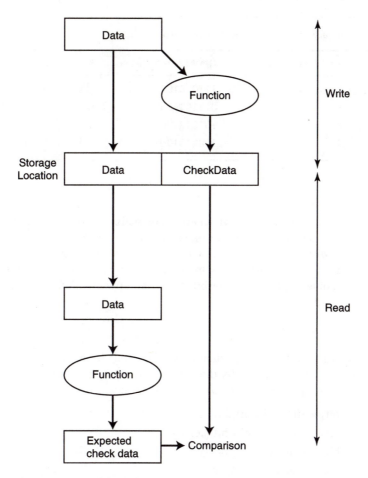

Figure 8.1 • Use of check data

according to this simple parity scheme and the change is undetectable. Table 8.1 shows some examples.

To sum up, when an odd number of bits are changed, the parity of the data changes to odd and we can detect that. If an even number of bits are changed, the simple parity scheme is not sufficient to detect it.

• 8.2.2 Hamming Codes

Hamming's scheme (Hamming 1950) uses multiple parity bits, each of which is derived from a different subset of the data bits. If a single bit is changed, there is enough information to enable us to determine which bit has changed (and therefore

● **TABLE 8.1** Detectable and Undetectable Data Corruption

Data + Parity	# of Bits Changed	New Stored Data	New Parity	Change Detected?
011010100	1	111010100	Odd	Yes
011010100	3	011101100	Odd	Yes
011010100	2	101010100	Even	No
011010100	4	100110100	Even	No

correct it). Thus, we have an **error-correcting code** (ECC). Most main memory modules in personal computers have circuitry for simple parity checking; memory modules with ECC are more expensive and a little slower.

How does Hamming's scheme work? Suppose we are storing and retrieving 8-bit data objects. If we number bits from one upwards, left to right, and denote the simple parity check as

$$bit_9 = f(bit_1, \dots bit_8)$$

then in the Hamming scheme, we have four independent parity checks. In the 12 stored bits, conceptually the 8 data bits are in positions 3, 5, 6, 7, 9, 10 , 11, and 12. The four parity bits are computed as follows:

$$bit_1 = f(bit_3,bit_5,bit_7,bit_9,bit_{11})$$
$$bit_2 = f(bit_3,bit_6,bit_7,bit_{10},bit_{11})$$
$$bit_4 = f(bit_5,bit_6,bit_7,bit_{12})$$
$$bit_8 = f(bit_9,bit_{10},bit_{11},bit_{12})$$

Hamming Code Example: Storage
If our data bits are 01101010, then we have

1	2	3	4	5	6	7	8	9	10	11	12
		0		1	1	0		1	0	1	0

The resulting parity bits are

$$bit_1 = f(bit_3,bit_5,bit_7,bit_9,bit_{11}) = f(0,1,0,1,1)\ = 1$$
$$bit_2 = f(bit_3,bit_6,bit_7,bit_{10},bit_{11}) = f(0,1,0,0,1)\ = 0$$
$$bit_4 = f(bit_5,bit_6,bit_7,bit_{12})\qquad = f(1,1,0,0)\quad = 0$$
$$bit_8 = f(bit_9,bit_{10},bit_{11},bit_{12})\qquad = f(1,0,1,0)\quad = 0$$

thus we store

1	2	3	4	5	6	7	8	9	10	11	12
1	0	0	0	1	1	0	0	1	0	1	0

If we change a single bit in the stored data, then when we read the data back and check it, we find that a unique combination of parity checks fails. Because the pattern of failures is unique, we can locate the error. Because there are only two possible values for a bit, we can correct the error.

Hamming Code Example: Retrieval
As an example of the error detection and correction, let us change bit 6 of our stored data so that it is now

1	2	3	4	5	6	7	8	9	10	11	12
1	0	0	0	1	0	0	0	1	0	1	0

When we read this data and check the parity groups, the results are

bit_1 $1 = f(0,1,0,1,1)$ OK
bit_2 $0 = f(0,0,0,0,1)$ fail $f(0,0,0,0,1)$ should be 1
bit_4 $0 = f(1,0,0,0)$ fail $f(1,0,0,0)$ should be 1
bit_8 $0 = f(1,0,1,0)$ OK

Adding the addresses of the incorrect parity bits (2 and 4) gives us the address of the bad bit (6). Why does this work? The columns of Table 8.2 show the binary representations of the numbers from 1 to 12 (least significant digit at the top), and thus how the parity groups with this additive property are determined.

For example, looking at the third row of Table 8.2 shows that the parity bit 4 is a check on those bits where the "4" digit in the binary representation is 1 (i.e., bits 5, 6, 7, and 12). The other parity groups are derived in a similar manner. Thus, if a

● **TABLE 8.2**   Parity Groups

	1	2	3	4	5	6	7	8	9	10	11	12
1	1	0	1	0	1	0	1	0	1	0	1	0
2	0	1	1	0	0	1	1	0	0	1	1	0
4	0	0	0	1	1	1	1	0	0	0	0	1
8	0	0	0	0	0	0	0	1	1	1	1	1

particular bit is changed, a unique pattern of parity bits fails—see column 6 for the example we used. This scheme is clearly extendible to larger numbers of data bits.

Limitations of Hamming Codes

The scheme outlined in the previous section works if no bits are altered or if a single bit is altered. (The assumption is that the probability of a bit being altered is very small and independent of other bits being altered, thus no-bit changes and one-bit changes are by far the two most likely cases.) To see that our scheme does not work in some other cases, let us change bits 2 and 4 in our stored data, which gives us the following.

1	2	3	4	5	6	7	8	9	10	11	12
1	1	0	1	1	1	0	0	1	0	1	0

The parity checks will show that bits 2 and 4 are wrong (as before, but this time because the parity bits themselves have been changed rather than a single data bit). If we assume that this indicates that bit 6 is wrong and we change it, we now have the following.

1	2	3	4	5	6	7	8	9	10	11	12
1	1	0	1	1	0	0	0	1	0	1	0

When we extract the eight data bits (01001010), we find that we have introduced an error rather than eliminated one.

We can improve the scheme somewhat by adding a 13th bit that is a parity check on the 12 bits. Therefore, we now have the following.

1	2	3	4	5	6	7	8	9	10	11	12	13
1	0	0	0	1	1	0	0	1	0	1	0	1

Now the algorithm for checking is:

```
Read 13 bits
N = sum of indexes of failing parity bits (bits 1, 2, 4, or 8)
    If (overall parity is OK)
        {
        // even number of bits have changed – possibly none
        If (N!=0) error – but can't fix it
        }
    else
        {
        // odd number of bits have changed
```

```
        If (1 < N < 13)
            change bit N
        Else error — but can't fix it
    }
```

Hamming Distance

The Hamming distance between two bit patterns of length K is the number of bit positions in which they are different. If we devise a coding scheme that uses N-bit **codewords** (binary strings) to represent symbols, then the Hamming distance of the scheme is the minimum distance between any two codewords.

In order to be able to detect up to d single-bit errors, the coding scheme must have a Hamming distance of at least $d + 1$. This ensures that even d changes to a valid codeword cannot change it into another valid codeword.

In order to be able to correct up to d single-bit errors, the code must have a Hamming distance of at least $2d + 1$. This means that making d changes to a codeword still leaves it closer to the correct codeword than to any other valid codeword.

The simple parity scheme of Section 8.2.1 has a Hamming distance of 2, thus we are able to detect single-bit errors but not correct any errors. The 13-bit scheme we devised earlier has distance 4, thus we can detect 2-bit errors and correct single-bit errors.

8.2.3 Block Check Data

In addition to checks on individual characters/bytes, we can derive check information from a block of data. The block of data might be a packet sent over a network, a block of data on a tape, or a sector stored on a disk. The block check data might be a **checksum**, which is a byte or two computed so that the sum of the data and the check byte(s) is some known quantity (e.g., zero). Alternatively, the block check information might take the form of a **cyclic redundancy check (CRC)**, computed as follows: As bits of the data block are written, they are also used (conceptually) as input to a shift register that is modified by feedback. The contents of the shift register are also written at the end of the data stream. When data are read back, the conceptual shift register is again driven, so we know what CRC to expect to read at the end.

Section 8.3 looks at the basic operation of a disk and at RAID technology. Some RAID configurations use the simple parity idea at a high level in mapping data to disks. Other configurations use Hamming codes. Most disk systems use some form of CRC in low-level data checking.

8.3 Disks, RAID, and Cache Memories

The moving-head disk is currently the most common secondary storage device. This section looks at how the moving-head disk works and notes its relative slowness and unreliability. Then we look at RAID ideas that improve reliability and/or performance. Finally, we look at cache memory, another performance-improving mechanism.

8.3.1 Disk Fundamentals

The earliest secondary storage devices were magnetic tapes. The main disadvantage of tape-based devices is that all data on the tape are not equally accessible; there is a large difference between the time required to access the data on the tape closest to the read/write head and the data farthest away. Efficient access is possible only if the data are to be processed in the same order in which they appear on the tape.

The problem of being able to access all data equally quickly has been largely solved by a variety of devices that rotate a recording surface at high speed past one or more read/write heads. A **track** is the projection of a given position of a read/write head onto the recording surface.[2] Access times to data are not exactly equal, but in the worst case, any data item is only a single revolution of the track away. Bits are written serially along tracks. Check information usually is stored together with the data.

The earliest spinning-track devices were drums—cylinders coated with magnetizable material. A drum rotated rapidly past a fixed row of read/write heads, thus causing tracks to be parallel circles of equal radius. For convenience, tracks were divided angularly into **sectors**, a sector being the smallest addressable unit of the drum. Because read/write heads were fixed, the main delay in reading from or writing to a drum was waiting for the appropriate sector to rotate around to the read/write position. Topologically similar to a drum,[3] a **fixed-head disk** has one or more rigid metal disks (**platters**). Platters typically are made of aluminum coated with a magnetizable material, for example, a mixture of chromic oxide and ferrous oxide. A fixed arm containing many read/write heads is positioned over each recordable surface, and tracks are concentric circles (see Figure 8.2).

Again, a significant part of reading and writing time is the wait for data to rotate around.

Drums and fixed-head disks are now rare; most disk drives can be classified as **moving-head**. In a moving-head drive, a single-read/write head per surface serves all the tracks on that surface moving to a particular track as required (see Figure 8.3).

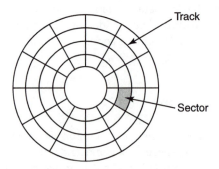

Figure 8.2 • Tracks and sectors on a disk

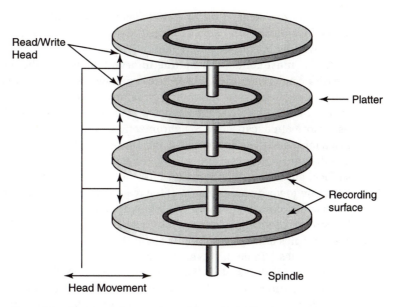

Read/Write Head

Platter

Recording surface

Spindle

Head Movement

Figure 8.3 • Platters, surfaces, and movable read/write heads

Generally, tracks are closer together in a moving-head system than in a fixed-head system, but there is a delay in reading and writing while the head moves to the appropriate track.

A floppy disk is contained in a plastic envelope with a window through which the read/write head accesses the recording surface. In contrast to the drums and hard disk drives, a floppy disk does not rotate continuously, rather only when a read/write operation is performed, and then at a much slower rate than a hard drive. Thus, access times tend to be significantly longer than for hard disks. Computer manufacturers are phasing out floppy disk drives from new systems.

A disk pack with more than one recording surface has cylinders of tracks. A **cylinder** is a set of tracks with the same radius. For example, cylinder 200 is made up of track number 200 on each of the recording surfaces. A disk drive with one read/write head per surface moves all the heads together, though on a normal drive only one of the heads can read or write at one time. If the heads are positioned at a particular track, then all the data in the particular cylinder are accessible with no further head movement. Electronic switching is then used to select the active head. Note that this switching is much faster than the mechanical movement of the read/write head and, for many purposes, can be considered instantaneous. Thus, if we have data on more than one track, it would be beneficial to store it cylinder by cylinder rather than surface by surface.

The time to read or write a sector includes the time to move to the correct track (**seek time**), the time for the appropriate sector to rotate around (**latency**), and the time to do the actual read or write. Delays are significant. The time to answer a query in a database system is largely dependent on the disk access times—time spent waiting for physical disk motions.

A disk must contain **formatting information** so that the recording locations on the disk can be identified. For this reason, new disks typically have to be formatted before use. Because a formatting program writes various pieces of information on each track of a disk, the capacity of a formatted disk is likely to be less than its unformatted capacity. Synchronization bits are written to enable the servo-mechanisms of the drive to detect and correct for fluctuations in the rotational speed of a disk during reading and writing. At the start of each sector there might be track, surface, and sector identification bits and status bits. This information allows the hardware to verify a movement of the read/write heads to a particular track.

Disk technology advances rapidly, particularly the density with which data can be stored. Two important disk manufacturers are Hitachi Global Storage Technologies and Fujitsu. Details about their products can be found at their respective websites.[4] Table 8.3 gives the parameters for what is, currently, a typical hard drive for a desktop system (Hitachi Deskstar 180GXP).

Manufacturers report that mean time between failures for their current drives is a few decades. This is clearly a theoretical estimate. In the author's experience, hard drive failures are not uncommon.

Ng (1998) outlines some of the ways in which disk technology may change and notes that not all changes will result in shorter access times. For example, packing tracks closer together may require a longer settling time after a head movement. The combination of data density on a track and rotation rate may increase to the point at which the rate that data passes under a read head exceeds the capacity of the channel sending it to the CPU. On the software side, disk capacity may exceed the largest disk that can be handled by the operating system file implementation technique.

● **TABLE 8.3**   Parameters of Deskstar 180GXP Disk Drive

Tracks per inch	72,000
Tracks per cylinder	6
Formatted capacity (Gb)	180
Bytes per sector	512
Maximum bits per inch (track)	632,000
Revolution time (ms)	8.33
Seek time (ms)	1.1(min.), 8.5(avg.), 15.0(max.)
Nonrecoverable errors	1 in 10^{14}

8.3.2 Read/Write Operations

A read/write operation can transfer one or many sectors of information. Because of the arrangement of recording surfaces and read/write heads, the time required for a particular operation (e.g., to access, read, and transmit a sector of data) involves five components:[5]

1. The time to select the appropriate surface
2. The time to move the read/write head to the appropriate track (seek delay)
3. The time for the required sector to rotate around to the location of the read/write head (rotational delay or latency)
4. The time to read the bytes from the disk surface
5. The time to transmit the bytes to the CPU

The user has no control over components 1, 4, and 5. The first is a purely electronic operation, and the time required is negligible. The fourth is dependent primarily on the amount of data read. The fifth depends on the busyness of the channel to the CPU; data may have to be buffered before being sent. We consider the second and third components in more detail.

Typically, the time required to move the read/write heads is a function of the number of cylinders over which the heads must move. However, as you can see from Table 8.3, the function is not linear. The time will have acceleration and deceleration components and a component representing the time during which the head is moving at maximum velocity. Note also that if we have a total of N cylinders and we pick starting and finishing cylinders at random, the average number of cylinders moved is $N/3$ (see Exercises). Other hardware configurations have been investigated. Deighton (1995) modeled the performance of a disk containing two read/write heads on each arm and found that optimal performance is achieved when the heads are placed $0.46N$ cylinders apart (N again being the total number of cylinders) and neither is allowed to move outside the track area. The average seek time is reduced by about 30 percent over single head-per-arm systems (typically from 15.1 to 10.7 ms on a large disk).

On average, the user must wait for a disk to make half a revolution for the required data to appear at the read/write position. Engineering advances have resulted in increased rotation rates. A rate of 3600 rpm used to be typical; the disk shown in Table 8.3 rotates at 5400 rpm, and disks are available that spin at 15,000 rpm. (Average latencies for these rates are approx 8.3, 5.5, and 2 ms, respectively.)

Data Placement

By means of its data placement strategy, an operating system has some control over delays due to head movement and rotation. If the data are to be processed in a predictable order, it is possible to take steps to minimize these delays.

To minimize head movement, it is better to treat a disk as a sequence of cylinders rather than as a sequence of surfaces. When processing a disk cylinder by cylinder, head movement occurs only after all data in one cylinder have been processed. Thus, there is minimal head movement. In contrast, when processing surface by surface, head movement occurs after each track is processed. If a disk has M platters, then the number of head movements when processing surface by surface is M times the number when processing cylinder by cylinder. We can go further and place frequently accessed data on cylinders near the middle of the disk, thus reducing the maximum head movement needed to get to that data from the current track.

Next, consider a number of data items that are to be placed on a particular track and processed in a known sequence. To minimize rotational delay, the items could be located in such a way that a sector containing the item is just coming under the read/write head at the time when it is required. It is likely that data so placed will not appear in consecutive physical sectors, but rather will appear in a hopscotch pattern.

An operating system will usually allocate disk space to files in **clusters** (e.g., an **allocation unit** might be a cluster of four adjacent sectors). This strategy reduces the time needed to read the file. However, on a typical disk, with the free space fragmented after many file creations and deletions, the clusters allocated to a particular file are likely to be noncontiguous. Disk defragmentation software rearranges the contents of a disk so that each file occupies contiguous space. It is a time-consuming operation, but one that normally results in faster file accessing.

Reliability and Speed
Disks are prone to failure that results in data loss. For example:

- Data can become irreparably corrupted while on the disk.
- Data can become inaccessible because of loss of formatting information.
- The read/write head can crash onto the recording surface.
- The power supply can fail.

RAID techniques (discussed next) configure two or more disks in order to improve reliability, performance, or both. Often it is possible to replace defective devices without halting the system (hot swap).

Why do we care how slow disks are? We care because disks are orders of magnitude slower than main memory. In the time required to read a disk sector (typically around 10 ms), we can make hundreds of thousands of accesses to main memory. It is often worth expending CPU time to save a single disk access. The enormous speed differences between the two types of memory influence the design of persistent data structures, which we examine in later chapters. Caching is a general technique that holds copies of frequently accessed data in local, small, fast memories to reduce the number of times we need to access a slower memory. Disk caching aims to reduce effective I/O times. We look at RAID systems and cache memories in the next two sections.

8.3.3 RAID

Originally RAID was an acronym for Redundant Array of Inexpensive Disks, but because individual disks are not necessarily cheap, and cheap disks are not necessarily very reliable, it was subsequently changed to Redundant Array of Independent Disks. More recently, some have proposed extending the disk-oriented techniques to nondisk storage media, in which case the acronym becomes Redundant Array of Independent Devices.

Although the principle predates its publication, many common RAID ideas were discussed in a paper written by Patterson et al. in 1988. The paper describes how improvements in CPU and memory were outpacing improvements in the performance of disk units. The authors proposed RAID as a solution. The original paper described five configurations. Three of them (RAID levels 1, 3, and 5) are practical and are available in commercial products. The other two configurations (RAID levels 2 and 4) are mainly of theoretical interest.

In effect, each RAID configuration makes an array of disks appear to be a single virtual disk. Thus, RAID is an alternative to SLED (Single Large Expensive Disk). Each configuration gives the virtual disk certain reliability and performance characteristics. Chen et al. (1994) discuss the reliability, performance, and cost of seven different disk array configurations. In the future, it is likely that the particular RAID level of a system will not be important; RAID systems will be characterized by factors such as reliability, scalability, serviceability, and price per usable megabyte.

The following sections look at the five RAID configurations of Patterson et al. (1988), as well as at other configurations that have been implemented. We will then speculate on how RAID might be extended to two dimensions.

RAID Level 1

RAID level 1 has mirrored disks; that is, each disk is duplicated. A write operation writes to both the main and check disk; a read operation can be done from either disk. In the event that one disk of a pair fails, it is highly likely that the other is available. To this end, it is important to make a disk and its mirror as independent as possible; this means providing separate power supplies, for example. Because of the duplication, the effective capacity of the disk system is 50 percent of its nominal capacity.

A variation on level 1 is to spindle-synchronize a disk and its mirror 180 degrees apart, as depicted in Figure 8.4.

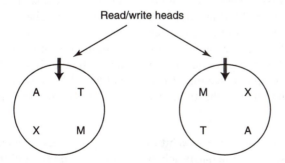

Figure 8.4 • Disks spindle-synchronized 180 degrees apart

Because both disks must be updated, average latency for a write is the larger of the two latency times, that is,

$$max(0.25R, 0.75R) = 0.75R$$

where R is the rotation time of a disk. When reading, the system can read from the first disk on which data become available, thus average latency for a read is the smaller of the two latency times:

$$min(0.25R, 0.75R) = 0.25R$$

Thus, on average, reads are faster and writes are slower than with a single disk in which average latency is $0.5R$ on both read and write.

Related to RAID level 1 are "unofficial" levels 0 and 10. In RAID level 0, data is "striped" across a group of disks. That is, sector 0 of the virtual disk is on physical disk 0, sector 1 is on disk 1, and so on. In a simple scheme, if we are striping across N disks, sector k of the virtual disk is found at

sector k/N on physical drive $k\%N$

This configuration is more reliable than a single large disk (we do not lose everything if a disk crashes) and may be faster if read/write operations to the individual disks can be done in parallel. RAID 10 usually means a combination of levels 1 and 0.[6] For example, there might be eight disks configured as four pairs. Data is striped four ways, and each disk in a pair is a mirror of the other. Thus, we have the speed benefits of RAID 0 and the increased reliability of RAID 1.

RAID Level 2

RAID level 2 interleaves across disks at the bit level. That is, individual bits of a byte to be stored are written to separate disks. This level uses Hamming code techniques (see Section 8.2.2); for example, there might be a group of eight data disks as well as four check disks. One bit of each byte is written to each data disk, and appropriate check bits are written to the check disks. When data are read and reassembled, RAID 2 can check the 12-bit group and, assuming that data from no more than one disk are bad, correct errors. Thus, a RAID 2 system can recover from the failure of an entire disk because no more that one bit per byte is affected. Storage utilization is better than RAID level 1; for eight data and four check disks it is 67 percent.

A RAID level 2 configuration can detect some errors that slip past a particular controller. However, in practice, the individual controllers will almost always be able to signal that an error has occurred on a particular disk (see Table 8.3), thus the elaborate cross-disk checking of RAID level 2 and the cost of additional disks are not outweighed by the ability to recover from a class of rare errors.

RAID Level 3

Like RAID 2, RAID level 3 uses bit interleaving, but this time with just a single parity disk. It uses a simple parity scheme rather than the Hamming code, and thus has

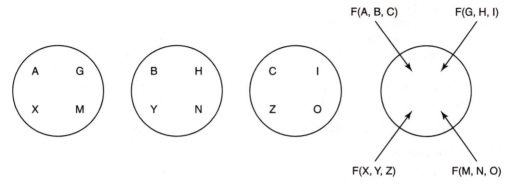

Figure 8.5 • RAID level 4

more choice over the number of disks than does RAID level 2. Although the disks operate in parallel, read and write operations are comparatively slow because all disks are involved. In a read, all disks have to be read to ensure that data checks are valid. In a write, all disks have to be written. If we have N disks, the fraction of space storing useful data is $(N - 1)/N$. However, the biggest problem with RAID 3 (and RAID 2) is the size of the smallest feasible transfer. If we assume that the smallest unit that can be transferred to and from a single disk is one sector, then with a bit-interleave scheme over $N - 1$ data disks, the smallest unit that can be read or written is $N - 1$ sectors.

RAID Level 4
RAID 4 interleaves at the sector level rather than at the bit level. It uses independent read/writes to the data disks, which solves the problem of the large minimum-transfer requirement. Sector interleaving means that, as in RAID 0, sector 0 (of our virtual big disk) is mapped to actual sector 0 on physical disk 0. Virtual sector 1 is mapped to sector 0 on physical disk 1, and so on. In general, sector k is mapped onto disk $k\%N$ (where N is the number of data disks).[7]

In addition to the data disks, there is a single check disk. The contents of sector I on this disk are a function of the sector Is on all the data disks (e.g., a simple parity). This is illustrated in the four-disk layout of Figure 8.5.

If a single disk fails, and we know which one it is, its data can be recovered by examining corresponding data on the other disks. Note how read and write operations proceed:

```
Read: Read from the appropriate disk (sector-level checks on the disk itself
         indicate if the data are bad).
      If the read was not successful
             read corresponding sectors from all the other disks to
             recover the data.
```

```
Write: Read the current contents of the sector to be written and also read
       the appropriate sector on the parity disk. (These reads can be done in
       parallel because they are from different disks.)
       Write two sectors (new data, new parity) also in parallel.
```

Note that we can determine the new value of the parity data if we know what the current parity data is and the old value of the data sector:

new parity = (old data XOR new data) XOR current parity

For example,

Old data: 01101000
Other data: 10010001
Current parity: 11111001

If the new data bits are 01110001, then we compute the new parity.

Old data XOR new data: 00011001
XOR current parity: 11100000 => new parity

We can verify that this is correct:

New data: 01110001
Other data: 10010001
New parity: 11100000

RAID Level 5

The problem with RAID level 4 is that the single check disk becomes a bottleneck in the system during write operations. All write operations have to read from and write to the check disk, thus reducing the degree to which write operations can be done in parallel. In a RAID 5 system, check information is dispersed evenly throughout the disks. For example, the check sector for the sector ks could be on disk $(N-1) - (k \% N)$. See Figure 8.6.

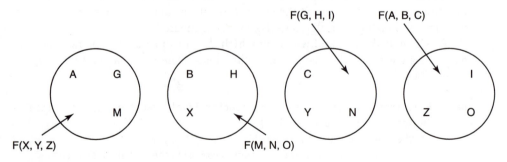

Figure 8.6 • RAID level 5

More parallelism is possible with RAID 5 than with RAID 4, with the same reliability. Suppose, for example, that we need to update two data sectors (A and B) and the corresponding parity sectors (P_A and P_B). In RAID 4, we know that the two parity sectors are on the same drive, so the process will take four time intervals. Table 8.4 shows a possible sequence of read and write operations.

When performing the same update on a RAID 5 system, we have three situations depending on whether the four sectors (A, B, P_A, P_B) are on two, three, or four disks. Possible sequences include those shown in Table 8.5, where R represents a read operation, W a write operation, and X' represents a modified sector X.

Thus we have the same storage utilization and reliability in RAID 5 as we had with RAID 4, and potentially more parallelism.

RAID Variations

RAID 6 (see Chen et al. 1994) differs from RAID 5 in that each group of data sectors generates two independent check sectors. This permits recovery from two disks failing at the same time; for example, when a second disk fails while we are recovering from an initial failure.

Different RAID levels can coexist on the same disk. AutoRAID (Wilkes et al. 1996) is a Hewlett-Packard two-level storage system. Write-active data are in the RAID 1 upper level, where writes are comparatively fast but storage utilization is poor. Write-inactive data are in the lower RAID 5 level, where access is slower but

● **TABLE 8.4** Updating Sectors A and B in a RAID 4 System

Time	Operation(s)
1	read(A) read(P_A)
2	write(A') write(P'_A)
3	read(B) read(P_B)
4	write(B') write(P'_B)

● **TABLE 8.5** Updating Sectors A and B in a RAID 5 System

Time	Four Disks	Three Disks	Two Disks
1	R(A), R(P_A), R(B), R(P_B)	R(A), R(B), R(P_B)	R(A), R(P_A)
2	W(A'), W(P_A'), W(B'), W(P_B')	W(A'), W(P_B'), R(P_A)	R(B), R(P_B)
3		W(P_A')	W(A'), W(P_A')
4		W(B')	W(P_B'), W(B')

storage utilization is better. Data migrate between levels. For example, the least recently written data are moved down to level 5 when there is a need for space in the mirrored level 1 storage; this migration is done as a background task when the disk is detected as being idle. A data unit moves from the lower to the higher unit when it is written. New disks can be added on the fly.

Tsai and Lee (1997) take the AutoRAID idea further and describe how a disk array can be divided into several partitions, each having different properties. They are particularly concerned with the performance of the system after a failure has occurred. Data are allocated to a partition depending on frequency of use.

Two-Dimensional RAID

The following describes two ways in which we might extend the RAID concept by considering disks in a two-dimensional rather than a one-dimensional array. This provides gains in reliability (we can tolerate more than one disk failing at a time), but at a cost of increased update times. Recall that RAID levels 4 and 5 require a single check sector to be updated when a data sector is updated. The configuration that we designate RAID level X requires two check sectors to be updated, and the configuration that we term RAID level Y requires three check sectors to be updated. To the author's knowledge, neither configuration has been implemented.

Level X In level X, we extend the ideas we have seen in RAID level 5 to two dimensions. First, consider Figure 8.7, which depicts the first few sectors of each disk in a six-disk RAID level 5 configuration. D represents a data sector and C represents a check sector. We see the dispersal of the check sectors.

Figure 8.8 shows how this idea of dispersed check data could be extended to two dimensions with 16 disks arranged in a (conceptual) four-by-four square.

In Figure 8.8, each check sector is a function of the data sectors in both its row and its column. Thus, in our example, each check sector is based on six data sectors. Note that each data sector is checked by two check sectors. Consequently, when a data sector is changed, two check sectors must be updated.

	Disk 1	Disk 2	Disk 3	Disk 4	Disk 5	Disk 6
Sector 1s	C	D	D	D	D	D
Sector 2s	D	C	D	D	D	D
Sector 3s	D	D	C	D	D	D
Sector 4s	D	D	D	C	D	D
Sector 5s	D	D	D	D	C	D
Sector 6s	D	D	D	D	D	C
Sector 7s	C	D	D	D	D	D

Figure 8.7 • RAID level 5

```
Sector 1s     C     D     D     D
              D     C     D     D
              D     D     C     D
              D     D     D     C


Sector 2s     D     C     D     D
              D     D     C     D
              D     D     D     C
              C     D     D     D
```

Figure 8.8 • RAID level X

If one data sector fails, we can recover its contents by looking at either of the two groups of which it is a member. If two data sectors fail, then in some cases (but not all—see Problems) each sector is the member of a group of which the other failing sector is not. Hence, by using those two groups we can recover the sectors separately. There are cases, however, when recovery is not possible. Suppose, for example, that the two failures are the two data sectors in the lower-right quadrant of the sector 1 diagram in Figure 8.8. We cannot recover either sector.

We can recover from some three-disk failures in a similar manner, but there are others that would prove fatal. Consider, for example, the failure of the top left-hand corner in the sector 1 diagram, (i.e., the failure of the first two sectors in the first row and the first two sectors in the first column). Each of the appropriate check sets has at least two bad disks, and hence are beyond repair.

Level X RAID has an additional overhead compared with RAID level 5 because a write operation affects two check sectors rather than one. But again, in some cases, operations on the check disks can be done in parallel, and there is the compensation of increased reliability.

Level Y   We can go further. Let us take the configuration of RAID level 4 and extend it to two dimensions. We term this level Y. We will have a check disk for each row of data disks and a check disk for each column. Thus, a 20-disk system might be configured as five rows of four disks each, as shown in Figure 8.9. As in a RAID 4 system, each disk is entirely data sectors (*Data*) or entirely check sectors (*Check*).

```
Data      Data      Data      Check
Data      Data      Data      Check
Data      Data      Data      Check
Data      Data      Data      Check
Check     Check     Check     Check
```

Figure 8.9 • RAID level Y

The disk in the lower-right corner is a check on the column of check disks and the row of check disks. A write to a data sector requires three check sectors to be updated—the row-check, the column-check, and the check-check sector (lower right-hand corner in Figure 8.9). The latter will be a bottleneck in the system, just as it was in RAID 4. If a read failure occurs, we read the corresponding sectors from the disks in the rest of the row (or the rest of the column, whichever is faster) to re-create the data.

Although level Y has more write overhead than level X, it can recover from a greater variety of multiple disk failures. For example, if two disks fail they must either be in two different columns or in two different rows. Thus, the column or row sets can be used to recover the data. We can also recover from the simultaneous failure of any three disks. There must be at least one row or column that has only one failure; we fix this first. This leaves two disks that must be in different rows or in different columns, and we fix them as shown earlier. We can recover from some, but not all, simultaneous failures of four or more disks. (Consider the case where four failing disks are at the corners of a rectangle.)

RAID systems can improve both reliability through redundancy and speed through parallelism. A more common way of achieving speed improvements is to use cache memories to reduce the number of times we need to do a physical read or write operation. We look at cache memories next.

● 8.3.4 Cache Memories

A typical computer system has many storage devices with different access times and storage costs. A trade-off usually exists between access time and cost per byte; faster memories are more expensive. In general, a **cache memory** is a small, fast, memory that is logically positioned in front of a slower, cheaper one. There may be cache memories at many points in the storage hierarchy. Consider the analogy of a desktop Rolodex card index and a set of phone books. The materials cost of the Rolodex is higher per entry than the phone books, but it has shorter access time. The cache operates in the same way in which we use a Rolodex. When a read request is made, we first search the cache. If the item is found there, we have the data. If it is not in the cache, then we get it from the slower memory and put a copy in the cache for future reference.

Read/Write Operations

Let us see how read and write operations work in the presence of a cache. A read is straightforward:

```
Read:  If not in cache
             copy data from slow memory to cache
       Give data to cpu
```

What about a write operation? There are two possibilities depending on how much time we wish to save and if we need be concerned about the cache and the slower memory being inconsistent. The **write-through strategy** keeps the two memories consistent but does not save any time:

```
Write (write-through):        If in cache
                                  update cache
                          Update slow memory
```

In our phone book analogy, when we find out that a number has changed, the write-through strategy updates both the phone book and the Rolodex. Thus, a write operation in a system with write-through cache is no faster (and may be slower) than in a system with no cache.

The **copy-back strategy** only updates the cache copy of a data item:

```
Write (copy-back):     If in cache
                          update cache and tag it "changed"
                       else  update main memory
```

In our phone book analogy, when we find out that a number has changed, the copy-back strategy updates only the Rolodex, but we make a notation on the card that this is a new number. Thus, a write operation in a system with copy-back cache may be faster than in a system with no cache. The version of a data item in the slower memory is updated only when the cache section is needed for other data (see the following Replacement Algorithm section) or when the cache is flushed for various reasons (e.g., system shutdown). This update might take place after several writes to a particular cache location. Note that data are lost if something (e.g., a power failure) prevents the new contents from being written to the slow memory.

Cache Effectiveness

A cache is effective because the different data elements in the slower memory are not used with the same frequency. Consider the phone book. A typical person probably uses a very small percentage of the listed numbers; the vast majority are never referenced. Further, of those that are used, some are used much more often than others. The net effect is that a cache, though relatively small, can hold a significant fraction of those portions of the slower memory that are in actual use. Time is saved because data brought into a cache are likely to be used repeatedly. We can define **hit ratio** as the proportion of read/write requests that are satisfied from the cache and therefore do not require operations on the slower memory.

Consider a disk. Not every sector is allocated to a file and, at a particular time, only a small number of the files on the disk are likely to be in use. Among the files that are in use, some are used more often than others; for example, if we are in a compile-edit cycle, the files containing the compiler, the editor, and the source code of the program will be in frequent use. Disk subsystems are usually sold with on-board cache. The ratio of disk size to cache size is typically between 2000:1 and 8000:1. A cache is most effective when the slower memory is used only by a single process. On a multiuser system, a disk cache will tend to contain information used by many concurrent processes.

One way in which a computer cache differs from our card index analogy is that it may perform anticipatory reads. For example, a request for location N in the slow memory may cause the cache to load locations $N, N + 1, \ldots, N + k$, anticipating that, given the nature of code segments and data structures, the additional data items will be needed in the future. Typically, about half the read requests on a particular disk are sequential; that is, they request the sector following the previous one requested. This cache read-ahead mode may be under user control. Read-ahead makes particular sense when we are caching a disk in which much of the reading time is waiting for the required sector to be under the read/write head. Reading a few extra sectors requires comparatively little additional time.

The DOS SMARTDRV software allows a PC user to establish a disk cache in main memory. The user can enable/disable write-behind (copy back), specify the size of the read-ahead buffer, and force the cache to be made clean (i.e., all changed data written to disk) before each DOS prompt.

Replacement Algorithm

What if the cache is full when we need to bring in new information? We need an algorithm to determine which section to overwrite. Ideally, we would like to be able to identify the section least likely to be needed in future. Typically, replacement algorithms use information about past usage in making a selection.

We have a similar problem in our card index. What if all the cards for which we have room are in use, yet we need to record another number? Which currently stored number do we get rid of to make room for the new one? Four possible replacement algorithms are summarized in Table 8.6.

The *Random* algorithm, though a low-overhead scheme, may well discard much-used information. The *FIFO* algorithm is not a good choice because often the first

● **TABLE 8.6** Cache Replacement Strategies

Algorithm	Section Discarded
Random	One chosen randomly
FIFO (First-In, First-Out)	The one that has been in the cache longest
LFU (Least Frequently Used)	The one that has been used least often
LRU (Least Recently Used)	The one that has been unused for the longest time

data items that were read into the cache are highly used (e.g., it might be a root-level directory block). The *LFU* algorithm is biased against information that has only recently come into the cache and also may require a tie-break mechanism. *LRU* is, in practice, the algorithm of choice. The reasoning is that if data items have been unused for some time, they are unlikely to be needed again soon.

What are the implications of a disk cache? A distinction can be made between a **logical data transfer** (a read or write request issued by a program) and a **physical data transfer** (an actual read from or write to the disk). If accesses to a file are "random," use of a cache is not likely to result in significant savings. However, a linear pass through the file is likely to be faster with a cache than without, and if there is a skewed distribution of file accesses, with some blocks highly used, we may achieve significant savings.

Most users are not concerned with low-level details of disk operations. They regard the disk as somewhere to store and retrieve files. In the next section, we look briefly at ways in which an operating system might store files on disks.

8.4 File Systems

8.4.1 Properties of a File System

A **file** is a named collection of data held on secondary storage. At the lowest level, it can be treated as a sequence of bytes. A **file system** consists of the files and the operating system utilities that enable users to create and manipulate them. System utilities permit users to perform actions such as creating, moving, removing, and renaming files and attaching them to programs. Typically, users can organize files into folders or directories (and subdirectories to an arbitrary depth). The directory entry for a file includes its name and data such as creation time, size, access permissions, and location.

8.4.2 Mapping Files to Disks

Four ways in which an operating system might organize files on disks are:

1. Contiguous storage
2. Linked storage
3. Index nodes
4. Directoryless

Recall that an allocation unit is a group of adjacent sectors.

Contiguous Storage
In the **contiguous storage** scheme, a file occupies contiguous allocation units. A directory entry must include the size of the file and a pointer to where it begins on

disk. Serial access—reading the file in a linear manner—is very efficient because the next sector needed is very close physically to the current sector. Random access—reading or writing an arbitrary part of the file—will also be fast because we can compute the address of the required sector given its file-relative address and the location of the start of the file.

However, a contiguous storage scheme is too restrictive. For example, to make a copy of a file, the operating system has to locate a contiguous empty space of the appropriate size. In addition, if a program opens a file for writing, where should the file be placed given that we do not know how big it will get? Over time, as files are created and deleted, the disk is likely to become fragmented; the free space will consist of many small, noncontiguous regions. If, for example, we have four free space regions of sizes 8, 6, 4, and 10, we cannot create a file larger than 10 even though the total free space is 28. To enable creation of the largest possible file, we need to run a defragmentation program that moves files so that the free space is in one contiguous region. Defragmentation can be a time-consuming operation because of the number of reads and writes required and the need to update pointers to files.

Linked Storage

In the **linked storage** scheme, a file is stored as a linked list of allocation units. The directory entry contains pointers to the beginning and to the end of the list. The end pointer enables append operations to be performed efficiently. The scheme is more flexible than the contiguous storage one; a file can occupy space anywhere on the disk. However, in the absence of file compaction (see Exercises), the blocks comprising a particular file are likely to be scattered over a disk, making serial access slow. In the absence of direct pointers to each allocation unit, direct access is very slow.

Index Nodes

An alternative to linked storage is for the directory entry to point to each allocation unit of the file. This speeds up random access. But how many pointer fields do we allow for? If we allow space for M pointers, then directory space is wasted if the file is smaller than M allocation units and we have a problem if the file is larger than M units. The Unix operating system has an elegant solution to this dilemma: It uses index nodes (**i-nodes**) between directory entries and the units of a file. The directory entry points to an i-node, and the i-node contains pointers to the units of the file (as well as other information such as the name of the owner of the file, permissions granted on the file, and time of last modification).

Because more than one directory entry can point to the same i-node, the same file can appear in multiple directories. The file may have different names in each directory. Figure 8.10 shows an example.

In directory *CS2*, the file is referenced as *Homework4*; in directory *MyHeaders*, the file is *Bintree.h*, and finally, in directory *FilesForReport*, it is accessible as

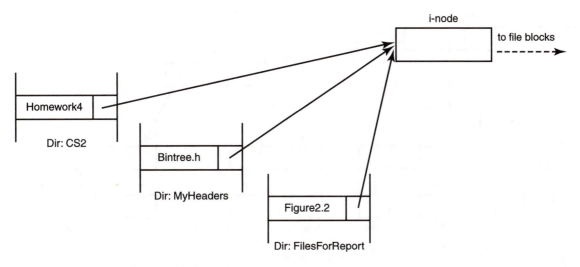

Figure 8.10 • File pointed to from multiple directories

Figure2.2. The i-node includes a count of the number of pointers to it; the file is not deleted until the count is zero.

The i-node normally contains pointers to each of the first N units of the file, enabling them to be accessed quickly. In addition, if the file is larger than N blocks, then there is a pointer to a block of M pointers that enable the next M units to be accessed indirectly. Finally, if the file is larger than $N + M$ units, then the last pointer in the i-node is a pointer to a block of pointers to blocks of pointers that enable the next P units of the file to be accessed doubly indirectly.[8] This is illustrated in Figure 8.11.

When the file is opened, the i-node is read into memory. A typical file is small, thus all its allocation units can be accessed quickly. Very large files can be accommodated by this scheme (see Exercises).

Directoryless

In a conventional file system, part or all of a file may become inaccessible because a directory component, an i-node, or a file allocation table has become corrupted, even though the file itself is intact. A file system devised by McGregor and Malone (1981) attempted to eliminate this problem.

Their scheme does not have any directories; instead, each allocation unit is hashed onto the disk using a unique key formed from the filename and the number of the unit within the file. This key is stored as part of the data in the allocation unit. For this purpose, the disk can be regarded as a linear array of allocation units. For example, if we are storing the 15th allocation unit of file *results*, then the key

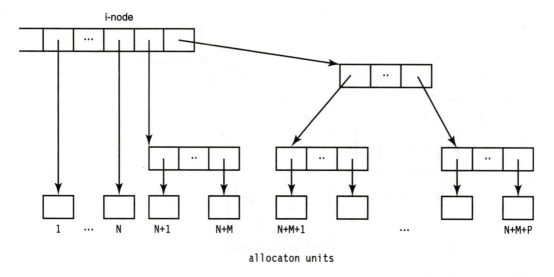

allocaton units

Figure 8.11 • I-node pointers and file allocation units

of this unit might be *results%%15*. Suppose that this string hashes to 397; in that case, we store the allocation unit on unit 397 on the disk.

Initializing the disk includes marking each allocation unit with a key that signifies that the unit is available. If the system determines that a particular allocation unit is physically unreliable, then it can be tagged with a "bad" key that causes the insert algorithm to regard it as in use and to place data elsewhere.

Direct access to a particular record in a file is fast. Disadvantages of this directory-less approach are:

- Space is required to store keys, particularly if the equivalent of subdirectories are permitted and implemented using long path names such as *Cs2/Homework/ BinaryTrees*.
- Operations such as getting a listing of the files currently on a disk take a long time.

8.4.3 Hierarchical File Systems

One definition of a hierarchical file system states that such a system permits subdirectories to an arbitrary depth. The term is also used to refer to a system in which there is a hierarchy of storage devices on which the operating system stores files with different access times and costs.[9] In order to achieve the best overall performance, an operating system moves files from faster to slower devices (and vice versa) depending on the usage of the files. Thus, in such a **hierarchical file system,** copies of frequently used files migrate to devices with shorter access times. If a file becomes inactive, then its copies on the faster devices are deleted, and eventually the only copy of it might be on an offline archive tape.

Chapter Summary

Although secondary storage devices enable persistent storage of data, transfers to and from such devices are orders of magnitude slower than to locations in primary memory, because almost all secondary storage devices are electromechanical devices rather than electronic. Some aspects of the transfer times can be influenced by the way data are arranged on the devices. Some RAID configurations and the use of cache memories can speed up effective access times and reduce the number of physical disk transfers. We shall see in Chapter 11 how some object implementations use main memory to reduce the number of logical disk transfers.

This chapter looked at low-level details of storage devices and the operating system interface that results when programmers are not concerned with the details of physical storage. The next chapter looks at file input/output from the programmer's perspective.

Exercises

1. A given disk has 512 bytes in each sector, 11 surfaces on which to record information, 200 tracks per surface, and 20 sectors on each track.

   a. What is the total capacity of the disk (in megabytes)?

   b. How many 120-byte logical records can be stored on 10 cylinders of this disk if we assume that no logical record can be split across a sector boundary?

2. A certain system holds two copies of a file containing 1000 records. On Disk A, the file is held with 10 records per sector. On Disk B, the sector size is smaller and only 5 records can be stored in a sector.

   Assume that in each case when a read is made from a disk, one sector is read. Assume that the disks have the same seek and rotation times. Assume that the disks are shared among many simultaneous users of a multiuser system.

   a. On which system is it likely to be faster to read the file in sequence (i.e., record 1, record 2, ..., record 1000)? Give reasons for your answer and state clearly any assumptions you make.

   b. On which system is it likely to be faster to read the entire file in random order (i.e., each record in the file is read exactly once, but the probability of the next record being in the same sector as the current one is negligibly small)? Give reasons for your answer and state clearly any assumptions you make.

3. A certain serial file occupies 100 disk sectors. On system A, the sectors are scattered over the disk. On system B, the sectors are all in the same cylinder. Each disk rotates 120 times a second; the average seek time is 20 ms; and it takes 1 ms to read a sector. How long would it take to read the file on each of the two systems?

4. The XYZ company makes disks that meet the following specifications:

   - 500 cylinders

   - 8 tracks per cylinder

- 15 sectors per track

- 512 bytes per sector

a.   What is the storage capacity of a disk?

b.   Why might the space available for user files be less than your answer to part a?

5. How long does it take to read a 960-cylinder disk, cylinder by cylinder? Each cylinder contains 5 tracks of 36 sectors. Within a cylinder, all of the sectors on surface 0 are to be read starting at sector 0, then all of the sectors of surface 1 starting at sector 0, and so on. You may need some or all of the following information to compute your answer.

- Time for one rotation of the disk: 16 ms

- Time to move from one cylinder to the adjacent cylinder: 10 ms

- Time to move from cylinder 0 to cylinder 959: 50 ms

- Time to switch between the tracks of a cylinder: 0 ms

State clearly any assumptions you make.

6. Suppose a disk drive were devised that had two read/write arms on opposite sides of the disk (i.e., 180 degrees apart). What advantages would such a disk have over a normal disk:

a.   If only one of the read/write arms can be active at any time?

b.   If only one read/write can happen at a time but the other arm may be positioning?

c.   If both can be active at the same time?

7. If the start and finish cylinders for a head movement are chosen randomly and the total number of cylinders is N, then the average number of cylinders moved tends to $N/3$ as N increases. Show why this is the case.

8. Suggest why an organization is likely to purchase a RAID level 5 product rather than a RAID level 4 product (and hence why nobody is manufacturing level 4 systems). Give examples as appropriate to illustrate your answer.

9. Compare and contrast a RAID level 3 system with a RAID level 5 system based on the following three actions:

a.   Successful (error-free) read operation

b.   Unsuccessful (but correctable) read including error correction

c.   Write operation

Consider, for example, the number of disks involved in each type of operation.

10. A 20-sector cache is associated with a 50,000-sector disk. Assume that 10 ms is required to load a sector from disk to cache, 0.01 ms is required to fetch data from the cache to main memory, and 0.0001 ms is required to determine if a copy of a sector is on the cache. Write a program to tabulate the average time required to perform a sector read

for each hit ratio from 49 to 99 percent in steps of 2 percent.

11. Consider the four cache replacement algorithms of Table 8.6.

    a. How could each be implemented for a Rolodex?

    b. What usage information (if any) would you need to maintain?

    c. Which algorithm would be the most appropriate for the Rolodex example? Give reasons for your choice.

12. The following is a list of addresses of disk sectors in the order in which they are read:

    10 18 11 10 19 30 31 18

    a. Suppose that the (initially empty) cache has room for four sectors. What is the hit ratio? Assume an LRU replacement algorithm.

    b. Suppose the (initially empty) cache has room for two groups of two sectors each. When a requested sector is brought into the cache, the sector with the next highest address is also brought in. What is the hit ratio in this case? Again assume an LRU replacement algorithm.

13. Suppose that it takes

    • A ms to check to see if a particular sector is in a disk cache

    • B ms to transfer a sector from disk to cache

    • C ms to transfer a sector from cache to main memory

    and that the hit ratio is D percent. Give an expression for the average access time to the disk. State clearly any assumptions you make.

    Using your formula, or otherwise, compute the effective access time to a disk when it takes 0.5 ms to check the cache, 12 ms to transfer a disk sector to cache, 1 ms to transfer a sector from cache to main memory, and the hit ratio is 60 percent.

14. Operating system A requires that files occupy adjacent sectors on a disk. A directory entry identifies the location of the first sector and the number of sectors in the file. Operating system B allows sectors of a file to be placed anywhere on a disk. The directory entry again points to the first sector. A few bytes at the end of a sector point to the next one in the file. For each of the two operating systems, give an advantage and a disadvantage of the way that it stores files.

15. Many operating systems permit the sectors that comprise a file to be physically scattered over the disk. A defragmentation program rearranges the contents of a disk so that the sectors comprising a particular file are physically adjacent. Explain why defragmenting a disk is likely to result in better disk performance (shorter access times) and why this might be particularly true if a disk cache is used.

16. Sketch a defragmentation algorithm for (a) the contiguous-block-allocation file system and (b) the linked-block file system. Assume that in each case, main memory can hold k

file blocks. Application of the algorithm should result in the free blocks forming a single contiguous area and, in each file, also occupying a single contiguous area.

17. Suppose that in a particular Unix system, i-nodes contain 13 pointers, file blocks are 512 bytes long, and pointers to disk blocks are 4 bytes long.

   a. What is the size of the largest possible file if the system uses direct pointers, indirection, and double indirection?

   b. What is the largest file size if triple indirection is also used (still a total of 13 pointers)?

Problems

1. In RAID configuration X, if certain pairs of disks fail, data will be lost. Analyze the example configuration in the text and determine characteristics of such pairs. If disks fail independently, what proportion of two-disk failures lead to data loss?

2. Given a RAID level 5 system with N disks, what is the probability that two successive write operations can be performed in parallel (i.e., require reads/writes on four different disks)? What is the smallest value of N for which this probability exceeds 0.5?

3. Generate a stream of integers representing the addresses of disk sectors requested by a program. (See Appendix A for ideas about random numbers.) Simulate the effect of a cache that can hold M sectors. Implement each of the four replacement algorithms discussed in Section 8.3.4 and determine the hit ratio. Your data stream should be realistic in that some numbers should occur less often than the average and some much more often. In addition, if N is the current number, there should be a high probability of the next being $N + 1$.

4. A certain file contains 21 records arranged in ascending key order. The records are large—only three fit into a disk sector. No record is split over two sectors. The file occupies adjacent sectors within a track on a disk. A user program performs a binary search on the file. What is the average number of physical reads required by such a search in each of the following three circumstances:

   a. There is no disk cache.

   b. The disk cache can hold one sector.

   c. The disk cache does read-ahead and can hold two sectors.

5. There are various instances in real life of an "80/20 rule"; for example, 80 percent of traffic in a town is on 20 percent of the streets, 80 percent of the borrowings from a library are accounted for by 20 percent of the books. Examine a file volume or partition and construct a histogram of file sizes (rounded to nearest block). Do you observe any instances of the 80/20 rule? If you can, look also at file creation time and last access time.

6. Suggest a way in which a conventional (erasable files) file system can be mapped onto a WORM (Write Once Read Many times) disk.

7. Suggest ways in which an operating system can encourage users to delete unused/unwanted files.

● References

Chen, P. M., E. K. Lee, G. A. Gibson, R. H. Katz, and D. A. Patterson. 1994. *RAID: High-Performance, Reliable Secondary Storage. ACM Computing Surveys,* 26 (2): 145–185.

Deighton, K. 1995. Average time to travel on two-headed, non-linear disks. *Computer Journal,* 38 (10): 811–817.

Hamming, R. W. 1950. Error detecting and correcting codes. *Bell System Technical Journal,* 29 (2): 147–160.

McGregor, D. R., and J. R. Malone. 1981. Design for a robust, simple and highly reliable filestore. *Software Practice and Experience,* 22 (9): 943–947.

Ng, S. W. 1998. Advances in disk technology: Performance issues. *Computer,* 31 (5): 75–81.

Patterson, D. A., G. Gibson, and R. H. Katz. 1988. A case for redundant arrays of inexpensive disks (RAID). *SIGMOD Record,* 17 (3): 109–116.

Tsai, W.-J., and S.-Y. Lee. 1997. Multi-partition RAID: A new method for improving performance of disk arrays under failure. *Computer Journal,* 40 (1): 30–42.

Wilkes, J., R. Golding, C. Staelin, and T. Sullivan. 1996. The HP AutoRAID hierarchical storage system. *ACM Transactions on Computer Systems,* 14 (1): 108–136.

● Notes

[1]In the case of disk storage, the **disk controller** computes and verifies the check data so that they are transparent to the CPU.

[2]The head may be movable.

[3]One difference between a drum and a disk is that the disk track radius varies. If each track contained the same number of sectors, then data storage would be less dense on outer tracks than on the inner tracks. Consequently, the tracks on most disks are grouped into zones (perhaps 20 or 30 tracks per zone). The tracks in a zone have the same number of sectors. The number of sectors is higher in outer zones.

[4]See *http://www.hgst.com* and *http://www.fujitsu.com.*

[5]If the disk is not constantly rotating, time is also needed to bring it up to speed.

[6]Some manufacturers refer to this configuration as RAID 6, using the next available number after the original five levels.

[7]In general, we could stripe groups of M sectors rather than one.

[8]Some implementations also have triple indirection.

[9]Our Rolodex example really has three levels. Some numbers are called so frequently that we keep them in our heads and don't even need to go to the Rolodex.

Files and Objects

9.1 Introduction

Chapter 8 looked at some ways in which an operating system could store files on disks. In this chapter, we look at a typical interface between a programming language and those files, and at how files are created and accessed from within a program. We look at lower-level details first, the nuts and bolts of file operations, and then examine how these details can be hidden inside a class definition to give users higher-level functions.

9.2 Programming Language Interface

In a programming language environment, it is common to have an entity that acts as an intermediary between a disk file and the main memory data elements into which we are reading or from which we are writing. The terminology for these entities varies from language to language. In C++, they are objects termed *streams*;[1] in Ada and Pascal, they are termed *file variables*; in FORTRAN, they are *unit numbers*. In what follows, we will use the C++ terminology and call them **file streams**.

9.2.1 File Streams

In a C++ program, three built-in file streams are provided: *cin* is an input file stream; *cout* and *cerr* are output file streams.[2] The user can define additional

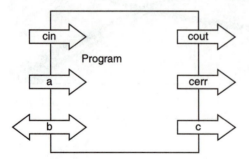

Figure 9.1 • Program and file streams

streams. Figure 9.1 depicts a program with the three built-in streams and three user-defined streams: *a*, *b*, and *c*.

Some streams, such as *a*, are created for input only. Some, such as *c*, are for output only. Some, such as *b*, are for both input and output.

9.2.2 Attaching and Detaching Files

Each programming language needs a mechanism by which a named file can be attached to a particular stream, as depicted in Figure 9.2.

Various languages (FORTRAN, Pascal, C++, and C, respectively) have commands such as:

```
open(unit=40, file='mydata', access=direct)
assign(infile, 'mydata'); reset(infile)
file1.open("mydata",ios::in)
fp = fopen("mydata", "rb")
```

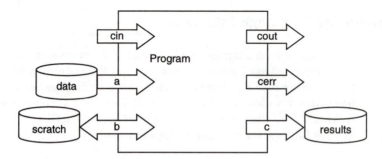

Figure 9.2 • Program with file streams and attached files

that attach file *mydata* for reading. Corresponding detaching commands are:

```
close (unit=40)
close (infile)
file1.close()
fclose(fp)
```

The detaching commands break the link between the file and the stream. This separation is necessary before the stream can be attached to a different file. If a file was attached for writing, then, in some environments, the detaching operation may also be responsible for ensuring that any data in output buffers in main memory are written to the disk file before the connection is broken.

Programs can be written in terms of the streams; the connection to actual files is done at run time. In most cases, the user can supply the name of the file to be used at run time rather than have this be a constant string in the program code.

In the following C++ program fragment, the program makes up to k attempts to attach to stream f a file with a name supplied by the user.

```
attempts_remaining = k;
while (attempts_remaining > 0)
{
      cout << "Filename: ";
      cin >> filename;
      f.open(filename,ios::in);
      attempts_remaining--;
      if (f.fail())
         cout <<  "could not open " << filename <<endl;
      else
         break;
}
if (!f.fail())
   { //   file is available for reading on stream f
    ...
   }
```

The program reads the user-entered filename into string variable *filename*; then it tries to open the specified file for reading.[3] The function *fail* of the stream object returns *true* (a nonzero value) if the attempt does not succeed. If the file is opened successfully, the program breaks out of the loop; otherwise, it gives an error message and repeats the loop. A file may fail to open for reading for a variety of reasons. For example, the file may not exist, the file may exist but the user is not allowed to open it, or the file may be openable but the program has reached a limit on the number of concurrently attached files.

File Names as Command Line Arguments

An alternative to inputting filenames while the program is running is to pass the filenames as arguments in a command line. Consider the following program (*echoprog.cc*).

```
#include <iostream.h>

int main (int argc, char* argv[])
{
    cout << "argc is: " << argc << endl;
    for (int i=0; i<argc; i++)
        cout << "argv[" << i << "] is " << argv[i] << endl;
    return 0;
}
```

The parameters of *main* are an integer *argc* (argument count) and an array of pointers to strings *argv* (argument vector). When the program is run, the operating system puts a count of the symbols on the command line into *argc* and pointers to the symbols into *argv*. The *echoprog.cc* program merely echoes that information. For example, when run as

```
echoprog one two three
```

the output is

```
argc is: 4
argv[0] is echoprog
argv[1] is one
argv[2] is two
argv[3] is three
```

More usefully, suppose we wish to have a program (*copylines*) that copies the first *N* lines of one file to another. A typical invocation of the program is

```
copylines 20 olddata newdata
```

Part of that program might be:

```
int main (int argc, char* argv[])
{
    if (argc != 4)
     {
```

```
        cerr << "Usage is: copylines N inputfile outputfile\n";
        exit(-1);
      }
    ifstream infile;          // stream for the input file
    ofstream outfile;         // stream for the output file
    int number_of_lines;      // number of lines to copy

    // open files - error checking omitted
    infile.open(argv[2]);       // using input file name
    outfile.open(argv[3]);      // using output file name

    number_of_lines = atoi(argv[1]);  // convert string to int
    // and so on ...

}
```

The program checks that it has been called with the correct number of arguments (four, including the name of the program itself), then it uses the argument strings in function calls to attach files to streams and to obtain *N*, the number of lines to copy.

Usually, the mechanisms by which data are read from the standard input (keyboard) and written to the standard output (screen) also permit reading from and writing to files attached to streams. Thus, if each of the following

```
cin.get(c)
cin >> c
```

gets a character from the keyboard and stores it into *char* variable *c*, then each of the following

```
infile.get(c)
infile >> c
```

reads in a similar manner from the file currently attached to stream *infile*.

9.2.3 Text Files and Binary Files

We know that data in main memory are represented in binary form. When such data (e.g., numeric data) are output to the screen, the data have to be converted by write/output routines into an appropriate stream of character codes. However, when writing data from main memory to a file, we have a choice. We can either convert the data into a stream of character codes and create a *text* file or simply copy the bytes from main memory and create a *binary* file. Each file type has its advantages.

Advantages of text files:

- Legible
- Editable with a text editor

Advantages of binary files:

- May be smaller than the corresponding text file
- Uniform size of items makes random access easier
- No conversion operations—I/O likely to be faster

In some programming environments, whether a file is interpreted as text or binary depends on the type of stream variable to which it is attached. In other environments, it may depend on the parameters of the function call that opens the file. In either case, each of the two file types is likely to have its own routines for performing data transfers.

Example Program with Text and Binary File Output
The following program creates two files, each containing the sequence of integers from −10 to +10. File A contains the integers written in text form, separated by single spaces. File B contains the numbers written as binary integers.[4]

```
#include <fstream.h>

int main()
{
  fstream out1, out2;

  out1.open("A",ios::out);  // no difference in the way
  out2.open("B",ios::out);  // that the files are opened

  for (int i=-10; i<11; i++)
    {
      out1 << i << " ";                      // text output
      out2.write( (void *) &i, sizeof(i));   // binary output
    }

  out1.close();
  out2.close();

  return 0;
}
```

The program was run in a Unix environment in which the utility *xd* displays the contents of a file in hexadecimal (thus, two characters per byte). Each line of the output from *xd* contains 16 bytes preceded by the address (also in hexadecimal) of the first byte. Here are results of calling *xd* with file A following a run of the previous program. The character code for a minus sign is *2d*, the code for a space is *20*, and codes for the digits are consecutive beginning at *30*.

A (54 bytes)

```
0000000 2d31 3020 2d39 202d 3820 2d37 202d 3620
0000010 2d35 202d 3420 2d33 202d 3220 2d31 2030
0000020 2031 2032 2033 2034 2035 2036 2037 2038
0000030 2039 2031 3020
0000036
```

Here is the result of running *xd* on file B. The system on which the program was run uses the two's complement number system and 4 bytes for each integer variable.

B (84 bytes)

```
0000000 ffff fff6 ffff fff7 ffff fff8 ffff fff9
0000010 ffff fffa ffff fffb ffff fffc ffff fffd
0000020 ffff fffe ffff ffff 0000 0000 0000 0001
0000030 0000 0002 0000 0003 0000 0004 0000 0005
0000040 0000 0006 0000 0007 0000 0008 0000 0009
0000050 0000 000a
0000054
```

Note that there is nothing in either file—no header bytes, for example—that indicate whether the file type is text or binary. Thus, when reading data from an existing file, a programmer must be careful to use the appropriate protocol.

9.2.4 Serial Access and Direct Access

Some programming languages make a distinction between files opened in a serial manner and files opened for direct (random) access. Historically, this difference between **serial files** and **direct access files** reflects the different properties of serial storage devices such as tapes and direct access storage devices such as disks. In both modes, a **file pointer** has information about the current reading/writing position in the file.[5] One difference between the two modes is that in direct access, there is a mechanism by which we can move the file pointer(s) to an arbitrary position in the file (we usually would do this immediately before a read or write operation), whereas serial access has no such mechanism, and the pointers advance as a side effect of reading and writing.[6]

Serial Access
Terminology varies, but in our interpretation of serial file processing, a file that has been opened in serial mode is open for reading or for writing but not for both. In

addition, it is not possible to position the file pointer explicitly at an arbitrary location in the file.

When a file is opened for reading, a file pointer is positioned at the beginning of the file. Reading proceeds in a serial manner through the file, and the pointer advances over an appropriate number of bytes as data are read. There is typically a mechanism that enables us to detect when the pointer has reached the end of the file. This mode of operation is comparable with how a tape is read. (In some environments, there is even a "rewind" operator that sets the pointer back to the beginning of the file.)

When a serial file is opened for writing, an empty file is created. This usually overwrites any existing file with the same name. As data are written, it is appended to the file; thus, the file pointer is always at the end of the file.

Note that if only reading or writing can be performed on a file, then in order to change its contents, we have to create a new file. We copy information from the old file to a new file and make appropriate changes to the data as it passes through main memory. This has the advantage of retaining the old version of the data file, but it is a slow process. However, if we have a data file that does not have to be up to date at all times, then it might be acceptable to batch the changes and to periodically merge them with the data file. An example of such a data file is a mailing list of subscribers to a monthly magazine. The data changes as new customers are added, customers are deleted, and other customer information changes (e.g., billing address or subscription expiration date), but perhaps the data file only needs to be updated once a month when mailing labels are printed.

Next are two example C++ programs that demonstrate serial file reading and/or writing. In the first example, we need to find which numbers in a file are greater than the average number. In the second example, we merge two ordered files of integers to create a third file.

Serial File Example: Finding the Average Number   We have a file of integers called *scores*. We wish to output (to the standard output) those numbers in the file that are greater than the average of the numbers in the file. In the program that follows, *infile* is the stream variable. The program reads the file twice: once to compute the average and then a second time to print the numbers that are greater than the average.[7]

```
#include <fstream.h>

int main()
{
     fstream infile;              // bi-directional "pipe"
     int N, count=0, sum=0;
     float average;

     infile.open("scores",ios::in);  // file opened for input only

     while ( !infile.eof() )  // more data?
       {
```

```
        infile >> N;        // get number
        sum +=N;            // add to total and
        count++;            // bump the count
    }

    infile.close();  // so we can re-open at the beginning

    average = float(sum)/float(count);

    infile.open("scores",ios::in);   // back at the beginning
    while ( !infile.eof() )
        {
          infile >> N;
          if (N>average) cout << N << endl;
        }
    infile.close();
    return 0;
}
```

Serial File Example: File Merging   Relatively straightforward software (see Exercises 1 and 2) can merge an ordered file of records (old master file) with a comparably ordered file of changes to those records (updates) and create a file of changed records (new master file). Our second example program solves a similar but simpler problem. We merge two ordered files to form a third. Each input file contains integers in ascending order ending with a recognizable sentinel value. The program writes the sentinel value to the end of the output file, thus enabling that file to be used in subsequent merge operations. If the input files (with sentinel 999) are:

```
One:    2 6 7 43 999
Two:    1 3 6 8 21 999
```

then the output will be:

```
1 2 3 6 6 7 8 21 43 999
```

The program keeps in memory one data item from each input file. At each iteration it outputs the smaller of the two items and replaces that item by the next one from the appropriate file. If one file but not the other has data remaining, the program writes and then replaces that data. The program iterates until there is no more data to be read.

```
#include <fstream.h>

#define sentinel 999

void getfrom (fstream& f, bool& finishedflag, int& number)
{
```

```
    // reads number from file on f
    // sets finishedflag to true if number is last in file

    f >> number;
    if (number==sentinel) finishedflag = true;
}

int main()
{
    fstream infile1, infile2, outfile;
    bool finished1 = false,    // flag - first file finished
    finished2 = false,         // flag - second file finished
    number1,                   // number from first file
    number2;                   // number from second file

    infile1.open("dataone",ios::in);    // error checks
    infile2.open("datatwo",ios::in);    // omitted for
    outfile.open("results",ios::out);   // brevity

    getfrom(infile1,finished1,number1);
    getfrom(infile2,finished2,number2);

    while ( !(finished1 && finished2) )
        {       // at least one file has unread data
            if (finished1)
                {       // no data on file 1, process file 2
                    outfile << number2 << endl;
                    getfrom(infile2,finished2,number2);
                }
            else if (finished2)
                    { // no data on file 2, process file 1
                    outfile << number1 << endl;
                    getfrom(infile1,finished1,number1);
                }
            else if (number1 < number2)
                    { // data on both, output smaller here
                    outfile << number1 << endl;
                    getfrom(infile1,finished1,number1);
                }
            else
                    { // or here
                    outfile << number2 << endl;
                    getfrom(infile2,finished2,number2);
                }
```

```
        }
// write terminator to output file
 outfile << sentinel << endl;
 outfile.close();
 infile1.close();
 infile2.close();
 return 0;
}
```

The function *getfrom* gets a data item from a specified file or sets a flag to indicate that there are no more data.

Direct Access

Direct access file processing requires a mechanism by which we can position a conceptual file pointer at an arbitrary point in the file. For example, the effect of function call *seek(i)* might be to position the file pointer at the *i*th byte or perhaps the *i*th record in the file. In addition, it is usually possible both to read from and to write to a file opened for direct access. Thus, we can position the pointer at an arbitrary record in the file, read the record into main memory, modify it, and then write the record back to the file, overwriting the old version without accessing the other records in the file. This mode of operation is comparable with how a disk works. With direct access to a file, we can modify it without creating a new file. Most of the persistent data structures that we look at in Chapters 11, 12, and 13 require that elements of a file be directly accessible.

The following is an example of direct access file processing. It is an interactive, menu-driven program that enables a user to perform simple operations on a file of records.

Direct Access File Example: Record Modification and Printing   We assume that the file is initially empty and that each record has three integer fields (designated *a*, *b*, and *c*). The program enables a user to change or print an arbitrary existing record and to add new ones at the end of the file.

The program loops accepting commands from the user. If the command is *q* (for quit), then the loop terminates. Three other commands permit operations on the file:

- *p:* In response to the *p* (for print) command, the program requests a record number and, if it is valid, opens the file for reading. It positions the file reading pointer to the appropriate point in the file, reads the record, prints the contents, and then closes the file.
- *c:* In response to the *c* (for change) command, the program requests a record number and, if it is valid, opens the file for both reading and writing. It reads an arbitrary record, and then allows a user to input a new value for any of the three fields. The record is then written back to the file, overwriting the old version, and the file is closed.

- *n:* In response to the *n* (for new) command, the program reads values for the three record fields, opens the file in append mode (which leaves the writing pointer at the end of the file), appends a new record to the file, and then closes the file.

Note how each of the different commands causes the file to be opened in a manner appropriate for the command and closes the file when finished.

```cpp
#include <fstream.h>
int main()
{
  fstream f;
  bool more = true;       // continue-processing flag
  int count = 0,          // number of records in the file
      N;
  char command, fieldname;
  struct {int a; int b; int c;} R;

  while (more)
   {
     cout << "command: ";
     cin >> command;

     switch(command)
     {
      case 'p': // print
               cout << "which record to print? ";
               cin >> N;
               if (N < count)                          // records numbered from 0 upwards
                 {
                   f.open("recordfile",ios::in);        // open file for reading
                   f.seekg(N * sizeof(R));              // position reading ptr at record N
                   f.read( (void *)&R, sizeof(R));      // get Nth record
                   f.close();
                   cout << R.a << R.b << R.c << endl;
                 }
               break;

      case 'c': // change
               cout << "which record to change? ";
               cin >> N;
               if (N < count)
                 {
                   f.open("recordfile",ios::in|ios::out); // open for reading and writing
```

```
                  f.seekg(N * sizeof(R));                 // reading pointer to record N
                  f.read( (void *)&R, sizeof(R));         // Nth record to memory
                  cout << "which new field? ";
                  cin >> fieldname;
                  switch (fieldname)
                    {
                      case 'a': cout << "a: "; cin >> (R.a); break;
                      case 'b': cout << "b: "; cin >> (R.b); break;
                      case 'c': cout << "c: "; cin >> (R.c); break;
                      default : cout << "Invalid field" << endl;
                    }
                  f.seekp(N*sizeof(R));                    // set writing ptr to record N
                  f.write( (void *)&R, sizeof(R));         // and put modified record back
                  f.close();
                }
             break;

      case 'n': // new record
                cout << "Enter values for 3 fields: ";
                cin >> R.a >> R.b >> R.c ;
                f.open("recordfile",ios::app);      // open file in append mode
                f.write( (void *)&R, sizeof(R));    // writing at the end of the file
                f.close();
                count++;
                break;

      case 'q': // quit
                more = false;
                break;

      default: cout << "Invalid command: " << command << endl;
     }
   }
 return 0;
}
```

Here is output from a run of the program.

```
command: n
Enter values for 3 fields: 9 1 1
command: n
Enter values for 3 fields: 1 2 3
```

```
command: n
Enter values for 3 fields: 4 0 5
command: n
Enter values for 3 fields: 6 7 7
command: p
which record to print? 4
command: p
which record to print? 3
677
command: p
which record to print? 0
911
command: c
which record to change? 2
which new field? b
b: 8
command: p
which record to print? 2
485
command: n
Enter values for 3 fields: 9 8 7
command: p
which record to print? 4
987
command: q
```

In this program, we see examples of low-level file operations—moving file pointers and transferring the correct number of bytes between main memory and the file. Earlier chapters demonstrated how a class definition can be used to hide implementation details of an abstract data type. It is natural to do this with secondary memory structures as well as those implemented in main memory. In the next section, we give a definition of a *BinaryFile* class that includes functions to perform simple record-oriented storage and retrieval operations on a file of records.

● 9.3 File Objects

In the final example of the previous section, we used *fstream* and its methods to manipulate the contents of a file. But we can do this kind of processing in non-object-oriented languages such as Pascal and FORTRAN. In C++, we can use the class mechanism to define a higher-level object and free the user from some of the low-level details evident in our random access example.

9.3.1 Binary File Requirements

In the definition of *BinaryFile* that follows,[8] we assume that the user wishes to perform operations on a file of fixed-size records. The template mechanism lets us specify the particular record type when we declare an instance of *BinaryFile*. The operations provided in our definition enable a user to

- Open and close a file
- Read and write records at arbitrary locations
- Write a record at the current position

As in many of our earlier class definitions, successful operations return *true* and unsuccessful ones return *false*.

9.3.2 File Mode

One of the parameters of the *open* method is an integer that determines the mode in which we open the file. We have used parameter values such as *ios::in* and *ios::out* in our examples. In general, the integer can be regarded as a composite of seven flags and, as you can see from Table 9.1, *in* and *out* are two of seven possible values.

Thus, a parameter such as *ios::in | ios::out* is actually the integer 96. The *status* variable in a *BinaryFile* object contains zero if there is no currently attached file; otherwise, it records the mode in which the file was opened. This enables us to perform some checks on the legitimacy of file operations.

9.3.3 *BinaryFile* Class Definition

The definition of *BinaryFile* should be regarded as a prototype; many extensions and improvements are possible, some of which are assigned as Exercises at the end of the chapter. The class definition of *BinaryFile* follows.

● **TABLE 9.1** File Opening Flags

Mode	Description	Value
noreplace	Open fails if file exists	1
nocreate	Open fails if file does not exist	2
trunc	If file exists, contents are discarded	4
app	Output written to end of file	8
ate	Open with file pointer at end of file	16
out	File open for output	32
in	File open for input	64

```
#include <fstream.h>

template <class TYPE>
class BinaryFile
{
  public:
    BinaryFile ()
        {     // constructor sets record length and file object status
        sizeRecord = sizeof(TYPE);
        status = 0;
        }
    ~BinaryFile()
        {     // destructor makes sure file stream is closed.
        close();
        status = 0;
        };
    bool open(char *filename, int state)
        {  // open file stream
        if (status != 0) return false;     // a file is already attached
        myFile.open(filename, state);
        if (myFile.fail()) return false;  // open attempt failed
        status = state;                    // remember open mode
        return true;                       // successful open
        }
    bool close ()
        {
        if (status==0) return false;      // no file attached
        myFile.close();   // close file stream
        status = 0;
        return true;
        }
    bool getRecord(int index, TYPE & record)
        {     // get record at index i
        if ( (status & ios::in) == 0 )
            return false;  // not opened for reading
        myFile.seekg(index * sizeRecord);
        // read expects a char * so cast below
        myFile.read( (void *) & record, sizeRecord);
        return true;
        }
    bool putRecord(int index, TYPE  record)
        {     // write record at index i
        if ( (status & (ios::out|ios::app|ios::ate)) == 0 )
```

```
            return false; // not open for writing
        myFile.seekp(index * sizeRecord);
        // write expects a char * so cast below
        myFile.write((void *) &record, sizeRecord);
        return true;
        }
    bool putRecord(TYPE  record)
        {     // write record at current position - useful for append
        if ( (status & (ios::out|ios::app|ios::ate)) == 0 )
            return false; // not open for writing
        // write expects a char * so cast below
        myFile.write((void *) &record, sizeRecord);
        return true;
        }

    private:
        fstream myFile;   // declare file stream for record's use
        int sizeRecord;   // size of struct to be stored set in constructor
        int status ;      // 0 if no file, otherwise file opening mode
};
```

● 9.3.4 Use of the *BinaryFile* Class

A program might contain the following structure definitions for student information and for library books:

```
struct sturecord { int idnum; char major[50]; };
struct lib_book_record {char title[40]; bool on_loan; int isbn; };
```

with corresponding temporary records for a student and for a book:

```
sturecord tempstudent;
lib_book_record tempbook;
```

and corresponding *BinaryFile* objects for a file of enrolled students and the library catalog:

```
BinaryFile<sturecord> enrolled;
BinaryFile<lib_book_record> catalog;
```

enabling us to read/write the student data and append to the catalog:

```
enrolled.open("student-data",ios::in|ios::out);
catalog.open("current-holdings",ios::app);
```

and get an arbitrary student record and append a new book:

```
enrolled.getRecord(57,tempstudent);
catalog.putRecord(max,tempbook);
```

Appendix C contains a listing of a program that uses the *BinaryFile* class and the output from a run of the program. The following is our interactive program from Section 9.2 rewritten to use the *BinaryFile* class.

```
#include <fstream.h>
#include "newbinfile.h"
struct rectype {int a; int b; int c;};

int main()
{
  bool more = true;        // continue-processing flag
  int count = 0,           // number of records in the file
      N;
  char command, fieldname;
  rectype R;
  BinaryFile<rectype> f;

  while (more)
   {
      cout << "command: ";
      cin >> command;

      switch(command)
      {
       case 'p': // print
               cout << "which record to print? ";
               cin >> N;
               if (N < count)                          // records numbered
                                                       // from 0 upwards
                 {
                   f.open("recordfile",ios::in);       // open file for reading
                   f.getRecord(N,R);                   // get Nth record
                   f.close();
                   cout << R.a << R.b << R.c << endl;
                 }
               break;
```

```
      case 'c': // change
              cout << "which record to change? ";
              cin >> N;
              if (N < count)
                {
                  f.open("recordfile",ios::in|ios::out); // open for
                                                          // reading and writing
                  f.getRecord(N,R);                       // get Nth record
                  cout << "which new field? ";
                  cin >> fieldname;
                  switch (fieldname)
                   {
                    case 'a': cout << "a: "; cin >> (R.a); break;
                    case 'b': cout << "b: "; cin >> (R.b); break;
                    case 'c': cout << "c: "; cin >> (R.c); break;
                    default : cout << "Invalid field" << endl;
                   }
                  f.putRecord(N,R);                       // put modified
                                                          // record back
                  f.close();
                }
              break;

      case 'n': // new record
              cout << "Enter values for 3 fields: ";
              cin >> R.a >> R.b >> R.c ;
              f.open("recordfile",ios::app);      // open file in
                                                  // append mode
              f.putRecord(R);                     // writing at the end
                                                  // of the file
              f.close();
              count++;
              break;

      case 'q': // quit
              more = false;
              break;

      default: cout << "Invalid command: " << command << endl;
      }
   }
   return 0;
}
```

9.4 Saving Transient Objects

9.4.1 Overview

If we want an object to have an existence beyond its normal lifespan in a program, we can implement its data in secondary memory. We will consider some file-based data structures in Chapters 11, 12, and 13. Alternatively, we can implement its data in main memory and arrange for the data to be saved to secondary storage and restored from secondary storage as appropriate. This provides us the speed advantage of main memory operations together with the persistence of secondary storage.

Saving and restoring the data can be more or less difficult depending on the complexity of the structure and whether we want the restored data structure to be exactly the same as the one we save, or just equivalent. For example, on saving a binary tree, we can preserve enough information to enable the shape of the tree to be re-created or we can just save the data content and not be concerned about restoring the tree to exactly its original shape. Similarly, when we save a hash table, we can record the locations of the data items or just the items themselves. If we save only the items, then when we restore the table by rehashing the items we may end up with a different table than the one we saved. This section looks at some aspects of saving transient objects.

9.4.2 Implementation

We could take one of two approaches to save a transient object:

1. Add two methods to the class that respectively save and restore the data. The user is responsible for invoking the methods where appropriate in the program.
2. Augment the constructor and destructor functions so that the destructor saves the object and the constructor restores it. This makes saving and restoring largely transparent to the user. However, this approach is not appropriate for some objects in a program, such as those passed as value parameters to a function.

In what follows, we illustrate the second approach. We assume that if the user associates a filename with an object, then the data components of the object are to be saved in that file, and that if the null filename (empty string) is associated with an object, then no saving is required.

Constructor
If the filename is null (its default value) or a file with the given name does not exist, we initialize the data structure as normal. If the specified file does exist, then we restore the data structure from the file. We should verify that the file contents are a valid representation of an object.

Destructor
If the filename is not null, we create a new file with the given name (overwriting one that may already exist) and save the data structure to the file. If the filename is null, no saving is done.

Example: map_hash_bounded
To illustrate how the augmented constructor and destructor might work, we use one of the classes from Chapter 5 that implements a map using a hash table. We will write the contents of the table to a text file and save it so that it can be re-created exactly. To make the symbol table persistent, two additions are required to the class definition of *map_hash_bounded*. First, a new data item is required in the private section:

- *filename:* Holds the name of the file associated with the object

  Second, two new functions are required in the private section:

- *readtag:* A function to read a tag from a file
- *writetag:* A function to write a tag to a file

  Additionally, objects that are stored in the table must have two associated methods:

- *saver:* Writes the contents of the object in a restorable form to a text file
- *restore:* Reads object contents from a text file

(Note that there is a better solution than using a text file—see Problems at the end of the chapter.) Given these requirements, here are the new constructor and destructor functions:

```
template <class Entry>
map_hash_bounded<Entry>::map_hash_bounded(int N=10,char fname[]="")
        {
        ifstream f;
        strcpy(filename,fname);  // save filename for later use
        if (strlen(filename) > 0) f.open(filename);
        if (strlen(filename) == 0 || f.fail())
            { // initialize empty because no file name given
              // or attempt to open the file failed.
              size=N;
              tags = new hashtag[size];
              entries = new Entry[size];
              for (int i=0;i<N;i++) tags[i]=empty;
            }
        else
            { // get data from file, size of table is first
              f >> size;
```

```
                tags = new hashtag[size];
                entries = new Entry[size];
                for (int i=0; i<size; i++)
                  {
                    tags[i] = readtag(f);
                    if (tags[i]==full) entries[i].restore(f);
                  }
                f.close();
              }
          }

template <class Entry>
map_hash_bounded<Entry>::~map_hash_bounded()
        { ofstream f;
          // use file name saved by constructor
          if (strlen(filename) > 0) f.open(filename);
          if (strlen(filename) > 0 && !f.fail())
            { // file name given and file successfully opened
              // save to file, size first
              f << size << endl;
              for (int i=0; i<size; i++)
                {
                  writetag(tags[i],f);
                  if (tags[i]==full)
                     entries[i].saver(f);
                  else
                     f << endl;
                }
              f.close();
            }
          // deallocate space
          delete[] tags;
          delete[] entries;
        }
```

The following program tests the enhanced hash table.

```
//  program to test object saving and restoration

#include "map_hash_bounded2.h"    // enhanced constructor and destructor
#include <fstream.h>

class sturec2
{
```

```
    public: sturec2 (int N=-1,char S[]="  ")
            { idnum = N; strcpy(major,S); }  // constructor: id and name
         int H (int N)
            { return idnum % N; }            // hash on id
         int operator == (sturec2 S)
            { return S.idnum==idnum; }       // == operator
         int operator < (sturec2 S)
            { return S.idnum<idnum; }        // < operator
         int operator > (sturec2 S)
            { return S.idnum>idnum; }        // > operator
          void show()
            { cout << "  " << idnum << " " << major ;}  // display components
          void saver(ofstream& f)
            { f << idnum << "  " << major << endl;} // save to stream f
          void restore(ifstream& f)
            { f >> idnum >> major; }                 // restore from stream f

    private: int idnum;
            char major[10];
};

void A(int callnumber)
{
  map_hash_bounded<sturec2> one(20,"hash.sav");  // this one will be saved
  map_hash_bounded<sturec2> two(10);             // this one will be lost

  sturec2 a(6,"Math"),b(5,"English"),c(12,"Physics"),d(8,"Chemistry");

  if (callnumber==1)
     { // put data in tables one and two
       one.insert(a);
       one.insert(b);
       two.insert(c);
       two.insert(d);
     }
  if (callnumber==2)
     { // see what is in tables
       cout << "Here is table one\n";
       one.showtable();    // should be restored from file
       cout << "Here is table two\n";
       two.showtable();    // should be empty
     }
}
```

```
main()
{
    // first call sets up entries
    A(1);
    // second call sees what is in objects now. Expect that
    // table one contents are preserved, table two contents lost.
    A(2);
}
```

In the program, *sturec2* is a simple class for storing and operating on student data. In line with our requirements, it includes *save* and *restore* functions.

Function *A* contains local declarations of two maps (hash tables) of student records. Map *one* has a filename associated with its declaration (*hash.sav*), so the contents will be saved to that file when the function terminates and the destructor is invoked. Map *two* has no filename, so its contents are lost on exit from the function.

The main program calls *A* twice. During the first call of *A*, data are stored in each map, and on exit from the function, map *one* is saved. During the second call to *A*, map *one* is restored from the file and the contents of both tables are printed.

Here is output from a run of the program. As you can see, data in the first map have been preserved; data in the second table have been lost.

```
% a.out

Here is table one
0
1
2
3
4
5     5 English
6     6 Math
7
8
9
10
11
12
13
14
15
16
17
18
```

19

```
Here is table two
0
1
2
3
4
5
6
7
8
9
%
```

Chapter Summary

Chapter 8 looked at characteristics of storage devices on which files are kept. This chapter examined files from a programmer's viewpoint. We considered file variables (streams), the difference between text and binary files, and the difference between serial and direct access modes. We saw that file variables are a common intermediate object between a file and main memory. If a file can be opened only in a serial manner, updating it can be time-consuming. Random/direct access is necessary to do efficient changes.

We saw that we can define a class of objects that lets us hide low-level details of transfers to and from a file. Finally, we looked at ways in which a transient object might be enhanced to make it persistent.

Exercises

1. How could the record modification program of Section 9.2.4 be made more general by allowing changes to be made to an already existing file? How could it be made more robust by checking user inputs?

2. We saw how a map implemented as a hash table can be saved to a file and restored. Provide an algorithm that will do the same for a map implemented as a binary tree. The tree should be saved in such a way that it should be possible to recreate both the shape and the contents of the tree from the information stored in the file. For a small example tree, show what the file that contains the tree contents looks like.

3. Show how a binary tree can be saved and restored if we do not care if the restored tree has the same shape as the original. However, the tree should not be degenerate after its restoration.

4. Show how a binary trie can be saved and restored exactly.

5. How would you save and restore a graph implemented using an adjacency matrix? Aim for your data file to be as small as possible.

6. Describe how you would enhance the definition of the class *BinaryFile* so that if a user has:

   BinaryFile X

   then *X.getnext(R)* puts into *R* the record following the one most recently read and *X.getprevious(R)* puts into *R* the record that precedes the one most recently read. Don't forget to take error conditions into account in your design.

7. Describe how you would enhance the definition of the class *BinaryFile* so that a user is able to make certain records in a file temporarily read-only. Thus, if a user has

   BinaryFile X

   then *X.readonly(k)* prevents record *k* from being written to until *X.readwrite(k)* removes the protection. If, in the meantime, the user attempts *X.putrecord(k, R)*, an error message should be generated.

8. Describe how you would enhance the definition of the class *BinaryFile* so that a user is able to "erase" record *i* in a file. An erasure should cause subsequent records to appear to be renumbered. For example, if we have a file of six records numbered 0 through 5:

   0 1 2 3 4 5

   and we erase record 3, then, from the users point of view, the remaining records are numbered 0 through 4, thus

   0 1 2   3 4

   Describe circumstances under which the erased space could be reused.

9. Add a method to *BinaryFile* that returns the number of records in the file.

10. Describe how you could modify *BinaryFile* so that it would not be possible to read beyond the current end of the file, although it would still be possible to write there.

11. Describe a way in which the contents of a *map_hash_unbounded* object (see Chapter 5) can be saved and restored. Recall that this class uses overflow lists.

● Problems

1. Assume there is a master file of keys (integers) arranged in ascending order and a second file of modifications to the master file. Each line in the modifications file is either an insertion record of the form

   I <key>

   or a deletion record of the form

   D <key>

   Records in the modifications file are also in ascending key order. Write a program that creates a new master file with the appropriate changes made. (See Appendix A for ideas about generating test data for your program.)

2. Extend your solution to Problem 1. This time, each line of the master file has a key value (as before) followed by a data value. There is a third type of record in the modifications file, namely,

   M <key> <newvalue>

   that indicates a new data value for the record with the given key value.

3. Complete and test the *copylines* program. Ensure that your program deals gracefully with invalid parameters.

4. Modify the *saver* and *restore* functions of class *sturec2* so that multiword majors (e.g., "Computer Science") work correctly.

5. Modify the enhanced constructor and destructor of *map_hash_bounded* so that they use two binary files (one for tags, one for table entries) rather than a single text file. This takes away the need for *readtag*, *writetag*, *saver*, and *restore*. The constructor should ensure that either both files exist or neither exist. If both exist, it should check that they are the same length (see Exercise 9).

6. Write a program that creates a text file of pseudo-random integers. A user supplies four inputs:

   a. The number of integers to be written

   b. The smallest integer that may be written

   c. The largest integer that may be written

   d. Whether duplicate integers are permitted

   Your program should perform "reasonableness" checks on the user inputs (e.g., to determine if it is impossible to generate appropriate data).

7. Implement a simple line-oriented text editor. The program reads the contents of a user-specified file into a data structure in main memory and then enables the user to perform simple operations on the structure. Example operations are insertion and removal of lines and global replacement of one string by another. A user should be able to save the contents of the data structure to an arbitrary file at any time during the editing process.

● Notes

[1]*ios* is a base class from which many classes are derived for handling a variety of input/output operations. Examples of derived classes are stream classes *fstream*, *ofstream*, and *ifstream*.

[2]Imagine the operator interacting with a computer system at a console; this is where we get console-input (*cin*), console-output (*cout*), and console-error (*cerr*).

[3]The second parameter of the *open* function indicates the mode in which the file will be attached. Some possibilities are *ios::in* (input), *ios::out* (output), *ios::inlios::out* (input and output), and *ios::app* (append).

[4]The second parameter of *write* is the number of bytes to be written. Function *sizeof* returns the number of bytes occupied by a variable. The first parameter of the file reading and writing

functions is normally a pointer to a character variable. Here we use a cast to make a generic pointer and keep the compiler happy.

[5]There may be two pointers, one for reading and one for writing.

[6]In C++, *seekg* (*g* for "get") moves the reading pointer and *seekp* (*p* for "put") moves the writing pointer.

[7]The *eof* function of *fstream* returns true when the file pointer is at the end of the file. In the expression that computes the average, we "cast" the integers *count* and *sum* to floating point in order to get a true rather than truncated result.

[8]Based on an original design by Mike Barnes.

Sorting

10.1 Introduction

Sorting a data set is not usually an end in itself. Sorting is usually done to improve the efficiency of other operations, such as collation, searching, or elimination of duplicate items in a collection. When data were stored primarily on serial devices such as magnetic tapes, there was a significant need for algorithms that would sort data into order (e.g., a batch of transactions would be sorted before being merged with a sequential master file). With the development of online transaction processing and direct access storage devices, there is less need for this type of operation. However, there are still operations that require sorting, and some for which sorting improves performance.[1]

If the data to be sorted can be held entirely in main memory, then the data are typically stored in linear storage and rearranged so that storage order corresponds to collation order. This is **internal sorting**. We briefly present, compare, and give C++ functions for four internal sorting algorithms in Section 10.2. Internal sorting algorithms are typically evaluated according to the number of key-comparisons that are made during the sort. This is because the effort involved in determining the relative ordering of pairs of items is usually the largest component of the running time of the algorithm.[2]

If the data set is too large to hold entirely in main memory, then we resort to **external sorting** methods in which some of the data are on secondary storage during sorting. The criteria for evaluating external sorting algorithms are different from those for internal sorting algorithms. We are usually concerned not with the number of key-comparisons, but rather with the number of input/output transfers because these typically account for most of the total sorting time. We look at ways in which external sorting can be done in Section 10.3.

10.2 Internal Sorting

This section summarizes the strategies and properties of typical internal sorting methods. It is worth noting that sorting algorithms can often be modified to solve related problems, such as finding the median or, in general, the kth largest item in a data set. We consider four algorithms in this section: Selection Sort, Heapsort, Mergesort, and Quicksort. We assume, without loss of generality, that the algorithm is to sort an array of integers into ascending order. In practice, the array might be of pointers to objects, and we rearrange the pointers rather than move the objects themselves. In general, the algorithms can sort objects of any type given a way to determine the relative order of two objects.

10.2.1 Selection Sort

Selection Sort is a very simple method in which the array has a sorted section and an unsorted section. In each pass through the unsorted section, the smallest item is found and moved into the sorted section. The algorithm can be classified as $O(N^2)$ because we have nested loops and the number of iterations in each is proportional to N (the number of elements to be sorted). If N doubles, we expect sorting time to quadruple. Parameters of the following C++ function enable a user to specify that the function is to arrange in ascending order the section of array T from T_{low} to T_{high}:

```
void selectionsort (int T[], int low, int high)
{
  int temp;
  for (int i=low; i<=high; i++)
      {
       // find smallest among T[i] .. T[high]
       int min=T[i];   // smallest so far
       int minind=i;   // index of smallest so far

       for (int j=i+1; j<=high; j++)
          if (T[j]<min) { min=T[j]; minind=j; }

       // now exchange it with T[i] if not already there
       if (i != minind)
          {
            temp=T[i];
```

```
                    T[i]=min;
                    T[minind]=temp;
                }
            }
        }
```

Note that the number of comparisons required to sort the array using Selection Sort does not depend on the initial array contents. It would perform just as many comparisons if the data were already sorted as it would if the data were in exactly the wrong order.

10.2.2 Heapsort

A full binary tree with nodes at h different levels contains $2^h - 1$ nodes. A binary tree with k nodes is **complete** if its nodes correspond to the nodes numbered 1 through k in the full binary tree of the same height. In other words, in a complete tree, each level (except possibly for the last one) is full, and the nodes in the last level are as far to the left as possible. The tree in Figure 10.1a is full, the tree in Figure 10.1b is complete, and the tree in Figure 10.1c is not complete.

We can represent a complete tree by an array in which the root is in element 1 and the children of the node in element M_i (if they exist) are in elements M_{2*i} and element M_{2*i+1}. Thus, an N-element complete tree occupies elements 1 through N of the array.

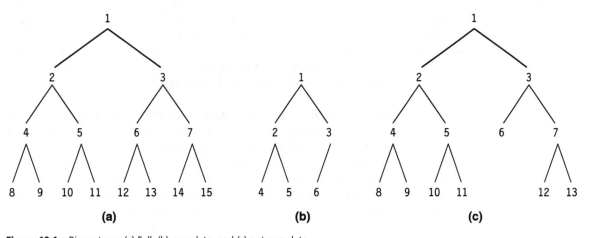

Figure 10.1 • Binary trees: (a) Full, (b) complete, and (c) not complete

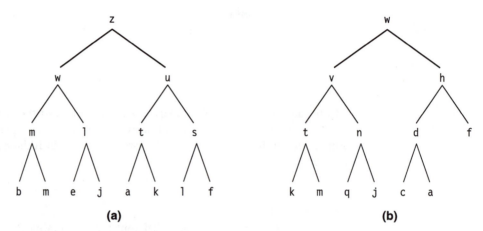

Figure 10.2 • Complete binary trees: (a) Max-heap and (b) non-max-heap

A **max-heap** is a complete binary tree in which the value in a node is not smaller than the value in either of its children.[3] A consequence of this definition is that no element is larger than the one in the root. In Figure 10.2, node values are represented by letters with the usual ordering ($a < b < \ldots < z$). The tree in Figure 10.2a is a max-heap; the tree in Figure10.2b is not a max-heap (see q and n).

Heapsort is a sorting algorithm that uses a max-heap.[4]

Heapsort Algorithm

Heapsort was devised by Williams (1964), who presented subprograms that used a min-heap. A sorting algorithm based on heaps can take a variety of forms. We could start with an empty array or we could start with the items to be sorted already in the array. Instead of extracting the items from the heap to an output stream, we could leave the array contents sorted. For compatibility with the other three internal sorting algorithms in this chapter, we assume that we start with the items to be sorted already in the array and that we end with the items in the array in sorted order.

There are two stages in our implementation of Heapsort. In the first, the array elements are formed into a max-heap. This floats the largest element to the top of the heap (element 1 of the array). In the second stage, we consider progressively smaller sections of the array, $1 \ldots N$, $1 \ldots N-1$, $1 \ldots N-2$, and so on. At each iteration we swap the root element with the last element of the section; this last element now contains its final value. Then we reduce the section size and make it into a heap again. The reheaping causes the next highest element to rise to the top. Thus our top-level algorithm is

```
Convert the complete tree to a heap.
For limit=N downto 2
  {
```

```
        Put largest element (root) into its final position,
        i.e., swap element [1] and element [limit]
        Reheap_elements (1,limit-1)
  }
```

Converting a Complete Tree into a Heap   The leaves of the tree are already heaps (of size 1). The first node we need to consider is the last nonleaf node. This is found at element $N/2$ in the array. Thus, the heap-formation part of the Heapsort algorithm is

```
for i = N/2 down to 1 reheap_elements(T,i,N)
```

where the *reheap_elements* function is

```
reheap_elements(int T[], int A, int limit)
  {
    if T[A] not a leaf
      {
        largerchild = index of child with larger value
        if T[A] < elements[largerchild]
          {
            swap (T[A],T[largerchild]);
            reheap_elements(T,largerchild,limit);
          }
      }
  }
```

Suppose, for example, that our initial array is the following permutation of the numbers 1 through 13.

```
12  2  5  10  1  7  8  9  4  3  6  11  13
```

Figure 10.3 shows the changes in the array contents as the array is formed into a heap. Note that elements 7 through 13 are leaves.

The tree in Figure 10.4a represents the first line of Figure 10.3 (the initial array), and the tree in Figure 10.4b represents the final line of Figure 10.3 showing the heap.

The Second Phase of Heapsort   During the second phase of Heapsort, we exchange the root element with element *limit* and then reheap elements 1 through *limit* − 1. The reheaping brings the largest element in the array segment into element 1. Figure 10.5 shows how the array changes during the second phase of the sort, starting with the array as heap (last line of Figure 10.3). Note how the largest

	1	2	3	4	5	6	7	8	9	10	11	12	13
Initial	12	2	5	10	1	7	8	9	4	3	6	11	13
$i = 6$	12	2	5	10	1	13	8	9	4	3	6	11	7
$i = 5$	12	2	5	10	6	13	8	9	4	3	1	11	7
$i = 4$	12	2	5	10	6	13	8	9	4	3	1	11	7
$i = 3$	12	2	13	10	6	11	8	9	4	3	1	5	7
$i = 2$	12	10	13	9	6	11	8	2	4	3	1	5	7
$i = 1$	13	10	12	9	6	11	8	2	4	3	1	5	7

Figure 10.3 • Heap formation

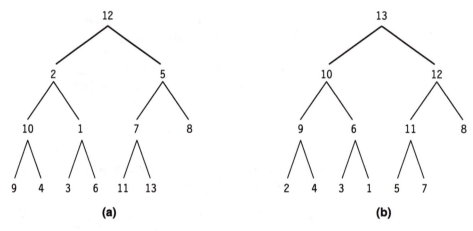

(a) (b)

Figure 10.4 • (a) Before and (b) after heap formation

element not in its final position is in element 1 and then is exchanged into its final position.

Performance of Heapsort

In initial heap formation, *reheap_elements* is called for each node that has a child. It can be shown that the time required for this phase is O(N). It takes work proportional to the height of the tree (O(log N)) to make the array into a heap again after a swap. We do this work N times during the sort phase. Thus, the work to sort the

Initial	13	10	12	9	6	11	8	2	4	3	1	5	7

limit=13	12	10	11	9	6	7	8	2	4	3	1	5	13

limit=12	11	10	8	9	6	7	5	2	4	3	1	12	13

limit=11	10	9	8	4	6	7	5	2	1	3	11	12	13

limit=10	9	6	8	4	3	7	5	2	1	10	11	12	13

limit=9	8	6	7	4	3	1	5	2	9	10	11	12	13

limit=8	7	6	5	4	3	1	2	8	9	10	11	12	13

limit=7	6	4	5	2	3	1	7	8	9	10	11	12	13

limit=6	5	4	1	2	3	6	7	8	9	10	11	12	13

limit=5	4	3	1	2	5	6	7	8	9	10	11	12	13

limit=4	3	2	1	4	5	6	7	8	9	10	11	12	13

limit=3	2	1	3	4	5	6	7	8	9	10	11	12	13

limit=2	1	2	3	4	5	6	7	8	9	10	11	12	13

Figure 10.5 • The second phase of Heapsort

array is $O(N \log N)$. Unlike Selection Sort, the number of key-comparisons required to sort the data depends on the initial ordering of the data. Unlike Mergesort (see Section 10.2.3), no auxiliary storage of any significant size is needed.

Heaps and Priority Queues

A heap is a good way to implement a priority queue (see Chapter 4). The head of the queue is the root of the heap. Adding a new item to a queue of N items is accomplished by placing the item at element $N + 1$ of the array, and then reheaping the array. Removal of the first item in the queue can be accomplished by replacing it by element N, and then reheaping elements $1 \ldots N - 1$. Both of these operations take time proportional to the height of the tree and are thus $O(\log N)$.

10.2.3 Mergesort

Mergesort uses a divide-and-conquer approach in which the two halves of the array are sorted separately and then merged together. The merge step typically requires additional storage. The algorithm can be expressed recursively; to sort half of the array, we first sort its two halves (quarters of the original), then merge them, and so on. The expected sorting time is O(*N* log *N*). To reduce overhead, we use a simple nonrecursive sort if the segment to be sorted is smaller than some threshold. The following implementation of the *merge* and the *mergesort* functions is simple rather than efficient.

```
void merge (int T[], int low, int middle, int high)
{ // pre: sorted are T[low..middle] and T[middle+1..high]
  // post: sorted are T[low..high]

  int i, left=low, right=middle+1;
  int *temp = new int[high+1];   // temporary storage

  for (i=low; i <= high; i++)
        if (left>middle)         { temp[i]=T[right]; right++;}
     else if (right>high)        { temp[i]=T[left]; left++;}
     else if (T[left]<T[right]) { temp[i]=T[left]; left++;}
                        else { temp[i]=T[right]; right++;}

  for (i=low; i <=high; i++) T[i]=temp[i];

  delete[] temp; // finished with temporary storage
}


void mergesort (int T[], int low, int high)
{
  if ((high-low) < 5)
    selectionsort(T,low,high); // or another nonrecursive sort
  else
     {
     int middle=(low+high)/2;
     mergesort(T,low,middle);
     mergesort(T,middle+1,high);
     merge(T,low,middle,high);
     }
}
```

• 10.2.4 Quicksort

Quicksort (Hoare 1961) is also a divide-and-conquer algorithm, and in some ways it is the inverse of Mergesort.

- Mergesort: Divide elements based on location, sort, and then merge.
- Quicksort: Divide elements based on value, and then sort.

The first stage in Quicksort is to partition the numbers in the array around a pivot element (P) such that all the numbers to the left of P are less than or equal to P, and all the numbers to the right of P are greater than P. Sorting the left and right partitions now yields a sorted array. Quicksort has an elegant recursive solution, and its behavior is typically $O(N \log N)$ because $O(N)$ work is required to partition at each of $\log N$ levels of recursion. However, pivot selection is crucial to this performance.

Pivot Selection

Ideally, when choosing P we would pick the median of the elements to be sorted, thus making the two partitions as equal in size as possible. However, we do not want to expend a lot of effort in finding this optimal value, because to do so would reduce the overall efficiency of the sort. It turns out that taking a minimal-effort approach and using either the first or the last element of the array as P has drawbacks. In cases in which the data are very nearly in the correct order, or very nearly in reverse order, the partitions will be very unequal in size. This will cause the number of levels of recursion to approach N rather than $\log N$, and, consequently, cause the behavior of the algorithm to degenerate to $O(N^2)$. The former case happens more often than you would expect by chance. Consider a file of names and addresses—a Boy Scout troop roster, for example. The list is kept in alphabetical order, but as new scouts join, their names are appended to the file which is then re-sorted periodically. When the re-sort is performed, a large part of the file is already in sorted order and the simple pivot selection strategy gives poor performance.

No pivot-selection strategy is immune to bad cases, but we can guard against the "already-sorted" case by making the pivot the median of three values: the first, the last, and the middle elements of the array. We use this strategy in the implementation that follows. As with Heapsort, we reduce overhead by invoking a nonrecursive sort if the partition size is less than some threshold.

```
int partition (int T[], int low, int high)
{
  // partitions the array from T[low] to T[high] and
  // returns the index of the pivot element

  int middle=(low+high)/2, upper=low, lower=high, temp;

  // order the first, last, and middle elements
  if (T[low]>T[middle]) exchange(T[low],T[middle]);
```

```
        if (T[low]>T[high]) exchange(T[low],T[high]);
        if (T[middle]>T[high]) exchange(T[middle],T[high]);

        // move median of 3 to beginning
        exchange(T[low],T[middle]);
        temp=T[low];                    // the pivot

        // now partition
        while (upper != lower)
         {
           while ( (upper < lower) && (temp <= T[lower]) ) lower--;
           if (upper != lower) T[upper] = T[lower];
           while ( (upper < lower) && (temp >= T[upper]) ) upper++ ;
           if (upper != lower) T[lower] = T[upper];
         }
        T[upper]=temp;  return upper;
      }

void quicksort (int T[], int low, int high)
{
     if ((high-low)< 5)               // arbitrary cut-off
        selectionsort(T,low,high);       // or other nonrecursive sort
     else
        {
           int pivot = partition(T,low,high);
           quicksort(T,low,pivot-1);
           quicksort(T,pivot+1,high);
        }
}
```

Figure 10.6a shows the top-level partitioning when the initial data are

13   2   5   10   1   7   12   9   4   3   6   11   8

meaning that the pivot will be 12 (the median of 13, 12, and 8). Figure 10.6b shows the partitioning when the initial data are

5   3   10   1   12   6   11   13   9   2   7   4   8

meaning that the pivot will be 8 (the median of 5, 11, and 8).

Note the imbalance in the sizes of the partitions in Figure10.6a when the element used as the pivot (12) is far from the median value of the data set (7).

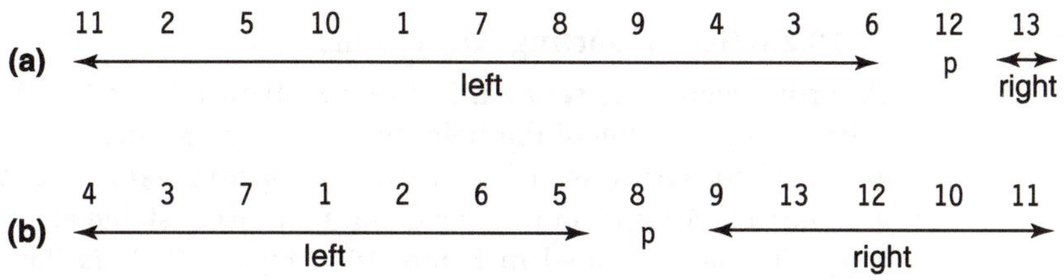

Figure 10.6 • Partitioned data

• 10.2.5 Comparison of Internal Sorting Algorithms

Arrays of random data ranging in size from 16 to 4096 elements were sorted using Selection Sort, Heapsort, Mergesort, and Quicksort. The number of times an array element was used in a comparison was counted. Table 10.1 gives the average number of comparisons (Ave.) and the standard deviation (σ) over 100 trials. In the cases of Mergesort and Quicksort (the two recursive algorithms), Selection Sort was used to sort subarrays with fewer than five elements. Note the greater standard deviations in Quicksort, reflecting its greater dependence on the data ordering.

• **TABLE 10.1** Comparison of Internal Sorting Algorithms

	Selection Sort		Heapsort		Mergesort		Quicksort	
N	Ave.	σ	Ave.	σ	Ave.	σ	Ave.	σ
16	120	0	81	3	51	2	69	3
32	496	0	223	4	133	2	186	7
64	2016	0	571	6	327	4	473	16
128	8,128	0	1,400	10	779	6	1,149	36
256	32,640	0	3,307	15	1,811	8	2,712	75
512	130,816	0	7,633	21	4,133	11	6,249	142
1024	523,776	0	17,319	31	9,288	16	14,198	290
2048	2,096,128	0	38,731	40	20,625	22	32,008	757
4096	8,386,560	0	85,655	65	45,337	33	70,470	1,244

10.2.6 Stable Sorting Algorithms

A sorting method is **stable** if it does not disturb the relative position of two items with the same value of the field by which we are sorting. A stable sort is useful if we need to sort a set of data by key_1 within key_2 (e.g., by *first_name* within *last_name*). We first sort by key_1, and then use a stable algorithm when sorting by key_2. This is illustrated in Figure 10.7. Figure 10.7a is the unsorted data, Figure 10.7b is the same data after sorting by first name, and Figure 10.7c is the data after subsequent sorting by last name with a stable algorithm. Note in Figure 10.7c that within a group of items having the same last name, ordering by first name has been preserved.

Stability of Quicksort   Quicksort is not stable; we can demonstrate this as follows. Suppose the pivot value (P) appears elsewhere in the array. For example, if we are sorting the elements of the following array by the integer value (rather than by the letter)

1	2	3	4	5	6
6_a	6_b	9_c	7_d	5_e	3_f

Sean	Baker
Kate	Finney
Lois	Antunez
Roger	Finney
Corey	Baker
Peter	Finney
Ray	Antunez
Andrew	Finney
Ed	Baker
Mildred	Antunez

(a)

Andrew	Finney
Corey	Baker
Ed	Baker
Kate	Finney
Lois	Antunez
Mildred	Antunez
Peter	Finney
Ray	Antunez
Roger	Finney
Sean	Baker

(b)

Lois	Antunez
Mildred	Antunez
Ray	Antunez
Corey	Baker
Ed	Baker
Sean	Baker
Andrew	Finney
Kate	Finney
Peter	Finney
Roger	Finney

(c)

Figure 10.7 • Sorting by field within field

and we are using element 1 as the pivot, then our top-level partitioning results in

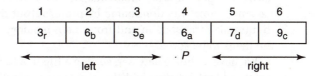

1	2	3	4	5	6
3_r	6_b	5_e	6_a	7_d	9_c

and the relative positioning of the two 6 values has changed irreversibly.

Stability of Heapsort   Heapsort is not stable either. Suppose our initial array is

1	2	3	4	5	6
10_a	10_b	8_d	3_m	6_p	5_r

representing

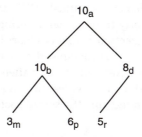

If we are sorting by the integer variables, this is already a heap. The first step in phase two of Heapsort is to move the root (10_a) to the last element of the array; thus, its position relative to 10_b is irrevocably altered. In contrast, Selection Sort (as represented by our C++ function) and Mergesort are stable.

10.3 External Sorting

In this section, we consider the problem of sorting a large file of items in which there are too many items to hold them in main memory simultaneously. We therefore consider **external sorting** algorithms, where at any time some of the data to be sorted are outside main memory. In contrast, the internal sorting algorithms of Section 10.2 keep all the data in main memory throughout the sorting process.

10.3.1 Overview

Criteria for evaluating external sorting algorithms are different from those for internal sorts. The efficiency of an algorithm for sorting an array in main memory is often expressed in terms of the number of times a comparison has to be made between a pair of array elements. However, the time required to execute an external sort is normally dominated by input/output time. It follows that we should aim to minimize transfers to and from main memory rather than comparisons between the items to be sorted.

We have a choice between sorting a file in situ (in its original position) and using a method that requires additional storage space. One advantage of in situ sorting is that it allows us to sort larger files with a given total storage capacity. A disadvantage is that a system that crashes during a sort may leave the file in a strange state. (This can be circumvented by making an offline copy before sorting.)

If we choose to sort a file in situ, then we may naturally turn to internal sorting algorithms and treat our file as an array of items. Clearly, this requires a direct-access file. We saw in Section 10.2 that Quicksort is one of the better internal sorting algorithms. Six and Wegner (1984) describe EXQUISIT, an algorithm based on Quicksort, which sorts a direct access file in situ. It requires that there be room in main memory for two file blocks. However, for good performance, the choice of pivot element is critical. EXQUISIT (and Quicksort, as we have seen) can perform very poorly if the initial ordering of records to be sorted is unfavorable.

This section presents algorithms that, although unspectacular, are safe. Their performance is guaranteed, independent of the ordering of the initial file. The algorithms considered are classified as **sort-merge**. Like Mergesort in Section 10.2.3, they sort by the divide-and-conquer technique of sorting subsections of the data set and then merging the sorted sections together.

Analogy

Consider the problem of sorting a large collection of books initially piled in a single stack from floor to ceiling. Your task is to create a single stack in which the books are ordered by ISBN. You have a small desk on which you can put six books at once and enough floor space to set up smaller stacks. One strategy is to use the desk as a sorting area and to make small stacks of six books each such that the books in a stack are in order. After the small stacks are created, the desk can be used in merging the stacks into larger and larger stacks until one stack contains all the books.

This is how external sorting algorithms based on Mergesort work. Thus, to sort an arbitrarily large file of items, we have a two-stage process:

1. **Sort stage.** Items are read from the input (unsorted) file, and sorted **partitions** (sometimes termed **runs** or **strings** of items) are written to output files. Items within a partition are in the desired final order.
2. **Merge stage.** Partitions generated in the sort stage are merged, producing longer and longer partitions. Merging stops when there is only one partition—the required sorted file.

The sort-merge approach works for external sorting because the sort stage can be adapted to available main memory. Furthermore, the merge stage needs space in memory only for one item from each of the partitions being merged. Each stage benefits from an increase in available main memory. The more memory there is, the longer the initial partitions are likely to be. Therefore, it is likely that fewer partitions will be generated from a given input file, and thus the merging stage requires fewer iterations. In addition, an increase in the number of partitions that can be merged at one time increases the merge order and also leads to a shorter merge phase. Note that with the sort-merge method, a file can be sorted in the extreme case that main memory can hold only two items. The capacity is large enough to produce partitions two items in length and to perform a two-way merge. Of course, in this case sorting would take a long time!

It is worth observing that the sort-merge algorithms require only serial files. External sorting can therefore be implemented using programming languages that support only serial files (such as Standard Pascal). (On early computers, which had tape drives but scarce disk space, much use was made of sorting algorithms of this type.)

10.3.2 Generating Sorted Partitions

Although there are many ways of producing partitions from an unsorted file, only the following three methods are considered here:

1. Internal sorting
2. Replacement selection
3. Natural selection

To compare the three algorithms, we show how each would process the following input file:

```
109  49  34  68  45   2  60  38  28  47  16  19  34  55
 98  78  76  40  35  86  10  27  61  92  99  72  11   2
 29  16  80  73  18  12  89  50  46  36  67  93  22  14
 83  44  52  59  10  38  76  16  24  85
```

Only the keys of the items are shown; the first item has key 109, the second 49, and so on. We will assume that main memory can hold M items. Keep in mind that our objective in this stage of the sort is to produce sorted partitions that are as long as possible.

Internal Sorting

The simplest strategy of all is to read M items at a time from the unsorted file, to sort them using an internal sorting method, and then to output them. Note that all partitions produced in this way, except perhaps for the last, will contain exactly M items. If $M = 5$, we get the following 11 partitions from our example data set.

```
34  45  49  68 109
 2  28  38  47  60
16  19  34  55  98
35  40  76  78  86
10  27  61  92  99
 2  11  16  29  72
12  18  73  80  89
36  46  50  67  93
14  22  44  52  83
10  16  38  59  76
24  85
```

Replacement Selection

The internal sorting strategy does not take advantage of any partial ordering that may exist in the input file. The replacement selection algorithm does exploit such ordering. Consider the following method for producing sorted partitions.

1. Read in *M* items from the unsorted file.
2. Output the item with the smallest key.
3. Replace the item with the next item in the input file. If the new item cannot be part of the current partition (i.e., if its key is smaller than that of the last item output), mark it "frozen." (Frozen items are ignored when searching for the item with the smallest key.) If there are any unfrozen items, return to Step 2.
4. Start a new partition. That is, unfreeze the frozen items and go to Step 2.

Two flags are associated with each item. One indicates whether the item has been written to the output. The other indicates whether the item is frozen; that is, whether it is usable in the production of the current partition. Although it is possible to combine these two flags into a single indicator, we leave them separated for clarity.

The following C++ program implements the replacement selection algorithm for a file of integers (details of two minor functions have been omitted to save space). The inner loop in the main function outputs integers to the current partition. Each cycle of the outer loop produces one partition; each partition is written to a separate output line.

```cpp
#include <fstream.h>

const int N = 5;

bool written[N], frozen[N];
int buffer[N];

int loc_smallest_unfrozen()
{ // finds index of smallest unfrozen integer in buffer
```

```
      // details omitted
    }


int loc_smallest_unwritten()
{ // finds index of smallest unwritten integer in buffer
  // details omitted
}

main(int argc, char *argv[])   // arguments are : input file, output file
{
  fstream in1;
  fstream out1;
  int last_key,s,i,endcount;

  // set flags and read initial buffer
  for (i=0; i<N; i++) written[i] = true;

  in1.open(argv[1],ios::in);             // open input file
  out1.open(argv[2],ios::out);           // open output file

  // read initial buffer
  i=0;
  while ( i<N && !in1.eof() )
    {
      in1 >> buffer[i];
      written[i]=false;
      i++;
    }

  // generate sorted partitions, one per output line
  while (!in1.eof())
    {
    // generate one sorted partition
    // initialize frozen flags
    for (i=0; i<N; i++) frozen[i]=written[i];

    while ( (s=loc_smallest_unfrozen()) != -1)
       { // write one record to sorted partition
         out1 << buffer[s] << " ";
         last_key = buffer[s];
         written[s] = true;
         frozen[s] = true;
```

```
        if (in1 >> buffer[s])
            {
             written[s] = false;
             if (buffer[s] >= last_key) frozen[s] = false;
            }
      }
   out1 << endl;  // end of partition
   }

// output any unwritten records in ascending order
endcount = 0;
while ( (s = loc_smallest_unwritten()) != -1 )
   {
     out1 << buffer[s] << " ";
      endcount++;
     written[s] = true;
    }
 if (endcount) out1 << endl;
 out1.close();
}
```

The replacement selection algorithm can take advantage of partial ordering of the items in the input file. The closer the input file is to the desired final order, the more often the replacement item can be used in the current partition. Hence, partitions will tend to be longer than those generated using internal sorting. It can be shown that the expected partition length when using replacement selection is $2M$ items [e.g., see Knuth (1973) and Bradley (1982)].

Here are the six partitions output from the replacement selection algorithm when applied to our example data. Again, it is assumed that main memory can hold five items and, in this case, the necessary flags, too.

```
34   45   49   60   68 109
 2   16   19   28   34   38   47   55   76   78   86   98
10   27   35   40   61   72   92   99
 2   11   16   18   29   50   73   80   89   93
12   14   22   36   44   46   52   59   67   76   83   85
10   16   24   38
```

Natural Selection

One of the disadvantages of the replacement selection algorithm is that toward the end of producing a partition, most of the main memory space is occupied by frozen items. These items cannot contribute to the current partition. The natural selection method devised by Frazer and Wong (1972) avoids this by having a "reservoir" on secondary storage into which frozen items are placed. The production of a partition now terminates when this reservoir overflows or the input file is exhausted.

The following C++ program implements natural selection for a file of integers. We assume that main memory can hold M items and that the reservoir can hold N items.

```cpp
// natural selection algorithm.

#include <fstream.h>

const int N = 10;   // main memory size
const int M = 10;   // reservoir size

fstream in1,out1;
bool written[N];
int buffer[N], reservoir[M];
int reservoir_count,next_rec;
bool holding;

int loc_smallest_unwritten()
{
  // get index of smallest unwritten or return -1 if none
  // details omitted
}


bool get_next (int& N)
{
  // get next input, if any. May be one in holding area
  int temp;

  if (holding)
      { N = next_rec; holding = false; return true; }
  if (in1 >> temp)
      { N = temp; return true; }
  return false;
}


main(int argc, char *argv[])
{
  int last_key,smallindex,i,temp;
  bool tryingtoreplace, moretodo=true, buffertowrite;
```

```
  if (argc!=3) {cerr <<  "Usage: program input-file output-file\n"; exit (-1); }

  // set flags and read initial buffer
  for (i=0; i<N; i++) written[i] = true;

  in1.open(argv[1],ios::in);          // open input file
  out1.open(argv[2],ios::out);        // open output file

  // initial buffer and flags
  i=0;
  while ( i<N && get_next(temp) )
   {
     buffer[i]=temp;
     written[i]=false;
     i++;
   }
reservoir_count = 0;

// generate sorted partitions, one per output line
while (moretodo)
    { // output from buffer and replace until
      //  all written or reservoir overflow or end-of-input

      buffertowrite = true;
      while (buffertowrite)
        {
          smallindex=loc_smallest_unwritten();
         if (smallindex != -1)
            {
             out1 << buffer[smallindex] << "  ";
             written[smallindex] = true;
             // try to replace
            tryingtoreplace = true;
            do
              { if (get_next(next_rec))
                  {
                  holding = true;
                  if (next_rec >= buffer[smallindex])
                    {
                      buffer[smallindex] = next_rec;
                         written[smallindex] = false;
                      holding = false;
```

```
                    tryingtoreplace = false;  // replaced
                  }
              else if (reservoir_count < M)
                    {
                      reservoir[reservoir_count] = next_rec;
                      reservoir_count++;
                      holding = false;
                    }
                  else  // reservoir full
                    {
                      tryingtoreplace=false;
                      buffertowrite = false;
                    }
                  }
            else tryingtoreplace = false; // eof
          } while (tryingtoreplace);
              }
        else buffertowrite = false;  // buffer all written
        }
      // if not all written flush buffer
      while ( (smallindex=loc_smallest_unwritten()) != -1)
          { out1 << buffer[smallindex] << " ";
            written[smallindex] = true;
          }
      out1 << endl;  // end of partition

      // copy any reservoir records to buffer
      if (reservoir_count>0)
   while (reservoir_count>0)
      { buffer[reservoir_count-1] = reservoir[reservoir_count-1];
            written[reservoir_count-1] = false;
            reservoir_count--;
          }
      else moretodo = false;  // reservoir empty
    }
 out1.close();
}
```

Frazer and Wong observed that when the reservoir and main memory have the same capacity and both can hold more than about 30 items, the expected partition length is about $M * e$ (i.e., $M * 2.718 \ldots$), hence the choice of name for the algorithm. The five partitions it generates for our example data with $M = 5$ and $N = 5$ are:

```
34  45  47  49  60  68  109
 2  16  19  28  34  38  40  55  61  76  78  86  92  98  99
10  11  16  27  29  35  50  67  72  73  80  89  93
 2  12  14  18  22  36  44  46  52  59  76  83  85
10  16  24  38
```

Comparison of Partition-Forming Algorithms

In general, we want partition-forming algorithms to generate long partitions so that the amount of merging required will be small. However, other factors might need to be considered when choosing an algorithm.

An advantage of using internal sorting to produce the initial partitions is that the partitions produced are all of the same length, except possibly for the last. This can simplify merging; the merging algorithm may be easier to develop if the size of each partition is predictable.

Replacement selection, on average, produces longer partitions than internal sorting. Although variability of partition length may complicate merging, it is simple to detect boundaries between partitions written to the same file.

Natural selection tends to produce longer partitions than either internal sorting or replacement selection. However, there are input/output transfers to and from the reservoir during initial partition formation. Neither of the other two methods incur this cost. Our aim is to minimize total sorting time, which in practice means minimizing the total number of input/output transfers. However, the reduction in merging brought about by having longer initial partitions may more than offset the number of reservoir transfers.

Table 10.2 shows the average partition length when a file of 10,000 unique integers was processed with a buffer size of 10. P represents a "sortedness" measure of the file.

Input files were generated by the following program that takes a parameter P. The numbers are generated in such a way that there is a probability $P/100$ that the next number in the file would be greater than the last. Thus, P is one measure of the sortedness of a file.

```
//  file generating program
#include <fstream.h>
#include <string.h>
#include <time.h>
#include <stdlib.h>

#define filesize 10000

main (int argc, char *argv[])
{
```

● **TABLE 10.2**   Average Partition Lengths vs. Sortedness Measure P

P	Internal Sorting	Replacement Selection	Natural Selection
0.0	10.0	10.0	10.0
0.1	10.0	10.3	10.4
0.2	10.0	10.8	11.0
0.3	10.0	12.1	12.6
0.4	10.0	14.7	16.1
0.5	10.0	20.5	24.9
0.6	10.0	36.0	51.0
0.7	10.0	88.5	149.3
0.8	10.0	303.0	714.3
0.9	10.0	3,333.3	5,000.0
1.0	10.0	10,000.0	10,000.0

```
long num, lastnum;
char filename[20];
float P = float(atoi(argv[1]))/100.0;

strcpy(filename,"RANDOM.");        // name of output file is RANDOM
strcat(filename,argv[1]);          // plus value of P e.g., RANDOM70
ofstream outfile(filename);

srand48 ( (unsigned) time(NULL) ); // initialize random number generator
lastnum = 0;
outfile << lastnum << endl;

for (int i=0; i<filesize-1; i++)
  {
    if ( (drand48() * 100.0) < P*100.0) // next number to be bigger?
        num = lastnum + int(drand48()*100.0) + 1;
    else
        num = lastnum - int(drand48()*100.0) - 1;
    outfile << num << endl;
    lastnum = num;
  }
outfile.close();
}
```

Note in Table 10.2 that the average partition length for the natural selection algorithm is at least as long as that for replacement selection for all values of P. If we take $P = 0.5$ as a typical file, then, as predicted, the average partition length for replacement selection is approximately $2 * N$, and for natural selection it is quite close to $e * N$. Figure 10.8 shows a graphical representation of the typical behavior of the three algorithms. N is the buffer size, T is the total number of items in the file, and P is the sortedness measure.

• 10.3.3 Distribution and Merging

Suppose that the sort stage produces R partitions. The optimal way of merging them is to have each partition in a separate file and then to perform a single R-way merge. However, in practice, there will be operational restrictions. The most likely of these is on the number of files that a program can have open at any time. Therefore, merging typically requires a series of **phases**. During each phase, items are read from one set of files and merged partitions are written to a second set of files. Many merging strategies exist, each having requirements regarding the distribution of the initial partitions. In this section, we will assume that at any time, we can have at most F files open for reading or writing. The larger the value of F, the faster merging is likely to proceed. A limit on the value of F is most likely to arise from an operating system restriction.

We will consider three distribution and merging strategies:

1. Balanced N-way merging
2. Optimal merging
3. Knuth-Gilstad algorithm

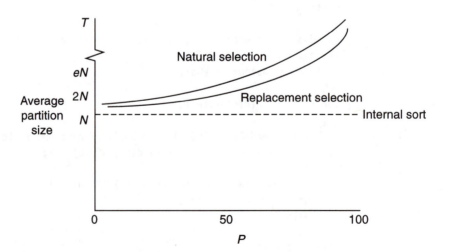

Figure 10.8 • Behavior of partition-forming algorithms

A measure of the efficiency of the merging stage of an external sorting algorithm is the number of **passes** over the data required to merge the partitions together. The number of passes is defined as follows:

$$Passes = \frac{Total\ number\ of\ record\ reads}{Total\ number\ of\ records\ in\ the\ file}$$

That is, the number of passes is the average number of times a record is read during the merging. For every read there is a corresponding write, thus the number of passes is a measure of the total input/output required.

Balanced N-Way Merge
In the balanced N-way merge, we compute $N = F/2$; that is, N is approximately half the limit on the number of attached files. The partitions generated by the partition-formation algorithm are distributed as evenly as possible onto N files. During each phase of the merge, records on N input files are read, and merged partitions are distributed cyclically onto N output files. At the end of a phase, the output files are closed and become the input files for the next phase. This merging strategy is balanced in the sense that each of the files in the input set contains approximately the same number of items. Here is a pseudo-C++ algorithm for the balanced N-way merge.

```
int N,            // size of one set of files (F-N is the size of the other)
    outsetsize,   // size of the output set
    base,         // the number, in the range 1..F of the first output file
    outfilenum,   // the number of the current output file
    partitioncount,  // count of partitions written during this phase
    sorted_file;  // number of the final sorted file

bool input_set_first, // used to differentiate between the input and output
                      // sets during merging

main()
{
  N = F % 2;            // N is roughly half F
  input_set_first = false;

  do {  // set up files
       input_set_first = !input_set_first
       if (input-set-first)
          {  open files 1 through N for reading
             open files N+1 through F for writing
             outsetsize = F - N;
             base = N + 1;
          }
```

```
        else
            {   open files 1 through N for writing
                open files N+1 through F for reading
                outsetsize = N;
                base = 1;
            }

        // perform a merging phase
        outfilenum = 0;
        partitioncount = 0;
        do {   // merge one partition from each input file onto
               // the file numbered (base+outfilenum)
                partitioncount++;
                outfilenum = (outfilenum + 1) % outsetsize;
            } while (more input on an input file);

        rewind input files and output files

    } while (partitioncount != 1);

    if (input_set_first)
        sorted_file = N+1;
    else sorted_file = 1;
}
```

The flag *input_set_first* is used to remember which of the two sets of files (the files numbered *N* or those numbered *N* + 1 through *F*) is currently the input. The value of *input_set_first* is established at the start of each phase. During a phase, items are read from the input files and merged partitions are written to the output files. Partitions are written cyclically to the output files in order to distribute them as evenly as possible. If exactly one partition is written out during a particular phase, then merging is complete. The value of *input_set_first* implicitly identifies the file containing the final sorted items.

Assume we have *R* = 20 initial partitions and *F* = 4 files. Table 10.3 shows how merging proceeds when using the balanced *N*-way algorithm with *F* = 4. In the table, *i* × *j* represents *i* partitions each containing *j* items.

Recall from our earlier discussion that, in practice, initial partitions will be long and will vary in length. However, so that we can compare the three merge algorithms in a simple way, we assume that each initial partition contains exactly one item. Initially, the 20 partitions are distributed evenly on files 1 and 2. Therefore, each of these two files is shown as 10 × 1.

In the first phase, files 1 and 2 are the input files and files 3 and 4 are the output files. In phase 1, partitions of length 1 are read and, because we are performing

● **TABLE 10.3** Balanced *N*-Way Merging				
	File 1	**File 2**	**File 3**	**File 4**
Initially	10 × 1	10 × 1		
After phase 1			5 × 2	5 × 2
After phase 2	3 × 4	2 × 4		
After phase 3			1 × 8, 1 × 4	1 × 8
After phase 4	1 × 16	1 × 4		
After phase 5			1 × 20	

two-way merging, partitions containing two items are produced. Ten partitions are produced and distributed over files 3 and 4. In phase 2, files 3 and 4 become the input files and files 1 and 2 become the output files. Partitions containing four items are produced, which are the result of merging partitions containing two items. Five partitions are produced in phase 2 and distributed over the two output files. The algorithm proceeds in this way until one phase, phase 5 in this example, produces exactly one partition.

Note that the balanced *N*-way merge algorithm, although simple, is far from the best strategy. We are performing only $(F/2)$-way merging instead of $(F - 1)$-way merging, which is the best we could do (there must always be at least one output file). In addition, depending on the number of initial partitions and the value of F, during certain phases partitions are liable to be copied from one file to another without being merged with anything. In our example, a partition of length 4 is copied from file 1 to file 3 during phase 3. During phase 4, the same partition is copied from file 3 to file 2.

The number of passes required by the balanced *N*-way merge algorithm is always the same as the number of phases because all the items are read in each phase. For our 20-partition example, therefore, there are five passes. We will see that this simple relationship between phases and passes does not hold for the other two algorithms.

Optimal Merge

The optimal merge algorithm was described by Lewis and Smith (1982). Initial partitions are written to separate files, and a record is kept of the length of each partition. Thus, we have a set of files, each containing one partition. As with the other algorithms, merging proceeds in a number of phases. During each phase, the $F - 1$ shortest partitions are read and merged, and the merged partition is written to an output file. The input files are then removed from the set of files, and the output file is added to the set. The process of merging is repeated until the set contains only one file. Table 10.4 shows how this algorithm operates on the 20 partitions of the earlier example; again we assume that each initial partition contains exactly one

● **TABLE 10.4** Optimal Merging

Phase	Input 1	Input 2	Input 3	Output	Reads
1	1:1	2:1	3:1	21:3	3
2	4:1	5:1	6:1	22:3	3
3	7:1	8:1	9:1	23:3	3
4	10:1	11:1	12:1	24:3	3
5	13:1	14:1	15:1	25:3	3
6	16:1	17:1	18:1	26:3	3
7	19:1	20:1	21:3	27:5	5
8	22:3	23:3	24:3	28:9	9
9	25:3	26:3	27:5	29:11	11
10	28:9	29:11		30:20	20
					Total 63

item and that $F = 4$. We use $x{:}y$ to represent file number x containing a partition of y records. Files 1 through 20 contain the original partitions; files numbered 21 and above are generated during the merging. For example, file 21, containing three items, is created in phase 1. In phase 7, file 21 is merged with files 19 and 20 to create file 27, containing five items. The number of passes required is 63/20, or 3.15.

The algorithm is not truly optimal because the input files in a phase may be very different in length. The effective merge order is reduced when input from some of the files has been exhausted. In addition, there may be fewer than $F - 1$ files left for the final phase (in the example of Table 10.4, there are only two inputs in phase 10).

Knuth–Gilstad Algorithm

The algorithm that we designate Knuth–Gilstad is based on one presented by Knuth (1973), which is a generalization of an algorithm presented by Gilstad (1960). The algorithm has neither of the disadvantages of the balanced N-way merge (low order of merge and running out of input) and does not require the record keeping of the optimal merge. However, it does require a more complex initial distribution of partitions. We will consider two algorithms, one for a special case and one for a general polyphase merge.

Table 10.5 shows how the merging of 31 partitions with $F = 4$ would proceed. (The number of partitions and their initial distribution are carefully chosen.) We assume again that each initial partition contains exactly one item. We use the notation introduced earlier for the balanced N-way example; that is, $i \times j$ represents i partitions each containing j items.

In phase 1, we produce partitions containing three items because we are merging partitions of length 1 from each of three files. We can produce only seven partitions

	File 1	File 2	File 3	File 4	Reads
Initially	13 × 1	11 × 1	7 × 1		
After phase 1	6 × 1	4 × 1		7 × 3	21
After phase 2	2 × 1		4 × 5	3 × 3	20
After phase 3		2 × 9	2 × 5	1 × 3	18
After phase 4	1 × 17	1 × 9	1 × 5		17
After phase 5				1 × 31	31
					Total 107

● **TABLE 10.5**   Knuth–Gilstad Merging

before we reach the end of file 3 and stop because one of the inputs is exhausted (we do not merge with fewer than the maximum number of inputs). This leaves six partitions unread on file 1 and four partitions unread on file 2. In phase 2, we produce partitions of length 5 because we are merging partitions of lengths 1, 1, and 3 from files 1, 2, and 4, respectively. We can produce only four such partitions before we reach the end of file 2 and stop. Merging proceeds in this way until phase 5 produces the sorted file. The number of passes required is 107/31, or about 3.45.

The general algorithm will be able to merge an arbitrary number of partitions. However, it will be convenient to consider first an algorithm that requires that the total number of partitions be one of a special set of numbers.

Special-Case Distribution   The difficulty with the Knuth–Gilstad algorithm is knowing how to distribute the initial partitions so that the algorithm can merge them optimally. To determine the initial distribution, we work back from the final one. Consider the case where $F = 4$; that is, in any phase there are three input files. We are concerned with the number of partitions on each of these input files. The final distribution is one partition on one file. Before the final phase, we must therefore have one partition on each of the input files. We denote this as

1   1   1

Three-way merging will then produce the final partition. Before the penultimate phase, we must have

2   2   1

so that when we merge, we produce one partition (before reaching the end of the shortest file). This, together with the two files with one partition remaining on them, gives us the 1 1 1 distribution. In general, if at any phase we want to produce

a b c

partitions, then the phase before must leave us with

$a + b$ $a + c$ a

partitions so that when we merge we produce

$a = \text{minimum}(a, a + b, a + c)$

partitions, leaving b partitions on one file and c partitions on another. Table 10.6 shows how this works when $F = 4$.

Thus, working back from the desired final configuration, we arrive at the distribution used in our example (13 partitions on the first file, 11 on the second, and 7 on the third).

You may observe that this merging method, when F is equal to 4, will work optimally if the total number of initial partitions is in the sequence

1   3   5   9   17   31 . . .

These numbers are part of a generalized Fibonacci sequence. The appropriate sequence when F equals 4 is the sequence of order 3, which is

1   1   1   3   5   9   17   31   57 . . .

Each of the first three terms is 1. Each succeeding term is the sum of the three that precede it. In general, the sequence $T_1, T_2, T_3, \ldots$ is defined

$$T_i = \sum_{k=i-F+1}^{i-1} T_k \quad i \geq F$$

$$T_i = 1 \qquad i < F$$

Special-Case Algorithm   In the special case, we know that the total number of initial partitions is a member of the appropriate Fibonacci sequence. We have seen how

● **TABLE 10.6**   Partition Distribution, $F = 4$

Produced by Phase	a	b	c	Total Partitions
Last	1	0	0	1
Last − 1	1	1	1	3
Last − 2	2	2	1	5
Last − 3	4	3	2	9
Last − 4	7	6	4	17
Last − 5	13	11	7	31

each term in the sequence is associated with a particular distribution of partitions. We have also seen how a distribution is derived from the distribution for the preceding term in the sequence. This suggests the following algorithm for distributing a number of partitions onto files. Again, we illustrate using $F = 4$.

We regard

1   0   0

as our first target distribution and write the first partition onto one of the three files. If a second partition is generated, then we know this target is no good and switch to the next target, that is

1   1   1

The second and third partitions are written to the two remaining input files. If a fourth partition is generated, then this target is also no good and we replace it with

2   2   1

The fourth and fifth partitions are written to files that are short of their target number of partitions. We know with this special-case algorithm that when the partitions are all distributed, some target distribution will have been matched exactly. Therefore, it does not matter to which of those files that are short of their quota we write a partition. Distribution of partitions proceeds in this way until there are no more.

Next, we consider a more general algorithm in which it is not necessarily the case that the total number of partitions to be merged is a member of the appropriate Fibonacci sequence.

General Distributing and Merging Algorithm   We have seen how distribution and merging works optimally if the number of partitions is a member of an appropriate Fibonacci sequence. If the total is not guaranteed to be a member of the sequence, a solution is to introduce **dummy partitions**. Dummy partitions do not occupy file space; in fact, they exist only as numbers in a table. We introduce sufficient dummy partitions to make the total number of partitions (real ones plus dummy ones) a term in the sequence.

The use of dummy partitions has consequences for the section of the sorting algorithm that merges partitions. It must be able to distinguish between dummy partitions and real ones. How are dummy partitions regarded in relation to the files containing real partitions? Note that during merging, the partitions toward the beginning of a file are read more often than those toward the end (consider Table 10.5). It makes sense, therefore, to treat the dummy partitions as if they appeared at the beginning rather than at the end of a file. In this way real input/output is minimized. For the same reason, it is desirable to spread the dummy partitions as evenly as possible over the files.

Here is a pseudo-C++ implementation of the Knuth–Gilstad polyphase sort-merge algorithm.

```cpp
int Target[F],    // the current target distribution
    Dummies[F],   // the number of dummies assumed on each file
    Pntr,         // indicates where the next initial partition should be written
    LEVEL;        // the number of merge phases needed

fstream FILE[F];  // for attaching files

main()
{

    // initialization
    Target[0] = Dummies[0] = 1;
    for (int i=1; i<F; i++) Target[i] = Dummies[i] = 0;
    Pntr = 0;
    LEVEL = 0;

    // ** generation and distribution of initial partitions on files 0 through F-2 **
    for (int i=0; i<F-1; i++) open file i for writing on FILE[i]

    // first partition
    generate a partition and write to FILE[Pntr]
    Dummies[Pntr]--;

    // any more partitions?
    while (not end-of-file(input))
        {
          if (Dummies[Pntr] < Dummies[Pntr+1])
              Pntr++;
          else if (Dummies[Pntr] == 0)
              { // revise target
                    LEVEL++ ;
                    int a = Target[0];
                    for (k = 0; k<F-1; k++)
                        {
                            Dummies[k] = a + Target[k+1] - Target[k];
                            Target[k] = a + Target[k+1];
                        }
                // reset pointer
                Pntr = 0;
                While (Dummies[Pntr]==0) Pntr++;
```

```
        }
    generate partition and write to FILE[Pntr];
    Dummies[Pntr]--;
    }

close files on FILE[0] ... FILE[F-2];
for (int i=0; i<F-1; i++) open file i on FILE[i] for reading
open file on FILE[F-1] for writing

// ** merge section **
while (LEVEL > 0)
    {
    // perform a merge phase
    do { Merge partitions from files on FILE[0] ... FILE[F-2] onto the file
            on FILE[F-1]
        } while not end-of-file(FILE[F-2])
    LEVEL--;
    // make changes for next phase
    rewind and close files on FILE[F-1] and FILE[F-2]
    open file on FILE[F-1] for reading
    open file on FILE[F-2] for writing
    // reallocate files to channels, make corresponding changes to D
    // so that output file is always on FILE[F-2]
    FILE[0],FILE[1], ..., FILE[F-1] = FILE[F-1],FILE[0], ..., FILE[F-2] respectively
    Dummies[0],Dummies[1], ..., Dummies[F-1]
                        = Dummies[F-1], Dummies[0], ..., Dummies[F-2] respectively
    }
// done. Sorted file is on FILE[0]
}
```

Variable *LEVEL* and tables *Target* and *Dummies* are used in the following way. During the distribution phase, the variable *LEVEL* records how many targets have been reached. When merging, *LEVEL* is decreased after each phase; when it reaches zero, we have finished. Table *Target* at any time holds a target distribution of partitions. Each target is a row similar to those in our example table. Table *Dummies* holds the number of dummy partitions required to bring the number of actual partitions on each file up to the appropriate quota in the target. Thus, as we put real partitions on the file, the elements of *Dummies* are decreased. If table *Dummies* contains all zeros, we have reached the current target. If, at this point, we have not yet come to the end of the input file, then the target is replaced as in the earlier special-case algorithm. The elements of *Dummies* are modified accordingly. Note that the real partitions are distributed across the files in such a way as to even out the number of dummy partitions.

In order to take dummy partitions into account, the merging process operates as follows for each merged partition produced.

```
if Dummies[k] > 0 for all k      ( 1 ≤ k ≤ F-2 )
    then {
          increase Dummies[F-1] by 1
          decrease Dummies[k] by 1  ( 1 ≤ k ≤ F-2 )
          }
    else
        {
        merge one partition from each FILE[k] where
              Dummies[k] = 0 ( 1 ≤ k ≤ F-2 )
        and decrease Dummies[k] by 1 where  Dummies D[k] > 0
        }
```

Figure 10.9 shows the results of the distribution phase of the polyphase algorithm. As with our traces of balanced N-way merging and optimal merging, we use 20 partitions and make F equal to 4. Note that because 20 is not a term in the modified Fibonacci sequence, 11 dummy partitions are required to bring the total to 31, the next term in the sequence. The real partitions, in the order in which they are generated, are denoted Ra, Rb, . . ., Rt. The figure also shows the final contents of tables *Target* and *Dummies*.

Figure 10.10 traces the merging stage of the polyphase algorithm as it merges the 20 partitions. Dummy partitions are shown (as D) in the positions that the merging algorithm assumes they occupy.

When real partitions are merged, we designate this by concatenating the partition identifiers. Thus, for example, *Rabi* represents the merge of Ra, Rb, and Ri and

4	4	3	0	Dummies

13	11	7	0	Target

File 1	File 2	File 3	File 4
Ra	Rb	Rc	
Rd	Re	Ri	
Rf	Rh	Rn	
Rg	Rk	Rq	
Rj	Rm		
Rl	Rp		
Ro	Rt		
Rr			
Rs			

Figure 10.9 • Distribution of 20 partitions, Knuth–Gilstad algorithm

	File 1	File 2	File 3	File 4	LEVEL
Initially	D	D	D		5
	D	D	D		
	D	D	D		
	D	D	Rc		
	Ra	Rb	Ri		
	Rd	Re	Rn		
	Rf	Rh	Rq		
	Rg	Rk			
	Rj	Rm			
	Rl	Rp			
	Ro	Rt			
	Rr				
	Rs				
After phase 1	Rg	Rk		D	4
(10 reads)	Rj	Rm		D	
	Rl	Rp		D	
	Ro	Rt		Rc	
	Rr			Rabi	
	Rs			Rden	
				Rfhq	
After phase 2	Rr		Rgk	Rabi	3
(9 reads)	Rs		Rjm	Rden	
			Rlp	Rfhq	
			Rotc		
After phase 3		Rrgkabi	Rlp	Rfhq	2
(12 reads)		Rsjmden	Rotc		
After phase 4	Rrgkabilpfhq	Rsjmden	Rotc		1
(11 reads)					
After phase 5					0
(20 reads)			Ra..t		

Figure 10.10 • Merging of 20 partitions, Knuth–Gilstad algorithm

is itself merged later. A total of 31 partitions are merged: 20 real partitions and 11 dummies. The number of passes required is

$$\frac{Total\ reads}{20} = \frac{10 + 9 + 12 + 11 + 20}{20} = \frac{62}{20} = 3.1$$

Note that only real reads are counted.

10.3.4 Comparison of Distribution and Merging Strategies

Balanced N-way merging is simple to implement but not very efficient. The algorithm designated as optimal is not the best in all cases, as we have demonstrated with our example, and has record-keeping space requirements proportional to the number of partitions. The Knuth–Gilstad algorithm also requires overhead space, but it is proportional to the order of the merge. Knuth (1973) offers extensive descriptions and analyses of sorting algorithms.

Chapter Summary

We first considered internal sorting where all the data can be held in memory at once. We noted that some algorithms are $O(N^2)$, whereas others, in the best cases, are $O(N \log N)$. We observed that algorithms vary in their sensitivity to initial data ordering and noted that some of the algorithms are stable, which is useful when sorting by one field within another.

We then examined external sorting algorithms and looked at algorithms that are based on Mergesort. In the first stage of the sort operation, comparatively small sections of the unsorted file are sorted. In the second stage, the sorted partitions are merged in a number of phases into a sorted file.

Sorted partitions can be generated from an unsorted file in many ways. We examined three methods: internal sorting, replacement selection, and natural selection. The methods differ in the extent to which they are able to take advantage of any partial ordering in the unsorted file and produce longer partitions. Longer partitions will require fewer partitions and less subsequent merging. However, extra storage, internal or external, is needed by the better algorithms.

Similarly, sorted partitions can be distributed and then merged in many ways. To minimize total sorting time, we try to minimize the number of input/output transfers. Balanced N-way merging was the first algorithm considered. It is simple but comparatively slow: Only half the available files are used for input during merging. Optimal merging allocates one partition to each of a number of files and then produces the sorted file by merging the smallest partitions into a new partition at each phase. An algorithm created by Knuth and Gilstad was the final one considered. It typically merges faster than the other two, but requires a relatively complex distribution of partitions based on the properties of a Fibonacci sequence.

Exercises

1. What simple modification to our implementation of Selection Sort would make it unstable?

2. Write a version of Selection Sort that identifies the *k*th highest value in a given section of an array.

3. The following array is in the process of being formed into a max-heap:

20	16	12	24	14	15	6	8	19

   Show what it looks like after the next change in its contents.

4. Write a version of Mergesort that finds the *k*th highest element in an array. Compare the strategy with that of adapting Quicksort to solve the same problem.

5. Devise an efficient sorting algorithm for the special case in which every element in an array is either 0 or 1. Alternatively, how would you sort a Boolean array?

6. Suggest a way in which one of the internal sorting algorithms could be modified to sort a two-dimensional array such that all the elements in row *I* are not greater than any element in row *J* (*I* < *J*), and elements in a particular row are sorted in ascending order.

7. Suppose it were only necessary that the elements in an array be in their correct quartiles; that is, the lowest-valued 25 percent of the elements are in the first 25 percent of the array elements, the next 25 percent by value are in the next 25 percent of the elements, and so on. Suggest a method for accomplishing this partial sorting.

8. Devise a sorting algorithm for the special case in which each element in an *N*-element array is a pointer to an object, and each object contains one of the integers 1 through *N* (no two objects having the same integer). The algorithm is to arrange the contents of the array so that element *I* points to the object containing the integer *I*.

9. One measure of the sortedness of an array is the percentage of pairs of its elements that are in the correct order. For example, $A[i] \le A[j]$ if $i < j$. Write a function that takes as parameters an array of integers A and the number of elements in A and returns this measure of its sortedness.

10. Suppose that we know that all N integers to be sorted are in the range X to Y. Devise an $O(N)$ sorting method. Why would this method not be preferred to the $O(N \log N)$ methods described in the chapter?

11. Would your $O(N)$ method of Exercise 10 extend to the sorting of noninteger types such as real numbers and strings? If so, how? If not, why not?

12. If the only sorting method you had available was an unstable one, how would you sort a list of records by $field_1$ within $field_2$ within $field_3$?

13. Suggest a way of finding the median of the values in an array using minimal additional storage and without rearranging its contents.

14. Sometimes we are interested in a partially sorted data set. For example, we might need to know the top 10 best-selling books or the 6 highest-grossing movies or the top 8 students by GPA.

    a. Modify the *selectionsort* function so that it takes an additional parameter *k* and stops after having identified the *k* highest items.

    b. Modify Quicksort similarly.

15. Each book published is assigned a unique International Standard Book Number (ISBN). Assume that whenever a bookstore sells a copy of a book, its ISBN is appended to a serial file. At the end of the week, the bookstore needs a list of the 10 best-selling books (ISBN and copies sold for each one) in descending order of copies sold. Outline how the list can be produced from a serial file that may contain hundreds of thousands of entries. (It is a very busy bookstore.) State clearly any assumptions you make.

16. Complete the definition of *loc_smallest_unfrozen* and *loc_smallest_unwritten* in the replacement selection program and test the program with your own input files.

17. A certain external sorting program forms initial partitions using internal sorting and merges the partitions using balanced *N*-way merging.

    a. Assuming that the input file contains *X* records, how many read operations are required in stage one (partition formation)?

    b. Assuming that main memory can hold exactly *M* records, give an expression for *P*, the number of initial partitions generated.

    c. Assuming that *F* files are used in the balanced merging (*F* is even), give an expression for *T*, the number of phases required to merge *P* partitions.

    d. Assuming that the system takes 0.01 seconds to perform a read or write operation and that processing time can be ignored, how long will it take to sort a file of 51,200 records if $M = 50$ and $F = 8$?

18. Write a program that reads a file of integers and reports the locations and lengths of (a) the longest sequence in ascending order and (b) the longest sequence in descending order. Your program should be general in that it should not assume that all the integers can be held in memory simultaneously.

19. Consider the following partition generating and merging strategy. *M* records are read from the unsorted file, sorted, and written to a file. The next *M* records are read, sorted, and merged with the first partition to form a partition of 2*M* records. Similarly, the next *M* records are read, sorted, and merged to form a partition of 3*M* records. We proceed in this way until the partition consists of the entire file to be sorted. Compare this strategy with balanced *N*-way merging. What is the total number of reads required by each method to sort a file of *X* records?

20. A certain sort program uses a total of five files in the distribution and merge stages of a sort-merge algorithm. It uses the Knuth–Gilstad algorithm. From a particular unsorted file, 49 partitions are generated.

    a. Will any dummy partitions be required? If so, how many?

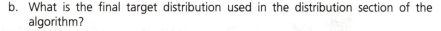

b. What is the final target distribution used in the distribution section of the algorithm?

c. How many phases are required to merge the partitions together?

d. How many passes are needed to merge the partitions? (Assume that all initial partitions are the same length.)

Problems

1. Write an "entry-comparison" function for use in sorting the entries in a phone book. Look at a real phone book for inspiration.

2. Modify Selection Sort so that the direction of the sweep through the unsorted section of the array alternates between ascending and descending. Thus, on the first pass, it places $A[1]$; on the second, $A[N]$; on the third, $A[2]$; and so on. Compare the performance of this modified algorithm with the original.

3. Suppose our unsorted array contains a permutation of the integers 1 through 10. Which permutation requires the largest number of comparisons during Heapsort? Which permutation requires the least? Do you observe a general pattern?

4. Investigate the performance of a Quicksort algorithm that picks the pivot element at random from the elements to be sorted. Compare it with the median-of-three strategy.

5. Investigate Shellsort (Shell 1959). Compare its performance with Selection Sort and Mergesort.

6. Investigate radix-sorting methods and discuss the circumstances under which they are superior to the four internal algorithms of Section 10.2.

7. We assumed in Section 10.2 that the number of item-comparisons was a good indication of the sorting time of an algorithm. Instead, measure the CPU time consumed by the algorithm and compare your results with those of Table 10.1.

8. Write a program that generates P random numbers representing the number of records in each of P partitions and then computes the number of passes and phases required by an "optimal" merge algorithm to merge the partitions into a single file (if we can have F files open at once). Run your program for $F = 2, 3, \ldots 10$ and $P = 64, 128, 192, \ldots 1024$.

9. Write a simulator that lets the user investigate the performance of external sorting algorithms. The user should be able to specify the values of the following parameters (as used in the chapter): M, N, F, partition-generating method, merging strategy, and the sortedness of the input (by some measure). The simulator should report (a) the total number of reads and writes (partition formation and merging reported separately), (b) the number of phases required to merge, and (c) the number of passes required to merge.

10. Devise and test an "antisorter" program (see note 1).

11. Look at the manual page for the sort package on your local computer system. What options does it provide? Is there a limit on the size of a file that may be sorted? Is the algorithm used stable? If you wish to sort a file of records by field B within field A, does this require two separate sorts?

● References

Bradley, J. 1982. *File and Data Base Techniques.* New York: Holt Rinehart and Winston, section 5.3.1.

Frazer, W. D., and C. K. Wong. 1972. Sorting by natural selection. *Communications of the ACM,* 15 (10): 910–913.

Gilstad, R. L. 1960. Polyphase merge sorting—An advanced technique. *Proceedings of the Eastern Joint Computer Conference,* 18: 143–148.

Hoare, C. A. R. 1961. Partition, Algorithm 64: Quicksort, and Algorithm 65: Find. *Communications of the ACM,* 4 (7): 321–322.

Knuth, D. E. 1973. *Sorting and Searching.* Vol. 3, *The Art of Computer Programming.* Reading, MA: Addison-Wesley, section 5.4.1.

Lewis, T. G., and M. Z. Smith. 1982. *Applying Data Structures*, 2d ed. Boston: Houghton Mifflin.

Shell, D. L. 1959. A high-speed sorting procedure. *Communications of the ACM,* 2 (7): 30–32.

Six, H. W., and L. Wegner. 1984. Sorting a random access file in situ. *Computer Journal,* 27 (2): 270–275.

Williams, J. W. J. 1964. Algorithm 232: Heapsort. *Communications of the ACM,* 7 (6): 347–348.

● Notes

[1]There are circumstances in which sorted data makes things worse (e.g., inserting such data into an initially empty search tree). In such circumstances, it would be useful to have an "antisorter" or scrambler program that would make a set of data as far removed from sorted order as possible.

[2]In certain sports leagues, the relative position of two teams may have to be determined by examining not only their overall records, but also the scores of games between them.

[3]A min-heap is similarly defined. A min-heap is a complete binary tree in which the value in a node is not larger than the value in either of its children.

[4]For descending order, use a min-heap.

Maps: Hash Files

11.1 Introduction

Chapters 5 and 6 examined ways to implement maps—with hash tables in Chapter
5 and with trees in Chapter 6. In this chapter and the next, we look at ways to
implement what might be termed *persistent maps*. The interface is the same as
with the transient version, but by making the implementation file-based, the map
is persistent.

This chapter looks at various kinds of hash files, the counterparts to the hash
tables of Chapter 5. (In the next chapter, we look at tree-structured files, the counterparts of the trees of Chapter 6.) Sections 11.2 and 11.3 look at fixed-length
files. Section 11.4 considers the differences between fixed-length files and files
that can change size. Sections 11.5 and 11.6 examine two particular types of
extensible files. Techniques that supplement the hash file with a data structure in
main memory are presented; these enhancements let us retrieve objects extremely
quickly but, in some cases, insertion of an object into a structure may take a long
time.

11.2 Hash Files

When we looked at hash tables in Chapter 5, we considered four design factors: bucket size, packing density, hash function, and overflow resolution. We look at the design of a hash file with a simple example that we will use throughout this section:

> A university administration wishes to store basic biographical information about students so that it can be retrieved very quickly. Student records are of fixed size: Each is 80 bytes long. Secondary storage devices on the university computer have sectors (physical records) that are 512 bytes long, and up to two sectors can be fetched in one read operation.

The four design factors are the same.

11.2.1 Bucket Size

We noted in Chapter 5 that when hashing is used in main memory, there was little reason to have a bucket size larger than 1. This is because we can access any element of main memory as quickly as any other; the next item in the current bucket can be accessed as quickly as an item in a different bucket. A disk drive is different. Having read a particular sector into memory, the items in that sector can be accessed very quickly compared with items on another sector that is only on the disk. Generally, we try to minimize overflow by making the bucket size as large as possible, but not so large that it requires more than one disk access to read or write a bucket. As bucket size increases, the probability of overflow decreases, but the time taken to search for an object in a bucket may increase. However, the cost of accessing a bucket element once the bucket is in main memory is normally small compared with the time required to fetch a bucket. If bucket search time is critical, there are fast techniques for storing and retrieving objects within a bucket. (Hashing is one example!)

Running Example

We can store six student records in one sector, so the system designers choose a bucket size of 12, which is the largest number of student records fetchable in a single read. The 32 bytes left over in each physical record after the six logical records are stored can be used for pointers, counters, and so on. For example, it would be desirable, on fetching a bucket, to know quickly how many records it contains.

11.2.2 Packing Density

The factors that determine the density of our hash file are the same as those that determined the packing density of our main memory hash table. There is a time-space trade-off. With lower density, operations may proceed faster but there will be more unused space. It is likely, however, that disk space in general is more plentiful than main memory.

Given the choices for bucket size and packing density, we can estimate the number of objects that will overflow the home buckets. What follows is the derivation of a formula that yields the expected percentage of overflows for a file with a given bucket size and packing density.

Assume that there are N home buckets, that each has a capacity of C objects, and that K objects are put into the file. The packing density is

$$\frac{K}{C \times N}$$

The probability of a given bucket receiving exactly I of the K objects is[1]

$$P(I) = C_{K,I} \times \left(\frac{1}{N}\right)^I \times \left(\frac{N-1}{N}\right)^{K-I}$$

Note that this assumes a uniform distribution of objects into buckets. Given this function P, the probability of exactly J objects overflowing from a given bucket with capacity C is $P(C + J)$. Thus, the expected number of overflows from a given bucket is

$$P(C + 1) + 2 * P(C + 2) + 3 * P(C + 3) + \ldots + (K - C) * P(K)$$

$$= \sum_{j=1}^{K-C} j \times P(C + j)$$

The expected number of overflows from all the N home buckets is therefore

$$N \times \sum_{j=1}^{K-C} j \times P(C + j)$$

which we can express as a percentage of the number of objects put into the file:

$$100 \times \frac{N}{K} \times \sum_{j=1}^{K-C} j \times P(C + j)$$

Note that any bias in the address transformation function toward particular addresses is likely to increase this percentage. We should thus regard the figure produced in this way as a minimum percentage. Given these formulas, we can plot expected overflow against packing density for a particular bucket size.

Table 11.1 shows the expected percentage overflow for various combinations of bucket size and packing density (*PD*). (In the calculations, the file was assumed to contain 200 objects.)

Running Example
The designers of the student record retrieval system aim to have about 30 percent of the file empty when all the expected student records have been loaded. Given the current and projected student population, the administration determines that the

● **TABLE 11.1**   Expected Overflows

Bucket Size	PD 50%	PD 55%	PD 60%	PD 65%	PD 70%	PD 75%	PD 80%	PD 85%	PD 90%	PD 95%
1	21.23	22.98	24.68	26.36	27.97	29.53	31.08	32.47	33.88	35.30
2	10.27	11.87	13.50	15.20	16.89	18.48	20.30	21.90	23.41	25.09
3	5.83	7.15	8.56	10.15	11.66	13.48	14.99	16.73	18.31	20.08
5	2.39	3.26	4.29	5.46	6.65	8.16	10.06	11.19	13.16	14.68
8	0.78	1.19	1.85	2.59	3.67	4.64	5.89	7.50	9.54	10.76
12	0.18	0.36	0.72	1.16	1.89	2.41	3.94	5.02	6.40	8.12
15	0.08	0.15	0.30	0.63	0.91	1.89	2.73	3.91	5.58	5.58
20	0.02	0.04	0.12	0.23	0.43	0.80	1.48	2.72	2.72	4.88

system should be capable of holding up to 60,000 student records at any time. The file will therefore contain

$$\lceil (60000 \,/\, 12) \; * \; (10 \,/\, 7) \rceil \quad = \quad 7143$$

home buckets. Given a packing density of 70 percent in conjunction with a bucket size of 12, the entry in Table 11.1 indicates that we can expect at least 1.89 percent of the records put in the file to overflow home buckets. Provisions must therefore be made for at least 1134 overflow records.

● 11.2.3 Hash Function

As noted in Chapter 5, it may be worth using a relatively time-consuming hash function if the result is fewer overflows, reducing expensive disk accesses rather than accesses to main memory. For example, if we can reduce overflows by employing a function that uses every byte of a 120-byte key rather than just the first and last byte, then it is probably worth doing.

Running Example

Student identification numbers are seven digits long and are of the form YYSDDDD, where YY is the last two digits of the year of application, S is the semester of application (2 = spring, 3 = summer, 4 or 5 = fall), and DDDD is an integer consecutively assigned from 0000 up within a semester. (Because more than 10,000 applications are received during the fall, two S digits are allocated to it and the number allocated after YY49999 is YY50000.)

In light of the discussion in Chapter 5, the designers decide to use a division operation on the student identification number to produce an address. Because 7143 (the number of buckets computed earlier) has a small factor (3), they increase the size of the address space to 7151, which is the next highest prime number. The remainder when dividing the five-digit SDDDD by 7151 should give an acceptable hash value.

11.2.4 Overflows

In dealing with overflow, our aim is to minimize the number of disk accesses when retrieving objects that do not fit in home buckets. Knuth (1973) compared retrievals done from files organized using open addressing (linear probe) with files in which overflow was handled by separate lists. Open addressing performed well unless the file was almost full. Chaining methods performed well but require extra space for pointers.

Recall from Chapter 5 the care that is needed if we use open addressing to resolve overflows and also need to delete objects. We could simply mark objects logically deleted and then, at some convenient time, rehash the entire file. Alternatively, we could take a little more time during each deletion and rehash appropriate nondeleted objects. Either solution may require many reads and writes and may incline us towards a closed addressing implementation.

Running Example

The university administrators want fast retrieval even in the worst case. The file designers decide to have overflow handled by separate chains. They decide to have a separate overflow area on each disk cylinder for the buckets on that cylinder. A separate set of cylinders is provided in case any of the primary overflow areas become full.

11.2.5 Main Memory Enhancements to Hash Files

We can use comparatively small data structures in main memory to save disk accesses. For example, if we are using open addressing, we can have a table in main memory that indicates for each bucket whether the bucket is empty, full, or neither empty nor full. In the insert algorithm, this allows us to detect that a bucket is full (and skip over it) without having to read from the disk, and also to determine that a bucket is empty and that we do not need to read it in order to insert an object into it. In the retrieval algorithm, the status information allows us to detect that a bucket is empty and that we can stop a search without further disk reads.

The remaining sections of this chapter look at implementations of a persistent map using variants of the hash file just presented. Each of the variants uses a data structure in main memory in addition to the buckets on the disk, and each guarantees retrieval of an object in a single file access. However, although retrievals are fast, insertions may be slow, and, in some circumstances, the insertion algorithm may not terminate successfully. In the structures described in Sections 11.5 and 11.6, the file is extensible: The number of buckets can grow and shrink as objects are inserted and deleted.

11.3 Table-Assisted Hashing

Larson and Kajla (1984) describe a file organization based on hashing that guarantees retrievals in one access to secondary storage. This is accomplished by means of a table in main memory that has one entry for each bucket in the hash file. (The table must be saved to disk when the hash file is closed and read into main memory when the hash file is opened.) As you will see, insertions into the file may take a long time, so the organization is good for applications in which retrievals are much more common than insertions. An example is the file of user passwords maintained by an operating system; it is accessed frequently to check log-ins and is added to relatively infrequently. Another example is a file of stock market data that is accessed very often by people enquiring about current stock prices. Additions to and deletions from this file will be much rarer than retrievals.

Table-assisted hashing requires mechanisms that will generate a sequence of bucket addresses and a parallel sequence of **signatures** from a key, thus

> Bucket addresses: Key → A_0, A_1, A_2, A_3, ...
> Signatures: Key → S_0, S_1, S_2, S_3, ...

Signatures are typically k-bit integers and are generated independently from the addresses.

Suppose, for example, that we are storing objects having a name as a key, and that a name may contain both uppercase and lowercase letters. The following is part of the definition of such an object (*testitem*) showing functions *A* and *S*. We assume that addresses are to be in the range 0 through *numaddresses* − 1 and that signatures are in the range 0 through *maxsig* − 1. (We will see later what signature value *maxsig* is used for.)

```
class testitem
{

public:  testitem(char N[]=" ", int v=99) {strcpy(key,N); value=v;}

    int A (int i, int numaddresses)
    {
    // returns ith address generated from key
    // numaddresses is the number of buckets/table entries 0..numaddresses-1
    // A0 = (1st character) + (last character) mod numaddresses
    // Ai = (A0 + i * length(key)) mod numaddresses

    int result = ( rank(key[0]) + rank(key[strlen(key)-1]) ) % numaddresses;
    while (i>0)
        {
            result = ( result + strlen(key) ) % numaddresses;
```

```
            i--;
        }
    return result;
    }




int S (int i, int maxsig)
{
    // returns ith signature generated from key
    // S0 = ((1st character) + ... + (last character)) mod maxsig
    // Si = (S0 + i * prime(length(key)) mod maxsig
    // prime(j) = jth prime number (for limited j)

    int primes[] = {2,3,5,7,11,13,17,19,23,29,31,37,41,43,47};
    int result = rank(key[0]);

    for (int j=1; j < strlen(key); j++)
        result = ( result + rank(key[j]) ) % maxsig;

    while (i>0)
        {
        result = ( result + primes[(strlen(key)-1) % 15] ) % maxsig;
        i--;
        }
    return result;
    }

private: char key [40];
        int value;
        int rank(char c)
        {
        if (c>='A' && c <='Z') return c-'A'+1;
        if (c>='a' && c <='z') return c-'a'+1;
        return -1;
        }
};
```

Table 11.2 shows the result of applying functions A and S to a small set of carefully chosen names. In each case, only the first five addresses (the A row) and the

		$i = 0$	$i = 1$	$i = 2$	$i = 3$	$i = 4$	...
TABLE 11.2 Address and Signature Values							
Fred	A	10	14	18	22	26	...
	S	2	9	16	23	30	...
Ferdinand	A	10	19	28	37	5	...
	S	13	5	28	20	12	...
Elsie	A	10	15	20	25	30	...
	S	19	30	10	21	1	...
Elise	A	10	15	20	25	30	...
	S	19	30	10	21	1	...
Indra	A	10	15	20	25	30	...
	S	15	26	6	17	28	...
Carog	A	10	15	20	25	30	...
	S	13	24	4	15	26	...
Butch	A	10	15	20	25	30	...
	S	23	3	14	25	5	...

corresponding signatures (the S row) are shown. We assume that *numaddresses* is 41 (thus A values are 0 through 40) and that *maxsig* is 31 (thus S values are 0 through 30).

Note that with our particular example functions, two keys that are permutations of each other, such as *Elise* and *Elsie*, will have the same sequence of addresses and the same sequence of signatures.

11.3.1 Insertions, Retrievals, and Deletions

We can implement a map using table-assisted hashing. The map will have two components: a file of buckets and a table of signature values. We introduce an implementation of a map with an informal examination of the insertion, retrieval, and deletion algorithms.

Insertions

When a map is created, the table entries are initialized to a value larger than the largest signature that function S can return. Typically, this will be *maxsig* (31 in our example). Suppose that each bucket in the file of buckets can hold three objects. Let us insert objects with the names shown in Table 11.2 in the order shown in that table. (The set of names has been chosen to produce many collisions; note, for instance, that the home bucket of each object is 10.)

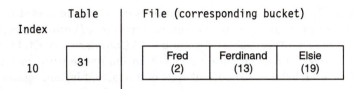

Figure 11.1 • Table and hash file after first three insertions

After inserting the first three objects, bucket 10 will be full. Figure 11.1 shows the relevant parts of the table and the file.

We assume that signatures for objects are stored with them in the buckets in order to save recomputation; signatures are shown in parentheses in the diagrams. Now what happens when we want to insert *Elise*? If an object hashes to a full bucket, then we do the following:

1. Look at the signatures that the objects (both those in the bucket and the new object) have for that bucket.
2. Add objects having the highest signature value (*HSV*) to a reinsert list.
3. Put the remaining objects back into the bucket.
4. Change the table entry for the bucket to *HSV*.

In order for an object to be eligible to be stored in a particular bucket, its signature for that bucket must be less than the corresponding table entry. Thus, the table entry acts as a form of barrier or threshold for the bucket. Changing the table entry to *HSV* as we do prevents the objects that we added to the reinsert list from going back into the bucket from which they were removed.

When we insert *Elise*, the algorithm identifies bucket 10 as the first suitable bucket. This bucket is full, so we find the highest signature among the four objects (*Fred, Ferdinand, Elsie,* and *Elise*). This is 19. Table[10] is set to 19, and objects with signature value 19 (*Elise* and *Elsie*) are moved to the reinsert list. Figure 11.2 shows what the file, table, and reinsert list now look like.

We could at this time process the objects in the reinsert list, but let us assume that we deal with each of the seven original objects first and come back to the reinsert list later. The next object (*Indra*) can be inserted into bucket 10. The one after

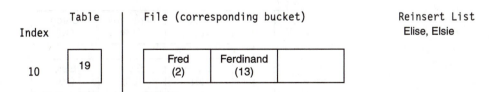

Figure 11.2 • Table, file, and reinsert list after four insertions

that (*Carog*) is also a candidate for bucket 10, but the bucket is now full again. We look at the signatures for the four objects (*Fred*, *Ferdinand*, *Indra*, and *Carog*). On this occasion, the highest signature is 15 (*Indra*), so Table[10] is set to 15 and *Indra* is removed from the bucket and put on the reinsert list, making room for *Carog*. Figure 11.3 shows the current state of the table, file, and reinsert list.

Butch is the next object to be inserted. When we insert *Butch*, we have to skip bucket 10 because *Butch*'s signature for bucket 10 is 23, and this is not lower than Table[10], which is 15. *Butch* ends up in bucket 15. Figure 11.4 shows what the table, file, and reinsert list now look like.

At this point, we have attempted to insert all seven objects, so we now process the objects in the reinsert list. Like *Butch*, *Elise* is not a candidate for bucket 10 and is placed in bucket 15. *Elsie* is treated in the same way, so we now have the configuration shown in Figure 11.5.

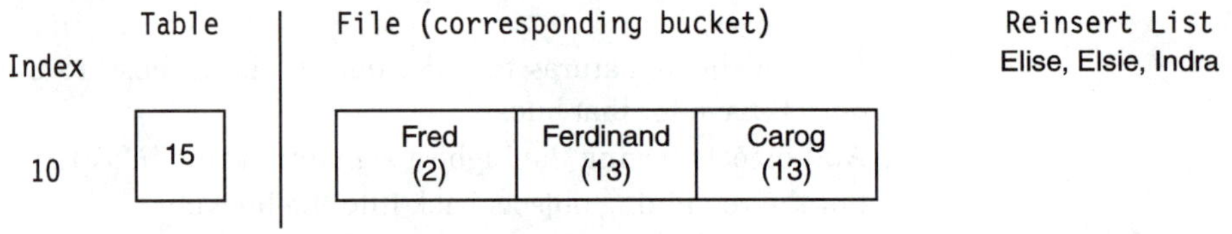

Table | File (corresponding bucket) | Reinsert List
Index | | Elise, Elsie, Indra

10 | 15 | Fred (2) | Ferdinand (13) | Carog (13)

Figure 11.3 • Table, file, and reinsert list after six insertions

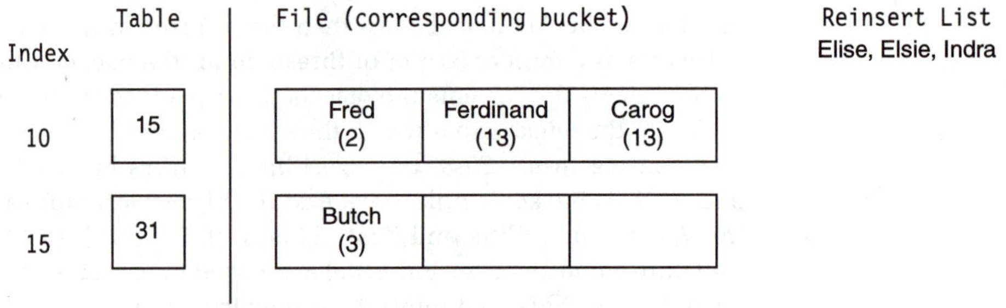

Table | File (corresponding bucket) | Reinsert List
Index | | Elise, Elsie, Indra

10 | 15 | Fred (2) | Ferdinand (13) | Carog (13)

15 | 31 | Butch (3)

Figure 11.4 • Table, file, and reinsert list after seven insertions

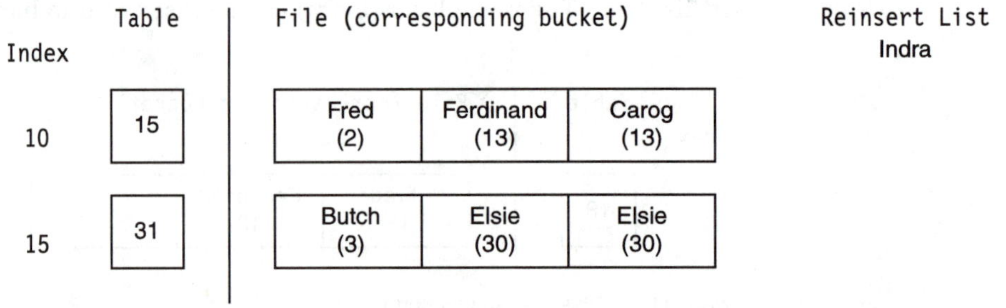

Table | File (corresponding bucket) | Reinsert List
Index | | Indra

10 | 15 | Fred (2) | Ferdinand (13) | Carog (13)

15 | 31 | Butch (3) | Elsie (30) | Elsie (30)

Figure 11.5 • Table and file during processing of reinsert list

When we process *Indra*, we find that 15 is the first suitable bucket. However, it is full, so we look at objects *Butch, Elise, Elsie*, and *Indra* and find the highest signature (30). We set Table[15] to 30 and move objects with that signature value (*Elise* and *Elsie*) to the reinsert list. This makes room for *Indra*, so the table, file, and reinsert list now look like Figure 11.6.

When we reinsert *Elise*, the first suitable bucket is 20. *Elsie* is treated in a similar fashion. The final table and file are shown in Figure 11.7.

Retrievals

Retrieval of objects from a table-assisted hash structure is very efficient. Both a successful and an unsuccessful search require only one file access. From the object to be retrieved, we generate addresses ($A_0, A_1, \dots$) and corresponding signatures ($S_0, S_1, \dots$), and stop when we find

$S_i < \text{Table}[A_i]$

or when we have determined that no such i exists. The object is a candidate for bucket A_i. Bucket A_i is the only bucket it can be in; if it is not in this bucket, it is not in the file.

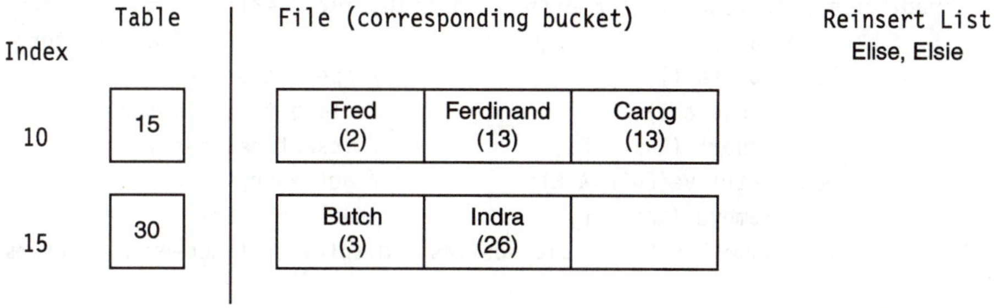

Figure 11.6 • Table and file after *Elise* and *Elsie* are moved back to the reinsert list

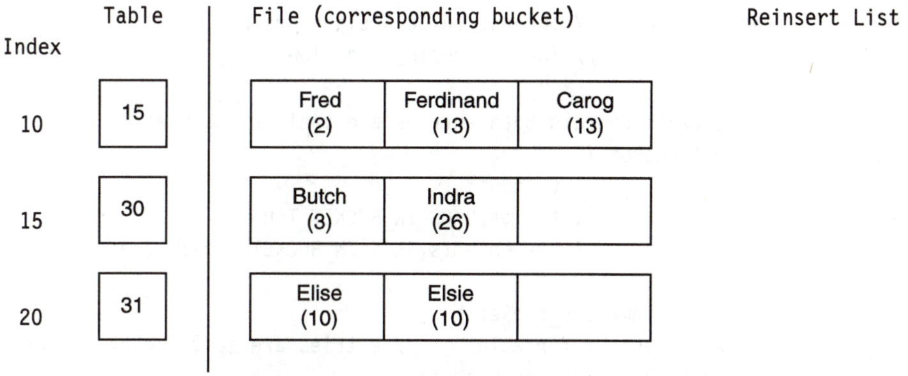

Figure 11.7 • Table and file after insertion of all objects from Table 11.2

Deletions

Larson and Kajla (1984) make no reference to deletions from a table-assisted hash file. However, it is not a difficult problem. Having found the object to be deleted (in one file access, see earlier discussion on retrievals), we mark it in some way. We can reserve an extra bit per object in the bucket for this purpose. Alternatively, we could keep a count (k) of nondeleted objects in the bucket and make sure that they occupy the first k locations. No changes are made to the table entries as a result of a deletion, and only one bucket is affected.

11.3.2 Implementation: *map_tah* Class

The following is the top level of a class definition for a map implemented using table-assisted hashing:

```
template <class Entry>
class map_tah
  { //
    // assumes Entry has functions a(I,range), s(I,range) and == defined

    public: map_tah(char filename[]="",int S=10, int MS=31); // constructor
            ~map_tah();                                        // destructor
            bool opentah();                   // open structure
            bool closetah();                  // close the structure
            bool insert (Entry E);            // insert new entry
            bool retrieve(Entry& E);          // get entry
            bool remove (Entry E);            // delete entry
            void show() ; // for diagnostics - display just non-empty buckets

    private: char tabfname[34],datfname[34];

            int size;     // number of buckets and table entries
            int maxsig;   // largest value a signature can have
            int HSV;      // for use during overflow

            // buckets contain both entries and their signatures
            struct bucket {
                    int count;
                    int sigs[RECS_IN_BUCKET_TAH];
                    Entry objects[RECS_IN_BUCKET_TAH];
                    };
            bucket mainmemory_bucket;
            BinaryFile<int> fortable;    // entries are just bucket numbers
            BinaryFile<bucket> forbuckets;
```

```
bool tablechanged;   // flag - do we need to save table?
int *thetable;       // table space dynamically allocated

stack<Entry> reinsertlist;

int candidate (int numbuckets, Entry E,
                         int& thesig); // find candidate bucket
void getbucket(int i) {forbuckets.getRecord(i,mainmemory_bucket);}
void putbucket(int i) {forbuckets.putRecord(i,mainmemory_bucket);}
void showbucket() ;          // simple display of contents
bool isinbucket(Entry E) ;   // search main memory bucket for E
void overwrite(Entry E);     // overwrite main memory with same key as E
bool roominbucket();         // is there space in main memory bucket?
int findhsv() ;              // find hsv in main memory bucket
void movetoreinsert(int HSV); // move objects to reinsert list
};
```

The class definition assumes that symbol *RECS_IN_BUCKET_TAH* has been appropriately defined as the number of objects in a bucket. Two files are used: a file of integers for the table and a file of buckets.

Opening and Closing the Structure
Most of what the constructor does is copy parameters: the basename of the files (*filename*), the size of the table (*S*), and the maximum signature values (*MS*). Each of the parameters has a default value. The *opentah* and *closetah* functions handle the opening and closing of the structure.

The *opentah* function checks to see if a pair of files already exists with the filename *filename.tbl* for the table and *filename.dat* for the buckets. If so, it checks that the files contain the same number of records and then loads the table from the file.[2] If no pair of files exists, then a table is initialized with the maximum signature and a file is filled with empty buckets. If only one file exists or the file contents are incompatible, then *opentah* exits, returning *false*.

When the structure is closed, the *tablechanged* flag is checked to see if the table needs to be written back to the file.

The definitions of the functions that open and close the structure follow.

```
template <class Entry>
bool map_tah<Entry>:: opentah()
{
 int goodopen=0;
 fstream temp,temp2;
 // see how many of the component files exist
 temp.open(tabfname,ios::in);
```

```
              if (!temp.fail()) goodopen++;
              temp2.open(datfname,ios::in);
              if (!temp2.fail()) goodopen++;

              if (goodopen==1)
                  { cerr << "one component not available\n";
                    return false;
                  }
              if (goodopen==2)  // files exist, check if OK
                    {
                    fortable.open(tabfname,ios::in|ios::out);
                    int A = fortable.numcomponents();
                    forbuckets.open(datfname,ios::in|ios::out);
                    int B = forbuckets.numcomponents();
                    // must be 1-to-1 correspondence between table entries and buckets
                    if (A==B && A>0)
                        { // components count match and are positive
                          size = A;
                          // allocate space for table
                          thetable = new int[size];
                          // and fill from file
                          for (int k=0; k<size; k++) fortable.getRecord(k,thetable[k]);
                          tablechanged=false;
                        }
                    else
                        {
                          cerr << "files incompatible - Table components: " << A
                              << " Bucket components: " << B << "\n";
                          return false;
                        }
                    }
              if (goodopen==0)  // no structure on disk yet
                  {
                    thetable = new int[size];
                    // make empty bucket for file initialization
                    mainmemory_bucket.count = 0;
                    // open files
                    fortable.open(tabfname,ios::in|ios::out);
                    forbuckets.open(datfname,ios::in|ios::out);

                    tablechanged=true;     //  forces table to be saved at end

                    // initialization of table and buckets
                    for (int k=0; k<size; k++)
```

```
            {
             thetable[k]=maxsig;
             forbuckets.putRecord(k,mainmemory_bucket);
            }
        }
}


template <class Entry>
bool map_tah<Entry>:: closetah()
{
  // save table if it has changed
  if (tablechanged)
        for (int k=0; k<size; k++) fortable.putRecord(k,thetable[k]);
  fortable.close();
  forbuckets.close();
}
```

Insertions, Retrievals, and Deletions
The following function, *candidate*, is used by the *insert*, *retrieve*, and *remove* functions. It returns the number of the bucket in which *Entry E* should be stored (or -1 if there is no such bucket). It uses functions *A* and *S* and the table. If there is a candidate bucket for *E*, then the signature of *E* for that bucket is passed back through parameter *thesig*.

```
template <class Entry>
int map_tah<Entry>:: candidate (int numbuckets, Entry E, int& thesig)
        {  // get address of candidate bucket or -1 if none
           // used by insert, retrieve, and remove
           // appropriate signature returned via thesig
           int i=0;
           int sig = E.S(i,maxsig), addr = E.A(i,size);
           bool more = true;

           while (thetable[addr] <= sig && more)
           {  // try next bucket
              i++;
              addr = E.A(i,size);
              if (addr == E.A(0,size))  // back to starting point?
                    more = false ;
                else sig = E.S(i,maxsig);
           }
```

```
                              if (more == false)
                                    return -1;
                              else {
                                    thesig=sig;
                                    return addr;
                              }
                        }
```

The condition for terminating the *while* loop is somewhat arbitrary. Although the sequence of addresses may begin to cycle, the corresponding signatures may be different during each repetition. Thus, for example, for a particular address, the second time it is generated, the corresponding signature may be lower than the first time, and an object may in fact be insertable if we let address generation continue. However, if we ignore address repetition, how do we know when to give up looking for a suitable bucket?

Insertions   We use a stack for the reinsert list; the *insert* algorithm begins by pushing the object to be inserted onto the stack and then continues processing stack items until the stack is empty. This way the insert operation is self-contained; there is no separate function required to handle reinsertions. However, there is no guarantee that the stack will become empty. As is usually the case with our insertion functions, if an object with the same key already exists, we overwrite it.

```
template <class Entry>
bool map_tah<Entry>:: insert (Entry E)
{
  // insert E into the structure - overwrite existing object with the same key
  Entry theitem;
  reinsertlist.push(E);  // push on reinsert list - to be popped momentarily
  int sigforstorage;

  while (!reinsertlist.empty())    // more objects to insert?
  {
   theitem = reinsertlist.top();  // get the first and
   reinsertlist.pop();            // remove from list

   int candidatebucket = candidate(size,theitem,sigforstorage);
   if (candidatebucket==-1)
        { // no candidate bucket found
          cerr << "cannot insert record\n";
          return false;
        }
```

```
        // get the candidate bucket
        getbucket(candidatebucket);

        if (isinbucket(theitem)) // already an object with the same key?
            { // overwrite in bucket
               overwrite(theitem);
               putbucket(candidatebucket);
            }

        else if (roominbucket())
            {// update bucket
            mainmemory_bucket.objects[mainmemory_bucket.count]=theitem;
            mainmemory_bucket.sigs[mainmemory_bucket.count]=sigforstorage;
            mainmemory_bucket.count++;
            putbucket(candidatebucket);
            }

        else
            {// do overflow steps
            // find highest sig
            HSV=sigforstorage;
            for (int k=0; k<mainmemory_bucket.count; k++)
                if (mainmemory_bucket.sigs[k]>HSV) HSV=mainmemory_bucket.sigs[k];
            // update table
            thetable[candidatebucket]=HSV;
            tablechanged = true;
            // put records on reinsert list
            movetoreinsert(HSV);
            if (sigforstorage==HSV)
                reinsertlist.push(theitem);   // if the new object has HSV
            else
                { // put new item into bucket
                mainmemory_bucket.objects[mainmemory_bucket.count]=theitem;
                mainmemory_bucket.sigs[mainmemory_bucket.count]=sigforstorage;
                mainmemory_bucket.count++;
                }
            putbucket(candidatebucket);
            }
    }
return true;
}
```

Saving Reads and Writes During an Insertion The following are three ways that we could save reads or writes during insertions:

● **TABLE 11.3** Signature-Dependent Actions for Example Insertion	
Signature	**Action**
≥ 50	Skip to next (*A*,*S*) pair—not allowed to be in this bucket.
> 40 and < 50	The object goes to the reinsert list and table[*i*] changes to its signature. Knowing the highest signature in the bucket and the fact that the bucket is full allows us to save a disk read in this case. No change to bucket.
= 40	The object, and the other objects with signature 40, are put on the reinsert list.
< 40	The object goes into the bucket and the two objects with signature 40 are moved to the reinsert list.

1. We can save an initial read from each bucket by maintaining information in main memory that indicates which buckets are empty. One way of doing this is to add a single-bit flag to each table entry.

2. On overflow, we can save a bucket write if there is exactly one object that overflows the bucket and that object happens to be the one not currently in the file. In this case, the bucket is unchanged.

3. For each bucket, we can hold in main memory the highest signature currently in each bucket and a full/not-full flag.

Consider the following example:

Suppose table[*i*] is 50, the bucket size is 4, and the signatures of the objects in bucket *i* are:

12 30 40 40

Regarding the new object to be inserted, we can identify four cases depending on the value of its signature for bucket *i*. The extra information held for each bucket allows us to save a disk read in one of the cases. (See Table 11.3.)

Retrievals   The *retrieve* function is comparatively simple.

```
template <class Entry>
bool map_tah<Entry>:: retrieve (Entry& E)
{
 int tempsig;
 int candidatebucket = candidate(size,E,tempsig);
 if (candidatebucket==-1)
     return false;
```

```
            else {
                    getbucket(candidatebucket);
                    // search the only bucket that can contain E
                    // overwrite parameter E if found
                    for (int k=0; k<mainmemory_bucket.count; k++)
                        if (E==mainmemory_bucket.objects[k])
                            { // key match found
                              E = mainmemory_bucket.objects[k];
                              return true;
                            }
                    return false;
            }
    }
```

If we have an additional bit in each table entry that indicates whether the corresponding bucket is empty or nonempty, we can avoid reading an empty bucket, and thus, in some cases, report that an object is not in the file without reading from the file at all!

Deletions   The *remove* function is also straightforward. We remove an object from a bucket rather than simply mark it deleted.

```
template <class Entry>
bool map_tah<Entry>:: remove (Entry E)
{
 int tempsig;
 int candidatebucket = candidate(size,E,tempsig);
 if (candidatebucket==-1)
      return false;  // not in file
      else {
            getbucket(candidatebucket);
            // search the only bucket that can contain E
            for (int k=0; k<mainmemory_bucket.count; k++)
              if (E==mainmemory_bucket.objects[k])
                {
                // remove from bucket & shuffle up remaining objects
                for (int j=k; j < mainmemory_bucket.count-1; j++)
                    {
                      mainmemory_bucket.objects[j]
                                      =mainmemory_bucket.objects[j+1];
                      mainmemory_bucket.sigs[j]=mainmemory_bucket.sigs[j+1];
                    }
                // adjust count
```

```
            mainmemory_bucket.count--;
            putbucket(candidatebucket);
            return true;
        }
    return false;
    }
}
```

Testing

We test the persistence properties of a *map_tah* object by running a sequence of three programs.

1. *Test5a:* Creates a persistent map object based on filename *example* (thus the components of the map are stored in files *example.dat* and *example.tbl)*. Each object in the map has a character array key and an integer nonkey field. Seven objects having the keys shown in Table 11.2 are inserted into the initially empty file.

2. *Test5b:* Opens the map created by *Test5a*. Removes an object (the one with key *Indra*), inserts a new object (with key *Anamari*), and modifies an object (changes the nonkey value of *Butch* from 55 to 30).

3. *Test5c:* Opens the file created by *Test5a* and modified by *Test5b* and displays its contents.

Here is the output from a run of the three programs, which is interspersed with listings of the directory entries for the files. Note from the file modification times how the second program modifies the bucket file but not the signature file.

```
$ test5a
10 15:  [Fred 60](2)[Ferdinand 23](13)[Carog 7](13)
15 30:  [Indra 200](26)[Butch 55](3)
20 31:  [Elsie 17](10)[Elise 49](10)
$ ls -l example*
-rw-r--r--   1 psmith    fac          6068 Oct 16 21:27 example.dat
-rw-r--r--   1 psmith    fac           164 Oct 16 21:27 example.tbl
$ test5b
10 15:  [Fred 60](2)[Ferdinand 23](13)[Carog 7](13)
15 30:  [Butch 30](3)
17 31:  [Anamari 45](12)
20 31:  [Elsie 17](10)[Elise 49](10)
$ ls -l example*
-rw-r--r--   1 psmith    fac          6068 Oct 16 21:28 example.dat
-rw-r--r--   1 psmith    fac           164 Oct 16 21:27 example.tbl
$ test5c
```

```
10 15:   [Fred 60](2)[Ferdinand 23](13)[Carog 7](13)
15 30:   [Butch 30](3)
17 31:   [Anamari 45](12)
20 31:   [Elsie 17](10)[Elise 49](10)
```

11.3.3 Periodic Maintenance

When a table entry changes, it gets smaller. This makes it more difficult for objects to get into the corresponding bucket and increases the probability of time-consuming or unsuccessful insertions. Performance can be restored by creating a new file and corresponding table (with entries at the maximum value). We write those objects not tagged for deletion to the new file.

11.4 Fixed-Length Versus Extensible Files

Up to this point, we have considered the hashing of fixed-length files. In our design process, we chose a bucket size and a packing density. In conjunction with an expected number of objects to be stored, this fixed the number of buckets allocated to the file (and in the case of table-assisted hashing, the size of the table). We assumed implicitly that the number of objects in the file at any time would not vary a great deal. In many applications, however, the number of objects in a file is likely to grow and shrink by large amounts.

Suppose that K is the number of objects stored in the file at any time, and K ranges between K_{min} and K_{max}. If we define *SPAN* as K_{max}/K_{min}, then fixed-size files in which the value of *SPAN* is large may cause problems. When K is close to K_{min}, space may be unacceptably underutilized; when K is close to K_{max}, the packing density is high, and storage and retrieval times may be long. Rehashing is one solution. When the number of objects in the file differs significantly from the original estimate, a new file of a more appropriate size can be created and the objects hashed into it using a suitably modified hash function. In practice, however, this is likely to be very time-consuming. In addition, the file is likely to be unavailable while rehashing is performed. This may be unacceptable in many applications.

A number of hashing techniques have been developed for organizing files with high *SPAN* values. We will consider two of them in the following sections. Each technique assumes that buckets can be allocated to a file from some pool and deallocated as required. This is a reasonable assumption; an operating system performs this type of space management as files are created and deleted. We classify the two techniques described in Sections 11.5 and 11.6 as implementations of **extensible files**, in contrast with conventional hashing, which uses fixed-length files. Each technique has methods for:

- Splitting a bucket when it becomes full
- Dispersing objects between old and new buckets

- Minimizing bucket accesses during retrieval
- Deleting objects from the file

The techniques we consider are Larson's dynamic hashing (1978) in Section 11.5 and the extendible hashing scheme devised by Fagin et al. (1979) in Section 11.6. (Note that we use the term *extensible* to describe a class of techniques, whereas Fagin et al. use the term *extendible* for their particular organization.) In each of these file organizations, the number of buckets in the file grows and shrinks relatively smoothly with the number of objects stored. There are no overflow buckets, and deletions can be quite simple. Retrievals, successful or not, typically require only one access to secondary storage. In what follows, we assume that buckets are of fixed size and that each has a capacity of C objects.

11.5 Dynamic Hashing

The main memory component of a dynamic hash file is a forest of binary trees. Each leaf points to a bucket on a disk. From the key of an object to be retrieved, we derive information that selects a tree and also a path from the root to a leaf in that tree. The leaf points to the only bucket that can possibly contain the object.

Initially, a file organized using Larson's (1978) dynamic hashing consists of N buckets. We have a hash function (H_0) that maps objects to be stored onto integers 1 through N (or equivalent). Each bucket is pointed to by a cell in main memory. Figure 11.8 depicts an initial file configuration when N is 10 and C is 3.

In Figure 11.8, the part of the structure above the dashed line is in main memory, and the part below the line is on disk. We term the main memory structure the **index**. (We consider indexes in general in later chapters.) The initial index has just one level, which we denote level 0.

11.5.1 Insertions, Retrievals, and Deletions

We will examine how each of the three fundamental operations works on a dynamic hash file.

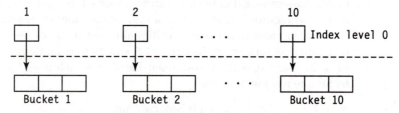

Figure 11.8 • Initial dynamic hash file

Insertions

Applying the hash function H_0 to the object to be stored yields the address of a level 0 index element. The appropriate bucket is identified by following the pointer contained in the index element. If there is room in the bucket, then the new object is inserted there.

If the bucket is full, then a new bucket is allocated to the file. The $C + 1$ objects (bucket contents plus the new object to be inserted) are distributed between the old and new buckets. In the index, the pointer to the old bucket becomes the parent of two leaves—an internal node in a binary tree. One leaf contains a pointer to the old bucket and the other contains a pointer to the new bucket. Figure 11.9 depicts the file from Figure 11.8 after bucket 2 has split.

As objects continue to be inserted into the file and splitting continues to occur, the index tends toward a forest of N binary trees. The roots of the trees are at index level 0.

The internal and external nodes can be represented very simply. The conventions proposed by Larson are as follows:

Internal node	0	parent_pointer	left_child_pointer	right_child_pointer

External node	1	parent_pointer	count_of_records	bucket_pointer

Two questions come to mind:

1. When dispersing objects between two buckets, how do we decide which object goes in which bucket?
2. Hash function H_0 brings us to the appropriate binary tree in the index. How do we decide which of the buckets pointed to by the leaves of that tree is the one to fetch?

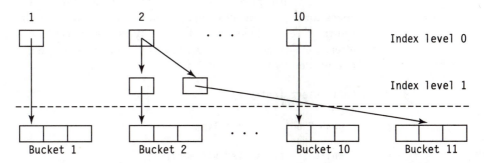

Figure 11.9 • File of Figure 11.8 after bucket 2 splits

Key	H_0(Key)	B(Key)
12	3	0110101000
13	4	1110010011
34	5	0111001011
174	5	1010100011
14	5	1100110011
24	5	0011111100
74	5	1010110101
244	5	1011000010
94	5	1010100111

● **TABLE 11.4** Keys: H_0(key) and B(key)

These questions are related. When deciding whether to put an object in the old bucket or in the new bucket, we must do so in a way that does not depend on the other objects in the bucket because conditions might be different when we search for the object later.[3] Larson's solution is to have a second function B that, given a key, returns an arbitrarily long binary string (i.e., a string in which each element is either 1 or 0). Table 11.4 shows typical keys, values of arbitrary H_0, and the first 10 bits of the strings generated by a function B (see Section 11.5.2 for details of how function B might work).

If the bucket being split is pointed to from a node at level I in the tree, then we use the value of the $(I + 1)$st digit of B(key) to determine if an object goes in the left (old) or right (new) bucket. For example, we could adopt the convention that 0 signifies left and 1 signifies right.

The following is a pseudo-C++ algorithm for the insert operation. We use the same technique here that we used in *map_tah*; that is, we add the item to be inserted to the reinsert list (stack) and then loop until that list is empty. The *insert* function returns *false* if space we try to allocate is not available. This might be disk space for a new bucket or main memory space for a new tree node. The function returns *true* if it is successful in emptying the reinsert list. As usual, if an object already exists having the same key as the one we are trying to insert, the old one is overwritten by the new.

```
bool insert (entry E)
{
  push E onto reinsert list

  while (reinsert list not empty)
    {
```

```
           pop item X from reinsert list

           // identify tree
           *node T = index [ X.HO(N) ];   // N is the number of index entries
           int I = 0;

           // traverse to leaf
           while (internal_node(T) )
               {
                  if (X.B(I) == 1)
                       T = T -> right
                  else  T = T -> left
                     I++
               }

           getbucket(T->bucketpointer)

             if (X in bucket)
                {    overwrite it
                     putbucket (T->bucketpointer)
                }
             else if (room in bucket)
                {    add X
                     putbucket (T->bucketpointer)
                }
             else
                {
                     allocate bucket; if none, return false
                     new leftnode = t->bucketpointer; if none, return false
                     new rightnode = t->rightnode; if none, return false
                     makeinternal(T,leftnode,rightnode)
                     move old bucket contents onto reinsert list
                     move X onto reinsert list
                }
           }
      return true;  // reinsert list empty
}
```

Example Sequence of Insertions   Consider what happens when we insert objects having the keys listed in Table 11.4 (in the order shown) into the structure of Figure 11.8.

Insert 12. Goes into bucket 3.
Insert 13. Goes into bucket 4.

Insert 34. Goes into bucket 5.

Insert 174. Goes into bucket 5.

Insert 14. Goes into bucket 5.

Insert 24. Bucket 5 is full. Assign another bucket to the file; assume this is bucket 11. Turn the pointer to bucket 5 into the parent of pointers to buckets 5 and 11. Arbitrarily label the pointer to 5 with 0 and the pointer to 11 with 1. Use the first digits of the *B* values (see Table 11.4) and assign:

34	to bucket 5	(0)
174	to bucket 11	(1)
14	to bucket 11	(1)
24	to bucket 5	(0)

Thus, we have the structure shown in Figure 11.10.

Insert 74. Goes into bucket 11.

Insert 244. Bucket 11 is full. Assign a new bucket (12) to the file. Turn the pointer to bucket 11 into the parent of pointers to buckets 11 and 12. Arbitrarily label the pointer to 11 with 0 and the pointer to 12 with 1. Use the second digits of the *B* values and assign:

174	to bucket 11	(0)
14	to bucket 12	(1)
74	to bucket 11	(0)
244	to bucket 11	(0)

We now have the structure shown in Figure 11.11.

Insert 94. Bucket 11 is full. Assign bucket 13 to the file. Turn the pointer to bucket 11 into the parent of pointers to buckets 11 and 13. Arbitrarily label

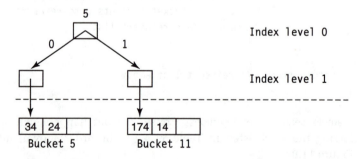

Figure 11.10 • Dynamic hash structure after split of bucket 5

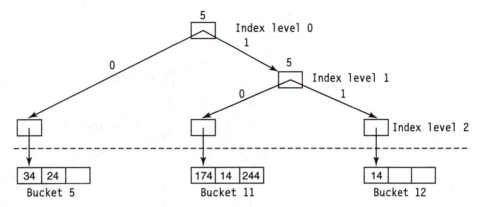

Figure 11.11 • Dynamic hash structure after split of bucket 11

the pointer to 11 with 0 and the pointer to 13 with 1. Use the third digits of *B* values and assign:

174	to bucket 13	(1)
74	to bucket 13	(1)
244	to bucket 13	(1)
94	to bucket 13	(1)

Unlucky 13! The bucket overflows (note that bucket 11 is empty). We assign bucket 14 to the file and turn the pointer to 13 into the parent of pointers to buckets 13 and 14. Label the pointer to 13 with 0 and the pointer to 14 with 1. Use the fourth digits of *B* values and assign:

174	to bucket 13	(0)
74	to bucket 13	(0)
244	to bucket 14	(1)
94	to bucket 13	(0)

Figure 11.12 shows what the structure now looks like.

Note that a result of the splitting strategy we used is that all objects in a bucket pointed to by a leaf node at index level J ($J > 0$) have the same first J bits of the B(key).

Retrievals

When searching for an object, we apply H_0 to the key to get the appropriate tree root. Then we use as many bits of the B(key) as are required to traverse the tree to a leaf. The combination of the two functions uniquely identifies a leaf in the forest of trees and hence a bucket in the file. The bucket identified in this way is the only one that can possibly contain the object we are looking for (c.f. table-assisted

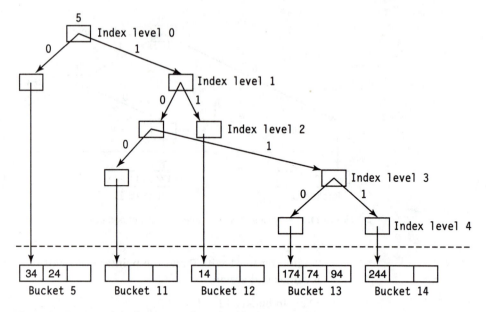

Figure 11.12 • Dynamic hash structure after split of buckets 11 and 13

hashing). If the object is not in there, it is not in the file at all. Here is a pseudo-C++ retrieval function.

```
bool retrieve (entry& E);
{
  // if structure contains an object with the same key as E, overwrite E with the object
  // and return true, otherwise return false.

  // identify tree
  *node T = index[ E.H0(N) ]; // N is the number of index entries
  int i = 0;

  while (internal_node(T))
      {
        if (E.B(i)==1)
            T = T -> right;
        else T = T -> left;
        i++;
      }
```

```
getbucket (T->bucketpointer);

// search the only bucket that can contain E
// overwrite parameter E if found
for (int k=0; k<mainmemory_bucket.count; k++)
      if (E==mainmemory_bucket.objects[k])
            { // key match found
              E = mainmemory_bucket.objects[k];
              return true;
            }
  return false;
}
```

Deletions

When deleting an object from a bucket, we can just shuffle the remaining objects and then exit. However, we should enable the file to shrink as well as expand, so we need to consider whether the bucket from which a deletion has been made has a **buddy bucket**. Bucket *A* is buddy to bucket *B* if the two buckets are pointed to by external nodes with the same parent. If the objects in two buddies combined will fit into a single bucket, then the objects can be put in one of the two buckets and the empty bucket deallocated from the file. The parent of the two leaves becomes a pointer to the remaining bucket. Here is a psuedo-C++ deletion function.

```
bool delete (entry E)
{
    // identify tree
    *node T = index [ E.HO(N) ]; // N is the number of index entries
    int i = 0;

    // traverse to leaf
    while ( internal_node(T))
            {
                if (E.B(i) == 1)
                    T = T -> right
                else  T = T -> left
                i++
            }

    getbucket(T->bucketpointer);

    if ( !object_in_bucket(E) ) return false; // object not found

    remove_from_bucket(E);
    putbucket(T->bucketpointer);              // put back updated bucket
```

```
while(true)
    {
        if (T->parent_pointer==nil) return true; // at top of index

        T = T->parent_pointer;
        // see if we can combine buddies
        if (  (count(T->left) + count(T->right)) > bucketsize)
            return true;    // no, so we are done

        copy_records(T->left,T->right);    // copy both to right child
        freebucket(T->left);               // and free up the left one
        makeexternal(T,T->left,T->right); // adjust the tree
    }
}
```

If we use this algorithm to delete the object with key 174 from the file shown in Figure 11.12, we can combine buckets twice. First we can combine buckets 13 and 14; this is shown in Figure 11.13a. Then we can combine buckets 11 and 14; this is shown in Figure 11.13b.

Dynamic hashing requires no periodic maintenance. However, free buckets must be obtainable when needed and must be returnable to a system pool. The deletion algorithm presented will always leave at least N buckets in the file (where N is the number of entries in the top level of the index). If necessary, we could modify the structure and algorithms so that more than one index entry could point to the same bucket.

11.5.2 Bitstring Function *B*

There are various ways of constructing the bitstring function B. One possibility is to use the key of the object being stored (or, in general, some function H_1 of the key) as the seed for a pseudo-random number generator. Each pseudo-random integer generated is then transformed into a binary digit. The transformation should produce 0 and 1 with equal probability; one possible transformation is to use the parity of the binary representation of the integer (i.e., the evenness or oddness of the number of 1s in the binary representation of the integer). Such a parity function is shown here and is employed in the following implementation of function *getbit* that was used to generate the bits in our earlier example table (Table 11.4). Recall that *getbit* is to return the ith bit in a bitstring generated from the key.

```
int parity (int N)
{
  // returns parity of N
  int sum=0;
```

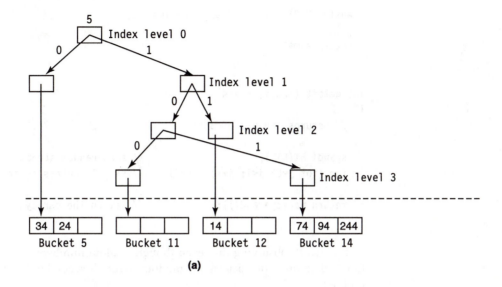

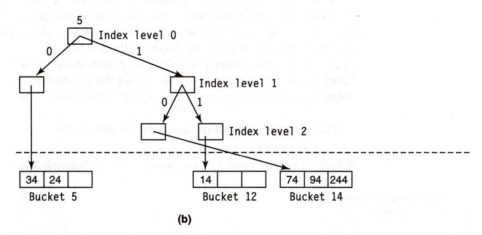

Figure 11.13 • (a) Structure of Figure 11.12 midway through the deletion of object with key 174. Buckets 13 and 14 have been combined. (b) Structure of Figure 11.12 after completion of the deletion. Buckets 11 and 14 have been combined.

```
        while (N>0) { sum += N&1;  N = N >> 1;  }

        return sum%2;
    }

    int getbit (int i, key K)
    {
        // returns ith bit of B(K)

        srand( H1(K) );                     // seed random stream with function of K
        for (int j=0; j<i; j++) rand();     // skip I numbers in the stream

        return parity(rand());              // return the parity of the next number
    }
```

It is worth observing that even though random numbers are involved, the function is deterministic because the random stream is seeded with a value based solely on the key.

Note that if function B is implemented in this way, a problem occurs on overflow if all objects to be distributed between the pair of buckets have the same value of the H_1(key). The result will be that the binary strings of the objects will be identical, and hence the objects can never be divided between two buckets. The system could monitor the number of different H_1(key) values in a bucket, but "operator intervention" may be necessary to prevent the *insert* algorithm from looping until either the supply of buckets or the supply of tree nodes is exhausted.

• 11.5.3 Implementation: *map_dynamich* Class

At the top level, the class definition for *map_dynamich* is very similar to the class definition for *map_tah*. The top level of *map_dynamich* follows.

```
template<class Entry>
class map_dynamich
{
// assumes entries have HO and B functions and == defined

public: map_dynamich(char filename[]="",int indexsz=4);  // constructor
        ~map_dynamich();                                 // destructor
        bool opendynamich();       // open structure
        bool closedynamich();      // close structure
        bool insert (Entry E);     // insert new entry
        bool retrieve (Entry& E);  // get entry
        bool remove (Entry E);
        void show(); // show index entries and buckets
```

```
private:int size;  // size of top level index
        stack<Entry> reinsertlist;
        int numbuckets;

     // index nodes have 4 fields:
     // isinternal (bool)  - indicates if node is internal or leaf
     // left, right (pointers to node) - used of internal
     // bucknumber (int) - used if leaf, bucket number pointed to
      struct node {bool isinternal; node *left; node *right; int bucknumber;};

      struct bucket {int count; Entry objects[RECS_IN_BUCKET_DYNH];};

      char idxfilename[34], datfilename[34];
      bool idxchanged;  // flag - do we need to save the index?

      node *index;        // array of nodes is dynamically allocated
      bool *bucketmap;    // as is the map of used/free buckets
      bucket mainmemory_bucket;

      fstream forindex;                 // for attaching text file to save index
      BinaryFile<bucket> forbuckets;    // for the buckets

      void getbucket(int i) {forbuckets.getRecord(i,mainmemory_bucket);}
      void putbucket(int i) {forbuckets.putRecord(i,mainmemory_bucket);}
      bool saveindex(char fname[]);     // save index to file
      void restoreindex(char fname[]);  // restore index from file
      int numlines(char fname[]);       // get the number of lines in file
      void traverse (node *T, int maxval);// traverse tree - identify buckets
      void printindexstring(int value, int d); // prints value as d digits
      void printtreeaux(node *T, int N, int depth); // prints index tree
      void deltree(node *T) ;                   // reclaim tree space
      void savetree(node *T);           // saves tree in pre-order
      void restoretree(node *&T);       // the inverse routine to restore
      int allocatebucket();             // find a new bucket
      void releasebucket(int i);        // make bucket available
      bool isinbucket(Entry E);         // search main memory bucket
      void overwrite(Entry E);          // replace old record by new with same key
};
```

Most of the differences between the two class definitions are due to the index now being a forest of trees instead of a table of integers. In addition, buckets are allocated and deallocated dynamically.

Bucket Allocation and Deallocation

In the absence of an interface to disk space allocation utilities, we simulate bucket allocation and deallocation. We have a file of buckets and a corresponding map that indicates if a particular bucket is in use. To deallocate a bucket, we simply identify it as free using the map entry. To allocate a bucket, we first see if there are any free buckets in the current file; if there are, the first one encountered is used. If all buckets are in use, the file and map are extended by one bucket. Thus, the file can never shrink below its high-water mark.

Insertions

The following insert function demonstrates the bucket-splitting protocol. As with *map_tah*, we make use of a reinsert list (which is actually a stack).

```
template <class Entry>
bool map_dynamich<Entry>::insert(Entry E)
{
  // insert E into the structure - overwriting any existing object with same key
  Entry theitem;

  reinsertlist.push(E); // push on reinsert list to be popped momentarily

  while (!reinsertlist.empty())     // more objects to insert?
    {
      theitem = reinsertlist.top(); // get the first and
      reinsertlist.pop();           // remove from list

    // HO identifies index entry
    node *X = &index[ theitem.HO(size) ];
    int currentbit,indexlevel;

    indexlevel=0;

  // traverse tree to leaf
    while ( (X->isinternal) )
      {
        currentbit = theitem.B(indexlevel);
        indexlevel++;
        if (currentbit==0) X=X->left; else X=X->right;
      }

    // get bucket pointed to by leaf
    getbucket(X->bucknumber);
```

```
// see if record with the same key
if (isinbucket(theitem))
  {
   overwrite(theitem);
   putbucket(X->bucknumber);
  }
// no - see if room for a new one
else if (mainmemory_bucket.count < RECS_IN_BUCKET_DYNH)
  {
   // room in bucket
   mainmemory_bucket.objects[mainmemory_bucket.count]=theitem;
   mainmemory_bucket.count++;
   putbucket(X->bucknumber);
  }
else
  {
   // overflow
   node *temp1, *temp2;
   int newbucknumber;

   newbucknumber = allocatebucket();
   if (newbucknumber==-1)
       {
        cerr << "insert: out of buckets\n";
        return false;
       }
  // external node becomes parent to 2 leaves
   temp1 = new node;
   if (temp1==0)
      {
       cerr << "insert: out of heap space\n";
       return false;
      }
   temp2 = new node;
   if (temp2==0)
      {
       cerr << "insert: out of heap space\n";
       return false;
      }
  // mark new nodes as leaves
   temp1->isinternal = false;
   temp2->isinternal = false;
```

```
      // one leaf points to old bucket, the other to the new bucket
       temp1->bucknumber = X->bucknumber;
       temp2->bucknumber = newbucknumber;
      // old node becomes their parent
       X->left = temp1;
       X->right = temp2;
       X->isinternal = true;
       idxchanged=true;          // index will need to be saved now
      // put records to be dispersed onto the reinsert list
       reinsertlist.push(theitem);
       for (int i=0; i<RECS_IN_BUCKET_DYNH; i++)
             reinsertlist.push(mainmemory_bucket.objects[i]);
      // clear both buckets
       mainmemory_bucket.count=0;
       putbucket(X->bucknumber);
       putbucket(newbucknumber); // to initialize new one with count of 0
       }
   }
  return true;
}
```

Deletions

The following function removes an object from the dynamic hash function implementation of a map; it includes code that consolidates the index tree, if possible.

```
template <class Entry>
bool map_dynamich<Entry>::remove(Entry E)
{
 node *Z, *X = &index[ E.HO(size) ];  // HO identifies tree
 stack<node*> S;                       // for going back up the tree
 int currentbit,indexlevel = 0;
 Entry tempentry;
 bucket mainmemory_bucket2;
 node tempnode;
 bool go_on,found = false;

 // go down tree to leaf
 while ( (X->isinternal) )
   {
     currentbit = E.B(indexlevel);
     indexlevel++;
```

```
          // stack pointers for going back up tree later.
          S.push(X);
          if (currentbit==0) X=X->left; else X=X->right;
        }

// get bucket pointed to by leaf
getbucket(X->bucknumber);
// see if object with same key as E is in ..
for (int k = 0; k<mainmemory_bucket.count; k++)
  if (mainmemory_bucket.objects[k]==E)
      {
        found=true;
        // remove, adjust count, put bucket back
        if (k!=mainmemory_bucket.count-1)
            {
              // exchange with last in bucket
              tempentry=mainmemory_bucket.objects[k];
              mainmemory_bucket.objects[k]=
                      mainmemory_bucket.objects[mainmemory_bucket.count-1];
              mainmemory_bucket.objects[mainmemory_bucket.count-1]=tempentry;
            }
        mainmemory_bucket.count--;
        putbucket(X->bucknumber);
      }
  if (!found) return false;
  // possible consolidation of tree follows
  go_on = true;
  while(go_on)
   {
    if (S.empty())
      go_on = false; // no parent
    else
      {// get pointer to parent
       Z=S.top();
       S.pop();
       // see if children are both leaves
       if (Z->left->isinternal || Z->right->isinternal)
           go_on = false;   // no
       else
           {
             // both are leaves, get the buckets
```

```
                        getbucket(Z->left->bucknumber);
                        mainmemory_bucket2=mainmemory_bucket;
                        getbucket(Z->right->bucknumber);
                        // if can consolidate
                        if (mainmemory_bucket.count+mainmemory_bucket2.count
                                  <=RECS_IN_BUCKET_DYNH
                           )
                           {
                             // do that here. Put records from
                             // mainmemory_bucket2 into mainmemory_bucket
                             for (int k=0; k<mainmemory_bucket2.count; k++)
                                 {
                                    mainmemory_bucket.objects[mainmemory_bucket.count]
                                               =mainmemory_bucket2.objects[k];
                                    mainmemory_bucket.count++;
                                 }
                             // get rid of redundant bucket
                             releasebucket(Z->left->bucknumber);
                             // put the bucket we added to back in file
                             putbucket (Z->right->bucknumber);
                             // node is now leaf
                             Z->isinternal = false;
                             // with pointer to added to bucket
                             Z->bucknumber = Z->right->bucknumber;
                             // return two leaves to heap
                             delete Z->right  ;
                             delete Z->left     ;
                             idxchanged=true;  // and flag index for saving
                           }
                       else
                          go_on = false; // buckets too big to combine
                     }
                  }
               }
          }
```

Retrievals

For completeness, the following retrieval function is presented. It is comparatively simple.

```
bool map_dynamich<Entry>::retrieve(Entry& E)
{
 // H0 identifies tree
```

```
node *X = &index[ E.HO(size) ];
int currentbit,indexlevel = 0;

// follow path to leaf
while ( (X->isinternal) )
  {
   currentbit = E.B(indexlevel);
   indexlevel++;
   if (currentbit==0) X=X->left; else X=X->right;
  }
getbucket(X->bucknumber);
// see if object with same key as E is in bucket. If so, overwrite E
for (int k = 0; k<mainmemory_bucket.count; k++)
  if (mainmemory_bucket.objects[k]==E)
      { E=mainmemory_bucket.objects[k];
        return true;
      }
return false;
}
```

11.5.4 Saving and Restoring the Index

Various techniques can be used to save a tree index [e.g., Frost (1979)]. In our implementation, we write a representation of the index to a text file. Each tree is saved to a separate line that begins with the number of the tree. A tree is saved in preorder (root, left subtree, right subtree, applied recursively). A leaf is represented by the number of the bucket it points to; an internal node is represented by the symbol I. Consider the index fragment shown in Figure 11.14.

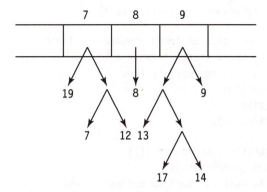

Figure 11.14 • Fragment of dynamic hash index

When this index is saved, the lines of the text file corresponding to the fragment of Figure 11.14 are:

```
7 I 19 I 7 12
8 8
9 I I 13 I 17 14 9
```

The following function, *opendynamich*, shows how an index stored on disk is checked and reconstructed in main memory (compare this with function *opentah* for the *map_tah* class).

```
template <class Entry>
bool map_dynamich<Entry>::opendynamich()
        {
        int goodopen=0;
        fstream temp1, temp2;

        // see how many of the component files exist
        temp1.open(idxfilename,ios::in);
        if (!temp1.fail()) goodopen++;
        temp2.open(datfilename,ios::in);
        if (!temp2.fail()) goodopen++;

        if (goodopen==1)
           {
           cerr << "one component not available\n";
           return false;
           }
        if (goodopen==2)
            {
            // files exist load and check?
            forbuckets.open(datfilename,ios::in|ios::out);

            // from index file get size of index = number of lines
            // each line of the index (text) file is a
            // representation of the appropriate tree
            size = numlines(idxfilename);
            index = new node[size];
            restoreindex(idxfilename);

            numbuckets = forbuckets.numcomponents();
            bucketmap = new bool[numbuckets];
            // assume initially that all buckets are not in use
            for (int i=0; i<numbuckets; i++) bucketmap[i] = false;
            // traverse index finding which are actually in use
```

```
    for (int i=0; i<size; i++) traverse(&index[i],numbuckets);

    idxchanged = false;
  }

if (goodopen==0)
  {
  // no pre-existing structures on file so set up
  numbuckets = size;
  index = new node[size];
  bucketmap = new bool[numbuckets]; // initial file same size as index

  // make bucket with zero count for initializing file
  mainmemory_bucket.count=0;

  forbuckets.open(datfilename,ios::in|ios::out);
  idxchanged = true;                    // to force save later

  // create the top-level index entries, the empty buckets and bucket
  // map values
  for (int i=0; i<numbuckets; i++)
    {
     index[i].isinternal = false;
     index[i].bucknumber=i;
     forbuckets.putRecord(i,mainmemory_bucket);
     bucketmap[i]=true;
    }
  }
return true;
}
```

Here is the *closedynamich* function.

```
template <class Entry>
bool map_dynamich<Entry>::closedynamich()
        {
          bool result = true;
          if (idxchanged)
            { // write new index file replacing the old one
              result = saveindex(idxfilename);
            }
          forbuckets.close();
          return result;
        }
```

Testing

Now, we test the persistence of the structure—the saving and restoring of the index and the insertion and deletion functions with a sequence of three programs. The index has 10 elements, and the objects stored in our *map_dynamich* object have an integer key and a nonkey array of characters.

- *Test7:* Stores 12 objects into an initially empty structure. The first nine objects have the example keys from Table 11.4. Note how the *show* function shows the bitstring corresponding to the path from root to leaf.
- *Test7a:* Opens the structure from disk and displays it. It also checks that the save and restore work.
- *Test7b:* Removes objects with keys 14, 34, and 104 to test the bucket consolidation.

Output from runs of the programs follows.

```
$ test7
show ..
subindex : 0
indexstring:     bucket : 0 : 0 :
subindex : 1
indexstring:     bucket : 1 : 0 :
subindex : 2
indexstring:     bucket : 2 : 1 : [ 12 cat ]
subindex : 3
indexstring:     bucket : 3 : 1 : [ 13 tac ]
subindex : 4
indexstring: 000  bucket : 4 : 2 : [ 74 toad ] [ 94 sinead ]
indexstring: 001  bucket : 12 : 2 : [ 24 frog ] [ 244 denis ]
indexstring: 01  bucket : 11 : 0 :
indexstring: 10  bucket : 10 : 3 : [ 34 dog ] [ 44 team ] [ 4 avail ]
indexstring: 11  bucket : 13 : 3 : [ 174 mouse ] [ 14 rat ] [ 104 sad ]
subindex : 5
indexstring:     bucket : 5 : 0 :
subindex : 6
indexstring:     bucket : 6 : 0 :
subindex : 7
indexstring:     bucket : 7 : 0 :
subindex : 8
indexstring:     bucket : 8 : 0 :
subindex : 9
indexstring:     bucket : 9 : 0 :
$
$ test7a
show ..
subindex : 0
indexstring:     bucket : 0 : 0 :
```

```
subindex : 1
indexstring:   bucket : 1 : 0 :
subindex : 2
indexstring:   bucket : 2 : 1 : [ 12 cat ]
subindex : 3
indexstring:   bucket : 3 : 1 : [ 13 tac ]
subindex : 4
indexstring: 000  bucket : 4 : 2 : [ 74 toad ] [ 94 sinead ]
indexstring: 001  bucket : 12 : 2 : [ 24 frog ] [ 244 denis ]
indexstring: 01  bucket : 11 : 0 :
indexstring: 10  bucket : 10 : 3 : [ 34 dog ] [ 44 team ] [ 4 availability ]
indexstring: 11  bucket : 13 : 3 : [ 174 mouse ] [ 14 rat ] [ 104 sad ]
subindex : 5
indexstring:   bucket : 5 : 0 :
subindex : 6
indexstring:   bucket : 6 : 0 :
subindex : 7
indexstring:   bucket : 7 : 0 :
subindex : 8
indexstring:   bucket : 8 : 0 :
subindex : 9
indexstring:   bucket : 9 : 0 :
$
$ test7b
show ..
subindex : 0
indexstring:   bucket : 0 : 0 :
subindex : 1
indexstring:   bucket : 1 : 0 :
subindex : 2
indexstring:   bucket : 2 : 1 : [ 12 cat ]
subindex : 3
indexstring:   bucket : 3 : 1 : [ 13 tac ]
subindex : 4
indexstring: 000  bucket : 4 : 2 : [ 74 toad ] [ 94 sinead ]
indexstring: 001  bucket : 12 : 2 : [ 24 frog ] [ 244 denis ]
indexstring: 01  bucket : 11 : 0 :
indexstring: 1  bucket : 13 : 3 : [ 174 mouse ] [ 4 availability ] [ 44 team ]
subindex : 5
indexstring:   bucket : 5 : 0 :
subindex : 6
indexstring:   bucket : 6 : 0 :
subindex : 7
indexstring:   bucket : 7 : 0 :
subindex : 8
```

```
indexstring:  bucket : 8 : 0 :
subindex : 9
indexstring:  bucket : 9 : 0 :
```

11.5.5 Storage Utilization

Larson (1978) analyzed expected storage utilization and showed it to be approximately 69 percent all of the time. However, as we have seen, additional space beyond that required for the buckets would normally be required to store the index when the file is not in use.

Dynamic hashing may have a hidden overhead. Because of the discontiguous way in which the index evolves, nodes on a path from a root to a leaf may be widely separated in main memory. In a virtual memory system, several page faults may be incurred during a tree traversal, and dealing with a page fault may require one or more disk accesses.[4] In addition, if the file is large, the index may be too big to fit in main memory, and at least the lower levels may have to be kept on secondary storage. Thus, access times are further increased.

Variations on dynamic hashing have been described by Scholl (1981). In one variation, overflow buckets are introduced and bucket splitting is deferred. In this way, storage utilization can be improved at a cost of longer average access times.

Next, we look at extendible hashing, which is similar to dynamic hashing but has a simpler index and only needs one hash function.

11.6 Extendible Hashing

The main memory component of an extendible hash file is a table with 2^k entries, each pointing to a disk bucket (more than one pointer may point to the same bucket). A k-bit **pseudokey**, derived from the key of the object being searched for, is used to index the table. The table entry points to the only bucket that can possibly contain the object.

The extendible hashing organization of Fagin et al. (1979) is similar to Larson's (1978) dynamic hashing in that a two-level organization is used. Whereas Larson's method uses, in effect, two hash functions (H_0 and B), extendible hashing uses a single hash function. The function operates on the key of an object and produces a bitstring denoted the pseudokey. (This function is comparable to Larson's function B.) Extendible hashing uses a **directory** and a set of "leaves." Each leaf consists of a bucket of objects and an integer header. The directory consists of a similar header $d(d \geq 0)$ and 2^d pointers (not necessarily distinct) to leaves. Figure 11.15 shows a typical configuration in which the header for the directory is 3 and the headers for the four leaves are 3, 3, 2, and 1, respectively.

The header of a particular leaf indicates the number of prefix bits that the pseudokeys of the bucket objects have in common. For example, the pseudokeys of the objects in the first bucket in Figure 11.15 start with the same three bits (000).

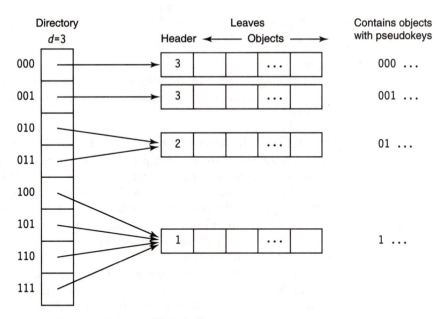

Figure 11.15 • A typical extendible hash file

Let us look at the three fundamental operations on an extendible hash file.

Retrievals

If $d = 0$, then there is only one directory entry, and we follow its pointer to the only bucket in the file. If d > 0, as will usually be the case, we use the first d bits of the pseudokey of the object we are looking for as an index into the directory. The directory entry yields a pointer to the appropriate leaf to search. For example, suppose that we are searching the file shown in Figure 11.15 for an object with key X, and that the pseudokey derived from X is 1010000100010. We use the first three bits of the pseudokey (because the directory header is 3) to form an index (101 = 5) into the directory. Entry 5 points to the fourth leaf, so this is where we search for an object with key X.

Extendible hashing improves on dynamic hashing because there is only one access to main memory when using the index, and therefore we risk incurring only one page fault in the directory/index part of the search.

If we want the structure to grow completely naturally, the initial file would contain just one leaf and the directory would have a single entry pointing to the leaf. The initial value of the directory header and the leaf header will be 0. However, we would usually choose to have an initial file containing N buckets. The value of d

will be $\lfloor \log_2(N-1) \rfloor + 1$ and the directory will have 2^d entries.[5] For example, if N were 50, d is 6, and the directory has 64 entries.

Insertions

To store an object, the first d bits of its pseudokey are used to access the directory, and the leaf pointed to is retrieved. Assume the leaf capacity is C objects. There are three cases:

1. There are currently fewer than C objects in the leaf. The new object is inserted.
2. The leaf is full and there are multiple pointers to it; that is, the header (T) for the leaf is less than the directory header (d). A new leaf is allocated to the file (as with dynamic hashing; the address of the new leaf is unimportant). The headers for the old leaf and the new leaf are both set to $T + 1$. The group of pointers pointing to the old leaf is split in two; half will point to the new leaf and half to the old leaf. The $C + 1$ objects are dispersed between the new and old leaf according to bit $T + 1$ of their pseudokeys.
3. The leaf is full and there is only one pointer to it; that is, the leaf header (T) is equal to the directory header (d). In this case, the size of the directory must be doubled so that it can differentiate between the old and new leaves. The value of d therefore increases by 1, and every entry in the old directory is duplicated in the new directory. The leaf that is overflowing is pointed to by two pointers and we proceed as in case 2. The creation of a new directory from the old one is a simple linear operation.

The way in which the index grows is one of the differences between dynamic hashing and extendible hashing. An insertion into a dynamic hashing structure typically adds at most two tree nodes to the index, so index growth is gradual. In contrast, an insertion into a dynamic hash structure may cause the index to double in size.

Consider the keys and pseudokeys shown in Table 11.5.

● **TABLE 11.5** Keys and Pseudokeys

Key	Pseudokey
a	1101 ...
b	0110 ...
c	0010 ...
d	1010 ...
e	0011 ...
f	0010 ...
g	1000 ...
h	1101 ...

d=0

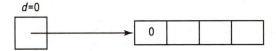

Figure 11.16 • Initial extendible hash structure

We will see how an initial structure consisting of a single directory entry and a single leaf changes as the objects having the keys shown in Table 11.5 are inserted. A leaf contains a header and up to three objects. Figure 11.16 depicts the initial structure.

The insertions of objects with keys *a*, *b*, and *c* are case 1 insertions. The resulting structure is depicted in Figure 11.17.

Inserting an object with key *d* is a case 3 insertion. First we double and duplicate the directory, yielding the structure of Figure 11.18a, then the pointers divide and the objects disperse, yielding the structure of Figure 11.18b.

Insertion of an object with key *e* is another case 1 insertion and yields the structure shown in Figure 11.19.

d=0

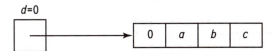

Figure 11.17 • Structure from Figure 11.16 after insertion of *a*, *b*, and *c*

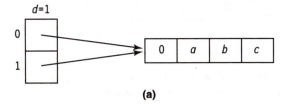

(a)

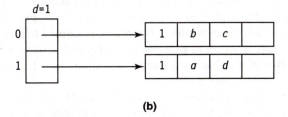

(b)

Figure 11.18 • (a) Structure of Figure 11.17 midway through insertion of object with key *d*; directory size has doubled. (b) Completion of insertion, pointers have divided.

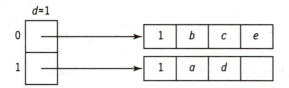

Figure 11.19 • Insertion of *e* into the structure from Figure 11.18

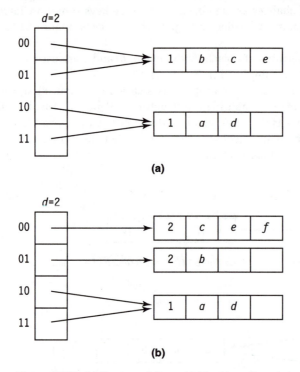

Figure 11.20 • (a) Structure of Figure 11.19 midway through insertion of object with key *f;* directory size has doubled. (b) Completion of insertion, pointers have divided.

When we now insert an object with key *f*, we get another case 3 insertion because the target leaf is full and there is only one pointer to it. Figure 11.20a depicts the first stage, in which the directory is doubled and duplicated. Figure 11.20b depicts the structure after division of pointers and dispersal of objects.

The insertion of an object with key *g* is another case 1 insertion. The structure now is as shown in Figure 11.21.

Finally, inserting *h* is a case 2 insertion (multiple pointers to a full bucket). The pointers are divided and the objects are dispersed without changing the size of the directory. The result is as shown in Figure 11.22.

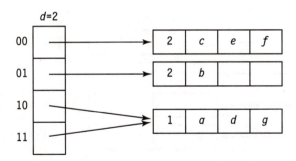

Figure 11.21 • Insertion of *g* into structure from Figure 11.20

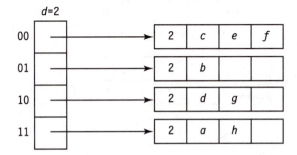

Figure 11.22 • Result of inserting *h* into the structure from Figure 11.21

Deletions

The buddy bucket concept that we saw in dynamic hashing is also part of the extendible file organization. Buddy buckets have the same header value (T), and the pseudokeys of the objects they contain have $T - 1$ prefix bits in common. For example, in Figure 11.22, the bucket containing *c*, *e*, and *f* and the bucket containing *b* are buddies. However, the bucket containing *b* and the bucket containing *d* and *g* are not buddies because they do not satisfy the prefix-bit condition. If space permits, buddy buckets can be combined after a deletion. The new header for the combined leaf will be $T - 1$. If all leaf headers are now less than the directory header, the directory can be halved in size, and the pointers adjusted.

If we delete any of the objects from the structure of Figure 11.22, we can combine buckets. The result of deleting *d* is shown in Figure 11.23a; Figure 11.23b shows the combined buddy buckets.

If we delete *b*, *c*, *e*, or *f* from the structure shown in Figure 11.23, bucket consolidation can be followed by dictionary halving. Figure 11.24a shows the removal of *e* from the bucket. Figure 11.24b shows bucket consolidation, and Figure 11.24c shows the reduction in the directory.

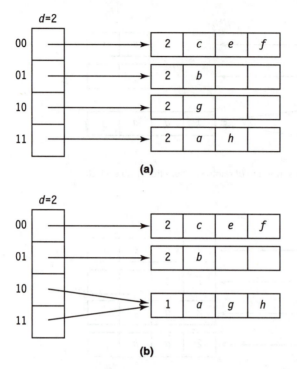

Figure 11.23 • (a) Structure of Figure 11.22 midway through deletion of object with key *d;* buddy buckets not yet combined. (b) Combination of deletion, buddy buckets combined.

11.6.2 Implementation: *map_exth* Class

As we would expect, the interface of an object of type *map_exth* is similar to those for objects of type *map_tah* and *map_dynamich*. In addition, the implementation of *map_exth* has much in common with the implementation of *map_dynamich*, such as the allocation and deallocation of buckets. At the same time, some functions are unique to *map_exth*, including those concerned with checking a directory structure that has been saved in a file (see Opening and Closing the Structure). The following is the top level of the class definition.

```
template<class Entry>
class map_exth
{
// assumes entries have pseudokey function

public: map_exth(char filename[]="",int dirsz=4, int numbucks=1); // constructor
        ~map_exth();                                               // destructor
        bool openexth();                    // open structure
```

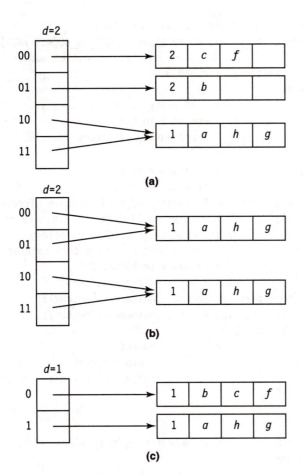

Figure 11.24 • Deletion of object with key e from the structure of Figure 11.23 (a) after removal of object (b) after combining buddy buckets and (c) after compaction of directory

```
      bool closeexth();            // close structure
      bool insert (Entry E);       // insert new entry
      bool retrieve (Entry& E);    // retrieve entry
      bool remove (Entry E);       // remove entry
      void show();                 // display current structure

private:int size;         // number of entries in directory
      int numbuckets;   // number of buckets in the file
      int dirheader;    // number of directory entries is 2^dirheader
      stack<Entry> reinsertlist;
      char dirfilename[34], datfilename[34];
```

```
bool dirchanged;    // flag - do we need to save directory?
struct bucket {int header; int count; Entry objects[RECS_IN_BUCKET_EXTH];};
BinaryFile<int> fordir;          // directory entries are bucket numbers
BinaryFile<bucket> forbuckets;   // for the buckets
bucket mainmemory_bucket;
int *map;                        // map of empty/non-empty buckets
int *directory;                  // power of 2 in size
int *temp;                       // for use during directory doubling

bool powerof2(int i) ;           // is i a power of 2?
int getpower(int i) ;            // i is 2^k, return k
void getextent(int v, int& first, int& length); // find range in directory
int trailingzeros (int N);       // how many trailing zeros in binary of N
bool goodrange(int v);           // is range of v valid in directory
bool dircheck(int limit);        // validity checks on directory entries
int buddy(int BN);               // find buddy to bucket BN
bool tablecanbehalved();         // can we halve the directory?
void getbucket(int i) {forbuckets.getRecord(i,mainmemory_bucket);}
void putbucket(int i) {forbuckets.putRecord(i,mainmemory_bucket);}
void releasebucket(int i) {map[i]=0;}
int allocatebucket();            // need a new bucket
bool isinbucket(Entry E);        // search main memory bucket
void overwrite(Entry E);         // replace old object by new one with same key
};
```

Retrievals

Here is the retrieval function. Note its simplicity relative to the retrieval function in *map_dynamich*.

```
template <class Entry>
bool map_exth<Entry>::retrieve(Entry& E)
{
 int index = E.pseudokey(dirheader); // dirheader is number of bits to use
 int bucknumber = directory[index];
 getbucket(bucknumber);
 for (int k = 0; k<mainmemory_bucket.count; k++)
   if (mainmemory_bucket.objects[k]==E)
        { E=mainmemory_bucket.objects[k];
          return true;
        }
 return false;
}
```

Insertions

The implementation of the insertion algorithm shows how we handle the three cases identified earlier.

```cpp
template <class Entry>
bool map_exth<Entry>::insert(Entry E)
{
  Entry theitem;
  int index,bucknumber,newbucket,first,last,numsame,numnew;

  reinsertlist.push(E); // push object on reinsert list to be popped soon

  while (!reinsertlist.empty())
    {
     theitem = reinsertlist.top();
     reinsertlist.pop();
     // dirheader indicates how long a pseudokey we need
     index = theitem.pseudokey(dirheader);
     bucknumber = directory[index];
     getbucket(bucknumber);

     // see if object with the same key
     if (isinbucket(theitem))
        {
          overwrite(theitem);
          putbucket(bucknumber);
        }
     // no - see if room for a new one
     else if (mainmemory_bucket.count<RECS_IN_BUCKET_EXTH)  // room in bucket
         { ** CASE 1 **
           mainmemory_bucket.objects[mainmemory_bucket.count]=theitem;
           mainmemory_bucket.count++;
           putbucket(bucknumber);
           }
        else

          {// overflow - will need new bucket
           newbucket=allocatebucket();
           if (newbucket==-1)
               {
```

```
                              cerr << "insert fails: out of disk buckets\n";
                              return false;
                            }

                    // if single pointer to overflowing bucket then directory doubles
                    if (dirheader==mainmemory_bucket.header)
                        { ** CASE 3 **
                        temp = directory;
                        directory = new int[2*size];
                        if (directory==0)
                            {
                             cerr << "insert fails: out of main memory\n";
                             directory = temp; // restore directory
                             return false;
                            }
                        dirheader++;
                        for (int i=0; i<size; i++)
                            {
                             directory[2*i] = temp[i];
                             directory[2*i+1] = temp[i];
                            }
                        dirchanged = true;
                        size = size * 2;
                        delete[] temp;
                        }

                    // now will have multiple pointers i.e. "case 2 insertion"
                    // find entries pointing to current bucket and change half to new one
                    // could change the following to call of getextent
                    // ** CASE 2 **
                    for (int i=0; i<size; i++)
                        { if (directory[i]==bucknumber) last=i;
                          if (directory[size-i-1]==bucknumber) first=size-i-1;
                        }
                    numsame=last-first+1;
                    numnew=numsame/2;
                    for (int i=first; i<first+numnew; i++) directory[i]=newbucket;
                    dirchanged = true;
                    // put objects on reinsert list
                    reinsertlist.push(theitem);
                    for (int i=0; i<RECS_IN_BUCKET_EXTH; i++)
                        {
                        reinsertlist.push(mainmemory_bucket.objects[i]);
```

```
                                  }
                          // and clear bucket
                          mainmemory_bucket.count=0;
                          // make sure bucket headers are OK after division of pointers
                          mainmemory_bucket.header++;
                          putbucket(bucknumber);
                          putbucket(newbucket);  // should serve to initialize new one
                          }
                      }
                  // reinsert list empty - we are done
                  return true;
                  }
```

Deletions
The code for the *remove* function includes calls to functions that determine if the
directory can be halved and that carry out the halving. Details of these two routines
are left as exercises.

```
template <class Entry>
bool map_exth<Entry>::remove(Entry E)
{
 int index = E.pseudokey(dirheader);
 int bucknumber = directory[index];
 bucket mainmemory_bucket2;
 Entry tempentry;
 getbucket(bucknumber);

 bool found=false,
      flag=true;     // for consolidation loop
 int i=0;
 while (i<mainmemory_bucket.count)
   {
     if (mainmemory_bucket.objects[i]==E)
         {
           found=true;
           if (i!=mainmemory_bucket.count-1)
             {
             // exchange with last in bucket
             tempentry=mainmemory_bucket.objects[i];
             mainmemory_bucket.objects[i]
                      =mainmemory_bucket.objects[mainmemory_bucket.count-1];
             mainmemory_bucket.objects[mainmemory_bucket.count-1]=tempentry;
             }
```

```
             mainmemory_bucket.count--;
             putbucket(bucknumber);
             break;
           }
      else i++;
 }
if (!found) return false;   // delete fails: object not found


// see if structure can be consolidated after the deletion

while (flag)
  {
    int potentialbuddy = buddy(bucknumber);
    if (potentialbuddy==-1)
        flag = false;   // no buddy => no consolidation
    else {
          // see if we can combine buckets
          getbucket(bucknumber);
          mainmemory_bucket2 = mainmemory_bucket;
          getbucket(potentialbuddy);
          if ( (mainmemory_bucket.count + mainmemory_bucket2.count)
                                            <=RECS_IN_BUCKET_EXTH
            )
            {
            // combine, deallocate, update index and headers?
            //
            for (int i=0; i<mainmemory_bucket2.count; i++)
              {
               mainmemory_bucket.objects[mainmemory_bucket.count]
                                  =mainmemory_bucket2.objects[i];
               mainmemory_bucket.count++;
              }
          mainmemory_bucket.header--;
          putbucket(bucknumber);
          releasebucket(potentialbuddy);
          for (int i=0; i<size; i++)
             if (directory[i]==potentialbuddy) directory[i]=bucknumber;
          dirchanged = true;
          if (tablecanbehalved())
              {
               // halve table
               temp = directory;
               directory = new int[size/2];
```

```
            dirheader --;
            for (int i=0; i<size; i+=2) directory[i/2]=temp[i];
            size /= 2;
            delete[] temp;
          }
      }
    else flag = false; // buckets too big to combine
    }
  }
return true;
}
```

Opening and Closing the Structure

Saving the index is simpler than saving the index in *map_dynamich*. When we open a pair of files containing the index and the buckets, the *openexth* function performs some checks (additional checks are possible) to see if the files represent a valid structure; for example, is the directory size a power of two? The locations occupied by a particular value in the directory are constrained. Consider the locations of the number 6 in the dictionary fragments of Figure 11.25. In Figure 11.25a, the region of 6 is not contiguous. In Figure 11.25b, the region is contiguous but not a power of two in size. In Figure 11.25c, the problem is that the region of 6 does not begin at a multiple of four (the size of the region). The fragment shown in Figure 11.25d is valid.

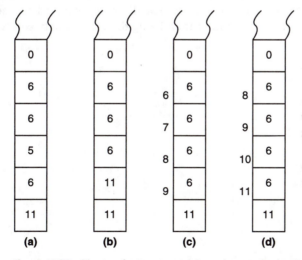

Figure 11.25 • Directory fragment containing pointers to bucket 6. (a) invalid: pointers are not contiguous, (b) invalid: size of pointer region is not a power of 2, (c) invalid: start index of pointer region is not a multiple of 4, (d) valid.

● TABLE 11.6 Test Objects for *map_exth*		
Key	**Nonkey**	**Pseudokey**
y	young	11111
i	ice	10001
j	john	11110
d	dog	01100
q	quince	10100
m	mouse	10001
g	gnu	11111
n	nice	10010
f	frog	00000
sj	stevejobs	11111

Testing

Table 11.6 shows the key fields, the nonkey fields, and the first five bits of the pseudokeys of the objects used in a small test of the implementation of *map_exth*.

The following output from the test program shows the contents of the directory and buckets after the objects in Table 11.6 were inserted in table order into an initially empty object of type *map_exth*. For each bucket, the program outputs the bucket number, the value of the header, a count of objects in the bucket, and then the objects themselves. The directory is large because on two occasions it splits, and objects, rather then being distributed between two buckets, all end up in one.

```
dirheader: 5
directory
dir:0 : 0
dir:1 : 0
dir:2 : 0
dir:3 : 0
dir:4 : 0
dir:5 : 0
dir:6 : 0
dir:7 : 0
dir:8 : 0
dir:9 : 0
dir:10 : 0
dir:11 : 0
dir:12 : 0
dir:13 : 0
```

```
dir:14 : 0
dir:15 : 0
dir:16 : 3
dir:17 : 3
dir:18 : 3
dir:19 : 3
dir:20 : 2
dir:21 : 2
dir:22 : 2
dir:23 : 2
dir:24 : 4
dir:25 : 4
dir:26 : 4
dir:27 : 4
dir:28 : 5
dir:29 : 5
dir:30 : 6
dir:31 : 1
bucket: 0 : 1 : 2 : [d dog][f frog]
bucket: 1 : 5 : 3 : [g gnu][y young][sj stevejobs]
bucket: 2 : 3 : 1 : [q quince]
bucket: 3 : 3 : 3 : [m mouse][i ice][n nice]
bucket: 4 : 3 : 0 :
bucket: 5 : 4 : 0 :
bucket: 6 : 5 : 1 : [j john]
```

The following output is from a program that displays the contents of the *map_exth* object after the object with key *sj* has been removed. Note the bucket consolidation and the reduction in the size of the directory.

```
dirheader: 3
dir:0 : 0
dir:1 : 0
dir:2 : 0
dir:3 : 0
dir:4 : 3
dir:5 : 2
dir:6 : 1
dir:7 : 1
bucket: 0 : 1 : 2 : [d dog][f frog]
bucket: 1 : 2 : 3 : [j john][g gnu][y young]
bucket: 2 : 3 : 1 : [q quince]
bucket: 3 : 3 : 3 : [m mouse][i ice][n nice]
```

● Chapter Summary

We have seen that hashing techniques used to organize tables in main memory can be extended to files in secondary storage. Information held in main memory can minimize the number of disk transfers needed in storage and retrieval operations. Assuming appropriate operating system support, the hash file can change in size to reflect changing numbers of objects in it. Some of the properties of the four methods we looked at are summarized in Table 11.7.

We can store and retrieve single objects by using information derived directly or indirectly from the keys. A retrieval operation returns either zero or one object. Although this is a good choice for many applications, sometimes we need:

- All objects with keys in a certain range
- All objects with a secondary key equal to X
- All objects in sequence

Because of scattering resulting from hashing the key, the techniques described in this chapter are not good for these operations.[6] In the next two chapters, we look at methods that are still reasonably fast for storage and retrieval of single objects and, in addition, make some of the other operations feasible.

● Exercises

1. A small publishing company keeps records on the books that it publishes. Each record includes a book's title and author. Records are 160 bytes long and are to be stored in a hash file on a disk with 1024-byte sectors. A unique five-digit integer is associated with each different book that is published. The company currently has 15,000 records and, to allow for future expansion, plans that the file be 50 percent full when all current records are in the file.

● **TABLE 11.7** Characteristics of Hashing Techniques

Hashing Method	Functions Required	File Size	Retrievals	Insertions	Main Memory
Normal	key → $A_0, A_1, \ldots$	Fixed	≥1 access	≥1 access	Nothing required
Table-assisted	key → $A_0, A_1, \ldots$ key → $S_0, S_1, \ldots$	Fixed	1 access	≥1 access (may not terminate)	Table of signatures
Dynamic	key → A key → $B_0, B_1, \ldots$	Variable	1 access	≥1 access (may not terminate)	Table of trees
Extendible	key → $B_0, B_1, \ldots$	Variable	1 access	≥1 access (may not terminate)	Table of bucket pointers

    a. What is the bucket size?

    b. How many buckets will the file contain?

    c. Outline a good hash function for this task.

2. Consider table-assisted hashing. Would it still work if the key of an object were used as its signature for all addresses?

3. a. In table-assisted hashing, what advantage might there be in storing, in main memory, the smallest signature currently in each bucket?

    b. If signatures are not stored in buckets, it is possible that there may be room for additional objects in the file. But, if signatures are not stored, how could we determine the *HSV* on overflow?

4. Suppose we change the condition under which the table-assisted hashing insertion algorithm terminates. We now continue trying addresses until we arrive back at A_0 with signature S_0. Currently, the algorithm terminates if we regenerate A_0, even if the signature is different. What will be the general effect of this change in terminating condition?

5. Augment the definition of *map_tah* so that a user can save the map to a pair of files different from those currently storing it.

6. When *map_tah::opentah* checks two existing files (one file of table entries, one file of buckets), it simply makes sure that they contain the same number of items. What other checks could it perform?

7. Consider the following extensible hash file:

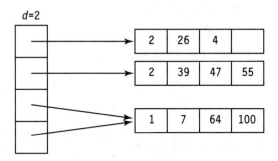

The (partial) pseudokeys of the objects currently in the file are as follows:

Key	Pseudokey	Key	Pseudokey
26	000...	4	001...
39	010...	47	011...
55	010...	7	101...
64	110...	100	101...

Consider the following six objects, which are among those to be inserted into the file.

Key	Pseudokey	Key	Pseudokey
71	000...	72	101...
73	010...	74	111...
77	001...	78	011...

a. Give an example of an object that could be inserted into the file and would not cause any change to the directory.

b. Give an example of an object that could be inserted into the file and would cause a change to the contents but not the size of the directory.

c. Give an example of an object that could be inserted into the file and would cause a change in both the size and contents of the directory.

d. For the object you chose as your answer to (c), show what the file looks like after this object has been inserted into the file shown.

8. In dynamic hashing, what are the implications of starting the index with a NULL pointer in each element and no buckets in the file? If there is a bad hash function such that value k never gets generated, then no bucket will ever be allocated for that index element. Are there disadvantages to this approach?

9. Suppose we have an initially empty table-assisted hash file with a capacity of 1200 objects on which we perform the following sequence of operations:

a. Insert a set of 1000 randomly selected objects.

b. Delete the 1000 objects.

c. Insert the same 1000 objects again.

d. Delete the 1000 objects again.

e. Insert a second (different) set of 1000 objects.

Rank operations (a), (c), and (e) by the time that you would expect them to take (from slowest to fastest). Give reasons for your ordering.

10. Larson's dynamic hashing technique uses binary trees in the index. What would be the consequences of using eight-way trees instead? In your answer, make reference to the hash functions, the bucket-splitting process, and expected storage utilization.

11. Larson's function B produces a random bitstring from the key. It can be implemented using pseudo-random numbers. Why would it probably be a mistake to use function H_0 rather than a second function H_1 to derive the seed from the key?

12. Every extendible file directory can be represented by an equivalent dynamic hashing binary tree. Suppose the current 16-entry directory is as shown as follows. Element 0 is on the left and element 15 on the right. Each directory entry is the number of the bucket pointed to. Draw the corresponding binary tree, labeling the branches appropriately.

7	8	4	4	2	5	1	1	3	3	3	3	6	6	9	10

13. Explain how it is possible that the process of inserting an object into an extendible file may not terminate successfully.

14. Fill in the body of the C++ function *double_dir* that follows. This function is used in the implementation of extendible hashing to perform directory updating in the case where the directory doubles in size. The routine is to put into *newdir* a pointer to a new array of directory entries (*direntrys*). The entries in this array are to be derived from *olddir*, which has *N* entries. The doubling is needed because bucket *I* is overflowing. The bucket newly added to the file is bucket number *X*. You do not need to be concerned with the contents of the buckets.

```
void double_dir (direntry olddir*, direntry newdir*&, int N, int I, int X)

    {



    }
```

15. Fill in the body of the C++ function *dir_check* that follows. This function checks to see if the size of an extendible hashing directory can be halved. Assume that bucket capacity is *C* objects and that *dir[i].size* gives the number of objects currently in the bucket pointed to from the *i*th directory entry. *dir_check* should return *true* if the directory can be halved, and *false* otherwise.

```
bool dir_check (direntry dir*, int N)

    {



    }
```

16. Exhaustion of what resource or resources may cause an insertion into a dynamic hash file to fail? What are the characteristics of an insertion that will inevitably fail?

17. Suppose we have a table-assisted hash file. Buckets are 512 bytes in size. The objects we wish to store are 63 bytes long. The number of buckets in the file is 3000. You have a choice between using 8-bit and 16-bit signatures. What factors would you take into account in making your choice?

18. Consider the following extendible hash file.

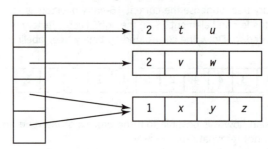

a. Which objects can be deleted from the file in the diagram and cause no change in the number of buckets and no change in the size of the directory?

b. Which objects can be deleted from the file in the diagram and may cause a change in the number of buckets in the file and a change in the size of the directory?

c. For one of the objects you have identified in your answer to (b), draw the file after that object has been deleted.

19. Assume that for a particular table-assisted hash file, the range of signatures that function S can generate is 0 through 63. Currently,

1. Table[25] contains 30

2. Bucket 25 is full; it contains 3 objects:

   B (with signature 20)

   Y (with signature 13)

   X (with signature 20)

Suppose that the object with key T hashes to bucket 25 and that we designate its signature for that bucket G.

a. What range of values of G would cause us to generate the next (A,S) pair for T?

b. What range of values for G would cause object T to go straight to the overflow list without affecting the bucket?

c. What range of values for G would cause objects to be bumped from bucket 25 to make room for T?

d. Suppose that the previous case occurs. Show the new contents of table[25] and the new contents of bucket 25.

20. In the *opendynamich* function, what additional checks would you include to ensure that the contents of the two files represent a valid dynamic hash structure?

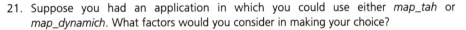

21. Suppose you had an application in which you could use either *map_tah* or *map_dynamich*. What factors would you consider in making your choice?

22. Suppose a dynamic hash file has an index of size one, thus we have no need for function *H* and use only function *B* to determine where an object is stored. This is now similar to extendible hashing using pseudokeys.

    a. What are the advantages of extendible hashing over this modified dynamic hashing?

    b. What are the disadvantages?

23. Suppose we read two files representing a saved extendible hash file. One file is the saved directory, and the other is the corresponding file of leaves. What checks would you perform on the two files to ensure that they represent a consistent structure?

24. In testing the *map_tah* object, we inserted an object with key *Anamari*. Explain how this object ended up in bucket 17.

Problems

1. Using your own or another implementation of table-assisted hashing, compare the time to insert and then retrieve *N* random objects when (a) signatures are stored in buckets and (b) signatures are recalculated on the fly. Tabulate your results for *N* = 64, 128, 256, ..., 8192.

2. Modify the *map_tah* class definition so that if there is not enough room in main memory to hold the table, the methods use a file instead.

3. Develop criteria for determining when a *map_tah* structure needs periodic maintenance. Implement your ideas so that the effects are transparent to a user.

4. Add to the *map_tah* class definition some of the bells and whistles described in the chapter. Run benchmark programs and measure the savings achieved, if any, on typical data sets and operations.

5. In table-assisted hashing, what would be the consequences of bumping out more objects than necessary when a bucket overflows? For example, we could bump out all the objects having either of the two highest signature values. Devise and implement experiments to test the effects of bumping out objects with either of the 2, 3, ..., *J* highest signatures.

6. Our current technique for saving the directory of a *map_exth* object is to write each element to a file record. The patterns of entries in the directory suggest that data compression algorithms might be applicable. Investigate methods for compressing the saved version of the directory. Implement and test one method.

7. Design, implement, and test copy constructors for *map_tah*, *map_dynamich*, and *map_exth*.

8. Devise experiments to compare the performance of *map_dynamich* and *map_exth*.

● References

Fagin, R., J. Nievergelt, N. Pippenger, and H. R. Strong. 1979. Extendible hashing—a fast access method for dynamic files. *ACM Transactions on Database Systems,* 4 (3): 315–344.

Frost, R. A. 1979. Algorithm 112—Dumping the index of a dynamic hash table. *Computer Journal,* 24 (4): 383–384.

Knuth, D. E. 1973. *Sorting and Searching.* Vol. 3, *The Art of Computer Programming.* Reading, MA: Addison-Wesley.

Larson, P.-A. 1978. Dynamic hashing. *BIT,* 18 (2): 184–201.

Larson, P.-A., and K. Kajla. 1984. File organization. Implementation of a method guaranteeing retrieval in one access. *Communications of the ACM,* 27 (7): 670–677.

Scholl, M. 1981. New file organizations based on dynamic hashing. *ACM Transactions on Database Systems,* 6 (1): 194–211.

● Notes

[1] If the hash function is uniformly distributed, we can make two assumptions. First, we assume that the probabilities associated with a record being inserted into a home bucket are independent. Second, we assume that the expected probability that a record will be inserted into one of N specific home buckets is $(1/N)$. Thus, the probability that a specific set of I records will be inserted into a given home bucket (e.g., bucket B) is $(1/N)^I$. As you can see, this is the second term in the expected probability expression. The third term is similar. It describes the expected probability that the remaining $K - I$ records will be inserted in different home buckets (not B). The term $((N - 1)/N)$ is the probability that a record will not be inserted into a particular home bucket.

So far we have been discussing the probability that I of K records will be inserted into a particular home bucket and that the remaining $K - I$ records will not be inserted into that bucket; that is $(1/N)^I * ((N - 1)/N)^{K-I}$. However, there are a number of ways that K records could be taken I at a time. This is the first term in the expression in the text:

$$C_{K,I} = \frac{K!}{I! \times (K - I)!}$$

In summary, the first term is the number of different ways I records could be inserted into a specific home bucket, and the remaining $(K - I)$ records are inserted into other home buckets.

[2] Other checks could be performed on the two files (see Exercises).

[3] It would be equivalent to remembering where you parked by remembering that you were between a white van and a red pickup.

[4] Typically, not all of the user's program is in main memory at any one time. If the program attempts to reference a location that is not currently in main memory, the operating system suspends the program until the required program section can be loaded from disk. This operation is transparent to the user.

[5]The floor function ⌊ ⌋ yields the largest integer less than or equal to its argument. Thus, $\lfloor 3.4 \rfloor$ is 3 and $\lfloor 6.0 \rfloor$ is 6.

[6]Order-preserving hashing is possible. For example, we could use Larson's dynamic hashing and the actual keys instead of functions of the keys. The first $\log_2 N$ bits of the key would be used to select an index entry, and the remaining bits would be used to traverse the tree rooted in the index entry. To preserve ordering, it appears that three conditions must be met:

1. The ordering of the trees must reflect the keys. That is, every record pointed to from the leaves of tree i must be greater than any record pointed to by tree $i - 1$.

2. The ordering of records within a tree must reflect key order. This means that if we do an in-order traversal of a tree, all the records in the bucket pointed to from the kth leaf must have keys greater than all records in the bucket pointed to by the $(k - 1)$st leaf.

3. Records must be ordered within a bucket.

The last condition could be waived if we were prepared to sort bucket contents when fetched. Retrievals of individual records are still possible in a single access. Sequential accessing is straightforward—a sequence of tree traversals. Range processing is also OK.

Problems. Larson's method uses hashing to even out distribution and, in effect, try to make the index trees as equal in size as possible. In our proposed order-preserving scheme, we could have a great variety in tree size and a larger number of internal nodes. However, if we know that all keys have the first M bits in common, we could strip out those bits from the key. For example, the 7-bit ASCII codes for the uppercase letters all start with 10.

Non-problems. The finite size of the key is not a problem. The key is unique, so we are guaranteed unique paths to leaves. One key being the prefix of another is not a problem; we can add an artificial "end-of-key" character.

Maps: File-Based Trees

12.1 Introduction

Hashing is an efficient technique for storage and retrieval of individual objects, given the primary key. However, when keys are hashed onto addresses, ordering of the keys is not usually retained (e.g., see the table of names in Chapter 5). Thus, hash-based techniques are not suitable for processing all objects in key order or for locating those objects having keys in a particular range. A **sequential file**, in which objects are stored in key order, is good for processing objects in sequence, but it is not a good structure if we wish to find a particular object quickly.

In this chapter and the next, we look at data structures that permit both sequential access to a file of objects and reasonably fast retrievals of individual objects. Some of the techniques involve indexing. The **index** added to a file may be functionally similar to the table of contents at the front of a book or like the index found at the end of a book. Both are retrieval aids and could be implemented as a separate structure or integrated into the file of objects.

Objects in a file being indexed usually are stored in key order, thus giving us an **indexed sequential file**. Indexes are often tree-structured, so we have a file organization similar to the one depicted in Figure 12.1.

Indexed file structures differ in the way that they deal with insertions into the file. In **static index** structures (Section 12.2), the structure of the index is fixed and is determined by the size and contents of the initial file. The file adapts in various

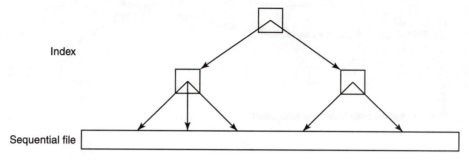

Figure 12.1 • Indexed sequential file

ways as insertions are made; for example, a certain amount of free space is left when the initial file is constructed. Typically, it is distributed evenly in the file. As long as insertions are well scattered, the contents of the index change moderately, and processing times are barely affected. However, if insertions are clustered in a relatively small subrange of the key space, then local free space is used up, overflow lists start to be used (look-aside pointers) and processing slows dramatically. Thus, our indexed file might look like Figure 12.2. Periodic file maintenance is required to restore performance. This may involve taking the file offline while it is reorganized.

In **dynamic index** structures (Section 12.3), the structure of the index adapts to changes to the file. This is depicted in Figure 12.3. Note the increase in the number of index levels.

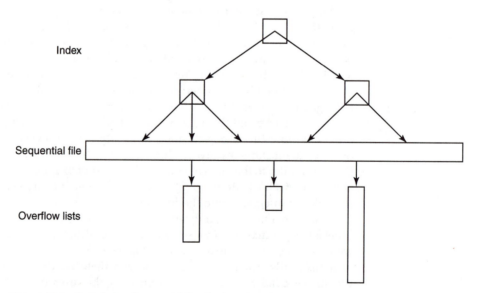

Figure 12.2 • Static indexed sequential file after insertions

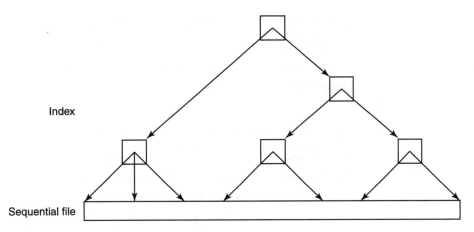

Figure 12.3 • Dynamic indexed sequential file after insertions

Indexing is also a useful technique when we need to find all objects having a particular value of a secondary (nonunique) key. We look at the indexing of secondary keys in Chapter 13.

12.2 Static Indexes

An early implementation of the static indexed sequential technique is IBM's ISAM (Indexed Sequential Access Method) file organization (IBM 1966). It is a disk-oriented structure.

12.2.1 ISAM

ISAM files have a hierarchy of indexes reflecting the hierarchy of structures within a disk. The lowest level is the **track index**; above that is the **cylinder index**; finally, there is the **master index**. The number of levels is fixed.

Example ISAM Structure
Assume in what follows that the disk holding the ISAM file has four recording surfaces. Thus, each cylinder contains four tracks. Assume that one track on each cylinder (this will usually be track 0) is used as a track index, and another is used as an overflow area for the cylinder. This leaves two prime **data tracks** per cylinder in which to store our data objects.

For each prime data track on a cylinder, there is an entry in the track index of the cylinder. We will assume that each entry has the four fields shown in Figure 12.4.

For each cylinder that holds user objects, there is an entry in the cylinder index. We will assume that each of these entries has the three fields depicted in Figure 12.5.

Surface number of the track	Highest key on track	Highest overflow key associated with the track	Pointer (surface/position) to overflow list

Figure 12.4 • Track index entry

Cylinder number	Highest key on cylinder	Number of the surface containing the track index

Figure 12.5 • Cylinder index entry

Track number	Highest key in cylinder(s) indexed from the track

Figure 12.6 • Master index entry

The master index is typically stored on the same cylinder as the cylinder index. We will assume that for each track in the cylinder index there is an entry in the master index. The information in a master index entry is shown in Figure 12.6.

Example ISAM Contents
Assume that the initial file contains objects with the following keys:

6 15 19 24 28 32 35 41 42 68 74 79 82 83 88 95 101 106

In the case of hash files (as we saw in Chapter 11) and in the case of B-trees (as we will see later in this chapter), there is a single insertion algorithm. A file is initially empty, and the insertion algorithm is used to add objects to it. ISAM files are different. An ordered set of objects is used to create the initial file and index structure. Appropriate index entries are created as objects and are loaded onto prime data tracks. Objects that are added to the file after this initial structure is built are processed in a different way.

Given the keys just presented, Figure 12.7 is a representation of the initial file.

Data cylinders do not need to be adjacent on the disk (though they might be for efficiency reasons), so we have chosen arbitrary cylinder numbers for the data. We assume that the tracks in a cylinder are numbered from 1 upwards and that the track index on each of the three is on track 1. Notice how the track index entries contain the track number and the highest key on that track together with two fields that are currently empty. The cylinder index occupies two tracks, so there is an entry for each of these tracks in the master index.

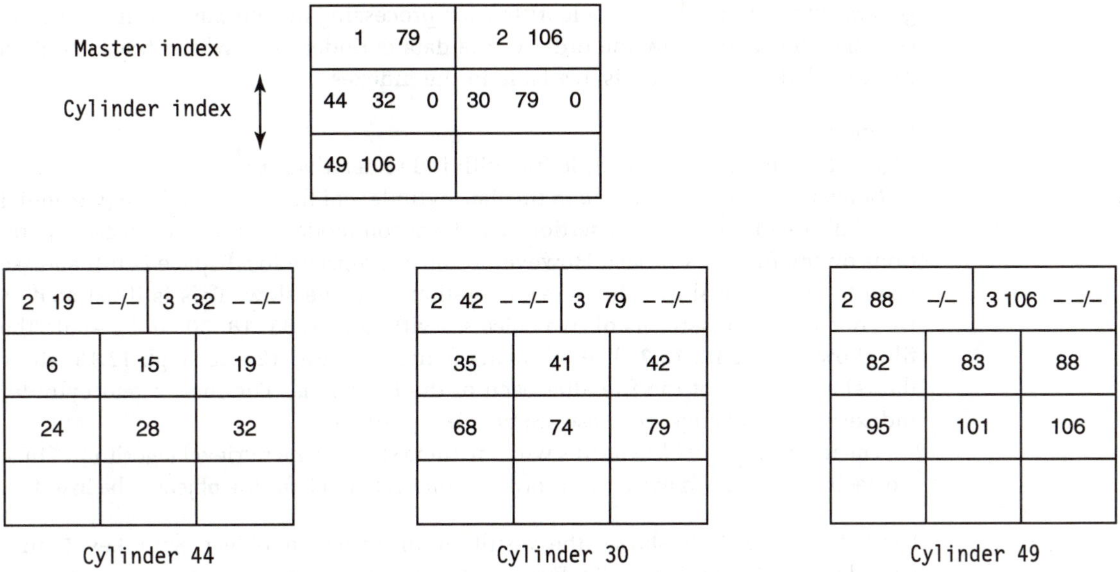

Master index	1 79	2 106
Cylinder index	44 32 0	30 79 0
	49 106 0	

2 19 --/--	3 32 --/--	
6	15	19
24	28	32

Cylinder 44

2 42 --/--	3 79 --/--	
35	41	42
68	74	79

Cylinder 30

2 88 --/--	3 106 --/--	
82	83	88
95	101	106

Cylinder 49

Figure 12.7 • Example ISAM file

Retrievals

Retrieval of an object begins with comparison of the target key with the entries in the master index. This shows us which track of the cylinder index we need to look at next. Suppose we are looking for an object with key 74 in the structure shown in Figure 12.7. Because the target is less than 79, the master index indicates that the next comparisons should be on track 1 of the cylinder index. Had the target key been in the range 79 to 106, our next search would have been on track 2. Note that if our search key is greater than 106, we can tell from the master index that it is not in the file.

The entries in the cylinder index identify the cylinder we should search. In our example, the entries on track 1 indicate that the search key (74) is too big to be found on cylinder 44 (the largest key there is 32) and may be on cylinder 30 (where the largest key is 79). The latter entry also shows that the track index for cylinder 30 is on track 0.

Information in a track index tells us the track with which our target key may be associated. In our example, we read the track index on cylinder 30, and it shows that key 74 is too big for data track 2 (the largest key there is 42) and may be on track 3 (where the largest key is 79). Our final search is therefore track 3 of cylinder 30.

If we do not find the key on the track identified by the track index, then it is not in the file. In our example, we find the key we are looking for on track 3.

If the master index is small enough to be held in main memory, we need to read only three tracks to retrieve any object. If a track is too large to read in one access, the design can be modified to use smaller units (e.g., sectors) while maintaining the general index hierarchy. An algorithm for processing all the objects in the file in sequence needs to know the order of the data cylinders and which tracks contain indexes. This information is available in the indexes.

Insertions

Figure 12.8 depicts our example file with index detail suppressed.

Some free space is available in the data cylinders of the sequential file (we depict this with - - -); as long as insertions can be accommodated in those spaces, operations on the file are still fast. However, if the appropriate local space is full and we need to use a global overflow area, operations become slow. This is illustrated as we consider the insertions of five objects—with keys 7, 33, 18, 20, and 1—into the file shown in Figure 12.7. The following figures (Figures 12.9 through 12.13) show the relevant parts of the file after each of the insertions. The master and cylinder indexes do not change, so these are not shown again.

The insertion algorithm begins with the same steps as the retrieval algorithm. Thus, we begin the insertion at the appropriate prime data track for the object to be inserted.

Insert 7   Figure 12.9 shows the result of inserting an object with key 7 into cylinder 44. Comparison with Figure 12.7 shows that in order to make room for the new object in sequence, the object with key 19 has been bumped from track 2 onto the overflow track. The track index reflects this change: 15 is now the highest key on the track. The highest key on the overflow list is 19 (can this ever change?); the notation following object 19 in the overflow track is an end-of-list marker. The last field in the track index entry denotes a pointer (track 4, position 1) to the list of objects that have been bumped from the track.

Insert 33   Inserting an object with key 33 into the file results in a similar change being made to cylinder 30. The resulting cylinder is shown in Figure 12.10.

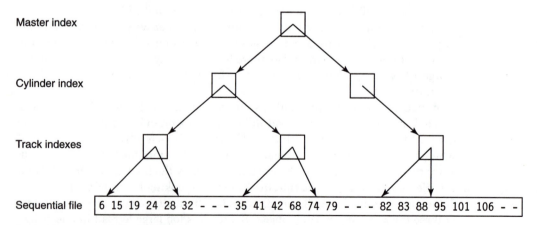

Figure 12.8 • Our example ISAM file

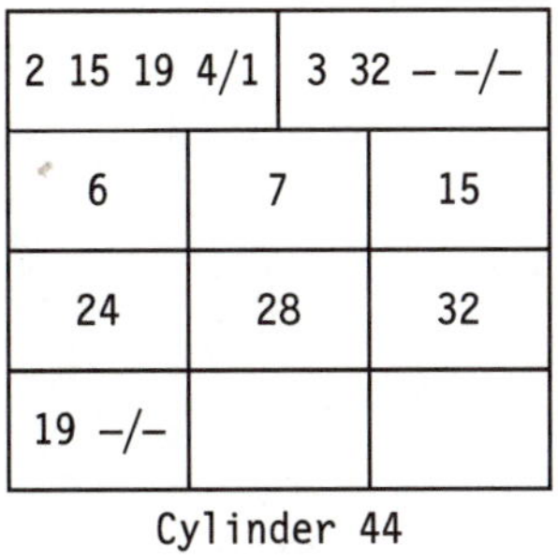

2 15 19 4/1	3 32 – –/–	
6	7	15
24	28	32
19 –/–		

Cylinder 44

Figure 12.9 • Cylinder 44 after insertion of an object with key 7

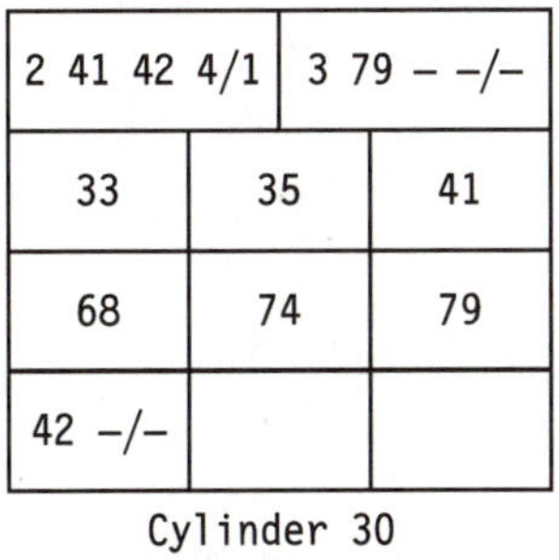

2 41 42 4/1	3 79 – –/–	
33	35	41
68	74	79
42 –/–		

Cylinder 30

Figure 12.10 • Cylinder 30 after insertion of an object with key 33

Insert 18   According to the higher-level indexes, an object with key 18 should be on the first track of cylinder 44—its key is less than the highest key (19) associated with track 1. However, we find that its key is larger than the highest key on this track, so it goes straight to the overflow list. The result is shown in Figure 12.11.

Physically, the object occupies the next free space in the overflow track. Logically, the list of overflow objects is in key order, so the notation after the object with key 18 denotes a pointer back to the overflowing object with key 19.

Insert 20   When we insert 20, the second data track of cylinder 44 overflows. The new cylinder 44 is depicted in Figure 12.12. Note that the free space on this cylinder is now exhausted.

Insert 1   We have a problem because the overflow track on cylinder 44 is full. The object (key 15) bumped from the prime data track has to go into a general overflow

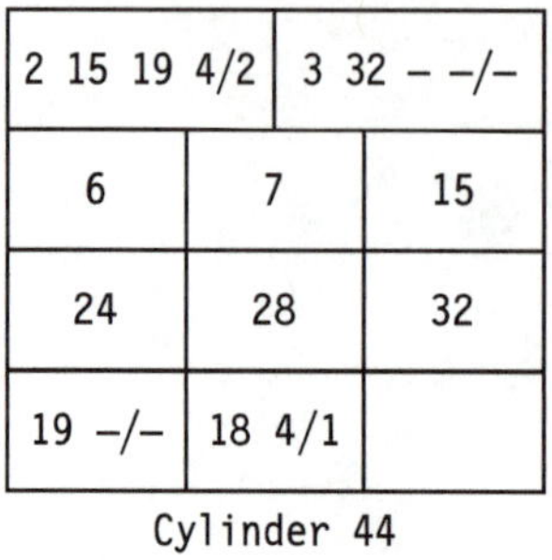

2 15 19 4/2	3 32 – –/–	
6	7	15
24	28	32
19 –/–	18 4/1	

Cylinder 44

Figure 12.11 • Cylinder 44 after insertion of an object with key 18

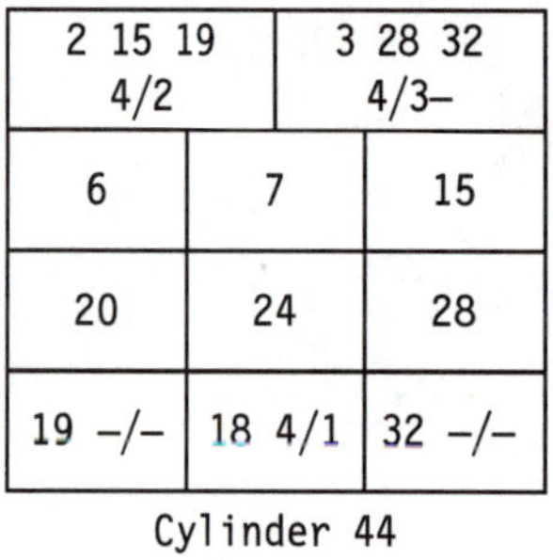

2 15 19 4/2	3 28 32 4/3–	
6	7	15
20	24	28
19 –/–	18 4/1	32 –/–

Cylinder 44

Figure 12.12 • Cylinder 44 after insertion of an object with key 20

cylinder; we arbitrarily pick 99 as the number of that cylinder. Figure 12.13 depicts the resulting structure.

Note that on cylinder 44 we have a pointer (in a track index entry) to cylinder 99, and that on cylinder 99 we have a pointer to cylinder 44. Thus, following this chain would require two disk head movements.

Deletions

When an object is deleted, we can simply tag it *deleted* (e.g., as in a hash table). This is a low-cost deletion strategy, but it does not improve the performance of the system. However, we can modify the insert algorithm to take advantage of any deleted space it comes across.

Alternatively, if retrievals are relatively frequent compared with deletions, it might be worth doing extra work to rearrange the file, particularly if this results in overflow lists that are faster to traverse. The action taken depends on whether the object being deleted is in a prime data track or in an overflow list.

• If the object being deleted is in a prime track having an overflow list, then reshuffle the track objects and bring back to the track the first overflowing object. Add

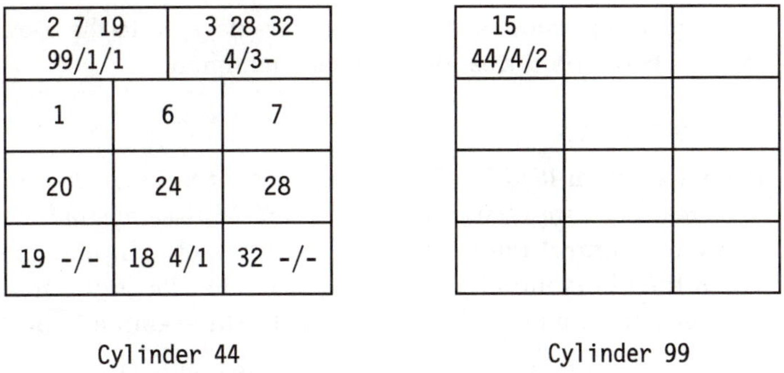

2 7 19 99/1/1	3 28 32 4/3–	
1	6	7
20	24	28
19 –/–	18 4/1	32 –/–

15 44/4/2		

Cylinder 44   Cylinder 99

Figure 12.13 • Overflow to general overflow area

the overflow node to the free list. If the node is on the cylinder and the cylinder has one or more objects in the general overflow area, use newly freed space to relocate one of them.

- If the object being deleted is in overflow list, delete it, mark the node free, and attempt to reuse the space as in the first option.

12.2.2 Periodic Maintenance

Sequential and random access operations are efficient provided that any overflows can be accommodated on the home overflow areas; that is, if each new object can be placed on the cylinder where it belongs. If this is the case, retrievals of single objects are as fast as when there are no overflows because the track index will tell us whether the next track to read is a prime data track or the overflow track. Sequential processing will be slower because after we have processed the objects on a prime data track, we may need to read the overflow track to get the next object in sequence. Thus, assuming no track cache, sequential processing can be up to two times slower than it was when there were no overflows.

If we need to use the global overflow area and the overflow lists span cylinders, as in the last case, then access times can be very long. Periodic maintenance is needed to restore performance. Typically this involves processing the objects in sequence and writing those not tagged for deletion to the prime data tracks of a new set of cylinders. Indexes are constructed as this writing is done.

12.3 Dynamic Indexes

In contrast with the static index structures that we looked at in Chapter 11, a dynamic index structure adapts as the contents of the indexed file change. IBM's VSAM (Virtual Storage Access Method) is such a system, and, particularly when contrasted with the ISAM structure of the previous section, it provides a gentle introduction to the idea of a dynamic index. We look at VSAM in the next section.

The remaining sections of the chapter are devoted to the B-tree and variations on it. Indexes based on B-tree ideas are very common.

12.3.1 VSAM

In contrast with ISAM, VSAM comprises virtual storage units that can be mapped onto real ones in a variety of ways. VSAM uses abstract data structures (**control areas** and **control intervals**) rather than direct mapping onto hardware elements. When the file is initially created, space is left for future insertions. Consider a set of objects having the same keys as our ISAM example in Section 12.2, that is:

6 15 19 24 28 32 35 41 42 68 74 79 82 83 88 95 101 106

Assume that a control interval (the smaller of the two units) can hold up to four objects and that a control area has up to four control intervals. Figure 12.14 is a representation of our initial VSAM configuration.

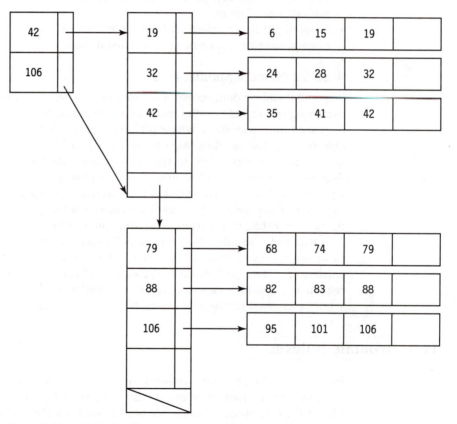

Figure 12.14 • Initial VSAM file

We have chosen to distribute free space in the initial file. We have used only 75 percent of each control interval and only 75 percent of the control intervals in a control area. Note that each pointer to a control interval is associated with a copy of the highest key of an object in that interval. These **sequence sets** comprise the lowest index level; they are linked to facilitate sequential processing of the file.

Insertions

Now consider the insertion of four objects with keys 4, 16, 37, and 34 into the structure shown in Figure 12.14.

Insert 4   The appropriate control interval has room for the new object. Figure 12.15 shows how the first control area has changed.

Insert 16   The interval into which the object should go is full, so the five objects are divided approximately equally into two intervals. The control area has room for the additional interval. Figure 12.16 shows the first control area after the insertion of the object.

Insert 37   There is again room in the appropriate control interval, so not much changes. Figure 12.17 shows the control area after the insertion of an object with key 37.

Insert 34   The appropriate control interval is full, so again we divide the five objects into two control intervals. But this time there is no spare control interval in the control area, so the five control intervals (the four existing ones and the one

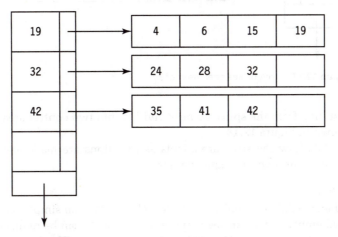

Figure 12.15 • First control area after insertion of 4

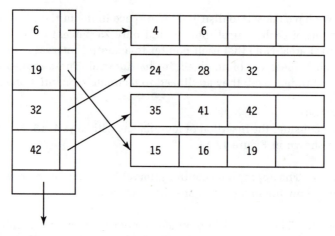

Figure 12.16 • First control area after insertion of 16

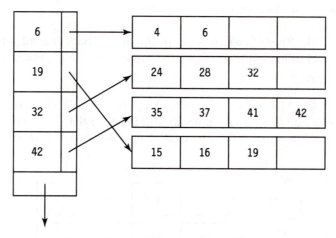

Figure 12.17 • Control area after insert of 37

resulting from the split) are now divided into two control areas. The final result is shown in Figure 12.18.

Note how the structure adapts as insertions are made and how sequencing is possible through the sequence sets.

Deletions

When we delete an object we have a choice. We can simply leave the space it occupied empty or we can see if space requirements can be reduced by combining two intervals into one and possibly two areas into one. The former strategy is faster, but may require the structure to occupy more space than necessary.

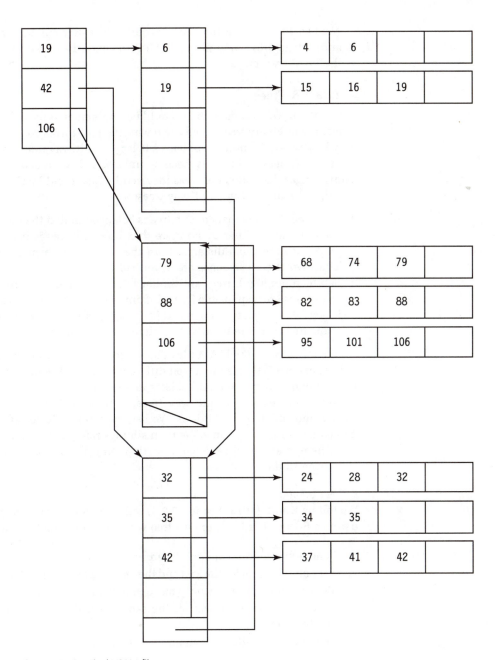

Figure 12.18 • Final VSAM file

Next we look at the B-tree data structure; the B-tree and its variants are very common file structures. We will see that a B-tree modifies itself in much the same way as the VSAM structure.

12.3.2 B-Trees

In Chapter 6, you saw how maps could be implemented using binary trees. Because branching in binary trees is only two way, the paths from root to leaves can become very long when the number of leaves is large. Multiway trees provide shorter paths from root to leaves, but may become unbalanced, with some paths being significantly longer than others. B-trees [devised by Bayer and McCreight (1972)] are balanced, self-maintaining, multiway trees:

- Balanced: We saw that an AVL tree is balanced in that the heights of the two subtrees of a node differ by no more than one. A B-tree is balanced in that all the leaves are the same distance from the root, an even more rigorous condition. Thus, worst-case searches are never bad.
- Self-maintaining: B-trees are similar to AVL trees in that insertion and deletion algorithms are responsible for maintaining the balance properties. When an object is inserted (or deleted), the insert (delete) algorithm may make significant changes to the tree structure in order to maintain the balanced property of the tree.

In contrast with the ISAM files that we looked at in Section 12.2, there is no initial file of objects that is processed differently from subsequent objects. We can start with an empty B-tree and add objects in any order.

B-trees are balanced multiway trees. A node of the tree may contain several objects and pointers to children. We use the term **child** to refer to the immediate descendant of a node; hence the term **siblings** refers to nodes having the same parent. The operations of retrieval, insertion, and deletion are guaranteed to be efficient even in the worst case.

B-Tree Definition

We follow Knuth (1973, Section 6.2.4) rather than Bayer and McCreight (1972) and define a B-tree of order M to be a tree with the following five properties:

1. No node has more than M children.
2. Every node, except for the root and the terminal nodes, has at least $\lceil M/2 \rceil$ children.[1]
3. The root, unless the tree only has one node, has at least two children.
4. All terminal nodes appear on the same level (i.e., they are the same distance from the root).
5. A node with K children contains $K - 1$ objects.

A B-tree can be used to hold an index to a set of objects rather than the objects themselves. In that case, an object in the B-tree typically consists of a key and a pointer to the main file that holds the rest of the object. We will consider this possibility in more detail later.

We can speak of a B-tree of order 8 ($M = 8$), a B-tree of order 197 ($M = 197$), and so on. The integer M imposes bounds on the "bushiness" of the tree. Although the root and terminal nodes are special cases, normal nodes have between $\lceil M/2 \rceil$ and M children and contain between $\lceil M/2 \rceil - 1$ and $M - 1$ objects. For example, a normal node in a tree of order 11 has at least 6 and not more than 11 children. The lower bound on node size ensures that the tree does not get too tall and thin, preventing slow searches. The upper bound on node size ensures that searches of an individual node will be fast. For example, when implementing the tree as a file of records, the upper bound allows us to define an appropriate record type to hold a node. The lower bound ensures that each node is at least half full and therefore that file space is used efficiently.

This definition determines only the structure of a B-tree; for a B-tree to be useful there must be some ordering of the objects in the tree. In what follows, we will make the following two assumptions:

1. Within a node of $K - 1$ objects, objects are numbered R_1, R_2, ..., R_{K-1}, and pointers to children are numbered P_0, P_1, ..., P_{K-1}. Thus, a typical node may be depicted as follows:

P_0	R_1	P_1	...	R_{K-1}	P_{K-1}

2. Objects in the subtree rooted in P_0 have keys less than the key of object R_1. Objects in the tree rooted in P_{K-1} have keys greater than the key of object R_{K-1}. Objects in the subtree rooted in P_i ($0 < i < K - 1$) have keys greater than the key of object R_i and less than the key of object R_{i+1}.

Figure 12.19 shows an example B-tree. In this and subsequent examples, we will assume that objects in the tree have keys that are single lowercase letters. For simplicity, we will show just the key fields, although typically objects will have non-key fields, too.

It is not always possible to determine the order of a B-tree by looking at it. The tree shown in Figure 12.19 must be at least order three because some nonroot nodes have three children. At the same time, it must be less than order five because some nodes have only two children. It is therefore a tree of order three or order four.

B-Tree Representation

Let us assume that the tree in Figure 12.19 is a B-tree of order four. Thus, each node contains a maximum of four pointers and three objects. Our concern is with persistent structures, so we are interested in how the tree can be mapped to a file of

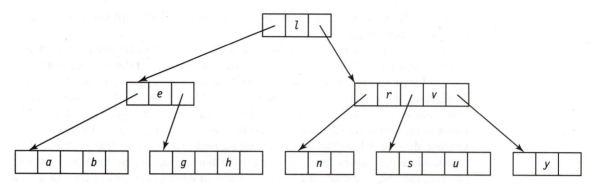

Figure 12.19 • Example B-tree

records. Figure 12.20 shows a possible file corresponding to the tree. We assume that the tree is not an initial tree, but rather the result of insertions and deletions; thus, there are "holes" in the file where nodes have been deleted.

Three features of this particular representation follow.

1. Each record in the file has an integer counter, an array holding up to three of whatever object type we are storing in the tree, and an array holding up to four pointers to other nodes. Here we implement a pointer as the record number of the record being pointed to (a value of −1 represents a null pointer).

2. The first record in the file is a header record. Its first pointer field points to a list of records representing free nodes. In a record representing a free node, the count of objects is zero, and the first pointer field points to the next free record. In Figure 12.20, record *n* is the last one in the free list.

3. The second pointer field in the header record points to the root record. Retrieval, insertion, and deletion algorithms need to know where the root is. The position of the root may change as the result of insertions and deletions (see the sections on B-Tree Insertion and B-Tree Deletion). The location of the root is typically read into main memory when the B-tree file is opened and written back to the file whenever it changes.

We present algorithms and performance figures for each of the search, insert, and delete B-tree operations in the following sections. The important aspect of the insert and delete operations is how they maintain the balanced property of the B-tree.

B-Tree Terminology
Adjacent siblings are two nodes that have the same parent and are pointed to by adjacent pointers in the parent. Thus, in the tree shown in Figure 12.19, (.*n*.) and (.*s.u.*) are adjacent siblings, whereas (.*n*.) and (.*y*.) are siblings but not adjacent sib-

Record#	Count	Objects 0	1	2	Pointers 0	1	2	3
0	0				3	1		
1	1	1			2	5		
2	1	e			7	12		
3	0				9			
4	1	n			-1	-1		
5	2	r	v		4	8	10	
6	0				11			
7	2	a	b		-1	-1	-1	
8	2	s	u		-1	-1	-1	
9	0				6			
10	1	y			-1	-1		
11	0				13			
12	2	g	h		-1	-1	-1	
n	0				-1			

Figure 12.20 • B-tree as file of records

lings. Adjacent siblings are pointed to by P_{i-1} and P_i (for some i) in the parent node. We will term object R_i the **separating object** for the two siblings. In Figure 12.19, adjacent siblings (.s.u.) and (.y.) are separated by an object with key v.

B-Tree Retrievals

The retrieval algorithm is simply a generalization of one that we might use for a binary search tree. When searching for an object with a given key, we start by examining the root node. We search the node for the required object. If the object is not found, comparisons with the keys in the node will identify the pointer to the subtree that may contain the object. If the selected pointer is null, then we are at the lowest level in the tree, and the object we are searching for is not present in the tree. If the pointer is not null, then we read the node pointed to—that is, the root node of the subtree—and repeat the operation. A C++ function for the search follows.

```
bool retrieve (Entry& Target, int root)
{
  // looks for object in tree with same key as Target. If found, overwrites
  // Target and returns true, otherwise returns false
  // Assumes < defined on objects
  // root is the number of the record containing the root

  node tempnode;
  int P = root;
  int numobjects;

  getnode(P,tempnode);
  numobjects = tempnode.numobjects;

  while (true)
   {
        if (Target < tempnode.objects[0]) P = tempnode.Pointers[0];

      else if (tempnode.objects[numobjects-1] < Target) P =
                      tempnode.Pointers[numobjects];

      else for (int i=0; i<numobjects-1; i++)
              {
                if ( !tempnode.objects[i] < Target
                   && !Target < tempnode.objects[i]
                  )
                  {
                    Target=tempnode.objects[i];
                    return true;
                  }

                if ( tempnode.objects[i] < Target
                   && Target < tempnode.objects[i+1]
                  )
                  {
                    P = tempnode.Pointers[i+1];
                    break;  // out of the loop searching the current node
                  }
              }

      if (P == -1) return false;  // reached lowest level, not found
      getnode(P,tempnode);        // get node at next level down
      numobjects = tempnode.numobjects; // continue search
   }
}
```

Assume the B-tree is of order M and that it contains N objects. Consider the null pointers in the terminal nodes.[2] An in-order traversal of a B-tree will alternate between null pointers and objects and will start and finish with a null pointer. Therefore, a tree with N objects has $N + 1$ null pointers. From the definition of the tree, all the null pointers are at the same level; assume that this is level h, where the root is considered to be level 1. Thus, in our example tree (Figure 12.19), null pointers are at level 3. The worst case when searching the tree will require h node reads—one at each level 1 through h. The tallest tree containing N objects occurs when the nodes are minimally full. In the case of the root, this means it contains two pointers; nonroot minimal nodes contain $\lceil M/2 \rceil$ pointers. We can now derive an expression for h in terms of N and M as follows.

We know that there are $N + 1$ null pointers, therefore

$$N + 1 \geq 2 * \lceil M/2 \rceil^{h-1}$$

Equality occurs if all nodes are minimally full. Rearranging the expression gives us

$$h \leq 1 + \log_{\lceil M/2 \rceil} [(N + 1)/2]$$

This gives us an upper bound on the height of a B-tree of order M containing N objects, and hence an upper bound on the number of node reads during a retrieval. The minimum number of node reads is clearly one. In this case, the object being searched for is found in the root.

B-Tree as Index

An alternative to storing a set of objects in a B-tree is to store just each object's key in the tree and a pointer to where the rest of the object is stored. Depending on the proportion of the object that the key comprises and on the types of operations required on the objects, this may save time. Consider the following partial analysis.

Suppose, for example, that we have 50,000 objects, each of which requires 120 bytes of storage. Of the 120 bytes, 20 bytes is a unique key. Physical records on our storage device are 1024 bytes long. Assume further that storing a pointer from one record to another on the storage device requires 4 bytes.

- Option A—B-tree of objects: The order of the B-tree (M) is nine. This is because nine pointers at 4 bytes each and eight objects at 120 bytes each is the largest number that will fit in a physical record (occupying 996 of the 1024 bytes). Using the formula derived earlier, the maximum height of the tree (and hence the largest number of node fetches required in a retrieval) is seven.
- Option B—B-tree as index: The order of the B-tree (M) in this case is 43 because we have 42 20-byte keys and 43 pointers occupying 1012 of the 1024 bytes. Applying the formula, we find that the maximum height of the tree is four, so we need no more than four node fetches to locate a key-pointer pair. An additional read is then required to fetch the nonkey part of the object; thus, the largest number of record fetches required in a retrieval is five.

This is just one point of comparison between the two options. A more complete analysis would also estimate retrieval times in the average case and also determine how long it would take to process objects sequentially. Note that in option B, the nonkey object components could be stored sorted by a second field.

Tree Balancing

Tree-balancing operations are required in two cases when performing insertions or deletions on a B-tree. In the insertion operation, a node can overflow because the definition of the tree imposes an upper bound on node size. We can resolve overflow by redistributing objects in existing nodes or by splitting the overlarge node. When deleting, however, we may have node underflow because a node may become smaller than the lower bound on node size. Underflow can be resolved either by redistribution or by **concatenation** of two nodes.

B-Tree Insertion

New objects are always inserted into a terminal node. In our diagrammatic representation of a B-tree (e.g., Figure 12.19), every null pointer represents an insertion point where a new object might go. In Figure 12.19, objects with keys greater than l but less than r would be inserted into the node containing n: to the left of n if less than n and to the right if greater than n. To determine the appropriate insertion point for a particular new object, the insertion algorithm starts by searching for the new object as if it were already in the tree. The search algorithm will bring us to the appropriate point in a terminal node.

Node Overflow   As stated earlier, a problem with inserting objects is that nodes can overflow because there is an upper bound to the size of a node. What if the node into which we have inserted an object now exceeds the maximum size? This situation can be resolved using **redistribution** or **splitting**. We talk about the possibility of redistributing objects in the section on B*-trees later in this chapter. Here we consider how a node might be split.

On overflow, the node is split into three parts. The middle object is passed upward and inserted into the parent, leaving two children behind where there was one before. Suppose that the order of the B-tree is M. The largest number of objects allowable in a node is therefore $M - 1$. Splitting an overfull node with M objects can be depicted as follows:

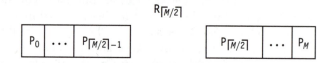

Figure 12.21 shows how, in addition to an object, a pointer to one of the two children is inserted into the parent. As usual, lowercase letters here represent objects; uppercase letters represent pointers. F is a pointer to a newly allocated node.

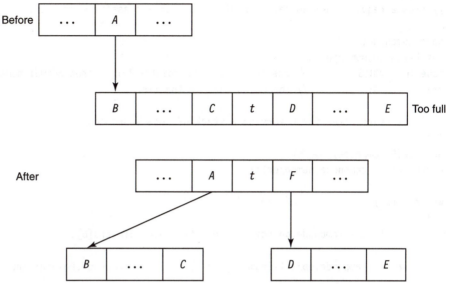

Figure 12.21 • Node splitting

Splitting may propagate up the tree because the parent into which we inserted an object may already have been at its maximum size; therefore, it will also split. If it becomes necessary for the root of the tree to split, then a new root is created that has just two children. This is a valid node because of the third property of a B-tree (see B-Tree Definition earlier). If the root splits, then the tree grows by a level. This is the only circumstance under which the height of a B-tree increases. We can regard the leaves as being the fixed level of a tree that grows up or down only at the top (root). Note that, in contrast to an AVL tree, for example, no explicit height-balancing operations are required in the insertion algorithm.

The following is a pseudo-C++ function for the insertion of a new object into a B-tree. The insertion algorithm assumes the existence of a stack of pointers to nodes and also a temporary node, called *TOOBIG*, in main memory. *TOOBIG* has room for one more object and one more pointer than the maximum node allowed in the B-tree. It is used as temporary working space when a node splits. Note that the algorithm may leave the tree in a strange state if it is unable to complete the insertion because a new node is required but none can be created (see Problems at the end of the chapter).

```
bool insert (Entry E, int& root)
{
  // if object with the same key as E is in the tree it is overwritten with E
  // otherwise E is inserted into the tree. Function returns false if cannot
```

```
// create required new space, otherwise true for successful operation.

node tempnode;
int P=root,Q,numobjects;
nodeplus TOOBIG;        // one object and one pointer larger then normal node
stack<int> S;           // for going back up the tree

// First search tree for E forming a stack of node addresses
S.push(P);
getnode(P,tempnode);
numobjects = tempnode.numobjects;

while (true)
  {
        if (E < tempnode.objects[0]) P = tempnode.Pointers[0];

    else if (tempnode.objects[numobjects-1] < E) P = tempnode.Pointers[numobjects];

    else for (int i=0; i<numobjects-1; i++)
           {
              if ( !tempnode.objects[i] < E && !E < tempnode.objects[i] )
                 {
                   tempnode.objects[i]=E; // overwrite existing object
                   putnode(P,tempnode);    // putting the modified node back
                   return true;            // successful exit
                 }

              if ( tempnode.objects[i] < E && E < tempnode.objects[i+1] )
                 {
                   P = tempnode.Pointers[i+1];
                   break;  // out of the loop searching the current node
                 }
           }

    if (P == -1) break;   // reached lowest level
    S.push(P);
    getnode(P,tempnode);
    numobjects = tempnode.numobjects;
  }
// Insert object E and pointer P into the tree
while(true)
    {
      if (!fullnode(tempnode))
```

```
        {
                insertinnode(tempnode,E,P);
                P = S.pop();                    // address of the node
                putnode(P,tempnode);            // put modified node back
                return true;                    // insert successful
        }
    else
        { // node full so split it
                copynode(tempnode,TOOBIG);
                insertinnode(TOOBIG,Rec,P);
                E = center_object(TOOBIG);
                tempnode = left_half(TOOBIG);
                P = S.pop();
                putnode(P,tempnode);
                P = getnewnodeaddress();
                if (P == -1) return false;  // insert fails - no new nodes available
                tempnode = right_half(TOOBIG);
                putnode(P,tempnode);
                if (!S.empty())
                        getnode(S.top(),tempnode);
                else
                    { // tree grows by a level
                    Q = getnewnodeaddress();
                    if (Q == -1) return false;  // insert fails - no new nodes
                                                // available
                    insertinnode(tempnode,root,E,P);
                    putnode(Q,tempnode);
                    root = Q;                    // new value for root
                    return true;                 // insert successful
                    }
        }
    }
}
```

The insertion algorithm starts by searching for the object to be inserted, which brings us to the appropriate terminal node in the tree. If we find an object having the same key as the object to be inserted, we overwrite the tree object and exit. During the search, whenever we move from a parent node to one of its children, we push the address of the parent node onto the stack. Later, this will enable us to move from a node to its parent by unstacking an address. The stack mechanism is adequate because the only nodes we are interested in are the direct ancestors of the terminal node where we start the insertion. Use of the stack means there is no need for any node to contain a pointer to its parent.

An insertion of an object into the current node can have two possible results. The insertion may occur without any maintenance operations being required or it may cause overflow.

1. Nonoverflow insertion: The current node is not full. In this case, we insert the object. We also insert an appropriate pointer so that the number of pointers in the node is still one greater than the number of objects. The algorithm terminates.

2. Overflow insertion: The current node is full. In this case, we copy it into the overlarge node *TOOBIG*, which has room for one more object and one more pointer than the maximum allowed in a tree node. We insert the new object and an appropriate pointer into *TOOBIG*, and then put the contents of *TOOBIG* back in the tree to effect the splitting operation. The center object is identified; if *M* is even, an arbitrary choice is made between the two central objects. Objects and pointers to the left of the center object are put back in the current node, the remainder of which is cleared. Objects and pointers to the right of the center object are put into a new node.[3] The center object and a pointer to the newly allocated node now have to be inserted into the parent of the current node. The algorithm therefore iterates until at some level no further splitting is needed. If the root has to split, the new root will contain, in addition to the object and pointer passed up from below, a pointer to the old root.

Consider the example B-tree in Figure 12.19 and the successive insertion of objects with keys *m*, *j*, *p*, and *d*. We will assume for our purposes that the tree is order three. It follows that the largest node can hold two objects and three pointers and that the smallest node can hold one object and two pointers. TOOBIG can hold three objects and four pointers.

Insert *m*: This is a simple insertion. The key is greater than *l* but less than *r*, so the object goes into the node with *n*. Because there is enough room in this node for a new object, the insertion algorithm finishes. Figure 12.22 shows the resulting tree.

Insert *j*: The object with key *j* should go into the node currently containing *g* and *h*. However, this node is at its maximum size, so objects *g*, *h*, and *j* are put into the *TOOBIG* node. The middle object (*h*) is then inserted into the parent node. The remaining objects form two children where there was one child before. The final result of inserting an object with key *j* is shown in Figure 12.23.

Insert *p*: When we insert an object with key *p* into our tree we find that node splitting occurs at two levels. Initially, *p* is put into *TOOBIG* with objects *m* and *n*. When this splits, object *n* is passed up to be inserted into the parent.

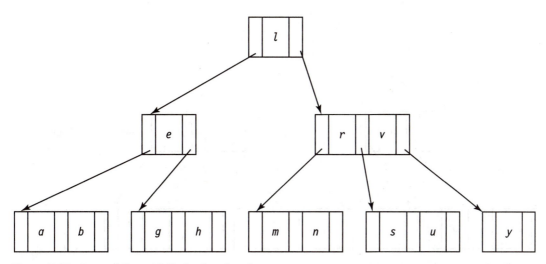

Figure 12.22 • B-tree of Figure 12.19 after insertion of *m*

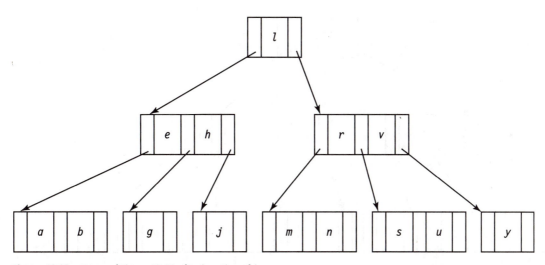

Figure 12.23 • B-tree of Figure 12.22 after insertion of *j*

However, the parent is already full, so *TOOBIG* holds the parent and object *n*, as depicted in Figure 12.24.

When *TOOBIG* is split, object *r* is passed up to the root. The final tree resulting from the insertion of *p* is shown in Figure 12.25.

Insert *d*: The insertion of the final example object into our tree causes splitting to occur all the way up to the root and the tree grows one level. Initially

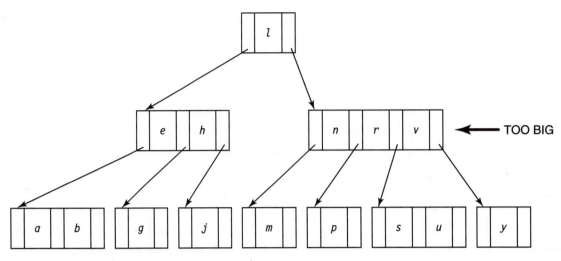

Figure 12.24 • B-tree of Figure 12.23 during insertion of *p*

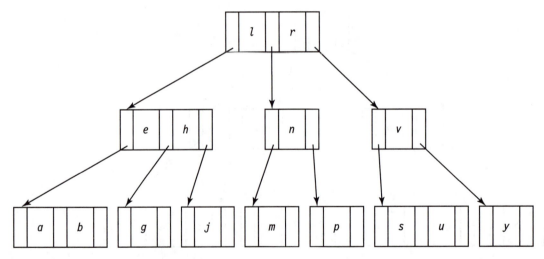

Figure 12.25 • B-tree of Figure 12.23 after insertion of *p* terminates

object *d* goes into *TOOBIG*, together with objects *a* and *b*. When *TOOBIG* splits, object *b* is passed up to the parent. However, because the parent is already full, its contents are copied with object *b* into *TOOBIG*, as depicted in Figure 12.26.

When *TOOBIG* splits again, object *e* is passed up to the root. Because the root is already full, *TOOBIG* is set up again, this time containing the old root and object *e*, as shown in Figure 12.27.

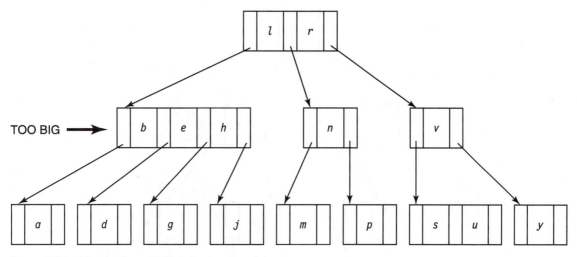

Figure 12.26 • B-tree of Figure 12.25 during insertion of *d*

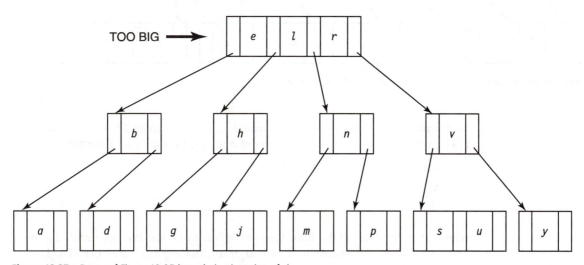

Figure 12.27 • B-tree of Figure 12.25 later during insertion of *d*

When *TOOBIG* splits for the final time, a new root is created and the tree grows by a level. The final tree is shown in Figure 12.28.

Performance of the Insertion Algorithm   The best case for the insertion algorithm is when there is room for the new object in the initial node. In this case, we have to read *h* nodes (where *h* is the height of the tree) and write one node.

The worst case is illustrated by our last example. If the tree is split all the way up to the root, then *h* + 1 new nodes are created (where *h* is the height of the tree

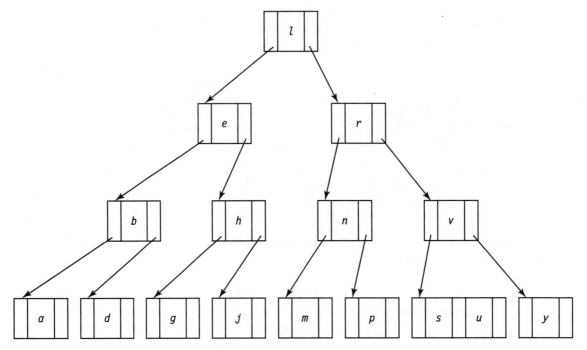

Figure 12.28 • B-tree of Figure 12.25 after completion of insertion of *d*

before insertion). That is, we must read h nodes and write $2h + 1$ nodes. Knuth (1973) reports that the average number of nodes split during an insertion is

$$\frac{1}{\left\lceil \dfrac{M}{2} \right\rceil - 1}$$

where M is the order of the tree. Thus, as M increases, the average number of node splits decreases. For example, if M is 9 or 10, the expected number of splits per insertion is 0.25. This drops to 0.02 when M is 101 or 102. The minimum and maximum number of node reads are both h because insertion is always initially into a terminal node. The minimum number of node writes is one when, as in the case of our first example, the object can be inserted in a lowest-level node. The maximum number of node writes is $2h + 1$, which occurs when the root splits and the tree grows a level.

An alternative to splitting as a means of resolving an overlarge node is to redistribute objects in a local area of the tree. If an adjacent sibling of the overlarge node has spare room, objects can be moved from one node to the other. Naturally, the ordering of objects in the tree must be preserved. We have not, however, included redistribution in the insertion algorithm. This is left as an exercise for the reader. Redistribution will, however, be discussed in the context of deletions from a B-tree.

B-Tree Deletions

As with the insert operation, we always start the delete operation at the lowest level of the tree. If the object we need to delete is not in a terminal node, then we replace it with a copy of its successor, that is, the object with the next-highest key. The successor will be in a terminal node (see our example trees). We then delete the successor object. (Note that using the predecessor rather than the successor would work just as well.)

A problem with deletions is that after an object has been removed from a node, we may have **underflow**; the node may be smaller than the minimum size. This situation can be resolved by means of redistribution or concatenation.

Redistribution is possible when an adjacent sibling of the node with underflow has objects to spare; that is, it contains more than the minimum number of objects. Redistribution involves moving objects among the adjacent siblings and the parent; thus, the structure of the tree is not changed, only the contents of nodes are changed. Concatenation, which is performed when redistribution is not possible, involves the merging of nodes and is the complement of the splitting process we saw with insertions. If concatenation is performed, the structure of the tree changes. Changes may propagate all the way to the root. In extreme cases, the root node is removed, and the tree shrinks by one level.

Here is a pseudo-C++ algorithm for the deletion of an object from a B-tree. The temporary node we use in this algorithm is called *TWOBNODE*. It is approximately twice the size of a normal node.

```
bool delete (Entry E, int& root)
{
  // deletes from the tree the object with the same key as E. Returns false
  // if no such object is in the tree, true otherwise.
  // If the height of tree decreases, value in root will change.

  node tempnode;
  bool searching = true;
  int P=root,numrecs;
  nodetimes2 TWOBNODE;              // twice as big as normal node
  stack<int> S;                     // for moving back up the tree

  // First search tree for E forming a stack of node addresses

  S.push(P);
  getnode(P,tempnode);
  numobjects = tempnode.numobjects;
```

```
while (searching)
  {
        if (E < tempnode.objects[0]) P = tempnode.Pointers[0];

    else if (tempnode.objects[numobjects-1] < E) P = tempnode.Pointers[numobjects];

    else for (int i=0; i<numobjects-1; i++)
          {
            if ( !tempnode.objects[i] < E && !E < tempnode.objects[i] )
               {
                 searching = false; // found the object to be deleted
                 break;
               }

            if ( tempnode.objects[i] < E && E < tempnode.objects[i+1] )
               {
                 P = tempnode.Pointers[i+1];
                 break;
               }
          }

    if (P == -1) return false;    // reached lowest level without finding object
    S.push(P);                    // more levels to search
    getnode(P,tempnode);
    numobjects = tempnode.numobjects;
  }

if (tempnode.Pointers[0] != -1)  // node is not a leaf
  {
    search for successor object of E (stacking node addresses)
    copy successor over E
    E = successor from leaf node
    P = pointer to node containing successor (tempnode holds contents of that node)
  }

// remove object and adjust tree
while (true)
  {
    remove E (object Rᵢ) and pointer Pᵢ from tempnode
    if (P == root || tempnode.objects >= appropriate_minimum)
      { putnode(P,tempnode);
        break;
      }
```

```
        else
            if (redistribution is possible) // A-sibling > minimum
              {
                    // redistribute
                    Copy "best" A-sibling, intermediate parent record, and
                        current (too small) node into TWOBNODE
                    Copy objects and pointers from TWOBNODE to "best"
                        A-sibling, parent and current node so that A-sibling
                        and current node are roughly equal size
                    Update file nodes.
                     return true;
              }
            else
              {

                    // concatenate with appropriate A-sibling
                    Choose best A-sibling to concatenate with
                    Put in the leftmost of current node and A-sibling
                        the contents of both nodes and copy of the
                                    intermediate parent record
                    Discard rightmost of the two nodes
                     Update file node
                    Intermediate object in parent now becomes E
                     P = S.pop()
                     getnode(P,tempnode)

              }
  }

// see if tree shrinks
getnode(root,tempnode);
if (tempnode.numobjects==0)
     {  // yes it does
        int new_root = tempnode.P[0];
        discardnode(root);
        root=new_root;
     }
return true;
}
```

The deletion algorithm starts by searching for the object to be deleted. As with the insertion algorithm, node addresses are put on a stack during the search to make it simple to later move from a node to its parent. If the object is not in a terminal node, then we cannot delete it directly. Instead, we move to its successor (stacking addresses again) and replace the object to be deleted by a copy of its successor.

Because of the structure of a B-tree, the successor of any object not at the lowest level will be in a terminal node. The redundant object is then deleted from the terminal node. Thus, in all cases, deletion involves removing an object from a terminal node. The successor of object R_i is the leftmost object in the subtree pointed to by P_i. It can be located by moving down the P_0 pointers in that subtree until the lowest level is reached.

In addition to removing the object from the current node, we also remove one of the adjacent pointers. In this way, the number of objects in the node will still be one less than the number of pointers. We choose, arbitrarily, to delete the pointer following the deleted object. If the new node size is not below the minimum, the algorithm terminates.

Node Underflow   We can deal with underflow either by redistribution or by concatenation. The problem of a too-small node usually can be resolved by redistributing objects in a local area of the tree. Redistribution is possible if either adjacent sibling contains more than the minimum number of objects. Conceptually, redistribution involves moving objects from the selected adjacent sibling through the parent to the too-small node. We assume in the algorithm the existence of a temporary main memory variable, *TWOBNODE*. This variable has to be big enough to hold the contents of the too-small node, one of its adjacent siblings, and an object from the parent. If *M*, the order of the tree, is odd, then *TWOBNODE* must be able to contain $1.5M - 1.5$ objects and $1.5M - 0.5$ pointers. If *M* is even, then the capacity must be $1.5M - 2$ objects and $1.5M - 1$ pointers.

Redistribution involves bringing into *TWOBNODE* the contents of the too-small node, one of its adjacent siblings, and the appropriate separating object from the parent. These objects and pointers are then redistributed in a way similar to the splitting of *TOOBIG* in the insertion algorithm. The central object from *TWOBNODE* is the one written back to the parent. The left and right halves remaining are written back to the two siblings.

Given a choice of sibling nodes to use, we might reasonably choose to use the one that will cause the new sizes of the two sibling nodes to be closest to 75 percent full. They would then be as far as possible from the two size bounds. We could thus hope to minimize the possibility, assuming insertions and deletions to be equally likely, of future time-consuming splitting, concatenation, or redistribution operations. To avoid additional node reads when deciding which sibling to use, parent nodes could hold, together with each pointer to a child, a count of the number of objects the child contains. However, although this would speed up the delete operation, maintaining the counts would be a considerable overhead in the insert operation.

Redistribution is not possible if the too-small node does not have an adjacent sibling node that is more than minimally full. In this case, we have to use concatenation. We merge the too-small node with one of its adjacent siblings and the appropriate separating object from the parent. The resulting node replaces the selected sibling, and the too-small node is discarded.

If we examine the properties of the B-tree, we see that concatenation is possible only in relatively rare circumstances. If M, the order of the tree, is odd, then concatenation is possible only if an adjacent sibling is minimally full; that is, if it contains $(M - 1)/2$ objects. If the sibling were larger than this, the node after concatenation would exceed the maximum size. If M is even, then concatenation is possible only if a sibling is minimally full or contains one object over the minimum. We are unlikely, therefore, to have a significant choice between siblings with which to concatenate. However, if there is such a choice, we could again choose the sibling that results in the size of the new node being furthest from the two extremes.

Concatenation of two children removes an object from the parent; the separating object that is used in forming the new node has to be deleted from the parent node. If the parent node becomes too small by this deletion, then the problem of resolving a too-small node has to be solved at the next level up. In the most extreme case, concatenation takes place all the way up the tree. It may be that we remove the only object in the root, leaving just a pointer. In this case, we can discard the root; the node pointed to by the pointer becomes the new root. This is the only way in which the height of a B-tree can decrease.

Consider the B-tree of Figure 12.29 and the successive deletion from it of objects with keys j, m, r, h, and b.

We will assume the tree to be of order five. It follows that the largest node can hold four objects and five pointers and the smallest node can hold two objects and three pointers. *TWOBNODE* can hold six objects and seven pointers.

Delete j: The first deletion is a simple one from the lowest level of the tree. The tree after the deletion is shown in Figure 12.30.

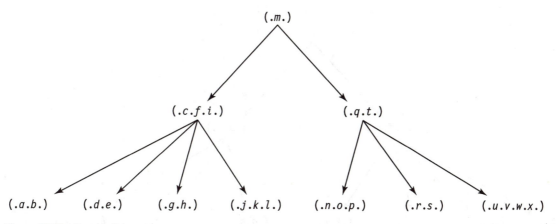

Figure 12.29 • Example B-tree

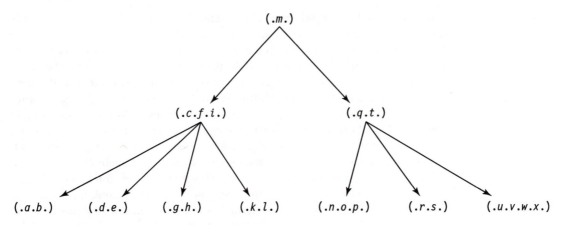

Figure 12.30 • B-tree of Figure 12.29 after deletion of *j*

Delete *m*: In this case, the object to be deleted is not at the lowest level in the tree, so we replace it with a copy of its successor (the object with key *n*), and then delete the lowest-level successor. The resulting tree is shown in Figure 12.31.

Delete *r*: Deletion of object *r* makes the resulting node too small; however, we can resolve the situation without altering the structure of the tree by redistributing objects because one of the adjacent siblings is more than minimally full. Objects in the two adjacent siblings, together with the separating object in the parent, are thus brought into *TWOBNODE* and redistributed. Figure 12.32 shows the tree after the initial deletion and the contents of *TWOBNODE*.

After redistribution, we get the tree shown in Figure 12.33.

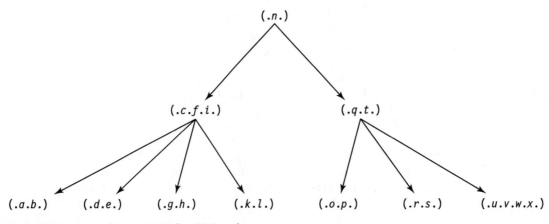

Figure 12.31 • B-tree of Figure 12.30 after deletion of *m*

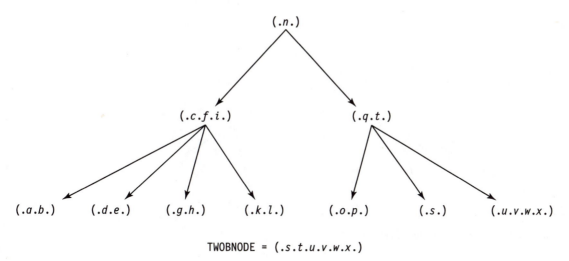

TWOBNODE = (.s.t.u.v.w.x.)

Figure 12.32 • B-tree of Figure 12.31 during deletion of *r*

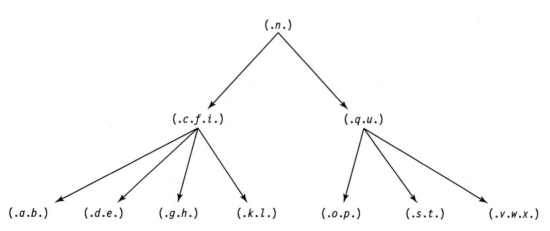

Figure 12.33 • B-tree of Figure 12.32 following redistribution

Delete *h*: When we delete the object with key *h*, the resulting node is again too small; however, in this case we cannot resolve it using redistribution because neither adjacent sibling has objects to spare. We therefore use concatenation. Objects and pointers from the too-small node and the separating object from the parent are inserted into an adjacent sibling. The too-small node is then discarded. The tree after initial deletion is shown in Figure 12.34.

The node with *g* is too small. We choose arbitrarily to concatenate with the (.k.l.) node, and the resulting tree is shown in Figure 12.35.

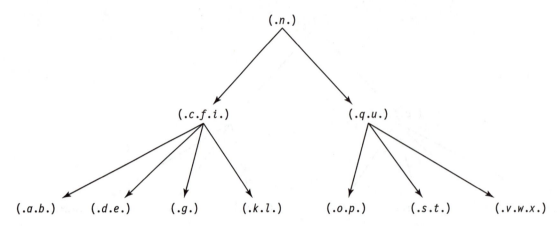

Figure 12.34 • B-tree of Figure 12.33 during deletion of *h*

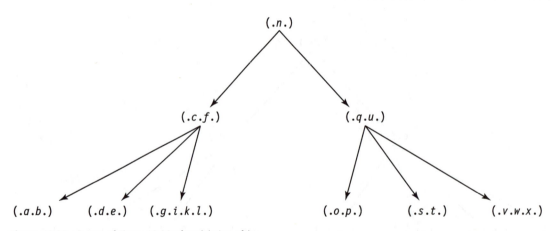

Figure 12.35 • B-tree of Figure 12.33 after deletion of *h*

Delete *b*: When the object with key *b* is deleted from the tree, we have under-flow. This is resolved using concatenation (node *.a.* with object *c* and node *.d.e.*). However, in this case, removing an object from the parent causes it in turn to become too small, as shown in Figure 12.36.

The too-small node cannot be resolved using redistribution because its only sib-ling (*.q.u.*) is minimally full. Therefore, concatenation takes place at this level, too. The result is shown in Figure 12.37.

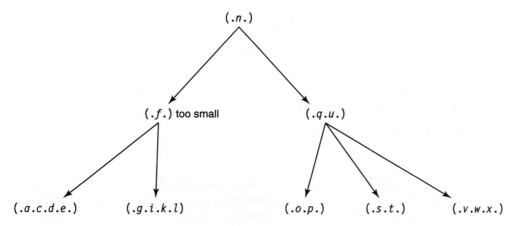

Figure 12.36 • B-tree of Figure 12.35 during deletion of *b*

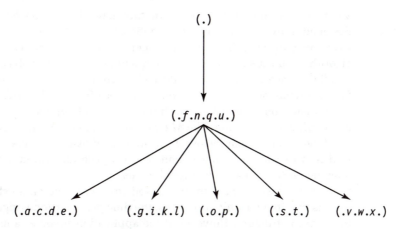

Figure 12.37 • B-tree of Figure 12.36 during deletion of *b*

Note now, however, that bringing an object down from the root causes the root to contain no objects. It can therefore be removed; the final tree is shown in Figure 12.38.

Performance of the Deletion Algorithm

The best case of the deletion algorithm is illustrated by our first example (i.e., when the object to be deleted is at the lowest level). In this case, we have to read h nodes (where h is the height of the tree) and write one node (to put back the modified node). The worst case, according to Bayer and McCreight (1972), occurs when concatenation occurs at all but the first two nodes in the path from the root to the lowest-level deletion node, the child of the root has underflow, and the root itself is modified. In this case, $2h - 1$ nodes are read, and $h + 1$ nodes are written. However,

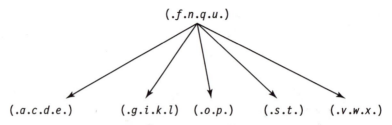

Figure 12.38 • B-tree of Figure 12.37 after deletion of *b*

because the majority of objects are at the lowest level, Bayer and McCreight report that, on average, during a delete operation the number of node reads is less than h + 1 + 1/k and the number of node writes is less than 4 + 2/k, where k is $\lceil M/2 \rceil - 1$.

12.3.3 Variations on the B-Tree

Variations on the B-tree data structure have been devised. Typically, each is designed to overcome some of the deficiencies of the B-tree, such as the comparatively poor space utilization, the frequency with which nodes are split by the insert algorithm, and the relatively slow sequential accessing of objects.

When space utilization in a B-tree is high, retrieval times are short. Techniques for improving the space utilization of a B-tree often involve deferring node splitting. Srinivasan (1991) describes a technique in which an overflow node is attached to an overflowing leaf node. The $M + r$ objects are held in sequence in the leaf and the overflow nodes. When the overflow node itself overflows, the two nodes are organized into two leaves and a parent object. Space utilization is never worse and is often better than in a conventional B-tree.

Costs are associated with the revised structure. Srinivasan shows that for applications that involve only insertions, the time per insertion is significantly higher for the revised structure. However, if the application involves a mixture of insertions and deletions, intermixed and with near equal probabilities, then the performance of the structure is comparable with the original B-tree.

The two most common variations on the B-tree structure are B*-trees, which arose from a suggestion by Bayer and McCreight (1972), and B+-trees, which were suggested by Knuth (1973). Compared with the B-tree, the B*-tree aims to (1) make insert and delete operations symmetric and (2) improve storage utilization. However, processing a group of objects in sequence in a B*-tree still requires a lot of tree traversal. The B+-tree speeds up sequential access by linking leaves together. In a B+-tree, the structure of nonleaf nodes is different from the leaf nodes. The index (nonleaf) levels contain only keys and pointers and are structured like the nodes of a B-tree (or B*-tree); the leaves contain the full objects ordered within each node. We look at B*-trees next and B+-trees in Section 12.3.5.

12.3.4 B*-Trees

Let us look at the retrieval, insertion, and deletion operations on B*-trees and compare B*-trees with B-trees.

B-Tree Retrievals*
The B*-tree performs searches in the same way as the B-tree.

B-Tree Insertions*
Bayer and McCreight (1972) considered making the insertion operation of a B-tree more efficient by reducing the number of occasions when a node had to be split. If the node into which we need to insert an object is full, we might, in certain circumstances, be able to solve the overflow problem by local redistribution of objects rather than by splitting the nodes. Here we consider three possible techniques for redistributing objects called *right-only*, *right-or-left*, and *right-and-left*. The names are derived from the adjacent sibling nodes involved.

- Right-only redistribution: The right-only redistribution process is similar to the redistribution in the B-tree deletion algorithm. The proposed algorithm examines the right sibling of the node that is too full (or the left sibling if there is no right one). Redistribution is possible if the sibling node is not full. Thus, we must split a node only if the sibling is full. When we do split, we distribute objects from the two adjacent siblings (one full, one overfull) into three nodes: the two siblings and a new node. One effect of this splitting strategy is that tree nodes will now be at least two-thirds full instead of at least half full, as in a B-tree.
- Right-or-left redistribution: Right-or-left redistribution is similar to right-only redistribution except when the right sibling is full. In this case, the left sibling is checked for possible redistribution. Nodes are split only when both siblings are full. Again, we distribute objects from two full nodes into three nodes. Right-or-left distribution postpones node splitting, so the resulting tree will contain nodes that are, on the average, fuller than with the right-only technique.
- Right-and-left redistribution: We could go further than the right-or-left redistribution. At the time a node is split in the right-or-left technique, we are likely to have copies of the three nodes and the two parent objects in main memory. These are the originally full node, its right and left siblings, and the separating objects in the parent node. At this point, we could redistribute three nodes into four. With this algorithm, the lower bound on node size would in most cases be raised to three-quarters full. However, not every node has two siblings, so the split routines involving the right or left sibling only would have to be employed occasionally.

We can compare the expected performance characteristics of the three possible redistribution techniques based on the number of reads and writes required on the B*-tree file under the following three assumptions. First, we assume that all nodes required will be available in main memory. Second, we assume that the necessary pre-conditions for the technique have been satisfied; for example, in the case of the right-and-left technique, we assume that the node has both a right and left sibling. Third, we assume that each technique has a roughly equal probability of propagating splits up the tree. Thus, in this comparison, we examine only the local effect of the three redistribution techniques on the sibling nodes; that is, we do not include rewriting the parent node in our metrics, because it is a constant. Table 12.1 shows the number of reads (R) and writes (W) required in the best and worst cases for each of the three techniques.

The best case for each technique is when the right sibling is not full. Two nodes are read and then written back. The worst case for the right-or-left technique, for example, is when the right sibling is full, and thus the left sibling must be read. The left sibling is full, so we have to split and write three nodes. Recall for comparison that a split-on-overflow strategy results in a one-read, two-writes case with nodes at least half full. What, then, are the advantages of local redistribution? There are two. First, the nodes are used more efficiently with a minimum capacity of $\lfloor (2M - 2)/3 \rfloor$ objects in the case of the first two techniques and $\lfloor (3M - 3)/4 \rfloor$ objects in the third case. Second, with redistribution, splitting does not propagate up the tree. Note, however, that the range of node size in a B*-tree is smaller than that in a B-tree of the same order. If the tree is volatile, there may consequently be more occasions on which underflow or overflow has to be resolved.

With these redistribution assumptions and analysis, the right-only redistribution technique seems preferable. The right-only technique is simple and gives the advantages of redistribution with little I/O overhead. Therefore, our further discussion will assume a right-only redistribution algorithm.

For an example of a case where node-splitting is necessary, assume that we have a B*-tree of order five, with the three nodes depicted in Figure 12.39 (objects with keys shown as ? are not relevant to the example).

Inserting an object with key o into the B*-tree will result in a merging and splitting sequence that transforms it into the tree shown in Figure 12.40.

However, the root node has no siblings. What happens if it needs to split? As before, the central object will become the new root, and the remaining parts of the old root will form the first level of the tree. However, to ensure that these children are not smaller than the new minimum size we defined, the upper bound on the

● **TABLE 12.1** Reads and Writes for Distribution Options

Redistribution	Best Case	Worst Case
Right only	2R 2W	2R 3W
Right or left	2R 2W	2R 3W
Right and left	2R 2W	2R 3W

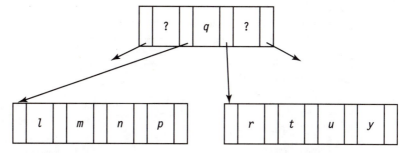

Figure 12.39 • B*-tree fragment

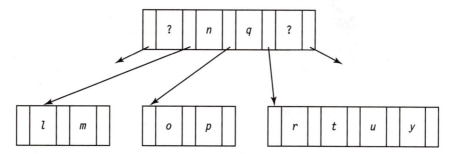

Figure 12.40 • B*-tree fragment of Figure 12.39 after insertion of *o*

root has to be modified. For a B*-tree of order M, the upper bound of the root node will now be $2 * \lfloor(2M - 2)/3\rfloor$ objects. When the root splits, it will leave two nodes each containing $\lfloor(2M - 2)/3\rfloor$ objects. Thus, we now have a tree with two different node capacities (root node and other nodes).

Knuth (1973, Section 6.2.4) termed the tree resulting from these modifications a B*-tree. A B*-tree of order M has the following five properties:

1. No node apart from the root has more than M children.
2. Every node, except for the root and the terminal nodes, has at least $\lfloor(2M - 2)/3\rfloor + 1$ children.
3. The root, unless the tree has only one node, has at least two children and at most $2 * \lfloor(2M - 2)/3\rfloor + 1$ children.
4. All terminal nodes appear on the same level; that is, they are the same distance from the root.
5. A node with K children contains $K - 1$ objects.

Table 12.2 shows maximum and minimum node sizes for root and nonroot nodes. The figures for a B-tree and a B*-tree are given for nonempty trees of order 20, 21, and 22.

	Formula	M = 20	M = 21	M = 22
● TABLE 12.2 Bounds on B-Tree and B*-Tree Nodes				
B-tree (order _M_)				
Min. objects (root)	1	1	1	1
Max. objects (root)	$M - 1$	19	20	21
Min. objects (nonroot)	$\lceil (M - 2)/2 \rceil$	9	10	10
Max. objects (nonroot)	$M - 1$	19	20	21
B*-tree (order _M_)				
Min. objects (root)	1	1	1	1
Max. objects (root)	$2 * \lfloor 2M - 2)/3 \rfloor$	24	26	28
Min. objects (nonroot)	$\lfloor (2M - 2)/3 \rfloor$	12	13	14
Max. objects (nonroot)	$M - 1$	19	20	21

B*-Tree Deletions

What do we do if a deletion leaves a node too small? As in the case of a B-tree, we can locally redistribute objects if an adjacent sibling has objects to spare. If there is no such sibling, we must concatenate nodes. Note that the only concatenation normally allowable is of three nodes into two. (The exception is when the only two children of the root are concatenated and the tree shrinks a level.) What happens, however, if we are dealing with a node at one end of a tree level? Such a node has only one adjacent sibling. See, for instance, node X in the examples in Figure 12.41.

We know that node W is minimally full; otherwise, redistribution would have been possible. However, we cannot necessarily concatenate V, W, and X. If V is not also minimally full, the result will be too large to fit into two nodes. One

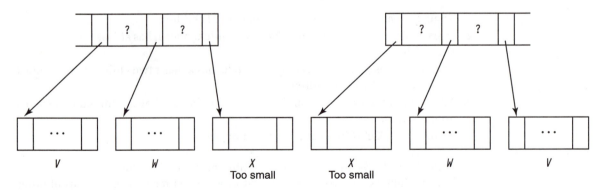

Figure 12.41 • B*-Tree Fragments

solution is to redistribute a single object so that W is now too small and X is minimally full. Now we have an instance of the more general case. Redistribution can be tried; if it turns out that V is minimally full, then V, X, and W can be concatenated.

Comparison of B-Tree with B-Tree*

The height (h) of a B*-tree of order M containing N objects is given in the following expression:

$$h \le 1 + \log_{\lceil (2M-1)/3 \rceil} (N+1)/2$$

For a particular M and N, searching a B*-tree is faster, on average, than searching a B-tree, due to the higher average branching factor. However, B-trees are better for applications in which insertions or deletions are more common than searches. B*-trees are thus better when searching is the most common tree operation.

Srinivasan (1991) provides data on B-tree space utilization. When deletions and insertions take place with equal probability, utilization is close to 59 percent. In the B*-tree, when both left and right siblings are examined on overflow, average utilization is around 87 percent.

• **12.3.5 B+-Trees**

Knuth (1973) proposed a B-tree variation that, for clarity, Comer (1979) designated the B+-tree. Objects in a B+-tree are held only in the terminal nodes of the tree. The terminal nodes are linked to facilitate sequential processing of the objects and are termed the **sequence set** (compare with VSAM). Nonterminal nodes are indexes to lower levels. Nodes in the index levels contain only key values and tree pointers. There is no need for terminal nodes to have tree pointer fields. Thus, terminal nodes have a different structure from nonterminal nodes. In fact, there is no reason why the index part of the tree should not be stored on a different device than the terminal nodes. Figure 12.42 depicts an example B+-tree.

Objects in terminal nodes are shown thus: [x=]. The = represents the nonkey fields. Nonterminal nodes contain keys and pointers; in those levels of the tree, we use notation similar to our B-tree and B*-tree examples.

The objects in the tree of Figure 12.42 are those in our first example B-tree (Figure 12.19). The objects were inserted into an empty B+-tree in arbitrary order; thus, the index structure shown in Figure 12.42 is just one of many possibilities.

Recall that terminal nodes contain complete objects whereas index-level nodes contain only keys. In addition, for efficiency, node capacity is likely to be a function of the physical record size. Therefore, it is likely that the order of a B+-tree index will be different from the capacity of the terminal nodes in its sequence set. Suppose, for example, that

- Physical records are 512 bytes long.
- User objects are 42 bytes long.

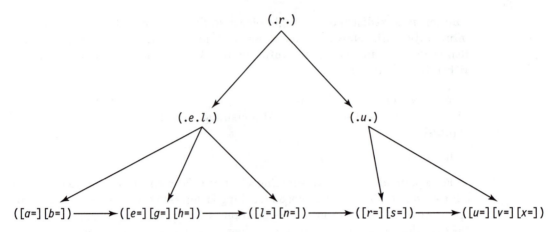

Figure 12.42 • Example B⁺-tree

- Keys of user objects are 8 bytes long.
- Pointers are 4 bytes long.

We can pack 12 objects into a 512-byte leaf node, leaving 8 bytes for the pointer to the next leaf node. In the index levels, we can have 42 8-byte keys and 43 tree pointers in each 512-byte node, and have 4 bytes free in which to store information such as the number of keys currently in the node.

The index levels could be structured as a B-tree or as a B*-tree. In what follows, we assume for simplicity that the index levels have a B-tree structure; thus, the properties of a B⁺-tree of order M are as follows:

1. The root node has either 0 or 2 through M children.
2. All nodes except the root and terminal nodes have at least $\lceil M/2 \rceil$ children and not more than M children.
3. All terminal nodes appear at the same level; that is, they are the same distance from the root.
4. A nonterminal node with K children contains $K - 1$ keys.
5. If the capacity of a terminal node is N objects and there is more than one terminal node, then each contains at least $\lceil N/2 \rceil$ objects.
6. Terminal nodes represent the sequence set of the data file and are linked together.

B⁺-Tree Capacity
If there are L index levels, then the maximum number of objects that can be held in a B⁺-tree as just defined is $N \times M^L$, and the minimum number is $\lceil N/2 \rceil \times 2 \times \lceil M/2 \rceil^{L-1}$.

For example, if L is 3 and we have the user objects of our example above ($M = 43$, $N = 12$), then the B⁺-tree contains as few as 5808 objects and as many as 954,084.

B+-Tree Insertions

If we need to insert an object into a leaf node that is full, we may be able to resolve the overflow by redistributing objects using an adjacent leaf. If this is not possible and we need to split a leaf, then we can make use of a temporary node (*TOOBIG*), as we did with a B-tree. We put a copy of the key of the central object in *TOOBIG* into the index. We then divide all the objects in *TOOBIG* between the old node and a new node. Thus, the central object will also be in one of the two halves after splitting. If an index node has to split, the algorithm is the same as for a conventional B-tree, and the central object (key) is passed up to the parent. Figures 12.43a through 12.43e depict the evolution of a B+-tree. It is only one of the possible ways in which our example tree might have evolved. We assume objects were inserted into an initially empty tree in the following sequence:

a u r n e s l v

For this example, we assume that terminal nodes can hold two or three objects and that index nodes can hold one or two keys.

Figure 12.43a shows the tree after only the first three objects have been inserted. Insertion of an object with key *n* causes the terminal node to split in two and the key *r* to be passed into the index. It is the first key in the index. This is shown in Figure 12.43b. Figure 12.43c shows the tree after objects with keys *e* and *s* have been inserted. Insertion of an object with key *l* causes another terminal node to split and a second key to be inserted into the index. This is shown in Figure 12.43d. Finally, insertion of an object with key *v* causes another terminal node to split, a key to be inserted into the index, and the root of the index to split. Now we have two index levels, as shown in Figure 12.43e.

B+-Tree Deletions

When an object is deleted from the B+-tree and no redistribution or concatenation is needed, no changes need be made to the index. Even if the key of the object to be deleted appears in the index, it can be left there as a separator. Figure 12.44 shows the B+-tree of Figure 12.42 after the deletion of an object with key *e*.

If, after a deletion, a leaf is too small, we may be able to redistribute objects with an adjacent sibling leaf. Deletions that result in redistribution of objects cause changes in the content but not the structure of the index levels. Figure 12.45 shows what happens if we delete the object with key *s* from the tree of Figure 12.44.

Finally, deletions that result in concatenation of terminal nodes also cause deletions from the index levels. Figure 12.46 shows the tree of Figure 12.45 after we delete the object with key *g*.

Comparison of B+ Tree with B-Tree

All searches in a B+-tree have to go down to the terminal nodes. However, because the index levels hold only keys rather than complete index objects, searching time

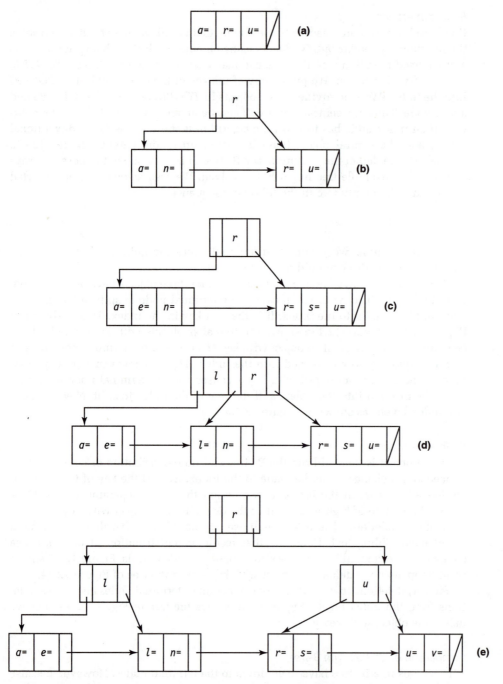

Figure 12.43 • Evolution of B+-tree (a) After initial 3 insertions (b) 4th insertion causes leaf node to split (c) after 6 insertions leaves are full (d) 7th insertion causes another leaf split and (e) final insertion causes splits in leaf level and index

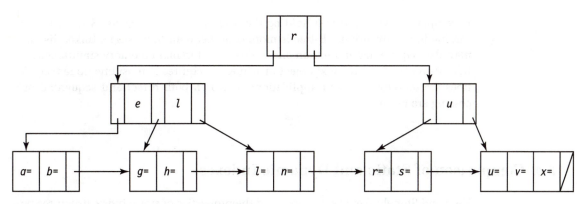

Figure 12.44 • B⁺-tree of Figure 12.42 after deletion of *e*

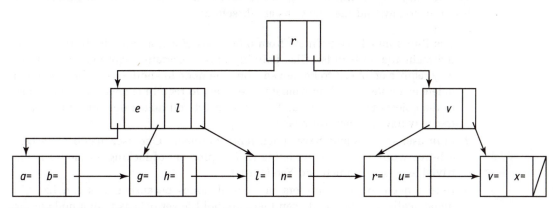

Figure 12.45 • B⁺-tree of Figure 12.44 after deletion of *s*

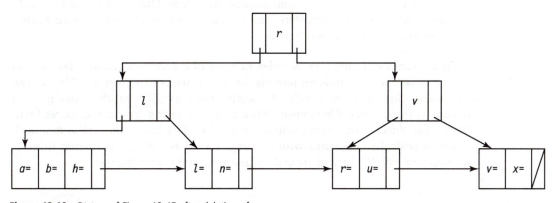

Figure 12.46 • B⁺-tree of Figure 12.45 after deletion of *g*

is comparable with a B-tree holding the same number of objects. Sequential processing in a conventional B-tree is more complex than traversing a linked list, and may also require that more than one node be held in main memory simultaneously. In a B+-tree, getting the next object in sequence requires at most one node read. B+-trees are therefore good in applications in which both direct and sequential processing are required.

12.4   Comparison of Static and Dynamic Indexes

Held and Stonebraker (1978) compared the properties of **static index** structures typified by ISAM with those of **dynamic index** structures typified by B-trees and VSAM. They suggest that although a dynamic structure is easier to reorganize, there is a price to pay, and that the costs are threefold:

1. The B-tree may have pointers from other files. For example, the B-tree may be the main file with index files pointing into it. Certain operations on a B-tree may require an object to be moved from one node to another (see the insert and delete examples). Such movements are likely to require changes to the pointers to the objects that are moved. Thus, the insert and delete operations on the B-tree may have hidden overheads.

2. Multiuser systems may have concurrency problems. One user may try to access a B-tree while another is updating it. The problem of locking out nodes is not trivial [e.g., see Lehman and Yao (1981)].

3. B-trees need explicit pointers in nonleaf nodes because nodes can be split dynamically. A B-tree node can therefore hold fewer objects than a node of the same total size that does not require such pointers. The branching factor is therefore smaller and the height of the tree likely to be greater than that of a static structure holding the same number of objects. Operations such as search, insert, and delete will therefore tend to take longer than they would for a static index to a file with no overflows.

In the same way that a book index or table of contents provides a fast way to access parts of a book, indexes provide fast access paths to objects in a file. We can create and destroy indexes without affecting the main file, but they may need to change as the indexed file changes. Primary key indexing typically involves identifying the object with a given primary key. Secondary indexing, similar to a book index, is typically concerned with locating all objects having a particular value of a secondary key. We look at secondary indexing in the next chapter.

● Chapter Summary

We considered solutions to the problem of being able to process objects in a collection in sequence while still being able to retrieve individual objects quickly by primary key. Adding an index to a sequential file increases the efficiency of retrieving individual objects and finding objects that have keys in a particular range. Indexed files differ in the way that the index does or does not change structure as the underlying file changes. This chapter looked at both static indexes and dynamic indexes.

Static indexes are based on an initial file, and the index structure remains static as the file expands. Although insertion and retrieval operations are initially efficient, performance of the structure may decline over time, requiring periodic maintenance.

A dynamic index adapts as the indexed file changes. Indexes are often tree-structured because search operations are efficient and sequential processing is normally easy. A B-tree is a multiway tree with bounds on the node size. The B-tree organization is particularly suitable because the search, insert, and delete operations are guaranteed to be efficient even in the worst case. We also compared the B-tree with two variations: B*-trees and B+-trees.

● Exercises

1. The ISAM organization described in this chapter distributes free space uniformly during the initial loading. Suggest why a method that takes key values into account when distributing space might perform better. Illustrate your answer with appropriate examples.

2. Suppose that an ISAM index entry holds the lowest key on a particular storage unit rather than the highest, as we have assumed. How would the retrieval algorithm change?

3. Show how you could find the number of objects in an ISAM file that have keys greater than x and less than y.

4. Compare an ISAM file with a sequential file having no index. Which operations are faster and which are slower using the ISAM file?

5. What is different about the treatment of index entries if we logically delete data objects from an ISAM file rather than physically delete them?

6. How could the ISAM insert algorithm be modified to take advantage of logically deleted entries?

7. If you were designing an ISAM package, which parameters would you let a user control?

8. Suppose you are designing a utility that checks the integrity of an ISAM file. What checks would you have your algorithm perform?

9. A certain system contains two files of objects. The files are identical except that in one (*File-1*) the objects are in random order and in the other (*File-2*) the objects are sorted in ascending order by primary key.

   a. Consider the creation of a B-tree using one of the two files. The tree is initially empty, and the objects are read one at a time from the file and inserted into the tree (using the primary key to decide where to place the object). Node overflow is resolved using splitting only (no object redistribution). Would the tree created from

File-1 be the same as the tree created from *File-2*? If not, what would be the main difference between the trees?

b. Suppose we modify our insert algorithm so that when a node overflows it redistributes objects if possible and only splits nodes if it cannot redistribute. Would the tree created from *File-1* be the same as the tree created from *File-2*? Give reasons for your answer.

10. Clustered insertions are a group of insertions with a small range of key values compared with the range of keys in the file. We saw that clustered insertions may cause an ISAM structure to perform poorly. Do they have the same effect on a B-tree?

11. A certain disk has a sector size of 512 bytes. Suppose that we are storing 110-byte objects in which the primary key is 10 bytes long. Suppose that pointers occupy 4 bytes. Consider a B$^+$-tree.

    a. How many objects fit in a leaf?

    b. What is the order of the index level tree?

    c. What is the largest number of objects in the leaves if we have just two index levels?

12. Discuss the advantages and disadvantages of having in each B-tree node a pointer to the parent node.

13. Derive expressions for (a) the minimum and (b) the maximum number of objects in a B-tree of order M with objects at L levels in the tree.

14. A B-tree of order six contains 17 objects. The keys of the objects are

    8, 13, 26, 28, 41, 49, 54, 67, 83, 84, 96, 107, 132, 146, 151, 154, 170

    The tree has three levels (the root and two levels beneath). Draw the tree. Draw it also as it appears after each operation in the following sequence:

    a. Delete the object with key 83.

    b. Delete the object with key 67.

    c. Delete the object with key 26.

15. The following is a B-tree of order three, with x's marking the locations of the objects.

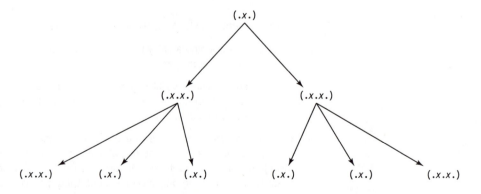

The tree holds objects with the following single-character keys:

P, Y, A, Q, F, W, J, T, B, L, M, D, U

a. Draw the tree, showing where each object would appear.

b. Draw the relevant parts of the tree as they would appear after each step in the following sequence of operations:

1. Insert object with key X.

2. Delete object with key Q.

3. Delete object with key M.

4. Insert object with key C.

16. What are the advantages and disadvantages of storing a file of objects as a B-tree as compared with simply having a B-tree index to the file?

17. Consider a file organized using table-assisted hashing and a file organized as a B-tree. Assume that in both files there are no two objects with the same key. What are the comparative advantages and disadvantages of the two organizations (a) when inserting objects into the file and (b) when retrieving objects from the file?

18. Modify the B-tree insertion algorithm so that it delays node splitting in a manner similar to B*-trees. It should prefer redistribution over splitting and not split if there is an adjacent sibling that is not full. However, when splitting, it should still only split one node into two.

19. Consider a situation in which a hash file of objects is being created and an index to the file (in the form of a B-tree) is also required. The objects are processed in ascending key order. The B-tree could be generated in parallel with the hash file, in which case the index entries would be inserted into the tree in ascending order. Alternatively, the tree could be generated after the hash file is complete. In this case, a sequential pass through the buckets of the hash file would generate index entries in random order.

What differences, if any, would the choice between these two strategies have on the efficiency of subsequent (a) insertions into, (b) deletions from, and (c) retrievals from the index?

20. Discuss the advantages and disadvantages of deleting objects logically rather than physically from a B-tree.

21. Compare and contrast a B-tree of order two with an AVL tree (see Chapter 6).

22. a. Devise an algorithm that finds the successor of an arbitrary object in a B-tree.

b. Devise an algorithm to find the predecessor of an object.

c. Describe how to enhance a map object implemented as a B-tree with methods that enable a user to move to (a) the successor and (b) the predecessor of the last object retrieved.

● Problems

1. Implement a *map_isam* class. Your class should include at least the following methods:

   create: Build the initial structure from a file of objects.

   insert: Insert a new object into an existing structure.

   retrieve: Find an object in the structure.

2. Add to your *map_isam* class a method that lets a user remove an object from the structure. A user should have the choice of whether to delete the object physically or logically.

3. Add code to your *map_isam* class that enables the structure to monitor the location of overflowing objects and the efficiency of retrievals. Implement triggers that cause a new file structure to be built from the old.

4. Three parameters of a B-tree are *L* (the number of levels at which objects are stored), *M* (the order of the tree), and *N* (the number of objects in the tree).

   a. Write a program that will prompt the user for values of any two of the three parameters and will output the bounds on the value of the third.

   b. Modify your program so that it is appropriate for B*-trees.

5. Devise an algorithm for traversing a B-tree, accessing the objects in ascending order. Generalize your solution so that it can output in sequence all objects with keys greater than K_1 and less than K_2, for arbitrary K_1 and K_2. Try to minimize the number of nodes visited. Implement your solution and ensure that it gives sensible output for any K_1 and K_2.

6. The B-tree insertion algorithm may leave the tree in a strange state if it exits because there is no new node available. Modify the algorithm so that if there are not enough new nodes to complete the insertion, the tree is left as it was before the insertion was attempted.

7. Suggest how concurrent access to a B*-tree could be managed. That is, assuming that allowable operations are insert, delete, retrieve, and modify, how can you determine the particular part of the tree that might be affected by a particular operation?

8. Write a complete class definition for a *map_btree* that allows a user to retrieve, insert, and remove objects. In addition, there should be a *retrieve_next* method that retrieves the object that is next in sequence after the last one retrieved.

● References

Bayer, R., and E. McCreight. 1972. Organization and maintenance of large ordered indexes. *Acta Informatica,* 1(3):173–189.

Comer, D. 1979. The ubiquitous B-tree. *ACM Computing Surveys,* 11(2):121–137.

Held, G. D., and M. R. Stonebraker. 1979. B-trees reexamined. *Communications of the ACM,* 21(2):139–143.

IBM Corporation. 1966. *OS ISAM Logic. Order Form GY28-6618.* White Plains, NY: IBM Corporation.

Knuth, D. E. 1973. *Sorting and Searching.* Vol. 3, *The Art of Computer Programming.* Reading, MA: Addison-Wesley.

Lehman, P. L., and S. B. Yao. 1981. Efficient locking for concurrent operations on B-trees. *ACM Transactions on Database Systems,* 6(4):650–670.

Srinivasan, B. An overflow technique to defer splitting in B-trees. *Computer Journal,* 34(5):397–405.

● Notes

[1]The ceiling function ($\lceil\ \rceil$) returns the smallest integer greater than or equal to its argument. Thus, $\lceil 3.4 \rceil$ is 4 and $\lceil 5.0 \rceil$ is 5.

[2]In the literature (Bayer and McCreight 1972; Knuth 1973), these pointers are often regarded as pointers to leaves.

[3]We assume that there is a mechanism for allocating new nodes to the tree. As we saw earlier, a file of node records is a reasonable implementation of the B-tree. We could keep a list of the records not currently used in the tree. When a new node is required by the insertion algorithm, one could be taken from the list. We will see later that the deletion algorithm sometimes discards nodes from the tree. They would be added to the free node list. Only if the list were empty would the insertion algorithm need to invoke mechanisms to extend the file.

Multimaps: Secondary Key Retrievals

13.1 Introduction

In Chapters 5, 6, and 12, we discussed the implementation of maps—containers of objects in which there is only one object with a particular key. The key in this case is a **primary key** because it uniquely identifies an object. We looked at both hash-based and tree-based map implementations. In this chapter, we are concerned with implementations of multimaps—containers in which there may be many objects associated with a particular key. The key in this case is termed a **secondary key**. If we interpret the idea of a multimap broadly, then many applications involve multimaps. You are probably familiar with search engines for the World Wide Web that enable you to find pages containing one or more key words. You may also have searched an online bookstore by author, title, or publisher. These are examples of secondary key retrieval; here are others:

A realtor wishes to retrieve from a file of objects all those representing properties with:

- Three bedrooms
- At least 1.5 bathrooms
- A swimming pool[1]

A college dean awarding scholarships needs a list of all students with:

- A GPA of at least 3.3
- U.S. citizenship
- A major in physics or math

A person buying a used car wishes to retrieve from a file of objects all those representing vehicles that:

- Are less than four years old
- Have fewer than 25,000 miles on the odometer
- Are blue or white in color
- Are not Fords

In contrast with primary key retrievals, the same secondary key value may be found in many objects in a container. Indexes are one way to locate the appropriate objects. In Chapter 12, you saw that the index component of an indexed sequential file (ISAM or B$^+$-tree), that is, a primary key index, is similar to the table of contents of a book. The index contains a subset of the items in the container in the same order as they appear in the container. This enables us to identify the region of the container that contains the item of interest. In contrast, an index that facilitates secondary key retrievals is more like the index of a book. It identifies the location(s) of particular data items. This chapter looks at ways to organize secondary key indexes and also examines a retrieval method that does not use indexes.

13.1.1 Indexed Versus Brute-force Searches

A secondary index provides a fast way to locate all objects with a particular attribute value; however, there is a price to be paid. Indexes take up space, and if the indexed collection of objects changes frequently, much time may be spent keeping the indexes up-to-date. The user has to weigh the cost of retrievals with and without a particular index against the cost of maintaining that index. Clearly the relative frequencies of retrievals and container modifications will be a factor. A brute-force search of the container may be satisfactory if a fast response to a query is not required, if the container is small, or if the data are so volatile that a lot of time would be spent in index maintenance. Text, for example, can be searched rapidly with string-matching algorithms (Hume and Sunday 1991).

13.1.2 The World Wide Web

Some searches, for example, those of the World Wide Web, cannot be accomplished in a reasonable time without indexes. Search engines use programs that traverse the Web, sending back information about pages and the terms they contain. The data are collected into indexes that are accessed when users perform searches. Because of the size of the Web and the speed with which its contents change, coverage represented by the indexes is likely to be incomplete and somewhat out-of-date.[2]

In a variety of ways, an entry in a typical secondary key index indicates the location of those objects having a particular attribute value. For example, the index entry may contain linked lists or bit maps. It is normally straightforward to combine data sets in order to satisfy multikey queries.

Although indexes are good for queries specifying exact matches, such as

find bedrooms = 3 and baths = 2

find GPA = 4.00

they are not such a good solution for queries involving ranges of attribute values, as in

find 100000 < price < 150000

find 2.50 < GPA < 2.70

because we would have to form the union of many different sets of objects. In the case of the GPA query, for example, we would find the union of the sets of objects with GPA = 2.51, objects with GPA = 2.52, objects with GPA = 2.53, and so on. Such **range queries** might be better handled if data were held in a multidimensional **grid file**. In Section 13.2, we look at a common secondary indexing technique and at a particular application of it. In Section 13.3, we look at grid files, including some grid file implementation issues.

13.2 Inverted Files

Throughout this section we use the extract from collection *CARS*, shown in Figure 13.1.

In the inverted file organization, we create an index for each field from which we wish to retrieve. The entries in a particular index are the values of that field that currently exist in the collection. Each index entry identifies those objects that have the particular value of the particular attribute. The set of indexes is an **inverted file**. It is so called because we can think of a file of objects as being like a function. Given an object number, it returns the attribute values of that object:

File(number) → (attribute,value), (attribute,value) ...

An example is

CARS(19) → (Manufacturer, Ford), (Model, Pinto),
            (Color, Red), (License, LUV2SKI)

A set of indexes represents the inverse function. We can give such indexes an (attribute,value) pair and have returned a list of the numbers of the objects with the specified attribute value:

File'(attribute,value) → number, number, ...

Thus, if we denote the set of indexes to *CARS* as *CARS'*, an example is

CARS'(Color,White) → 1, 4, 7, 11, 16, ...

Inverted files are common in document retrieval systems in which documents are stored together with key words or index terms indicative of their content. Users

Object #	Manufacturer	Model	Color	License
1	Ford	Pinto	White	HORS4ME
2	VW	Bug	Red	SKIBNY
3	BMW	322i	Black	DADIOU1
4	Ford	Mustang	White	VALEGRL
5	Ford	Pinto	Blue	RATFACE
6	VW	Rabbit	Black	910VCD
7	Ford	Pinto	White	PACMAN
8	VW	Rabbit	Blue	BYE4NOW
9	BMW	320	Red	CMEGO
10	Ford	Mustang	Blue	DPGURU
11	Audi	5000	White	OU2LNCH
12	VW	Jetta	Black	1GWN821
13	VW	Bug	Green	BUG4AJS
14	Ford	Mustang	Red	SURVIVR
15	Honda	Civic	Green	COMPSCI
16	BMW	320	White	4AUH20S
17	BMW	322i	Blue	GOTTAGO
18	Ford	Tempo	Black	L8AGAIN
19	Ford	Pinto	Red	LUV2SKI
20	Ford	Mustang	Green	MYWHLS

Figure 13.1 • Part of the *CARS* collection

of information retrieval systems typically express requests in the form of Boolean expressions. For example, to find information about the health hazards of computer terminals, a user might enter:

find (hazard or danger) and (terminal or monitor or screen or display)

The user wants documents that have been indexed by the term *hazard* or *danger* and also by one of the terms *terminal*, *monitor*, *screen*, or *display*. The user interface is usually more sophisticated, however. For example, the user can typically find out how many documents are indexed with a particular term and can ask for a list of more precise or more general terms. Users may be able to form sets of documents and include references to them in queries. In the next section, we will look at the design of a particular document retrieval system that illustrates one way to retrieve documents containing an arbitrary phrase.

We can define the degree of inversion of a collection to be the percentage of object fields that are indexed. If the collection is 100 percent inverted, then every attribute is indexed. Figure 13.2 shows part of the inverted file index for the *CARS* collection of Figure 13.1.

The names of attributes form a linked list. Each element in this list points to a list of values of the attribute. Each of these values in turn points to a list of object numbers.

In practice, it might be advantageous to use something other than the number of an object as a pointer to it. This is because there are likely to be many pointers to a particular object, and hence many changes required to position-dependent pointers if the object changes its position within the container. For instance, we have seen that when containers are implemented using table-assisted hashing or B-trees, objects may move from one physical record to another. The primary key is a possible position-independent pointer, but use of it would slow down accessing because of the need at some stage to translate the key to an address.

If the main file is 100 percent inverted, it is redundant for certain purposes because the inverted file contains the same information. For example, from a complete *CARS'* file we can recreate *CARS*.

13.2.1 Implementation of Indexes

The inverted file organization causes a problem with maintaining variable-length lists for each attribute value. This is one of the major problems of multimap indexing. Four ways in which we might implement the lists are simple lists, bit maps, lists of bit maps, and graph structures.

Simple List of Object Numbers

For merging purposes, the list will probably be kept ordered. An alternative to storing object numbers is to store the differences between successive object numbers. That is, instead of storing

Ford: 1, 4, 5, 7, 10, 14, 18, 19, 20

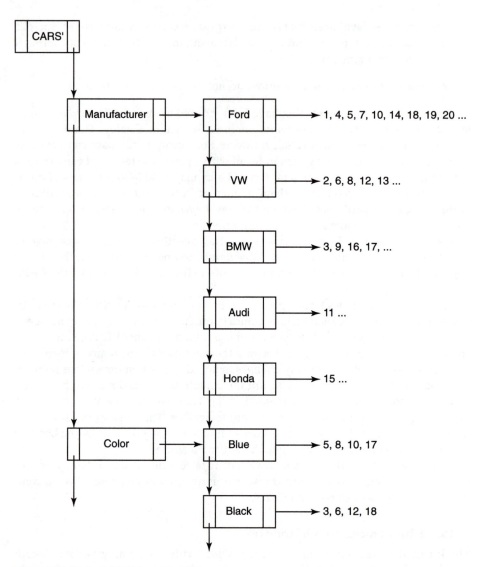

Figure 13.2 • Part of *CARS'*: Inverted *CARS*

we store

Ford: 1, 3, 1, 2, 3, 4, 4, 1, 1

Data compression techniques will probably be effective on such a list because of the skewed distribution of data values; for example, we could store differences using variable-length codes, with shorter codes for the more frequent numbers.

Bit Map

A **bit map** (or **bit vector**), in the context of indexes, is an array of bits with as many elements as there are objects in the container being indexed. Each bit indicates whether the corresponding container object has a particular attribute value. Figure 13.3 shows the (partial) bit maps for the manufacturer attribute of our *CARS'* file.

Sparse bit maps (where there are very few ones) can be stored in a compressed form.

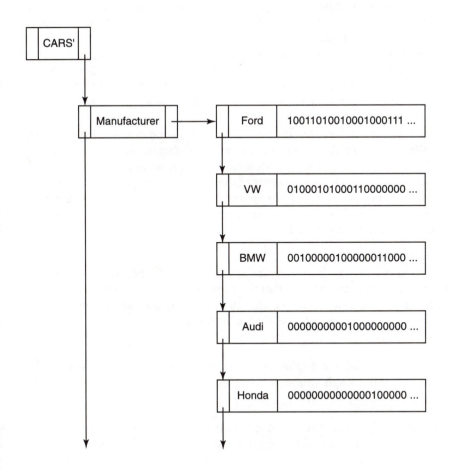

Figure 13.3 • Partial bit maps for *CARS'*

List of Bit Maps

A disadvantage of bit maps is the need to replace the maps by larger maps when the indexed container expands. A solution is to combine bit maps with linked lists; for example, the index entry could point to a linked list of bit maps. Each list element might be 8 bytes long, representing a block of 256 container objects. As the size of the container grows, we add elements to the lists as needed. Each new list element represents another 256 objects. A variation on this idea is to add a field to each list element indicating which section of the container it represents. If a particular container section has no objects with a particular attribute value, there will be no element for it in the corresponding linked list.

Graph Structure

We can save space in a pointer-based index structure if we combine those list elements that point to the same container object. Thus, each container object is represented in the index collection by a single node that is on as many lists as there are indexed attributes. (We therefore have a graph structure.) Figure 13.4 shows a small fragment of the graph structure for our *CARS* file.

A node will have, for each indexed attribute, a pointer to the next node representing a container object with the same value of that attribute. It is convenient if each node also contains a pointer back to the owner of the list, that is, the index entry for the particular attribute value. Figure 13.5 shows the possible contents of a node in general.

Consider how the problem of finding green Fords might be solved using the graph structure. We choose, arbitrarily, one of the two attributes, for example, *manufacturer*. We follow the manufacturer pointers from the first node pointed to by *Ford*. At each node visited, we check the owner of the *color* attribute to see if it is *green*.

Depending on the type of retrieval required, combining the various nodes for a container object into a single node, as in Figure 13.4, may reduce the number of accesses needed to the index structure.

Comparisons Between Bit Maps and Graphs

At first sight, uncompressed bit maps may appear to have higher storage costs than graph structures. However, suppose that the indexed container contains M objects, that P different attributes are indexed, and that the attributes have an average of N different values. The storage required for the bit maps is

$M \times N \times P$ bits

Assuming that we are combining nodes as just described, the storage for the comparable part of the graph structure (M nodes) is

$M \times (2P + 1)$ pointers = $2MP + M$ pointers

Roughly speaking, if the number of different values of an attribute (N) is less than the number of bits required to hold two pointers, then a set of bit maps occu-

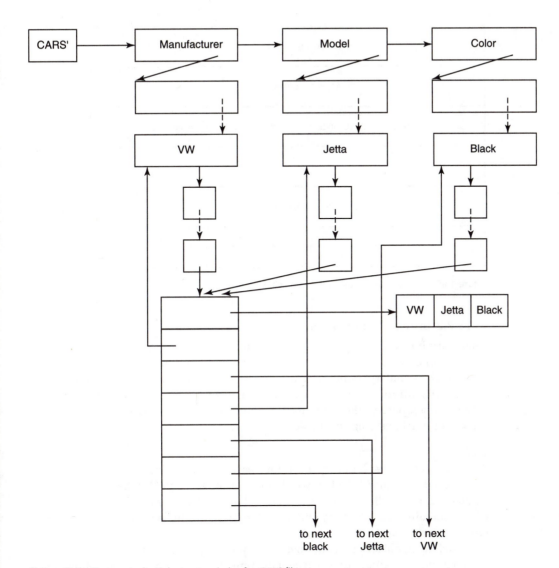

Figure 13.4 • Fragment of graph structure index for *CARS* file

pies less space than the comparable graph structure. A hybrid system might be a preferred compromise; bit maps would be used for attributes with few different values, and lists would be used for attributes with many different values.

The biggest advantage of bit maps is the speed with which simple set operations can be performed on conventional hardware. Most computers have machine-level instructions for performing logical operations on bit patterns. In contrast, list merging is comparatively slow.

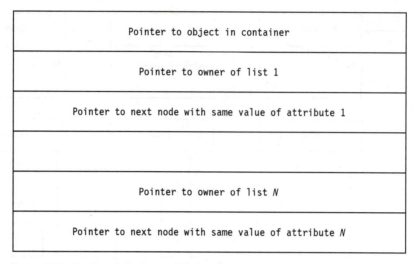

Figure 13.5 • Graph node for inverted file implementation

13.2.2 Index Maintenance

Secondary indexes, like primary indexes, must at all times reflect the contents of the container being indexed. Whereas there is only one primary index, there may be several secondary indexes. Thus, maintenance of correct index entries may become a significant overhead. In this section, we consider how bit maps and graph structures compare in the amount of maintenance required. We also look at some aspects of reliable storage of linked structures.

Updating

An inverted file must be updated in three cases: (1) when we delete an object from the indexed container, (2) when we insert a new object, and (3) when we change the value of an indexed attribute. In the case of an insertion or a deletion, all indexes for the container have to be modified. In the case of a single attribute modification, only one index has to be updated.

To delete an object in a container, we could simply mark it deleted (i.e., a logical deletion). The alternative is to actually remove it (i.e., a physical deletion), making necessary changes to the container structure. Logical deletion is simpler. A disadvantage of physical deletion is that remaining objects may change position in the container and thus require changes in pointers to them. Whatever type of deletion we perform on the container, we must perform the same type on any bit map indexes. However, in the case of a linked list index, we can use either physical or logical deletion on the list. An advantage of physical deletion is the reduction in list length; this makes subsequent traversals shorter.

For some insertions, we may be able to reuse logically "deleted" objects in the container, in which case there is no problem in updating a bit map. However, depending on the implementation, bit maps might be awkward to deal with if the container increases in size. Every bit map would have to be lengthened. Adding objects to a graph structure is, of course, not a problem. However, if the elements of a list are kept in sequence, lengthy traversals may be necessary.

If we change the value of an attribute (e.g., the color of a used car from green to red), the changes in a bit map index are very small. We simply clear the appropriate bit in one list (green) and set it in another (red). If the index is a graph structure, however, we must release the node from one inverted attribute list and add it to another.

Both the insertion of a new object and a change in an attribute value might introduce an attribute value not previously represented in the container. In the case of a bit map, we must create a new map with exactly one bit set; in the case of the graph structure, there will be a new list with exactly one node.

Reliability

Secondary storage tends to be more vulnerable to data corruption than primary storage. Some of the data structures we have described can be rendered useless if a critical pointer is damaged. We might therefore consider methods of making the structures more robust, that is, less likely to be damaged irreparably. A general technique might be to provide two or more paths to any object. A maintenance program can check the integrity of access paths. A damaged path can be detected in a number of ways. For example, an object addressed by a pointer may be missing information identifying it as part of the container. If a damaged path is detected, we can possibly use another route and repair it. This recovery principle suggests that use of a double-linked circular list is preferable to a single-linked list.

Double linking a list need not require additional storage. If we represent a node from a conventional double-linked list as:

where *A* is the pointer to the *previous* node, *B* is the pointer to the *next* node, and *t* is the node data, then the following shows how the two pointers can be combined into one:

f(*A*,*B*) represents some function of *A* and *B* from which each can be recovered given the other. (Exclusive-or is a candidate function.) Arriving at this node from *A* (the address of the *previous* node in the list), we can extract from f(*A*,*B*) the value of *B* (the address of the *next* node to visit). Similarly, we can move from right to left. Thus, double linking is achieved using only one pointer field. In summary, path duplication leads to a more robust list structure and can be achieved with no additional storage.

13.2.3 Simple Query Processing

In Chapter 4, we saw an algorithm that evaluated infixed arithmetic expressions such as

$(A + B) * (C - D * E)$

The algorithm required:

- A mechanism (e.g., a symbol table) to determine the value of an operand
- A mechanism to determine the priority of an operator
- A stack of numbers (operands)
- A stack of operators

We can use essentially the same algorithm to process queries such as

manuf = VW and (color = red and model = bug or color = black and model = jetta)

Our operands in this case are not numbers, but sets of (pointers to) objects being indexed. Consequently, our stack of operands is a stack of sets. We need a mechanism that will take an (attribute,value) pair such as (color, red) and return the appropriate set of pointers.

Our operators are the Boolean *not*, *and*, and *or* with appropriate priorities. Conventionally, the priority of *not* is greater than that of *and*, which in turn is greater than that of *or*. When we apply an operator, we apply the operation to the top one or two sets at the top of the stack. For example, if the operator is *and*, we replace the top two sets by the result of the intersection operation applied to them; if the operator is *or*, the appropriate operation is union. See Chapter 3 for details of set operations. Implementation of the *not* operator may be more complex; see the following section.

If the expression is well formed, then when the evaluation terminates there should be a single set on the stack—the set of (pointers to) objects satisfying the query.

The Not Operator
Consider a query such as

manuf = Ford and not color = black

The effect of applying the unary *not* operator is to replace the set at the top of the stack by its inverse. But this may be impractical. First, if we define the inverse of A as $U - A$, where U is the universal set, it may be difficult to determine what U is. Second, the inverse set may be extremely large. Consider the following two ideas:

1. Every set on the operand stack has a single bit flag that indicates whether it represents itself or its inverse. Now the effect of unary *not* is to change the

value of the flag of the top stack item. We need to generalize the definition of our intersection and union operations to work with "inverted" sets. See Exercises.

2. Eliminate use of the unary *not* and replace it by a new operator *andnot* (or perhaps *butnot*). Thus, our example query becomes

manuf = Ford andnot color = black

Applying an *andnot* operator requires performing a set difference on the top two sets.

13.2.4 Application of Inverted Files

In this section, we look at one way in which full-text retrieval can be accomplished through the use of inverted files. The indexing technique is based on that of IBM's STAIRS (STorage And Information Retrieval System) (IBM 1973).

The following indexing scheme enables users to retrieve documents containing combinations of words with conventional queries such as

Retrieve anti-trust and (Microsoft or AT&T)

In addition, it enables retrievals of documents containing an arbitrary phrase as in

Retrieve "split pea soup"

Furthermore, it supports specialized queries such as

Matrix

|

Dictionary

|

Occurrence file

|

Index

|

Documents

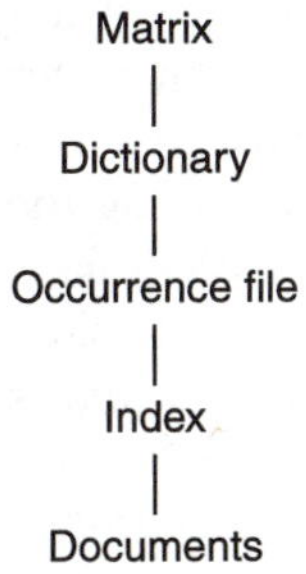

Figure 13.6
File hierarchy

Retrieve Nixon w/s Watergate	[*Nixon* and *Watergate* in the same sentence]
Retrieve Lakers w/3 victory	[*Lakers* within three words of *victory*]
Retrieve graph pre/3 structure	[*graph* in the three words preceding *structure*]
Retrieve/abstract fusion	[documents where *fusion* is in the abstract]

In contrast with many document retrieval systems, STAIRS indexes every word occurrence in the text. Most document retrieval systems index a few selected key words or discard those words found on a "stop list" of common words such as *and*, *of*, *the*, and *if*. STAIRS can thus be classified as a full-text document retrieval system.[3] In this section, we give a brief description of the file structures that enable queries such as those just listed to be answered. The five levels of data structures/files are depicted in Figure 13.6.

Documents

The lowest level in the structure, the *Documents* file (or files), contains the machine-readable documents. The only additions required to the text of a document are tags for each paragraph such as TITLE, TEXT, ABSTRACT, and so on. In addition, the document contains end-of-sentence codes that the system can recognize.

Index

The index has one entry for each document. The entry contains information such as a pointer to the document, protection codes (who is allowed to access the document), and the date of entry to the system. The three file levels above the index can thus refer to a document by a unique number: the position of its entry in the index.

Occurrence File

The occurrence file contains one record for each word occurrence in the document collection. The information recorded for each word occurrence is:

Document number	Paragraph code	Sentence number	Position in sentence

The entries in the occurrence file are ordered so that all records for a particular word are contiguous. Within this grouping, records are sorted in the order of the four fields just shown. As you can imagine, this is a large file.

Dictionary

The dictionary contains an entry for each different word in the document collection (including such common words as *the*, *of*, and *in*). Summary information, such as the number of times the word occurs and the number of different documents in which it occurs, is stored together with the word.

Matrix

Large dictionaries in book form usually have a thumb index, which enables a user to find an alphabetical section rapidly. The matrix takes this one step further. It has 26*27 entries, each of which identifies the start of a section of the dictionary for words beginning with a particular pair of letters. (The 27th entry is a space character, thus allowing one-letter words to be indexed.) A consequence of having the matrix is that there is no need to store the first two letters of words in the dictionary.

Figure 13.7 depicts fragments of the top three levels of an example file collection.

We assume in Figure 13.7 that the first dictionary word beginning with *ma* is located at record 2341 in the dictionary. Hence, the *ma* entry in the matrix is 2341. Looking at record 2341 in the dictionary fragment, we see that the word is *macabre*. Only the tail of the word (*cabre*) is stored here in the first field of the dictionary record.

The other fields of record 2341 indicate that the word *macabre* occurs in one document a total of six times, and that the first occurrence record for the word is at position 4987 in the occurrence file. Similarly, the word *(ma)inframe* is found a total of 109 times in 20 documents; the occurrence records for the 109 occurrences start at record number 12,131 in the occurrence file.

Looking at the occurrence file, we see that the first occurrence of *mainframe* is the 7th word of the 14th sentence of document two in a text paragraph. The last occurrence is word eight of the seventh sentence of document 89 (also in a text

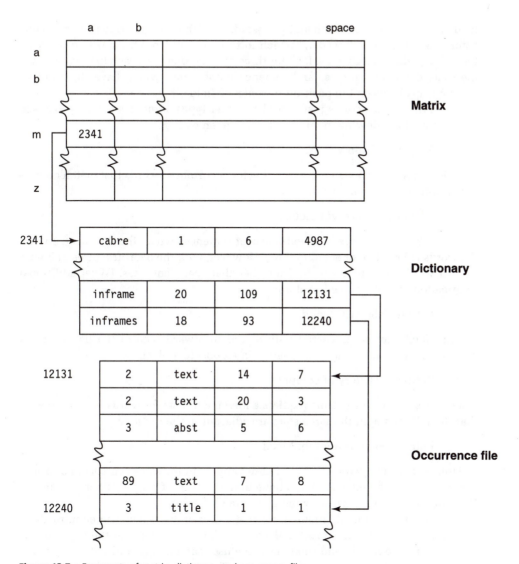

Figure 13.7 • Fragments of matrix, dictionary, and occurrence files

paragraph). To merge occurrence lists efficiently, occurrence records are ordered by position-in-sentence within sentence number within document number.

Answering Queries
Using the indexes exemplified by Figure 13.7, how do we find all documents containing a particular phrase? Consider, for instance, the phrase "fast breeder reactor." We perform a three-way merge on the occurrence lists of the three words. We wish

to identify sentences in which all three words occur and the position of "fast" is one before the position of "breeder," which in turn is one before the position of "reactor." Thus, when merging, we look for three records, one from each list, which have the same document number and sentence number and which have the required relationships between the position-in-sentence fields.

Given the file structures just described, other types of queries can be processed efficiently. The following include examples given earlier.

1.   Retrieve Nixon w/s Watergate

This requires a two-way merge looking for occurrence records that match on document number and sentence number.

2.   Retrieve Lakers w/3 victory

In this two-way merge, we would accept sentences where the distance between the words is less than or equal to three. However, with the data structures of Figure 13.7, it would be difficult to find matches that span sentences. (What additional information would we need to store?)

3.   Retrieve/abstract fusion

This query can be processed with a straightforward scan of the list of occurrences of *fusion* looking for occurrences in an *abst* text block.

4.   Retrieve "History of comput*"

Occurrences of word stems requires a merging of lists for words beginning with that stem. Words with the same stem are adjacent in the dictionary.

5.   Retrieve Fatigue and not Metal

Users can specify words that should not appear in the same sentence. For example, a user could be interested in fatigue in the context of people rather than metal. Extension to the usual two-way merge is straightforward.

An advantage of the file hierarchy is that a user of the system can enquire about the vocabulary of the document collection without going beyond the top two levels. By using the matrix and dictionary, the user can quickly find out how often a word occurs and in how many documents. The user may then wish to refine the search terms to provide more or less output. In response to a query, the system can report the number of documents satisfying it, taking into account protection codes, without having to go to the documents themselves.

13.2.5 Weaknesses of Inverted Files

Inverted files are a good way of answering many types of multiterm queries that are Boolean expressions involving equality operators, such as:

find Major = English and Age = 21 and GPA = 4.0
find (Color = Green or Color = Blue) and Make = Ford and Year = 1996

However, consider a query such as:

find Age > 20 and GPA < 2.0

If we have only the inverted files to work with, we would have to merge many sets to get the desired set of objects. In addition, if the container being indexed has many indexed attributes and is volatile, a large overhead may be incurred when we insert and delete objects because we have to make changes to the indexes. Grid files have been proposed as an alternative way of answering multiterm queries. We consider grid files next.

13.3 Grid Files

Nievergelt, Hinterberger, and Sevcik (1984) describe a secondary key accessing technique using grids that performs well on both stable and volatile files. We give an overview here and consider implementation issues in Section 13.3.3. See the original source for more details.

The design aims of the grid file organization are fourfold:

1. Point queries: A **point query** is a query in which a value is supplied for each key attribute. An example for the *CARS* collection in Figure 13.1 is:

   find Manufacturer = VW, Model = Jetta, Color = Black, License = 1GWN821

   It is denoted a point query because by specifying a value of each attribute, it identifies a single point in the multidimensional attribute space. The response to such a query is simply an indication of whether the specified object exists in the collection. The first design aim is that the processing of a point query be efficient, specifically, that no more than two accesses to secondary storage would be required to answer such a query.

2. Range queries: The second design aim is that processing of range queries and partially specified queries should be efficient. Two examples of such queries are:

   find Manufacturer = VW, Model = Bug, D < license < X
   find Manufacturer = Ford, Color = Green

3. Dynamic adaptation: The third design aim is that the data structure should adapt smoothly to insertions and deletions.

4. Symmetry: The final design aim is that all key fields, whether primary or secondary, should be treated equally. (Compare this with the inverted file organization, in which the location of an object typically depends on the primary key only.)

It is possible to devise a data structure that meets the four design aims. Suppose that our objects have k attributes (in the case of the *CARS* file, $k = 4$). Consider the

k-dimensional space defined by the k sets of possible values for these attributes. Extending the concept of a bit map, we can conceive of a k-dimensional bit matrix. Dimension i of this matrix has as many elements as attribute i has different values. If a particular element of the k-dimensional matrix is set to one, this indicates that an object exists with the corresponding set of k attribute values. If the bit is zero, then no such object exists. Note that the matrix of bits is therefore a complete representation of the collection of objects.

Although we have not specified how it might be stored, this data structure is likely to satisfy the four design aims: Processing point queries involves examination of a single matrix element (surely possible with two or fewer disk accesses); processing range queries involves processing all elements in a particular j-dimensional matrix ($j \leq k$); insertions and deletions are carried out by setting and clearing appropriate single elements of the matrix; and all dimensions of the matrix are treated equally.

The k-dimensional matrix, however, is a proof-of-concept rather than a practical data structure. In practice, the matrix is likely to require too much storage. For example, if the objects in our collection have five attributes and each attribute has 1000 possible values, the matrix will have 10^{15} elements. Even with 1 bit per element, that is still 125 terabytes for a very modest object specification. The grid file organization that we discuss next can be regarded as an approximation of the matrix.

13.3.1 The Grid File Concept

In the grid file structure, the size of the matrix is reduced by imposing a grid on the k-dimensional space. (This also eliminates some of the problems of mapping attributes such as names and colors onto indices.) Each of the k dimensions may be partitioned. For example, we could partition a GPA attribute (range 0.00 to 4.00) at 1.5, 2.5, and 3.2. Thus, a GPA of 2.7 falls into the third partition. The partition points are held in **linear scales**, one for each dimension.

However, by superimposing the grid, we have lost the one-to-one correspondence between matrix elements and potential objects. Each element of the **grid array**, instead of representing a single potential object, now represents many potential objects. Instead of each element being a single bit, it is a pointer to a bucket in which objects with appropriate field values will be held. Thus, the grid file has three components: *linear scales*, *grid array*, and *file of buckets*. The linear scales can be held in memory while the file is open; however, the grid array will typically be too large to hold completely in memory.

Figure 13.8 depicts a typical grid file. In order to keep multidimensional diagrams legible, we will use just two dimensions in our example. We assume that objects have just two attributes: student ID number and GPA. Our initial file contains seven such objects.

The linear scales show the value(s) at which each dimension is partitioned. There is one partition point on the GPA axis and two on the ID number axis; thus, we have a two-by-three grid array.

Linear scales: GPA: 2.70
                                  ID number: 7900000 , 8200000

Grid array   2.70

	1	4
7900000		
	3	3
8200000		
	2	5

File of buckets

Bucket #	Record count					Ref. count
1	1	742-1111	2.56			1
2	1	854-1234	2.34			1
3	2	801-1111	2.95	812-2222	2.30	2
4	2	764-1234	2.90	784-4321	3.10	1
5	1	832-9999	3.20			1

Figure 13.8 • Typical grid file

Each element of the grid array points to a bucket. If multiple pointers lead to a particular bucket, they must form a k-dimensional rectangle within the grid array; no L-shaped regions are permitted, for example. The bucket pointed to by an array element is the only bucket in the file where objects with the corresponding attribute values are stored. For example, in the file in Figure 13.8, the object representing a student with GPA < 2.70 and ID number > 8200000 can only be in bucket 2.

For convenience, a bucket contains both a count of the number of records it contains and a count of the number of pointers (references) to it. The reason for the latter will become clearer later when we consider insertions and deletions.

Does this approximation to the bit matrix satisfy the four design aims?

The First Design Aim
A point query should be answerable in no more than two accesses to secondary storage. Consider the query

Does student with ID number 8149876 have GPA = 2.54?

We are asking if there exists an object with ID number 8149876 and GPA 2.54. We first map each of the two attribute values onto partitions using the linear scales. In our example, 8149876 maps onto the second partition in the *ID number* dimension and 2.54 maps to the first partition in the *GPA* dimension. Thus, assuming that dimensions are indexed from zero upwards, the appropriate element of the grid array is element [1][0]. Now we access this element.[4] Given the sizes of the dimensions of the array, we can compute the position of an arbitrary element and, if necessary, fetch it from a disk file containing the array. A second disk access uses the pointer found in the array element and retrieves bucket 3. This is the only bucket we need to fetch. Thus, no matter how large the file or how many attributes objects have or how many objects there are in the file, we can retrieve a particular object in no more than two accesses. The first design aim is satisfied.

The Second Design Aim

It should be possible to process range and partially specified queries efficiently. Such queries typically involve processing a *j*-dimensional rectangle of the grid array ($j \leq k$). Consider the following query:

gpa > 3.0 and 769-999 < id number < 850-0000

We first map the constants in the query onto partitions using the linear scales. (It is worth noting that the constants in a query are unlikely to coincide with the partition points.) This defines what we might term the "query space." A strategy now is to form two sets of buckets:

1. The first set consists of those buckets where, for each bucket, all the pointers to that bucket are from grid array elements that fall entirely within the query space. Objects in these buckets must satisfy the query; we do not need to check them one by one.
2. The second set consists of those buckets where, for each bucket, there is at least one pointer from a region of the grid array that is partly inside the query space and partly outside. Objects in these buckets have to be checked one by one against the query.

The two sets can be formed by scanning rectangular areas of the grid array. Processing range and partial queries is still efficient. For more details see Section 13.3.3.

The Third Design Aim

The organization should adapt smoothly to insertions and deletions. To see if this aim has been achieved, we consider insertion and deletion techniques in the next section.

The Fourth Design Aim

All fields should be treated equally. The grid file treats all fields equally; the organization is symmetric.

13.3.2 Insertions and Deletions

Let us see how objects are inserted into and removed from a grid file.

Insertion Algorithm

The insertion algorithm begins by locating the appropriate bucket for the object to be inserted. This is done in the same way that point queries are processed. When the bucket is accessed, one of three cases may arise. (You may notice that this is similar to extendible hashing, discussed in Chapter 11.)

Case 1   The bucket has room for the new object. We insert the object and update the count of objects in the bucket. The grid array does not change.

Case 2   The bucket we wish to insert into is full but there is more than one pointer to it. For this to be the case, then, on at least one dimension, at least two adjacent grid array elements must point to this bucket (because the region pointing to the bucket must be rectangular). Therefore, on at least one dimension we can split the group of pointers to the bucket approximately in half. We add a bucket to the file and reassign about half the pointers from the old bucket to the new bucket in such a way that both buckets are pointed to by *k*-dimensional rectangles. Reference counts in the two buckets are set appropriately. The new object and the ones in the overflowing bucket are placed in the appropriate buckets. We could accomplish this dispersal by putting the object causing the overflow and the contents of the old bucket on a reinsert list. In Case 2 we change the contents but not the shape of the grid array.

Case 3   The bucket we wish to insert into is full, and there is only one pointer to it from the grid array. We need to refine the grid. This involves adding a new grid line running through the array element that points to the overflowing bucket. We need to determine which dimension to refine and the value of the new partition point. We could choose dimensions in a cyclic manner, skipping those dimensions in which the linear scale has reached its maximum length (if there is such a thing). When we refine the appropriate interval in the chosen dimension we could (a) bisect it or (b) choose as the partition point the value that will divide the objects to be reinserted as near equally as possible. If we choose option a, we may find that all the objects fall on one side of the line and a further refinement is necessary. In the case of the first (last) partition in a dimension, we may have to choose option b anyway unless some lower (upper) bound is known for attribute values. As a result of the grid refinement, the grid array gets larger, the mapping of the grid array changes, certain pointers will be duplicated, and reference counts will change.

After grid refinement, we have multiple pointers to the overflowing bucket and complete the insertion as in Case 2. In Case 3 we change both the shape and the contents of the grid array.

Here is a pseudocode algorithm for inserting an object into a grid file.

```
while (more objects to insert into file)
{
 Get an object
 Map attributes of the object to indices using linear scales
 Look up grid array entry
 Fetch bucket
 if (count_of_objects_in_bucket < bucketmax)
    {
      // Case 1
      Insert object in bucket
      Increment count for bucket
    }
    else {
           // bucket overflow
           Allocate new bucket to bucket file

           // see if we need to refine grid
           if (bucket to insert into has 2 or more pointers to it)
                  {
                   // No - Case 2
                   Pick one of the dimensions with adjacent
                     intervals pointing to the bucket
                   Assign approximately half the rectangle of pointers
                     to the new bucket
                  }
              else
                  {
                   // Yes - Case 3
                   Choose a dimension
                   Divide interval of this dimension that points to bucket
                   Update linear scale
                   Expand grid array and write/copy elements as appropriate
                  }

           Add old bucket contents to list of objects to be inserted
             into the file
           Clear old bucket
          }
    Put bucket back in file
}
```

Initial Grid File
What does an initial grid file look like? One possibility for the initial grid file is to assume nothing about the distribution of attribute values and to start with empty linear scales, a single element grid array, and a single (empty) bucket. Alternatively, we could examine the attributes of the objects to be put into the file and determine points at which attribute values could be partitioned. The dimensions of the initial grid array and the number of initial buckets then follow easily.

Example Insertion Sequence
Consider the insertion into the file from Figure 13.8 of objects with (ID number, GPA) values of:

    (830-1234, 2.40)
    (814-9999, 3.00)
    (782-1111, 2.85)

Insert (830-1234, 2.40)   This object maps to element [2][0] of the grid array, which points to bucket 2. There is room in this bucket for the object. The new file is shown in Figure 13.9.

Insert (814-9999, 3.00)   This object maps to element [1][1] of the grid array, which points to bucket 3. The bucket is full, but the reference count indicates that it is pointed to by more than one element of the grid array. We allocate a new bucket to the file and divide into two groups the pointers that point to the old one. We distribute the objects according to the existing partition. Figure 13.10 shows the new file.

Insert (782-1111, 2.85)   This object maps to element [0][1] of the grid array, which points to bucket 4. The bucket is full, and the reference count indicates that it is pointed to by only one element of the grid array. We refine the grid. We will partition the GPA attribute and select 3.00 as the new partition point based on the objects to be reinserted. Figure 13.11 shows the new file.

Deletion Algorithm
Having deleted an object from a bucket, we may be able to reduce the number of buckets in the file by combining two into one. (Any buckets freed in this way are added to a free list.) Recall that the section of the grid array that points to a particular bucket must be rectangular. Thus, if the objects pointed to by a $(k-1)$-dimensional rectangle of the grid array can all be stored in a single bucket, then we can do so and make all pointers in the rectangle point to that bucket. This is the reverse of a Case 2 insertion.

If a $(k-1)$-dimensional plane is duplicated adjacently, we can remove a partition point from the appropriate linear scale and collapse the array by one in that dimension. This is the reverse of a Case 3 insertion.

Linear scales: GPA: 2.70
                          ID number: 7900000 , 8200000

Grid array   2.70

	1	4
7900000	3	3
8200000	2	5

File of buckets

Bucket #	Record count					Ref. count
1	1	742-1111	2.56			1
2	2	854-1234	2.34	830-1234	2.40	1
3	2	801-1111	2.95	812-2222	2.30	2
4	2	764-1234	2.90	784-4321	3.10	1
5	1	832-9999	3.20			1

Figure 13.9 • Grid file of Figure 13.8 after insertion of (830-1234, 2.40)

Linear scales: GPA: 2.70
                          ID number: 7900000 , 8200000

Grid array   2.70

	1	4
7900000	3	6
8200000	2	5

File of buckets

Bucket #	Record count					Ref. count
1	1	742-1111	2.56			1
2	2	854-1234	2.34	830-1234	2.40	1
3	1	812-2222	2.30			1
4	2	764-1234	2.90	784-4321	3.10	1
5	1	832-9999	3.20			1
6	2	801-1111	2.95	814-9999	3.00	1

Figure 13.10 • Grid file of Figure 13.9 after insertion of (814-9999, 3.00)

Linear scales: GPA: 2.70 , 3.00
ID number: 7900000 , 8200000

Grid array   2.70 3.00

	2.70	3.00	
7900000	1	4	7
	3	6	6
8200000	2	5	5

File of buckets

Bucket #	Record count					Ref. count
1	1	742-1111	2.56			1
2	2	854-1234	2.34	830-1234	2.40	1
3	1	812-2222	2.30			1
4	2	764-1234	2.90	784-4321	2.85	1
5	1	832-9999	3.20			2
6	2	801-1111	2.95	814-9999	3.00	2
7	1	784-4321	3.10			1

Figure 13.11 • Grid file of Figure 13.10 after insertion of (782-1111, 2.85)

However, we may not wish to pack objects into the fewest possible number of buckets because this may increase the probability of having to split them again later on (c.f., B-trees). In addition, finding the best possible merge by scanning rectangles in the grid array is likely to be time-consuming, particularly if the grid array is held in secondary memory. Hence, we may just restrict ourselves to combining at most two buckets as the result of a deletion. One of these will clearly be the bucket from which we have just removed an object. How do we select the other (if any)?

Many possible selection strategies exist. Complex ones may require many fetches of grid blocks to look at object counts in buckets (perhaps this would be a reason to store those counts in the grid array itself). The strategy we choose may depend on how critical space is and how file size is expected to change. The following is a very simple strategy. If the bucket from which we just deleted an object has only one pointer to it and a neighbor in any of the *k*-dimensions also has only one pointer to it and can be combined with the current one, we do so.

Here is a pseudocode algorithm for this simple deletion strategy.

```
Map attributes of the object to indices using linear scales
Look up grid array entry
Fetch bucket
Remove object from bucket
newsize = new bucket size
Put bucket back in file

If (bucket has only 1 pointer to it)
   {
     dimension_index = 1
     stop = false
     repeat {
              if (bucket pointed to by grid array neighbor
                 in dimension dimension_index has only 1
                          pointer
                 and (size(neighbor) + newsize) <= bucketmax
                )
                {
                  copy neighbor contents to bucket
                  adjust object count
                  adjust reference count
                  adjust pointers
                  deallocate neighbor to free list.
                  stop = true
                }
              else dimension_index = dimension_index + 1
          }
     until (stop or dimension_index > k)
   }
```

Based on the discussion here and in the previous section, grid files may be considered to adapt smoothly to insertions and deletions (design aim 3).

13.3.3 Grid File Implementation

In this section, we give details of some of the techniques that might be used in grid file implementation and in the insertion, deletion, and retrieval algorithms. Some of the algorithms were devised for an implementation of a three-dimensional grid. They should be easily generalizable to k dimensions.

Mapping the Grid Array onto a File
We assume for generality that the grid array is so large that it must be stored in a file. When accessing or updating the grid array, we need to be able to find the loca-

tion of an arbitrary element in a single access to the file and also deal with refinements of the grid in which a partition splits, causing the array to grow. We will consider three-dimensional arrays here.

Given array *Size* ($Size_1$ . . . $Size_3$) holding the sizes of the three dimensions and assuming:

- That each dimension is indexed from zero upwards
- That the grid array is stored in row-major order (i.e., 000, 001, 002, etc.)
- That the first record in the grid array file is numbered zero

then the number of the record holding $GridArray_{pqr}$ is returned by a call to function *indextoposition*, defined as follows:

```
int indextoposition(int p, int q, int r, int Size[])
    {
            return  ( p * Size[2] * Size[3])
                  + ( q * Size[3])
                  +   r
    }
```

We may need the inverse mapping; that is, we may need to determine which element of the grid array is mapped onto file record *Pos*. The three indices are assigned by a call to the function *positiontoindex*, defined as follows:

```
void positiontoindex(int Pos, int& p, int& q, int& r, int Size[])
    {
      p = (Pos / (Size[2] * Size[3]));
      Pos = Pos - ( p * Size[2]*Size[3]);
      q = Pos / Size[3];
      r = Pos - q * Size[3];
    }
```

Case 2 Insertions

Questions: If a bucket pointed to by $GridArray_{pqr}$ overflows, and we know from the reference counter that the bucket is pointed to by more than one element of the grid array,

1. How do we find the elements of the array that point to it?
2. How do we change the array so that half the pointers point to the old bucket and half to a new one?

Answer: Two algorithms can be devised to solve these problems.

1. We scan backwards and forwards in each of the k dimensions starting at the location that we know points to the bucket. We know that the section of the grid

array pointing to a bucket is a *k*-dimensional rectangle, so by means of this scan we find the bounds of the rectangle.

The following function *scandown* returns the lower bound (in dimension *dimension_index*) of the rectangle of pointers to bucket *bucketid* given the *start* index. We assume function *get* retrieves a record from the grid array file.

```
int scandown (int dimension_index, int start, int bucketid)
{
  int  ptr=start, entry;
  bool stop=false;

      do { ptr--;
          if (ptr < 0)
                stop = true;
          else switch (dimension_index)
                {
                  case 1: entry=get(gridarray,indextoposition(ptr,j,k,Size));
                          break;
                  case 2 : entry=get(gridarray,indextoposition(i,ptr,k,Size));
                          break;
                  case 3 : entry=get(gridarray,indextoposition(i,j,ptr,Size));
                }
         } while (stop == false && entry == bucketid);

      return ptr + 1;
  }
```

Suppose, for instance, that bucket X is overflowing and that we accessed bucket X via $GridArray_{pqr}$. We then find lower bounds *mini*, *minj*, and *mink* on the rectangle of pointers to X as follows:

```
mini = scandown(1,p,X);
minj = scandown(2,q,X);
mink = scandown(3,r,X);
```

We can define a similar function *scanup* and find upper bounds on the rectangle as follows:

```
maxi = scanup(1,p,X);
maxj = scanup(2,q,X);
maxk = scanup(3,r,X);
```

Note that the last call is redundant because given $2k - 1$ index values, we can compute the value of the remaining one because of the reference count in the bucket that tells us the total number of elements that point to the bucket.

2. We can divide the rectangle of pointers by using an existing partition point in exactly one of the dimensions that has more than one index in the rectangle. For example, we might test as follows:

```
if (maxi – mini) >0
        {
          // can divide pointers along this dimension
          int divisioni = (maxi+mini)/2
          for all j
          for all k
              for i from mini to divisioni
                  {
                          gridarray[i][j][k] = new value
                          update counters and so on
                  }
        }
else if (maxj – minj) > 0  ...   and so on
```

Case 3 Insertions

The following is an example of a Case 3 insertion (where the grid is refined) that shows how the grid array is modified. We use a two-dimensional example for clarity. Figure 13.12 shows the array (both conceptual and file representations). Suppose that bucket 5 is overflowing and that we refine the grid along the "x" (horizontal) axis as shown.

Further assume that bucket 9 is the next one allocated to the file. Figure 13.13 shows how the grid array may change (5 and 9 could be interchanged) and its corresponding implementation in the grid array file.

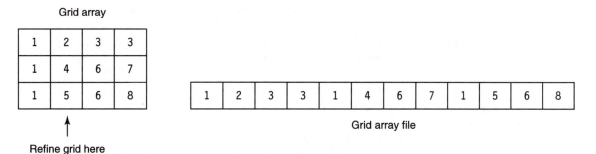

Figure 13.12 • Grid array before grid refinement

Grid array

1	2	2	3	3
1	4	4	6	7
1	5	9	6	8

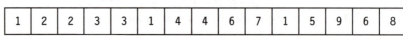

Grid array file

Figure 13.13 • Grid array after grid refinement

Here is an algorithm for updating the file that holds the grid array as required by a Case 3 insertion. We assume that *put(gridarray,I,J)* puts value *J* at record number *I* in the grid array file.

```
/*
    dimension_index - the dimension to be refined
    splitinterval - within the dimension, the interval to be duplicated
    otherd1, otherd2 - the indexes, in the non-split dimensions, of
                        the new value to be put in the array
    newbuck - the new value in the array (pointer to new bucket)
    Size - array holding size of dimensions of the (expanded) grid array
    Oldsize - array holding size of dimensions of the (old) grid array
    old, new — temporary indexes to the file of buckets
*/
    // remember old dimensions
    Oldsize = Size;
    Size[dimension_index]++;

    // extend file
    append product(size)-product(oldsize) records

    // copy elements to new positions duplicating the plane
    for (int i=Size[1]-1; i ≥ 0; i--)
    for (int j=Size[2]-1; j ≥ 0; j--)
    for (int k=Size[3]-1; k ≥ 0; k--)
      {
        new = indextoposition (i,j,k,Size);
        switch (dimension_index)
          {
          case 1: if (i <= splitinterval)
                        old = indextoposition (i,j,k,Oldsize);
                    else old = indextoposition (i-1,j,k,Oldsize);
```

```
                          break;
            case 2: if (j <= splitinterval)
                        old = indextoposition (i,j,k,Oldsize);
                    else old = indextoposition (i,j-1,k,Oldsize);
                    break;
            case 3: if (k <= splitinterval)
                        old = indextoposition (i,j,k,Oldsize);
                    else old = indextoposition (i,j,k-1,Oldsize);
        }
     if (old != new)
        { // copy element from position old to position new
          temp = get(gridarray,old);
          put(gridarray,new,temp);
        }
  }
// now put new value into an array element
switch(dimension_index)
  {
    case 1:newplace = indextoposition(splitinterval,otherd1,otherd2,Size);
             break;
    case 2:newplace = indextoposition(otherd1,splitinterval,otherd2,Size);
             break;
    case 3:newplace = indextoposition(otherd1,otherd2,splitinterval,Size);
  }
put(gridarray,newplace,newbuck);
```

Reference Counts

We need to know the number of grid array elements that point to an arbitrary bucket. It seems sensible, for consistency and space reasons, to keep this count in the bucket itself. How is this count changed by insert operations?

In a Case 2 insertion, the k-dimensional rectangle of pointers is partitioned into two k-dimensional rectangles. As this is done, a count is kept of the number of pointers to the new bucket. This count is the reference count for the new bucket and is subtracted from the reference count in the old bucket.

In a Case 3 insertion, the grid is refined (see previous section). We can modify the algorithm that duplicates a $(k-1)$-dimensional plane so that it keeps a list of the numbers of the buckets that have increased counts. The modification is to the elements of the *switch* statement, for example:

```
case 1: if (i ≤ splitinterval)
        {
             old = indextoposition (i,j,k,Oldsize);
             if (i == splitinterval)
```

```
            {
                temp = get(gridarray,old);
                addtolist(temp);
            }
        else old = indextoposition (i-1,j,k,Oldsize);
    }
```

Before inserting the new bucket number into an element of the grid array, delete the value found in that element from the list. For efficiency, sort the resulting list and compress N instances of b to a pair (N,b). Traverse the list and for each (N,b) pair add N to the reference count of bucket b.

Retrievals from a Grid File

Earlier, we saw that one reason for using a grid file instead of inverted files was because the latter are not very good for processing range queries. Here we present a method for answering range queries from a grid file.

The first step is to determine the appropriate region of the grid array based on the query. Then the corresponding buckets can be retrieved. Query processing is more or less complex depending on the power of the query language. In what follows, we will assume a simple language in which all queries define a k-dimensional rectangle (query space) within the attribute space.

For each dimension, there will be four indexes of interest (A,B,C,D). Roughly speaking, A is the smallest index we need to consider and D is the largest; there may be a subrange $B \ldots C$ within $A \ldots D$. If a query constant coincides with a partition point in a particular dimension, then D will be one greater than what at first sight seems to be necessary. Unless we are at the end of a dimension, B will be $A + 1$ and C will be $D - 1$.

For example, suppose we have a numeric attribute with eight partition points dividing the dimension into nine regions, as shown in Figure 13.14.

Here are examples of queries and the corresponding values of A, B, C, and D.

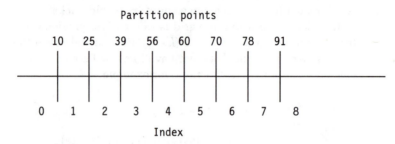

Figure 13.14 • Partition points and indexes

```
Query                                          A   B   C   D

attribute > 30 & attribute < 78                2   3   6   7
attribute > 62                                 4   5   8   8
attribute < 66                                 0   0   4   5
attribute > 24 & attribute < 65                1   2   4   5
attribute = 57                                 3   4   4   5
```

Query Processing   Assume we have a simple query language in which typical terms are:

gpa < 2.9

major = *   (* = "don't care")

For each term we:

1. Initialize search parameters.
2. Set up parameters for the array scan (based on the query term).
3. Scan (using search parameters) and set up sets of bucket addresses.
4. Search some or all of the buckets using the query term as necessary.

Initialization   The initialization in the three-dimensional case is:

```
iA = iB = 0;   iC = iD = Size[1]-1
jA = jB = 0;   jC = jD = Size[2]-1
kA = kB = 0;   kC = kD = Size[3]-1
```

This initialization means that if a query does not mention a particular dimension, we scan over the entire range of that dimension.

Setting Search Parameters   We assume that legal query specifications for a given attribute are sensible combinations of the following five constructions:

1. Nothing specified: No change is made to search parameters.
2. * (wild card): No change is made to the search parameters.
3. = *value:* Using the linear scale, set B and C search parameters equal to the appropriate index; set A to $\max(B - 1,1)$ and D to $\min(C + 1, Size[dimension] - 1)$.
4. < *value:* Affects C and D parameters. If *value* is the upper bound of a partition, set C to the index of the partition and D to $\min(C + 1, Size[dimension] - 1)$. Otherwise, set D to the index of the partition and C to $\max(D - 1,1)$.
5. > *value:* Affects A and B parameters. If *value* is the lower bound of a partition, then set B to the index of the partition and A to $\max(B - 1,1)$. Otherwise, set A to the index of the partition and B to $\min(A + 1, Size[dimension] - 1)$.

Here are three example queries illustrating the constructions; the second and third are equivalent.

gpa = 2.00, id number > 792, id number < 795-0000
gpa > 3.95, id number = *
gpa > 3.95

Scan and Set up Bucket Addresses   When we scan the grid array, we first form two sets of bucket addresses. One set (*ASET*) contains the numbers of those buckets in which all objects are known to satisfy the query. The second set (*BSET*) contains addresses of buckets in which the contents have to be checked object by object because some objects may not satisfy the query. Then we use the sets to process the buckets. Using sets, rather than lists, for example, ensures that we do not fetch the same bucket more than once, even if there are multiple array pointers to it. Here is an algorithm for creating the two sets of bucket addresses:

```
set<int> ASET, BSET;

for (int i = iA; i <= iD; i++)
for (int j = jA; j <= jD; j++)
for (int k = kA; k <= kD; k++)
 {
    temp = get (gridarray,indextoposition(i,j,k,size))
    if      ( i >= iB ) && ( i <= iC )
       and ( j >= jB ) && ( j <= jC )
       and ( k >= kB ) && ( k <= kC )
          add_to_set(ASET,temp);
    else add_to_set(BSET,temp);
 }

ASET = ASET - BSET;
```

To see how this works, consider Figure 13.15, which shows a fragment of a two-dimensional grid array and some of the bucket numbers it contains and, superimposed, the query space derived from the query:

$73 < X \le 113$ and $1750 < Y < 2390$

Dashed lines represent the boundaries of the query space where they differ from grid lines.

After the triple-nested loop, *ASET* is [9 10 20] (these are the buckets pointed to from the four grid array elements that are entirely within the query space), and *BSET* is [6 7 8 10 12 13 18 20] (these are the buckets pointed to from array elements on the fringe of the query space). After the set difference operation, *ASET* becomes [9]; this

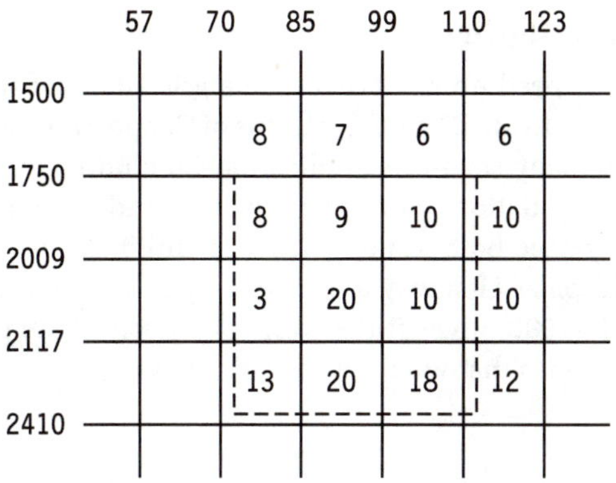

Figure 13.15 • Partial grid and query space

is the only bucket that has all its pointers entirely within the query space, and hence the only one containing objects that we do not need to check against the query.

Process Bucket Contents   Finally, we process the bucket contents.

```
for (i in ASET)
   { get (bucketfile,i);
     return all objects in the bucket;
   }
for (i in BSET)
   { get (bucketfile,i);
     return those objects satisfying the query;
   }
```

A Better Term-Processing Algorithm   This algorithm works but may fetch unnecessary buckets—bucket 7, for example. A better approach might make two changes. First, change the bounds so that if a query constant coincides with a partition point, we do not go one element beyond. Second, make *ASET* a list (*ALIST*). Having formed *ALIST*, compare the reference counts of those buckets with the number of times it appears in the list. If they are the same, then there is no need to check the bucket contents because we have found the only pointer(s) to the bucket; otherwise, they must be checked, because somewhere outside the query space there is another pointer. Applying this revised algorithm to the example above results in:

ALIST: 9 10 10 20

BSET: [8 10 3 13 18 20 12]

The reference counts for the buckets in *ALIST* are 9:1, 10:4, 20:2. Thus, 10 and 20 are removed from *ALIST* and added to *BSET* if they are not already members.

13.3.4 Data Declustering

It may be possible to speed up retrievals from a grid file by distributing buckets over multiple disks. (Recall the RAID configurations of Chapter 8.) Large, multidimensional data sets are used in many scientific applications, including long-term measurements of the atmosphere, simulations of airplane wakes, and geographic information systems. Users typically need both fast responses to multidimensional range queries and efficient use of disk space. One way to reduce response time is to maximize disk parallelism. Moon et al. (1996) investigated various aspects of the problem in an attempt to identify good strategies that would work for data sets of any size.

Declustering

Declustering is a technique that stores different grid file buckets on different disks so that they may be retrieved in parallel. We need a declustering algorithm that determines the disk on which the bucket pointed to from $GridArray[i_1][i_2]\ldots[i_k]$ is to be stored. The algorithm should make use of all the k indices. Given that a particular bucket can be pointed to from more than one grid array element, we also need a means to choose between two or more candidate disks (see *Tie-Breaking* later in this section).

Three possible declustering algorithms are:

1. Disk modulo (DM): The number of the disk on which we store the bucket pointed to from $GridArray[i_1][i_2]\ldots[i_k]$ is $(i_1 + i_2 + \ldots + i_k)$ modulo N, where N is the number of disks.
2. Exclusive-or (Exor): Exor is similar to DM except that we exclusive-or the indices rather than add them; thus, we store the bucket pointed to from $GridArray[i_1][i_2]\ldots[i_k]$ on disk number $(i_1 \oplus i_2 \oplus \ldots \oplus i_k)$ modulo N.
3. Hilbert curve (HC): A Hilbert curve is a space-filling curve that travels through a k-dimensional space visiting each point exactly once and never crossing itself. It is thus a means for giving a linear ordering to the points in the space. Figure 13.16 shows Hilbert curves for two-by-two and eight-by-eight two-dimensional grids. In the HC scheme, the buckets are allocated on a round-robin basis as the curve is traversed through the grid array. Thus, the disk number is $HC(i_1, i_2, \ldots i_k)$ modulo N where HC is an appropriate mapping function.

Tie-Breaking

As we have seen in our earlier examples, a rectangle of grid array elements may point to the same bucket. Our declustering function likely will yield different bucket numbers for different elements of this rectangle. How do we determine which disk gets the bucket in such cases? Here are four strategies for choosing between the candidate buckets:

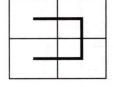

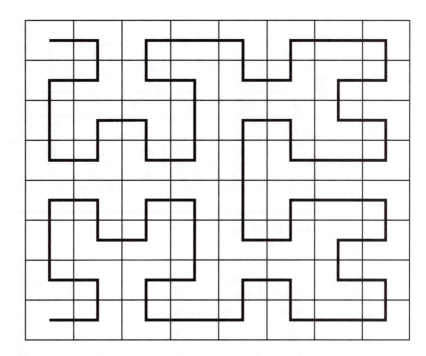

Figure 13.16 • Hilbert curves

1. Random: Select one of the candidate disks at random.
2. Most frequent: Choose whichever disk is most frequently identified when the declustering algorithm is applied to the elements of the rectangle. If there is still a tie, select one at random.
3. Data balancing: Look at all the tie-breaking cases across the entire grid array and use a global strategy that results in the number of buckets required on each disk being as equal as possible.
4. Area balancing: Again, break ties globally, but this time allocate buckets in such a way that the volume of the attribute space represented on each disk is as equal as possible.

Comparison of Bucket Allocation Methods
Suppose we have the grid array shown in Figure 13.17 and five disks on which to distribute buckets.

Assume rows and columns in the grid array are numbered from 0 upwards with element [0][0] in the top left-hand corner, thus *GridArray*[0][4] contains 25.

13	13	13	7	25	15	15	16
14	14	3	11	33	2	2	17
14	14	3	31	12	2	2	18
26	9	9	9	5	10	10	10
26	9	9	9	29	22	22	23
21	21	4	27	28	30	1	34
8	8	4	0	24	6	32	32
8	8	4	19	19	19	19	20

Figure 13.17 • Example grid array

Consider bucket 14, for example. It is in *GridArray*[1][0], *GridArray*[1][1], *GridArray*[2][0], and *GridArray*[2][1]. Here is how these four pairs of indexes are treated by our three declustering functions:

- DM: Applying DM to the four sets of indexes yields: $(1 + 0) \bmod 5 = 1$, $(1 + 1) \bmod 5 = 2$, $(2 + 0) \bmod 5 = 2$, $(2 + 1) \bmod 5 = 3$. Disk 2 is the most frequent, so bucket 14 would be assigned to disk 2 using this scheme.
- Exor: Similarly, applying the Exor function we get: $(1 \oplus 0) \bmod 5 = 1$, $(1 \oplus 1) \bmod 5 = 0$, $(2 \oplus 0) \bmod 5 = 2$, $(2 \oplus 1) \bmod 5 = 3$. We need to break the tie, so we will choose (randomly) disk 3.
- HC: The indexes of the grid array elements (mod 5) on the Hilbert curve (see Figure 13.16) are 2, 3, 4, and 2. Of these, 2 is the most frequent, so using this scheme, bucket 14 would be assigned to disk 2.

Table 13.1 shows how each of the buckets of Figure 13.17 would be allocated to a disk under the three declustering schemes. In the table, bucket numbers marked with an asterisk are those requiring a tie-break; we use tie-breaking scheme 2. The superscript *r* by a disk number indicates that it was selected randomly.

Declustering Experiments

Moon et al. (1996) used three data sets in their experiments. In the first (designated "uniform"), the data were so evenly distributed that only a very small number of buckets were pointed to from more than one element of the grid array. In the second data set ("hotspot"), in the center of the data space, buckets had single pointers, and the average number of pointers to a bucket increased towards the edges of the data space. In the third data set ("correlated"), data points were very dense (resulting in buckets with single pointers) along one axis of the data space.

● **TABLE 13.1** Bucket Allocation

Bucket	DM	Exor	Hilbert	Bucket	DM	Exor	Hilbert
0	4	0	1	18	4	0	0
1	1	3	4	19*	2^r	2^r	4^r
2*	2^r	2^r	3^r	20	4	0	2
3*	4^r	0^r	3	21*	0^r	4^r	1^r
4*	3	4^r	0	22*	4^r	2^r	0^r
5	2	2	1	23	1	3	2
6	1	3	0	24	0	2	1
7	3	3	0	25	4	4	1
8*	2	1^r	2^r	26*	4^r	3^r	3^r
9*	1^r	1^r	4	27	3	1	2
10*	4^r	4^r	1^r	28	4	1	3
11	4	2	2	29	3	0	2
12	1	1	0	30	0	0	4
13*	0^r	1^r	4^r	31	0	1	1
14*	2	3^r	2	32*	2^r	0^r	1^r
15*	0^r	1^r	0^r	33	0	0	2
16	2	2	1	34	2	2	3
17	3	1	2				

The bucket size in the experiments was 4K. The number of disks on which buckets were stored varied from 4 to 32. One thousand multidimensional queries were generated randomly, and the time required to retrieve the results was measured.

Among the tie-breaking algorithms, data balancing generally gave better results and had a side benefit of better space utilization. Declustering algorithms (with data balancing) were not consistently ranked. For small numbers of disks, DM gave the best performance, whereas for larger numbers of disks, the HC method gave best results.

● **Chapter Summary**

A multimap is a structure that associates more than one object with a particular key. One way to locate the objects having a particular key value is to use indexes. Multikey indexing involves finding all objects with particular combinations of key values. This contrasts with primary key indexing, discussed in Chapters 5, 6, and 12, where we were concerned with maps rather than multimaps and with finding one object with a particular (unique) primary key.

One approach to multikey retrieval is to create indexes that identify all occurrences of a particular attribute value. Thus, we get inversions of the container. One disadvantage of inverted files is the maintenance problem; that is, the extent of the updating required when the objects are added, removed, or modified. Another disadvantage is the amount of computation involved in answering range queries.

Grid files are an alternative way of satisfying multikey queries. In effect, a representation of the k-dimensional key space is partitioned into grid blocks that point to buckets of objects. The grid file organization adapts smoothly to insertions and deletions and allows both point queries and range queries to be answered efficiently. Performance on large data sets can be improved by dispersing the buckets over multiple disks.

● Exercises

1. Suppose the state highway patrol wants to retrieve records for all vehicles matching a partially known plate, such as

   2??B5?7

   Would index files help? If so, describe the files you would create. Assume each plate has a maximum of seven alphanumeric characters.

2. A library wants to record information about books and borrowers in such a way that it is possible to determine very quickly:

   a. Those books (if any) currently on loan to a given borrower

   b. Whether a particular book is on loan and, if so, who the borrower is

   Describe the files you would create to support such a query program. Show how these two types of queries would be answered using your files.

3. When completing a crossword puzzle, a solver may sometimes have partial information about a word. For example, a seven-letter word with second letter T, third letter O, and sixth letter G might be represented:

   - T O - - G -

   It would be convenient to have a program that listed those words in a dictionary that match a pattern of this form. Design appropriate files and a program that would find matching words quickly.

4. Suggest how a collection of wallpaper patterns might be indexed and searched.

5. Suppose we had two separate document collections, each having a four-level hierarchy of indexes (index, occurrence file, dictionary, and matrix). Describe a way in which the two collections could be merged into one.

6. Suppose we have two indexes representing the locations in a container of objects with attributes A and B, respectively. Each index is implemented as a linked list of bit maps. Each bit map represents a 256-object section of the container and has an associated integer k representing the location of the object represented by the first bit.

a. Sketch an algorithm for performing a *union* operation on the indexes.

b. Sketch an algorithm for performing an *intersection* operation on the indexes.

7. Given the index representation of Exercise 6 for an attribute *C*, give an algorithm for modifying the index

a. When object *j* acquires attribute *C*

b. When object *j* loses attribute *C*

8. Assume that the 20 cars of Figure 13.1 is the entire data set. Trace the processing of the following queries using the algorithm of Section 13.2.3.

a. find color = white or color = black and manuf = Ford or manuf = BMW

b. find manuf = Ford and not (color = red or color = blue)

c. find not (manuf = Ford or manuf = BMW) and color = white

9. Assume that we represent the set of objects not having attribute *A* by means of an "inverse" set; that is, we tag the set of objects having *A* and denote the result *A'*. Fill in the missing five entries in the following table showing how union and intersection operators can be implemented when either or both operands might be an inverse set.

Operands	A B	A' B	A B'	A' B'
Union	A ∪ B			(A ∩ B)'
Intersection	A ∩ B			

10. What are the consequences of having grid file buckets that can hold only one record?

11. Is there redundancy in the grid file organization? If there was a power failure and linear scales were lost, could they be restored using the grid array and grid blocks? What if the lengths of the scales were known but not the contents?

12. You have been asked to write a program that checks the consistency of a grid file organization. (Recall that such an organization has three components: linear scales, grid array, and file of buckets.) Describe the checks that you would have your program do.

13. Explain why retrieval of a single record, given only its primary key, is very slow if records are stored using the grid file organization.

14. Consider the grid file shown in Figure 13.11. Show how it changes after each step in the following sequence of operations:

Insert object (750-1212, 3.25)

Insert object (804-0022, 2.80)

Insert object (844-7777, 2.12)

15. Consider Table 13.1. Explain how the entries for each of the following buckets was derived:

a. Bucket 31

b. Bucket 25

   c. Bucket 17

● Problems

1. Create a large *CARS* file (adding other attributes if you wish). Write and test a program that enables users to pose Boolean queries on the file. Your query language should include the *not* operator.

2. Design, implement, and test a spider program that traverses the Web and sends back data from the pages that it encounters.

3. Research the design of a search engine of your choice. Find out as much as you can about the indexes that it uses.

4. Devise a method for compressing sparse binary strings representing inverted indexes. Implement and test operators that perform union and intersection operations on indexes represented by the compressed list. The result of an operation should be compressed or uncompressed, whichever is smaller.

5. You have been given a set of machine-readable documents and the task of creating the five levels of STAIRS files. Describe your solution to the problem.

6. The grid file organization was devised as an approximate implementation of the bit matrix. Although the bit matrix is impractical because it is so big, it will also normally be very empty. That is, at any time very few of its elements will be 1. An alternative to the grid file is to represent the bit matrix itself using sparse matrix techniques. How would you implement a sparse bit matrix? How would your solution compare with the corresponding grid file? Compare the two under the following headings:

   a. Amount of space needed

   b. Time needed to process a point query

   c. Time needed to insert an object

7. Suppose disk space is at a premium and that following a deletion from a grid file we want to combine buckets if at all possible. Outline a general deletion algorithm that does this.

8. Research Hilbert curves and design an implementation of the function HC described in Section 13.3.4.

9. Using the algorithms in the chapter, or from elsewhere, design and implement a grid file organization that enables you to insert objects representing vehicles (similar to those in the *CARS* file), remove objects, and retrieve by an attribute value or combination of attribute values.

● References

Blair, D. C., and M. E. Maron. 1985. An evaluation of retrieval effectiveness for a full-text document-retrieval system. *Communications of the ACM,* 28(3):289–299.

Hume, A., and D. Sunday. 1991. Fast string searching. *Software—Practice and Experience,* 21(11):1248.

IBM Corporation. 1973. *STAIRS, Storage and Information Retrieval System.* Stuttgart, Germany: IBM Corporation. General Information Manual GH 12.5107.

Moon, B., A. Acharya, and J. Saltz, 1996. Study of scalable declustering algorithms for parallel grid files. *Proceedings of the 10th International Parallel Processing Symposium*, Honolulu, HI, April 1996, pp. 434–440. See also *Technical Report CS-TS-3589*, Department of Computer Science, University of Maryland, College Park, MD.

Nievergelt, J., H. Hinterberger, and K. L. Sevcik. 1984. The grid file: An adaptable, symmetric, multikey file structure. *ACM Transactions on Database Systems,* 9(1):38–71.

● Notes

[1]An actual system used by California realtors enables users to specify values for a list of about 80 attributes.

[2]The reader may have experienced "link rot"—a link returned by a search engine pointing to a page that does not exist anymore.

[3]Full-text systems do have disadvantages. See, for example, Blair and Maron (1985).

[4]In our grid file diagrams, we assume that the top left-hand element of the array is [0][0] and that [*i*][*j*] refers to row *i*, column *j*.

14

Persistent Structures and Databases

14.1 Introduction

The material in this final chapter is intended to be a capstone to Part Two of the book, as well as the chapters on persistent objects, and also to give a brief look at database systems. In Section 14.2, we consider the problem of choosing the appropriate persistent structure for a particular application and present a methodology that may be useful in making the choice. In Section 14.3, we look briefly at database systems, in particular at what makes a database different from a collection of files. Database systems embody some of the implementation-independent ideas that we have discussed in the context of objects. Finally, in Section 14.4 we look very briefly at object databases.

14.2 Selection of Persistent Structure

In this section, we review the data structures used in earlier chapters to implement persistent maps and multimaps and suggest factors that software designers might consider when choosing among them for a particular application. We end the section with a back-of-the-envelope technique that might be a useful tool in making such a choice.

● **TABLE 14.1**   File Structures Examined in Part Two of the Text

Chapter	Structure(s)
11	Hash, table-assisted hash, dynamic hash, extendible hash
12	Sequential, indexed-sequential, B-tree, B*-tree, B+-tree
13	Inverted file, grid file

14.2.1 Summary of Structures

We have considered (directly or by implication) the 11 structures listed in Table 14.1.

The problem in choosing a file structure to hold persistent objects is finding the best match between the requirements of the application and the properties of the structure. In Chapters 11, 12, and 13, we presented different file organizations oriented toward single-key and multiple-key processing.

Maps: Single-Key File Processing
In single-key file processing, objects are stored and retrieved according to the value of a single key, typically the primary key. Common accessing requirements are retrieval of a single object with a particular primary key and the retrieval of all objects in primary key order. Table 14.2 shows four file organizations and their suitability for these accessing requirements.[1]

The "none" entry under *Organization* corresponds to a 12th file type, such as to a serial nonsequential file or to a direct-access file in which objects are placed in arbitrary locations. If fast query processing is not required and a large proportion of the objects read in a scan of a file are used, then a sequential organization is adequate. Files organized using hashing are suitable in cases in which independent individual retrievals are performed and fast response is needed. That is, the result of a query is either one object or none, and there is no correlation between one

● **TABLE 14.2**   Properties of Four File Organizations

Organization	Single Record by Primary Key	All Records in Primary Key Order
None	Slow	Very slow
Sequential	Slow	Fast
Hashed	Fast	Very slow
Indexed sequential	Moderate	Fast

retrieval and the next. An indexed file organization is also an appropriate organization for this kind of retrieval.

Files organized using hashing are not useful if it is necessary to find all objects with a key in a particular range. To satisfy such a request efficiently, the system must be able to process objects in key sequence. Sequential files are one solution. However, if only a small section of a file is to be retrieved, then it is desirable to be able to find the beginning of that section quickly. Indexed sequential files are thus more appropriate.

Multimaps: Multikey File Processing

If objects must be retrievable by more than one key, then the primary key organizations listed in Table 14.2 are not the best solution because they are asymmetric in their treatment of the keys of an object. We considered multiple-key retrievals in Chapter 13. Inverted file organizations are a common method of performing such retrievals, but they are not best suited to range queries and, in addition, updates can be time-consuming. Grid files are in some ways a better way of performing multikey retrievals. First, existence queries can be answered in no more than two disk accesses. Second, the index structure adapts smoothly to main file insertions and deletions. Third, all fields are treated equally.

14.2.2 Factors in Structure Selection

The following are some of the factors that a user may consider when evaluating candidate file organizations:

- Time
- File-use ratio
- Space
- Volatility

We consider each in turn in the following sections.

Time

Under the heading of *time*, we need to consider the programming time required to develop and maintain file-processing software. A more complex file organization may require more time to develop file access and maintenance software. In addition, there may be hidden software development and maintenance times.

If a particular organization requires that updates be processed in a particular sequence, then the time required to sort those updates must also be included in its cost. Some file structures require monitoring and periodic maintenance; this requires yet more processing time.

File-Use Ratio

The **file-use ratio** of a file in a particular run of an application program can be defined as the number of objects used divided by the number of objects in the file.

If the ratio is high, indicating that most of the objects in the file are used, then a serial file or a sequential file organization may be acceptable. If the ratio is low, then a better choice would be an organization in which it is possible to focus quickly on the needed objects, with minimal accesses of those that are not needed.

Complicating factors arise, however, when using a file-use ratio analysis. Consider an application that, when run, uses 30 percent of the logical objects in a file. If the file is organized as a hash file, then, in principle, only the 30 percent of objects in the file need be accessed. However, in practice, overflow resolution may make the percentage of objects accessed higher than 30 percent. Depending on the blocking factor (number of logical objects per physical record), the percentage of physical records accessed may be higher still. However, if the file is organized sequentially, then a large proportion of the objects must be read (depending on the position of the last object processed). In addition, there may be processing required (e.g., sorting) so that the accesses are made in sequential order. It is difficult to say that if the file use ratio exceeds X percent, a serial organization should be used. Obviously, when the file-use ratio is low, say between 5 and 10 percent, then an organization permitting direct access to objects is likely to be better. Each application is likely to be unique, however, and a simple simulation will probably give useful indicators on which to base an informed decision.

Space

When computing space requirements, the designer should take both primary and secondary storage into account. Many file organizations require space in addition to that used by the objects themselves. Table 14.3 gives some examples.

Hashing, for example, may be ruled out if space on secondary storage is at a premium. In addition, certain organizations we have considered, such as dynamic hashing and grid files, work best if certain tables are in main memory. These organizations may not be feasible on some configurations even if a large amount of disk space is available.

● **TABLE 14.3** File Structure Overheads

Organization	Overhead
B-tree	Pointers to nodes. Average node utilization is approximately 60%.
Grid file	Linear scales, grid array. Unused space in buckets.
Dynamic hash file	Index trees. Average bucket utilization is approximately 69%.
Table-assisted hash file	Table. Unused space in buckets.
Fixed hash file	Unused space in buckets. Maybe pointers for overflow.

In addition to the space taken up by the file itself, space may be needed during an update operation if the file is not updated in situ. Even though such space is likely to be needed only temporarily, it must be available when required.

Volatility

How often are the contents of the file changed? If the file changes frequently, an organization with many indexes may require much processing in order to keep the indexes current. It is useful to distinguish between two types of changes: (1) those that add objects to and delete objects from a file and (2) those that modify existing objects. Considering the number of objects in the file, is there real growth or only growth if the space occupied by deleted objects is not reused? Some organizations such as B-trees adapt as deletions are made. Others, such as ISAM, may not and may require periodic runs of a file-rewriting program to maintain efficiency. How often are there changes to the components of objects? Are some components more volatile than others? For example, consider seven components that might be found in a student object

birth date, sex, name, major, address, class year, gpa

From left to right they are increasingly likely to change. In some instances it may be worthwhile splitting objects in two and establishing two files, one containing objects with the volatile components and the other containing corresponding objects with the more stable components.

14.2.3 A Selection Methodology

It is clear that several factors have a bearing on the choice of a file organization for a particular application. The following is a simple, three-step, back-of-the-envelope approach to determining which structure might be the most suitable.

1. Consider the application and the environment in which the application runs, determine which characteristics of a file structure are important, and determine how important each is. Give each a weight (e.g., on a scale from 1 to 10). For example, a characteristic might be *disk space overhead*. If we have an environment in which disk space is plentiful, we may not be concerned with this aspect of a file structure and give it a comparatively low weight.
2. Identify candidate file structures and give each a score for each of the characteristics identified in Step 1. For example, table-assisted hashing would score highly under *retrieval time*, but not highly under *insertion time*.
3. Compute a weighted score for each candidate file structure by combining the weights and the scores.

Applying the Method

A magazine publisher maintains data on its subscribers, of which there are about 10,000. Once a week the data are used to print labels for issues of the magazine. In a typical week, the publisher makes about 350 changes to the file: new subscribers, changes of address, cancellations, and renewals. Changes can be batched; it is not essential that the file be up-to-date at all times. A few times a week a customer will make a telephone inquiry about his or her account. Disk space is somewhat at a premium on the current system. The publisher needs to determine which file structure to use to store the objects representing customers.

Step 1   Given the description of the application and the environment, the aspects of a file structure listed in Table 14.4 might be deemed to be important.

We have assigned each aspect a weight on a scale of 1 to 10 (10 being most important). For example, calls from customers regarding accounts are relatively rare, and as far as customer relations are concerned, it does not matter if it takes 5 seconds rather than 0.5 seconds to retrieve the appropriate object from the file.

Step 2   Let us suppose that the publisher has narrowed the choice down to four file structures that are readily available for the system. These structures are ISAM, sequential, B+-tree, and table-assisted hash. Table 14.5 shows possible ratings given to each organization under each of the headings from Table 14.4.

● TABLE 14.4   Aspects and Weights for Subscriber Database

Aspect	Weight
Space utilization (disk space at a premium)	7
Sequential access (label printing)	9
Retrieval of single objects (phone enquiries)	5
Insertions (new customers)	9
Deletions (cancellations)	5
Modifications (renewals, address changes)	7

● TABLE 14.5   Ratings for File Structures

Organization	Space	Sequential	Single	Insert	Delete	Modify
ISAM	8	9	9	8	9	9
Sequential	10	10	3	5	5	5
B+-tree	6	10	9	8	8	9
Table-assisted hash	6	1	10	7	9	9

For example, retrieval of a single object from a table-assisted hash file is very fast, whereas insertion of a new object into a sequential file is comparatively slow.

Step 3   Combining the ratings from Table 14.5 with the weights from Table 14.4 yields the weighted scores for each file organization shown in Table 14.6.[2]

Thus, on the basis of these figures, given our earlier assumptions, ISAM is the most suitable structure for the application.

In the next section, we look briefly at database systems—systems that evolved out of file systems and that aim to avoid some of the disadvantages of file processing.

14.3 Comparison of Files and Databases

The term *database* is sometimes used very loosely to refer to any collection of data. More precisely, a **database** is a collection of data shared between applications. Suppose, for example, that a college library, academic record office, and financial aid office each require a collection of data pertaining to students. Rather than each office maintaining a separate file structure, each could access a common database. Redundancy would be reduced. A **database management system** (DBMS) is software that facilitates access to the data and provides program–data independence. Examples of DBMSs are Access, Ingres, and Oracle.

By program–data independence, we mean that user programs are insulated from changes in the logical and physical arrangements of the data. Thus, the user can perform operations on the data using a query language or subprogram calls in a high-level language and need not be concerned with the logical or physical arrangement of the actual data. The user need not know whether the data are stored as a hash file or as a B-tree, for example. The DBMS achieves this insulation by mapping **views**. The application program view of data is mapped onto the actual storage arrangements. Changes can be made to the organization of shared data without those changes requiring modifications to the programs that use it; only the mapping of views performed at run time by the DBMS changes. It is this sharing and independence that distinguishes a database from a collection of files.

● **TABLE 14.6** File Structure Scores

Organization	Weighted Score
ISAM	362
Sequential	280
B+-tree	352
Table-assisted	272

Sometimes we may have a choice between using a DBMS or using a collection of integrated files. The following discussion presents some of the advantages and disadvantages of using integrated files.

14.3.1 Advantages of Using Integrated Files

There are five main advantages to using an integrated file-processing environment compared with a database management system. First, because file-based programming is relatively straightforward, the information technology staff does not need to use advanced programming techniques. Thus, software personnel may be more readily available and less expensive to hire. Second, there is no added expense in terms of purchasing and maintaining software to handle the file–program interface. Third, it is relatively easy to maintain the integrity of a set of files against system failure. Fourth, because of the relatively simple interface between a program and a file, transfers are relatively efficient. Finally, limited concurrent access makes recovery from crashes relatively simple.

14.3.2 Disadvantages of Using Integrated Files

There are four main disadvantages to using an integrated file-processing environment rather than a DBMS. First, there is a large degree of dependence between programs and data. Programs are not insulated from changes in the logical and physical organization of data. Second, answering new requests or producing one-of-a-kind reports is difficult when using files (most DBMSs, however, have an interactive **query language**). Third, only a limited degree of concurrent access is usually possible. If a program has a file open for writing, other programs are usually prevented from reading any part of it. Finally, in an integrated file environment, mechanisms for communicating data modifications across applications tend to be external to rather than part of the file system itself. In a multiuser environment, it is difficult to control, document, and disseminate changes to file structures. Data integrity is not maintained by the system, but rather is the responsibility of application programs.

14.3.3 Data Independence

Data independence is desirable because it reduces costs and increases the flexibility of data processing. Logical data independence is achieved by buffering the applications from the logical database. Physical data independence is achieved by buffering the logical database from the physical database (direct access storage devices).

Logical Data Independence
Logical data independence means that changes in the logical database structure have a minimal effect on application programs. It is desirable because of the costs involved in software maintenance. Without logical data independence, certain application programs would have to be modified and recompiled every time the logical database was reorganized; for example, changed from a hash file to a B^+-tree.

Logical databases are reorganized for many reasons, including the need to store additional fields in specific objects, reorganization of the institution using the database, and the need to improve database efficiency.

Physical Data Independence
Physical data independence means that changes in the physical storage of the database have minimal effect on the logical database. A database administrator might change a physical database to accommodate new storage hardware or restructure it to increase efficiency. For example, as discussed earlier, the volatile components of an object could be stored separately from the nonvolatile ones. Recompilation of the logical/physical mapping module reduces the likelihood that reorganization of the physical storage will necessitate reorganization of the logical database.

14.3.4 Database Models

Historically, the majority of database systems have been classified as *hierarchical, network*, or *relational* according to the fundamental way in which they model data. Most recent development has been in the relational model, so we emphasize that here.

Hierarchical Model
The hierarchical data model organizes data according to associations that are represented as trees. Such a tree is called a **hierarchical definition tree**. A **hierarchical database** is a collection of records (nodes) connected in a forest of disjoint trees. Each database tree includes a root record and its descendant records. The hierarchical data model has three advantages. First, the tree structure is easy to conceptualize; thus, a schema for a database can be easily understood. Second, the restriction of having only an ancestor–descendant association between different record types results in a small set of data manipulation commands sufficient for record processing. Third, the restricted linkage allowed among record types facilitates implementation of hierarchical database management systems.

Unfortunately, the restricted linkage that gives the hierarchical model its advantages is also the cause of its major disadvantage. The model cannot adequately represent the true semantics among entities that have *M:N* (many-to-many) associations. Examples of entities that have many-to-many associations are students and classes and parts and suppliers. Furthermore, few sets of naturally occurring objects are associated in a hierarchical fashion. Thus, the hierarchical model forces the database designer to use multiple, redundant database trees to represent nonhierarchical associations.

Network Model
The network database model represents the associations among record types in a graph structure. Thus, a record type may have numerous associations with other record types. Clearly, the network structure is less restricted than the hierarchical

data model and is more powerful than the hierarchical model in terms of expressing the associations that may exist among different entities. Unfortunately, it still cannot implement *M:N* associations directly.

The major disadvantage of the network data model is its complexity and structure. To write application programs that process data stored in the network, the programmer must know the logical structure of the database. This places a heavy burden on the programmer.

Relational Model

The relational model was proposed by Codd (1970). It has a certain elegance and simplicity compared with the network and hierarchical models. For this reason it is widely used. Formally, a **relation** is a subset of the cross-product of *N* domains and can be represented by a table with *N* columns. It can also be thought of as a set of points in *N*-dimensional space. Tables are simple in structure, and there are no pointers from one table entry to another. A major advantage of the relational model is that it can directly represent *M:N* associations. For example, Table 14.7 represents a relation with data about students and classes.

Consider the relation of Table 14.8, containing information from a parts catalog.

● **TABLE 14.7** Representation of a Student-Classes Relation

Student	Class
Bill	Math
Bill	Physics
Cindy	Math
David	Physics

● **TABLE 14.8** A Relation with Apparent Redundancy

Part #	Part Name	Price	Supplier	Supplier Phone
1	Hammer	10	Acme	555-1234
1	Hammer	10	ToolsRUs	555-4096
2	Wrench	12	WrenchCity	555-8866
3	Screwdriver	5	Acme	555-1234
3	Screwdriver	5	ToolsRUs	555-4096
4	Drill	35	Acme	555-1234

Intuitively, it would seem that there is redundancy in this relation that might lead to problems. In fact, this is the case. Although it is often discussed in the context of the relational model, the problem of update anomalies and associated data normalization has wider application. We look at data normalization in Appendix B.

The means by which data are manipulated in a relational database often falls into one or more of the following categories:

- Natural language
- Query by forms
- Relational calculus
- Relational algebra

Natural Language Some World Wide Web sites permit users to enter queries in natural language.[3] Some translate the query into SQL (a nonprocedural query language) and apply it to a database. For example, if we have a database containing data about winners of Oscars, then we could pose queries such as:

Who won Oscar for best actor in 1951?

How many acting Oscars has Jack Nicholson won?

When did Meryl Streep last win an Oscar?

Query by Forms An approach to entering queries is to have a user "fill in the blanks" in a form derived from the data being queried. For example, Figure 14.1 represents a form filled in to represent the first of our example queries.

Figure 14.2 shows two forms that would be submitted (and their results combined) in order to answer the second query.

Relational Calculus Relational calculus is nonprocedural in the sense that the user specifies the properties of the information to be delivered rather than the detailed steps by which the information is to be derived. The DBMS analyzes the request and performs the necessary operations. An example query is the following, which returns from relations *supplier* and *parts* the phone numbers of suppliers who supply hammers.[4]

```
retrieve supplier.phone where supplier.itemno=parts.itemno
                      and parts.name="Hammer"
```

Year	Best Picture	Best Actor	Best Actress	Best Supporting Actor	Best Supporting Actress
1951		<Print>			

Figure 14.1 • Example of query by forms

Year	Best Picture	Best Actor	Best Actress	Best Supporting Actor	Best Supporting Actress
<count>				Jack Nicholson	

Year	Best Picture	Best Actor	Best Actress	Best Supporting Actor	Best Supporting Actress
<count>		Jack Nicholson			

Figure 14.2 • Another example of query by forms

Query languages based on relational calculus are found in most commercial relational DBMS.[5]

Relational Algebra   Relational algebra is a procedural language in which the user specifies operations to be performed on relations. However, the specifications contain no references to access paths. In other words, the specification is independent of logical and physical organization of how the relations are actually stored. Relational algebra was devised by Codd (1972). Relational algebra and calculus have been shown to be equivalent [e.g., see Klug (1982)].

Selection and projection are monadic relational operators; each operates on a relation and returns a relation as its result. If two sets of N-tuples[6] are relations on the same collection of domains, then normal set operations such as union, intersection, and difference can be applied to them. On the other hand, the *join* operator defined in the following list can be applied to two dissimilar relations.

• Selection: Selection is the simplest of the relational algebra operators. It can be thought of as picking out one or more rows from a table. The general form is:

result = Relation <u>where</u> <condition>

The result relation is a subset of the original *Relation* and contains those tuples for which the specified condition is true.
• Projection: Whereas selection processes a relation by rows, projection can be thought of as processing the relation by columns. The general form is:

result = Relation [domain, domain, ... domain]

The result relation is almost the result of selecting the specified columns from *Relation*. It is not quite a column selection because there will be no duplication

of rows in the result. Thinking in terms of the *N*-dimensional space mentioned earlier will show how the projection is actually obtained.
- Join: The join operator is dyadic and comes in several forms. We denote the most general of them as follows:

```
result = join R1,R2 where <condition>
```

Every tuple in the result is a concatenation of a tuple from *R1* with a tuple from *R2*. Two tuples are concatenated if the specified condition holds.[7] A statement in relational algebra equivalent to the calculus query above is

```
(join supplier,(parts where name="Hammer") where itemno=itemno)[phone]
```

The simplest implementation of the join operator would take each tuple in *R1* in turn and examine its relationship with each tuple in *R2*, but this would require $M * N$ tuple-tuple evaluations. Ways have been proposed for implementing a join more efficiently. For example, the number of comparisons could be reduced if it were possible to access tuples in sequence by an attribute used in the join.

Comparison of Database Data Models

A data model is understandable if users can easily comprehend the associations represented by the model. A data model's understandability is primarily affected by the explicitness of the connections between associated record types and by the simplicity of the associations. Thus, the hierarchical data model is easy to understand because the only association allowed between different record types is that of parent–descendant. The network data model, on the other hand, is less understandable due to the numerous set associations allowed. The relational data model is the least understandable because the associations among relations are not explicitly represented; rather, they exist through shared attributes.

A model's understandability is also related to its representational power. Representational power is the ability of a data model to establish 1:1, 1:*N*, and *M:N* associations between record types. All three data models can easily represent 1:1 and 1:*N* associations. Their ability to represent *M:N* associations, however, differs greatly. The hierarchical model has the worst representational power. A hierarchical model must represent *M:N* associations indirectly as two 1:*N* associations in different database trees. This reduces its understandability for *M:N* associations. The network data model has better representational power, but cannot directly represent *M:N* associations. It must establish an intermediate record type and two set declarations. This obscures the underlying *M:N* dependency. The relational model has the best representational power because it can directly represent *M:N* associations. Although the *M:N* association is directly representable, it is not easily understood in the relational model because the associations are not explicitly stated.

The hierarchical and network models are roughly equivalent in their space efficiency. Their storage space is well utilized because they implement associations by pointers rather than data values. In addition, application programs can exploit the pointer linkages and currency pointers to minimize time for transactions. The relational model is not as efficient in time and space. This is because associations are stored by redundant attribute values, not pointers. Transactions can take a long time in the relational model because associations must be derived dynamically.

The application programmer's ease of use of the data manipulation language for the three models also varies. Both the hierarchical and network model are more difficult to use than the relational model. Data manipulation for hierarchical and network DBMSs are procedural. Application programmers must know both how the functional database is declared and how it is stored in order to develop efficient applications. Furthermore, navigation through the network with its many currency pointers can be difficult to comprehend. With the "functional" relational calculus, application programmers request information in terms of information content, not associational linkage.

In summary, the hierarchical and network data models (1) are more understandable, (2) have less representational power, (3) are more space and time efficient, and (4) are more difficult to use than the relational model.

The relational model is well suited to storing and retrieving data that can be represented as fields of records; it is not good for manipulating complex objects. We look at what are termed **object databases** very briefly in the next section.

14.4 Object Databases

We have seen that the object-oriented approach enables us to devise software components and use them without being concerned with implementation details. We have also seen that database systems insulate programs from details of logical and physical organization of data. If we were to try to combine these ideas into databases of objects, we might consider beginning with the relational model, but there are limitations to that model.

14.4.1 Weaknesses of the Relational Model

Entries in tables that represent relations must be atomic. Although it is possible to decompose a complex object (e.g., a clock, a car, or an integrated circuit) into atomic components and store them in appropriate relations, this makes it difficult to manipulate the object as a whole. How do we represent the information that tells us how to assemble an object from the entries in diverse relations? Typically, this information must be stored in additional relations. In addition, in SQL we need to use the join operation, and the list of tables to use must be built into the join query.

14.4.2 Alternatives to the Relational Model

We could set aside the advantages of database systems (sharing, minimal redundancy) and store objects to and retrieve them from files. This is what we have been doing with the file structures in Chapters 11, 12, and 13. However, it is not necessary to give up the sharing and transparency advantages of DBMSs. We could extend the relational model and permit nested relations. We could allow a relation component to be a relation itself. The query language would also have to be extended—nested SQL perhaps—and a subquery could yield a list to be used in a clause in the main query. However, even better is a new paradigm: the object database management system.

14.4.3 Object Database Management Systems

Object database management systems (ODBMSs) are an alternative to files and to conventional DBMSs for storing and manipulating objects. Data are stored in an ODBMS in the same format as it is held in main memory; there is no need for an object-to-relation translation tool, so complex data structures can be stored directly. Typically, each object has a unique unchanging object identifier (OID) generated by the system. ODBMSs will generally support inheritance. In a combination of database ideas and object-oriented ideas, an ODBMS must provide

- Persistent storage for objects
- A language for class definition and object manipulation
- A query language
- Concurrency control to enable many simultaneous users of the database to operate without interfering with each other
- Crash recovery

Now a user can write in an object-oriented language such as C++ or Java rather than a database sublanguage. It is unlikely that ODBMSs will replace relational DBMSs. Although the former is more suitable for data with complex structures, an enterprise may well have both kinds of database systems and move data between them as needed.

Chapter Summary

In the first part of the chapter, we briefly reviewed the persistent data structures that we covered in Part Two of the text. We listed some factors (such as time and volatility) that should be considered when making a choice between structures. A simple weighted-score system was presented that might be useful in making a choice.

We also looked at the differences between a database and a collection of files. A database management system facilitates sharing of data and insulates application programs for structural changes in the data. We looked briefly at database models, particularly the relational model, and then at the concept of an object database.

Exercises

1. A large manufacturing company has given you the task of devising an organization structure for its file of parts records. Each record in the file contains information about a particular part. The fields include number (which is unique), description, price, and quantity on hand (QOH). There are about 10,000 records. The file is accessed in a number of ways:

    a. Twice a year a catalog is produced containing the information in the parts records in ascending order of part number.

    b. Once a day the QOH field of about 100 records is increased to reflect deliveries made from the manufacturing plant.

    c. Several times during an hour the QOH field of a record is decreased as shipments are made out of the warehouse.

    d. Many times an hour customers make telephone enquiries about a part, referring to it either by part number or by description.

    Describe how you would organize the file, including any index files you would create. Give reasons for your choice of organization. State clearly any assumptions you make.

2. Suppose that the organization of Exercise 1 makes weekly changes to its catalog; it adds some new parts and deletes some obsolete ones. Would your solution to Exercise 1 be different? Give reasons for your answer.

3. Consider the three organizations that collect data on students: college library, academic record office, and financial aid office.

    a. What data might all three have in common for a particular student?

    b. For each office, what information might it have that would not be of interest to the other two?

4. Give an example of data that are naturally hierarchical, and that therefore might be well-suited to a hierarchical DBMS.

5. Suppose we have the following three relations: *Student-Class*, *Class-Instructor*, and *Instructor-Room*.

Student	Class
Bill	Math
Bill	Biology
Brandon	CS
Brandon	Math
Lynn	English
Lynn	Math
Sue	CS

Class	Instructor
Math	Euler
Biology	Crick
CS	Knuth
English	Shaw

Instructor	Room
Euler	123
Crick	444
Knuth	123
Shaw	808

Show how the answers to each of the following queries could be obtained using relational algebra. The only constants in your operations should be those that appear in the query itself.

a. The names of the students taking Math

b. The names of the students taught by Knuth

c. The courses taught by the instructors in room 123

d. The names of the students who are taking both Math and CS

Problems

1. Research techniques for performing fast join operations between two relations. Identify the fastest known algorithm.

2. Suppose that secondary storage were free. Would this change the way in which files are organized?

3. In the text, we mentioned the concept of a simulator to enable a user to see how various file structures might behave over the lifetime of an application. You have been asked to design such a simulator. Sketch a design of how it might work.

4. Find a DBMS on a system to which you have access. Does it use one of the three database models? Is so, which? What mechanisms are available to pose one-off queries? What interfaces are available to high-level languages?

References

Codd, E. F. 1970. A relational model of data for large shared data banks. *Communications of the ACM,* 13(6):377–387.

Codd, E. F. 1972. Relational completeness of data base sublanguages. In *Courant Computer Science Symposia No. 6: Data Base Systems*, ed. R. Rustin. 65–98. Englewood Cliffs, NJ: Prentice-Hall.

Klug, A. 1982. Equivalence of relational algebra and relational calculus query languages having aggregate functions. *Journal of the ACM,* 29(3):699–717.

● Notes

[1]Informally, our categories of very slow, slow, adequate, and fast might correspond to times proportional to N^2, N, log N, and 1, respectively, for a file of N records.

[2]The score for ISAM, for example, is

$$= (8 \times 7) + (9 \times 9) + (9 \times 5) + (8 \times 9) + (9 \times 5) + (9 \times 7)$$

$$= 56 + 81 + 45 + 72 + 45 + 63$$

$$= 362$$

[3]At the time of writing, EasyAsk sells a natural language interface tool.

[4]We assume two relations:

supplier (phone, itemno, ...)

parts (itemno, name, ...)

[5]There are limits on the power of relational calculus. A common example of this concerns a managerial hierarchy. Suppose we have an *employee* relation in which each employee tuple contains the employee name and the name of the employee's immediate supervisor. Although it may be trivial to find those supervised directly by employee X, it is beyond the power of relational calculus to find all those supervised by X either directly or indirectly.

[6]*N*-tuple is the generalization of pair, triple, quadruple, and so on.

[7]The *equijoin* operation is a special case of the join operation. Two tuples are concatenated if they have equal values of common attributes. The equijoin operator inevitably produces column duplication in the result. It is therefore convenient to define a variant that, in some ways, is the most useful form of the join operation. This *natural join* also joins two tuples if common attributes are equal, but discards duplicate occurrences of identical columns.

A

Random Numbers and Data Generation

A source of random numbers is useful in simulations and in algorithm analysis. True randomness is almost impossible to achieve on a deterministic computer system. However, there are sources of random bits [e.g., Marsaglia (1995) has 4.8 billion] that can be formed into integers of arbitrary size. Most programming environments provide a means to generate pseudo-random numbers. However, developing a pseudo-random number generator (PNG) that will pass a battery of tests (Marsaglia 1995) is nontrivial. Park and Miller (1988) describe a portable generator and also give examples of bad generating functions.

A.1 Single-Seed PNG

The numbers emitted by a PNG are only pseudo-random, because if you know the generating algorithm, you can predict what the next number will be. A typical PNG produces a sequence of numbers $(A_1, A_2, A_3, ...)$ generated from a **seed** as follows:

A_0 = seed mod *Modulus*

$A_i = (A_{i-1} * Multiplier + Increment)$ mod *Modulus* $(i > 0)$

The range of the numbers in this case is from zero to *Modulus* − 1. (The function may be available in a form that returns a real number $x: 0 \leq x < 1.0$.) Thus, starting with a particular seed (and keeping the same *Multiplier*, *Increment*, and *Modulus* parameters) the stream will always be the same. This repeatable property is useful during program testing.

Often a programming environment will contain two functions. One function loads the seed from a parameter or from a semi-random source such as the system clock, and the second returns the next A_i.

A.2 Multiseed PNG

Marsaglia (2003) draws attention to applications where it is required to select a subset of items in such a way that all subsets have an equal chance of being selected. Examples are selection of jury pools and devices that create a lottery ticket for a customer. In such cases, single-seed PNGs are inadequate if the number of possible seed values is less than the number of possible subsets. For example, in a lottery game where users pick six numbers from 51, the number of possible subsets (tickets) is approximately 18 million; only 65,536 of these could be picked by a PNG with a 16-bit seed.

Marsaglia proposes the use of multiseed PNGs. In essence, these comprise N streams of pseudo-random numbers seeded independently from each other. Numbers are extracted cyclically from the streams to give us a single stream. The following code (with some annotations added) is from Marsaglia (2003). Marsaglia shows how the code should be modified for several other values of N.

```
static unsigned long Q[1024];  /* array size is N */

unsigned long CMWC(void)
 {
  /* complimentary-multiply-with-carry method */

  unsigned long long t,
                     a=123471786LL;  /* constant depends on N */

  static unsigned long c=362436,     /* any nonnegative < a */
                       i=1023;       /* N-1 */

  unsigned  long x, r=0xfffffffe;

  i = (i+1) & 1023  ;  /* which stream to pick from, cyclic 0..N-1 */
  t = a * Q[i] + c;
  c = (t >> 32);
  x = t + c;
  if (x < c) { x++; c++; }

  return (Q[I] = r-x);
 }
```

The seeds are placed in Q before the first call of *CMWC*.

A.3 Example Applications of Single-seed PNGs

Following are four complete C++ programs illustrating uses of the built-in single-seed PNGs. In the programs, *rand()* is a function call that returns a nonnegative integer in a very large range. The function *srand()* is the initialization function (we call it with the current system time).

A.3.1 Example 1: A Uniform Distribution

We generate a stream of numbers uniformly in the range 0 to 10. In the following program, we initialize the number stream using the system clock. Using the mod operator we obtain random integers in the range 0 to 10. We generate 1100 such numbers and keep a table of how often each of the possible numbers is generated.

```
#include <iostream.h>
#include <stdlib.h>
#include <time.h>

main()
{ int i;
  int counters [11];
  for (i=0; i<11; i++) counters[i]=0;

  srand(  (unsigned)time(NULL) );

  for (i=0; i<1100; i++)
      counters[ rand() % 11 ]++;

  for (i=0; i<11; i++)
      cout << i << " " << counters[i] << endl;
}
```

The following table shows the frequency with which each of the 11 numbers appeared in a typical run of the program.

Number	0	1	2	3	4	5	6	7	8	9	10
Frequency	92	106	100	102	109	94	93	109	87	113	95

• A.3.2 Example 2: Unique Integers

We can generate a sequence of unique numbers by generating the first number randomly, then adding a random amount (at least one) to the previous number. Consider the following program.

```
#include <iostream.h>
#include <stdlib.h>
#include <time.h>

const N = 50;
const M = 17;

main()
{ int i, number;

    srand(  (unsigned)time(NULL) );

    number = rand() % N;
    cout << number << endl;

    for (i=1; i< 10; i++)
        {
          number = number + 1 + rand() % M;
          cout << number << endl;
        }
}
```

We choose *M* and *N* depending on the range of numbers we want. For example, if we need 1000 numbers in the range 0 to 18,000, we might set *N* to be 50 (thus the first number is 0 to 49), and set *M* to be 35. The average interval between numbers should be 17.5 or so.

The output from a typical run of the program (where the average difference will be about 8) is

```
36
44
58
73
89
102
110
113
115
131
```

If we intend these numbers to be primary keys in testing an implementation of a map, then we may not want them to be ordered (if the map is tree-based). In that case, we could pass them through an "antisorter" program.

A.3.3 Example 3: Nonuniform Distribution

If we roll two die and sum the numbers, numbers in the middle of the range 2 to 12 occur more often because there are more ways in which they can be formed. If we plot the frequencies with which the numbers occur, we would expect a bell-shaped curve. We can sum two calls of *rand()* and get a similar effect. In the following program, we have two subexpressions, each of which can be in the range 0 to 5. The distribution of the differences between the subexpressions is similar to the die pair distribution.

```
#include <iostream.h>
#include <stdlib.h>
#include <time.h>

main()
{ int i,temp;
  int counters [11];

  for (i=0; i<11; i++) counters[i]=0;

  srand(  (unsigned)time(NULL) );

  for (i=0; i<1100; i++)
     {
       temp = rand() % 6 - rand() % 6;    // -5 to +5
       counters[ temp+5 ]++;
     }

  for (i=0; i<11; i++)
       cout << i-5 << " " << counters[i] << endl;
}
```

The following table shows the frequency with which each of the 11 numbers appeared in a typical run of the program.

Number	−5	−4	−3	−2	−1	0	1	2	3	4	5
Frequency	40	52	101	110	150	201	152	120	86	60	20

• A.3.4 Example 4: Matching a Distribution

We may wish our generated numbers to reflect some previously observed data. For example, we simulate read requests to a disc unit in order to test cache algorithms. First, we record actual requests, then in our simulation use a stream of numbers with approximately the same distribution.

Imagine a line in which segments correspond to the data values and the length of a segment is proportional to the frequency with which that data value was observed. If we generate a random point on the line, we just need to determine which segment it falls into.

Suppose our observed frequency distribution of numbers is

Number	0	1	2	3	4	5	6	7	8	9	10
Observed	4	5	2	6	0	2	7	3	0	8	3

Thus, we want our generated numbers to be in the range 0 to 10, and for about three-fortieths of our numbers to be 7, one-fifth of the numbers to be 9, and so on. In the following program, the observed frequency of i is held in $F[i]$, and the sum of the observed frequencies (40 in our example) is in *SumFreq*.

The program generated 4000 numbers, therefore we would expect the number generated in each interval to be roughly 100 times the observed. The following table shows the frequency with which each of the 11 numbers was generated in a typical run of the program.

Number	0	1	2	3	4	5	6	7	8	9	10
Observed	**4**	**5**	**2**	**6**	**0**	**2**	**7**	**3**	**0**	**8**	**3**
Generated	400	486	180	627	0	187	701	316	0	810	293

```
#include <iostream.h>
#include <stdlib.h>
#include <time.h>

main()
{ int i,j,temp,sum;
  int counters [11];
  int F[11] = { 4,5,2,6,0,2,7,3,0,8,3 };
  int Sumfreq = 40;

  for (i=0; i<11; i++) counters[i]=0;

  srand(  (unsigned)time(NULL) );
```

```
for (i=0; i<4000; i++)
   {
     temp = rand() % Sumfreq;
     j = 0;
     sum = F[j];
     while (temp>=sum)
        { j = j + 1;
          sum = sum + F[j];
        }
     counters[j]++;
   }

for (i=0; i<11; i++)
     cout << i << " " << counters[i] << endl;
}
```

References

Marsaglia, G. 1995. *The Marsaglia Random Number CD-ROM with the Diehard Battery of Tests of Randomness.* Tallahassee: Florida State University. Also available at www.stat.fsu.edu/pub/diehard.

Marsaglia, G. 2003. Seeds for random number generators. *Communications of the ACM,* 46(5): 90–93.

Park, S. K., and K. W. Miller. 1998. Random number generators: Good ones are hard to find. *Communications of the ACM,* 31(10): 1192–1201.

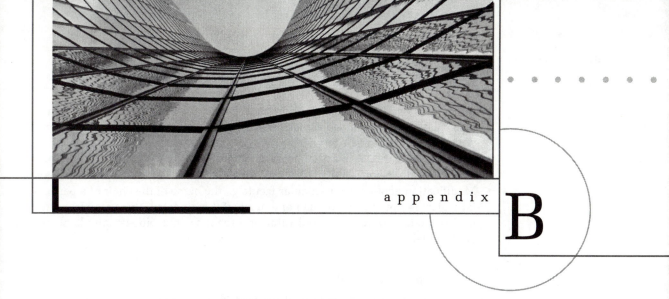

B

Data Normalization

B.1 Introduction

A **normal form** (NF) is a set of criteria that must be met by a set of record types. Several progressively more rigorous normal forms have been defined. We consider the first (1NF), second (2NF), third (3NF), Boyce–Codd (BCNF), fourth (4NF), and fifth (5NF) normal forms. Typically, a normal form is more rigorous than the one before it. For example, for a set of record types to satisfy the requirements of 3NF, it must satisfy all the requirements of 2NF and additional criteria.

B.1.1 Update Anomalies

Our motivation for making the data meet the criteria for a normal form is that it reduces the instances of **update anomalies**. An update anomaly can be one of three types: insertion, deletion, or modification. These are illustrated with the following data.

Student	Major	Department Chair
Bill	Math	Newton
Nancy	Chemistry	Boyle
Fred	Chemistry	Boyle
Anne	Psychology	King
Mike	Psychology	King
Victor	Chemistry	Boyle

- Insertion anomaly: Assuming we do not allow empty or null entries, we cannot insert data unless we have values for all three fields. So, if a new major begins with a department chair but no students, we cannot record it.
- Deletion anomaly: We may delete more data than we intended. For example, if the only Math major is removed, we lose the name of the Math department chair.
- Modification anomaly: A particular fact (e.g., the name of the chair of a particular major) is stored in more than one place. If it is updated, there may be a time during the update when the old value and the new value appear simultaneously in the table.

B.1.2 Running Example

We look at how normalization might proceed in the context of designing a set of record types for a small example application. Our data concern managers in a multinational corporation. The corporation has departments in various cities across the world. (We assume for the purposes of this example that city names and region names are unique. See Exercises.) Our first attempt at designing a record type is to have one record for each city as follows:

city, region, country, {(dept$_1$ manager$_1$), (dept$_2$ manager$_2$) ...}

Here are some example records.

City	Region	Country	(Dept Manager) ...
Boston	MA	USA	(Sales Bird) (R&D Orr)
Manchester	England	UK	(Sales Cantona) (Manufacturing Best)
New York	NY	USA	(R&D Ruth) (Sales Messier) (Legal Strawberry)

Note that the last field of our record type is open ended. It is an arbitrarily long list of the names of the departments and their managers in the particular city.

B.2 First Normal Form (1NF)

To be in first normal form (1NF), all fields must be atomic (i.e., cannot be decomposed into simpler elements.) This results in what is often called a **flat file**. Our last field, the list of managers, is not atomic. To make our unnormalized data conform with the requirements of 1NF, we have to eliminate the open-ended field. Thus, our revised record type is:

city, region, country, dept, manager

and if a city has five departments there will be five records, one for each department. Our three original records become seven.

City	Region	Country	Dept	Manager
Boston	MA	USA	Sales	Bird
Boston	MA	USA	R&D	Orr
Manchester	England	UK	Sales	Cantona
Manchester	England	UK	Manufacturing	Best
New York	NY	USA	R&D	Ruth
New York	NY	USA	Sales	Messier
New York	NY	USA	Legal	Strawberry

You may realize that this record type, like our earlier student example, may result in update anomalies. But we are not finished yet.

B.3 Functional Dependencies

Next, we introduce the idea of one field *determining* another. We say that field X determines field Y (and that Y is **functionally dependent** on X) if knowing the X value tells us what the Y value must be. We use the following notation for X determining Y:

$$X \rightarrow Y$$

Sometimes the **determinant** (on the left of the arrow) is a combination of fields. For example, we may only know C when we know both A and B. We write this as

$$(A,B) \rightarrow C$$

In addition, we can abbreviate

$$J \rightarrow K$$
$$J \rightarrow L$$

as

$$J \rightarrow K,L$$

In our example, we make the assumption that the same city does not house two departments of the same type. Thus (*city,dept*) is the (composite) key of our record type. Given the usual semantics of our fields, the dependencies are:

(city,dept) → manager
city → region
region → country
city → country

Now we can define second normal form.

B.4 Second Normal Form (2NF)

To be in second normal form (2NF), the data must be in 1NF and, in addition, all nonkey fields must be dependent on the whole of the primary key. Note that this means that 2NF can only be violated if we have a composite key, and is violated if we have a nonkey field that is dependent on only part of the key.

Our example data violates 2NF because *region* and *country* are dependent only on *city*. To make our 1NF-normalized data conform with the requirements of 2NF, we split it into two record types:

1. city dept manager
2. city region country

Our example data are now organized as

City	Dept	Manager
Boston	Sales	Bird
Boston	R&D	Orr
Manchester	Sales	Cantona
Manchester	R&D	Best
New York	R&D	Ruth
New York	Sales	Messier
New York	Legal	Strawberry

City	Region	Country
Boston	MA	USA
Manchester	England	UK
New York	NY	USA

Sometimes it is useful to represent dependencies diagrammatically. In our dependency graphs, we will enclose the primary key field(s) in a box and use arrows for dependencies. Our 1NF data can be represented thus:

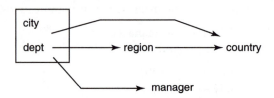

Normalization often requires decomposing a record type into two or more record types. This helps with anomalies but (1) may increase storage requirements and (2) may make certain operations more time-consuming. For example, to print the names of the managers and the cities in which they work, we now have to correlate two tables rather than make a simple pass through one.

Every time we have a dependency, there is a particular type of fact that we may wish to store. If Y is dependent on X, then we may wish to store the fact that a particular X value is associated with a particular Y value. Generally, what we are trying to do with normalization is to make sure that we can add, change, and delete facts independently of each other.

Consider the following.

X	Y	Z
a	m	r
b	t	w
c	g	q
a	m	w
c	g	w

What can we deduce about the dependencies between X, Y, and Z? Unless this set of records represents the only possible records, we can deduce nothing. The fact that records having the same value of X have the same value of Y in our sample cannot lead us to conclude anything about the general relationship between X and Y. Dependencies follow from the semantics of the domains, not from particular record instances. In order to normalize, we must know the dependencies.

B.5 Third Normal Form (3NF)

To be in third normal form (3NF), the data must be in 2NF and, in addition, there must be no dependencies between nonkey fields.

Third normal form prohibits dependencies between nonkey fields because wherever there is a dependency, there is potentially a fact we would like to store. If we permit dependencies between nonkey fields, we are unable to add and remove those facts unless there is also an associated primary key value.

Our (*city*, *region*, *country*) table violates 3NF. The primary key is *city*, the nonkey fields are *region* and *country*, but *region* determines *country*. The dependency graph is:

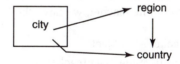

To make our data satisfy 3NF, we replace our second table by two tables:

1. City region
2. Region country

Our example data are now

City	Region
Boston	MA
Manchester	England
New York	NY

Region	Country
MA	USA
England	UK
NY	USA

Note that these record types would allow us to record the fact that Delaware is in the United States (for example) without needing to know of any cities there.

It turns out in our example that the final normalized data consists only of two-column tables that clearly cannot be decomposed further. This is not always the case. Fully normalized record types may have many fields.

First, second, and third normal forms were proposed in a paper by Codd.[1] Sometime later it was discovered that anomalies might still arise with data that are in third normal form. Examples of other normal forms are given in the following sections. However, as you will see, example violations are sometimes contrived. In practice, it is usually sufficient to make data conform to 3NF requirements.

B.6 Boyce–Codd Normal Form

Suppose we wish to record information about teachers, the subjects they teach, and the pupils enrolled in their classes. We propose a three-field record

teacher   subject   pupil

If each teacher teaches only one subject and a pupil only takes a particular subject from one teacher, we have the following dependencies:

teacher → subject
(pupil, subject) → teacher

The primary key must be composite because no single field is unique. In addition, (*teacher, subject*) is not unique, and if we make (*teacher, pupil*) the key we violate 2NF. That leaves us with (*pupil, subject*) as the primary key. Our record type must therefore satisfy 3NF because there is only one nonkey field. But the nonkey (*teacher*) determines part of the key (*subject*). So we could not record a particular *teacher-subject* combination unless we knew the name of a student. The dependency graph is:

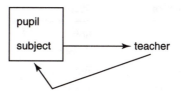

To satisfy Boyce–Codd normal form (BCNF), the data must be in 3NF and, in addition, every determinant must be a candidate key.

In our example, *teacher* is not a candidate key. In order to satisfy BCNF we split our data into two record types:

1. teacher   subject
2. pupil   teacher

In the first type, *teacher* is the primary key. In the second type, there is a composite key.

B.7 Fourth Normal Form (4NF)

Fourth normal form (4NF) is concerned with **multivalued dependencies**. We denote by

$X \twoheadrightarrow Y$

the fact that X **multidetermines** Y. In contrast with functional dependencies, this means that there is a set of Y values (rather than a single Y value) associated with a particular value of X. Some examples:

state $\twoheadrightarrow$ city

course $\twoheadrightarrow$ section

student $\twoheadrightarrow$ course

Sometimes multivalued dependencies can be a problem. Suppose we have a set of three-field records:

franchise   store   product

and multivalue dependencies

franchise $\twoheadrightarrow$ store

franchise $\twoheadrightarrow$ product

The semantics of the record collection are that all stores operated by a particular franchise must stock all products associated with the franchise. Thus, if we have the following four records

Franchise	Store	Product
7-11	Bob's	Cheese-its
7-11	Carol's	Slurpee
Stop'n'go	Ted's	Jawbreakers
Stop'n'go	Alice's	Diet Coke

then we must also have the following four records

7-11	Bob's	Slurpee
7-11	Carol's	Cheese-its
Stop'n'go	Ted's	Diet Coke
Stop'n'go	Alice's	Jawbreakers

Updating a file with these semantics is problematic. Inserting a record may require the insertion of other records. Deleting a particular record may require others to be deleted. Note that the above record type is all key and satisfies BCNF. Our (somewhat simplified) version of 4NF requires the two multivalued dependencies to be stored separately.

To be in fourth normal form (4NF), the data must be in BCNF and, in addition, if $A \twoheadrightarrow B$ is in R, then all (other) components of R are functionally dependent on A.

Thus, our data would be stored in two tables:

1. franchise   store
2. franchise   product

B.8 Fifth Normal Form (5NF)

The final normal form we consider is a catch-all. To be in fifth normal form (5NF) the data cannot be decomposable into simpler record types without loss of information. Naturally we must exclude trivial cases where the new record types have the same key as the old one and differ only by each having a subset of the nonkey fields.

To see how 5NF works, consider the following examples of the record type *ASSIGNMENTS*.

Profname	Department	Course
Jones	Math	FORTRAN
Jones	CS	FORTRAN
Brown	EE	Num. Methods
Brown	Math	Num. Methods
Brown	CS	Logic
Abbott	CS	Num. Methods
Abbott	Math	FORTRAN
Cowan	EE	Digital Circuits
Cowan	CS	FORTRAN

Assume that departments offer courses in many topic areas, and that professors, being highly versatile, can teach many types of courses for many departments. With no semantic constraints on the attributes, we need all three fields in one record type. The composite primary key is the combination of all three fields. The record type cannot be decomposed further: It is in 5NF.

Now consider the effect of adding a semantic constraint that says that if a professor teaches a certain course and he teaches for a department that offers that course, then he must teach the course for that department.

Under these conditions, we can represent the three-field *ASSIGNMENTS* record type by three two-field record types with less redundancy. First note that the previous set of records violates the new constraints. Here is a revised *ASSIGNMENTS*.

Profname	Department	Course
Jones	Math	FORTRAN
Jones	CS	FORTRAN
Brown	EE	Num. Methods
Brown	Math	Num. Methods
Brown	CS	Logic
Brown	*CS*	*Num. Methods*
Abbott	*CS*	*FORTRAN*
Abbott	CS	Num. Methods
Abbott	Math	FORTRAN
Abbott	*Math*	*Num. Methods*
Cowan	EE	Digital Circuits
Cowan	CS	FORTRAN

The three records in italics have been added to meet the new constraints. For example, Brown teaches for the EE, Math, and CS departments and teaches Num. Methods and Logic. The CS department offers a course in Num. Methods so, to meet the constraint on entries, Brown is assigned to teach it.

Our revised record specification (with the additional constraints) is not in 5NF because we can represent the same information by the three two-field record types (*AFFILIATIONS, EXPERTISE,* and *OFFERINGS*) that follow.

AFFILIATIONS

Profname	Department
Jones	Math
Jones	CS
Brown	CS
Brown	EE
Brown	Math
Abbott	CS
Abbott	Math
Cowan	EE
Cowan	CS

EXPERTISE

Profname	Course
Jones	FORTRAN
Brown	Num. Methods
Brown	Logic
Abbott	FORTRAN
Abbott	Num. Methods
Cowan	FORTRAN
Cowan	Digital Circuits

OFFERINGS

Department	Course
Math	FORTRAN
Math	Num. Methods
CS	FORTRAN
CS	LOGIC
CS	Num. Methods
EE	Num. Methods
EE	Digital Circuits

Note that we need all three of the two-field record types. Check this by eliminating in turn each of the three record types and see what three-field records you derive by combining the remaining two record types. You should find that in each case you get invalid records, that is, records not in the revised *ASSIGNMENTS*. For example, if we eliminate the *OFFERINGS* record type, we might deduce erroneously from *EXPERTISE* and *AFFILIATIONS* that Cowan teaches FORTRAN for the EE department.

Summary

We have seen that problems can arise if errors are made when grouping attributes into objects. We saw examples of insert, delete, and modification anomalies. The normalization process described here is a technique for minimizing anomalies.

Exercises

1. The Acme Tool Company buys tools from various suppliers and resells them to customers. Here is a fragment of their "database."

Part #	Part Name	Supplier #	Supplier Name	Quantity in Stock	Buy Price	Sell Price
10	Hammer	200	Ace Tools	30	$40	$45
10	Hammer	250	Jim's Tools	30	$42	$45
20	Wrench	200	Ace Tools	24	$25	$29
20	Wrench	300	Bob's Metal	24	$23	$29

   a. Draw a dependency diagram for this data. State clearly any assumptions you make.

   b. In what normal form is the data currently?

   c. If your answer to b is not BCNF, then show how the data can be rearranged so that it is in BCNF.

2. For each of the following five record specifications, the primary key and the dependencies are given. For each specification, (a) give the highest normal form that the specification is in (1NF, 2NF, 3NF, or BCNF), and, (b) if the specification is not in BCNF, give equivalent specifications that are.

   a. *R1* (e,f,g,h) primary key is *e*

      $e \rightarrow f, g, h$

      $f \rightarrow g$

   b. *R2* (m,n,o) primary key is *m*

      $m \rightarrow n, o$

   c. *R3* (i,j,k,l) composite primary key is (i,j,k)

      $j \rightarrow k$

      $(i,j,k) \rightarrow l$

    d. *R4 (p,q,r,s)* composite primary key is *(p,q)*

      (p,q) → r,s

      r → s

    e. *R5 (a,b,c,d)* composite primary key is *(a,b)*

      (a,b) → c

      b → d

3. How does our running normalization example change if we, more realistically, recognize that names of cities and regions are not unique in the world? (Still assume that country names are unique.)

4. Why is Boyce–Codd normal form not violated when a nonkey attribute determines the key? Compare the following record types.

    a. *R1 (a,b,c,d)*   key is *(a,b)*

      Dependencies: *(a,b) → c,d*   *c → b*

    b. *R2 (t,u,v,w)*   key is *t*

      Dependencies: *t → u,v,w*   *u → t*

    c. *R3 (p,q,r,s)*   key is *(p,q)*

      Dependencies: *(p,q) → r,s*   *r → p*   *r → q*

5. Normalize the following record type.

    R: (a, b, c, d, e, f) key is *a*

      a → b, c, d, e, f

      b → a

      c → f

6. Suppose we have *R: (a, b, c, d)* and dependencies

    a → b, c, d

    b → c

    c → d

    a. What normal form is *R* in?

    b. Give a fully normalized version.

7. For each of the following five record specifications, the primary key and the dependencies are given. For each specification, (a) give the highest normal form that the

specification is in (1NF, 2NF, 3NF or BCNF), and, (b) if the specification is not in BCNF, give equivalent specifications that are.

a. *R1 (e,f,g,h)*   key is *e*

$e \rightarrow f, g, h$

$f \rightarrow g$

b. *R2 (m,n,o)*   key is *m*

$m \rightarrow n, o$

c. *R3 (i,j,k,l)* composite key is *(i,j,k)*

$j \rightarrow k$

$(i,j,k) \rightarrow l$

d. *R4 (p,q,r,s)* composite key is *(p,q)*

$(p,q) \rightarrow r,s$

$r \rightarrow s$

e. *R5 (a,b,c,d)* composite key is *(a,b)*

$(a,b) \rightarrow c$

$b \rightarrow d$

8. The dean has asked you to design a set of records to hold information about students, the classes they are taking, the professors that teach the classes, and so on. Here (in no particular order) is a list of the 14 attributes involved:

student-id	ticket-number
course-number	prof-name
class-start-time	class-finish-time
student-name	prof-office
prof-phone	course-title
course-units	classroom
student-address	student-phone

Assuming that the attributes have their usual meaning, show how you would group these into record types. The data should be normalized but have as few record types as possible. In your solution, identify primary keys and foreign keys. (Hint: Start with an intuitive grouping of the fields, then check for violations of normal forms.)

9. For each of the following entity specifications, the primary key and dependencies are given. For each specification, indicate whether it is in BCNF. If it is not in BCNF, (a) show why it is not and (b) give equivalent specifications that are in BCNF.

   a. (A,B,C,D) key is (A,B)

   Dependencies: $(A,B) \rightarrow D$ $(A,B) \rightarrow C$ $B \rightarrow A$

   b. (A,B,C,D) key is (A,B)

   Dependencies: $(A,B) \rightarrow D$ $(A,B) \rightarrow C$ $C \rightarrow B$

   c. (A,B,C,D) key is (A,B)

   Dependencies: $(A,B) \rightarrow D$ $(A,B) \rightarrow C$ $C \rightarrow D$

10. For each of the following statements, indicate if it is true or false. If you think it is false, provide a counterexample.

    a. Any record type that is all-key must be in at least 3NF.

    b. If the minimal primary key for a record type is a composite key, then the specification includes a multivalued dependency.

    c. Any table can be decomposed into tables of a higher normal form.

    d. Any record type with a noncomposite key must be in 2NF.

    e. If $A \rightarrow B$ and $B \rightarrow C$, then $A \rightarrow C$.

11. What is the difference between a functional dependency $(X \rightarrow Y)$ and a multivalued dependency $(p \twoheadrightarrow q)$?

    Describe why it might be a problem if a table contains two independent multivalued dependencies.

12. For each of the following entity specifications, the primary key and dependencies are given. For each specification, indicate whether or not it is in BCNF. If it is not in BCNF, show why it is not and give equivalent specifications that are in BCNF.

    a. $R1$ (b, e, a, c, h) key is (b,e)

    Dependencies: $(b,e) \rightarrow a,c,h$ $c \rightarrow h$ $a \rightarrow b$

    b. $R2$ (s,u,r,f) key is (s,u)

    Dependencies: $(s,u) \rightarrow r,f$ $u \rightarrow f$

    c. $R3$ (n,o,w) key is n

    Dependencies: $n \rightarrow o,w$ $w \rightarrow o$

d.   *R4 (t,u,v,w)*   key is *t*

Dependencies: $t \rightarrow u,v,w$ $u \rightarrow t$

e.   *R5 (a,b,c,d,e,f)*   key is *a*

Dependencies: $a \rightarrow b,c,f,d,e$ $b \rightarrow a$ $c \rightarrow f$

NOTES

[1]Codd, E. F. 1970. A relational model of data for large shared data banks. *Communications of the ACM,* 13(6): 377–387.

Test of File Object

This appendix provides a program that tests the class *BinaryFile*, which was defined in Chapter 9. The class definition is in the included file *binfile.h*.

Imagine a program with a file attached on the left and a file attached on the right. The test program defines two record types and files of the record types. The record types are as follows:

- *leftrecord:* Contains an integer and a 20-character string
- *rightrecord:* Contains four integers

The menu-driven main program enables a user to quit the program (*q*) and perform six operations on the files. Each operation is triggered by a single-character command as follows:

    a: Create the left file (10 records) with random data
    b: Create the right file (five records) with zeros
    c: List the contents of the left file
    d: List the contents of the right file
    e: Left-to-right transfer—divide the integer among the four integers.
    f: Right-to-left transfer—sum the four integers into the destination integer

Following the program listing is the output from a run of the program.

```
#include <iostream.h>
#include <stdio.h>    // for sprintf
#include <stdlib.h>   // for rand
```

```cpp
#include <iomanip.h>  // for setw

#include "binfile.h"  // for class definition

char leftname[20],rightname[20];

// the record declarations

struct leftrecord  { int key; char descript[20]; };
struct rightrecord { int quarters[4]; };

// the two file objects

BinaryFile<leftrecord> left;
BinaryFile<rightrecord> right;

// temporary records

leftrecord templeft;
rightrecord tempright;

// create 10 simple records and write them out to the left
void Createleft()
{
  cout << "file name for left: ";
  cin >> leftname;
  left.open(leftname,ios::out);
  for (int i=0; i<10; i++)
    {
      templeft.key = rand();
      sprintf(templeft.descript, "item # %d", i);
      left.putRecord(i,templeft);
    }
  left.close();
}

// create 5 empty records and write to the right file.
void Createright()
{
  cout << "file name for right: ";
  cin >> rightname;
  right.open(rightname,ios::out);
  for (int i=0; i<4; i++) tempright.quarters[i]=0;
  for (int i=0; i<5; i++)
```

```
        {
          right.putRecord(i,tempright);
        }
    right.close();
}

// show current contents of left file
void Listleft()
{
  left.open(leftname,ios::in);
  for (int i=0;i<10;i++)
      {
        left.getRecord(i,templeft);
        cout << setw(7) << templeft.key << "   "
            << templeft.descript <<  endl;
      }
  left.close();
}


// show current contents of right file
void Listright()
{
  right.open(rightname,ios::in);
  for (int i=0;i<5;i++)
      {
        right.getRecord(i,tempright);
        cout << "Right record # " << i  << "      ";
        for (int j=0; j<4; j++)
            cout << setw(5) << tempright.quarters[j];
        cout << endl;
      }
  right.close();
}

void righttoleft()
{
  int recright,recleft;

  right.open(rightname,ios::in);
  cout << "which right record: ";
  cin >> recright;
  right.getRecord(recright,tempright);
  right.close();
```

```
      left.open(leftname,ios::in|ios::out);
      cout << "which left record: ";
      cin >> recleft;
      left.getRecord(recleft,templeft);
      templeft.key=0;
      for (int i=0;i<4;i++) templeft.key+=tempright.quarters[i];
      left.putRecord(recleft,templeft);
      left.close();
}

void lefttoright()
{
   int recright,recleft;

   left.open(leftname,ios::in);
   cout << "which left record: ";
   cin >> recleft;
   left.getRecord(recleft,templeft);
   left.close();
   for (int i=0;i<4;i++) tempright.quarters[i]=templeft.key/4;
   right.open(rightname,ios::in|ios::out);
   cout << "which right record: ";
   cin >> recright;
   right.putRecord(recright,tempright);
   right.close();
}


void menu()
{
   cout << "a: create left b: create right c: list left d: list right"
        << endl;
   cout << "e: left-to-right transfer f: right-to-left transfer" << endl;
}




int main ()
{

   char command;
```

```
menu();
cout << "Command: ";
cin >> command;
while (command != 'q')
  {
   switch (command)
    {
     case 'a': //"open left 10 record - random
             Createleft();
                break;
     case 'b': //"open right 5 records - zeros
                Createright();
                break;
     case 'c': //"list left 10
                Listleft();
                break;
     case 'd': //"list right 5
                Listright();
                break;
     case 'e': //left to right transfer
                lefttoright();
                break;
     case 'f': //right to left transfer
                righttoleft();
                break;
     default : cout << "Bad command: " << command << endl;
    }
    menu();
    cout << "Command: ";
    cin >> command;
  }
}
```

Here is the output from a run of the program.

```
a: create left b: create right c: list left d: list right
e: left-to-right transfer f: right-to-left transfer
Command: a
file name for left: leftfile
a: create left b: create right c: list left d: list right
e: left-to-right transfer f: right-to-left transfer
Command: b
file name for right: rightfile
a: create left b: create right c: list left d: list right
```

```
e: left-to-right transfer f: right-to-left transfer
Command: c
  16838  item # 0
   5758  item # 1
  10113  item # 2
  17515  item # 3
  31051  item # 4
   5627  item # 5
  23010  item # 6
   7419  item # 7
  16212  item # 8
   4086  item # 9
a: create left b: create right c: list left d: list right
e: left-to-right transfer f: right-to-left transfer
Command: d
Right record # 0        0     0     0     0
Right record # 1        0     0     0     0
Right record # 2        0     0     0     0
Right record # 3        0     0     0     0
Right record # 4        0     0     0     0
a: create left b: create right c: list left d: list right
e: left-to-right transfer f: right-to-left transfer
Command: e
which left record: 8
which right record: 1
a: create left b: create right c: list left d: list right
e: left-to-right transfer f: right-to-left transfer
Command: d
Right record # 0        0     0     0     0
Right record # 1     4053  4053  4053  4053
Right record # 2        0     0     0     0
Right record # 3        0     0     0     0
Right record # 4        0     0     0     0
a: create left b: create right c: list left d: list right
e: left-to-right transfer f: right-to-left transfer
Command: f
which right record: 3
which left record: 5
a: create left b: create right c: list left d: list right
e: left-to-right transfer f: right-to-left transfer
Command: c
  16838  item # 0
   5758  item # 1
  10113  item # 2
```

```
17515  item # 3
31051  item # 4
    0  item # 5
23010  item # 6
 7419  item # 7
16212  item # 8
 4086  item # 9
```
a: create left b: create right c: list left d: list right
e: left-to-right transfer f: right-to-left transfer
Command: f
which right record: 1
which left record: 9
a: create left b: create right c: list left d: list right
e: left-to-right transfer f: right-to-left transfer
Command: c
```
16838  item # 0
 5758  item # 1
10113  item # 2
17515  item # 3
31051  item # 4
    0  item # 5
23010  item # 6
 7419  item # 7
16212  item # 8
16212  item # 9
```
a: create left b: create right c: list left d: list right
e: left-to-right transfer f: right-to-left transfer
Command: q

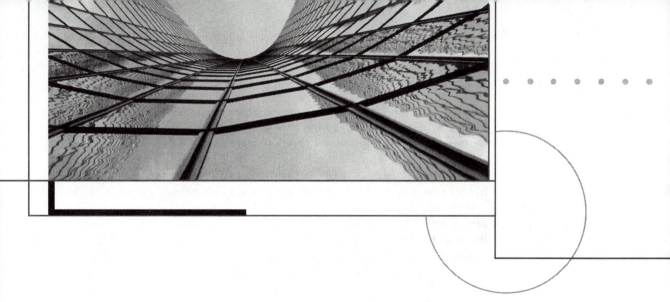

Glossary

This glossary includes definitions of the terms introduced in bold in the text. Other related terms have also been included. A useful resource is the *Dictionary of Algorithms and Data Structures* at www.nist.gov/dads.

Activity network   A network in which an activity is associated with each edge or with each vertex.

Acyclic   A graph that does not contain a cycle.

Address   Where to find an item; the address of an item might be the number of a byte in main memory or the number of a sector on a disc.

Address space   A set of valid addresses.

Adjacency list   When used to represent a graph, such a list holds information about the vertices directly connected to a particular vertex.

Adjacency matrix   A way to represent the connectivity of a graph; for example, matrix entry $M[i][j]$ holds information about the connection between vertices V_i and V_j.

Adjacent siblings   In a multiway tree, two nodes that have the same parent node and are referenced by adjacent pointers in the parent.

Allocation unit   The amount of disk space assigned at one time by the operating system during file creation.

Arc   In a graph, a link between two vertices that has a direction associated with it.

Associative memory   A memory in which the elements are accessed by content rather than by address.

Base class   An object class definition from which other definitions are derived.

Base type   The type over which a set is defined. All members of the set are of the type. All possible values of the type are either in the set or not in the set.

Batch updating   A file updating process in which transactions are collected and an update program is run periodically. This contrasts with processing the transactions immediately.

Binary search tree   A binary tree in which data are ordered systematically to facilitate searching.

Binary tree   A tree in which each parent node has at most two children.

Bit map (bit vector, bit list)   A one-dimensional array of bits used to indicate whether each of a set of objects has a particular property. Useful for inverted indexes in which an attribute has a limited set of values.

Block   Often synonymous with the physical record, that is, the unit of transfer between a secondary storage device and main memory.

Blocking factor   The number of logical records packed into a physical record (block).

Boyce–Codd dependency   The functional dependency of part of a key attribute on a nonkey attribute.

bpi (bits per inch)   A measure of recording density; typically, it refers to the number of bits in an inch of a track (tape or disk).

Breadth-first search   A search that works outwards from the starting point, exhausting the closest space before looking further away.

Bucket   In the context of a hash file, the unit of a file having a particular address.

Buddy bucket   In dynamic hashing, two buckets are buddies if they are pointed to by external nodes with the same parent. In extendible hashing, buddy buckets are pointed to from adjacent entries in the directory.

Bushiness   The number of children a tree node has.

Cache memory   A relatively small, fast memory designed to reduce the number of accesses required to an associated larger but slower memory.

Candidate key   A field or combination of fields that will uniquely identify a record in a file. A candidate key is a potential primary key.

Chaining   In hashing, a technique for handling overflowing entries that links them together. See also *closed addressing*.

Checksum   Information computed from and stored with data values; used to detect read/write errors.

Child node   In a tree, a node pointed to directly from a particular node.

Circular list   A list in which the last element points back to the first.

Closed addressing   The collection of hash overflow resolution methods in which overflow records are found by following pointers rather than calculating addresses. See also *chaining*.

Cluster   In a file system, a group of disk sectors allocated and deallocated as a unit. See also *allocation unit*.

Clustering   A defect of the linear probe overflow technique for hashing in which records tend to bunch together in a sequence of full buckets.

Codeword   A binary string representing a symbol.

Collision   Occurs in hashing when two logical records hash to the same address.

Complete binary tree   A binary tree in which each level is full except possibly for the last. If the last is not full, then its nodes are as far to the left as possible.

Complete graph   A graph in which every edge/arc that might exist does exist.

Composite key   A candidate key comprising more than one attribute.

Concatenation   Joining together; concatenation of adjacent sibling nodes is used in B-trees as a solution to node underflow.

Connected graph   A graph having no isolated subgraphs.

Constructor   A function called automatically when an object is created.

Content-addressable memory   A memory in which the elements are accessed by content rather than address. See *associative memory*.

Contiguous storage   In a file system, a space allocation method that stores a file in consecutive and adjacent allocation units.

Control area   Larger unit of storage in Virtual Storage Access Method.

Control interval   Smaller unit of storage in Virtual Storage Access Method.

Copy-back strategy   In a cache, a strategy whereby changes to a cache item are not written immediately to the slower memory.

Critical path   A path through an activity-on-edge network in which an increase in the time taken by any activity on the path increases the overall time required to complete the total activity.

Cycle   In a graph, a path that starts and finishes at the same vertex.

Cyclic   A graph that contains a cycle.

Cyclic redundancy check   A form of check data for a data block, for example, a disk sector; bits derived from the data are added to the block.

Cylinder   A set of tracks (one on each surface) having the same radius on a multi-surface disk pack. All tracks in a cylinder can be referenced without movement of the read/write heads.

Cylinder index   In ISAM, an index with an entry for each cylinder on which data are stored.

Database   A collection of integrated files designed to serve multiple applications.

Database management system (DBMS)   A collection of programs that allows the creation and maintenance of a database. A DBMS should insulate user programs from the physical database. A DBMS handles mapping from program perspectives to actual storage.

Data track   In ISAM, a disk track containing elements of the sequential file (as opposed to index entries).

Declustering   A technique for implementing a grid file in which buckets are dispersed over multiple disks.

Degree   In a graph, the number of edges attached to a vertex.

Deletion anomaly   When a deletion operation removes more information than was intended.

Depth-first search   A search technique that examines child nodes before sibling nodes. Such a search checks extremes before exhausting the local space. Compare with *breadth-first search*.

Deque A linear data structure in which items can be added and removed at either end.

Derived class When the definition of a class is based on another (base) class.

Destructor function A function called automatically when an object ceases to exist.

Determinant Attribute(s) on which some other attribute is fully functionally dependent.

Diameter The length of the longest path between any two vertices in the graph.

Direct-access file A file in which all records are equally accessible at any time.

Directed graph A graph in which there is a direction associated with links between edges.

Directory In a file system, a file holding information about a set of files. In the extendible hashing file organization, a directory points to leaves (buckets) that hold records.

Disk controller Hardware responsible for the low-level operation of a device such as a disk (or set of disks).

Double hashing A hashing technique used to reduce clustering. In double hashing, the linear probe step size is the result of a second function applied to the key.

Double-linked list A list in which a node points both to its successor and to its predecessor.

Double rotation An operation on an AVL tree to restore its height-balanced properties; involves two rotations around nodes.

Dummy partition In the Knuth–Gilstad sorting algorithm, this is a partition that exists only as a number in a table. It is used to make the algorithm perform optimally.

Dynamic index An index that may change shape as the indexed file is modified.

Edge A directionless link between two vertices in a graph. See also *arc*.

Error-correcting code A set of codewords so designed that some corruptions of a codeword can be detected and corrected.

Eulerian cycle A cycle in a graph that traverses each edge in the graph exactly once.

Eulerian path A path in a graph that traverses each edge in the graph exactly once.

Extensible file A file that can change size dynamically (shrinking as well as growing). Sometimes called a dynamic file.

External sorting Sorting in which, at any time, some (usually most) of the data being sorted are in secondary (external) memory rather than primary memory.

Field A named component of a record that can be manipulated independently of other components.

File A named collection of data almost always held on a secondary storage device.

File pointer Part of a high-level language interface to a file. It references the current accessible byte.

File stream In a high-level language, an object to which a file can be attached (and from which it can be detached). Stream methods enable transfer of data to and from the file.

File system   Collection of files maintained for users by an operating system.

File-use ratio   The proportion of records in a file used in a run of an application program.

Fixed head disk   An unmoving read/write head on a data storage device. Because each track has a separate read/write head, the heads do not need to move.

Flat file   A file in which the fields of records are simple atomic values. Relational databases require flat files.

Folding   In a hash function, the action of superimposing sections of a bitstring.

Formatting information   Data written to a secondary storage medium so that it can subsequently hold retrievable data.

Foreign key   A field in a record type that is the primary key of a second record type.

Full binary tree   A binary tree in which each level contains the maximum possible number of nodes.

Full functional dependency   Attribute Y is fully functionally dependent on a set of attributes X if it is functionally dependent on the whole of the set X and not on any proper subset of X.

Functionally dependent   A record attribute Y is functionally dependent on attribute X if, when two records have the same value of X, they must have the same value of Y.

Garbage collector   A system utility that reclaims memory blocks that were previously allocated by a user program but are now inaccessible.

Graph   A set of vertices and a set (possibly empty) of links between them.

Grid   An orthogonal partitioning of a space resulting from partitions on each dimension.

Grid array   Part of the grid directory that holds pointers to buckets.

Grid block   A subdivision of a space partitioned by a grid.

Grid directory   In a grid file organization, a k-dimensional structure that keeps track of the assignment of buckets to grid blocks.

Grid file   A file structure permitting efficient processing of range queries in multi-dimensional space.

Hamiltonian cycle   A cycle in a graph that visits each vertex in the graph exactly once.

Hamiltonian path   A path in a graph that visits each vertex in the graph exactly once.

Hash function   A function that maps a set of keys onto a set of addresses.

Hash table   A data structure in which entries are placed by means of a hash function.

Hashing   A storage and retrieval technique that uses a hash function to map records onto store addresses.

Height   In a tree, the length of the longest path from the root to a leaf.

Hierarchical database   A database in which record types are related in a tree-like structure.

Hierarchical definition tree A component of a hierarchical database that specifies the relationship between record types.

Hierarchical file system A file system in which files reside on a variety of media with different access and cost properties.

Hit ratio The proportion of read/write requests that can be satisfied from a cache memory.

Home buckets In a hash file, the buckets with addresses that can be produced by the hash function.

In-degree In a directed graph, the in-degree of a vertex is the number of arcs that terminate at that node.

Index Typically, a data structure of (key,address) pairs used to decrease file access times.

Indexed sequential file A sequential file supplemented by an index that speeds up access to records when the key value is known.

Indexing A technique for reducing storage and retrieval times by using an index to point to data areas.

Inheritance In object-oriented programming, a mechanism by which new classes can be defined in terms of existing classes.

i-node An index node in the Unix file system. Contains pointers (both direct and indirect) to blocks of a file as well as information about the file as a whole, such as the date of last access.

Insertion anomaly When partial information (usually incomplete records with no key) cannot be stored because of the record types available.

Internal sorting Sort methods that assume that the data to be sorted will fit entirely in main memory.

Inverted file An index from which the records in the main file with a particular attribute value can be determined.

Iterator A pointer-like object used to move through a data structure that frees the user from low-level details of how to move from one entry to the next.

Key A field or set of fields by which a record may be accessed. See also *composite key*.

Key space The set of values for a key.

Knight's tour A connected sequence of knight moves around a chess board in which each square is visited exactly once.

Latency In general, waiting time; often used to mean the delay in a disk transfer while the appropriate sector rotates to a read/write position.

Leaf A tree node without children.

Linear probe A method of searching for free space (to resolve overflow in hashing) by examining file/table entries at fixed intervals. A type of open addressing.

Linear scales Part of the grid directory in the grid file organization. Linear scales hold the partition points of a domain.

Linked storage A data structure in which elements contain pointers to other elements.

List   A collection of objects in which an item is accessible from its predecessor (single-linked list) or from both its predecessor and successor (double-linked list).

Locking   A technique for preventing conflicting concurrent operations on a data item.

Logical data independence   The insulation of user programs from changes in the logical database; achieved by using functional databases.

Logical data transfer   An apparent transfer between main memory and secondary memory.

Logical organization   The organization of data from the point of view of a user as opposed to organization on storage devices.

Logical representation   A user application's conception of data.

Logical track   A disk can be viewed as a series of logical tracks mapped onto physical tracks. This may be the view of a utility that can remap around faulty disk areas.

Map   An abstract data structure that stores and retrieves items by primary (unique) key.

Master index   In ISAM, the top level of the index.

Max-heap   A heap (complete binary tree) in which the value in a parent node is greater than or equal to the values in any child node.

Memo function   A function that remembers previously computed (parameter, result) pairs.

Memory leak   In a system without garbage collection, a memory block that becomes inaccessible to a user program and is not returned to the free space area.

Min-heap   A heap (complete binary tree) in which the value in a parent node is less than or equal to the values in any child node.

Minimum spanning tree   Of the spanning trees in a graph, the one with the smallest sum of weights on its edges.

Modification anomaly   When a modification results in inconsistent data (loss of data integrity).

Moving head   A read/write head in a storage device that serves more than one track. It must therefore be capable of moving from track to track.

Multidetermines   In an entity specification, X multidetermines Y if, whenever two entities have the same value of X, their Y values must be drawn from the same set of values.

Multigraph   A graph in which it is permissible to have more than one edge/arc between a particular pair of vertices.

Multikey retrieval   Retrieval of records by specifying values for secondary keys.

Multimap   A data structure that associates one or more items with a particular key.

Multiset   A set in which the same item may appear more than once.

Multivalued dependency   If X multidetermines Y, then whenever two records have the same value of X, their Y values must be drawn from the same set. See also *functionally dependent*.

Network   A graph in which a value or weight is associated with each edge.

Node   An element of a linked structure such as a list or tree.

Node-splitting   An action taken in response to an overflow. The contents of a node are divided. Typically involves adding a new node to the data structure.

Normal form   A set of conditions defined on a record/entity specification.

Normalization   The design process for generating entity specifications (logical record specifications) to minimize both data redundancy and update anomalies; generates entity specifications that conform to normal forms.

Object   An encapsulation of an entity that includes state and behavior.

Object database   A database capable of holding nonatomic items.

Object-oriented design   A software development technique that focuses on identifying objects and their inter-relationships.

Open addressing   Overflow resolution technique for hashing in which overflow records are placed and located by address calculation rather than by linked storage.

Operator overloading   Use of a single symbol to represent operations with different operand types. For example, the symbol * could represent multiplication operations defined for integers, floating point numbers, and matrices.

Out-degree   In a directed graph, the out-degree of a vertex is the number of arcs that begin at that vertex.

Overflow   Occurs when an insertion is attempted into a bucket or node that is full.

Packing density   The proportion of reserved space actually occupied by data.

Parent   In a tree, the node that immediately precedes the current node in the path from the root.

Partition   In external sorting, a subsection of the data being sorted (in this context, a synonym for run and string).

Partially functional dependency   The functional dependency of attribute Y on only a part of composite key X.

Pass   In external sorting, a measure of the number of read operations required to merge sorted data.

Path   In a graph, a path is a sequence of edges in which the end point of one edge is the beginning of the next.

Periodic maintenance   Action required on a data structure from time to time in order to restore some level of performance.

Persistence   A characteristic of a data item. A persistent item typically has an indefinite lifetime.

Phase   In external sorting, a stage during which the assignment of input and output files remains constant.

Physical data transfer   An actual data transfer that takes place between main memory and secondary memory.

Planar graph   A graph that can be drawn on a two-dimensional plane with no edges crossing.

Platter   The rotating, plate-like component of a disk drive on which data are recorded.

Point query A completely specified query; that is, a query in which a single value is specified for each key attribute. (A query to determine whether or not such a record exists.)

Precedence graph A graph in which the existence of an edge from V_i to V_j typically indicates that the entity represented by V_i has precedence over the entity represented by V_j.

Primary clustering In hashing using a linear probe, the tendency for records to bunch in a subset of the buckets because of the overlaying of overflow sequences.

Primary key A field or combination of fields that uniquely identifies a record in a file.

Priority queue A queue in which items are held not in order of arrival, but in order of some attribute.

Proper subset A is a proper subset of B if A is a subset of B and there is at least one item in B that is not in A.

Pseudo-key A sequence of bits generated from a record key in the extendible file organization.

Query language Usually a nonprocedural language in which users of a DBMS express transactions (updates as well as queries).

Queue A linear structure in which items are added at one end and removed at the other; thus, a First-In-First-Out (FIFO) structure.

Range query A query that, in part, specifies a range of values that an attribute must satisfy (e.g., 2.5 > GPA < 3.5).

Record A collection of fields that can be manipulated as a single entity.

Recurrence relation The specification of a sequence in which a member is defined in terms of earlier members (e.g., $T(n) = 2T(n/2) + n - 1$).

Redistribution In a B-tree, a solution to node overflow or underflow in which records are redistributed among the nodes, but there is no change in the number of nodes.

Reentrant knight's tour A knight's tour with the property that an additional move will return the knight to the starting square.

Relation A subset of the cross-product of one or more sets of attribute values.

Root The only node in a tree that has no parent.

Rotation In an AVL tree, a local change viewed as a rotation around a node; part of the process of maintaining height-balance properties.

Run In external sorting, a subsection of the data being sorted (in this context, a synonym for partition and string).

Secondary clustering In hashing using open addressing, the bunching of records in particular buckets because all records hashing to the same home bucket follow the same sequence of overflow buckets.

Secondary key A field of a record by which we may wish to retrieve the record but whose value is not unique to a particular record. See also *primary key*.

Sector An angular division of a disk or, particularly, a disk track.

Seed An initial value from which a sequence of pseudo-random numbers is derived.

Seek time The time that a disk needs to move the read-write heads to the appropriate track.

Separating record In a multiway tree, the record between pointers to adjacent siblings.

Sequence set Linked terminal nodes of a B$^+$-tree; also linked structure in VSAM.

Sequential file A file in which items are stored in order of some key.

Serial access file A file in which a record is accessible only after the preceding records have been processed.

Set An unordered collection of values of some base type. Every possible member of the base type is either in the set or not in the set.

Sibling node Two nodes are siblings if they have the same parent.

Signature A bitstring generated from a record key in table-assisted hashing.

Single rotation In an AVL tree, an operation involving three nodes that rotates data around one of them.

Single-valued dependency A single-valued dependency of Y on X means that a value of X determines a single value of Y. Compare with *multivalued dependency*.

Skip list A linear list augmented with pointers that enable algorithms to skip over some elements of the list.

Skip table The Boyer–Moore string searching algorithm uses a skip table to determine the distance that a pattern can be moved down the string following a character mismatch.

Sort-merge A sorting strategy in which subsections of the data are sorted and then the sorted subsections are merged together.

Spanning tree A subset of the edges in a graph that forms a tree and includes all the vertices of the graph.

Sparse array An array in which a large percentage of the elements have the same value (typically zero).

Splitting Dividing a node; a solution to node overflow in a B-tree.

Stable sort A sorting algorithm that preserves the relative positions of two items having the same value of the sort key.

Stack A linear structure in which items are added and removed at the same end; thus, a Last-In-First-Out (LIFO) structure.

Static index An index that does not change shape as the indexed file is modified.

String In external sorting, a subsection of the data being sorted (in this context, a synonym for partition and run).

Subset Set A is a subset of set B if all members of A are members of B.

Subtree A tree that is the child of a particular node.

Symbol table A data structure holding items in which the key field is typically a string; used frequently in language processing.

Synonyms Two keys that hash to the same value.

Tail recursion A form of recursion in which the recursive call is the last action performed.

Template In C++, a mechanism that permits objects of various types to be created from a single class definition.

Ternary tree A tree in which a node may have up to three children.

Topological ordering An ordering of the vertices of a graph where the existence of an edge V_{ij} means that V_i precedes V_j in the ordering.

Track The projection onto a recording surface of a position of a read/write head; the positions where data can be stored on a disk or tape.

Track identification bits Bits written during disk formatting to identify tracks.

Track index The lowest level of index in ISAM; typically one entry for each data track.

Transaction An operation performed on a set of data. Queries, insertions, deletions, and modifications are typical transactions.

Transient A transient data item is one having has a definite lifetime, perhaps the execution of a subprogram.

Transitive closure Instance in which graph G has the same vertices as G and an edge V_{ij} if there is a path from V_i to V_j in G.

Transitive dependencies If Y is dependent on X, and Z is dependent on Y, then Z is transitively dependent on X.

Tree A nonempty tree has a root node to which are attached zero or more subtrees that are themselves trees.

Tree traversal A systematic (often recursive) visiting of nodes in a tree.

Trie A tree-based data structure in which each level holds only part of the key rather than complete key.

Trivial dependency The dependency of an attribute on itself.

Unconnected graph A graph having one or more isolated subgraphs.

Underflow In the context of B-trees (and variations), a situation that occurs when the number of records in a node falls below a minimum.

Undirected graph A graph in which there is no direction associated with any of the links that connect vertices.

Update anomaly An undesirable side effect caused by an insertion, deletion, or modification.

Vertex A graph element comparable to a node in a tree.

Write-through strategy A strategy that may be adopted in the maintenance of a cache memory so that when a cache item is written to, the same change is made to the appropriate item in the slower memory.

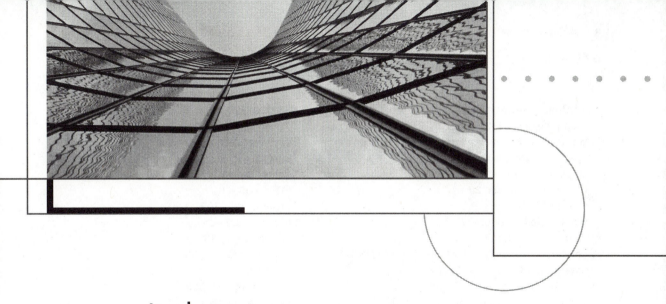

Index

Outstanding New Titles:

Computer Science Illuminated, Second Edition
Nell Dale and John Lewis
ISBN: 0-7637-0799-6
©2004

Programming and Problem Solving with C++, Fourth Edition
Nell Dale and Chip Weems
ISBN: 0-7637-0798-8
©2004

Programming and Problem Solving with Java
Nell Dale, Chip Weems,
and Mark R. Headington
ISBN: 0-7637-0490-3
©2003

C++ Plus Data Structures, Third Edition
Nell Dale
ISBN: 0-7637-0481-4
©2003

Databases Illuminated
Catherine Ricardo
ISBN: 0-7637-3314-8
©2004

Applied Data Structures with C++
Peter Smith
ISBN: 0-7637-2562-5
©2004

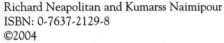

Foundations of Algorithms Using Java Pseudocode
Richard Neapolitan and Kumarss Naimipour
ISBN: 0-7637-2129-8
©2004

Foundations of Algorithms Using C++ Pseudocode, Third Edition
Richard Neapolitan and Kumarss Naimipour
ISBN: 0-7637-2387-8
©2004

Artificial Intelligence Illuminated
Ben Coppin
ISBN: 0-7637-3230-3
©2004

Managing Software Projects
Frank Tsui
ISBN: 0-7637-2546-3
©2004

The Essentials of Computer Organization and Architecture
Linda Null and Julia Lobur
ISBN: 0-7637-0444-X
©2003

Readings in CyberEthics, Second Edition
Richard Spinello and Herman Tavani
ISBN: 0-7637-2410-6
©2004

A Complete Guide to C#
David Bishop
ISBN: 0-7637-2249-9
©2004

C#.NET Illuminated
Art Gittleman
ISBN: 0-7637-2593-5
©2004

A First Course in Complex Analysis with Applications
Dennis G. Zill and Patrick Shanahan
ISBN: 0-7637-1437-2
©2003

Discrete Mathematics, Second Edition
James L. Hein
ISBN: 0-7637-2210-3
©2003

http://www.jbpub.com/

JONES AND BARTLETT PUBLISHERS
BOSTON   TORONTO   LONDON   SINGAPORE

1.800.832.0034

Take Your Courses to the Next Level

Turn the page to preview new and forthcoming titles in Computer Science and Math from Jones and Bartlett...

Providing solutions for students and educators in the following disciplines:

- Introductory Computer Science
- Java
- C++
- Databases
- C#
- Data Structures

- Algorithms
- Network Security
- Software Engineering
- Discrete Mathematics
- Engineering Mathematics
- Complex Analysis

Please visit http://computerscience.jbpub.com/ and http://math.jbpub.com/ to learn more about our exciting publishing programs in these disciplines.

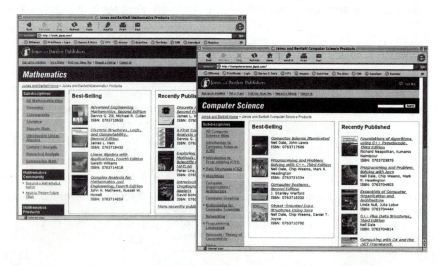